United Nations Conference on Trade and Development

# INFORMATION ECONOMY REPORT 2006

## The development perspective

Prepared by the UNCTAD secretariat

### UNITED NATIONS
New York and Geneva, 2006

# Note

Symbols of United Nations documents are composed of capital letters with figures. Mention of such a symbol indicates a reference to a United Nations document.

---

The designations employed and the presentation of the material in this publication do not imply the expression of any opinion whatsoever on the part of the Secretariat of the United Nations concerning the legal status of any country, territory, city or area, or of its authorities, or concerning the delimitation of its frontiers or boundaries.

---

Material in this publication may be freely quoted or reprinted, but full acknowledgement is requested, together with a reference to the document number. A copy of the publication containing the quotation or reprint should be sent to the UNCTAD secretariat at: Palais des Nations, CH-1211, Geneva 10, Switzerland.

---

The English version of the full report and the English, French and Spanish versions of its Overview section are currently available on the Internet at the address indicated below. Versions in other languages will be posted as they become available.

---

www.unctad.org/ecommerce

UNCTAD/SDTE/ECB/2006/1

UNITED NATIONS PUBLICATION

Sales No. E.06.II.D.8

ISBN 92-1-112700-9

# Foreword

At last year's concluding phase of the World Summit on the Information Society, the international community set itself an ambitious but achievable agenda. The Summit made a commitment to ensuring that information and communication technologies (ICTs) are employed to support a truly global, open and inclusive information society that benefits people everywhere.

Much work lies ahead to better understand the dimensions of the digital divide and its effects on development. However, the basic diagnosis is well established. People in developing countries need easier and cheaper access to ICTs. They need enhanced ICT skills to better employ these technologies in their homes, schools and jobs. And they need the freedom to create, share and exchange information and knowledge of all kinds.

UNCTAD's *Information Economy Report 2006: The Development Perspective* analyses the specific requirements of ICT and e-business strategy-setting in a developing-country context. It also considers the design and assessment of pro-poor e-strategies as well as the usefulness of national ICT policy reviews. Finally, it evaluates the development implications of crucial technology and business trends such as web services and service-oriented architectures – trends that first emerged in the developed world but that, in an increasingly networked economy, need to be considered by developing countries.

This Report was prepared as Governments, non-governmental organizations and the UN system continue to implement the World Summit's outcome. It is designed to help policymakers in developing countries make informed choices in the field of ICT and e-business. I am therefore pleased to recommend it to the growing ICT-for-Development community and, more generally, to anyone interested in promoting sustainable development for all.

Kofi A. Annan
Secretary-General of the United Nations

# Acknowledgements

The *Information Economy Report 2006* was prepared under the overall direction of Peter Fröhler, Officer-In-Charge of UNCTAD's Division for Services Infrastructure for Development and Trade Efficiency (SITE). It was written by a team led by Geneviève Féraud, Chief of the ICT and E-Business Branch, and consisting of the following UNCTAD staff members – Carolin Averbeck, Cécile Barayre, Dimo Calovski, Scarlett Fondeur Gil, Angel González Sanz, Muriel Guigue, Rouben Indjikian, Diana Korka, Carlos Moreno, Marta Pérez Cusó and Susan Teltscher – and with the collaboration of Roberto Zachmann from the International Labour Organization.

Pilar Borque Fernández, Marie Kamara and Ximena Laurie provided administrative support.

Diego Oyarzun designed the cover and formatted the charts, and the text was edited by Graham Grayston.

The UNCTAD team acknowledges the contribution of Filip Miodrag, Lawrence Solum and Ian Walden, consultants. The team also wishes to thank the following individuals for the information, comments and feedback they provided regarding various aspects of the Report: Mohamed Abida, Virginia Acha, John Caulker, Nancy Hafkin, Sophia Huyer, Pieter Kapteijn, Djalma Petit, Madanmohan Rao, David Rose and Sacha Wunsch-Vincent. UNCTAD appreciates the sharing of statistical data by ITU, OECD and Eurostat.

Research assistance was provided by Malte Lierl and Okke Wiersma during their internship with UNCTAD.

# Contents

# List of boxes

# List of charts

Chart                                                                                                   Page

Chart

# List of Tables

Table Page

Table Page

# List of abbreviations

| | |
|---|---|
| **ADNOC** | Abu Dhabi National Oil Company |
| **APC** | Association for Progressive Communications |
| **APDIP** | Asia Pacific Development Information Programme |
| **API** | American Petroleum Institute, USA |
| **API** | application program interface |
| **Aramco** | Arabian American Oil Company, Saudi Arabia |
| **ASEAN** | Association of Southeast Asian Nations |
| | |
| **B2B** | business-to-business |
| **B2C** | business-to-consumer |
| **BOP** | balance of payments |
| **BPEL** | Business Process Execution Language |
| **BPEL4WS** | Business Process Execution Language for Web Services |
| | |
| **CAGR** | compound annual growth rate |
| **CBO** | community-based organization |
| **CCA** | common country assessment |
| **CERA** | Cambridge Energy Associates Inc., USA |
| **CIS** | Commonwealth of Independent States |
| **CPC** | Central Product Classification |
| | |
| **DNS** | domain name server/system |
| **DESA** | Department for Economic and Social Affairs |
| **DSL** | digital subscriber line |
| | |
| **ebXML** | Electronic Business using eXtensible Markup Language |
| **ECA** | Economic Commission for Africa |
| **ECDR** | E-Commerce and Development Report |
| **ECLAC** | Economic Commission for Latin America and the Caribbean |
| **EDI** | electronic data interchange |
| **EIA** | Energy Information Administration, USA |
| **EIA** | Enterprise Integration Application |
| **ERP** | enterprise resource planning |
| **ESCAP** | Economic and Social Commission for Asia and the Pacific |
| **ESCWA** | Economic and Social Commission for Western Asia |
| **EU** | European Union |
| **EU15** | The 15 countries members of the European Union until May 2004 |

| | |
|---|---|
| **EU25** | The current member countries of the European Union |
| **Eurostat** | Statistical Office of the European Communities |
| | |
| **FATS** | Foreign Affiliates Trade Statistics |
| **FCC** | Federal communications Commission |
| **FDI** | foreign direct investment |
| **FLOSSPOLS** | Free/Libre/Open Source Software Policy Support |
| **FOC** | Forum of Conscience |
| **FOSS** | free and open source software |
| **FTTP** | fibre-to-the-premises |
| **FTP** | file transfer protocol |
| | |
| **GAPTEL** | Grupo de Análisis y Prospectiva del sector de las Telecomunicaciones (Spain) |
| **GATS** | General Agreement on Trade in Services |
| **GEM** | Gender and Evaluation Methodology |
| **GDP** | gross domestic product |
| | |
| **HTML** | hypertext transfer markup language |
| **HTTP** | HyperText Transfer Protocol |
| **HTTPS** | HTTP over SSL |
| | |
| **ICANN** | Internet Corporation for Assigned Names and Numbers |
| **ICE** | International Commodity Exchange |
| **ICTs** | information and communication technologies |
| **ICT4D** | ICT for Development |
| **ICT4P** | ICT for Poverty Reduction |
| **IDRC** | International Development Research Centre |
| **IEA** | International Energy Agency |
| **IER** | Information Economy Report |
| **IFP** | Institut français du pétrole |
| **IFPI** | International Federation of Phonogram and Videogram Producers |
| **IGF** | Internet governance forum |
| **IICD** | International Institute for Communication and Development |
| **IMF** | International Monetary Fund |
| **IOC** | international oil company |
| **IOS** | inter-organizational system |
| **IP** | Internet protocol |
| **ISIC** | International Standard Industrial Classification |
| **ITC** | Indian Tobacco Company |
| **ITU** | International Telecommunication Union |

| KOC | Kuwait Oil Company |
| --- | --- |
| **LAN** | local area network |
| **LDC** | least developed country |
| **mb/d** | million barrels per day |
| **MOWS** | Management of Web Services |
| **MUWS** | Management Using Web Services |
| **NGO** | non-governmental organization |
| **NIOC** | National Iranian Oil Company |
| **NOC** | national oil company |
| **OASIS** | Organization for the Advancement of Structured Information Standards |
| **ODI** | Overseas Development Institute |
| **OECD** | Organization for Economic Co-operation and Development |
| **OIES** | Oxford Institute of Energy Studies, UK |
| **OIL** | Oil India Ltd |
| **ONGC** | Oil and Natural Gas Corporation Ltd, India |
| **OPEC** | Organization of the Petroleum Exporting Countries |
| **OPIS** | Operational Program for the Information Society (Greece) |
| **Orbicom** | International Network of UNESCO Chairs in Communications |
| **OSI** | open systems interconnection model |
| **OSS** | open source software |
| **OU** | Open University |
| **PC** | personal computer |
| **PPP** | purchasing power parity |
| **PRSP** | Poverty Reduction Strategy Paper |
| **RIPE NCC** | Réseaux IP européens network coordination centre |
| **Rosneft** | Russian oil company, Russian Federation |
| **SAR** | Special Administrative Region |
| **SIDA** | Swedish International Development Agency |
| **Sinopec** | China Petroleum & Chemical Corporation |
| **SGML** | Standard Generalized Markup Language |
| **SMEs** | small and medium-sized enterprises |
| **SMS** | short message service |
| **SMTP** | Simple Mail Transfer Protocol |
| **SOA** | Service-oriented architecture |

| | |
|---|---|
| **SOAP** | Simple Object Access Protocol |
| **Sonatrach** | Société nationale de transport et commercialisation des hydrocarbures, Algeria |
| **SPE** | Society of Petroleum Engineers, USA |
| **SSL** | secure socket layer |
| **Surgutneftegas** | Surgut oil and gas company, Russian Federation |
| | |
| **TCP** | Transmission control protocol |
| **TCP/IP** | Transmission Control Protocol on top of the Internet Protocol |
| **TNK** | Tuimenskaya Neftyanaya Compania (Tiumen Oil Company), Russian Federation |
| | |
| **UDDI** | Universal Description Discovery and Integration |
| **UK** | United Kingdom |
| **UN/CEFACT** | United Nations Centre for Trade Facilitation and Electronic Business |
| **UN** | United Nations |
| **UNCPC** | United Nations Central Product Classification |
| **UNCTAD** | United Nations Conference on Trade and Development |
| **UNDAF** | United Nations Development Assistance Framework |
| **UNESCO** | United Nations Educational, Scientific and Cultural Organization |
| **UNDP** | United Nations Development Programme |
| **UPS** | uninterruptible power supply |
| **US** | United States |
| | |
| **VAN** | Value Added Network |
| **VoIP** | Voice over Internet protocol |
| **VSAT** | very small aperture terminal |
| | |
| **W3C** | World Wide Web Consortium |
| **WGIG** | Working Group on Internet Governance |
| **WS** | Web services |
| **WSDL** | Web Services Description Language |
| **WSFL** | Web Services Flow Language |
| **WSIS** | World Summit on the Information Society |
| **WSRM** | Web Services Reliable Messaging |
| **WSS** | Web Services Security |
| **WS-SX** | Web Services Secure Exchange |
| **WSTF** | Web Services Transaction Framework |
| | |
| **XLANG** | XML LANguage (an XML-based language for defining business processes from Microsoft) |
| | |
| **XML** | Extensible Markup Language |

# EXPLANATORY NOTES

The term "dollars" ($) refers to United States dollars unless otherwise stated. The term "billion" means 1,000 million.

Two dots (..) indicate that the data are not available or are not separately reported.

A hyphen (-) indicates that the amount is nil or negligible.

Because of rounding, details and percentages do not necessarily add up to totals.

# OVERVIEW

Global economic processes, including international trade, are increasingly influenced by the creation, dissemination, accumulation and application of information and knowledge. Development can no longer be understood without full consideration of the widespread effects of information and communication technologies (ICTs) and their applications to enterprise activities. UNCTAD's *Information Economy Report 2006* has been produced, like its predecessors in the E-commerce and Development Report series, with the intention of helping bring to the forefront of the international agenda the implications for developing countries of the changes that ICT and e-business are bringing about in the productive, commercial and financial spheres. The Report is also intended to support the efforts of developing countries to overcome the challenges they face as they strive to narrow the digital divide and to enable their enterprises to become more competitive through the adoption of ICTs and e-business. To do so, the Report analyses the specific policy challenges facing developing countries, proposes possible means to address them and identifies and disseminates existing international best practice.

The first question to be considered is the extent to which developing countries are active participants in today's global information economy. This problem presents several dimensions. The most obvious one has to do with the differences in the level of access to ICTs between developed and developing countries. From a development point of view, one must also investigate how and to what extent the enterprises of developing countries are adopting ICTs and e-business, and whether their patterns of adoption and use are (or should be) different from those of their counterparts in developed countries. It is then necessary to examine the internal divides in developing countries that limit the chances that groups such as the poor, rural communities and women will be able to benefit from ICTs in terms of better economic opportunities. The participation of developing countries in international trade in ICT goods and services is another fundamental aspect of their involvement in the global information economy. Lastly, one should try to quantify the impact of ICTs at the micro and macro levels, particularly with regard to their effects on growth and economic development. All these questions are treated in chapter 1 of this Report, which presents the only

internationally comparable statistical information available about e-business in developing countries, as well as in chapter 5, which examines in more detail the impact of ICTs on employment in developed and developing countries. Chapter 5, which has been produced by the International Labour Organization in close collaboration with UNCTAD, also demonstrates the usefulness of addressing related development issues through inter-agency cooperation.

Notwithstanding the magnitude of the issues involved, one has to acknowledge the efforts made by Governments in developing countries in recent years to bring the benefits of ICTs to their people. Today, many developing countries have formulated and implemented national ICT plans and policies setting out a road map for a national information society and for integration into the global knowledge-based economy. But how can countries determine whether they are still following the pre-defined strategy, and what needs to be done to revise and adapt existing policies to meet their goals? There are no international guidelines for developing countries to assess their national ICT strategies and plans. Chapter 2 proposes a model ICT policy review framework for developing countries and encourages Governments to carry out such reviews. In this regard, it is particularly important that the effects of ICT policies on the poor be fully taken into account before they are implemented. That is the reason why chapter 3 presents a framework that policymakers can use to design pro-poor ICT interventions in developing countries, or to assess their value in terms of their impact on poverty.

The impact of ICTs and e-business on the economic prospects of developing countries extends well beyond the more obvious examples of e-commerce or e-government applications. As general-purpose technologies, ICTs have the potential to enhance efficiency in most areas of economic activity. For example, chapter 4 of the Report looks into the effects of ICTs on the production and distribution of oil from two standpoints: first, how ICTs are making the exploitation of oil resources more effective (with a possible positive effect on supply); and second, how ICT applications in oil distribution can help alleviate the effects on oil-importing developing countries of rises in oil prices.

Effective decision-making in the field of ICT and e-business, with regard to either public policies or business competitive strategies, requires a sound understanding of the principles and dynamics that govern the interaction between technologies and the economic, legal and social environments of the developing countries in which those technologies are implemented. These interactions provide the focus of the last three chapters of the *Information Economy Report 2006*. Chapter 6 shows how, for technological as well as business strategy reasons, service-oriented architecture technologies and particularly Web services are likely to represent a major milestone in the evolution of e-business. Enterprises in developing countries should be aware of the latest trends in these technologies and consider the most appropriate strategies for their gradual adoption. Chapter 7 explains how the layered

structure of the Internet is one of the main reasons for the success of this technology and how it is in the interest of developing countries that the potential of the Internet as an equalizer in international competition is not eroded by suboptimal governance. In particular, the chapter makes it clear that optimal governance measures are those that respect the principle of minimal Internet layer crossing — that is, that policy should be implemented at the Internet layer that is closest to the problem that is intended to be dealt with. Chapter 8 closes the Report with an examination of the recently adopted United Nations Convention on the Use of Electronic Communications in International Contracts, which will help developing countries establish a legal framework for e-business that follows international best practice and enables and facilitates e-business transactions at the national and international levels.

# A Call for Action

A long and intense period of international dialogue on the issues of ICT for development came to a fruitful conclusion with the closing of the second phase of the World Summit on the Information Society (WSIS) in Tunis in November 2005. Stakeholders are now engaged in the translation into practical actions of the programme and principles that were adopted in the two phases of the Summit. The amount of work that needs to be done is formidable, the time available is short, and the challenges of a multistakeholder decision-making process are complex.

UNCTAD is fully committed to contributing to this endeavour within the scope of its mandate and expertise. In addition to its participation in several WSIS lines of action, UNCTAD has entered into a partnership with the International Labour Organization and the International Trade Centre, with the objective of addressing key issues of e-business and e-employment. The first activity of the partnership was the joint organization of the first facilitation meeting on "E-business and e-employment", which took place in May 2006. The meeting recognized the key role of stakeholders from Governments, civil society, academia and the private sector in shaping, promoting and implementing related projects and programmes. Another example of inter-agency cooperation to support ICTs for development is the joint organization of an UNCTAD–UNITAR seminar

on free and open source software (FOSS). The event, held on 29 August 2006 at the UN in New York, examined the role of FOSS in economic and social development as well as its use in the UN system. Ensuring the full participation of all developing countries in the global information economy will require the active involvement and support of the whole international community, including bilateral and multilateral donors.

The great potential of ICTs as catalysts of social and economic development is clearly recognized. ICT dissemination and adoption in developing countries are supported by many donors as a powerful means to facilitate the achievement of major development goals in the areas of health, education, governance and others. A comprehensive approach to supporting ICT-for-development actions should pay adequate attention to the adoption of ICTs and e-business by the enterprises of developing countries. There is a growing amount of evidence from developed and developing countries that the adoption of ICTs by enterprises helps accelerate productivity growth, which is essential for supporting income and employment generation. More widespread adoption of ICTs in the productive sectors of developing countries should also accelerate innovation and thus enhance the competitive position of developing countries.

In addition to the support of national and international development cooperation organizations, ICT and e-business for development initiatives have much to gain from South–South cooperation. This gives developing countries the possibility to share knowledge and capacity-building resources in an area in which a growing number of developing countries have achieved world-class expertise. UNCTAD actively supports South–South initiatives in the field of ICTs. An example of this was the signing of a Memorandum of Understanding with the Government of Brazil for capacity-building work in the field of FOSS in Africa.

In the final analysis, global knowledge sharing is also the fundamental purpose of this Report, whose chapters are summarized in the next few pages.

# 1. ICT Indicators for Development: Trends and impact

In 2005, the Internet and its applications continued to spread through societies and economies around the globe. Mobile communications are growing rapidly in developing countries, which are now far ahead of developed countries in terms of absolute number of subscribers. This makes mobile phones the only ICT in which developing countries have surpassed developed countries in terms of users. But penetration rates in developing economies continue to be well below those of developed countries. In some developed countries, the penetration rate is over 100 per cent, while in several dozen developing countries it is under 10 per cent. Schemes to make mobile telephony more affordable account for much of the growth in developing countries. For example, in 2004 almost 88 per cent of mobile subscribers in Africa used prepaid services that were tailored to low-income markets.

Although developed economies have lost some of their share of total Internet users to developing countries, they still account for more than half of Internet users worldwide. The digital divide between developed and developing economies is maintained in terms of Internet penetration. The average penetration for developing economies is boosted by the case of selected countries with exceptionally high penetration, such as the Republic of Korea. Approximately one third of developing economies have a penetration rate of less than 5 per cent. Africa has the highest growth rates in terms of Internet users, since many countries start from very low levels, but it has the lowest penetration rates.

Internet access by enterprises is nearly universal in most developed countries, with penetration rates reaching almost 100 per cent among large enterprises. Internet access by enterprises in the developing world is less uniform, reflecting a very broad range of penetration rates. There is, however, a positive correlation coefficient of 0.54 between Internet penetration and ownership of websites by enterprises with Internet access. This suggests that the level of ICT knowledge in the economy might also be an important determinant of Internet use by enterprises, since setting up a website demands more than basic computer literacy.

With regard to the type (or mode) of Internet access, there are large differences between developed countries, where broadband is growing rapidly, and developing countries, where dial-up is still prevalent. This changing nature of Internet modes of access is a new dimension of the international digital divide. In rich countries, broadband subscribers increased by almost 15 per cent in the last half of 2005, reaching 158 million. In particular, enterprise broadband connectivity grew significantly in the EU, from 53 per cent in 2004 to 63 per cent in 2005. Broadband increases the capacity of enterprises to engage in more sophisticated e-business processes and deliver through the Internet, thus maximizing the benefits of ICTs. It is estimated that broadband could contribute hundreds of billions of dollars a year to the GDP of developed countries in the next few years, and has been compared to utilities such as water and electricity.

The growth of broadband is largely due to competition and declining prices, but it also depends on the available infrastructure. In many developing countries, because of the lack of economies of scale, the incentive to expand broadband infrastructure outside urban areas is low. Wireless technology and satellites can help circumvent the cost of infrastructure for sparsely populated, remote or rural areas. Governments have an important role to play in improving access to broadband through infrastructure and policy. Government policy can either encourage or be a disincentive to competition, and thus have an impact on availability and prices. For example, while the Government of the Republic of Korea enforces competition and encourages new entrants in the telecommunications market, the United States has allowed growing consolidation of the industry. The result is that there is a wider choice and better offers for customers in the Republic of Korea than there are for customers in the United States.

Online sales and purchases are now commonplace in all developed economies, but vary across industries and countries. In the OECD countries, the share of enterprises purchasing online ranged between 20 and 60 per cent in 2004. Enterprises in developing countries are increasingly conducting e-commerce, but available data do not confirm the developed country trend that online purchases are more frequent than online sales. This can be partly explained by an overrepresentation of certain sectors in surveys, as is the case for the manufacturing sector in Argentina and Kazakhstan, or other business activities in the real estate sector in the case of Romania. As regards the manufacturing sector, the reason for the lower incidence of online purchases could be that in some emerging markets intermediate goods B2B is less developed than final products B2B. Information from developing countries on the use of e-business for internal business processes is very limited, but data on the use of the Internet for business applications seem to confirm the trend from developed countries in terms of the gap between SMEs and large enterprises, with some exceptions.

Data on the ICT sector show that, generally speaking, following the contraction in the early 2000s, developed countries experienced an increase in both value added and employment in the ICT sector in 2003. This increase in demand and supply in the developed countries' ICT sector opened up new prospects for developing country business partners. In 2003, the ICT sector represented 5.5 per cent of total business employment in developed countries and was a source of employment growth. ICT sector employment grew by over 8 per cent annually between 1995 and 2003, which represented an additional 1 million people employed. The majority (66 per cent) of those working in the ICT sector were employed in the services sectors, a figure that corresponds to the high share of services in a typical developed economy. Among the developing countries for which data are available, the Republic of Korea, Malaysia and the Philippines show a very large share of ICT employment in their business sector (above the OECD average). One explanation could be that in some developing countries the size of the business sector is still small and most developments in the private market are based on new technologies.

Exports of ICT-enabled services grew faster than total services exports during 2000–2003, thus creating new export opportunities for developing countries. In 2003, this was mainly due to the above-average 20 per cent growth rate of developing countries' exports, surpassing developed countries' performance. Developed countries' contribution to world ICT-enabled service exports remained high in 2003, at around 83 per cent. During 2000–2003, developing countries lagged behind the world compound annual growth rate, but some had exceptionally high growth rates. Developing and transition countries' exports of ICT-enabled services originated mostly in Asia (77 per cent), followed by America (10 per cent), Africa (7 per cent) and South-East Europe and the Commonwealth of Independent States (6 per cent). While currently the top 10 exporters of ICT-enabled services are all from developed countries, China and India will soon make their way into the top 10 rankings. In 2003, the $836 billion value of the ICT-enabled sectors represented about 45 per cent of total services exports, compared with only 37 per cent in 1995.

An analysis based on foreign affiliates' flows demonstrates that trade in the ICT-enabled services carried out through the foreign affiliates of multinational companies largely exceeds conventional export and import flows as measured by the IMF Balance of Payments statistics. Furthermore, developing and transition economies have increased their commercial presence abroad. An analysis in relative terms shows that in most cases ICTs boost service exports more than sales through foreign affiliates. However, large exports of ICT-enabled services are also likely to be sold more through foreign affiliates. Developing countries' exports would benefit from improved access to foreign markets under all WTO GATS modes of delivery.

Computer and information exports are the most dynamic ICT-enabled service sector, particularly in the developing economies. Between 1995 and 2004, computer and information services exports grew six times faster than total services exports. The share of developing countries in this export sector increased from 4 per cent in 1995 to 20 per cent in 2003, with the highest growth since 2000. This is partly explained by the corresponding low-level regulatory environment in the WTO. Continued trade liberalization in this sector would need to take into account developing countries' concerns about the movement of natural persons (Mode 4). Additionally, developing countries should seek improved market access commitments under the other modes of delivery in order to boost the potential for South–South trade in services.

Calls for the measuring of ICT impact on development have been an essential and persistent feature in the discussion on ICT measurement and the collection of statistical indicators. The chapter shows that most research on the impact of ICTs at the firm level revealed a positive impact on firm performance and increased market share, if complemented by organizational changes, the upgrading of skills and innovation. Age and size of the companies, as well as quality and speed of the Internet connection, also play a role. Other critical factors concern the regulatory environment in which the firm operates, the structure of the industry sector and the degree of competition in the market. Hence, to optimize impact, firm-level ICT strategies

need to be introduced in conjunction with other changes in the management of firms.

ICT access and use can contribute to productivity growth in both developed and developing countries. UNCTAD research on measuring the impact of ICTs on GDP in developing countries has revealed a positive contribution even in poorer countries. But countries that already have a certain level of ICT uptake and education seem to benefit most from the new technologies. Therefore, Governments need to create an enabling environment, through their national ICT plans and policies, to promote ICT diffusion among economic and social actors.

## 2. Reviewing National ICT Policies for the Information Economy

During the past decade, ICTs have become part of many developing countries' development plans and poverty reduction strategies. Governments have formulated ICT strategies or "master plans" and set objectives to ensure the effective deployment and use of ICTs in their country, for the benefit of their citizens and enterprises. As of June 2006, out of 181 developing and transition countries and territories, almost a half (44 per cent) had already adopted a national ICT plan and a fifth were in the process of preparing one.

But so far, only a few developing country policymakers have carried out a comprehensive assessment of their national ICT plans. Reviewing the status of their ICT policies would help them better understand the policy challenges and opportunities presented by ICTs for the information economy and quantify the main achievements regarding the implementation of their ICT policy measures as foreseen in the national ICT plan. It would also allow them to identify critical success factors and best practices as well as reasons for failure, which is important for adjusting and reforming the ICT policies.

However, there are no international guidelines for developing countries to define and implement an ICT policy review (such as, for example, what the OECD offers to its member countries through the ICT peer review process). Therefore, as part of its ongoing work on ICT policies and on ICT measurement for economic development and trade, UNCTAD has developed a model framework for carrying out national ICT policy reviews.

This chapter presents the **UNCTAD model ICT policy review framework** for developing countries. It outlines the three major components of the framework, using selected best practice country examples and successful ICT policies from developing countries. The first component is the review of the global ICT environment, which provides an overview of a country's ICT uptake, focusing on the status of ICT penetration and use for different economic actors. Its second component is the assessment of the main components of the ICT policy framework, which examines in depth the national ICT policies that have been put in place by the Government, including the components of a national ICT plan, priority actions, concerned sectors, targets and relevant projects. The last component consists of the assessment of the institutional framework and the implementation mechanisms, which considers the adequacy of the established implementation mechanisms and institutional framework and the extent to which changes have to be made to implement the policies contained in the ICT master plan.

The proposed framework is a generic model that could be used as a basis by developing countries. It will have to be adapted to the needs of each country, and could include additional elements to reflect specific national aspects not covered by the model. As part of its technical cooperation activities, UNCTAD carries out complete national ICT policy reviews at the request of member States and subject to the availability of funds.

# 3. Pro-Poor ICT Policies and Practices

ICTs are supporting poverty alleviation efforts across the world. Radio allows women in post-war Sierra Leone to express their concerns and advocate regarding their needs. Information kiosks in Bolivia are enhancing the negotiation position of agricultural producers because they can now access market price information.

In 2000, Governments committed themselves to halving poverty. Misconceptions about ICT and poverty should not cut short the much-needed contribution that ICTs can make to that end. This chapter provides policymakers, practitioners and the donor community with an understanding of how ICTs can contribute to poverty reduction and an overview of recommended pro-poor ICT policies and programmes.

Poverty alleviation means taking development efforts a step further to specifically enhance the capabilities of the poor. In a similar fashion, ICTs contribute to poverty reduction by complementing specific pro-poor activities (for example, by supporting women's advocacy efforts in Sierra Leone), directly enhancing poor livelihoods (for example, by providing access to market information in Bolivia) or reducing barriers to poverty reduction (including disinformation or corruption). ICTs for poverty reduction mean taking ICTs for development efforts one step further to enhance the capabilities of the poor using ICTs as an instrument.

Today, there is a common understanding that ICTs are a necessary but insufficient tool for poverty alleviation. Basic infrastructure, skills and political will, for example, are also needed. Reality shows that different technologies have different contributions to make to poverty reduction and that, in order to be effective, pro-poor ICT efforts must be embedded in poverty reduction initiatives (including national development strategies) and best practices (such as multistakeholder and participatory approaches). Support is needed at all levels, and sustainability concerns, although necessary, should not crowd out financial resources. Efforts should be made to scale up and replicate best practices, while policies and programmes must be context-specific. Finally, only through a focused dialogue and research on pro-poor ICTs will technologies bring poverty alleviation.

Having identified how ICT policies and programmes can contribute to poverty alleviation, one may ask what barriers policymakers and practitioners face in effectively pursuing pro-poor ICT endeavours. Recommended ICT policies and practices often do not materialize for various reasons. International debates and commitments (including the World Summit on the Information Society) are not focused on ICT for poverty reduction. And any broad commitments have yet to be translated into policy and practice. Contested discourses continue to influence policies and practices – failure to alleviate poverty is in the detail, not in the broad commitments. Experience shows that implementation of ICT programmes is the most challenging part. For instance, while multistakeholder approaches have many virtues, their practical implementation is not one of them – working with other organizations is not easy. Moreover, scaling up successful best practices involves more than replicating good projects: it requires another level of commitment. The cross-cutting nature of ICTs, as well as the limited availability of quantitative measurement and qualitative assessments of ICT for poverty alleviation, renders these efforts invisible. Institutionally, there is little accountability or incentive to coordinate ICT strategies and poverty reduction policies. More fundamentally, the question of how power imbalances are dealt with remains unsatisfactorily unanswered.

. UNCTAD offers a **Pro-poor ICTs Framework** to examine to what extent an ICT policy or programme is pro-poor. The framework (expanded from Rao's 8 Cs Framework for Analysis and Planning ICT interventions) helps policymakers understand, question and propose pro-poor ICT interventions. It questions key areas for meeting the needs of the poor, such as connectivity (is the technology accessible and affordable?), community (who benefits from the intervention?), capital (are there sufficient financial resources?) and coherence (is the ICT strategy/programme coherent with the development strategies?).

On the basis of these reflections, ICT policymakers and practitioners are encouraged to focus on ICTs for poverty reduction by promoting a better understanding of pro-poor ICTs (including the follow-up to the World Summit on the Information Society) and to make ICTs work for the poor by adopting best practices in ICT policies and interventions. They may also consider supporting approaches, including participation and decentralization, that enable the poor to be heard and to participate.

Other recommendations are to mainstream ICTs effectively into national and sectoral poverty reduction policies and into development assistance programmes, with an awareness of the cross-cutting nature of pro-poor ICTs; and also to promote the scaling up of successful programmes by providing an enabling environment as well as encouraging the development of pro-poor ICT networks and organizational capacities.

Finally, UNCTAD can support developing countries in carrying out poverty and gender analysis of ICT policies, and undertaking country reviews of policies and programmes across sectors and issues areas, and also support the collection of data disaggregated by sex, age, education and geography to help identify who is not benefiting from ICTs.

# 4. ICTs in the Oil Sector: Implications for Developing Economies

Oil is playing a major role in the world energy balance and the demand for it will continue to increase in the foreseeable future. Ensuring that the supply of oil from existing and new oilfields and other fossil energy sources is forthcoming will be the main challenge for the petroleum industry and one of the means of avoiding future energy crises. Meanwhile, tight market conditions, including a lack of enough spare productive capacities in oil production and refining, are keeping prices high and making upgrading and improving of the oil supply chain an urgent task. Given the capital-intensive and skill-based nature of the oil industry, a key instrument for facilitating its modernization is ICTs. More intensive and efficient use of the latter is increasingly mainstreamed into the industry practices in both developed and developing economies. Moreover, computing, measuring and communicating devices embedded in modern oil technologies are making them more information-intensive. Consequently, the oil sector could be considered an integral part of the information economy.

As the production of oil is mainly concentrated in developing and transition economies where the oil industry technology standards are similar to those in developed countries, the impact of ICTs on improving the economic performance of the oil sector is affecting the production of crude oil in all those countries. ICT and related key technology-driven efficiency gains happen in both the upstream stages (exploration and production of crude oil) and the downstream stages (transportation, refining of crude oil and distribution of oil products) of the global petroleum industry. ICTs impact the effectiveness of the petroleum industry and offer opportunities for its further diversification, especially in the oil-exporting developing and transition economies. They also offer possibilities for improving the production and distribution of oil products in oil-importing countries as part of sustainable development models.

Avoiding potential deterioration and oil supply shocks can be achieved only within a framework of well-defined and coordinated policies and practices that include the use of ICTs as a tool for integrating and optimizing business processes in both upstream and downstream operations. To improve the use of ICTs and new technologies the national oil-exporting companies of the oil-exporting developing countries should continue investing in ICT-related know-how and business processes. In addition to undertaking their own R&D, they should establish close relations with oil service companies and oil technology and ICT-related vendors, as well as oil industry consultants and experts. Stipulating technology transfer clauses in the production sharing or other arrangements with international oil companies could also be a part of their strategies. Governments, for their part, should encourage both national and foreign operators to use state-of-the-art technologies. As a result, oil companies will make the necessary investments in new ICTs and other oil-related technologies while extracting crude oil or producing oil products in those countries.

The benefits of using ICTs to reduce the unit costs of distribution of oil products are especially important for oil-importing developing countries that have no means of compensating for the increases in the cost of oil by increasing their exports or switching to alternative energy sources, or by introducing effective conservation measures. It is equally apparent that well-designed international energy cooperation efforts should include financial and technological support measures for those countries.

# 5. ICTs, Enterprises and Jobs: What Policies?

Jobs are an essential poverty eradication tool because they are the source of income both for the population through wages and for Governments through taxation. ICTs are important contributors to business performance. Since enterprises are the source of jobs, policymakers must develop strategies to promote ICT-using competitive enterprises (particularly small and medium-sized ones) that generate decent work.

The "digital divide" is the result of social and economic inequalities within and between countries. A major concern is to adopt corrective policies so that this divide does not prolong and deepen existing socio-economic inequalities. Chapter 5 reviews some of the factors that explain why ICTs have considerable effects on labour markets, how technology brings about changes in the structure of the economy and how the introduction of automation at the "factory" (or production) level has shifted employment away from production to managerial and other non-production employment and to the services sector. In addition, the chapter argues that there is scant evidence to prove that a significant amount of work previously done in high-cost areas is being displaced to low-labour-cost economies. On the other hand, employment levels of skilled workers in many developing countries tend to show a trend towards labour market segmentation similar to that in the developed economies. In all these countries there is evidence of a rise in either the employment or the wage levels of skilled workers and a fall in these same factors for others: there is considerable empirical evidence that skill-biased employment is related to technological change.

Those enterprises that fail to adapt to the structural changes associated with globalization and ICTs may be marginalized if they fail to recognize the competitive advantage offered by technology and the economies of scale that are associated with larger markets. Moreover, it is increasingly clear that economic activity will increasingly be network-driven. Several paths can be taken to achieve social and economic progress through ICTs. With regard to the first, enterprises must be able to fully exploit the benefits of ICTs. This implies ensuring that firms achieve productivity increases through their investments in these technologies: managers and entrepreneurs must be able to develop the processes and create the organizations that will make efficient use of investments in ICTs.

Unless the workforce has the necessary skills to adapt and be creative, enterprises will not be able to enhance their productivity and innovation. Throughout chapter 5 it is noted that ICTs are changing the nature of many tasks that have little to do directly with computers. Thus, the emphasis should not be placed exclusively on elusive "computer literacy". New production processes and enterprises require five fundamental skills: literacy, numeracy, the capacity to learn, the capacity to communicate clearly and the capacity to work in teams.

Taking the time and making the effort to explain to the labour force the work-related implication of investments in technology help to enlist their assistance and allay their fears. This can be achieved through dialogue, through social security and through training. Freedom of association and the possibility of initiating dialogue between employers and workers are central to this aim.

# 6. Service-Oriented Architecture and Web Services Technologies: Trends and Implications for E-Business in Developing Countries

The growing adoption of e-business practices reinforces global production and distribution models that emphasize cooperation and rapid information exchange among business partners. This means that competitiveness, including for enterprises in developing countries, is becoming more and more dependent on their ability to use ICTs to integrate themselves into value networks at regional and global levels.

In this business environment, web services (WS) technologies, which enable automated interaction over the Internet between computers that handle a business process, become particularly relevant. A very simple example of how web services can be used for e-business could be a service in an SME's website that automatically updates a catalogue's prices in several currencies by checking periodically the latest exchange rates from a financial news service. Of course, the same logic can be applied to a much more complex scenario involving any combination of business processes.

Systems operating in this way depend on the functionalities that other systems make available to them. Ideally, the level of dependence should be kept as low as possible in order to maximize the chances that different systems can interact with each other. Achieving such low levels of dependence is called "loose coupling", which is the goal pursued by Service-Oriented Architectures (SOA). SOA can be defined as a distributed software model in which modular, loosely coupled applications can be found, used and combined over a network.

SOA are built on open standards such as the eXensible Markup Language (XML) and Simple Object Access Protocol (SOAP), thus providing broad interoperability among different vendors' solutions. This means that an enterprise can implement WS without having any knowledge of the consumers of those services. Open standards ensure that the criteria and decisions are truly service-oriented and are not biased towards one platform or another. Without open standards the possibilities that SOA give enterprises to combine, replace and mix the components of their IT systems without the need to create specific code to interconnect them would not materialize.

Standard setting is therefore of the utmost importance for the development of SOA and WS technologies. These processes currently take place essentially outside the public sphere, through entities such as the Organization for the Advancement of Structured Information Standards (OASIS), the World Wide Web Consortium (W3C) and the Web Services Interoperability Organization (WS-I). The operations of these organizations have not always been controversy-free, as the competitive strategies of some of the major technology companies have affected their attitudes to and involvement in the standard-setting bodies. This is particularly true with regard to the intellectual property rights policies of the various actors involved. However, as the technological and market situation has evolved, a reasonable division of labour seems to have been achieved among the standard-setting organizations.

The adoption of WS technologies will be increasingly necessary in order to maintain competitiveness in several sectors and industries, some of which are important for the economies of developing countries. For example, the ICT-producing sector, in which developing countries have a significant and growing share of world trade, is rapidly adopting WS technologies. It can be expected that this trend will be replicated in a wide range of manufacturing activities of considerable importance in the developing world, including areas such as textile and apparel. Other sectors where SOA and WS could have a positive impact include retail banking, insurance, distribution services, transport and logistics operations, business process outsourcing and tourism. Developing countries should also consider the vast potential that WS and SOA technologies offer for the implementation of e-government services.

SOA and WS will facilitate deeper levels of inter-business collaboration. This could open up opportunities for developing country enterprises, for example by facilitating their participation in global supply chains or by making business process outsourcing more attractive. Enterprises in developing countries should also take advantage of the scalability of these technologies, which enables enterprises facing constraints in their IT budgets or in their human resources to gradually implement them. In any case, it is important to bear in mind that the pertinence of a change towards SOA and WS approaches is not a matter of mere IT policies, but of overall business strategy

From the practical point of view, an enterprise considering whether to invest in a WS implementation should address several issues. One of them is the kind of relationship it has with the business partners that are most likely to use the proposed WS. This refers to the content of the business relationship and to its time horizon. Another question to ask is how data are going to be shared and who is going to handle a given segment of a business process, and how. There are also decisions to be made about the way in which the WS are going to be implemented: what processes are to be automated and whether/how WS are to be extended to other business processes. Finally, there is the fundamental question of how the WS implementation is to be managed so that in the end the enterprise has made its knowledge base larger and enhanced its competitiveness.

In designing their strategy to implement SOA and WS technologies, enterprises in developing countries would be well advised to give full consideration to FOSS solutions. The value of implementing an SOA increases more than proportionally to the number of WS that are available in it. Commercial solutions require the payment of fees that are proportional to the computing resources that run them. All this means that going for a truly comprehensive SOA implementation that connects all the enterprise's services and applications can be rather expensive. If one or several of the

many FOSS solutions that are available is chosen, this restriction is lifted and as many services and applications can be added to the SOA infrastructure as makes business sense. Furthermore, the use of FOSS generates significant positive externalities that help advance the information economy in developing countries.

# 7. The Layered Internet Architecture: Governance Principles And Policies

A vast array of human activities, many of them of a commercial nature, are increasingly moving to the Internet. This move is accompanied by associated politics and, consequently, by the need to govern. Even our governing organizations have moved online. With the Internet's outstanding growth, organized society cannot ignore it or leave it ungoverned. The issue is no longer whether to govern, but how and on the basis of what principles.

In asking this question it is useful to review what it is that has made the Internet become the preferred data network and network applications platform. The answer has more to do with enabling and empowering than a set of technical features or the way in which a thing is used. What is opaque is that the empowering principles of the Internet are embedded in the technical specification of the TCP/IP suite – the Internet protocol – and to the majority of lay users they seem to represent just that: a set of features. However, the contributions of Lawrence Lessig, Yochai Benkler, Kevin Werbach, and Lawrence Solum and Minn Chung and others have provided an improved transparency by translating the technical principles of the Internet into conceptual notions such as the *code thesis*, the *end-to-end principle*, the concept of *network neutrality* and the *layers principle*.

These principles describe the Internet as a layered, open and accessible network that focuses on efficiently transferring data as its sole functionality. Any functionality beyond getting data from the sender to the recipient is built into an application that runs on top of the network. Below the applications, various layers of applications and protocols ensure that the data travel correctly within their primary network and to recipients on other networks. Four layers are commonly identified, from a non-technical point of view:

- The physical layer – wire, optic fibre;
- The logical layer – where the TP/IP suite is lodged;
- The application layer – where the functionalities that we as users see are implemented; and
- The content layer – text, graphics, audio, video, etc.

In this sense, the Internet is a "stupid network" that does not care what the data are or where they are going. Also, it does not discriminate as to what applications use it – web browser, e-mail clients or voice-over-Internet applications – nor does a developer need permission from the network, or its owners or managers, to develop an application to give away or sell. Finally, the Internet does not discriminate as to what content these applications create and move between users. This has made the Internet into one of the most powerful, yet democratic, technologies in human history.

Indeed, many of the showpiece Internet success stories, such as the World Wide Web, Yahoo, Google, Skype, Amazon and eBay, were developed by ambitious entrepreneurs or scientists, and not by mainstream industry corporations. In this sense, it is entirely conceivable that the next Internet "killer application" may come from a developing or transition economy. Beyond its role as a communications network of networks, the Internet has established itself as an innovation platform, precisely because of its open and accessible nature. While deliberating on the future of Internet governance, Governments should consider whether any proposed policy enhances these fundamental characteristics or contributes to their deterioration.

The best way to handle this task is to establish one or several referential principles that would serve as a qualifying test for policy proposals, in particular whether there is any intent to codify policy into regulation. This chapter proposes the so-called layers principle as a policy reference. The layers principle requires that Internet governance policy and regulation avoid interfering with and changing the layered nature of the Internet architecture. This principle can be decomposed into two arguments: the principle of layer separation and the principle of minimization of layer crossing.

The principle of layer separation states that the separation between Internet layers as designed in the Internet's basic technological architecture must be maintained. This means that policy or regulation that would require a particular layer of the Internet to differentiate the handling of data on the basis of information available only at another layer should be disallowed. The principle of minimizing layer crossing states that governing authorities primarily develop policy for a particular layer to be implemented precisely at that same layer. However, as this may not always be feasible, policymakers should minimize the distance

between the layer at which policy aims to produce an effect and the layer directly targeted by the policy. While the layers principle may be sufficient to provide a policy check in most cases, Internet governance authorities should consider policy proposals by referencing them to the other complementary Internet principles listed above.

The WSIS debate on Internet governance was assigned to the Working Group on Internet Governance (WGIG) and continues, after the WSIS, with the work of the Internet Governance Forum (IGF). The WGIG succeeded in mainstreaming the Internet governance debate and established solid guidelines for the continuation of this process by the IGF. While much has been accomplished, it is yet to be seen whether the process will succeed in establishing convergence between the technological and political communities in order to establish a common set of principles for governance that takes into account political and social needs while at the same time preserving the technological advantages of the Internet as both an open data network and an innovation platform.

# 8. Laws and Contracts in an E-Commerce Environment

Most legal systems have developed over many years and comprise a myriad of laws and regulations as well as judicial decision-making. While laws and regulations rarely expressly require the use of paper, they often use terminology that seems to presume the use of paper and other physical acts. Concerns had been expressed that existing paper-based legal systems might be unable to accommodate e-commerce and could lead to uncertainty which would hamper global electronic trade. As a consequence, when organizations shift from paper-based communication techniques to electronic methods, there is often uncertainty about how existing laws will treat data messages in terms of validity, enforceability and admissibility. Although there is a general consensus that e-commerce is not taking place within a legal vacuum for which a totally new legal framework needs to be created, it is also acknowledged that there is a need to adapt the existing laws and regulations to accommodate electronic commerce. Many Governments have amended or supplemented existing laws in order to increase legal certainty and boost the trust of both business and consumers in e-commerce.

This chapter examines the legal nature of communications and data messages in electronic commerce. Considerable international harmonization has been achieved in this field, based on a series of initiatives by the United Nations Commission on International Trade Law (UNCITRAL). The most significant of these was the adoption of the United Nations Convention on the Use of Electronic Communications in International Contracts, which was formally adopted by the General Assembly in November 2005 and opened for signature in January 2006.

The provisions of that Convention address three main topics, which comprise the focus of the chapter: legal validity, form requirements and regulating the contract creation process.

A fundamental legal concern that a person will have when communicating electronically is, will such communications be considered valid? Legal validity concerns arise from a number of different sources. First, it may simply be an issue in terms of the trading partner to whom a message is being sent: will the party accept my electronic message and act on it? Second, there will be concerns as to whether communications that pass between trading partners, but which are also required to be made by law, such as tax invoices, will be an acceptable record for the public authority with responsibility for regulatory supervision. Third, communications that are made directly with public authorities, namely e-government applications, raise issues concerning the possibility and validity of sending such communications electronically. Fourth, there is the need for electronic communications to be acceptable in a court of law in the event of a dispute arising between trading partners or a claim being made by a third party affected by the electronic communication. The Convention is designed to contribute to the resolution of all of these different validity concerns.

Legal systems abound with terms and phrases that, while not expressly excluding the use of electronic communications, were clearly used in reference to physical documents and processes, such that legal uncertainties exist as to whether electronic alternatives

are acceptable. The UNCITRAL Model Law on Electronic Commerce in 1996 and the subsequent Model Law on Electronic Signatures address such form requirements in considerable detail. These are replicated, in whole or part, in the Convention.

Generally, most electronic commerce legislation leaves in place underlying contract law on such issues as contract formation, enforceability, terms and remedies. There are a few instances, however, where there has been supplementation of that law, specifically in areas where there is a perceived need to deal with the unique aspects of electronic commerce, specifically the process of communicating: sending and receiving messages. The Convention sets out rules for this communication process, thus providing some certainty for trading partners.

Finally, some policy recommendations are made, which constitute a checklist of issues for developing countries to consider when embarking on law reform designed to facilitate electronic commerce.

# Chapter 1

# ICT INDICATORS FOR DEVELOPMENT: TRENDS AND IMPACT

## A. Introduction

In 2005, the Internet and its applications continued to penetrate societies and economies around the globe. Mobile communications continued their steep growth in developing countries, which are now far ahead of developed countries in terms of absolute number of subscribers. Mobile phones also continue to be the only ICT indicator where developing countries have surpassed developed countries. Despite this growth, penetration rates in many developing countries remain low, especially among least developed countries (LDCs). The Internet users' curve continues to flatten in most developed countries; at the same time, broadband is experiencing an unprecedented growth in rich countries, providing them with unexpected opportunities for economic growth and job creation. This flies in the face of reality in many developing countries, where SMEs depend on slow, low-quality connections unsuitable for most e-business applications.

The increasing availability of comparable data on the use of ICTs in developing countries permits a more informed discussion on the evolution of the information economy in those countries. Enterprises in developing countries are increasingly conducting e-commerce, but available data do not confirm the developed country trend that online purchases are more frequent than online sales. For example, about 28 per cent of enterprises in Qatar effect online purchases and almost 35 per cent effect online sales; this is also the case in Argentina, China and Romania. In terms of using ICT for e-business, the use of intranets and extranets remains low in comparison with developed countries.

Trade in ICT-enabled services has experienced above-average growth rates during the past five years, thus creating new export opportunities for developing countries. For example, as this chapter will show, between 1995 and 2004, computer and information services exports grew six times faster than total services exports. The share of developing countries in

this export sector increased from 4 per cent in 1995 to 20 per cent in 2003, with the highest growth since 2000.

Central to the debate on ICT for development is the availability of evidence on the impact of ICTs on productivity and growth in developing countries. While an increasing amount of research has become available, showcasing a positive impact in developed countries, limited research on developing countries indicates that those countries that have reached a certain level of ICT uptake benefit most from the new technologies.

These issues and others will be examined in this chapter of the report. It provides an overview of trends and indicators on the use of ICTs by different actors in society and the economy, as well as its impact on development, growth and trade. As in previous issues of the Information Economy Report, section B will first present basic access and use indicators, such as Internet users and mobile phone subscribers, as well as the scope and development of e-commerce and other e-business applications. In addition to presenting trends, facts and figures, it will examine how specific ICTs can impact and have impacted on enterprises in developing countries, in particular with regard to the growth of broadband availability and use.

Section C will take the reader from the individual and firm-level trends and analyses to the sectoral and industry levels. It will focus on the ICT industry sector, presenting available data on people employed by the sector, as well as its value-added contribution to the economy.

In section D, the focus will shift to ICTs and international trade. Last year's Information Economy Report examined the evolution of international trade in ICT goods. This year we will look at how ICTs have impacted on services trade, in particular in developing countries. The section will first present major trade flows and markets, most dynamic sectors and different modes of providing ICT-enabled services, including through offshoring. Then the reader's attention will be drawn to a broader analysis of ICT-related services trade, using foreign affiliates' inward and outward flows. It will finish with a snapshot of computer and information services, one of the most rapidly growing services export sectors, and present relevant WTO commitments.

Section E will discuss approaches to measuring the impact of ICTs on productivity and growth. It will first summarize the latest research findings in this area, and then present the results from recent UNCTAD work on measuring the impact of ICTs on GDP growth in developing countries.

As usual, the chapter's scope is defined by the availability of comparable statistical data. The data presented are based on sources that include the ITU for ICT access indicators, UNCTAD for ICT use data on enterprises and on the ICT sector for developing countries, the OECD and Eurostat for enterprise data for their members, and the IMF and UNCTAD for data on international trade in services and foreign affiliate sales, respectively.

The availability of data from developing countries is increasing gradually. In the past few years, the international community has made a major effort to raise awareness among developing country policymakers so that they include ICT measurement in their national ICT policy agenda; this effort is now starting to bear fruit. The Partnership on Measuring ICT for Development, which was launched during UNCAD XI in 2004, and which comprises 11 international organizations, continues to play a critical role in this process. Box 1.1 describes recent activities in which the Partnership has engaged and its role in the WSIS follow-up process.

## B.   ICT access and use by individuals, households and enterprises

This section looks at the latest available data on selected indicators of ICT access and use, which are part of the list of core indicators agreed upon under the aegis of

---

### Box 1.1

### Partnership on Measuring ICT for Development: Entering phase II

ICT policymaking, research and analysis, as well as strategic e-business decision-making, benefits considerably from reliable and compa- rable statistical data on ICT access, use and impact. Since 2004, the members of the Partnership on Measuring ICT for Development, which include the ITU, the OECD, UNCTAD, the UNESCO Institute for Statistics, the UN ICT Task Force, the World Bank, the UN Regional Com- missions (ECA, ECLAC, ESCAP and ESCWA) and Eurostat, have actively promoted the production of ICT statistics in developing countries. During the first phase of the Partnership (June 2004 – December 2005), a number of activities were carried out to create awareness among policymakers about the importance of ICT statistical indicators, to take stock globally on the status quo of data availability, and to develop a set of core ICT indicators that could be collected by all countries.

The World Summit on the Information Society (WSIS) and its two phases (Geneva 2003 and Tunis 2005) provided an ideal framework for promoting such activities and reaching out to the ICT policy community. The IER 2005 presented in detail the objectives, activities and achievements of the Partnership during its initial phase. It culminated in WSIS Tunis (November 2005), where the Partnership organized a parallel event on "Measuring the Information Society". At that event, the set of core statistical indicators for the information society agreed upon in Geneva at a global WSIS Thematic Meeting in February 2005 was launched through the publication "Core ICT Indicators". At the invitation of the Summit organizers, the outcome of the event was reported to the WSIS Plenary on 17 November 2005.

As a result of the work of the Partnership, the final WSIS outcome documents prominently feature the issue of indicators. The WSIS Tunis Agenda for the Information Society calls for periodic evaluation based on appropriate indicators and benchmarking, and using an agreed methodology, including that developed by the Partnership on Measuring ICT for Development. It furthermore invites the international com- munity to strengthen the ICT-related statistical capacity of developing countries, which is also a key objective of the Partnership.

Now that the Partnership has entered its second phase (January 2006 – December 2007), its main focus is on enhancing capacities in developing countries to produce comparable ICT statistics. To that end, members of the Partnership engage in various technical assistance activities, such as advisory missions, development and delivery of training, and the organization of more focused workshops to exchange best practice and advance ICT measurement at the regional and national levels. The Partnership continues its work on methodology and the development of new core indicators in areas such as education and government.

*For further information, see http://measuring-ict.unctad.org.*

---

## Box 1.2

## Comparability of enterprise data from developing countries

Whenever possible, the enterprise data from national surveys presented in this chapter have been adjusted to exclude micro-enterprises and ensure that their sectoral composition roughly represents the economic weight of each sector. But the lack of standardization and comparability of most national surveys in developing countries is still a problematic issue in measuring worldwide ICT trends. Also, in many developing countries small-scale agriculture and the informal sector account for a large part of the economy and might not be reflected in the surveys. Consequently, surveys from developing countries also tend to contain less information about the overall economic importance of information technologies than surveys from developed countries. This in turn renders comparisons between developing and developed countries more difficult.

Another comparability issue occurs with respect to the indicators on the activities carried out on the Internet by enterprises. Measured as a proportion of the enterprises with Internet access, some of these indicators can be higher in developing countries than in developed countries; this might seem counter-intuitive. However, it could be because in less developed economies Internet access itself already creates a selection bias in favour of enterprises with a particular affinity for ICT and e-business use, while in more developed economies Internet access tends to be more universal. For that reason, e-commerce and e-business usage indicators are presented here both as a share of enterprises with Internet access and as a share of all enterprises surveyed.

Table 1.20 in the statistical annex shows the most recent data on ICT use in businesses received from selected developing countries, which have been used in severasl of the charts and tables of Chapter 1. Some of the figures reflect sample survey results only and not the whole target population. Several surveys also covered enterprises with 0-9 employees, but data on these enterprises are not included in table 1.20. The metadata on the different country surveys are contained in the notes to table 1.20.

---

the Partnership on Measuring ICT for Development (see box 1.1). It will highlight trends in these indicators, which serve for the basic evaluation of the level of connectivity of individuals, households and enterprises in developing countries, as well as determine the use made of ICTs. This general picture of the status of ICT access and use in developed and developing countries is based on data from national statistical offices and other relevant sources, including the ITU, the OECD, Eurostat and UNCTAD. Enterprise data from developing countries should be interpreted with caution (see box 1.2).

### 1.  Mobile phones

Mobile phones are the only ICT in which developing countries have surpassed developed countries in terms of users (see table 1.1). Furthermore, mobile phones have economic importance for many users in developing countries, as they are enablers of business, in particular for micro-entrepreneurs. The relevance of mobile phones to small businesses in developing countries was examined in last year's Report (UNCTAD, 2005). The economic benefits of mobile phone use are a factor of the growth in the number of mobile phone subscribers in developing countries. The evolution and the growing share of developing economies in the worldwide mobile market can be seen in chart 1.1. Tables 1.14

### Chart 1.1

### Mobile phone subscribers by level of development

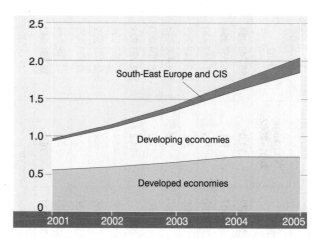

*Source:* UNCTAD calculations based on the ITU World Telecommunication Indicators Database, 2006.

and 1.15 in the statistical annex show mobile phone subscribers and penetration figures by country.

Trends from recent years continued during 2005:

- While developing Asia has the largest number of new subscribers from 2004 to 2005, African countries present the highest growth (see

Table 1.1 – Mobile phone subscribers by region and level of development

| | 2001 | % change 2001–2002 | 2002 | % change 2002–2003 | 2003 | % change 2003–2004 | 2004 | % change 2004–2005 | 2005 |
|---|---|---|---|---|---|---|---|---|---|
| **World** | 964 119 871 | 21.0 | 1 166 240 364 | 21.3 | 1 414 414 774 | 24.3 | 1 758 549 494 | 23.5 | 2 171 179 091 |
| **Developed economies** | 553 458 217 | 9.4 | 605 557 394 | 10.0 | 666 179 919 | 11.0 | 739 337 908 | 9.5 | 809 906 208 |
| Asia | 80 719 160 | 8.3 | 87 452 320 | 6.5 | 93 154 960 | 5.9 | 98 661 436 | 3.9 | 102 545 000 |
| Europe | 319 166 809 | 9.2 | 348 642 226 | 9.5 | 381 887 975 | 10.6 | 422 428 940 | 9.7 | 463 582 325 |
| North America | 140 152 248 | 10.2 | 154 438 848 | 12.8 | 174 190 984 | 14.1 | 198 771 532 | 11.6 | 221 828 884 |
| Oceania | 13 420 000 | 12.0 | 15 024 000 | 12.8 | 16 946 000 | 14.9 | 19 476 000 | 12.7 | 21 950 000 |
| **Developing economies** | 388 336 523 | 34.2 | 521 231 021 | 30.5 | 680 373 258 | 31.5 | 894 661 980 | 31.3 | 1 174 964 724 |
| Africa | 26 074 181 | 45.4 | 37 900 998 | 40.7 | 53 321 307 | 51.2 | 80 614 609 | 67.4 | 134 941 820 |
| Asia | 278 237 655 | 37.4 | 382 401 952 | 31.0 | 501 040 238 | 27.5 | 638 902 652 | 25.2 | 799 936 437 |
| Latin America and the Caribbean | 83 860 436 | 20.1 | 100 733 425 | 24.8 | 125 758 637 | 39.0 | 174 831 094 | 37.0 | 239 588 382 |
| Oceania | 164 251 | 18.5 | 194 646 | 30.0 | 253 076 | 23.9 | 313 626 | 58.8 | 498 085 |
| **South-East Europe and CIS** | 22 325 131 | 76.7 | 39 451 949 | 72.0 | 67 861 597 | 83.5 | 124 549 606 | 49.6 | 186 308 159 |

*Source:* UNCTAD calculations based on the ITU World Telecommunication Indicators Database, 2006.

Table 1.2 – Mobile phone penetration by region and level of development

| | 2001 | % change 2001–2002 | 2002 | % change 2002–2003 | 2003 | % change 2003–2004 | 2004 | % change 2004–2005 | 2005 |
|---|---|---|---|---|---|---|---|---|---|
| **World** | 15.6 | 19.5 | 18.7 | 19.8 | 22.4 | 22.9 | 27.5 | 22.0 | 33.6 |
| **Developed economies** | 58.0 | 8.8 | 63.1 | 9.4 | 69.0 | 10.3 | 76.2 | 8.9 | 83.0 |
| Asia | 60.5 | 8.0 | 65.3 | 6.3 | 69.4 | 5.7 | 73.3 | 3.7 | 76.1 |
| Europe | 67.2 | 8.8 | 73.1 | 9.1 | 79.7 | 10.2 | 87.8 | 9.4 | 96.1 |
| North America | 43.5 | 9.1 | 47.5 | 11.7 | 53.1 | 13.0 | 60.0 | 10.6 | 66.3 |
| Oceania | 58.0 | 10.7 | 64.2 | 11.5 | 71.6 | 13.7 | 81.4 | 11.5 | 90.8 |
| **Developing economies** | 8.0 | 32.3 | 10.5 | 28.7 | 13.6 | 29.7 | 17.6 | 29.5 | 22.8 |
| Africa | 3.0 | 42.3 | 4.2 | 37.7 | 5.8 | 48.0 | 8.6 | 63.9 | 14.1 |
| Asia | 8.1 | 35.7 | 11.0 | 29.4 | 14.2 | 26.0 | 17.9 | 23.7 | 22.1 |
| Latin America and the Caribbean | 15.5 | 18.4 | 18.3 | 23.1 | 22.5 | 37.1 | 30.9 | 35.2 | 41.8 |
| Oceania | 1.6 | 16.3 | 1.9 | 27.7 | 2.4 | 21.8 | 3.0 | 56.2 | 4.6 |
| **South-East Europe and CIS** | 6.7 | 77.2 | 11.9 | 72.5 | 20.6 | 84.0 | 37.9 | 49.9 | 56.8 |

*Source:* UNCTAD calculations based on the ITU World Telecommunication Indicators Database, 2006.

table 1.1) as a group, departing from a low base, followed by South-East Europe and CIS countries.[1]

- Among African countries, South Africa, Nigeria, Egypt and Morocco continue to be the leaders in terms of the region's number of subscribers.

- The penetration rate in developing economies continues to be well below that of developed countries (table 1.2). In some developed countries, the penetration rate is over 100 per cent, while in several dozen developing countries it is under 10 per cent. However, the gap in terms of mobile phone penetration has diminished over time between developed and developing countries.

In 2005, the worldwide number of mobile phone subscribers passed the 2 billion mark, with Asia accounting for more than 40 per cent of them. Private research estimates that by the end of 2006, the number of global mobile phone subscribers will be approximately 2.6 billion.[2] In developed countries the growth in the mobile phone industry will come from the increased offer and use of innovative services, from SMS and roaming to Internet access and music downloads. For example, it is expected that more than one third of Europeans will have Internet-enabled phones by 2010 (Kelley and McCarthy, 2006), although more than three quarters of Europeans that currently have mobile phones with Internet access do not use them for that purpose. There are, however, encouraging signs of potential growth, such as the fact that mobile phones accounted for 40 per cent of business-to-consumer (B2C) music downloads in 2005 worldwide, led by Europe and Asia (IFPI, 2006).[3]

Schemes to make mobile telephony more affordable account for much of the growth in developing countries. For example, in 2004 almost 88 per cent of mobile subscribers in Africa used pre-paid services that were tailored to low-income markets (ITU, 2006). The growth of mobile telephony in Asia is due to a highly competitive market, which has led to lower prices for calls and mobile devices (handsets). In fact, enhanced competition positively affects mobile teledensity in developing countries in general (World Bank, 2006).

Mobile connectivity sidesteps some important obstacles to other types of connectivity, but most notably to the deployment of fixed-line infrastructure, which can be hampered by, among other things, cost and the remoteness of certain areas. In Africa, mobile phones have proved so successful that in many cases they have replaced fixed lines.

## 2. Internet

*Individual users*

Between 2004 and 2005, the number of Internet users worldwide, as well as Internet penetration, continued to grow, as shown in tables 1.3 and 1.4.[4] Tables 1.16 and 1.17 in the statistical annex show the number of Internet users and Internet penetration figures by country. As is the case with mobile phones, previous trends have continued:

- Although developed economies have lost some of their share of total Internet users, they still account for more than half of Internet users worldwide (see chart 1.2), more than a third of whom are in the United States.

- The digital divide between developed and developing economies is maintained in terms of Internet penetration. The average penetration for developing economies is boosted by the case of selected countries with exceptionally high penetration, such as the Republic of Korea or small islands. Approximately one third of developing economies have a penetration rate of less than 5 per cent.

- The gender digital divide is apparent, but more and better data are needed in order to understand its magnitude, especially in developing countries (see box 1.3).

- In 2005, Asia accounted for nearly 40 per cent of all Internet users, almost a third of whom were in mainland China. In fact, China is second only to the United States in terms of the number of Internet users worldwide. Although mainland China's penetration rate is only 8.6 per cent, Macao (China) and Hong Kong (China) have penetration rates of 36.9 per cent and 50.1 per cent, respectively. Taiwan Province of China has the very high penetration rate of 58.1 per cent. But the regional leaders in terms of penetration are the Republic of Korea (69.0 per cent) and Japan (66.6 per cent). Central Asian

## Chart 1.2

### Internet users
### by level of development

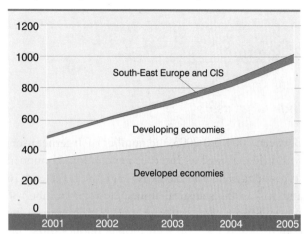

*Source:* UNCTAD calculations based on the ITU World Telecommunication Indicators Database, 2006.

countries have the lowest pene tration rates in the region.

- In 2005, Africa had the highest growth rates in terms of numbers of Internet users, since many countries start from very low levels, but it has the lowest penetration rate after Oceania. South Africa, Egypt and Nigeria account for approximately 14 per cent of African users each. South Africa and Egypt also have above average penetration rates with respect to the region.

- In Europe, almost 59 per cent of Internet users live in four Western European countries (Germany, United Kingdom, Italy and France).[5] The Russian Federation accounts for more than 60 per cent of users in SEECIS.

- In Latin America and the Caribbean, Brazil and Mexico accounted for over 60 per cent of Internet users in 2005. Another 25 per cent of users were located in Argentina, Chile, Colombia, Peru and Venezuela, all in South America. However, there were very high growth rates for Caribbean island countries and Central America. In terms of penetration, Caribbean islands also show the highest rates in the region, and Brazil has the highest penetration rate among the larger countries, at 19.5 per cent. It should be noted that a survey by the Brazilian Government conducted in August and September 2005 reported that 24.4 per cent of the population had accessed the Internet in the previous three months, usually at work or at home (Brazilian Internet Steering Committee, 2006).

### *Enterprise access to the Internet*

Internet access by enterprises is nearly universal in most developed countries (see table 1.5), with penetration rates reaching almost 100 per cent among large enterprises. Certain economic sectors are more connected than others, particularly the financial sector,

---

## Box 1.3

## Gender and Internet use

Men are more likely to use the Internet than women in OECD countries, with the exception of Finland and the United States (OECD, 2005a). In the EU, 38 per cent of European women regularly use the Internet (at least once a week), as opposed to 49 per cent of men.[1]

While there are gaps of similar magnitude in Internet access between men and women in some developing countries (for example, 4 per cent in Brazil), in most of those countries the gaps are more substantial, for example in Djibouti, Guinea, India, Nepal and Turkey. It would appear that the lower the penetration of ICT in developing countries, the larger the differences in gender access, with women at a disadvantage, but there are several exceptions (Orbicom, 2005). For example, the Netherlands and Mexico both have 40 per cent of female Internet users, but overall penetration in the Netherlands is 60 per cent, as opposed to less than 5 per cent in Mexico. In such cases there are cultural and social influences on the ability of women to access ICT, frequently country-specific ones, and policies to address the gender digital divide must take these influences into consideration.

The availability of data on individual access to the Internet disaggregated by gender is very limited. It is important to increase the availability and quality of disaggregated data on individual access to ICT, including the Internet, since such data can serve to assess public and private efforts to bridge national digital divides, such as the Republic of Korea's higher education programme to promote the participation of females in the ICT workforce (World Bank, 2005). In this connection, chapter 3 of this Report highlights the need for disaggregated data by gender, region and age in order to effectively inform pro-poor ICT policies and practices.

---

[1] Individual access data is not available for France, Ireland, Malta and Norway.

## Table 1.3 Internet users by region and level of development

| | 2001 | % change 2001–2002 | 2002 | % change 2002–2003 | 2003 | % change 2003–2004 | 2004 | % change 2004–2005 | 2005 |
|---|---|---|---|---|---|---|---|---|---|
| **World** | **490 773 008** | **25.7** | **618 038 617** | **16.3** | **717 381 946** | **19.0** | **854 041 719** | **19.5** | **1 020 614 866** |
| **Developed economies** | **342 797 199** | **15.5** | **395 818 444** | **7.8** | **426 734 196** | **12.5** | **479 924 204** | **10.7** | **531 289 219** |
| Asia | 50 700 000 | 20.7 | 61 220 000 | 4.8 | 64 140 000 | 5.0 | 67 360 000 | 32.4 | 89 173 852 |
| Europe | 125 172 191 | 17.6 | 147 263 444 | 14.8 | 169 124 796 | 13.1 | 191 273 204 | 7.4 | 205 412 718 |
| North America | 157 463 008 | 11.1 | 174 927 000 | 2.9 | 180 059 400 | 14.4 | 205 941 000 | 6.7 | 219 758 649 |
| Oceania | 9 462 000 | 31.1 | 12 408 000 | 8.1 | 13 410 000 | 14.5 | 15 350 000 | 10.4 | 16 944 000 |
| **Developing economies** | **139 154 246** | **49.3** | **207 776 692** | **28.3** | **266 677 707** | **26.6** | **337 645 107** | **30.6** | **441 132 301** |
| Africa | 6 478 700 | 66.8 | 10 805 156 | 45.4 | 15 711 500 | 47.7 | 23 213 421 | 52.5 | 35 389 128 |
| Asia | 102 951 221 | 48.8 | 153 198 459 | 29.2 | 197 894 654 | 26.4 | 250 121 471 | 26.4 | 316 233 484 |
| Latin America and the Caribbean | 29 581 925 | 47.2 | 43 547 477 | 21.2 | 52 783 353 | 21.2 | 63 976 215 | 39.3 | 89 135 132 |
| Oceania | 142 500 | 58.3 | 225 600 | 27.7 | 288 200 | 15.9 | 334 000 | 12.1 | 374 557 |
| **South-East Europe and CIS** | **8 821 563** | **52.4** | **13 443 481** | **78.3** | **23 970 043** | **52.2** | **36 472 408** | **32.1** | **48 193 346** |

*Source:* UNCTAD calculations based on the ITU World Telecommunication Indicators Database, 2006.

## Table 1.4 Internet penetration by region and level of development
(Internet users per 100 inhabitants)

| | 2001 | % change 2001–2002 | 2002 | % change 2002–2003 | 2003 | % change 2003–2004 | 2004 | % change 2004–2005 | 2005 |
|---|---|---|---|---|---|---|---|---|---|
| **World** | **7.9** | **24.2** | **9.8** | **14.9** | **11.3** | **17.6** | **13.2** | **18.1** | **15.6** |
| **Developed economies** | **35.9** | **14.8** | **41.2** | **7.2** | **44.2** | **11.8** | **49.4** | **10.1** | **54.4** |
| Asia | 38.0 | 20.4 | 45.7 | 4.5 | 47.8 | 4.8 | 50.1 | 32.1 | 66.1 |
| Europe | 26.3 | 17.2 | 30.9 | 14.4 | 35.3 | 12.7 | 39.8 | 7.0 | 42.5 |
| North America | 48.9 | 10.0 | 53.8 | 1.9 | 54.8 | 13.3 | 62.1 | 5.7 | 65.7 |
| Oceania | 40.9 | 29.7 | 53.0 | 6.9 | 56.6 | 13.2 | 64.1 | 9.2 | 70.1 |
| **Developing economies** | **2.8** | **47.2** | **4.2** | **26.5** | **5.3** | **24.8** | **6.6** | **28.8** | **8.5** |
| Africa | 0.7 | 63.3 | 1.2 | 42.4 | 1.7 | 44.7 | 2.4 | 49.3 | 3.6 |
| Asia | 3.0 | 46.9 | 4.4 | 27.6 | 5.6 | 24.8 | 6.9 | 24.9 | 8.7 |
| Latin America and the Caribbean | 5.5 | 45.1 | 7.9 | 19.5 | 9.5 | 19.6 | 11.3 | 37.5 | 15.5 |
| Oceania | 1.4 | 55.4 | 2.2 | 25.5 | 2.8 | 13.9 | 3.2 | 10.3 | 3.5 |
| **South-East Europe and CIS** | **2.6** | **52.8** | **4.0** | **78.8** | **7.2** | **52.5** | **11.0** | **32.5** | **14.6** |

*Source:* UNCTAD calculations based on the ITU World Telecommunication Indicators Database, 2006.

# Table 1.5 Internet penetration and website ownership, by enterprises in selected countries, 2004

*Enterprises with 10 or more employees*

| | Share of enterprises using the Internet | Share of enterprises with a website | |
|---|---|---|---|
| | | % of all enterprises | % of enterprises with Internet access |
| Japan (2003)[a] | 97.5 | 78.4 | 80.4 |
| Denmark | 97.4 | 80.9 | 83.1 |
| Iceland (2003) | 97.4 | 68.5 | 70.3 |
| Finland | 97.1 | 75.4 | 77.6 |
| Belgium | 96.0 | 67.6 | 70.4 |
| Sweden | 95.9 | 82.1 | 85.6 |
| Brazil (2005) | 95.1 | 56.2 | 59.1 |
| Germany | 94.1 | 72.4 | 76.9 |
| Rep. of Korea | 94.0 | 53.3 | 56.7 |
| Canada | 93.9 | 63.9 | 68.0 |
| Austria | 93.7 | 70.8 | 75.6 |
| Argentina[b] | 93.6 | 57.2 | 61.1 |
| Switzerland (2002)[c] | 92.0 | 64.0 | 69.6 |
| Ireland | 91.8 | 59.5 | 64.8 |
| Singaporc (2005) | 91.0 | 68.3 | 75.0 |
| Morocco (2005) | 90.6 | 46.7 | 51.5 |
| Australia[d] | 90.2 | 49.4 | 54.8 |
| Czech Republic | 90.1 | 60.9 | 67.6 |
| Netherlands | 88.5 | 65.5 | 74.1 |
| Italy | 87.4 | 44.1 | 50.5 |
| Greece | 87.4 | 49.0 | 56.0 |
| Spain (2003) | 87.4 | 39.7 | 45.5 |
| United Kingdom | 86.6 | 66.3 | 76.5 |
| Norway | 85.5 | 61.5 | 71.9 |
| Poland | 85.0 | 43.8 | 51.5 |
| Luxembourg (2003) | 85.0 | 58.4 | 68.7 |
| Hong Kong (2005) | 84.8 | 40.5 | 47.8 |
| New Zealand (2001)[c] | 84.3 | 41.7 | 49.5 |
| France (2003) | 82.9 | 26.3 | 31.7 |
| Hungary | 77.5 | 34.7 | 44.7 |
| Portugal | 77.3 | 29.4 | 38.1 |
| Slovakia | 71.3 | 46.7 | 65.5 |
| Costa Rica[e] | 69.9 | 10.3 | 14.7 |
| Macao (China) (2003) | 69.1 | 17.8 | 25.8 |
| Qatar (2005) | 68.4 | 67.8 | 99.0 |
| Russian Federation[f] | 68.2 | 24.0 | 35.2 |
| China (2005)[g] | 67.6 | 22.3 | 33.0 |
| Panama (2002) [h] | 65.7 | .. | .. |
| Thailand (2005)[i] | 64.1 | 32.7 | 51.0 |
| Andorra | 63.0 | 30.8 | 48.9 |
| Bulgaria | 62.6 | 24.3 | 38.9 |
| Philippines (2001)[j] | 62.4 | .. | .. |
| Cuba | 60.0 | 17.6 | 29.4 |

| | | | |
|---|---|---|---|
| **Mexico (2003)** | 55.4 | 7.2 | 13.0 |
| **Romania** | 52.3 | 19.9 | 38.0 |
| **Moldova**[g] | 51.6 | .. | .. |
| **Kazakhstan (2005)** | 45.5 | 8.4 | 18.5 |
| **Belarus (2005)**[g] | 37.6 | 10.2 | 27.2 |
| **Ukraine (2003)**[g] | 28.0 | .. | .. |
| **Kyrgyzstan (2005)**[k] | 25.1 | 8.4 | 33.2 |
| **Cameroon (2005)** | 25.1 | 12.1 | 48.3 |
| **Chile (2003)**[g] | 20.3 | 8.6 | 42.6 |
| **Azerbaijan (2005)** | 8.3 | 2.8 | 33.7 |
| **Paraguay (2002)**[b,h] | 5.7 | .. | .. |

**Notes:**

[a] Enterprises with 100 or more employees.

[b] Survey of the manufacturing sector only.

[c] Enterprises with 5 or more employees.

[d] Website includes a presence on another entity's web site.

[e] Enterprises with 10-249 employees.

[f] Enterprises with 50 or more employees.

[g] A breakdown by number of employees is not available, so the figure could include micro-enterprises with 0-9 employees.

[h] Provisional figures.

[i] Enterprises with 16 or more employees.

[j] Refers to establishments with average total employment of 20 or more.

[k] Of enterprises with computers.

*Source:* OECD (2006); UNCTAD e-business database (2006).

wholesale trade and real estate, renting and business services industries.[6, 7] In the EU, overall Internet access by enterprises with 10 or more employees is very high at 91 per cent, with Scandinavian countries showing the highest penetration rates (Finland with 98 per cent, Denmark with 97 per cent and Sweden with 96 per cent).[8] Slovenia also has very high penetration at 96 per cent.

Internet access by enterprises in the developing world is less uniform, reflecting a very broad range of Internet penetration rates. There is, however, a positive correlation coefficient of 0.54 between Internet penetration and ownership of websites by enterprises with Internet access.[9] This suggests that the level of ICT knowledge in the economy might also be an important determinant of Internet use by enterprises, since setting up a website demands more than basic computer literacy. Even more, it could matter that the characteristics of a country's economy and the structure of the enterprise sector result in differing predispositions for Internet use by enterprises. Enterprises involved in more knowledge-intensive production tend to have a greater demand for Internet access and so do larger enterprises compared with smaller firms.

Concerning the type or mode of Internet access, there are substantial differences between developed

countries, with an ever-increasing share of broadband connections, and developing countries, where dial-up is still prevalent (see chart 1.3). The changing nature of Internet modes of access is another dimension of the international digital divide. Broadband access deserves special attention for its potential to enable more sophisticated e-business, positively impacting on competitiveness and productivity at the firm level, this in turn having an impact on economic growth. The next section will take a more detailed look at this issue.

## 3.   Broadband spread and its potential

Access to the Internet via broadband is important for the development of countries' information societies.[10] Apart from the speed, the main characteristics of advanced broadband technologies that make them so desirable for developing countries wishing to advance technologically are that they are ever-present, always on, flexible, less costly and more secure. Individuals are able to obtain more services and a richer experience from the Internet, with greater ease; enterprises are able to add value to their online interactions with customers and suppliers and make them more efficient; and Governments are able to enhance the e-government experience for their citizens. Some of the current broadband

## Chart 1.3

## Modes of Internet access by enterprises in selected developing countries, 2005 or latest available year

*Enterprises with 10 or more employees*

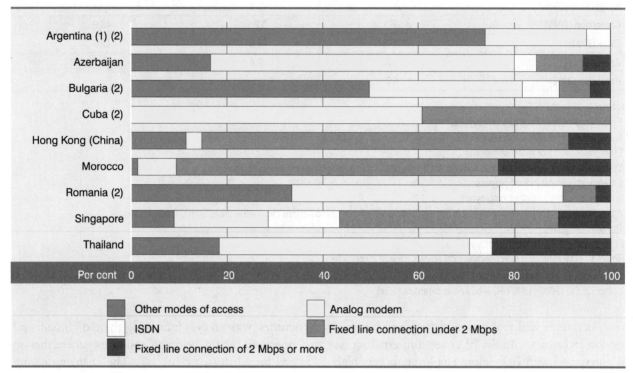

**Notes:**

(1) Survey of the manufacturing sector only.
(2) Reference year 2004.
*Source:* UNCTAD e-business database, 2006

trends (tables 1.18 and 1.19 in the statistical annex show data for selected countries on broadband subscribers and penetration) are as follows:

- Broadband is increasingly available worldwide (38 per cent of all Internet subscribers in 2004) (ITU, 2006), although some countries and regions have more affordable and thus more rapidly growing broadband connections.

- In the OECD countries (most of which, but not all, are classified as developed) broadband subscribers increased by almost 15 per cent in the last half of 2005 to 158 million. In terms of broadband penetration, the leaders were Iceland and the Republic of Korea, both with more than 25 per cent penetration. At the other end of the scale, Slovakia, Mexico, Turkey and Greece have less than 3 per cent penetration each.

- The United States has the largest total number of broadband subscribers at 49 million, with a penetration of 16.3 per cent. Although broadband becomes more common and continues to rapidly gain ground over dial-up at the household level, the United States is still lagging behind most of Western Europe and some Asian countries (Lopez, 2006).

- All non-OECD developing economies for which data on broadband are available have been showing very low penetration rates, with varying growth rates. The only exceptions are in Asia. The Special Administrative Regions of China (Hong Kong and Macao), as well as Taiwan Province of China, have a relatively small subscriber base but penetration rates of 23.6 per cent, 14.8 per cent and 20.2 per cent, respectively. This is the reverse of the situation in mainland China, which had the largest number of broadband subscribers among developing economies, but very low penetration (2.9 per cent). The Republic of Korea and Singapore continued to be outliers in 2005, with 25.5 per cent and 15.4 per cent penetration, respectively.

Growth in broadband access and penetration in recent years (see chart 1.4), particularly in developed countries, is due to competition and declining prices. In OECD countries, for example, users paid on average $9.42 less in 2004 than in 2002 for a 514 Kbp increase in their DSL connection (OECD, 2005c). On the other hand, the monthly charge for a broadband connection in low-income countries can be more than 10 times that of high-income and middle-income countries (World Bank, 2006).[11] It should be noted that the United States is lagging slightly behind other developed countries owing to insufficient competition, since choice of local access to broadband is usually limited to a few providers. Developed countries have also progressed in terms of the available connection speed. While the basic broadband is defined as equal to, or greater than 256 Kbps, most countries already offer minimum speeds of 512 Kbps. In France, Japan and Sweden, premium DSL services at 10 Mbps or more are available for residential users (OECD, 2005b).

## Chart 1.4

### Broadband penetration in selected economies (%)

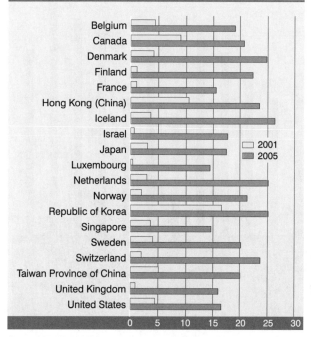

*Source:* ITU World Telecommunication Indicators database, 2005.

Apart from market factors such as pricing, offers and competition, broadband expansion depends on the available infrastructure. In 2005, 62 per cent of broadband Internet subscribers in OECD countries used DSL, 31 per cent used Cable Modem and 7 per cent used other types of connection.[12] In the European Union, DSL represents 80 per cent of all broadband subscriptions. The development of broadband by building on pre-existing networks in the EU15 has determined the prevalence of DSL. In the new EU member countries, where there are lower levels of PC and fixed-line penetration, broadband development could build on other types of network, such as cable, and even mobile or wireless.[13] The latter are particularly interesting for improving access in rural areas, where they can make better economic sense.[14] Previous infrastructure has also led to the prevalence of cable in the United States (65 per cent of broadband connections). Other broadband technologies are less prevalent, with some country exceptions, such as Japan with a high proportion of fibre-to-the-premises (FTTP), and Persian Gulf countries with their fibre optic backbone.

In many developing countries, because of the lack of economies of scale and infrastructure, the incentive to expand broadband outside urban areas is diminished. Wireless technology and satellites can help circumvent the cost of infrastructure for remote or rural areas, or for areas without a critical mass of users. Such is the case of eChoupal in India (see box 1.4), which uses very small aperture terminals (VSAT).[15] VSAT satellites may offer developing countries the possibility of increasing the availability of bandwidth and reducing its cost (UNCTAD, 2005). Some countries have no choice but satellite, such as Uganda, which currently lacks connections to submarine fibre optic cable systems.[16]

Governments have an important role to play in improving access to broadband through infrastructure and policy. In the Republic of Korea, the Government's vision of development through the ICT sector and ICT-enabled services is dependent on broadband deployment. The European Union's i2010 strategy focuses on promoting broadband networks, which are considered crucial for e-business, economic growth and employment. It aims to reduce the digital divide between urban and rural areas in Europe (27 per cent penetration among households in densely populated areas as opposed to 15 per cent in sparsely populated areas), including through public funding grants to invest in broadband infrastructure. For example, such funding was endorsed for Latvia in 2006, with the aim of promoting economic development of its rural areas.[17]

Government policy can either encourage or be a disincentive to competition, and thus have an impact on availability and prices. For example, while the Government of the Republic of Korea enforces competition and encourages new entrants in the telecommunications market, the United States has allowed growing consolidation of the industry. The result is that there is a wider choice and better offers for customers in the Republic of Korea than there are for United States customers.

Prominent researchers have warned that the United States will lose its competitive edge in technology if it does not come up with a national policy to promote broadband uptake and competition.[18] In response, at the time of the drafting of this report, the United States Senate had started hearings to review broadband legislation (the Communications, Consumers' Choice, and Broadband Deployment Act of 2006), which could increase competition in broadband services and provide incentives to bring broadband to unserved areas of the country.

Finally, Governments can promote not only supply of, but also demand for, broadband. In Europe, although 62 per cent of rural households could subscribe to broadband (the infrastructure is available), only 8 per

cent do so (ECTA, 2006). Governments could take measures to aggregate local demand, develop relevant content and services, and enhance skills. In Spain, for example, a Government observatory has suggested that public policies to promote digital literacy, and the inclusion of ICTs in education and administration, should be a priority for encouraging the development of broadband in that country (GAPTEL, 2004).

### Enterprise access to broadband

Some broadband trends among enterprises are highlighted below:

- Enterprises in OECD countries are increasingly adopting broadband platforms to connect to the Internet, and affordable broadband connectivity has been linked to the increased use of ICTs by SMEs (OECD, 2004).

- In the EU, where 63 per cent of enterprises have broadband access, there are prospects for continued growth and broadband has had a positive impact on certain economic activities, particularly business process outsourcing. Enterprise broadband connectivity grew

## Chart 1.5

## Enterprise broadband penetration in selected EU countries

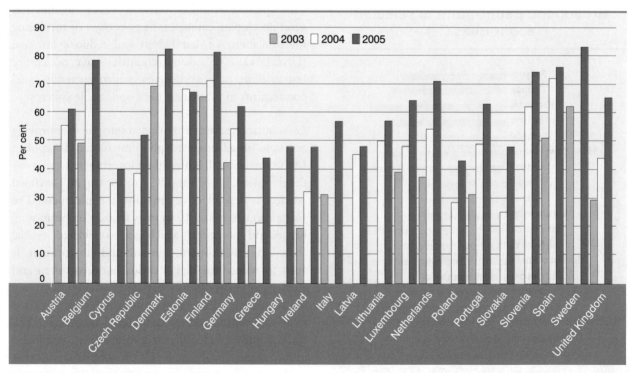

**Notes:** Missing columns reflect data not available.
*Source:* Eurostat, 2006.

significantly (from 53 per cent in 2004 to 63 per cent in 2005), with the highest penetration in Scandinavia (83 per cent in Sweden, 82 per cent in Denmark and 81 per cent in Finland) and the lowest penetration in Cyprus (40 per cent) (see chart 1.5).

- As both an OECD country and a developing economy, the Republic of Korea remains an exceptional case in enterprise broadband penetration. It was the leader among OECD member States and worldwide, with 92 per cent of enterprises having a broadband connection. Singapore is the other exception, as broadband Internet access among enterprises has overtaken narrowband: 55 per cent for all enterprises, with the percentage rising to 77 per cent for enterprises with 10 or more employees (IDA, 2005).

- For other developing economies, Internet modes of access other than broadband are still the norm, in particular dial-up modems, and there is still no clear picture regarding the growth rate of broadband access among enterprises.

While enterprises' access to the Internet adds value by improving their connectivity with suppliers and clients, and making them available to a wider market, including international markets, broadband increases the capacity of enterprises to deliver through the Internet. Corporate analysts estimate that broadband could contribute hundreds of billions of dollars a year to the GDP of developed countries in the next few years, and liken it to water and electricity as "the next great utility" (Whisler and Saksena, 2003). There is growing recognition that broadband can help enterprises maximize the benefits of ICTs and conduct e-business (including optimizing internal business processes).

For example, a German study estimates that if in the coming years broadband growth in Germany is maintained at an annual rate between 15 and 25 per cent, the deployment of new services and economic activities could result in the creation of 265,000 jobs and in GDP growth of up to 46 billion euros by 2010 (Fornefeld et al., 2006). Studies in the United Kingdom indicate that enterprises that use broadband are more likely to have multiple business links, and enterprises with more links tend to have higher labour productivity (Clayton and Goodridge, 2004).

A study in the United States indicates that broadband clearly has a positive economic effect (Gillett et al.,

2006).[19] Researchers linked broadband adoption at the community level to quicker growth in employment, and in the number of enterprises in IT-intensive sectors and overall. However, they also acknowledge that more study and better data are needed at the enterprise level in order to measure the impact of broadband on business and of ICT on national economic performance. Such data should reflect not only the availability of ICT (supply side), including broadband, but also how it is adopted and used (demand side).

However, in certain developing regions, such as Western Asia, most enterprises still need to become aware of the potential of broadband and related applications, and of the offers of application service providers (ESCWA, 2005).

## What are the sectors that stand to benefit more from broadband?

Broadband can enable or enhance the adoption of certain applications that have an impact on enterprise productivity. Broadband is much faster than dial-up Internet access, it is always on, and does not block telephone lines. In particular, broadband enhances existing multimedia applications, for example by broadening access to online video content, but it can be expected that new applications and business models could continue to emerge as broadband access grows. VoIP is an example of a broadband service with cost-saving potential for firms (and individuals) that is slowly gaining ground. However, in some cases, such as Singapore, it appears that there is not much difference between the types of Internet applications used by companies with broadband access as opposed to those enterprises that have slower access (IDA, 2005).

Several Governments, for example in the European Union, promote the enhanced use of broadband in the health sector, government, education, and the farm and food sectors (mainly in rural areas). The eChoupal case (see box 1.4), in India, is a good example of broadband adoption being relevant and beneficial to a non-ICT-intensive economic sector such as the agroindustry. However, it is those industries that make more use of multimedia applications or that have digital products that are the first to benefit from the enhanced experience that can be enabled by broadband. For example, the online music business has experienced recent significant growth worldwide, from $380 million in 2004 to $1.1 billion in 2005, with prospects for continued growth (IFPI, 2006). In the EU, 70 per cent of consumers that downloaded music from

## Box 1.4

## Broadband for enterprise efficiency in India: The eChoupal[1]

The role of broadband in India's offshore ICT-enabled services sector is well known. But it also holds significant promise for enterprise competitiveness in other economic sectors, including those that are anchored in rural areas, such as agriculture. Domestic efficiencies driven by ICT also have an impact on export competitiveness. The eChoupal project (www.echoupal.com), of the Indian corporation ITC, one of India's largest exporters of agricultural products, is a success story in this sense. It successfully used ICT to increase the efficiency of its agricultural supply chain, reduce costs, eliminate intermediaries, and improve price transparency and produce quality. The eChoupal has created shareholder value for the ITC Corporation while bringing economic and other benefits to small farmers.

The eChoupal started in June 2000 by integrating a computer with an Internet connection to six choupals (a traditional community gathering in farming villages) of soybean farmers in Madhya Pradesh, in Central India. A simple portal gave farmers access to information that significantly improved their work, and which until then was unavailable (local weather forecasts, crop price lists in nearby markets, better sowing techniques). The immediate benefits in terms of productivity encouraged farmers to sell directly to the ITC Corporation, which could pay a better price for a better product. The Corporation's warehouses that collected the crop eventually also served to sell to the farmers inputs such as fertilizers, agrichemicals, and seeds, with the Corporation also offering them credit and insurance.

Training was provided to eChoupal hosts (usually literate farmers, with a respected, prominent place in the community).

The eChoupal set-up is as follows:

- PC with operating system platform and multimedia applications;
- UPS and solar-energy battery back-up;
- Printer;
- VSAT connection of up to 256 Kbps;
- Approximately $6,000 investment in hardware, communication, software, staff, training and travel;
- Approximately $100 of yearly maintenance.

The ITC Corporation is recovers its investment within one to three years of deployment thanks to efficiency gains in the supply chain. Since the eChoupal's initial deployment, ITC's market share has grown from 8 to 12 per cent, and procurement costs have decreased by 2.5 per cent. At the same time, farmers have been able to obtain prices for their crops that are on average 2.5 per cent higher than through traditional channels, by improving their knowledge of market prices, their crop yields and decreasing waste.

The success of the soybean eChoupal encouraged the ITC Corporation to expand to other commodities. As at May 2006, the Corporation reported that the eChoupal programme had reached "more than 3.5 million farmers growing a range of crops — soybean, coffee, wheat, rice, pulses, shrimp — in over 31,000 villages through 5372 kiosks across seven states (Madhya Pradesh, Karnataka, Andhra Pradesh, Uttar Pradesh, Maharashtra, Rajasthan and Kerala)" (www.itcportal.com). The eChoupal aims to reach 100,000 villages by the year 2010.

The use of broadband in the eChoupal programme has made possible an unprecedented level of interactivity between the ITC Corporation and its suppliers that helps build and consolidate direct commercial relationships, improves terms of business, and encourages the exchange of ideas to enhance the quality of the product.

---

[1] For further details on the eChoupal see Annamalai and Rao (2003) and chapter 8 in Austin and Bradley (2005).

online music vendors to their personal computers had broadband at home (Jennings, 2006). SMEs in ICT-enabled services will clearly depend on broadband. But in other sectors, medium-sized enterprises will be more likely to implement e-business applications dependent on broadband than small companies.

Broadband adoption in the EU appears to be more relevant for the IT services, publishing, pharmaceutical, automotive and aerospace sectors (E-Business Watch, 2005). Future broadband applications could be in marketing and sales, and for certain types of worker, broadband will facilitate working from home. In the European manufacturing industry, broadband is a key

enabler of online procurement, which helps enterprises manage their supply chain. Supply-chain integration and the streamlining of procurement processes are common objectives in those industries for which e-business solutions are attractive. Online procurement has become a part of everyday business and is one of the most frequently adopted e-business applications.

## 4.   E-commerce

More and more enterprises worldwide are conducting e-commerce, understood as placing and receiving orders online. The bulk of e-commerce worldwide occurs between businesses (B2B), although business-to-consumer trade (B2C) is growing steadily among developed countries. In the United States, B2B accounted for 93 per cent of all e-commerce in 2004 (US Census Bureau, 2006), with B2B defined as transactions by manufacturers and merchant wholesalers. The volume of European B2B online trade has increased, with almost half of firms' purchases occurring online (European Commission, 2005b).

The diffusion of e-commerce depends on a variety of factors. Critical for the decision to purchase online are the availability of products on the Internet, which must be suitable for online commerce, and a supply price that is less than or equal to the sum of the market price of conventionally sold items, the difference in transaction costs, and the difference in risk premiums between e-commerce and conventional transactions. The technological, organizational and environmental contexts are also important for enterprises to decide whether to sell their products online (Zhu et al., 2006). Limitations include capital and human capital shortages, lack of complementary infrastructure, lack of regulatory and security frameworks, and issues of trust in online business practices. Moreover, less widespread Internet use in developing countries usually means a small relative size of the domestic market for Internet sales.

Online sales and purchases are now commonplace in all developed economies, but vary across industries and countries. In the OECD countries, in 2004, the share of

enterprises purchasing online ranged between 20 and 60 per cent averaged over the entire economy in 2004.[20] The share of enterprises selling their products online ranged between 10 and 20 per cent. Enterprises from the real estate sector, renting and business activities, as well as the wholesale and retail sectors, are more likely than other industries to purchase online, while online

## Chart 1.7

### Enterprises in selected EU countries placing orders online

Enterprises with 10 or more employees.

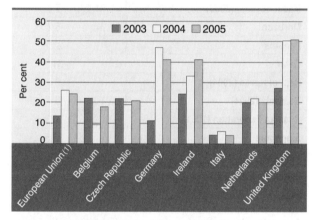

**Notes:** (1) 2003 refers to EU15; 2004 and 2005 refer to EU25.
*Source:* Eurostat (2006).

selling is generally most prevalent in manufacturing, wholesale and retail trade, and tourism. Among EU countries, an average of 12 per cent of enterprises received orders online, and 24 per cent placed orders online, although there were wide differences among countries (see charts 1.6 and 1.7).[21]

In other sectors, demand appears to be a principal constraint on increased electronic transactions, as customers prefer conventional sales channels. Furthermore, manufacturing and wholesale tend to be dominated by larger firms, for which necessary investments in e-commerce infrastructure are easier to afford.

The levels of online purchasing and selling also vary greatly among developing countries (see table 1.6). Contrary to the usual pattern throughout the developed economies, in which online purchases outnumber online sales, data from some developing and transition countries show the opposite situation. This can be partly explained by an overrepresentation of certain sectors in surveys, as is the case for the manufacturing sector in Argentina and Kazakhstan, or other business activities in the real estate sector (ISIC Rev. 3.1 category K74) in the case of Romania. As regards

## Chart 1.6

### Enterprises in selected EU countries receiving orders online

Enterprises with 10 or more employees.

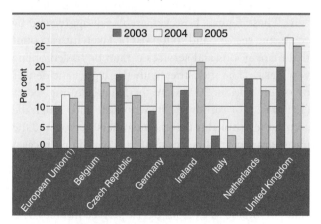

**Notes:** (1) 2003 refers to EU15; 2004 and 2005 refer to EU25.
*Source:* Eurostat (2006).

## Table 1.6

## E-commerce in selected economies, 2005 or latest available year

| | Selling online<br>% of all enterprises | Purchasing online<br>% of all enterprises | Delivering online<br>% of all enterprises |
|---|---|---|---|
| Argentina (2004)[a] | 37.4 | 36.5 | 4.5 |
| Brazil | 27.1 | 28.5 | .. |
| Bulgaria (2004) | 2.9 | 7.0 | 1.1 |
| Cameroon | .. | .. | 1.7 |
| Chile (2003)[b] | 1.2 | 1.8 | .. |
| China[b] | 9.1 | 8.1 | 7.2 |
| Kazakhstan | 13.1 | 13.7 | .. |
| Kyrgyzstan[c] | .. | .. | 1.6 |
| Macao (China) (2003) | 7.4 | 8.9 | .. |
| Morocco | 5.2 | 9.0 | 9.0 |
| Panama[d] | 23.1 | 29.7 | .. |
| Qatar | 34.9 | 28.3 | .. |
| Rep. of Korea (2004) | 6.8 | 23.9 | .. |
| Romania (2004) | 5.4 | 2.6 | 1.9 |
| Russian Federation (2004) [e] | 20.2 | 23.2 | 4.3 |
| Singapore | 13.5 | 30.8 | .. |
| Thailand[f] | 7.2 | 8.7 | .. |

Enterprises with 10 or more employees.

**Notes:**
[a] Survey of the manufacturing sector only.
[b] A breakdown by number of employees is not available, so the figure could include micro-enterprises with 0-9 employees.
[c] Of enterprises with computers.
[d] Provisional figures.
[e] Enterprises with 50 or more employees.
[f] Enterprises with 15 or more employees.

*Source:* UNCTAD e-business database, 2006

the manufacturing sector, the reason for the lower incidence of online purchases would require further research on e-commerce at the different stages of the value chain, but it could be that in some emerging markets B2B is less developed for intermediate goods than for final products.

There is much room for growth regarding the weight of e-commerce in the total turnover of economies, even in developed countries. For example, online sales represented only 2 per cent of all sales in Australia, and 1 per cent in Canada (OECD, 2005a). However, aggregated industry data show that in manufacturing industries, hotels, and the wholesale and retail trade, online sales represent a higher share of the total turnover than in other sectors. In the United States, the aggregated value of e-commerce in the manufacturing, wholesale and retail trade, and selected services sectors, accounts for nearly 10 per cent of the total revenue of those sectors; online sales play a particularly important role in manufacturing and in the wholesale and retail trade (see chart 1.8).

In the European Union, online sales account for an estimated 2.5 per cent of the gross output value of goods and services in 2005, although there are notable differences among countries. There are clear leaders, such as Ireland (10.1 per cent of all sales), Denmark (4.4 per cent in 2004), the United Kingdom (4.1 per cent) and Germany (3.1 per cent), while in several other EU economies the share of online sales was close to zero. These figures, however, are not disaggregated by economic sectors, and so it must be taken into account that many goods and services cannot be traded online very easily. The industries with the higher incidences of online sales in 2005 were the manufacturing sector (13 per cent of turnover), the wholesale and retail trade sector, the hospitality (hotels and others) sector, and the transport sector (8 per cent of turnover in each case) (see chart 1.9). Furthermore, less than one third of the EU enterprises that sold online also received online payments. Although there are virtually no data on the value of online sales from developing economies, it is not disputed that it accounts for a very small share of overall sales.

## Chart 1.8

### Online sales as a proportion of total turnover in the United States, selected industries

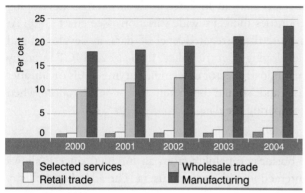

*Source:* US Bureau of Census (2006).

## Chart 1.9

### Online sales as a proportion of total turnover in the EU

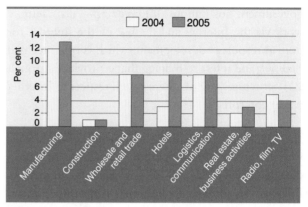

*Source:* Eurostat, 2006.

## Chart 1.10

### Enterprises using intranet, 2005 or latest available year

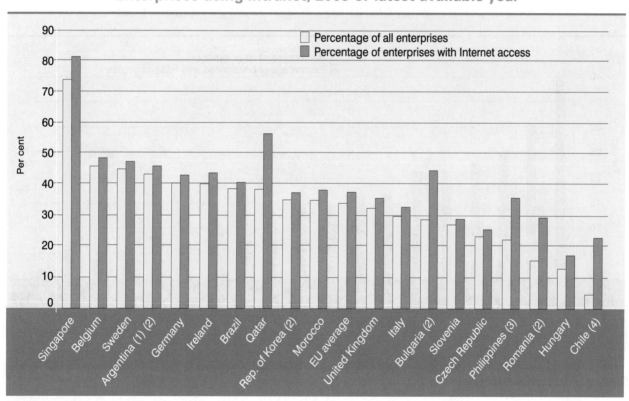

Enterprises with 10 or more employees.

**Notes:**

(1) Survey of the manufacturing sector only.
(2) Reference year is 2004.
(3) Reference year is 2001. Refers to establishments with average total employment of 20 or more.
(4) Reference year is 2003. A breakdown by number of employees is not available, so the figure could include micro-enterprises with 0-9 employees.

*Source:* UNCTAD e-business database, 2006 and Eurostat (2006).

## 5.   Other e-business

Other e-business refers to the use of the Internet for *internal business processes* and for interactions with government institutions (*e-government*). Also, remote work via the Internet and the use of the Internet for human resources development, which is often termed *e-learning* and refers to training that is provided through ICT structures, are of interest with respect to Internet use in enterprises.

In 2003, sharing and editing documents collaboratively was the by far most important e-business activity in developed countries (30–40 per cent of enterprises), followed by online applications supporting human resource management (15–30 per cent of enterprises).[22] There are no available data on such e-business activities from developing countries. Therefore, the presence of an intranet is used as a proxy in order to compare

developing countries and developed countries (in this case, the EU). An intranet indicates the existence of the technical prerequisites for carrying out internal business processes online. Accordingly, 34 per cent of enterprises (excluding the financial sector) in the EU had an intranet in 2005. Across developing countries there are wide variations (see chart 1.10). At a more disaggregated level of data, in developed and developing countries alike, firm size and ICT intensity per industry sector determine varying levels of intranet use and should be taken into consideration when comparing the data.

The use of an extranet can indicate a more evolved e-business capability from an intranet, since it allows interaction with external users. The added complexity means that usually there are fewer enterprises using extranets than intranets (see chart 1.11). Trends for extranet use for either developed or developing countries are still to be established, since the available

### Chart 1.11

### Enterprises using extranet, 2005 or latest available year

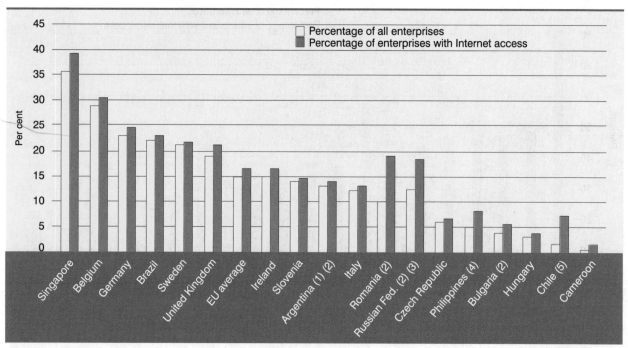

Enterprises with 10 or more employees.

**Notes:**

(1) Survey of the manufacturing sector only.
(2) Reference year is 2004.
(3) Enterprises with 50 or more employees.
(4) Reference year is 2001. Refers to establishments with average total employment of 20 or more.
(5) Reference year is 2003. A breakdown by number of employees is not available, so the figure could include micro-enterprises with 0-9 employees.

*Source:* UNCTAD e-business database, 2006 and Eurostat, 2006

time series is too short. In the EU, however, there was a slight growth in the proportion of enterprises with an extranet from 12 per cent in 2004 to 15 per cent 2005.

Enterprises can use the Internet for other e-business activities, such as e-banking and e-government. They can also provide customer services, although there are varying definitions of what these services cover (whether they involve a transaction or simply the availability of certain online content), and deliver digital products, but data on these activities are still very limited. Among the small set of developing economies for which information is available, some countries appear to have a demand constraint on Internet banking (when enterprises with Internet access have rates similar to those of developed countries, but the overall participation is low) or a supply constraint (when among the enterprises with

Internet access, Internet banking is not widespread) (see chart 1.12).

With respect to the use of the Internet for interaction with public authorities (e-government), the behaviour of enterprises often differs a great deal from the behaviour of households in the same country. In developed countries, where Internet access penetration among enterprises is nearly universal, neither the number of available online public services nor the Internet penetration rates in the population seem to matter significantly for enterprise use rates. Within the European Union, both the availability of online public services and Internet penetration are lower in the new member States, which nevertheless rank highest with respect to the diffusion of online transactions with government institutions among the enterprises (European Commission, 2005a, p. 23).

## Chart 1.12

## Enterprises using the Internet for Internet banking or accessing other financial services, 2005 or latest available year

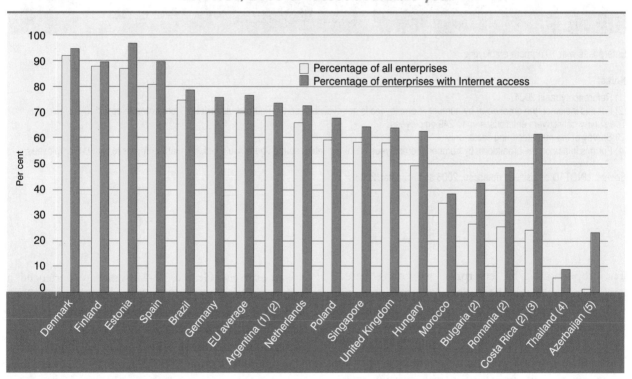

Enterprises with 10 or more employees.

**Notes:**

(1) Survey of the manufacturing sector only.

(2) Reference year 2004.

(3) For this indicator, the breakdown by number of employees is not available, so the figure could include micro-enterprises with 0-9 employees. The survey only covers enterprises up to 249 employees.

(4) Enterprises with 16 or more employees.

(5) For this indicator, the breakdown by number of employees is not available, so the figure could include micro-enterprises with 0-9 employees.

*Source:* UNCTAD e-business database, 2006 and Eurostat, 2006

## Chart 1.13

## Enterprises using the Internet for transactions with public authorities, 2005 or latest available year

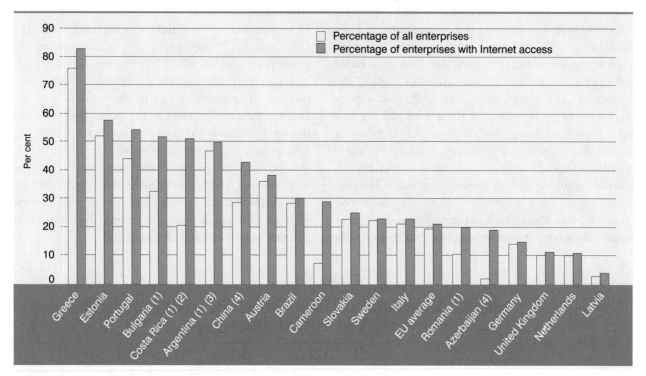

Enterprises with 10 or more employees.

**Notes:**

(1) Reference year is 2004.
(2) For this indicator, the breakdown by number of employees is not available, so the figure could include micro-enterprises with 0-9 employees. The survey only covers enterprises up to 249 employees.
(3) Survey of the manufacturing sector only.
(4) For this indicator, the breakdown by number of employees is not available, so the figure could include micro-enterprises with 0-9 employees.

*Source:* UNCTAD e-business database, 2006 and Eurostat, 2006

The proportion of EU enterprises with more than 10 employees in all but the financial sectors interacting with government institutions over the Internet for full electronic case handling was 19 per cent in 2005, 16 per cent in 2004 and 12 per cent in 2003 (EU-15). This reflects, on EU average, a continuing diffusion of e-government practices in the private sector. However, the diffusion of this form of e-government differs remarkably from country to country. While the diffusion of e-government practices among enterprises continues to increase in the EU average, this is not a universal trend for all individual member States. This is certainly also a result of the fact that the introduction of online transaction procedures is often economy-wide at discrete points in time, but concerns only clearly defined but possibly also varying subsets

of enterprises. Greece, for instance, experienced a significant jump from 40 to 70 per cent between 2003 and 2004, reflecting the committed promotion of e-government by the Greek authorities in its Operational Program for the Information Society (OPIS) (Boufeas, Halaris and Kokkinou, 2004). Far more widespread than online transactions with public authorities is the use of the Internet for obtaining government information.

The figures available for developing and transition countries deliver a mixed picture. In some cases, such as Azerbaijan, Bulgaria and Cameroon, the number of enterprises using the Internet to obtain government information does not exceed the number of enterprises actually completing transactions with government institutions online.

## Chart 1.14

## Enterprises using the Internet to obtain information from public authorities, 2005 or latest available year

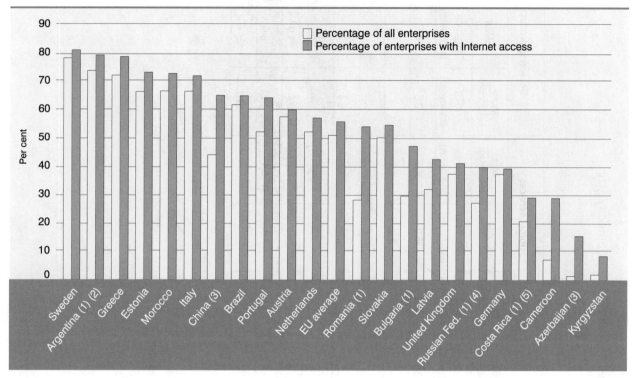

Enterprises with 10 or more employees.

**Notes:**

(1) Reference year is 2004.
(2) Survey of the manufacturing sector only.
(3) For this indicator, the breakdown by number of employees is not available, so the figure could include micro-enterprises with 0-9 employees.
(4) Enterprises with 50 or more employees.
(5) For this indicator, the breakdown by number of employees is not available, so the figure could include micro-enterprises with 0-9 employees. The survey only covers enterprises up to 249 employees.

*Source:* UNCTAD e-business database, 2006 and Eurostat, 2006

As regards other Internet uses facilitating business operations, the most popular forms of e-business are always those that will generate returns and profitability, or add value to the business, which in turn depends on the specific circumstances in a country or region. New data have been made available by Eurostat on remote work and e-learning implementation in European enterprises. In 2005, in 19 per cent of the enterprises surveyed in the EU some employees were working from a distance, using the Internet to connect with their company (16 per cent in 2004). Remote work is spearheaded by the Scandinavian countries. Also, up until 2005 on average 21 per cent of enterprises with more than 10 employees in the EU made use of e-learning techniques. For all EU member States these figures have been increasing or remaining roughly equal over the past few years.

SMEs constitute the majority of enterprises and employment in developing countries, and thus their access to and use of ICTs deserves special attention.[23] The Internet can provide SMEs with market and trade information, and reduce the cost of communication with customers and suppliers. SMEs can also use ICTs for e-business applications, although they have a lower capacity than large enterprises to adopt ICTs, usually owing to fewer resources for ICT investment and also because of less accessibility to e-business know-how.

Although there is not much difference in the penetration of ICTs such as the Internet between SMEs and large enterprises in developed countries, as a general rule there is a gap in their use of e-business applications. The gap between SMEs and large enterprises tends to widen the more complex the application. Although

## Table 1.7
## Use of the Internet for e-business activities broken down by company size, 2005 or latest available year

| | Internet banking | | | E-government | | | Online customer services | | | Delivering products online | | |
|---|---|---|---|---|---|---|---|---|---|---|---|---|
| | Micro-enterprises (0–9 employees) | SMEs (10–249 employees) | Large enterprises (250 or more employees) | Micro-enterprises (0–9 employees) | SMEs (10–249 employees) | Large enterprises (250 or more employees) | Micro-enterprises (0–9 employees) | SMEs (10–249 employees) | Large enterprises (250 or more employees) | Micro-enterprises (0–9 employees) | SMEs (10–249 employees) | Large enterprises (250 or more employees) |
| **Argentina (2004)[a]** | 25.0 | 67.0 | 82.6 | 12.5 | 44.6 | 59.6 | 19.4 | 35.3 | 36.6 | 2.8 | 4.5 | 4.2 |
| **Bulgaria (2004)** | .. | 25.6 | 56.8 | .. | 31.4 | 65.2 | .. | 3.5 | 8.4 | .. | 1.1 | 2.7 |
| **Kazakhstan** | .. | .. | .. | .. | .. | .. | 10.0 | 17.8 | 31.7 | .. | .. | .. |
| **Kyrgyzstan[b]** | | .. | .. | .. | .. | .. | .. | .. | .. | 0.4 | 1.4 | 4.2 |
| **Morocco[c]** | 8.1 | 33.0 | 50.0 | .. | .. | .. | .. | .. | .. | .. | .. | .. |
| **Romania** | 5.2 | 24.4 | 58.9 | 0.3 | 10.0 | 21.8 | 1.0 | 3.0 | 5.4 | 0.4 | 1.9 | 2.4 |
| **Russian Fed. (2004)[d]** | .. | .. | .. | .. | .. | .. | .. | .. | .. | 1.2 | 3.4 | 5.6 |
| **Singapore** | 25.0 | 57.7 | 63.0 | .. | .. | .. | .. | .. | .. | 16.0 | 35.6 | 53.0 |

**Notes:**
[a] Survey of the manufacturing sector only.
[b] Of enterprises with computers.
[c] Survey does not cover enterprises with fewer than 5 employees.
[d] Micro-enterprises refer to 0-49 employees; SMEs refer to 50-199 employees; large enterprises refer to +199 employees

*Source:* UNCTAD e-business database, 2006.

the reasons for this vary depending on the economic sectors and among countries, SMEs might also find that e-business applications for internal business processes might not be suitable for their size and industry,[24] or are not affordable. For example, only 9 per cent of EU enterprises with 10 to 49 employees use Enterprise Resource Planning systems (ERPs), as opposed to 59 per cent of enterprises with more than 250 employees (E-Business Watch, 2005).

Information from developing countries on the use of e-business for internal business processes is very limited, but data on the use of the Internet for business applications seem to confirm the trend in developed countries in terms of the gap between SMEs and large enterprises, with some exceptions (see table 1.7). It should be noted that, unlike most developed countries, several developing countries collect data on Internet e-business in micro-enterprises (0–9 employees), which are important actors in their economies and societies.

## C.   The ICT sector

This section presents trends related to two indicators on the ICT sector as identified by the core list of ICT indicators of the Partnership on Measuring ICT for Development (2005). More specifically, it shows ICT employment and value-added corresponding to the manufacturing and service industries capturing, transmitting or displaying data and information electronically. The two indicators measure the size of the ICT sector within the business sector both as a contribution to employment and as a share in production. The statistics presented in this section use data from the OECD and UNCTAD. The ICT sector is based on the OECD definition.[25]

Generally speaking, the data show that after the contraction in the early 2000s, developed countries experienced an increase in both value added and employment in the ICT sector in 2003. This increase in demand and supply in the developed countries' ICT sector opened up new prospects for developing country business partners.

*Business sector workforce in the ICT sector*

In 2003, the ICT sector represented 5.5 per cent of total business employment in developed countries and was a source of employment growth (OECD,

2006). ICT sector employment grew by over 8 per cent annually between 1995 and 2003, which represented an additional 1 million people employed. The European Union accounted for 37 per cent of total employment, the United States for around one third and Japan for 15 per cent (OECD, 2004). The majority (66 per cent) of those working in the ICT sector were employed in the services sectors, a figure that corresponds to the

## Chart 1.15

## Share of ICT sector workforce in total business sector workforce

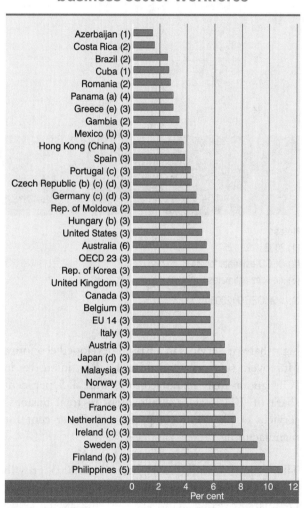

**Notes:**
(1) 2005.
(2) 2004.
(3) 2003.
(4) 2002.
(5) 2001.
(6) 2000.
(a) Preliminary data.
(b) Based on employees figures.
(c) Rental of ICT goods (ISIC Rev.3 7123) not available.
(d) ICT wholesale (ISIC Rev.3 5150) not available.
(e) Telecommunication services (ISIC Rev.3 642) included postal services.
*Source:* OECD (2006) and UNCTAD e-business database, 2006

## Chart 1.16

## Share of ICT-related occupations in the total economy, 2003

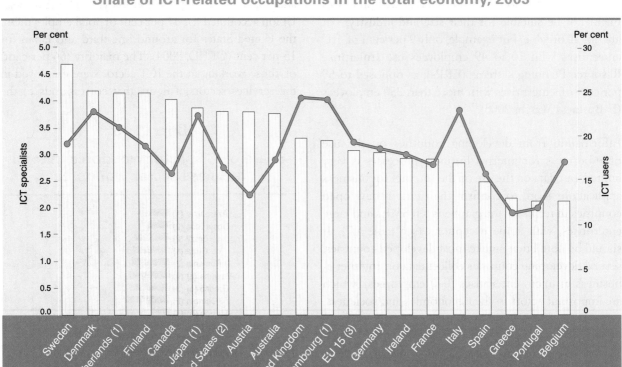

**Notes:**

(1) 2002.

(2) OECD estimate for 2003.

(3) includes estimates.

*Source:* OECD (2005a).

high share of services in a typical developed economy. Moreover, services tended to be less intensive in ICT labour than manufacturing, with a 5 per cent share of ICT service employment in total business services employment compared with 7 per cent for manufacturing.

The countries with the highest 1995–2003 growth in ICT sector employment were Finland, Norway, Denmark, Sweden, Hungary and the Netherlands. The ICT intensity of business sector employment varied in 2003 between 10 per cent (Finland) and 3 per cent (Greece). Ireland and Japan had the most ICT-intensive manufacturing employment, while Sweden and Finland had the most ICT-intensive business services employment (with 10 per cent or more each).

These findings complement chapter 5 of this report, which analyses the evolution of the manufacturing workforce and the business service workforce and their contribution to global employment growth. It argues that the employment levels and the wages of

skilled workers are rising in most countries, as a result of ICT-induced technological change.

Among the developing countries for which data are available, the Republic of Korea, Malaysia and the Philippines show a very high share of ICT employment in their business sector (above the OECD average) (chart 1.15). One explanation could be that in some developing countries the size of the business sector is still small and most developments in the private market are based on new technologies.

The core indicator on ICT employment presented above measures occupation in the industries identified as belonging to the ICT sector. Alternative measures of ICT contribution to employment can take into account the occupations that use ICTs to various degrees across all industries (OECD, 2004). Chart 1.16 shows a comparison of two alternative ICT employment indicators: ICT specialists and ICT users.[26] When these definitions are used, the 2003 ranking of countries changes slightly. The country with the highest proportion of ICT skills (users and specialists) in total occupations is the United Kingdom with 28 per cent. Greece and Portugal have again a lower specialization in ICT skills, with only 14 per cent. Sweden has the highest share of ICT specialists (4.7 per cent).

Interestingly, the correlation between the two alternative occupation indicators is only moderate (0.4 out of 1); this suggests that the countries with the most specialized ICT workforce are not necessarily the ones with the highest numbers of ICT users.

## Value added in the ICT sector

In developed countries, the ICT value added to the business sector picked up between 2000 and 2003, to reach over 9 per cent in 2003, closely matching the 2000 performance. Services accounted for over two thirds of the ICT sector, but were on average less ICT-intensive than manufacturing. For example, in Ireland and the United Kingdom the share of ICT in total business services value-added was the highest, with more than 11 per cent, while similar values for manufacturing reached above 20 per cent in Finland. Among ICT services, telecommunications had a particularly large share of value added in Greece, the Netherlands and Ireland (more than three quarters). The highest 1995–2003 growth rates were calculated for Finland, Hungary, the Netherlands and Norway.

Taking into consideration available data from selected developing countries, chart 1.17 gives a more global picture of the ICT value added to the business sector. Among the developing countries, the Philippines, Malaysia and the Republic of Korea stand out with above OECD-average contributions of ICTs to the business sector. Value-added figures by sector suggest that the business sector in these countries is highly ICT-intensive.

As in the case of the findings on employment, the ICT sector is very unevenly distributed across countries. Evidence suggests that while on average, the developed countries have a higher share of ICT value-added, some developing countries report even higher values.

Although not directly comparable to the two core indicators on the ICT sector, in China the "information industry"[27] contributed 7.5 per cent value-added to the GDP in 2004 (OECD, 2006). The high growth rate of this indicator in 2004 (30 per cent) suggests that China developed rapidly a leading position in the production of certain ICTs. The industry has a value

### Chart 1.17

### Share of ICT sector value-added in business sector value-added

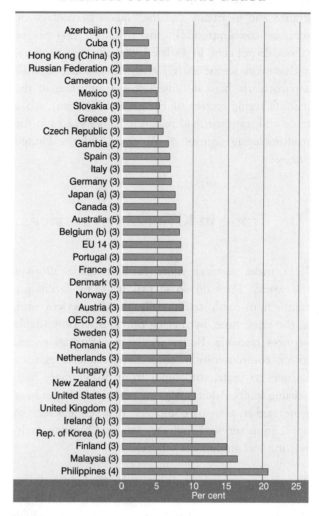

**Notes**:
(1) 2005
(2) 2004
(3) 2003
(4) 2001
(5) 2000
(a) ICT wholesale (ISIC Rev.3 5150) not available.
(b) rental of ICT goods (ISIC Rev.3 7123) not available.
*Source:* OECD (2006) and UNCTAD e-business database, 2006

added estimated at $118 billion, of which 60 per cent derives from the electronics and information industry and 40 percent from the communications industry. The communications industry in particular experienced high growth as shown by the post and telecommunications value added of $40.1 billion in 2003 as compared with $13.6 billion in 1997.

As suggested by data on a set of additional statistics, services contributed increasingly to the manufacturing value-added, with important consequences for outsourcing. Between the early 1970s and the mid-1990s this evolution reflected the outsourcing of manufacturers' service activities previously produced in-house (OECD, 2003). Japan, the United States, Australia, France and Germany had the highest percentage of services consumption in the manufacturing sector (above 25 per cent) in the late 1990s. Business services, a champion sector in ICT-enabled outsourcing, had a particularly high intermediate consumption in the manufacturing sectors of France and Germany, while trade and transport had relatively higher shares in the manufacturing sectors of Australia and the United States.

## D.   Trade in ICT-enabled services

ICTs make services more easily tradable all over the world. They do so in two ways: by facilitating transactions with traditionally traded services and, at the same time, by making previously non-tradable services tradable. Better access to information and lower communication costs have reduced existing barriers to trade, sometimes from prohibitively high starting levels. Additionally, the new technologies have generated an array of completely new services such as application service providers, data warehousing, web-hosting and multimedia services.

The decline in trade costs in services has given rise to new international business opportunities, notably for developing countries. The "slicing-up of the value-added chain" (Krugman, 1995) has been extended to also take into account the services industry and the delocalization to lower-cost markets. More standardized services such as customer services, human resource management or software consultancy no longer have to be provided in house. Through outsourcing and offshoring,[28] services can be provided from a distance by more cost-effective suppliers. At the international level, the result is a deeper specialization that is bound to benefit all parties involved, with more productivity-driven gains on the outsourcers' side, and more employment-driven gains in the host country. Developing countries that are receivers of offshoring are given the possibility to complement their development policies with a services-based strategy.

Estimates of IT and business process outsourcing and offshoring are reflected only to a small extent in developing countries' statistics of trade in ICT-enabled services. Outsourcing and offshoring of ICT-enabled services have a substantial growth potential and some countries are not yet involved in the process. According to Chakrabarty, Ghandi and Kaka (2006), by 2005 service providers had captured only 10 per cent of the potential market to be offshored, valued at $300 billion. The United States was the world's leading offshorer, responsible for an estimated 70 per cent of the offshored market (McKinsey Global Institute, 2003). Additionally, offshoring continued to have a relatively small proportion in the balance-of-payments statistics of trade in services. The value of offshored IT and business service activities represented only about 5 per cent of the world exports of ICT-enabled services in 2001 (OECD, 2005b).

World exports of ICT-enabled services had an accelerated growth in 2003. This was mainly due to the above-average 20 per cent growth rate of developing countries' exports, for the first time surpassing developed countries' performance after the slow down in 2000. However, developing countries only exported 16 per cent of world ICT-enabled services in 2003, with a small decline from the 18 per cent they accounted for in 2000.

Which are the main exporters and importers of ICT-enabled services? To what extent and in what way can ICTs enhance developing countries' export capacity in services? The answers to these questions encompass the full complexity of exporting and importing operations in which outsourcing and offshoring play a limited role. This section tries to answer the above questions and provides developing countries with the necessary information to be able to evaluate their export growth potential in ICT-enabled services.

The first part proceeds with a conventional analysis of trade in ICT-enabled services. It focuses on trends, values, driving sectors and leading countries, while highlighting the development perspective of ICT-enabled services trade.

The second part takes into account the more comprehensive framework of trade in services by delivery modes (cross-border, consumption abroad, commercial presence and presence of natural persons). This approach follows the logic set out by the WTO General Agreement on Trade in Services (GATS), which allows trade policymakers to liberalize services according to the above-mentioned modes of service delivery. Within this framework, the second part looks at the effects of ICTs on delivery modes. It shows that ICTs brought about a more substantial boost in services delivered across borders and by consumption abroad as opposed to those delivered through commercial presence. This finding is in line with ICTs' cost reduction and trade liberalization effects.

The last part concentrates on computer and information services, as the most dynamic ICT-enabled service component. A detailed presentation of the WTO GATS commitments corresponding to this sector helps to build the link between countries' positions and opportunities within the WTO negotiations on liberalization.

## 1.   Trends of exports and imports: An analysis of the BOP data

### ICT-enabled services definition

To date, global definitions of ICT-enabled services still oscillate between broader and narrower frameworks. While clearly some services are more closely related to ICT use and adoption, it is not obvious where to draw the line between sectors. Building on the balance-of-payments (BOP) standard services classification, the *E-commerce and Development Report 2002* identified seven

sectors that were mostly influenced by the adoption of ICTs. Following the same approach and definition, the present analysis considers the ICT-enabled services as the highlighted BOP components in table 1.8.

Box 1.5 summarizes information on data sources, data availability and classifications.

### ICTs facilitate trade in services

Exports of ICT-enabled services grew faster than total services exports during 2000–2003 (chart 1.18). Over this period, every percentage increase in the world exports of services was accompanied by a 1.6 per cent rise in ICT-enabled services exports. As a result, in 2003 the $836 billion value of the ICT-enabled sectors represented about 45 per cent of total services exports. This share has had a steady positive evolution over the past years, rising from approximately 37 per cent in 1995. A similar trend was found for "other services",[29] with a rising share in total service exports by a closely matching 6 percentage points over the 1995–2003 period, from 44 to 50 per cent.

## Table 1.8

## Components of ICT-enabled services

| Balance-of-payments standard classification components of services | | ICT-enabled services |
|---|---|---|
| **Transportation** | | |
| **Travel** | | |
| **Other services**[a]: | Communication services | Include postal, courier and telecommunications services |
| | Construction services | |
| | Insurance services | Include life insurance, pension funding, freight insurance, other direct insurance, reinsurance and auxiliary services |
| | Financial services | Include financial intermediation and auxiliary services |
| | Computer and information services | Include computer, news agency and other information provision services |
| | Royalties and licence fees | Include franchises and similar rights, plus other royalties and licence fees |
| | Other business services | include merchanting,[b] trade-related, operational leasing, legal, accounting, management consulting and public relations, advertising, market research and public opinion polling, research and development, architectural, engineering, agricultural, mining, and other on-site processing and services between related enterprises[c] |
| | Personal, cultural and recreational services | Include audiovisual and related services plus education and health services provided online or onsite. |
| | Government services | |

**Notes:**
[a] This is not a standard component but is provided by the IMF as total services minus transportation and travel.
[b] E.g. commodity arbitrage and wholesale trading.
[c] E.g. payments between subsidiaries and the parent companies to cover overhead expenses.
*Source:* IMF CD-ROM and UNCTAD (2002).

## Box 1.5

## Note on balance-of-payments data availability

The balance-of-payments trade in services data is gathered by the International Monetary Fund and provided usually by national central banks. The different service sectors are categorized following the standardized Extended Balance of Payments Services Classification. Many developing countries (e.g. South Africa, Thailand, Swaziland, India, Indonesia) and some developed countries (e.g. Denmark and Switzerland) do not provide complete data sets for all relevant ICT-enabled service sectors. Therefore, the analysis of ICT-enabled services, as defined here, was sometimes complemented with data on the "other services" category, for which reporting was more consistent. Within the "other services" category, ICT-enabled service exports represent about 85 to 90 per cent, the rest being allocated between "construction" and "government services" exports. 2003 was the latest year with available data for all the major exporters of ICT-enabled services.[1]

Comparing ICT-enabled service exports' share in total services with the "other services'" share reveals different trends only for the 1999–2000 period (chart 1.18). One interpretation is that, for this specific period of time, the growth of ICT-enabled services was rather due to an improvement in developing countries' data reporting. For example, that year corresponded to a change in the classification base on which Indian data were reported to the IMF.[2] Also, other countries provided more detailed sectoral data starting with the year 2000. Therefore, this chapter focuses on the 2000–2003 evolution.

The lack of internationally comparable price data for services prevents the comparison of real trade flows. Moreover, data on trade in services are limited to global flows. Often the bilateral flows of trade in ICT-enabled services are not published. Exceptionally, for some countries bilateral trade in services data are gathered by the OECD.[3]

[1] 2004 data were missing for most developing countries of Asia.
[2] Computer and information services started to be reported separately from other business services.
[3] OECD Statistics on International Trade in Services: http://caliban.sourceoecd.org/vl=16644019/cl=18/nw–1/rpsv/~4260/v239n1/s4/p1.

## Chart 1.18

### ICT-enabled services' share in total worldwide services exports

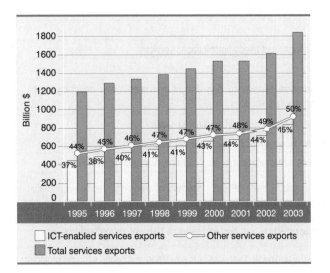

**Notes:** Percentage figures represent the yearly share of the ICT-enabled services (below)/"other services" (above) in total services exports. "Other services" are the following: communication, construction, insurance, financial, computer and information, royalties and licence fees, other business, personal, cultural and recreational and government services.

*Source:* IMF BOP data.

The faster growth of the ICT-enabled cluster within services trade confirms that these services are more easily tradable. Empirical research quantifies the positive effect of ICTs on services trade. Using United States bilateral balance-of-payments trade data from 14 service sectors, Freund and Weinhold (2002) estimated that a 10 per cent increase in the number of Internet host sites[30] in a partner country brought about a 1.7 percentage point boost in the country's exports to the United States. The sample covered United States imports and exports from a panel of 31 partner countries, including 17 developing ones, from 1995 to 1999. The same analysis showed that ICTs' effects on trade are visible on both the import and the export side with a similar impact and intensity.

While it is true that improved access to and use of ICTs have the potential to boost trade in services, there are other factors that play an equally important role both in international trade and in offshoring. ICTs cannot be used only as "plug and play" technologies. The legal and regulatory environment, the level and type of education of the people, the transparency of the political system and various cultural aspects can scale up ICTs' impact on trade. For that purpose, Governments have to ensure that the right ICT strategies are put in place, then evaluated and eventually redesigned to extend access to, and efficient use of, ICTs.[31]

## Table 1.9

## Trends in world services trade

| | 2003 BOP data aggregation (billion $) | Annual growth rates (%) | | | | |
|---|---|---|---|---|---|---|
| | | 1999–2000 | 2000–2001 | 2001–2002 | 2002–2003 | 2003–2004 WTO (2005) estimates |
| Transport | 397.3 | 7.1 | -1.7 | 4.1 | 13.9 | 23 |
| Travel | 520.4 | 4.0 | -2.8 | 4.7 | 10.2 | 18 |
| Other services | 919.1 | 6.5 | 2.4 | 7.2 | 16.2 | 16 |

**Note:** "Other services" are communication, construction, insurance, financial, computer and information, royalties and licence fees, other business, personal, cultural, recreational and government services.

*Source:* IMF BOP data, UNCTAD calculations and WTO (2005) estimates for the 2004 values.

In 2002, the expansion of services exports was driven by the "other services" category, corresponding to the ICT-enabled cluster. However, during 2003 and 2004 the "transportation" and "travel" exported values picked up as well (table 1.9). Moreover, WTO (2005) estimates suggest that the latter may have outpaced the "other services" growth rate in 2004. Real trade flows could not be compared because price data for services were not available for most countries. However, according to the same source, price increases rather than volume were the main cause of the change in exports' sectoral growth pattern. For example, higher oil prices may have led to a greater number of "transportation" services exports.

### Developed countries still in the lead

As shown by the linear trends in chart 1.19, both developed and developing countries have seen their ICT-enabled services exports expand over the past ten years (1994–2004).[32] This growth gained momentum in the aftermath of the year 2000. However, developed countries were still leading the global market of ICT-enabled services (as for total services in general) in terms of both value and growth rates. Developed countries' contribution to world ICT-enabled service exports remained high in 2003 at around 83 per cent. During 2000–2003, developing countries lagged behind the world compound annual growth rate (CAGR) of 10 per cent, with 7 per cent annually. Among the developing economies, some had exceptionally high growth rates. Over the same period, South-East Europe and the Commonwealth of Independent States (SEECIS) achieved the highest growth rate (19 per cent annually), but their ICT-enabled exports only amounted to 1 per cent of the global value.

An analysis of developed countries' exports of ICT-enabled services reveals that the European Union 15 (EU-15) as a group was the world's largest and most dynamic exporter in 2003 (chart 1.20). The European Union still featured as a major world trader even when the high share of intra-EU-15 trade is subtracted. Moreover, during 2000–2003, the EU-15 improved its competitive position mainly outside the European markets. Estimations using Eurostat data show that the share of intra EU-15 trade in "other services'" exports had declined in recent years, to reach 52 per cent in 2003. It follows that most of the growth

## Chart 1.19

### ICT-enabled services exports, by broad development categories

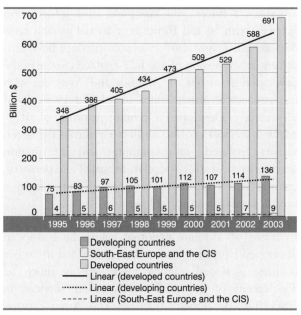

*Source:* IMF BOP data.

## Chart 1.20

## ICT-enabled services exports of developed countries

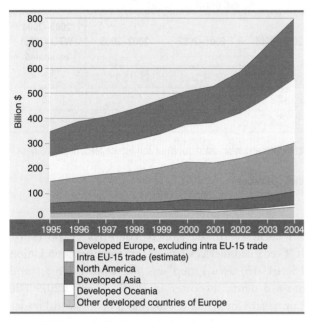

**Note:** The share of intra EU-15 trade was approximated by the Eurostat estimations corresponding to the "other services" exports.
*Source:* IMF BOP data and Eurostat.

in EU-15's exports of ICT-enabled services went to outside markets, where the European exporters improved their position to the disadvantage of their competitors. At the same time, the EU-15 markets of ICT-enabled services were increasingly catered for by other exporters, including those from developing countries.

The EU-15's exports of ICT-enabled services with the highest four-year (2000–2003) increases were insurance services and computer and information services, with 30 and 16 per cent annual growth rates respectively. Exports of insurance services have also driven the expansion of the ICT-enabled cluster in the developed countries of America and Asia, but with less substantial growth rates of 14 and 19 per cent respectively. Developed Oceania's exports of ICT-enabled services evolved moderately across the seven sectors analysed, with computer and information services in the lead (10 per cent annually) and personal, cultural and recreational services suffering from a pronounced downturn (-19 per cent).

In terms of absolute exported value, the European developed countries were rather specialized in "other business services", which made up as much as 55 percent of the their ICT-enabled services in 2003. The developed American and Asian exports were concentrated more in royalties and licence fees,

with an approximately 29 per cent market share for both regions, as against only 6 per cent in the EU-15. Developed Oceania had a more balanced market structure across the seven sectors, with relatively higher shares of the communication and computer and information services.

Table 1.21 in the statistical annex shows country exports and growth rates of ICT-enabled services from 2000 to 2003.

### Developing countries' export recovery in 2003

In 2003 developing countries' exports of ICT-enabled services recorded an annual growth rate of 20 per cent, surpassing developed countries' performance (17 per cent) for the first time since the 2000 dot-com crash. Developing countries took longer to regain high dynamics in their ICT-enabled services exports, but trade statistics suggest a strong recovery after the 2000-2003 period.

Developing and SEECIS countries' exports of ICT-enabled services came mostly from Asia (chart 1.22), which held the lion's share with 77 per cent. It was followed by America with around 10 per cent, Africa with 7 per cent and the SEECIS with around 6 per cent of ICT-enabled services exports in the sample of developing and transition economies.

Asian developing economies' exports of ICT-enabled services taken together had moderate growth rates over 2000–2003 (8 per cent CAGR). However, chart 9 reflects the large imbalance in growth rates between India and China on the one hand (22 per cent CAGR) and the other developing Asian economies on the other hand (3 per cent CAGR). Past figures show that the ICT-enabled services exports of India and mainland China taken together grew faster and recovered more rapidly in the aftermath of 2000. Despite this past imbalance, in 2003 all Asian developing countries' exports of ICT-enabled services experienced a significant increase, suggesting that more recently all were able to benefit. The exceptional 2003 growth rates are also related to the South–South trade opportunities and the positive economic developments, particularly in China and India. The Asian exported services expanded faster than the world average in the computer and information and royalties and licence fees sectors.

The SEECIS region accounted for one of the highest compound annual growth rates over the period 2000–

## Chart 1.21

## ICT-enabled services exports of developing countries

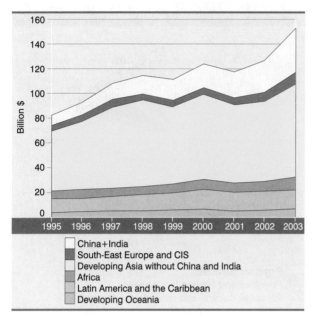

Source: IMF BOP data.

2003 (19 per cent). Three sectors had particularly high growth rates: computer and information, personal, cultural and recreational, and insurance services.

Notable also was Africa's constantly increasing annual growth rate of approximately 8 per cent. After a period of negative growth in 2000–2003, Latin America and Carribean exports of ICT-enabled services picked up again in 2004 to regain the 2000 values. Owing to lack of data, the service exports of developing Oceania cannot be assessed.

### ICT-enabled service exports by sectors

ICTs persistently reshape services industry boundaries and as a side effect, they make classification attempts look obsolete or sometimes overlapping. On the balance-of-payments classification scale, the "other business services"[33] represented the highest share of ICT-enabled services, with a quarter of the world exported value of all services (chart 1.22). However, this category decreased in importance as a share of total ICT-enabled services from 61 per cent in 1995 to 54 per cent in 2003.

The positive trend in the ICT-enabled cluster was also found in most of the seven sectors analysed. Three sectors were exceptionally dynamic: computer and information, insurance[34] and financial services.

Computer and information services recorded the highest growth rate in the sample.[35] Over the nine years taken into consideration (1995 to 2003), every percentage point increase in total services exports was accompanied by an almost 5 per cent rise in "computer and information" exports.

## Chart 1.22

## Share of ICT-enabled services sectors in the export market, 2003

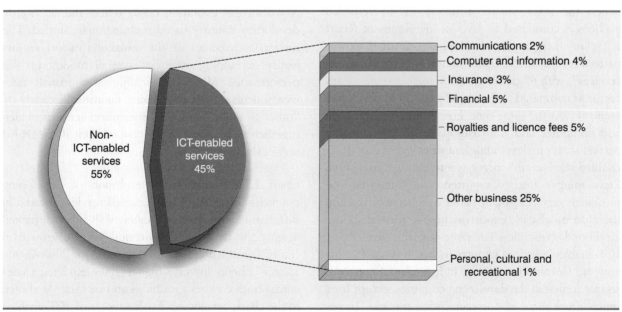

Source: IMF BOP data and UNCTAD calculations.

## Chart 1.23

### Share of ICT-enabled services sectors in the export market, developed and developing countries, 2003

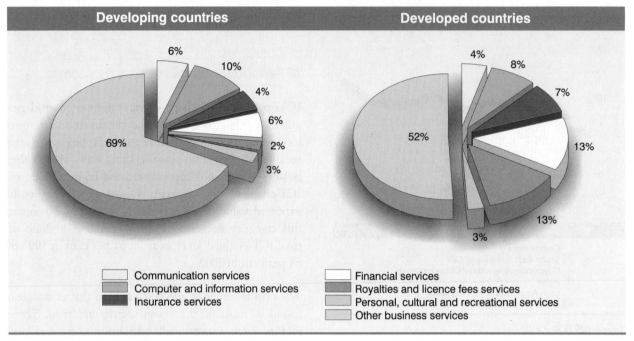

*Source:* IMF BOP data and UNCTAD calculations.

While before the year 2000, financial services recorded the second highest growth rates, in the aftermath of the dot-com crash, world exports in this sector had not recovered their 2000 value by 2003. The development of insurance services showed the reverse image of financial exports, with modest increases before 2000 and a strong recovery afterwards, culminating in the highest 2002 growth rate of all ICT-enabled services (48 per cent).

When the 2003 market structure of ICT-enabled services is compared by level of development (chart 1.23), it emerges that developing countries' export pattern is much more concentrated in "other business services", with 69 per cent of the market share in this sector as compared with only 52 per cent in developed countries. At the same time, however, communication and computer and information services had higher market shares in developing countries' exports of ICT-enabled services; this suggests a relative specialization. Developing countries exported fewer financial and insurance services and royalties and licence fees and therefore most world exports in these sectors came from developed economies. The same year, the structure of ICT-enabled services exports in South–East Europe and the Commonwealth of Independent States was similar to that in the developing countries, except for a much larger share of communication services (16 per cent of ICT-enabled services exports).

During 2000–2003, developing countries continued to specialize in computer and information services, with a 33 per cent compound annual growth rate (CAGR).[36] Royalties and licence fees were the other service sector where developing countries' exports attained above-average increases for the same period of time. While holding only a small 2 per cent of their export market share, credits corresponding to royalties and licence fees grew at 18 per cent CAGR in favour of developing economies' balance of payments. Arguably, this evolution could reflect the activity of developing country-based multinationals abroad. The moderate dynamics of the remaining export sectors justify developing countries' overall modest growth performance. More specifically, lower growth rates were calculated for developing countries' exports of "other business" and communication services, which together represented 75 per cent of their ICT-enabled services market.

Chart 1.24 compares the evolution of developing countries' exports of ICT-enabled services located in different regions. Each sector's CAGR is benchmarked against the developing countries' average growth in the ICT-enabled cluster (6.7 per cent for 2003–2000). Larger spheres indicate higher 2003 exported values across both country groupings and sectors. As shown in the chart, developing Asia's exports of ICT-enabled services grew mainly through the computer and information sector, which had acquired both a large export market value and a high growth rate. Unlike in other developing regions, exports of royalties, licence fees and insurance services have complemented the growth of Asian ICT-enabled services.

A different story is revealed by a similar analysis of the Latin American and Caribbean economies. There, despite a confirmed above-average performance of the computer and information sector, the other ICT-enabled services still lagged behind in terms of growth rate. However, early 2004 export figures show that Latin America and the Caribbean recovered the 2000 value in terms of ICT-enabled service exports, with a significant increase in computer and information, personal, cultural, recreational and "other business" services.

Africa stands out with a highly dynamic evolution of its personal, cultural and recreational exports, as well as its financial services exports[37] (chart 1.24). This happened against the background of a relatively

## Chart 1.24

## Developing countries' exports of ICT-enabled services, 2000–2003

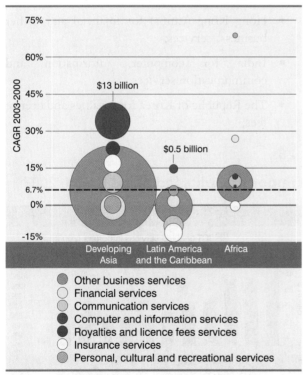

**Note:** The size of the spheres represents the exported value in 2003. Larger spheres stand for larger exports of a given region and of a given sector. The figure of 6.7 per cent is the benchmark given by developing countries' average 2003–2000 CAGR of all ICT-enabled services exports.

*Source:* IMF BOP data and UNCTAD calculations.

smaller size of the ICT-enabled service sector in Africa. The export expansion was sustained by a good growth performance of "other business services", the sector with the largest export market share. Insurance was the main weak export sector of both American and African developing countries as shown by the deteriorating growth rate.

Table 1.22 in the statistical annex shows 2003 country exports of ICT-enabled services by sectors.

### Main exporters and importers

ICT use played a positive role in enhancing both imports and exports of services. In most countries analysed, increases in ICT-enabled exports were accompanied by similarly sized rises in ICT-enabled imports.

Despite this observation, the developed countries of Europe and America remained on average the world net exporters of ICT-enabled services, while most developing countries were still net importers. Communication services were the only notable exception where developing countries as a group and by geographical locations (America, Africa, Asia, Oceania and South-East Europe) were net exporters, while developed countries tended to be net importers. Overall, Asian developing countries also managed to build up a net exporter position in computer and information, financial and "other business" services. The developed countries of Europe were the only net exporters of insurance services, while developed America had an uncontested net exporter position in royalties and licence fees and personal, cultural and recreational services.

Chart 1.25 identifies developed countries' ICT-enabled service imports with the largest values and the highest growth rates.[38] As suggested before, developed countries' high growth rates in exports of insurance and computer and information services corresponded to similarly high rates in imports of these sectors. European countries appeared again to be more dynamic importers of ICT-enabled services than their other developed counterparts. As a distinct feature, Europe had a higher and faster growing demand for communication service imports. On the other hand, the developed countries of Asia and Oceania stood out with faster growing imports of financial services.

Comparison of the top ten importers and exporters of ICT-enabled services shows imports to be more evenly distributed across the leading countries (chart

## Chart 1.25

### Developed countries' imports of ICT-enabled services, 2000–2004

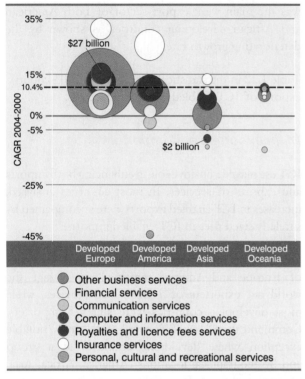

**Note:** The size of the sphere represents the imported value in 2004. Larger spheres stand for larger imports of a given region and larger imports of a given sector. The figure of 10.4 per cent is the benchmark given by developed countries' average 2004–2000 CAGR of all ICT-enabled services imports.

*Source:* IMF BOP data and UNCTAD calculations.

1.26). In 2003 the United States remained the world's largest exporter of ICT-enabled services, while Japan remained the largest importer. The developed European countries entering the two rankings, both on the import and on the export side, had higher growth rates. Among them, Ireland stood out as one of the countries with the highest growth rates in ICT-enabled services trade. Hong Kong (China) was the only developing economy featuring among the top ten exporters of ICT-enabled services. No developing economy achieved a similar performance in terms of imports, despite the average developing country being in a net importer position. This suggests that most trade in ICT-enabled services was carried out between developed country partners.

Adding China and India to the top ten rankings presented in chart 1.26 shows how close these countries have come to the world's largest exporters and importers. Their high growth rates also imply that should trade continue to evolve at the same pace, China and India will soon make their way into the top 10 rankings.

On the basis of each sector's ranking, there were eight developing economies among the top ten exporters of the different ICT-enabled service sectors:

- China for "other business" services;

- Hong Kong (China) for financial and "other business" services;

- India for computer, information and communication services;

- The Republic of Korea for royalties and licence fees;

## Chart 1.26

### Top 10 ICT-enabled services exporters and importers, plus India and China, 2003

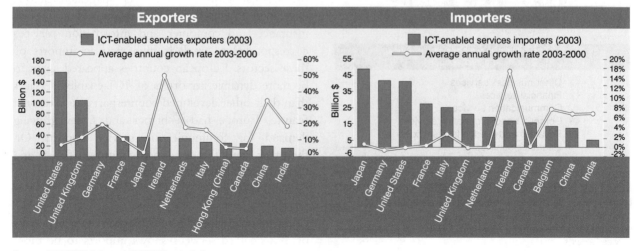

*Source:* IMF BOP data and UNCTAD calculations.

## Chart 1.27

## Republic of Korea: Bilateral imports and exports of "other commercial services"

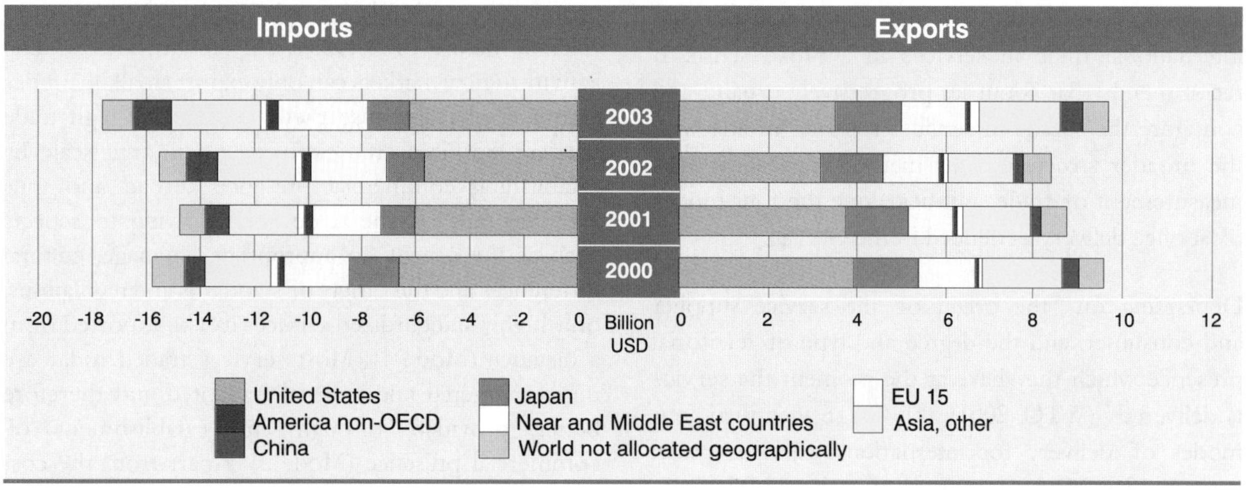

*Source:* OECD balance-of-payments data.

- Malaysia and Turkey for personal, cultural and recreational services;

- Singapore for financial and insurance services;

- Mexico for insurance services.

From a dynamic perspective, in the ICT-enabled service sectors, higher export growth rates often matched with higher import increases. While firms in some developing countries have already specialized in exporting large sector-specific values, higher imports of other ICT-enabled services benefited their consumers.

### Regional trade in ICT-enabled services

ICTs' role as trade facilitators is further enhanced when complemented with trade policy actions and favourable external factors. Regional trade agreements, as well as existing cultural awareness and affinities between geographically close countries, can compound ICTs' effect of reducing trade barriers. Unfortunately, bilateral trade in services data covering developing countries' flows are available only for very few countries.

Most trade in ICT-enabled services takes place between developed countries. For example, in 2002, the latest year for which bilateral data were available, 85 per cent of EU-15's imports of services and 64 per cent of Japan's came from OECD countries. In the same year, only 2 per cent of the European Union's imports of services and 11 per cent of Japan's came from India, China, Taiwan Province of China and Hong Kong

(China) taken together. However, the high growth rates for developing countries' exports and imports suggest the great potential of South–South trade in this field.

The Republic of Korea is one of the few developing countries for which bilateral trade data are available. Its exports and imports of "other commercial services"[39], by its main trade partners, are shown in chart 1.27. The evolution of China is noteworthy on both the imports' and the exports' side, as an emerging world major buyer and supplier. The Republic of Korea's imports from China increased by an annual 22 per cent CAGR between 2000 and 2003 and attained the fastest growth rate among its import partners. China's exports market share in the Republic of Korea improved by 4 percentage points from 5 to 9 per cent. This value was still far below the calculated 52 per cent of intra-EU-15 "other business services" trade in the regional group with the highest degree of trade integration.

## 2.  The broader concept of ICT-enabled trade in services

When analysing trade in ICT-enabled services, one can take into account the more broadly established concept of international trade in services. This not only comprises trade flows between resident and non-resident entities as registered in the International Monetary Fund Balance-of-Payments (IMF BOP) statistics, but also covers other modes of delivering services abroad. The approach is based on the recommendations of the Manual of International Trade in Services Statistics (2002), co-developed by UNCTAD.[40] The manual sets out an internationally accepted framework for reporting statistics of international trade in services in a broad sense. It recommends that countries progressively expand and configure their trade in services statistics in line with the broader structure. This methodology allows the measurement of trade statistics along the four modes of service delivery as defined in the GATS.

Depending on "the origin of the service supplier and consumer, and the degree and type of territorial presence which they have at the moment the service is delivered" (WTO, 2001), the GATS identified four modes of delivery for international services trade: cross-border (Mode 1), consumption abroad (Mode 2), commercial presence (Mode 3) and presence of natural persons (Mode 4). The data sources for international trade in services statistics, detailed by modes of delivery, are presented in table 1.10.

Box 1.6 presents information on the data sources, data availability issues and classifications for the foreign affiliates' trade statistics (FATS).

The composition of international trade in services is dominated by deliveries through forms of commercial presence (Mode 3) (see estimates in table 1.10). The prominence of Mode 3 can be explained by the non-tradable nature of services. Private firms expanding activity in new markets can only export small quantities across borders because they have to face high trade barriers. Services are exported on a large scale by establishing commercial presence abroad and thus avoiding part of the trade costs. Owing to aspects such as the use of an appropriate language, cultural differences and the variety of standards and regulations, only highly standardized services can be exported from a distance (Mode 1). Most services traded today are market-targeted and culturally adapted and therefore better provided through the establishment of commercial presence (Mode 3). Apart from the cost issue, only large and efficient firms can afford to set up foreign affiliates abroad, while the smaller firms have to opt for other contract arrangements to ensure service delivery in foreign markets. Most Mode 3 deliveries originate in developed countries and go hand in hand with a certain level of capital export. However, foreign investment data show that developing and SEECIS countries' role in this field has increased substantially in recent years (UNCTAD, 2005). Moreover, ICTs

## Table 1.10. Statistical coverage by modes of supply

| WTO GATS Classification | Practical example | Sources of statistics | Estimated share in world trade in services |
|---|---|---|---|
| **Mode 1** **Cross-border supply** | An Indian software consultant providing services electronically to a British consumer in the UK | Balance of payments: *transportation* (most of), *communications services, insurance services, financial services, royalties and licence fees;* part of *computer and information services, other business services,* and *personal, cultural, and recreational services* | 35% |
| **Mode 2** **Consumption abroad** | An Indian software consultant providing services to a British consumer in India | Balance of payments: *travel* (excluding goods bought by travellers); repairs to carriers in foreign ports (goods); part of *transportation* (supporting and auxiliary services to carriers in foreign ports) | 10–15% |
| **Mode 3** **Commercial presence** | An Indian software consultancy resident in the UK and providing services to a local British consumer | Foreign Affiliates Trade Statistics (FATS) | 50% |
| **Mode 4** **Presence of natural persons** | An Indian software consultant temporarily employed by a firm located in the UK and providing services to the locals | Balance of payments: part of: *computer and information services; other business services; personal, cultural and recreational services;* and *construction services;* FATS (supplementary information): foreign employment in foreign affiliates' balance of payments (supplementary information): labour-related flows. | 1–2% |

*Source:* Manual of International Trade Statistics (2002) for the statistical coverage; International Trade Statistics (WTO, 2005) for the estimated share in world trade and Wunsch-Vincent (2005) adapted for examples.

## Box 1.6

## Sales by foreign affiliates in the service sector: Data considerations

When the broader definition of international trade in services is applied, not all relevant flows are recorded statistically in the same way. The main distinction occurs along the line of residence. Transactions between residents and non-residents appear in the IMF Balance-of-Payments (BOP) statistics and are usually referred to as exports and imports. Sales made by foreign affiliates of transnational companies (considered resident in the host country) are recorded separately under the Foreign Affiliates Trade Statistics[1] (FATS). For some economies, separate supplementary data on the value of services supplied by professionals temporarily working abroad is also recorded under the FATS.

Following the Manual of International Trade Statistics' description, the IMF BOP exports and imports of ICT-enabled services correspond to Mode 1, Mode 2 and marginally Mode 4[2] deliveries. The sales of foreign affiliates correspond to Mode 3 deliveries[3] and are referred to as outward and inward flows. Most foreign affiliates' trade statistics follow the ISIC Rev.3 classification. Using the established correspondence between BOP and FATS classifications (The Manual, 2002), equivalents of the ICT-enabled service aggregate were constructed for sales through commercial presence[4] (Mode 3).

FATS availability is limited to some developed countries and data are only provided separately, in a decentralized manner by national institutions. Additionally, among the 24 countries that publish foreign affiliates' trade statistics,[5] only a few have separate data on services. In this chapter the analysis of Mode 3 ICT-enabled service trade was restricted to data from Austria, Canada, Finland, France, Germany, Japan, Portugal and the United States.

---

[1] For example, the US Bureau of Economic Analysis defines the sales of services through foreign affiliates of multinational companies as sales in international markets through the channel of direct investment.

[2] Services delivered electronically could fall under both Mode 1 and Mode 2 obligations, although an agreement has not been reached on this issue. For a detailed discussion see the WTO's secretariat note on «Technical Issues Concerning Financial Services Schedules», S/FIN/W/9, 29 July 1996.

[3] However, FATS underestimate Mode 3 deliveries for two reasons. First, the WTO and FATS definition do not match perfectly. A certain percentage of foreign ownership is required for a company to appear as a foreign affiliate in the FATS data, while no such limitation applies to the WTO Mode 3 definition. Second, FATS in the tertiary sector only cover businesses registered as services and therefore do not take into account sales of foreign affiliates registered in the primary or secondary sectors, which sell services occasionally (The Manual of International Trade Statistics, 2002).

[4] The broad International Standard Industrial Classification (ISIC Rev 3) categories included as ICT-enabled services were trade, post and communications, finance (including insurance), business activities, and community, social and personal services.

[5] Austria, Belgium, Luxembourg, Denmark, Finland, France, Germany, Ireland, Italy, Portugal, Sweden, United Kingdom, Norway, Canada, United States, Japan, China, India, Singapore, Madagascar, Slovenia, Czech Republic, Hungary and Poland (UNCTAD FDI/TNCs database (www.unctad.org/fdistatistics )).

---

can lower transaction costs and thus increase services' tradability across borders.

The persistence of Mode 3 as the primary delivery mode in international services trade relates also to the existence of relatively higher trade barriers in the other modes. For example, service deliveries through the movement of natural persons abroad are substantially limited by migration regulations. Section 3 looks into the WTO sector-specific market access commitments for computer and information services.

The value of services traded through Modes 2, 3 and 4 overtakes Mode 1 deliveries (65 per cent against 35 per cent) also because of the proximity problem. In most cases, the delivery of services relies heavily on a close interaction between consumer and provider. Mode 1, cross-border supply, is the only case where services are delivered from a distance.[41]

### Why is the analysis by modes of delivery useful for developing countries?

The modes of trading services internationally have distinct features as described before, but their final result is the same: foreign services are supplied in domestic markets. Corresponding to services delivered through forms of commercial presence (Mode 3), foreign affiliates' sales are an additional source of trade information for policymakers. Like the BOP registered exports and imports, services can thus also be supplied abroad as outward and inward sales of foreign-owned companies.

When compared, the sales of foreign affiliates and the BOP trade data provide trade policymakers with meaningful results. Three considerations are introduced below.

### Chart 1.28

## Domestic and international outsourcing

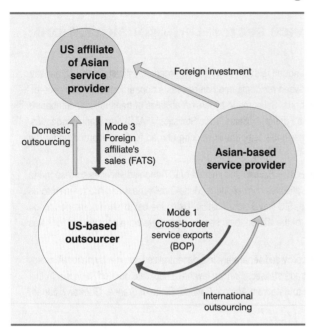

*Source:* UNCTAD.

First, through their policy actions, developing countries can choose the right balance between exports and imports on the one hand and foreign affiliates' sales on the other. Deliveries through foreign affiliates have different socio-economic consequences when compared with the export-import activities. By definition, selling services through forms of commercial presence depends on the amount of foreign investments from the sending to the receiving country. Subject to the particular local context, the presence of foreign-owned affiliates in the territory of a host country gives rise to new opportunities and threats. For example, better job opportunities, additional tax revenues and technology transfers could serve as a trade-off with host Governments' difficulty in regulating foreign companies and the weakened competitiveness of the domestic suppliers.

Second, the comparison of services imports and exports with foreign affiliates' inward and outward flows can provide a valuable insight, particularly in the context of outsourcing. In this way different aspects of the services internationalization story are taken into account: the foreign investment side and the exporting side. For example, a US firm deciding to outsource part of its service activities can choose as its business partner an Asian-based transnational company with commercial presence in the United States. In this example, the BOP statistics do not record the resulting service transaction, since the Asian foreign affiliate would be resident in the host country. However, the FATS typically register this type of domestic outsourcing to a foreign-owned firm. For a graphical illustration see chart 1.28.

Last, but not least, foreign investment and trade often go hand in hand, with consequences for the development of the service sector. Empirical studies have proved that the investment development path and

### Chart 1.29

## United States' imports and inward foreign affiliates' sales of private services

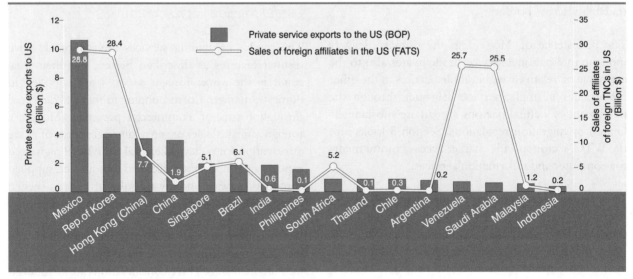

**Note:** Private services include all the service transactions of private entities.
*Source:* US Bureau of Economic Analysis data.

the trade development path are closely interconnected (Dunning et al., 2001). Increased exports in a particular sector often go together with a higher participation of that sector in both inward and outward foreign direct investment. This link is reinforced in the services industry, where suppliers and consumers often need to meet face to face.

Chart 1.29 shows to what extent deliveries through the Mode 3 channel were relevant for a group of selected developing economies. The calculations used data on the total private services imports and inward foreign affiliates' sales in the United States for the year 2001 (the latest data available). As illustrated by the chart, private services delivered through affiliates of developing-country-based trans-nationals exceeded the value imported across borders from the same developing countries. Detailed sectoral data were not available for most developing countries selected in the chart and therefore a similar analysis corresponding to the ICT-enabled service cluster could not be conducted. Also, the breakdown of existing FATS by sending country only captured observations with regard to some developing country partners. However, it is calculated that in 2001 approximately 88 per cent of the US total inward foreign affiliates' sales of services were ICT-enabled. At the same time, the ICT-enabled services represented about 18 per cent of total US private services imports.

The question addressed in the following section is how ICTs influence the composition by delivery modes of international trade in services and what are the implications for the developing countries.

## The internationalization of the service industry

A large share of the globally produced services is not traded in the conventional way, but rather sold abroad through commercial presence. BOP statistics show a relatively constant evolution of the share of services in total world exports, which has stayed at approximately 20 per cent during the past ten years. UNCTAD estimates[42] that total BOP trade in services expanded with a 10 per cent growth rate in 2005, but slightly lagged behind the trade in goods growth rate (table 1.11). While it could be considered that commodity price increases boosted the value of trade in goods, for trade in services only nominal trade flows could be compared since internationally comparable services price data are not available.

The relatively low share of services in total exports has been contrasted against the much higher share of services in national GDP composition. Services represented 72 per cent of developed countries' GDP, 52 per cent of developing countries' output and 57 per cent of Central and Eastern European countries' GDP according to UNCTAD (2003) estimates. Using BOP data as the basis for trade in services evaluation suggests that services evolve into an international business only on a small scale.

Foreign direct investment (FDI) statistics, however, tell a different story. While departing from fairly low figures in 1990, services' share in the composition of foreign investments has increased spectacularly during the last decade. According to UNCTAD (2004), the world has witnessed a shift of foreign investment composition towards services for both developed and developing country investors. Services accounted for about 60 per cent of total global FDI inward stock in 2002, rising from less than half in 1990. An increasing value of FDI came from the developed and transition economies, together with an increase in South–South FDI flows. There are thus signs that the service industry did become more international mainly through foreign investments.

The substantial increase in service-related foreign investments was also reflected in foreign affiliates' sales (Mode 3). Foreign investments in services generated

## Table 1.11

## Trends in world trade

| World exports | UNCTAD estimates for 2005 (billion $) | Annual growth rates (%) | | | | | |
|---|---|---|---|---|---|---|---|
| | | 1999–2000 | 2000–2001 | 2001–2002 | 2002–2003 | 2003–2004 | 2004–2005 |
| Goods | 10 278.3 | 12.8 | -4 | 4.7 | 15.9 | 20.5 | 13.8 |
| Services | 2 439.9 | 5.6 | 0.4 | 6.3 | 14.6 | 18.3 | 10.1 |

*Source:* IMF BOP data and UNCTAD calculations.

## Chart 1.30

### United States' outward services transactions

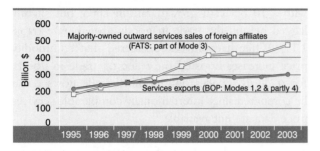

**Note:** The FATS sales referred to here are not limited to majority-owned foreign affiliates' sales.

*Source:* US Bureau of Economic Analysis; IMF BOP data.

ICT-enabled services represented more than 55 per cent of the global figure in 2004.

ICTs can boost services trade in all the delivery modes because they lower transaction costs. For example, the value of foreign affiliates' sales has also been boosted by the recent surge of mergers and acquisitions (United States Department of Commerce, 2003). However, since the value delivered through commercial presence also necessitates capital investment and thus an additional financial effort, ICTs' effect on Mode 3 trade should be more moderate. Therefore, ICTs can bring about a change in the structure of international service deliveries. More specifically, improved access to and use of ICTs should favour Modes 1 and 2 over Mode 3 deliveries. This change would benefit the developing countries with reduced commercial presence abroad.

higher and more dynamic sales of foreign affiliates than the traded value registered in the BOP. In the United States, the ratio of majority-owned foreign affiliates' sales to BOP trade followed a steadily increasing trend from 0.8 in 1987 to 1.6 in 2003 for outward transactions and from 0.8 to 1.7 for inward transactions (chart 1.30). The same trend and a higher share of FATS services sales vis-à-vis BOP service exports were found in the developed countries with growing exports.[43] Canada, Finland, France, Germany and Portugal had both higher and faster growing majority-owned foreign affiliates' outward sales of services than the BOP exports (1995/1997 to 2002). Austria had more service exports than outward sales, but the trend of the ratio was similar to that of the other countries. These countries' exports (BOP) of

To check whether ICT-enabled services were increasingly delivered across borders and through consumption abroad (through Modes 1 and 2), the analysis relied on individual country data. Chart 1.31 presents the data analysis and results for the United States. There were similar findings for the majority-owned foreign affiliates' sales in Canada (1999 to 2002), France (1999 to 2001), Germany (1995 to 2003) and Portugal (1997 to 2003). These countries exported 49 per cent of world ICT-enabled services in 2003 and recorded positive growth rates in the aggregate sector.

The share of ICT-enabled services in total services exports increased in the United States by 15 percentage points over a seven-year period (1995–2002). As highlighted in the first part of this section, the same

## Chart 1.31

### Share of ICT-enabled services in total US outward service flows

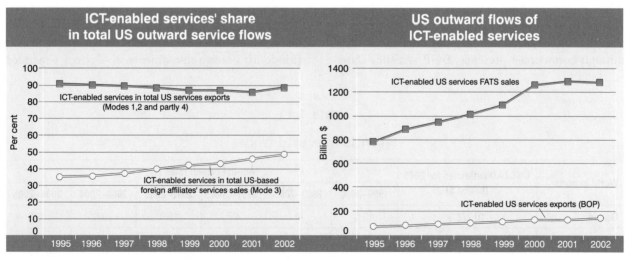

*Source:* US Bureau of Economic Analysis data.

trend was found at the global level, where the share of ICT-enabled services exports also improved. On the other hand, US ICT-enabled Mode 3 sales grew at a slower pace than the total outward sales of US-based foreign affiliates. Chart 1.31 illustrates the two slowly converging shares of ICT-enabled services within total US exports and, respectively, total US foreign affiliates' sales. The opposite happened in absolute terms, where the ICT-enabled services delivered through commercial presence remained considerably larger and expanded faster than the exports of ICT-enabled services. Results suggest that, given the global context of surging Mode 3 deliveries and the relatively slower evolution of BOP trade flows, the trends of the ICT-enabled sectors had a compensating effect that favoured Mode 1 and 2 exports.

Exceptions were Japan and Finland (1995 to 2002), where exports of ICT-enabled services experienced fluctuating and declining growth rates respectively. For Japan the shares of ICT-enabled services in exports and outward sales had a parallel evolution, while for Finland the two calculated shares diverged.

It appears therefore that the countries which specialized in ICT-enabled service exports over the period analysed have also seen an increase in the corresponding sales of home-based multinationals. ICT-enabled service sales through commercial presence grew faster than exports for most countries analysed. The same applied for trade in services in general. However, if the general trend of trade in services is accounted for separately, ICT-enabled services were increasingly delivered cross-border and through consumption abroad (Modes 1 and 2) rather than through commercial presence (Mode 3). This result applied particularly to countries with an increasing trend towards ICT-enabled service exports.

## Chart 1.32

## Growth of computer and information services exports

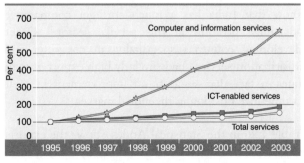

Source: IMF BOP data and UNCTAD calculations.

## Chart 1.33

## Exports of computer and information services, by level of development

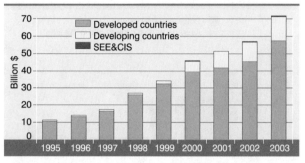

Source: IMF BOP data and UNCTAD calculations.

The lack of data prevented a similar analysis of the developing countries' exports and outward sales. However, as confirmed by empirical studies (Dunning et al., 2001), developing countries with growing ICT-enabled service exports should also be able to improve their competitive position in the sector's outward sales of foreign affiliates. Moreover, the developing countries with less commercial presence abroad could increasingly specialize in ICT-enabled service exports.

## 3.    Sector focus: Computer and information services

### Exports and imports

Compared with the 1995 value, in 2003 global computer and information service exports multiplied six times and grew six times faster than total ICT-enabled services (chart 1.32). The spectacular expansion of export statistics in this service sector has been greatly helped by developing countries' growth rates. In 2003, developing countries' exports of computer and information services were thirty times greater than their 1995 value. Developing countries' share in computer and information exports increased from 4 per cent in 1995 to 20 per cent in 2003, reaching the highest growth of all ICT-enabled service sectors since 2000 (chart 1.33).

Most of developing countries' exports of computer and information services originated in Asia. Export growth rates were positive for developing countries from America and Africa as well, even if the Asian developing countries again had the most substantial increases.

## Chart 1.34

## Top 10 exporters and importers of computer and information services, 2003

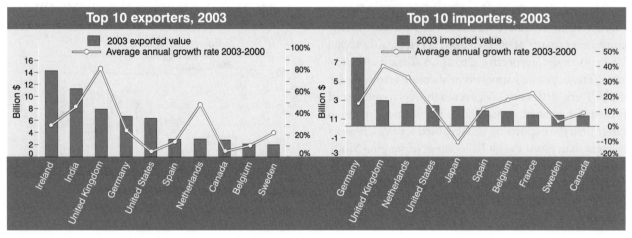

*Source:* IMF BOP data and UNCTAD calculations

In absolute value, the largest exporters and importers of computer and information services were still mainly the developed countries (chart 1.34). The only notable exception was India, which exported in 2003 the second highest value of computer and information services, worth $ 11.4 billion. With an annual average growth rate of 47 per cent, over a period of only three years (2000–2003) India surpassed the United States. Unlike in the case of the other large exporters' performance, Indian imports significantly lagged behind the exports' growth rate over the same period, by 45 percentage points, reaching in 2003 total imports worth only $659 million. A similar case was Ireland, the world's largest exporter in this sector, with $14.2 billion exports as opposed to only $371 million imports in 2003.

## Chart 1.35

## Top 10 developing economy exporters of computer and information services

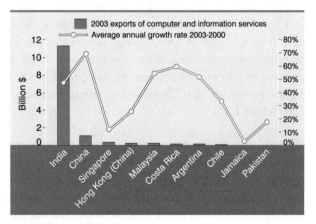

*Source:* IMF BOP data and UNCTAD calculations.

The developed European countries were among the largest and most dynamic exporters of computer and information services. The performance of Germany, the United Kingdom and the Netherlands in terms of both exports and imports of computer and information services was particularly significant.

In Asia and America, developed countries' imports in the sector had a below-average development and even a negative growth rate in Japan. Trade data show that Europe, developed Oceania and developing Asia were the largest and most dynamic markets for the computer and information services trade. In 2003, China imported $1 billion worth of computer and information services, which almost doubled its 2000 figure. At the same time, China was also the second largest developing exporter in this service sector, with $1.1 billion.

The top ten list of developing country exporters of computer and information services shows the uncontested leadership of India (chart 1.35). Even when scaling exports to the size of the economy, trade specialization indices (revealed comparative advantage) show that India has a much stronger comparative advantage position in this service sector.[44] Other developing countries specializing in computer and information services had similarly high export growth rates, a fact that suggests an improvement in their competitive position in the global market.

Table 1.26 in the Statistical Annex shows the exports of computer and information services by country from 2000 to 2003.

## WTO liberalization commitments

The dynamic evolution of computer and information services and their particular relevance to developing countries' exporters justify an analysis of the corresponding WTO commitments in the sector. In 2003, 99.6 per cent of world exports of computer and information services originated from WTO members. Moreover, in this sector developing and transition countries participated substantially in determining the current level of market access commitments. Out of 90 WTO members with specific commitments for computer and related services, 52 per cent were developing economies and 10 per cent were from South-East Europe and the Commonwealth of Independent States. These figures can be contrasted with a majority of more than three quarters of developing and transition economies among WTO members.[45]

Services are classified differently in the IMF Extended Balance of Payments and the WTO schedules of commitments.[46] The Manual of Trade in Services Statistics (2002) established a correspondence between the two classification systems. The BOP computer and information sector corresponds largely to the WTO computer and related services.[47] Annex III gives a detailed description of the type of services included in the WTO computer and related sector, based on the provisional United Nations Central Product Classification.

Services have been subject to multilateral trade negotiations since 2000. Despite continuous negotiations on services in the WTO, at the time of completing this report (July 2006) the outcome of the negotiations remained unresolved. During 1998–2006, seventeen new members joined the WTO and all made specific commitments with regard to computer and related services. Therefore, the information presented in this chapter corresponds to both the WTO members' market access commitments as submitted in the 1995 lists and the acceding countries' additional commitments.

Among the sectors negotiated in the WTO, the computer and related services sector is one of the most liberalized, largely owing to the low-trade barrier environment in this sector at the time of the Uruguay Round. However, as is generally the case for service sectors, the level of liberalization varies greatly by modes of delivery. For example, while most developed countries committed to full market access for computer and related services delivered through Modes 1 to 3 (cross-border, consumption abroad and commercial presence), significantly less was achieved for the movement of natural persons (Mode 4).

WTO GATS market access commitments represent the upper bound to the level of protectionism that policymakers can exercise in a domestic market. More liberal conditions may apply for trade in computer and related services either for regional trade partners or on a more general basis. For this reason, the WTO level of commitments in services is a deficient proxy for the actual level of trade liberalization achieved within a member economy.

Charts 1.36 and 1.37 show the global level of commitments for market access liberalization in the computer and related service cluster, by comparing Mode 1 and Mode 3. With a few exceptions (Georgia, Indonesia, Pakistan and China) WTO members have agreed to bind all the five subsectors of computer and related services with the same commitments.[48] Annex IV shows WTO members' market access commitments under Modes 1 and 3 for computer and related services.

Sectoral commitments were categorized between three options: full, partial or no market access. Alternatively, WTO members could also choose not to include the computer and related sector in their lists of specific commitments. Such a choice resulted also in the absence of any binding commitment of market access for foreign service providers.[49]

The geographical representation of countries shows a very large participation by the European countries in the negotiations on this sector. Almost all the European economies are members of the WTO, and committed to open their markets for computer and related services. In contrast, only 20 per cent of the African WTO members included this sector in their list of commitments. The countries of Oceania have limited participation in the WTO, while Asia and America made up half of the existing commitments in the sector. On average, half of the developing WTO members included computer and related services in their lists. Brazil, Chile, Egypt, Thailand, Morocco and Macao (China) are among the WTO members with no commitments in the sector.

Computer and related services benefit from full free access to all developed WTO members' markets when delivered cross-border, through consumption abroad or through commercial presence. It follows that 83 per cent of the world exports of computer and information

## Charts 1.36 and 1.37

## WTO market access commitments for computer and related services

### (Mode 1)

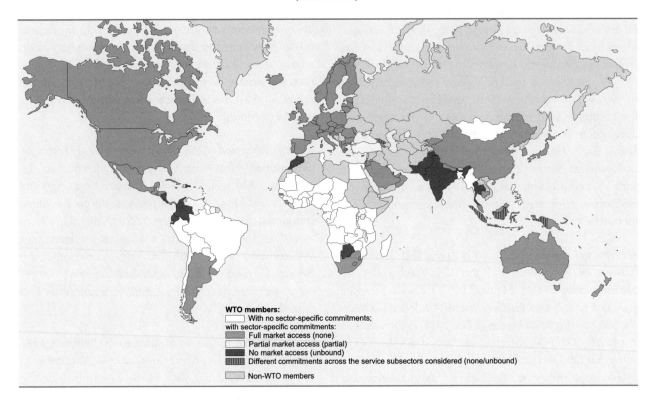

### (Mode 3)

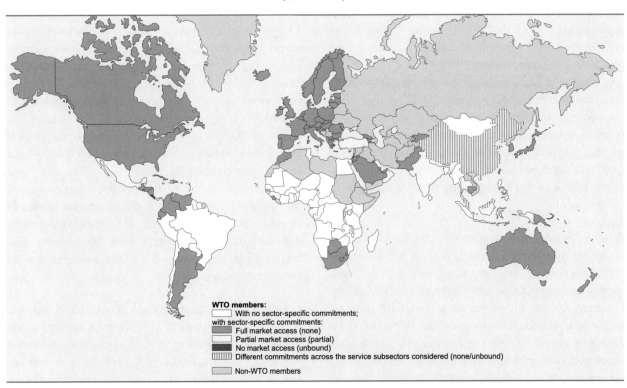

services in 2003 came from WTO members with full cross-border market access commitments. The WTO members permitting full access through commercial presence in their markets also exported 82 per cent of the global value of this service sector.

Developing WTO members made less liberal market access commitments. Only two thirds of them committed to open markets for computer and related services delivered cross-border (Mode 1). One third allowed only partial market access through forms of commercial presence. Half of the developing countries chose a combination of Mode 1 and Mode 3 full commitments. Costa Rica, India, Indonesia, Thailand and Turkey were the only WTO members with partial or no market access commitments on computer and information services for across-border consumption abroad deliveries.

Service provision through the movement of natural persons is still qualified by specific domestic require-ments in most countries (in 93 per cent of all commitments). The same applies to South-East European countries and the Commonwealth of Independent States. The lack of free trade commit-ments under Mode 4 seriously hinders the provision of services through the movement of natural persons.

A continued services liberalization process will have to tackle at least three aspects of the computer and related sector.

First, not all countries have included this sector among their market access commitments and, additionally, some subsectors were omitted. WTO members are continuing negotiations on services, which could eventually lead to a comprehensive sectoral coverage of the entire computer and related service cluster subject to the same type of regulations.[50] However, developing countries have to consider world prices, and weigh carefully their need for access to computer and related services, against making commitments that may inhibit the development of their own productive capacities in this sector.

Secondly, more liberalization could be required with regard to the movement of natural persons (Mode 4). In the computer and related services sector full market access has already been achieved in respect of developed countries for Modes 1, 2 and 3. From a developing country point of view, more service liberalization under Mode 4 needs to be examined. India has been the main advocate of this position with both multilateral and sector-specific proposals.[51]

Developing countries' better endowment in ICT human skills rather than ICT capital could justify their relative specialization in Mode 4 trade rather than Mode 3. Moreover, empirical evidence shows that in the case of India in particular, a substantial presence of IT specialists in the United States led to a significant increase in overall trade flows between India and the United States (Herander and Saavedra, 2005). At present, most developed country commitments with regard to Mode 4 refer only to specialists employed by foreign affiliates. Therefore, they can only be exploited marginally by those developing countries with less commercial presence abroad.

Thirdly, developing countries could also seek to pursue mutual liberalization with other developing countries under all modes of delivery in the context of South–South trade negotiations, whose potential has been highlighted previously in this chapter.

Last, but not least, developing countries with commercial presence abroad should build up comprehensive development strategies to take into account Mode 3 deliveries. As suggested by data findings for some of the large exporters of ICT-enabled services, the sales of foreign affiliates seem to play an essential role in the internationalization of the services industry.

## E.    Measuring ICT impact

Calls for measuring ICT impact on development have been an essential and persistent feature in the discussion on ICT measurement and the collection of statistical indicators. After all, how important is it to know how many enterprises have access to the Internet, when we do not know how their use of Internet-based technologies has changed the way they operate or interact with the global economy, or whether this has led to job losses or the creation of new jobs?

Therefore, an increasing amount of research is emerging on quantitatively measuring[52] the impact of ICTs on social and economic development, including firm productivity and national GDP growth. This kind of empirical research has been made possible by the increasing availability of comparable statistical indicators on ICT access and use. So far, most of the work has been based on developed countries' data. But with the gradual increase in the availability of comparable data from a number of developing countries, similar analysis will be possible in the near future.

This section will first briefly discuss different approaches to measuring the economic impact of ICTs using both aggregate and micro-level data, drawing primarily on developed countries' studies. Then it will present the latest research results from UNCTAD's work on measuring the impact of ICTs on GDP growth in developing countries. While it will not answer all questions related to the impact of ICT on development, it provides a starting point for this growing field of research, which will be extended in future editions of the Information Economy Report.

## 1.  Measuring ICT impact using aggregate data

Measuring the economic impact of ICTs on growth and productivity has been the subject of intense investigation during the last decade. The interest was mainly stirred by the unusually long period of expansion experienced in the United States (1992–2000). One approach was to focus on the ICT sector and measure its productivity gains within the GDP of the country, using aggregate-level data (Jorgenson, Ho and Stiroh, 2005). The hypothesis here is that the greater the size of the sector producing ICT goods and services, the larger the positive impact of ICT on growth. This positive effect would be mainly justified by the rapid technological progress and very strong demand characterizing the ICT sector in most OECD countries. Estimation results show that the largest contributions of ICT manufacturing were achieved in Finland, Ireland and the Republic of Korea, by adding almost 1 percentage point to aggregate multi-factor productivity growth in the 1995–2001 period (OECD, 2003). The analysis shows the leaders of the new technological wave to be on average in the forefront of economic expansion.

This type of analysis identifies a strong causal relationship, but it has the disadvantage of only focussing on ICT-producing countries. Also, it ignores to a large extent the differences in the use of ICTs as inputs to other industries. In addition, it does not provide suggestions on how less technologically advanced countries should proceed to catch up with the information economy leaders. For example, according to the comparative advantage notion of conventional trade theory, an efficient allocation of resources would prevent at least some countries from specializing in ICT production. If this were the case, a focus on producing more ICT goods and services

could even hinder developing countries from growing and catching up.

Another common approach to measuring ICT and growth focuses on ICT inputs and the role of the ICT-using sector. It estimates the impact of ICT-related capital investments on overall capital deepening and the corresponding increases in labour productivity (Waverman, Meschi and Fuss, 2005). It is expected that the higher the ICT-related capital investment, the greater the gains in per capita GDP. The theoretical background of this type of models is based on the Solow growth model (Solow, 1957), which compares the impact on growth of ICT-related capital investment as opposed to non-ICT capital investments. National studies based on this approach have estimated the impact of ICT investments on per capita GDP growth at a magnitude of between 0.2 per cent for France and Japan and 1.4 per cent for the Republic of Korea.

The main challenge of this analysis is related to the differences between countries' national accounts statistical data with regard to ICT and non-ICT capital investments. Also, the analysis cannot be reproduced in a global context as the data are not available for developing countries. Moreover, the approach has been criticized for underestimating the ICT contribution to growth by ignoring the potential network effects and the knowledge spillover supposedly generated by ICT technologies. Finally, aggregate-level data provide few insights into the underlying causes that affect firm performance.

## 2.  Measuring ICT impact using micro-data

With the increasing availability of data at the firm level, more and more studies are emerging that aim to capture the extent to which the efficient use of ICTs by firms contributes to multi-factor productivity growth and firm performance more generally (OECD, 2005d). Put differently, ICT assets can be used more or less efficiently depending on the regulatory environment, the structure of the industry sector and the degree of competition in the market. In a sample of 13 OECD countries, firm-level data showed that the use of ICTs can help firms increase their market share, expand their product range, better adapt their products to demand, reduce inventories and help them integrate activities throughout the value chain (OECD, 2003). Some of the key findings emerging from these firm-level studies are that:[53]

- Among ICTs, networking technologies have the highest positive impact on firm performance;

- ICT impacts emerge over time; and

- Effective ICT use is closely linked to innovation, skills and organizational change.

These positive changes are reflected in higher productivity gains for the firms adopting more complex ICT strategies. The advantage of using micro-data is that the analysis can be linked to other firm-specific characteristics or data such as skills.

Preliminary research results from a micro-data-based Canadian study suggest that firms both progress and regress from one e-business stage to another over time and that larger firms are more likely to move up the e-business ladder than SMEs (Statistics Canada, 2006). A recent Finnish study on ICT impact in firms found that a computer increases average workers' productivity by 24 per cent and that computer portability and LAN connections add additional important effects (32 per cent and 14 per cent respectively) (Maliranta and Rouvinen, 2004). The impact was found to be much greater in younger companies than in older ones.

Researchers from the United Kingdom have extensively used micro-data to measure the impact of ICTs on firm productivity (Bloom, Sadun and van Reenen, 2006; Clayton, 2006; Crespi, Crisculo and Haskel, 2006; Farooqui and Sadun, 2006). They revealed positive and significant productivity effects across all economic

sectors, with strong links to other variables such as organizational structure, skills, age and size, as well as broadband availability. The impact of broadband on productivity has been the subject of a number of recent studies which revealed positive and significant links (see section B of this chapter).

## 3.    Impact of ICTs on GDP growth in developing countries[54]

Most of the above-mentioned research on measuring ICT impact has focused on developed countries, primarily for reasons of statistical data availability.[55] To extend the work on ICT impact measurement to developing countries, UNCTAD carried out in 2005 empirical research on the macroeconomic impact of ICTs with a special focus on developing countries and using the Orbicom infodensity model as a basis (Orbicom, 2005). The analysis is based on the Infodensity composite index developed by the Orbicom Digital Divide Initiative, which defines Infodensity as "representing the ICT productive function of an economy", composed of ICT-enhancing capital and labour (Orbicom, 2003). The choice of this index over other available indexes[56] was motivated primarily by the fact that it includes — apart from ICT capital — a proxy for measuring ICT skills, which are considered critical to a country's ability to absorb and effectively use ICTs. A short description of the infodensity methodology is provided in annex II.

## Chart 1.38

## GDP per capita and infodensity in 1995 and 2003

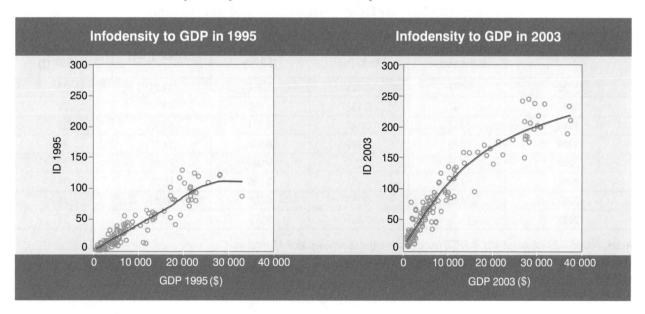

---

## Box 1.7

## An empirical model for estimating ICT impact on GDP growth

UNCTAD's analysis was built on the derivations of the neoclassical growth model (Solow, 1957) extended to include government policy variables. The empirical model uses the framework of Barro (1997) for the analysis of growth across countries. Accordingly, differences in the relative growth rates across countries are explained by the targeted level of output, as determined by policymakers' choices. Technological innovation is driving sustained long-run growth in this model as an external factor. Barro and Sala-i-Martin (1995) provide a more complex endogenous growth setting in which, even if only leading-edge countries discover new ideas and the other countries simply imitate,[1] in the long run all output growth rates converge towards the levels chosen by policymakers. Their setting confirms that government action to improve ICT use can help developing countries to grow faster even when they do not lead innovation in ICT.

Following this analysis, the empirical model developed is shown in the following equation:

$$\log(GDP_{percapita})_{t,i} = a_0 + a_1 PopulationGrowth_{t,i} + a_2(\frac{GCF}{GDP})_{t,i} + a_3 OPENNESS_{t,i} + a_4 Inflation_{t,i} + a_{5,t}$$

The per capita GDP growth rate is represented here as a function of five variables: the annual population growth rate, the gross capital formation weighted by the GDP (as a proxy for investment), a classical index of openness (as a proxy for trade), an annual inflation index calculated from the GDP deflator, and the Infodensity index (ID).

The $a_{5,t}$ coefficient measures how sensitive GDP is to changes in Infodensity. In other words, if $a_{5,t}$ is equal to 0.3, a 1 per cent increase in the Infodensity index of a country would, on average, bring about a 0.3 per cent increase in per capita GDP.

---

[1] Technological innovation is endogenous.

---

The goal of the UNCTAD analysis was to estimate whether a relative measure of ICT uptake can justify differences in output growth on a more global scale. Given the scarcity of data on ICT investment for developing countries, a general growth accounting framework was chosen. Rather than capturing the impact of ICT-related capital investments, the analysis inquires into whether a greater stock of ICT capital and labour helps boost economic growth. The channels through which this is expected to take place are mainly network and spillover effects.

The model uses available statistical data from 153 countries to proxy the diffusion and uptake of ICTs. The panel data consist of a mix of developed and developing countries, with a substantial prevalence of developing countries, covering the period from 1995 to 2003.

## Table 1.12

## Impact of ICT on GDP growth (global estimates)

| Sample year | Number of countries in the sample | GDP elasticity to ID (%) | GDP per capita mean ($ PPP) | ID mean (*100) | Marginal effect of ID on GDP ($) |
|---|---|---|---|---|---|
| 1996 | 147 | 0.125 | 7 654 | 41.21 | 23 |
| 1997 | 147 | 0.132 | 8 039 | 48.67 | 22 |
| 1998 | 147 | 0.142 | 8 284 | 55.90 | 21 |
| 1999 | 146 | 0.199 | 8 537 | 64.57 | 26 |
| 2000 | 146 | 0.236 | 9 060 | 73.08 | 29 |
| 2001 | 146 | 0.262 | 9 386 | 80.00 | 31 |
| 2002 | 143 | 0.310 | 9 565 | 87.10 | 34 |
| 2003 | 135 | 0.327 | 9 572 | 97.35 | 32 |

**Notes:** Pooled SUR estimation with an AR(3) process, convergence achieved after 17 iterations
Unbalanced panel with 901 observations, 132 countries and 9 years.
$a_0$ = 6.97
R-squared 0.729682

What follows illustrates, first, the linkage between the levels of GDP per capita in purchasing power parity (PPP) terms and ICT levels. Then, on the basis of a growth accounting model that includes data on investment, trade, population growth and inflation, it presents a summary account of the results of measuring the impact of ICTs on economic growth, in particular in developing countries.

### Correlation between ICTs and GDP

ICT uptake is found to be highly correlated with per capita GDP at purchasing power parity (PPP) (chart 1.38). The correlation coefficients tend to decline slightly over time – from around 0.95 (1995) to 0.9 (2003). At the same time, the ICT–GDP relationship appears to have grown more robust, with the 2003 values more evenly distributed along the regression line. This confirms the strong linkage between the level of ICT advancement of a country and per capita GDP.

The graphs also show that the fitted lines are steeper for 2003 data than for 1995 data. This suggests that, on average, GDP levels are more responsive to changes in ICT uptake today than nine years ago.

### Impact of ICT on GDP growth

A strong correlation between two variables is not sufficient to prove a causal relationship. ICT uptake and GDP per capita may simply go hand in hand; it does not necessarily mean that an increase in the ICT level will bring about stronger GDP growth. Therefore,

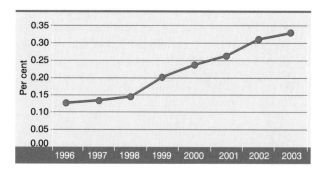

**Chart 1.39**

**GDP elasticity to infodensity**

a panel data estimate was run to measure the impact of ICTs on per capita GDP within a more comprehensive growth model framework, taking into consideration data on investment, trade, population growth and inflation (box 1.7).

Results illustrate the impact of ICTs on economic growth (table 1.12). Here, the model explains approximately 73 per cent of the variation in GDP per capita growth rates across time and countries. Moreover, ICTs have a positive effect on income growth.[57] In addition, the estimated elasticity coefficients put into perspective the relationship between the variables growth rates rather than their levels. Merely having a good ICT level but very slow ICT growth rates can be reflected in slower GDP growth rates. The estimation of the elasticity coefficient is therefore more suitable for capturing the relationship between the ICT and GDP growth rates.

Over time, the elasticity coefficients experience an upward trend, as anticipated in the previous graphical

**Table 1.13**

**Impact of ICT on GDP growth, by country groups (estimated coefficients)**

| Year | Group A (%) | Group B (%) | Group C (%) | Group D (%) | Group E (%) |
|---|---|---|---|---|---|
| 1995 | 0.140 | 0.251 | 0.070 | 0.089 | 0.099 |
| 1996 | 0.145 | 0.250 | 0.080 | 0.091 | 0.101 |
| 1997 | 0.150 | 0.256 | 0.092 | 0.095 | 0.107 |
| 1998 | 0.155 | 0.257 | 0.094 | 0.097 | 0.103 |
| 1999 | 0.167 | 0.252 | 0.102 | 0.102 | 0.103 |
| 2000 | 0.176 | 0.266 | 0.111 | 0.108 | 0.100 |
| 2001 | 0.182 | 0.272 | 0.116 | 0.116 | 0.106 |
| 2002 | 0.182 | 0.271 | 0.120 | 0.123 | 0.105 |
| 2003 | n.a | n.a | n.a | 0.130 | 0.112 |
| R-squared | 0.230 | 0.310 | 0.190 | 0.090 | 0.080 |

analysis in chart 1.38. They increase from 0.1 in 1996 to 0.3 in 2003 (chart 1.39). In other words, a 1 per cent increase in the Infodensity index of a country resulted on average in a 0.1 per cent increase in per capita GDP in 1996 and in a 0.3 per cent increase in 2003. As suggested earlier, the elasticity coefficients proxy the degree to which the ICT-related inputs have been incorporated into the production processes of a given country.

### Impact by country groups

Finally, the model was run separately for five different country groups with different levels of ICT uptake. This is based on the assumption that economic growth has not been equally sensitive to changes in the ICT indicators across different levels of ICT performance. Therefore, countries have been sorted according to their 2003 Infodensity performance and categorized into five groups (A to E), in a decreasing order (see annex II, table 1.24, for country classification).

Compared with the overall estimation results, group estimates are less significant statistically (table 1.13). Accordingly, the model fits best the countries in Group B, where it explains approximately 30 per cent of the variation in the income growth rate. Despite efficiency limitations, elasticity coefficients exhibit a similar upward trend found in the global analysis. Results also suggest that Group B countries benefit most from increases in ICT growth rates over the nine years, having the highest coefficients (ranging from 0.25 to 0.27). Moreover, it seems that over time, Groups C, D and E could catch up, given the upward trend of the corresponding coefficients. Also, in contrast with Groups A and B, Groups C, D and E have relatively low coefficients (chart 1.40). The slightly lower results of Group A countries compared with Group B countries suggest that in countries with high ICT endowment the

effect is somewhat levelling off, although it continues to increase over time.

The more moderate results for the least-ICT-endowed countries are a potential indicator of an insufficient or inefficient incorporation of ICTs into the production processes of those countries. Market rigidities (such as difficult access to credit, lower degree of technological advances diffusion, lower rates of enrolment in higher education resulting in limited high-skilled labour endowments, etc.) could limit a more efficient incorporation of ICTs into the production process in countries of Groups C to E and thus might prevent them from taking full advantage of their ICT-related investments. Another explanation could be stronger spillover and network effects. Countries with a higher ICT stock could theoretically benefit from a higher level of interaction of their domestic ICT networks, thus creating added value at very low cost and achieving higher productivity gains.

To conclude, the results of the empirical analysis showed that ICT adoption can make an important positive contribution to gains in per capita income — even in poorer countries. ICTs as measured by the Infodensity index can contribute to the GDP per capita (PPP) growth rate with an increase of 0.1 to 0.3 percentage points. However, the best results are retrieved from group estimations for the intermediate level of ICT uptake. In other words, countries with similar shares of world GDP and ICT uptake seem to be benefiting most from the opportunities provided by ICTs. Since human capital is a central component of the Infodensity index, the results strongly reflect the level of skills and education available in the countries, as a key determinant for the impact of ICTs on development.

## F.  Conclusions and recommendations

This chapter has provided an overview of the latest trends in ICT access and use globally, and specifically in the developing world. It has included a description of the evolution of core ICT indicators such as Internet and mobile phone use, as well as the role of broadband in promoting the information economy. The chapter has also analysed the role of ICTs in developing countries' services trade, and presented research results that aimed to measure the economic impact of ICTs. On the basis of this comprehensive discussion of global ICT developments, the following will — in

**Chart 1.40**

**Country group elasticities**

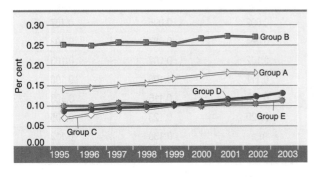

a summary fashion — draw some key conclusions and provide suggestions for policymakers in developing countries.

## The diffusion of ICT in developing countries still needs government intervention

ICT diffusion in developing countries should address connectivity in both urban and rural areas, where private providers might be discouraged to go because of costs associated with geographical hurdles or the absence of a critical mass of customers. Mobile phones and other wireless technologies present a viable alternative solution to connectivity problems in developing countries. To reduce the economic isolation of rural and remote areas, wireless communications should be encouraged actively by Governments where telecommunications incumbents could take the lead.

## Broadband is crucial for developing an information economy

Broadband Internet access makes it possible to conduct more sophisticated e-business, and is essential for conducting such business at the international level. This will become increasingly evident in developing countries, as the rapid growth in broadband penetration in OECD countries shed further light on the technology gap. The use of broadband for e-business has a positive impact on competitiveness and productivity at the firm level, which in turn has an impact on macroeconomic growth.

## Demand is as important as supply to broadband deployment

National ICT policies must address both the supply and the demand sides of broadband deployment, with special attention to SMEs. Broadband deployment should match demand, but demand can be encouraged through the development of content and skills, as well as by ensuring an enabling environment through an adequate regulatory framework and security.

## The ICT sector could be an important source of employment and growth

Following the contraction in the year 2000, ICT-sector value-added and employment grew in developed countries in 2003. This increase in demand and supply in the developed countries' ICT sector opens up new prospects for developing country business partners. Industrial and trade policies in ICT-producing developing countries should therefore support the creation of business opportunities in ICT-related industries.

## ICTs continue to facilitate trade in services

ICT-enabled service exports continued to grow faster than total service exports, thus confirming ICTs' role in facilitating services trade. Developing countries contributed with less than one fifth to the global exported value of ICT-enabled services and took longer to recover in the aftermath of 2000. However, in 2003, developing countries' exports picked up again and exceeded the average growth rate. Asian exporters in general and mainland China and India in particular performed better in terms of both absolute value and dynamics.

## South–South trade potential: Evidence from Asia

Developed countries remained the main exporters and importers of ICT-enabled services, although they traded to an increasing extent with transition/SEECIS and developing partners. Given the lack of bilateral data, the potential of South–South trade in ICT-enabled services could not be thoroughly assessed. The Republic of Korea's exports and imports of services suggest a growing contribution of regional trade in the developing countries' balance of payments.

## ICTs boost countries' exports more than multinationals' sales

In the ICT-enabled sectors, trade carried out through the foreign affiliates of multinational companies exceeds by a large extent the conventional export and import flows. Furthermore, developing and transition economies have increased their commercial presence abroad. An analysis in relative terms shows that in most cases ICTs boost service exports more than sales through foreign affiliates. However, large exports of ICT-enabled services are also likely to sell more through their foreign affiliates. Developing countries' exports would benefit from improved access to foreign markets under all WTO modes of delivery.

## Computer and information services trade needs further liberalization

Computer and information exports are the most rapidly growing ICT-enabled service sector, particularly in the developing economies. This may be explained by, inter alia, the correspondingly low regulatory environment in the WTO. Continued trade liberalization in this sector would need to take into account developing countries' concerns about the movement of natural persons (Mode 4). Additionally, developing countries should seek improved market access commitments under the other modes of delivery to boost the potential for South–South trade in services.

## ICT impact on firms is best when complemented with other changes

Research on the impact of ICTs at the firm level revealed a positive impact on firm performance and increased market share if it is complemented by organizational changes, the upgrading of skills and innovation. The age and size of the companies, as well as the quality and speed of the Internet connection, also play a role. Other critical factors are the regulatory environment in which the firm operates, the structure of the industry sector and the degree of competition in the market. Hence, to optimize impact, firm-level ICT strategies need to be introduced in conjunction with other changes in the management of the firms.

## ICT impact on growth is highest once a critical threshold of ICT uptake is reached

ICT access and use can contribute to productivity growth in both developed and developing countries. UNCTAD research on measuring the impact of ICTs on GDP in developing countries revealed a positive contribution even in poorer countries. But countries that already have a certain level of ICT uptake seem to benefit most from the new technologies. Therefore, Governments need to create an enabling environment through their national ICT plans and policies, so as to promote ICT diffusion among economic and social actors (see chapter 2).

## Measuring ICT impact sho uld focus on micro-level data

Research on measuring the impact of ICT on development is still in its infancy. However, with the increasing availability of reliable and comparable statistical data, further work will be possible. In particular, there is a need to carry out micro-data analysis to identify the extent to which ICTs change the performance of SMEs in developing countries. Another important advantage of using micro-data is that the analysis can be linked to other firm-specific characteristics or data such as skills. National statistical offices, the producers of such data, are in the best position to carry out this analysis, as an input to national ICT policymaking.

## More and better data are crucial for assessing the information economy

Finally, research on ICT trends and impact on development will benefit significantly from improved data. Measuring the information society should therefore be an integral component of national ICT plans and policies. This requires close cooperation between policymakers and statistical offices, and among stakeholders in the national statistical system. Since the development of comparable data is a long-term process, even countries with relatively less advanced information societies should start the process early in order to have some initial data in the medium term that will allow them to assess the impact of ICT on their social and economic development.

# Annex I
# STATISTICAL ANNEX

Table 1.14
Mobile phone subscribers:
Economies by level of development and by region

| | 2001 | % change 2001–2002 | 2002 | % change 2002–2003 | 2003 | % change 2003–2004 | 2004 | % change 2004–2005 | 2005 |
|---|---|---|---|---|---|---|---|---|---|
| DEVELOPED ECONOMIES | | | | | | | | | |
| ASIA | | | | | | | | | |
| Israel | 5 900 000 | 7.4 | 6 334 000 | 2.6 | 6 500 000 | 10.6 | 7 187 500 | 8.5 | 7 800 000 |
| Japan | 74 819 160 | 8.4 | 81 118 320 | 6.8 | 86 654 960 | 5.6 | 91 473 936 | 3.6 | 94 745 000 |
| EUROPE | | | | | | | | | |
| Andorra | 29 429 | 11.4 | 32 790 | 58.3 | 51 893 | .. | .. | .. | 64 560 |
| Austria | 6 541 000 | 3.0 | 6 736 000 | 5.3 | 7 094 502 | 12.6 | 7 989 955 | 2.1 | 8 160 000 |
| Belgium | 7 697 000 | 5.3 | 8 101 777 | 6.2 | 8 605 834 | 6.1 | 9 131 705 | 3.6 | 9 460 000 |
| Cyprus | 314 355 | 32.9 | 417 933 | 32.0 | 551 752 | 16.1 | 640 515 | 12.2 | 718 842 |
| Czech Republic | 6 947 151 | 23.9 | 8 610 177 | 12.8 | 9 708 683 | 10.9 | 10 771 270 | 9.3 | 11 775 878 |
| Denmark (incl. Faroe Islands) | 3 984 652 | 13.1 | 4 508 461 | 6.6 | 4 805 917 | 7.5 | 5 165 546 | 6.7 | 5 511 878 |
| Estonia | 651 200 | 35.3 | 881 000 | 19.2 | 1 050 241 | 19.6 | 1 255 731 | 15.1 | 1 445 300 |
| Finland | 4 175 587 | 8.2 | 4 516 772 | 5.1 | 4 747 126 | 5.1 | 4 988 000 | 4.9 | 5 231 000 |
| France | 36 997 400 | 4.3 | 38 585 300 | 8.0 | 41 683 100 | 6.9 | 44 551 800 | 7.9 | 48 058 400 |
| Germany | 56 126 000 | 5.3 | 59 128 000 | 9.6 | 64 800 000 | 10.1 | 71 316 000 | 11.1 | 79 200 000 |
| Gibraltar | 9 797 | 24.2 | 12 167 | 30.7 | 15 900 | 15.7 | 18 392 | .. | .. |
| Greece | 7 963 742 | 17.0 | 9 314 260 | 11.0 | 10 337 000 | 6.8 | 11 044 232 | -9.1 | 10 042 633 |
| Greenland | 16 747 | 19.0 | 19 924 | .. | .. | .. | .. | .. | .. |
| Guernsey | 31 539 | 16.0 | 36 580 | 13.5 | 41 530 | 5.5 | 43 824 | .. | .. |
| Hungary | 4 967 430 | 38.6 | 6 886 111 | 15.4 | 7 944 586 | 9.9 | 8 727 188 | 6.8 | 9 320 000 |
| Iceland | 248 131 | 5.0 | 260 438 | 7.4 | 279 670 | 4.2 | 291 372 | 4.3 | 304 001 |
| Ireland | 2 970 000 | 1.0 | 3 000 000 | 16.7 | 3 500 000 | 8.0 | 3 780 000 | 11.4 | 4 210 000 |
| Italy | 51 246 000 | 5.8 | 54 200 000 | 4.7 | 56 770 000 | 10.5 | 62 750 000 | 14.0 | 71 535 000 |
| Jersey | 61 417 | .. | .. | .. | 81 200 | .. | .. | .. | .. |
| Latvia | 656 835 | 39.6 | 917 196 | 33.0 | 1 219 550 | 26.0 | 1 536 712 | 21.8 | 1 871 602 |
| Liechtenstein | 11 000 | 3.7 | 11 402 | 119.3 | 25 000 | 2.0 | 25 500 | .. | .. |
| Lithuania | 1 017 999 | 61.6 | 1 645 568 | 31.9 | 2 169 866 | 57.7 | 3 421 538 | 27.2 | 4 353 447 |
| Luxembourg | 409 064 | 15.6 | 473 000 | 14.0 | 539 000 | .. | .. | .. | .. |
| Malta | 239 416 | 15.6 | 276 859 | 4.7 | 289 992 | .. | .. | .. | 323 980 |
| Netherlands | 12 200 000 | 0.8 | 12 300 000 | 9.7 | 13 491 000 | 9.9 | 14 821 000 | 6.8 | 15 834 000 |
| Norway | 3 766 431 | 3.8 | 3 911 136 | 6.4 | 4 163 381 | .. | .. | .. | 4 754 453 |
| Poland | 10 004 661 | 38.9 | 13 898 471 | 25.2 | 17 401 222 | 32.7 | 23 096 064 | 26.7 | 29 260 000 |

## Table 1.14 (Continued)

| | 2001 | % change 2001–2002 | 2002 | % change 2002–2003 | 2003 | % change 2003–2004 | 2004 | % change 2004–2005 | 2005 |
|---|---|---|---|---|---|---|---|---|---|
| Portugal | 7 977 537 | 6.9 | 8 528 900 | 17.6 | 10 030 000 | 2.7 | 10 300 000 | 11.1 | 11 447 670 |
| San Marino | 15 854 | 5.7 | 16 759 | 0.8 | 16 900 | .. | .. | .. | .. |
| Slovakia | 2 147 331 | 36.1 | 2 923 383 | 25.8 | 3 678 774 | 16.2 | 4 275 164 | 6.2 | 4 540 374 |
| Slovenia | 1 470 085 | 13.4 | 1 667 234 | 4.3 | 1 739 146 | .. | .. | .. | 1 759 232 |
| Spain | 29 655 728 | 13.1 | 33 530 996 | 11.0 | 37 219 840 | 3.8 | 38 622 584 | 7.0 | 41 327 911 |
| Sweden | 7 177 000 | 10.8 | 7 949 000 | 10.7 | 8 801 000 | 5.7 | 9 302 000 | -9.3 | 8 436 500 |
| Switzerland | 5 275 791 | 8.7 | 5 736 303 | 7.9 | 6 189 000 | 1.4 | 6 275 000 | 9.1 | 6 847 000 |
| United Kingdom | 46 283 000 | 7.3 | 49 677 000 | 6.7 | 52 984 000 | 15.3 | 61 100 000 | .. | .. |
| **NORTH AMERICA** | | | | | | | | | |
| Canada | 10 649 000 | 11.5 | 11 872 000 | 11.4 | 13 228 000 | 13.3 | 14 984 396 | 10.8 | 16 600 000 |
| United States (incl. Puerto Rico and Guam) | 129 535 848 | 10.1 | 142 566 848 | 11.3 | 158 721 984 | 15.8 | 183 787 136 | 9.7 | 201 650 000 |
| **OCEANIA** | | | | | | | | | |
| Australia | 11 132 000 | 13.0 | 12 575 000 | 14.1 | 14 347 000 | 14.7 | 16 449 000 | 12.0 | 18 420 000 |
| New Zealand | 2 288 000 | 7.0 | 2 449 000 | 6.1 | 2 599 000 | 16.5 | 3 027 000 | 16.6 | 3 530 000 |
| **DEVELOPING ECONOMIES** | | | | | | | | | |
| **AFRICA** | | | | | | | | | |
| Algeria | 100 000 | 300.0 | 400 000 | 260.3 | 1 441 400 | 224.9 | 4 682 690 | 191.7 | 13 661 000 |
| Angola | 86 500 | 50.3 | 130 000 | 156.0 | 332 800 | 182.5 | 940 000 | 16.4 | 1 094 115 |
| Benin | 125 000 | 75.0 | 218 770 | 8.0 | 236 175 | .. | .. | .. | 75 063 |
| Botswana | 316 000 | 37.7 | 435 000 | 20.2 | 522 840 | 7.8 | 563 782 | 46.0 | 823 070 |
| Burkina Faso | 76 000 | 48.7 | 113 000 | 100.9 | 227 000 | 75.3 | 398 000 | 43.8 | 572 200 |
| Burundi | 30 687 | 69.5 | 52 000 | 23.1 | 64 000 | .. | .. | .. | 153 000 |
| Cameroon | 417 295 | 68.1 | 701 507 | 53.5 | 1 077 000 | 42.7 | 1 536 594 | 47.0 | 2 259 000 |
| Cape Verde | 31 507 | 36.3 | 42 949 | 24.2 | 53 342 | 23.3 | 65 780 | 24.2 | 81 721 |
| Central African Rep. | 11 000 | 14.5 | 12 600 | 217.5 | 40 000 | 50.0 | 60 000 | .. | .. |
| Chad | 22 000 | 55.5 | 34 200 | 90.1 | 65 000 | 89.2 | 123 000 | 70.7 | 210 000 |
| Comoros | .. | .. | .. | .. | 2 000 | .. | .. | .. | 16 065 |
| Congo | 150 000 | 47.9 | 221 800 | 48.8 | 330 000 | 16.3 | 383 653 | 27.7 | 490 000 |
| Côte d'Ivoire | 728 545 | 41.0 | 1 027 058 | 24.7 | 1 280 696 | 19.6 | 1 531 846 | 43.0 | 2 190 000 |
| Democratic Republic of the Congo | 150 000 | 273.3 | 560 000 | 78.6 | 1 000 000 | .. | .. | .. | 2 746 000 |
| Djibouti | 3 000 | 400.0 | 15 000 | 53.3 | 23 000 | .. | .. | .. | .. |
| Egypt | 2 793 800 | 60.9 | 4 494 700 | 29.0 | 5 797 530 | 31.8 | 7 643 060 | 78.3 | 13 629 602 |
| Equatorial Guinea | 15 000 | 113.3 | 32 000 | 29.7 | 41 500 | 33.7 | 55 500 | 74.6 | 96 900 |
| Eritrea | .. | .. | .. | .. | .. | .. | 20 000 | 102.2 | 40 438 |
| Ethiopia | 27 500 | 83.2 | 50 369 | 94.2 | 97 827 | 82.0 | 178 000 | .. | .. |
| Gabon | 150 000 | 86.2 | 279 289 | 7.4 | 300 000 | 63.1 | 489 367 | 32.8 | 649 807 |

## Table 1.14 *(Continued)*

| | 2001 | % change 2001–2002 | 2002 | % change 2002–2003 | 2003 | % change 2003–2004 | 2004 | % change 2004–2005 | 2005 |
|---|---|---|---|---|---|---|---|---|---|
| Gambia | 55 085 | 81.5 | 100 000 | .. | .. | .. | 175 000 | 41.4 | 247 478 |
| Ghana | 243 797 | 58.6 | 386 775 | 105.7 | 795 529 | 113.1 | 1 695 000 | 4.1 | 1 765 000 |
| Guinea | 55 670 | 63.1 | 90 772 | 22.8 | 111 500 | .. | .. | .. | 189 000 |
| Guinea-Bissau | .. | .. | .. | .. | 1 275 | .. | .. | .. | 67 000 |
| Kenya | 600 000 | 97.9 | 1 187 122 | 34.0 | 1 590 785 | 60.1 | 2 546 157 | 81.1 | 4 611 970 |
| Lesotho | 57 000 | 69.9 | 96 843 | 4.8 | 101 474 | 56.7 | 159 000 | 54.1 | 245 052 |
| Liberia | 2 000 | .. | .. | .. | 47 250 | .. | .. | .. | 160 000 |
| Libyan Arab Jamahiriya | 50 000 | 40.0 | 70 000 | 81.4 | 127 000 | .. | .. | .. | .. |
| Madagascar | 147 500 | 10.5 | 163 010 | 74.0 | 283 666 | 17.7 | 333 888 | 51.1 | 504 660 |
| Malawi | 55 730 | 54.4 | 86 047 | 57.0 | 135 114 | 64.4 | 222 135 | 93.3 | 429 305 |
| Mali | 45 340 | 16.1 | 52 639 | 365.3 | 244 930 | 63.3 | 400 000 | 117.4 | 869 576 |
| Mauritania | 110 463 | 123.8 | 247 238 | 41.9 | 350 954 | 48.9 | 522 400 | 42.7 | 745 615 |
| Mauritius | 272 416 | 27.8 | 348 137 | -6.3 | 326 033 | 56.4 | 510 000 | 39.9 | 713 300 |
| Mayotte | .. | .. | 21 700 | 65.9 | 36 000 | 5.6 | 38 000 | .. | .. |
| Morocco | 4 771 739 | 29.9 | 6 198 670 | 18.7 | 7 359 870 | 26.9 | 9 336 878 | 32.7 | 12 392 805 |
| Mozambique | 152 652 | 66.9 | 254 759 | 71.0 | 435 757 | 62.5 | 708 000 | 72.3 | 1 220 000 |
| Namibia | 106 600 | 40.7 | 150 000 | 49.1 | 223 671 | 27.9 | 286 095 | 73.0 | 495 000 |
| Niger | 2 126 | 683.1 | 16 648 | 360.0 | 76 580 | 93.6 | 148 276 | 102.3 | 299 899 |
| Nigeria | 400 000 | 302.0 | 1 607 931 | 95.9 | 3 149 473 | 190.4 | 9 147 209 | 103.3 | 18 600 000 |
| Reunion | 421 100 | 16.3 | 489 800 | 15.4 | 565 000 | .. | .. | .. | .. |
| Rwanda | 65 000 | 26.8 | 82 391 | 58.7 | 130 720 | 6.1 | 138 728 | 109.0 | 290 000 |
| Sao Tome and Principe | .. | .. | 1 980 | 143.4 | 4 819 | .. | .. | .. | 12 000 |
| Senegal | 301 811 | 51.0 | 455 645 | 26.4 | 575 917 | 78.5 | 1 028 061 | 68.3 | 1 730 106 |
| Seychelles | 36 683 | 21.9 | 44 731 | 10.1 | 49 229 | 0.0 | 49 230 | 15.8 | 57 003 |
| Sierra Leone | 26 895 | 149.1 | 67 000 | 69.0 | 113 214 | .. | .. | .. | .. |
| Somalia | 85 000 | 17.6 | 100 000 | 100.0 | 200 000 | 150.0 | 500 000 | 0.0 | 500 000 |
| South Africa | 10 787 000 | 27.0 | 13 702 000 | 23.0 | 16 860 000 | 15.7 | 19 500 000 | 59.0 | 31 000 000 |
| Sudan | 103 846 | 83.7 | 190 778 | 176.4 | 527 233 | 98.9 | 1 048 558 | 89.4 | 1 986 000 |
| Swaziland | 55 000 | 23.6 | 68 000 | 25.0 | 85 000 | 32.9 | 113 000 | 77.0 | 200 000 |
| Syrian Arab Republic | 200 000 | 100.0 | 400 000 | 196.3 | 1 185 000 | 97.9 | 2 345 000 | 25.8 | 2 950 000 |
| Togo | 95 000 | 78.9 | 170 000 | 29.4 | 220 000 | .. | .. | .. | 443 635 |
| Tunisia | 389 208 | 47.6 | 574 334 | 233.9 | 1 917 530 | 85.8 | 3 562 970 | 59.4 | 5 680 726 |
| Uganda | 283 520 | 38.7 | 393 310 | 97.3 | 776 169 | 50.1 | 1 165 035 | 30.9 | 1 525 125 |
| United Republic of Tanzania | 426 964 | 78.0 | 760 000 | 36.9 | 1 040 640 | 57.6 | 1 640 000 | .. | .. |
| Zambia | 121 200 | 14.8 | 139 092 | 73.3 | 241 000 | 24.5 | 300 000 | 145.0 | 735 000 |
| Zimbabwe | 314 002 | 7.9 | 338 779 | 7.3 | 363 365 | 9.4 | 397 500 | 75.8 | 699 000 |

## Table 1.14 (Continued)

| | 2001 | % change 2001–2002 | 2002 | % change 2002–2003 | 2003 | % change 2003–2004 | 2004 | % change 2004–2005 | 2005 |
|---|---|---|---|---|---|---|---|---|---|
| **ASIA** | | | | | | | | | |
| Afghanistan | .. | .. | 25 000 | 700.0 | 200 000 | 200.0 | 600 000 | 100.0 | 1 200 000 |
| Bahrain | 299 587 | 29.8 | 388 990 | 13.9 | 443 109 | 46.6 | 649 764 | 15.2 | 748 703 |
| Bangladesh | 520 000 | 106.7 | 1 075 000 | 27.0 | 1 365 000 | 217.0 | 4 327 516 | 108.0 | 9 000 000 |
| Bhutan | .. | .. | .. | .. | 7 998 | 122.6 | 17 800 | 112.6 | 37 842 |
| Brunei Darussalam | 137 000 | .. | .. | .. | .. | .. | .. | .. | .. |
| Cambodia | 223 458 | 70.1 | 380 000 | 31.2 | 498 388 | .. | .. | .. | 1 062 000 |
| China | 144 820 000 | 42.2 | 206 004 992 | 31.0 | 269 952 992 | 24.0 | 334 824 000 | 17.5 | 393 428 000 |
| Dem. People's Rep. of Korea | .. | .. | .. | .. | .. | .. | .. | .. | .. |
| Hong Kong (China) | 5 776 360 | 10.7 | 6 395 725 | 14.9 | 7 349 202 | 10.9 | 8 148 685 | 6.0 | 8 635 532 |
| India | 6 431 520 | 97.3 | 12 687 637 | 106.1 | 26 154 404 | 80.8 | 47 300 000 | 60.7 | 76 000 000 |
| Indonesia | 6 520 947 | 79.4 | 11 700 000 | 60.7 | 18 800 000 | 59.6 | 30 000 000 | 56.4 | 46 909 972 |
| Iran (Islamic Rep. of) | 2 087 353 | 4.8 | 2 186 958 | 54.4 | 3 376 526 | 27.3 | 4 300 000 | 68.0 | 7 222 538 |
| Iraq | .. | .. | 20 000 | 300.0 | 80 000 | 617.5 | 574 000 | .. | .. |
| Jordan | 865 627 | 40.9 | 1 219 597 | 8.7 | 1 325 313 | 20.3 | 1 594 513 | .. | .. |
| Kuwait | 877 920 | 39.8 | 1 227 000 | 15.7 | 1 420 000 | 40.8 | 2 000 000 | 19.0 | 2 379 811 |
| Lao PDR | 29 545 | 86.7 | 55 160 | 103.5 | 112 275 | 81.9 | 204 191 | 212.6 | 638 202 |
| Lebanon | 766 754 | 1.1 | 775 104 | 5.8 | 820 000 | 8.3 | 888 000 | 11.5 | 990 000 |
| Macao (China) | 194 475 | 42.0 | 276 138 | 31.8 | 364 031 | 18.8 | 432 450 | 23.2 | 532 758 |
| Malaysia | 7 385 240 | 25.3 | 9 253 387 | 20.2 | 11 124 112 | 31.4 | 14 611 902 | 33.8 | 19 545 000 |
| Maldives | 18 894 | 121.8 | 41 899 | 58.6 | 66 466 | 70.4 | 113 246 | 35.5 | 153 393 |
| Mongolia | 195 000 | 10.8 | 216 000 | 47.7 | 319 000 | .. | .. | .. | 557 207 |
| Myanmar | 22 671 | 111.6 | 47 982 | 38.6 | 66 517 | 38.3 | 92 007 | 99.4 | 183 434 |
| Nepal | 17 286 | 26.6 | 21 881 | 130.2 | 50 367 | 255.6 | 179 126 | 38.9 | 248 820 |
| Oman | 324 540 | 43.2 | 464 896 | 27.7 | 593 450 | 35.6 | 805 000 | 65.6 | 1 333 225 |
| Pakistan | 742 606 | 128.7 | 1 698 536 | 41.6 | 2 404 400 | 108.9 | 5 022 908 | 154.3 | 12 771 203 |
| Palestine | 300 000 | 6.7 | 320 000 | 50.0 | 480 000 | 103.0 | 974 345 | 12.3 | 1 094 640 |
| Philippines | 12 159 163 | 26.5 | 15 383 001 | 46.3 | 22 509 560 | 46.3 | 32 935 876 | -0.4 | 32 810 000 |
| Qatar | 177 929 | 49.9 | 266 703 | 41.2 | 376 535 | 30.2 | 490 333 | 46.2 | 716 763 |
| Rep. of Korea | 29 045 596 | 11.4 | 32 342 492 | 3.9 | 33 591 760 | 8.9 | 36 586 052 | 4.8 | 38 342 323 |
| Saudi Arabia | 2 528 640 | 98.0 | 5 007 965 | 44.5 | 7 238 224 | 26.8 | 9 175 764 | 44.9 | 13 300 000 |
| Singapore | 2 991 600 | 11.8 | 3 344 800 | 4.0 | 3 477 100 | 11.0 | 3 860 600 | 13.6 | 4 384 600 |
| Sri Lanka | 667 662 | 39.5 | 931 580 | 49.6 | 1 393 403 | 58.7 | 2 211 158 | 52.0 | 3 361 775 |
| Taiwan Province of China | 21 786 384 | 12.0 | 24 390 520 | 5.8 | 25 799 840 | -11.8 | 22 760 144 | -2.6 | 22 170 702 |
| Thailand | 7 550 000 | 113.5 | 16 117 000 | 54.3 | 24 864 020 | 10.1 | 27 379 000 | .. | .. |
| Turkey | 19 572 896 | 19.2 | 23 323 118 | 19.6 | 27 887 536 | 24.5 | 34 707 548 | 25.6 | 43 608 965 |
| United Arab Emirates | 1 909 303 | 27.2 | 2 428 071 | 22.4 | 2 972 331 | 23.9 | 3 683 117 | 23.1 | 4 534 480 |
| Viet Nam | 1 251 195 | 52.0 | 1 902 388 | 44.1 | 2 742 000 | 80.9 | 4 960 000 | 81.5 | 9 000 000 |

## Table 1.14 *(Continued)*

| | 2001 | % change 2001–2002 | 2002 | % change 2002–2003 | 2003 | % change 2003–2004 | 2004 | % change 2004–2005 | 2005 |
|---|---|---|---|---|---|---|---|---|---|
| Yemen | 152 000 | 170.4 | 411 083 | 70.3 | 700 000 | 53.1 | 1 072 000 | 86.6 | 2 000 000 |
| **LATIN AMERICA AND THE CARIBBEAN** | | | | | | | | | |
| Antigua and Barbuda | 25 000 | 52.8 | 38 205 | .. | .. | .. | 54 000 | .. | .. |
| Argentina | 6 741 791 | -2.6 | 6 566 740 | 19.4 | 7 842 233 | 72.3 | 13 512 383 | 63.6 | 22 100 000 |
| Aruba | 53 000 | .. | .. | .. | .. | .. | .. | .. | .. |
| Bahamas | 60 555 | 101.1 | 121 759 | -4.5 | 116 267 | 60.0 | 186 007 | .. | .. |
| Barbados | 53 111 | 83.0 | 97 193 | 44.0 | 140 000 | 43.0 | 200 138 | 3.0 | 206 190 |
| Belize | 39 155 | 32.1 | 51 729 | 16.8 | 60 403 | 61.8 | 97 755 | -4.8 | 93 089 |
| Bermuda | 13 333 | 125.0 | 30 000 | 33.3 | 40 000 | 22.5 | 49 000 | .. | .. |
| Bolivia | 779 917 | 31.2 | 1 023 333 | 25.0 | 1 278 844 | 40.8 | 1 800 789 | 34.5 | 2 421 402 |
| Brazil | 28 745 768 | 21.3 | 34 880 964 | 32.9 | 46 373 264 | 41.5 | 65 605 000 | 31.4 | 86 210 000 |
| Cayman Islands | 17 000 | .. | .. | .. | .. | .. | .. | .. | .. |
| Chile | 5 271 565 | 22.3 | 6 445 698 | 16.7 | 7 520 280 | 27.2 | 9 566 581 | 10.5 | 10 569 572 |
| Colombia | 3 265 261 | 40.8 | 4 596 594 | 34.6 | 6 186 206 | 68.1 | 10 400 578 | 109.6 | 21 800 000 |
| Costa Rica | 326 944 | 53.7 | 502 478 | 54.9 | 778 299 | 18.6 | 923 084 | 19.3 | 1 101 035 |
| Cuba | 8 579 | 108.1 | 17 851 | 98.1 | 35 356 | 114.4 | 75 797 | 77.4 | 134 480 |
| Dominica | 7 710 | 57.9 | 12 173 | 73.3 | 21 099 | 98.3 | 41 838 | .. | .. |
| Dominican Rep. | 1 270 082 | 33.9 | 1 700 609 | 24.8 | 2 122 543 | 19.4 | 2 534 063 | 43.0 | 3 623 289 |
| Ecuador | 859 152 | 81.7 | 1 560 861 | 53.6 | 2 398 161 | 89.5 | 4 544 174 | 37.5 | 6 246 332 |
| El Salvador | 857 782 | 3.6 | 888 818 | 29.4 | 1 149 790 | 59.4 | 1 832 579 | 31.6 | 2 411 753 |
| French Guiana | 75 320 | 15.9 | 87 300 | .. | .. | .. | 98 000 | .. | .. |
| Grenada | 6 414 | 17.8 | 7 553 | 459.9 | 42 293 | 2.4 | 43 313 | .. | .. |
| Guadeloupe | 292 520 | 10.6 | 323 500 | .. | .. | .. | 350 000 | .. | .. |
| Guatemala | 1 146 441 | 37.6 | 1 577 085 | 29.0 | 2 034 776 | 55.7 | 3 168 256 | .. | .. |
| Guyana | 75 320 | 15.9 | 87 300 | 35.9 | 118 658 | 21.3 | 143 945 | 73.7 | 250 000 |
| Haiti | 91 500 | 53.0 | 140 000 | 128.6 | 320 000 | 25.0 | 400 000 | .. | .. |
| Honduras | 237 629 | 37.4 | 326 508 | 16.2 | 379 362 | 86.4 | 707 201 | 81.2 | 1 281 462 |
| Jamaica | 635 000 | 87.0 | 1 187 295 | 34.8 | 1 600 000 | 37.5 | 2 200 000 | 22.7 | 2 700 000 |
| Martinique | 286 120 | 11.8 | 319 900 | .. | .. | .. | 349 000 | .. | .. |
| Mexico | 21 757 560 | 19.2 | 25 928 266 | 16.1 | 30 097 700 | 27.8 | 38 451 136 | 23.4 | 47 462 108 |
| Netherlands Antilles | .. | .. | .. | .. | 200 000 | 0.0 | 200 000 | .. | .. |
| Nicaragua | 164 509 | 44.2 | 237 248 | 96.7 | 466 706 | 58.3 | 738 624 | 51.5 | 1 119 379 |
| Panama | 475 141 | 10.7 | 525 845 | 58.6 | 834 031 | 2.6 | 855 852 | 58.0 | 1 351 924 |
| Paraguay | 1 150 000 | 45.0 | 1 667 018 | 6.2 | 1 770 345 | -0.1 | 1 767 824 | 6.7 | 1 887 000 |
| Peru | 1 793 284 | 28.6 | 2 306 944 | 27.0 | 2 930 343 | 39.7 | 4 092 558 | 36.4 | 5 583 356 |
| Saint Kitts and Nevis | 2 100 | 138.1 | 5 000 | .. | .. | .. | 10 000 | .. | .. |
| Saint Lucia | 2 700 | 430.1 | 14 313 | .. | .. | .. | 93 000 | .. | .. |

## Table 1.14 *(Continued)*

| | 2001 | % change 2001–2002 | 2002 | % change 2002–2003 | 2003 | % change 2003–2004 | 2004 | % change 2004–2005 | 2005 |
|---|---|---|---|---|---|---|---|---|---|
| Saint Vincent and the Grenadines | 7 492 | 33.2 | 9 982 | 530.2 | 62 911 | -9.5 | 56 950 | 24.0 | 70 620 |
| Suriname | 87 000 | 24.6 | 108 363 | 55.5 | 168 522 | 26.3 | 212 819 | 9.4 | 232 785 |
| Trinidad and Tobago | 256 106 | 41.3 | 361 911 | 34.3 | 485 871 | 33.3 | 647 870 | 23.5 | 800 000 |
| Uruguay | 519 991 | -1.2 | 513 528 | -3.1 | 497 530 | 20.6 | 600 000 | .. | .. |
| Venezuela | 6 472 584 | -0.1 | 6 463 561 | 8.5 | 7 015 735 | 20.0 | 8 420 980 | 48.4 | 12 495 721 |
| Virgin Islands (U.S.) | 41 000 | .. | .. | .. | .. | .. | .. | .. | .. |
| **OCEANIA** | | | | | | | | | |
| American Samoa | .. | .. | .. | .. | .. | .. | .. | .. | .. |
| French Polynesia | 67 300 | 33.7 | 90 000 | .. | .. | .. | .. | .. | 87 000 |
| Kiribati | 395 | 25.3 | 495 | 6.3 | 526 | .. | .. | .. | .. |
| Marshall Islands | 489 | 12.9 | 552 | 8.3 | 598 | .. | .. | .. | .. |
| Micronesia (Fed. States of) | .. | .. | 100 | 5 769.0 | 5 869 | 117.8 | 12 782 | .. | .. |
| Nauru | 1 500 | .. | .. | .. | .. | .. | .. | .. | .. |
| New Caledonia | 67 917 | 17.8 | 80 000 | 21.4 | 97 113 | 19.9 | 116 443 | 15.3 | 134 265 |
| Northern Marianas Islands | .. | .. | .. | .. | .. | .. | .. | .. | .. |
| Palau | .. | .. | .. | .. | .. | .. | .. | .. | .. |
| Papua New Guinea | 10 700 | 40.2 | 15 000 | .. | .. | .. | .. | .. | 26 000 |
| Samoa | 2 500 | 8.0 | 2 700 | 288.9 | 10 500 | .. | .. | .. | 24 000 |
| Solomon Islands | 967 | 3.3 | 999 | 48.9 | 1 488 | .. | .. | .. | 6 000 |
| Tonga | 236 | 1321.2 | 3 354 | .. | .. | .. | .. | .. | .. |
| Tuvalu | .. | .. | .. | .. | .. | .. | .. | .. | .. |
| Vanuatu | 350 | 1300.0 | 4 900 | 59.2 | 7 800 | 34.7 | 10 504 | 20.8 | 12 692 |
| **TRANSITION ECONOMIES** | | | | | | | | | |
| **SOUTH-EAST EUROPE AND CIS** | | | | | | | | | |
| Albania | 392 650 | 116.7 | 851 000 | 29.3 | 1 100 000 | .. | .. | .. | .. |
| Azerbaijan | 730 000 | 8.8 | 794 000 | 33.1 | 1 057 000 | 68.7 | 1 782 900 | 25.8 | 2 242 000 |
| Belarus | 138 329 | 234.4 | 462 630 | 141.7 | 1 118 000 | .. | .. | .. | 4 097 997 |
| Bosnia and Herzegovina | 444 711 | 68.4 | 748 780 | 40.2 | 1 050 000 | .. | .. | .. | 1 594 367 |
| Bulgaria | 1 550 000 | 67.6 | 2 597 548 | 34.8 | 3 500 869 | 35.1 | 4 729 731 | 32.0 | 6 244 693 |
| Croatia | 1 755 000 | 33.3 | 2 340 000 | 9.1 | 2 553 000 | .. | .. | .. | 2 983 900 |
| Georgia | 301 327 | 67.1 | 503 619 | 41.2 | 711 224 | 18.2 | 840 600 | 73.6 | 1 459 180 |
| Kazakhstan | 582 000 | 76.5 | 1 027 000 | 29.6 | 1 330 730 | 107.3 | 2 758 940 | 79.6 | 4 955 200 |
| Kyrgyzstan | 27 000 | 96.6 | 53 084 | 160.5 | 138 279 | 117.0 | 300 000 | 80.6 | 541 652 |
| Rep. of Moldova | 225 000 | 50.3 | 338 225 | 40.7 | 475 942 | 65.4 | 787 000 | 38.5 | 1 089 800 |
| Romania | 3 845 116 | 32.9 | 5 110 591 | 37.8 | 7 039 898 | 45.1 | 10 215 388 | 30.7 | 13 354 138 |
| Russian Federation | 7 750 499 | 127.2 | 17 608 756 | 107.3 | 36 500 000 | 103.9 | 74 420 000 | 61.2 | 120 000 000 |
| Serbia and Montenegro | 1 997 809 | 37.7 | 2 750 397 | 32.1 | 3 634 613 | 30.1 | 4 729 629 | 10.6 | 5 229 000 |

## Table 1.14 *(Continued)*

| | 2001 | % change 2001–2002 | 2002 | % change 2002–2003 | 2003 | % change 2003–2004 | 2004 | % change 2004–2005 | 2005 |
|---|---|---|---|---|---|---|---|---|---|
| Tajikistan | 1 630 | 709.8 | 13 200 | 260.7 | 47 617 | .. | .. | .. | 240 000 |
| TFYR Macedonia | 223 275 | 63.6 | 365 346 | 112.4 | 776 000 | .. | .. | .. | 1 250 000 |
| Turkmenistan | 8 173 | 0.0 | 8 173 | 12.4 | 9 187 | .. | .. | .. | .. |
| Ukraine | 2 224 600 | 66.0 | 3 692 700 | 76.0 | 6 498 423 | 111.4 | 13 735 000 | 25.3 | 17 214 280 |
| Uzbekistan | 128 012 | 46.0 | 186 900 | 71.7 | 320 815 | 69.6 | 544 100 | 32.3 | 720 000 |

*Source:* UNCTAD calculations based on the ITU World telecommunication Indicators Database, 2006.

## Annex I

## Statistical Annex

## Table 1.15

## Mobile phone penetration: Economies by level of development and by region

Mobile phone subscribers per 100 inhabitants

| | 2001 | % change 2001–2002 | 2002 | % change 2002–2003 | 2003 | % change 2003–2004 | 2004 | % change 2004–2005 | 2005 |
|---|---|---|---|---|---|---|---|---|---|
| DEVELOPED ECONOMIES | | | | | | | | | |
| ASIA | | | | | | | | | |
| Israel | 90.7 | 5.3 | 95.5 | 0.6 | 96.1 | 9.0 | 104.7 | 7.9 | 113.0 |
| Japan | 58.8 | 8.3 | 63.7 | 6.7 | 67.9 | 5.4 | 71.6 | 3.3 | 74.0 |
| EUROPE | | | | | | | | | |
| Andorra | 36.9 | 8.5 | 40.0 | 54.1 | 61.6 | .. | .. | .. | .. |
| Austria | 81.1 | 2.5 | 83.1 | 4.8 | 87.2 | 11.7 | 97.4 | 2.5 | 99.8 |
| Belgium | 74.7 | 4.8 | 78.2 | 6.1 | 83.0 | 6.5 | 88.3 | .. | .. |
| Cyprus | 45.6 | 28.2 | 58.4 | 31.4 | 76.8 | 3.3 | 79.4 | 8.5 | 86.1 |
| Czech Republic | 67.9 | 24.9 | 84.9 | 13.6 | 96.5 | 9.2 | 105.3 | 9.4 | 115.2 |
| Denmark | 74.0 | 12.7 | 83.3 | 6.0 | 88.3 | 8.8 | 96.1 | 4.8 | 100.7 |
| Estonia | 45.5 | 42.8 | 65.0 | 19.6 | 77.7 | 23.5 | 96.0 | 13.3 | 108.8 |
| Faroe Islands | 54.3 | 18.4 | 64.4 | 18.9 | 76.5 | .. | .. | .. | .. |
| Finland | 80.4 | 7.9 | 86.7 | 4.9 | 91.0 | 5.1 | 95.6 | 4.2 | 99.7 |
| France | 62.3 | 3.8 | 64.7 | 7.6 | 69.6 | 5.9 | 73.7 | 7.8 | 79.4 |
| Germany | 68.1 | 5.2 | 71.6 | 9.6 | 78.5 | 10.1 | 86.4 | 10.8 | 95.8 |
| Gibraltar | 35.6 | 21.9 | 43.5 | 28.4 | 55.8 | .. | .. | .. | .. |
| Greece | 75.2 | 12.5 | 84.5 | 6.7 | 90.2 | 11.5 | 100.6 | -10.2 | 90.3 |
| Greenland | 29.9 | 17.7 | 35.2 | .. | .. | .. | .. | .. | .. |
| Guernsey | 56.1 | 16.4 | 65.3 | 13.9 | 74.4 | .. | .. | .. | .. |
| Hungary | 48.8 | 39.1 | 67.9 | 15.7 | 78.5 | 13.0 | 88.8 | 4.0 | 92.3 |
| Iceland | 86.5 | 4.6 | 90.4 | 7.0 | 96.8 | 2.8 | 99.4 | 4.0 | 103.4 |
| Ireland | 77.4 | -1.4 | 76.3 | 15.3 | 88.0 | 7.5 | 94.5 | 7.4 | 101.5 |
| Italy | 88.3 | 8.7 | 96.0 | 2.2 | 98.1 | 10.3 | 108.2 | 13.8 | 123.1 |
| Jersey | 70.4 | .. | .. | .. | 92.3 | .. | .. | .. | .. |
| Latvia | 27.9 | 41.0 | 39.4 | 33.5 | 52.6 | 27.8 | 67.2 | 20.7 | 81.1 |
| Liechtenstein | 32.8 | 2.6 | 33.7 | 116.5 | 72.9 | .. | .. | .. | .. |
| Lithuania | 29.2 | 62.2 | 47.4 | 32.7 | 62.8 | 58.1 | 99.3 | 28.0 | 127.1 |
| Luxembourg | 93.1 | 14.0 | 106.1 | 12.6 | 119.4 | .. | .. | .. | .. |
| Malta | 61.1 | 14.5 | 69.9 | 3.7 | 72.5 | .. | .. | .. | 80.8 |
| Netherlands | 75.8 | .3 | 75.9 | 9.1 | 82.8 | 10.3 | 91.3 | 6.4 | 97.1 |
| Norway | 83.3 | 3.2 | 85.9 | 5.8 | 90.9 | .. | .. | .. | 102.9 |

## Table 1.15 *(Continued)*

| | 2001 | % change 2001–2002 | 2002 | % change 2002–2003 | 2003 | % change 2003–2004 | 2004 | % change 2004–2005 | 2005 |
|---|---|---|---|---|---|---|---|---|---|
| Poland | 25.9 | 39.0 | 36.0 | 25.3 | 45.1 | 32.9 | 59.9 | 26.8 | 75.9 |
| Portugal | 77.2 | 6.2 | 82.0 | 17.6 | 96.4 | 6.1 | 102.3 | 6.7 | 109.1 |
| San Marino | 58.7 | 5.7 | 62.1 | 0.8 | 62.6 | .. | .. | .. | .. |
| Slovakia | 39.9 | 22.5 | 48.9 | 17.9 | 57.7 | 37.1 | 79.1 | 6.3 | 84.1 |
| Slovenia | 73.7 | 13.4 | 83.5 | 4.3 | 87.1 | .. | .. | .. | 89.4 |
| Spain | 73.4 | 11.2 | 81.6 | 6.9 | 87.2 | 7.7 | 93.9 | 3.1 | 96.8 |
| Sweden | 80.5 | 10.3 | 88.9 | 10.3 | 98.0 | 5.3 | 103.2 | -9.6 | 93.3 |
| Switzerland | 72.8 | 8.2 | 78.8 | 7.4 | 84.6 | 0.1 | 84.6 | 8.4 | 91.8 |
| United Kingdom | 77.0 | 9.1 | 84.1 | 8.4 | 91.2 | 12.8 | 102.8 | .. | .. |
| **NORTH AMERICA** | | | | | | | | | |
| Canada | 34.2 | 10.3 | 37.7 | 10.4 | 41.7 | 13.3 | 47.2 | 9.0 | 51.4 |
| United States | 45.0 | 8.6 | 48.9 | 11.7 | 54.6 | 11.7 | 61.0 | 10.9 | 67.6 |
| **OCEANIA** | | | | | | | | | |
| Australia | 57.3 | 11.7 | 64.0 | 12.7 | 72.2 | 14.5 | 82.6 | 10.6 | 91.4 |
| New Zealand | 59.0 | 5.4 | 62.2 | 4.3 | 64.8 | 19.6 | 77.5 | 13.0 | 87.6 |
| **DEVELOPING ECONOMIES** | | | | | | | | | |
| **AFRICA** | | | | | | | | | |
| Algeria | 0.3 | 294.2 | 1.3 | 255.1 | 4.5 | 219.0 | 14.5 | 187.2 | 41.6 |
| Angola | 0.6 | 45.9 | 0.9 | 148.5 | 2.3 | 188.1 | 6.7 | 2.8 | 6.9 |
| Benin | 1.9 | 69.4 | 3.2 | 4.5 | 3.4 | .. | .. | .. | 1.0 |
| Botswana | 18.8 | 34.5 | 25.3 | 17.5 | 29.7 | 5.7 | 31.4 | 48.5 | 46.6 |
| Burkina Faso | 0.7 | 45.1 | 0.9 | 96.0 | 1.9 | 60.5 | 3.0 | 45.6 | 4.3 |
| Burundi | 0.4 | 66.4 | 0.7 | 20.8 | 0.9 | .. | .. | .. | 2.0 |
| Cameroon | 2.7 | 63.7 | 4.4 | 49.5 | 6.6 | 42.3 | 9.4 | 46.8 | 13.8 |
| Cape Verde | 7.1 | 33.9 | 9.5 | 22.0 | 11.6 | 19.9 | 13.9 | 15.7 | 16.1 |
| Central African Rep. | 0.3 | 9.5 | 0.3 | 203.4 | 1.0 | 58.7 | 1.5 | .. | .. |
| Chad | 0.3 | 51.4 | 0.4 | 85.1 | 0.8 | 72.8 | 1.4 | 55.1 | 2.2 |
| Comoros | .. | .. | .. | .. | 0.3 | .. | .. | .. | 2.0 |
| Congo | 4.8 | 39.4 | 6.7 | 40.3 | 9.4 | 6.6 | 10.0 | 21.9 | 12.3 |
| Côte d'Ivoire | 4.5 | 39.8 | 6.2 | 23.6 | 7.7 | 17.7 | 9.1 | 33.1 | 12.1 |
| Democratic Republic of the Congo | 0.3 | 272.5 | 1.1 | 78.2 | 1.9 | .. | .. | .. | 0.9 |
| Djibouti | 0.5 | 390.9 | 2.3 | 50.6 | 3.4 | .. | .. | .. | .. |
| Egypt | 4.3 | 54.3 | 6.7 | 26.5 | 8.4 | 29.3 | 10.9 | 68.6 | 18.4 |
| Equatorial Guinea | 3.2 | 98.5 | 6.3 | 20.6 | 7.6 | 43.2 | 10.9 | 76.0 | 19.3 |
| Eritrea | .. | .. | .. | .. | .. | .. | 0.5 | 97.3 | 0.9 |
| Ethiopia | 0.0 | 77.8 | 0.1 | 88.6 | 0.1 | 74.3 | 0.2 | .. | .. |

**Table 1.15** *(Continued)*

| | 2001 | % change 2001–2002 | 2002 | % change 2002–2003 | 2003 | % change 2003–2004 | 2004 | % change 2004–2005 | 2005 |
|---|---|---|---|---|---|---|---|---|---|
| Gabon | 11.9 | 80.8 | 21.5 | 4.4 | 22.4 | 61.3 | 36.2 | 29.7 | 47.0 |
| Gambia | 4.3 | 76.6 | 7.5 | .. | .. | .. | 12.0 | 36.3 | 16.3 |
| Ghana | 1.2 | 54.5 | 1.9 | 100.3 | 3.7 | 112.1 | 7.9 | 0.7 | 8.0 |
| Guinea | 0.7 | 61.2 | 1.2 | 21.5 | 1.4 | .. | .. | .. | 2.4 |
| Guinea-Bissau | .. | .. | .. | .. | 0.1 | .. | .. | .. | 5.0 |
| Kenya | 1.9 | 96.6 | 3.8 | 33.1 | 5.0 | 56.5 | 7.9 | 71.4 | 13.5 |
| Lesotho | 2.6 | 69.4 | 4.5 | 4.4 | 4.7 | 89.2 | 8.8 | 54.6 | 13.7 |
| Liberia | 0.1 | .. | .. | .. | 1.4 | .. | .. | .. | 4.9 |
| Libyan Arab Jamahiriya | 0.9 | 40.6 | 1.3 | 82.2 | 2.3 | .. | .. | .. | .. |
| Madagascar | 1.0 | 7.6 | 1.0 | 69.4 | 1.7 | 7.4 | 1.9 | 45.4 | 2.7 |
| Malawi | 0.5 | 53.6 | 0.8 | 56.3 | 1.3 | 39.8 | 1.8 | 85.1 | 3.3 |
| Mali | 0.4 | 13.6 | 0.5 | 355.3 | 2.3 | 59.8 | 3.6 | 112.7 | 7.7 |
| Mauritania | 4.2 | 118.1 | 9.2 | 38.4 | 12.8 | 37.5 | 17.5 | 38.6 | 24.3 |
| Mauritius | 22.7 | 26.7 | 28.8 | -7.2 | 26.7 | 54.9 | 41.4 | 38.5 | 57.3 |
| Mayotte | .. | .. | 13.5 | 59.2 | 21.6 | 5.6 | 22.8 | .. | .. |
| Morocco | 16.4 | 27.8 | 20.9 | 16.8 | 24.4 | 27.8 | 31.2 | 26.1 | 39.4 |
| Mozambique | 0.9 | 63.0 | 1.4 | 67.0 | 2.4 | 58.6 | 3.7 | 65.1 | 6.2 |
| Namibia | 5.8 | 37.1 | 8.0 | 45.3 | 11.6 | 22.4 | 14.2 | 71.3 | 24.4 |
| Niger | 0.0 | 648.4 | 0.1 | 339.6 | 0.6 | 91.7 | 1.2 | 79.9 | 2.1 |
| Nigeria | 0.3 | 291.4 | 1.3 | 90.7 | 2.6 | 181.7 | 7.2 | 96.5 | 14.1 |
| Reunion | 57.6 | 14.4 | 65.9 | 13.4 | 74.7 | .. | .. | .. | .. |
| Rwanda | 0.8 | 23.3 | 1.0 | 54.4 | 1.6 | 5.1 | 1.6 | 96.2 | 3.2 |
| Sao Tome and Principe | .. | .. | 1.3 | 141.8 | 3.2 | .. | .. | .. | 7.6 |
| Senegal | 3.1 | 46.9 | 4.5 | 23.0 | 5.6 | 78.9 | 9.9 | 49.2 | 14.8 |
| Seychelles | 45.2 | 18.3 | 53.4 | 11.3 | 59.5 | 2.2 | 60.8 | .. | .. |
| Sierra Leone | 0.5 | 148.1 | 1.4 | 68.3 | 2.3 | .. | .. | .. | .. |
| Somalia | 0.9 | 17.2 | 1.0 | 64.3 | 1.7 | 150.0 | 4.2 | 0.0 | 4.2 |
| South Africa | 24.2 | 24.5 | 30.1 | 20.6 | 36.4 | 18.6 | 43.1 | 51.5 | 65.4 |
| Sudan | 0.3 | 78.7 | 0.6 | 172.8 | 1.6 | 91.8 | 3.0 | 80.4 | 5.5 |
| Swaziland | 5.4 | 22.2 | 6.6 | 23.6 | 8.1 | 28.2 | 10.4 | 85.6 | 19.4 |
| Syrian Arab Republic | 1.2 | 95.2 | 2.3 | 189.2 | 6.8 | 90.6 | 12.9 | 20.4 | 15.5 |
| Togo | 2.0 | 74.4 | 3.5 | 26.1 | 4.4 | .. | .. | .. | 7.2 |
| Tunisia | 4.0 | 45.9 | 5.9 | 230.5 | 19.4 | 84.7 | 35.9 | 57.1 | 56.3 |
| Uganda | 1.2 | 33.9 | 1.6 | 90.4 | 3.0 | 43.9 | 4.4 | 21.3 | 5.3 |
| United Republic of Tanzania | 1.3 | 73.6 | 2.2 | 33.6 | 2.9 | 47.7 | 4.4 | .. | .. |
| Zambia | 1.1 | 11.6 | 1.3 | 68.4 | 2.2 | 27.6 | 2.7 | 129.4 | 6.3 |
| Zimbabwe | 2.7 | 6.7 | 2.9 | 6.1 | 3.1 | -0.5 | 3.1 | 91.1 | 5.9 |

## Table 1.15 *(Continued)*

| | 2001 | % change 2001–2002 | 2002 | % change 2002–2003 | 2003 | % change 2003–2004 | 2004 | % change 2004–2005 | 2005 |
|---|---|---|---|---|---|---|---|---|---|
| **ASIA** | | | | | | | | | |
| Afghanistan | .. | .. | 0.1 | 829.2 | 1.0 | 141.4 | 2.4 | 99.4 | 4.8 |
| Bahrain | 46.0 | 25.7 | 57.9 | 10.3 | 63.8 | 37.7 | 87.9 | 17.1 | 103.0 |
| Bangladesh | 0.4 | 103.7 | 0.8 | 25.1 | 1.0 | 186.2 | 2.9 | 119.5 | 6.3 |
| Bhutan | .. | .. | .. | .. | 1.1 | -29.7 | 0.8 | .. | .. |
| Brunei Darussalam | 40.1 | .. | .. | .. | .. | .. | .. | .. | .. |
| Cambodia | 1.7 | 65.8 | 2.8 | 27.9 | 3.5 | .. | .. | .. | 7.5 |
| China | 11.0 | 45.4 | 16.0 | 30.3 | 20.9 | 22.0 | 25.5 | 17.3 | 29.9 |
| Dem. People's Rep. of Korea | .. | .. | .. | .. | .. | .. | .. | .. | .. |
| Hong Kong (China) | 85.9 | 9.7 | 94.2 | 14.5 | 107.9 | 6.1 | 114.5 | 7.1 | 122.6 |
| India | 0.6 | 94.5 | 1.2 | 103.2 | 2.5 | 76.8 | 4.4 | 57.5 | 6.9 |
| Indonesia | 3.1 | 76.9 | 5.5 | 58.5 | 8.7 | 54.2 | 13.5 | 56.2 | 21.1 |
| Iran (Islamic Rep. of) | 3.2 | 3.5 | 3.3 | 52.2 | 5.1 | 21.0 | 6.2 | 68.6 | 10.4 |
| Iraq | .. | .. | 0.1 | 289.2 | 0.3 | 591.5 | 2.2 | .. | .. |
| Jordan | 16.7 | 37.2 | 22.9 | 5.6 | 24.2 | 17.4 | 28.4 | .. | .. |
| Korea (Rep. of) | 61.4 | 10.7 | 67.9 | 3.4 | 70.2 | 8.4 | 76.1 | 4.3 | 79.4 |
| Kuwait | 38.6 | 34.5 | 51.9 | 10.1 | 57.2 | 34.8 | 77.1 | 14.9 | 88.6 |
| Lao P.D.R. | 0.5 | 81.9 | 1.0 | 98.4 | 2.0 | 78.5 | 3.5 | 205.3 | 10.8 |
| Lebanon | 22.9 | -0.8 | 22.7 | 3.2 | 23.4 | 6.8 | 25.0 | 10.6 | 27.7 |
| Macau (China) | 44.5 | 40.4 | 62.5 | 29.8 | 81.2 | 14.1 | 92.6 | 25.1 | 115.8 |
| Malaysia | 30.9 | 22.1 | 37.7 | 17.1 | 44.2 | 32.9 | 58.7 | 28.0 | 75.2 |
| Maldives | 6.9 | 117.3 | 14.9 | 55.4 | 23.2 | 49.0 | 34.5 | .. | .. |
| Mongolia | 8.1 | 9.5 | 8.9 | 46.0 | 13.0 | .. | .. | .. | 21.1 |
| Myanmar | 0.0 | 107.5 | 0.1 | 35.9 | 0.1 | 36.3 | 0.2 | .. | .. |
| Nepal | 0.1 | 24.0 | 0.1 | 125.6 | 0.2 | 227.4 | 0.7 | 31.7 | 0.9 |
| Oman | 13.1 | 39.9 | 18.3 | 24.6 | 22.8 | 20.1 | 27.4 | 89.4 | 51.9 |
| Pakistan | 0.5 | 123.2 | 1.2 | 38.1 | 1.6 | 105.6 | 3.3 | 151.0 | 8.3 |
| Palestine | 9.1 | 1.8 | 9.3 | 43.2 | 13.3 | 99.3 | 26.4 | 11.8 | 29.6 |
| Philippines | 15.5 | 24.5 | 19.4 | 43.5 | 27.8 | 43.5 | 39.8 | -0.9 | 39.5 |
| Qatar | 27.9 | 42.5 | 39.7 | 34.2 | 53.3 | 48.6 | 79.2 | 16.3 | 92.2 |
| Saudi Arabia | 11.8 | 93.0 | 22.8 | 40.8 | 32.1 | 14.7 | 36.8 | 47.0 | 54.1 |
| Singapore | 72.4 | 10.9 | 80.3 | 3.1 | 82.9 | 8.0 | 89.5 | 13.3 | 101.4 |
| Sri Lanka | 3.6 | 37.9 | 4.9 | 47.2 | 7.2 | 58.5 | 11.5 | 41.2 | 16.2 |
| Taiwan Province of China | 97.2 | 11.4 | 108.3 | 5.4 | 114.1 | -12.4 | 100.0 | -2.6 | 97.4 |
| Thailand | 12.3 | 111.3 | 26.0 | 54.2 | 40.1 | 10.0 | 44.2 | .. | .. |
| Turkey | 28.6 | 17.3 | 33.5 | 17.7 | 39.4 | 21.7 | 48.0 | 24.1 | 59.6 |
| United Arab Emirates | 54.7 | 18.2 | 64.7 | 13.7 | 73.6 | 15.1 | 84.7 | 19.1 | 100.9 |

## Table 1.15 (Continued)

| | 2001 | % change 2001–2002 | 2002 | % change 2002–2003 | 2003 | % change 2003–2004 | 2004 | % change 2004–2005 | 2005 |
|---|---|---|---|---|---|---|---|---|---|
| Viet Nam | 1.5 | 51.8 | 2.3 | 43.9 | 3.4 | 78.5 | 6.0 | 77.7 | 10.7 |
| Yemen | 0.8 | 161.7 | 2.1 | 64.8 | 3.5 | 48.8 | 5.2 | 84.4 | 9.5 |
| **LATIN AMERICA AND THE CARIBBEAN** | | | | | | | | | |
| Antigua and Barbuda | 32.3 | 51.7 | 49.0 | .. | .. | .. | 70.1 | .. | .. |
| Argentina | 18.1 | -3.5 | 17.5 | 18.3 | 20.7 | 67.9 | 34.8 | 64.7 | 57.3 |
| Aruba | 50.0 | .. | .. | .. | .. | .. | .. | .. | .. |
| Bahamas | 19.7 | 97.8 | 39.0 | -6.0 | 36.7 | 60.0 | 58.7 | .. | .. |
| Barbados | 19.8 | 82.5 | 36.1 | 43.7 | 51.9 | 42.3 | 73.9 | 3.8 | 76.7 |
| Belize | 15.2 | 23.3 | 18.8 | 9.0 | 20.5 | 83.0 | 37.5 | -7.9 | 34.5 |
| Bermuda | 20.6 | 123.6 | 46.2 | 32.5 | 61.2 | 29.2 | 79.0 | .. | .. |
| Bolivia | 9.4 | 30.2 | 12.3 | 24.0 | 15.2 | 32.0 | 20.1 | 31.4 | 26.4 |
| Brazil | 16.7 | 19.9 | 20.1 | 31.0 | 26.3 | 38.1 | 36.3 | 27.4 | 46.2 |
| Cayman Islands | 38.0 | .. | .. | .. | .. | .. | .. | .. | .. |
| Chile | 34.2 | 25.1 | 42.8 | 15.3 | 49.4 | 25.7 | 62.1 | 9.2 | 67.8 |
| Colombia | 7.6 | 39.2 | 10.6 | 33.1 | 14.1 | 63.9 | 23.2 | 106.5 | 47.8 |
| Costa Rica | 8.2 | 52.2 | 12.5 | 49.3 | 18.7 | 16.4 | 21.7 | 17.1 | 25.4 |
| Cuba | 0.1 | 107.4 | 0.2 | 97.4 | 0.3 | 114.1 | 0.7 | 78.4 | 1.2 |
| Dominica | 9.9 | 57.5 | 15.6 | 72.9 | 27.0 | 118.4 | 58.9 | .. | .. |
| Dominican Rep. | 15.7 | 26.6 | 19.9 | 23.2 | 24.5 | 17.8 | 28.8 | 41.1 | 40.7 |
| Ecuador | 6.7 | 80.0 | 12.0 | 52.5 | 18.3 | 88.2 | 34.4 | 37.1 | 47.2 |
| El Salvador | 13.4 | 2.7 | 13.8 | 25.8 | 17.3 | 60.0 | 27.7 | 26.5 | 35.0 |
| French Guiana | 44.6 | 11.9 | 49.9 | .. | .. | .. | 53.6 | .. | .. |
| Grenada | 6.4 | 11.1 | 7.1 | 428.1 | 37.6 | 11.8 | 42.1 | .. | .. |
| Guadeloupe | 67.9 | 9.5 | 74.3 | .. | .. | .. | 79.0 | .. | .. |
| Guatemala | 9.8 | 34.0 | 13.1 | 25.7 | 16.5 | 51.5 | 25.0 | .. | .. |
| Guyana | 8.7 | 14.7 | 9.9 | 34.5 | 13.4 | 40.5 | 18.8 | 77.4 | 33.3 |
| Haiti | 1.1 | 52.5 | 1.7 | 127.8 | 3.8 | 23.4 | 4.7 | .. | .. |
| Honduras | 3.6 | 34.1 | 4.9 | 14.5 | 5.6 | 81.0 | 10.1 | 76.1 | 17.8 |
| Jamaica | 24.3 | 86.0 | 45.2 | 33.9 | 60.6 | 35.7 | 82.2 | 23.9 | 101.8 |
| Martinique | 74.0 | 11.0 | 82.1 | .. | .. | .. | 88.4 | .. | .. |
| Mexico | 21.9 | 17.4 | 25.8 | 14.4 | 29.5 | 24.3 | 36.6 | 21.0 | 44.3 |
| Netherlands Antilles | .. | .. | .. | .. | 89.9 | .2 | 90.1 | .. | .. |
| Nicaragua | 3.2 | 44.2 | 4.6 | 86.8 | 8.5 | 55.0 | 13.2 | .. | .. |
| Panama | 16.4 | 6.7 | 17.5 | 53.0 | 26.8 | 0.8 | 27.0 | 55.2 | 41.9 |
| Paraguay | 20.4 | 41.3 | 28.8 | 3.5 | 29.9 | -1.6 | 29.4 | 4.3 | 30.6 |
| Peru | 6.9 | 25.5 | 8.6 | 23.9 | 10.7 | 38.9 | 14.8 | 34.5 | 20.0 |
| Saint Kitts and Nevis | 4.6 | 135.0 | 10.7 | .. | .. | .. | 20.0 | .. | .. |

## Table 1.15 *(Continued)*

| | 2001 | % change 2001–2002 | 2002 | % change 2002–2003 | 2003 | % change 2003–2004 | 2004 | % change 2004–2005 | 2005 |
|---|---|---|---|---|---|---|---|---|---|
| Saint Lucia | 1.7 | 422.7 | 8.9 | .. | .. | .. | 62.0 | .. | .. |
| Saint Vincent and the Grenadines | 6.5 | 31.0 | 8.5 | 519.7 | 52.9 | -11.0 | 47.1 | 26.1 | 59.3 |
| Suriname | 18.5 | 23.0 | 22.8 | 53.9 | 35.0 | 38.4 | 48.5 | 6.9 | 51.8 |
| Trinidad and Tobago | 19.7 | 41.2 | 27.8 | 34.1 | 37.3 | 32.9 | 49.6 | 23.6 | 61.3 |
| Uruguay | 16.2 | -1.5 | 15.9 | -3.4 | 15.4 | 20.2 | 18.5 | .. | .. |
| Venezuela | 26.2 | -2.1 | 25.6 | 6.5 | 27.3 | 17.8 | 32.2 | 45.2 | 46.7 |
| Virgin Islands (U.S.) | 37.5 | .. | .. | .. | .. | .. | .. | .. | .. |
| **OCEANIA** | | | | | | | | | |
| Fiji | 9.9 | 10.2 | 11.0 | 21.3 | 13.3 | .. | .. | .. | .. |
| French Polynesia | 27.9 | 31.3 | 36.7 | .. | .. | .. | .. | .. | 34.0 |
| Kiribati | 0.5 | 23.3 | 0.6 | 4.5 | 0.6 | .. | .. | .. | .. |
| Marshall Islands | 0.9 | 11.2 | 1.0 | 6.7 | 1.1 | .. | .. | .. | .. |
| Micronesia (Fed. States of) | .. | .. | 0.1 | 5752.7 | 5.4 | 111.7 | 11.5 | .. | .. |
| Nauru | 13.0 | .. | .. | .. | .. | .. | .. | .. | .. |
| New Caledonia | 31.0 | 15.3 | 35.7 | 18.7 | 42.4 | 18.4 | 50.2 | 12.9 | 56.7 |
| Northern Marianas Islands | .. | .. | .. | .. | .. | .. | .. | .. | .. |
| Palau | .. | .. | .. | .. | .. | .. | .. | .. | .. |
| Papua New Guinea | 0.2 | 35.9 | 0.3 | .. | .. | .. | .. | .. | 0.4 |
| Samoa | 1.4 | 6.9 | 1.5 | 285.0 | 5.8 | .. | .. | .. | 13.0 |
| Solomon Islands | 0.2 | .5 | 0.2 | 38.8 | 0.3 | .. | .. | .. | 1.3 |
| Tonga | 0.2 | 1 316.9 | 3.4 | .. | .. | .. | .. | .. | .. |
| Tuvalu | .. | .. | .. | .. | .. | .. | .. | .. | .. |
| Vanuatu | 0.2 | 1 263.3 | 2.4 | 55.0 | 3.8 | 28.9 | 4.8 | 20.3 | 5.8 |
| **TRANSITION ECONOMIES** | | | | | | | | | |
| **SOUTH-EAST EUROPE AND CIS** | | | | | | | | | |
| Albania | 12.7 | 117.2 | 27.6 | 29.6 | 35.8 | .. | .. | .. | .. |
| Armenia | 0.7 | 179.8 | 1.9 | 60.3 | 3.0 | 121.4 | 6.7 | 26.4 | 8.4 |
| Azerbaijan | 9.1 | 6.8 | 9.8 | 31.1 | 12.8 | 65.1 | 21.1 | 26.3 | 26.7 |
| Belarus | 1.4 | 235.8 | 4.7 | 142.6 | 11.3 | .. | .. | .. | 42.0 |
| Bosnia and Herzegovina | 11.7 | 67.6 | 19.6 | 39.6 | 27.4 | .. | .. | .. | 40.8 |
| Bulgaria | 19.6 | 68.5 | 33.1 | 35.6 | 44.9 | 34.6 | 60.4 | 33.8 | 80.8 |
| Croatia | 40.1 | 33.3 | 53.5 | 9.1 | 58.4 | .. | .. | .. | 65.6 |
| Georgia | 6.1 | 68.5 | 10.2 | 42.4 | 14.5 | 14.0 | 16.6 | 96.9 | 32.6 |
| Kazakhstan | 3.6 | 77.9 | 6.4 | 30.6 | 8.4 | 113.2 | 17.9 | 86.6 | 33.4 |
| Kyrgyzstan | 0.5 | 94.0 | 1.1 | 159.2 | 2.7 | 109.8 | 5.8 | 78.7 | 10.3 |
| Rep. of Moldova | 6.2 | 50.8 | 9.3 | 41.2 | 13.2 | 39.9 | 18.5 | 40.4 | 25.9 |
| Romania | 17.2 | 36.6 | 23.5 | 38.5 | 32.5 | 41.2 | 45.9 | 34.2 | 61.5 |

**Table 1.15** *(Continued)*

|  | 2001 | % change 2001–2002 | 2002 | % change 2002–2003 | 2003 | % change 2003–2004 | 2004 | % change 2004–2005 | 2005 |
|---|---|---|---|---|---|---|---|---|---|
| Russian Federation | 5.3 | 127.5 | 12.0 | 107.5 | 24.9 | 107.0 | 51.6 | 62.0 | 83.6 |
| Serbia and Montenegro | 18.7 | 37.2 | 25.7 | 31.7 | 33.8 | 33.1 | 45.0 | 42.3 | 64.0 |
| Tajikistan | 0.0 | 689.2 | 0.2 | 251.5 | 0.7 | .. | .. | .. | 3.7 |
| TFYR Macedonia | 10.9 | 62.0 | 17.7 | 110.3 | 37.2 | .. | .. | .. | 61.5 |
| Turkmenistan | 0.2 | -0.3 | 0.2 | 12.0 | 0.2 | .. | .. | .. | .. |
| Ukraine | 4.6 | 67.6 | 7.7 | 78.1 | 13.6 | 109.0 | 28.5 | 29.8 | 37.0 |
| Uzbekistan | 0.5 | 44.2 | 0.7 | 69.5 | 1.3 | 64.1 | 2.1 | 31.8 | 2.7 |

*Source:* UNCTAD calculations based on the ITU World Telecommunication Indicators Database, 2006.

# Annex I
## Statistical Annex
### Table 1.16
## Internet users: Economies by level of development and by region

| | 2001 | % change 2001–2002 | 2002 | % change 2002–2003 | 2003 | % change 2003–2004 | 2004 | % change 2004–2005 | 2005 |
|---|---|---|---|---|---|---|---|---|---|
| DEVELOPED ECONOMIES | | | | | | | | | |
| ASIA | | | | | | | | | |
| Israel | 1 800 000 | 11.1 | 2 000 000 | 25.0 | 2 500 000 | 28.0 | 3 200 000 | .. | .. |
| Japan | 48 900 000 | 21.1 | 59 220 000 | 4.1 | 61 640 000 | 4.1 | 64 160 000 | 32.9 | 85 290 000 |
| EUROPE | | | | | | | | | |
| Andorra | .. | .. | .. | .. | 10 049 | 9.5 | 11 000 | 99.3 | 21 922 |
| Austria | 3 150 000 | 6.0 | 3 340 000 | 11.7 | 3 730 000 | 4.6 | 3 900 000 | 2.6 | 4 000 000 |
| Belgium | 3 200 000 | 6.3 | 3 400 000 | 17.6 | 4 000 000 | 5.0 | 4 200 000 | 14.3 | 4 800 000 |
| Cyprus | 150 000 | 40.0 | 210 000 | 19.0 | 250 000 | 19.2 | 298 000 | 9.4 | 326 000 |
| Czech Republic | 1 500 000 | 73.3 | 2 600 180 | -7.9 | 2 395 000 | 7.6 | 2 576 000 | 7.1 | 2 758 000 |
| Denmark (incl. Faroe Islands) | 2 320 000 | 4.1 | 2 415 500 | 3.9 | 2 509 000 | 9.9 | 2 757 000 | 4.7 | 2 887 000 |
| Estonia | 429 656 | 3.3 | 444 000 | 35.1 | 600 000 | 11.7 | 670 000 | 3.0 | 690 000 |
| Finland | 2 235 320 | 13.1 | 2 529 000 | 1.2 | 2 560 000 | 4.7 | 2 680 000 | 4.5 | 2 800 000 |
| France | 15 653 000 | 15.4 | 18 057 000 | 20.5 | 21 765 000 | 9.0 | 23 732 000 | 10.2 | 26 154 000 |
| Germany | 26 000 000 | 7.7 | 28 000 000 | 17.9 | 33 000 000 | 6.7 | 35 200 000 | 6.5 | 37 500 000 |
| Gibraltar | 6 179 | .. | .. | .. | .. | .. | 6 295 | .. | .. |
| Greece | 915 347 | 62.3 | 1 485 281 | 15.7 | 1 718 435 | 13.8 | 1 955 000 | 2.4 | 2 001 000 |
| Greenland | 20 000 | 25.0 | 25 000 | 24.0 | 31 000 | 22.6 | 38 000 | .. | .. |
| Guernsey | 25 000 | 20.0 | 30 000 | 10.0 | 33 000 | 9.1 | 36 000 | 8.3 | 39 000 |
| Hungary | 1 480 000 | 8.1 | 1 600 000 | 50.0 | 2 400 000 | 12.5 | 2 700 000 | 11.1 | 3 000 000 |
| Iceland | 172 000 | 8.5 | 186 600 | 4.5 | 195 000 | 15.7 | 225 610 | 14.4 | 258 000 |
| Ireland | 895 000 | 23.1 | 1 102 000 | 14.3 | 1 260 000 | -4.9 | 1 198 000 | -4.3 | 1 146 700 |
| Italy | 15 600 000 | 26.9 | 19 800 000 | 15.6 | 22 880 000 | 18.8 | 27 170 000 | 3.1 | 28 000 000 |
| Jersey | .. | .. | .. | .. | 20 000 | 35.0 | 27 000 | .. | .. |
| Latvia | 170 000 | 82.4 | 310 000 | .. | .. | .. | 810 000 | 27.2 | 1 030 000 |
| Liechtenstein | 15 000 | 33.3 | 20 000 | 0.0 | 20 000 | 10.0 | 22 000 | .. | |
| Lithuania | 250 000 | 100.0 | 500 000 | 39.1 | 695 700 | 39.1 | 968 000 | 26.2 | 1 221 749 |
| Luxembourg | 160 000 | 3.1 | 165 000 | 3.0 | 170 000 | 59.3 | 270 810 | 16.3 | 315 000 |
| Malta | 70 000 | 14.9 | 80 410 | 19.4 | 96 022 | 16.3 | 111 634 | 14.0 | 127 247 |
| Netherlands | 7 900 000 | 3.8 | 8 200 000 | 3.7 | 8 500 000 | 17.6 | 10 000 000 | 20.6 | 12 060 000 |
| Norway | 1 319 400 | 6.0 | 1 398 600 | 13.2 | 1 583 300 | 13.2 | 1 792 000 | 89.7 | 3 400 000 |
| Poland | 3 800 000 | 133.7 | 8 880 000 | 1.0 | 8 970 000 | 0.3 | 9 000 000 | 11.1 | 10 000 000 |
| Portugal | 1 860 400 | 21.9 | 2 267 200 | 17.9 | 2 674 000 | 10.4 | 2 951 000 | -0.4 | 2 939 000 |
| San Marino | 13 850 | 3.5 | 14 340 | 1.0 | 14 481 | 3.6 | 15 000 | .. | .. |
| Slovakia | 674 039 | 28.0 | 862 833 | 59.5 | 1 375 809 | 65.4 | 2 276 055 | 9.8 | 2 500 000 |

## Table 1.16 *(Continued)*

| | 2001 | % change 2001–2002 | 2002 | % change 2002–2003 | 2003 | % change 2003–2004 | 2004 | % change 2004–2005 | 2005 |
|---|---|---|---|---|---|---|---|---|---|
| Slovenia | 600 000 | 25.0 | 750 000 | 6.7 | 800 000 | 18.8 | 950 000 | 14.7 | 1 090 000 |
| Spain | 7 388 000 | 6.3 | 7 856 000 | 24.6 | 9 789 000 | 46.4 | 14 332 800 | 5.5 | 15 119 000 |
| Sweden | 4 600 000 | 11.4 | 5 125 000 | 10.3 | 5 655 000 | 20.2 | 6 800 000 | 1.3 | 6 890 000 |
| Switzerland | 2 800 000 | 7.1 | 3 000 000 | 13.3 | 3 400 000 | 2.9 | 3 500 000 | 5.7 | 3 700 000 |
| United Kingdom | 19 800 000 | 26.3 | 25 000 000 | 4.1 | 26 025 000 | 8.0 | 28 094 000 | 1.5 | 28 515 000 |
| **NORTH AMERICA** | | | | | | | | | |
| Canada[a] | 14 000 000 | 8.6 | 15 200 000 | 15.8 | 17 600 000 | 13.6 | 20 000 000 | 0.0 | 20 000 000 |
| United States (incl. Puerto Rico and Guam) | 143 463 008 | 11.3 | 159 727 000 | 1.7 | 162 459 400 | 14.4 | 185 931 000 | .. | .. |
| **OCEANIA** | | | | | | | | | |
| Australia | 7 700 000 | 36.4 | 10 500 000 | 7.6 | 11 300 000 | 15.0 | 13 000 000 | 9.2 | 14 190 000 |
| New Zealand | 1 762 000 | 8.3 | 1 908 000 | 10.6 | 2 110 000 | 11.4 | 2 350 000 | 17.2 | 2 754 000 |
| **DEVELOPING ECONOMIES** | | | | | | | | | |
| **AFRICA** | | | | | | | | | |
| Algeria | 200 000 | 150.0 | 500 000 | 30.0 | 650 000 | 130.8 | 1 500 000 | 28.0 | 1 920 000 |
| Angola | 20 000 | 105.0 | 41 000 | 104.9 | 84 000 | 104.8 | 172 000 | 2.3 | 176 000 |
| Benin | 25 000 | 100.0 | 50 000 | 40.0 | 70 000 | 42.9 | 100 000 | 325.0 | 425 000 |
| Botswana | 50 000 | 20.0 | 60 000 | 0.0 | 60 000 | 0.0 | 60 000 | 0.0 | 60 000 |
| Burkina Faso | 19 000 | 31.6 | 25 000 | 92.0 | 48 000 | 10.8 | 53 200 | 21.4 | 64 600 |
| Burundi | 7 000 | 14.3 | 8 000 | 75.0 | 14 000 | 78.6 | 25 000 | 60.0 | 40 000 |
| Cameroon | 45 000 | 33.3 | 60 000 | 66.7 | 100 000 | 70.0 | 170 000 | 47.1 | 250 000 |
| Cape Verde | 12 000 | 33.3 | 16 000 | 25.0 | 20 000 | 25.0 | 25 000 | 0.0 | 25 000 |
| Central African Rep. | 3 000 | 66.7 | 5 000 | 20.0 | 6 000 | 50.0 | 9 000 | 22.2 | 11 000 |
| Chad | 4 000 | 275.0 | 15 000 | 100.0 | 30 000 | 16.7 | 35 000 | 14.3 | 40 000 |
| Comoros | 2 500 | 28.0 | 3 200 | 56.3 | 5 000 | 60.0 | 8 000 | 150.0 | 20 000 |
| Congo | 1 000 | 400.0 | 5 000 | 200.0 | 15 000 | 140.0 | 36 000 | 38.9 | 50 000 |
| Côte d'Ivoire | 70 000 | 28.6 | 90 000 | 55.6 | 140 000 | 14.3 | 160 000 | 25.0 | 200 000 |
| Democratic Republic of the Congo | 6 000 | 733.3 | 50 000 | .. | .. | .. | 112 500 | 25.0 | 140 625 |
| Djibouti | 3 300 | 36.4 | 4 500 | 44.4 | 6 500 | 38.5 | 9 000 | 11.1 | 10 000 |
| Egypt | 600 000 | 216.7 | 1 900 000 | 57.9 | 3 000 000 | 30.0 | 3 900 000 | 28.2 | 5 000 000 |
| Equatorial Guinea | 900 | 100.0 | 1 800 | 66.7 | 3 000 | 66.7 | 5 000 | 40.0 | 7 000 |
| Eritrea | 6 000 | 50.0 | 9 000 | 5.6 | 9 500 | 426.3 | 50 000 | 40.0 | 70 000 |
| Ethiopia | 25 000 | 100.0 | 50 000 | 50.0 | 75 000 | 50.7 | 113 000 | 45.1 | 164 000 |
| Gabon | 17 000 | 47.1 | 25 000 | 40.0 | 35 000 | 14.3 | 40 000 | 67.5 | 67 000 |
| Gambia | 18 000 | 38.9 | 25 000 | 40.0 | 35 000 | 40.0 | 49 000 | .. | .. |
| Ghana | 40 000 | 325.0 | 170 000 | 47.1 | 250 000 | 47.2 | 368 000 | 9.1 | 401 310 |
| Guinea-Bissau | 4 000 | 250.0 | 14 000 | 35.7 | 19 000 | 36.8 | 26 000 | 19.2 | 31 000 |
| Kenya | 200 000 | 100.0 | 400 000 | 150.0 | 1 000 000 | 5.5 | 1 054 920 | 5.3 | 1 111 000 |

**Table 1.16** *(Continued)*

| | 2001 | % change 2001–2002 | 2002 | % change 2002–2003 | 2003 | % change 2003–2004 | 2004 | % change 2004–2005 | 2005 |
|---|---|---|---|---|---|---|---|---|---|
| Lesotho | 5 000 | 320.0 | 21 000 | 42.9 | 30 000 | 43.3 | 43 000 | .. | .. |
| Liberia | 1 000 | .. | .. | .. | .. | .. | .. | .. | .. |
| Libyan Arab Jamahiriya | 20 000 | 525.0 | 125 000 | 28.0 | 160 000 | 28.1 | 205 000 | .. | .. |
| Madagascar | 35 000 | 57.1 | 55 000 | 28.2 | 70 500 | 27.7 | 90 000 | 11.1 | 100 000 |
| Malawi | 20 000 | 35.0 | 27 000 | 33.3 | 36 000 | 28.2 | 46 140 | 13.8 | 52 500 |
| Mali | 20 000 | 25.0 | 25 000 | 40.0 | 35 000 | 42.9 | 50 000 | 20.0 | 60 000 |
| Mauritania | 7 000 | 42.9 | 10 000 | 20.0 | 12 000 | 16.7 | 14 000 | 42.9 | 20 000 |
| Mauritius | 106 000 | 17.9 | 125 000 | 20.0 | 150 000 | 20.0 | 180 000 | .. | .. |
| Mayotte | .. | .. | .. | .. | .. | .. | .. | .. | .. |
| Morocco | 400 000 | 75.0 | 700 000 | 42.9 | 1 000 000 | 250.0 | 3 500 000 | 31.4 | 4 600 000 |
| Mozambique | 30 000 | 66.7 | 50 000 | 66.0 | 83 000 | 66.3 | 138 000 | .. | .. |
| Namibia | 45 000 | 11.1 | 50 000 | 30.0 | 65 000 | 15.4 | 75 000 | .. | .. |
| Niger | 12 000 | 25.0 | 15 000 | 26.7 | 19 000 | 26.3 | 24 000 | 20.8 | 29 000 |
| Nigeria | 115 000 | 265.2 | 420 000 | 78.6 | 750 000 | 136.0 | 1 769 661 | 182.5 | 5 000 000 |
| Reunion | 120 000 | 25.0 | 150 000 | 20.0 | 180 000 | 11.1 | 200 000 | 10.0 | 220 000 |
| Rwanda | 20 000 | 25.0 | 25 000 | 24.0 | 31 000 | 22.6 | 38 000 | 31.6 | 50 000 |
| Sao Tome and Principe | 9 000 | 22.2 | 11 000 | 36.4 | 15 000 | 33.3 | 20 000 | .. | .. |
| Senegal | 100 000 | 5.0 | 105 000 | 114.3 | 225 000 | 114.2 | 482 000 | 12.0 | 540 000 |
| Seychelles | 9 000 | 30.4 | 11 736 | 2.2 | 12 000 | 66.7 | 20 000 | 5.0 | 21 000 |
| Sierra Leone | 7 000 | 14.3 | 8 000 | 12.5 | 9 000 | 11.1 | 10 000 | .. | .. |
| Somalia | 85 000 | 1.2 | 86 000 | 4.7 | 90 000 | .. | .. | .. | 90 000 |
| South Africa | 2 890 000 | 7.3 | 3 100 000 | 7.3 | 3 325 000 | 7.2 | 3 566 000 | 43.0 | 5 100 000 |
| Sudan | 150 000 | 100.0 | 300 000 | 212.3 | 937 000 | 21.7 | 1 140 000 | 145.6 | 2 800 000 |
| Swaziland | 14 000 | 42.9 | 20 000 | 35.0 | 27 000 | 33.3 | 36 000 | .. | |
| Syrian Arab Republic | 60 000 | 508.3 | 365 000 | 67.1 | 610 000 | 31.1 | 800 000 | 37.5 | 1 100 000 |
| Togo | 150 000 | 33.3 | 200 000 | 5.0 | 210 000 | 5.2 | 221 000 | .. | 300 000 |
| Tunisia | 410 000 | 23.3 | 505 500 | 24.6 | 630 000 | 32.5 | 835 000 | 14.2 | 953 770 |
| Uganda | 60 000 | 66.7 | 100 000 | 25.0 | 125 000 | 60.0 | 200 000 | 150.0 | 500 000 |
| United Republic of Tanzania | 60 000 | 33.3 | 80 000 | 212.5 | 250 000 | 33.2 | 333 000 | .. | .. |
| Zambia | 25 000 | 109.7 | 52 420 | 109.8 | 110 000 | 110.0 | 231 000 | .. | .. |
| Zimbabwe | 100 000 | 400.0 | 500 000 | 60.0 | 800 000 | 2.5 | 820 000 | 22.0 | 1 000 000 |
| **ASIA** | | | | | | | | | |
| Afghanistan | ... | .. | 1 000 | 1900.0 | 20 000 | 25.0 | 25 000 | 20.0 | 30 000 |
| Bahrain | 100 000 | 22.8 | 122 794 | 22.2 | 150 000 | 1.8 | 152 721 | 1.5 | 155 000 |
| Bangladesh | 186 000 | 9.7 | 204 000 | 19.1 | 243 000 | 23.5 | 300 000 | 23.3 | 370 000 |
| Bhutan | 5 000 | 100.0 | 10 000 | 50.0 | 15 000 | 33.3 | 20 000 | 25.0 | 25 000 |
| Brunei Darussalam | 35 000 | .. | .. | .. | 48 000 | 16.7 | 56 000 | 16.1 | 65 000 |
| Cambodia | 10 000 | 200.0 | 30 000 | 16.7 | 35 000 | 17.1 | 41 000 | .. | .. |
| China | 33 700 000 | 75.4 | 59 100 000 | 34.5 | 79 500 000 | 18.2 | 94 000 000 | 18.1 | 111 000 000 |

## Table 1.16 *(Continued)*

| | 2001 | % change 2001–2002 | 2002 | % change 2002–2003 | 2003 | % change 2003–2004 | 2004 | % change 2004–2005 | 2005 |
|---|---|---|---|---|---|---|---|---|---|
| Dem. People's Rep. of Korea | .. | .. | .. | .. | .. | .. | .. | .. | .. |
| Hong Kong (China) | 2 601 300 | 12.2 | 2 918 800 | 10.1 | 3 212 800 | 8.3 | 3 479 700 | 1.3 | 3 526 200 |
| India | 7 000 000 | 136.9 | 16 580 000 | 11.5 | 18 481 044 | 89.4 | 35 000 000 | 71.4 | 60 000 000 |
| Indonesia | 4 200 000 | 7.1 | 4 500 000 | 79.6 | 8 080 000 | 38.9 | 11 226 143 | 42.5 | 16 000 000 |
| Iran (Islamic Rep. of) | 1 005 000 | 215.2 | 3 168 000 | 51.5 | 4 800 000 | 14.6 | 5 500 000 | 27.3 | 7 000 000 |
| Iraq | 12 500 | 100.0 | 25 000 | 20.0 | 30 000 | 20.0 | 36 000 | .. | .. |
| Jordan | 234 000 | 31.4 | 307 469 | 44.4 | 444 000 | 41.8 | 629 524 | .. | .. |
| Kuwait | 200 000 | 25.0 | 250 000 | 126.8 | 567 000 | 5.8 | 600 000 | 16.7 | 700 000 |
| Lao PDR | 10 000 | 50.0 | 15 000 | 26.7 | 19 000 | 10.0 | 20 900 | 23.9 | 25 900 |
| Lebanon | 260 000 | 53.8 | 400 000 | 25.0 | 500 000 | 20.0 | 600 000 | 16.7 | 700 000 |
| Macao (China) | 101 000 | 13.9 | 115 000 | 4.3 | 120 000 | 25.0 | 150 000 | 13.3 | 170 000 |
| Malaysia | 6 346 650 | 23.6 | 7 842 000 | 10.2 | 8 643 000 | 14.3 | 9 879 000 | 11.5 | 11 016 000 |
| Maldives | 10 000 | 50.0 | 15 000 | 13.3 | 17 000 | 11.8 | 19 000 | .. | .. |
| Mongolia | 40 000 | 25.0 | 50 000 | 185.6 | 142 800 | 40.1 | 200 000 | 34.2 | 268 300 |
| Myanmar | 10 000 | 150.0 | 25 000 | 12.0 | 28 002 | 127.4 | 63 688 | 22.5 | 78 010 |
| Nepal | 60 000 | 33.3 | 80 000 | 25.0 | 100 000 | 20.0 | 120 000 | -6.3 | 112 500 |
| Oman | 120 000 | 50.0 | 180 000 | 16.7 | 210 000 | 16.7 | 245 000 | 16.3 | 285 000 |
| Pakistan | 500 000 | 100.0 | 1 000 000 | 700.0 | 8 000 000 | 25.0 | 10 000 000 | 5.0 | 10 500 000 |
| Palestine | 60 000 | 75.0 | 105 000 | 38.1 | 145 000 | 10.3 | 160 000 | 51.9 | 243 000 |
| Philippines | 2 000 000 | 75.0 | 3 500 000 | 14.3 | 4 000 000 | 10.0 | 4 400 000 | .. | .. |
| Qatar | 40 000 | 75.0 | 70 000 | 101.1 | 140 760 | 17.2 | 165 000 | 32.7 | 219 000 |
| Rep. of Korea | 24 380 000 | 7.8 | 26 270 000 | 11.2 | 29 220 000 | 8.1 | 31 580 000 | 4.5 | 33 010 000 |
| Saudi Arabia | 1 016 208 | 39.6 | 1 418 880 | 5.7 | 1 500 000 | 5.7 | 1 586 000 | .. | .. |
| Singapore | 1 700 000 | 23.5 | 2 100 000 | 1.7 | 2 135 034 | 13.4 | 2 421 782 | .. | .. |
| Sri Lanka | 150 000 | 33.3 | 200 000 | 25.0 | 250 000 | 12.0 | 280 000 | .. | .. |
| Taiwan Province of China | 7 820 000 | 37.1 | 10 720 000 | 9.5 | 11 740 000 | 4.0 | 12 210 000 | 8.2 | 13 210 000 |
| Thailand | 3 536 019 | 35.7 | 4 800 000 | 25.6 | 6 030 000 | 15.6 | 6 971 500 | 1.6 | 7 084 200 |
| Turkey | 3 500 000 | 22.9 | 4 300 000 | 39.5 | 6 000 000 | 70.3 | 10 220 000 | 56.6 | 16 000 000 |
| United Arab Emirates | 976 000 | 20.4 | 1 175 516 | -5.6 | 1 110 207 | 11.6 | 1 238 464 | 12.8 | 1 397 207 |
| Viet Nam | 1 009 544 | 48.6 | 1 500 000 | 106.5 | 3 098 007 | 104.8 | 6 345 049 | 68.8 | 10 710 980 |
| Yemen | 17 000 | 488.2 | 100 000 | 20.0 | 120 000 | 50.0 | 180 000 | .. | .. |
| LATIN AMERICA AND THE CARIBBEAN | | | | | | | | | |
| Antigua and Barbuda | 7 000 | 42.9 | 10 000 | 40.0 | 14 000 | 42.9 | 20 000 | 45.0 | 29 000 |
| Argentina | 3 650 000 | 12.3 | 4 100 000 | 10.5 | 4 530 000 | 35.8 | 6 153 603 | 11.5 | 6 863 466 |
| Aruba | 24 000 | .. | .. | .. | .. | .. | .. | .. | .. |
| Bahamas | 16 923 | 254.5 | 60 000 | 40.0 | 84 000 | 10.7 | 93 000 | 10.8 | 103 000 |
| Barbados | 15 000 | 100.0 | 30 000 | 233.3 | 100 000 | 50.0 | 150 000 | 6.7 | 160 000 |

**Table 1.16** *(Continued)*

| | 2001 | % change 2001–2002 | 2002 | % change 2002–2003 | 2003 | % change 2003–2004 | 2004 | % change 2004–2005 | 2005 |
|---|---|---|---|---|---|---|---|---|---|
| Belize | 18 000 | 38.9 | 25 000 | 20.0 | 30 000 | 16.7 | 35 000 | 8.6 | 38 000 |
| Bermuda | 30 000 | .. | .. | .. | 36 000 | 8.3 | 39 000 | 7.7 | 42 000 |
| Bolivia | 180 000 | 50.0 | 270 000 | 14.8 | 310 000 | 29.0 | 400 000 | 20.0 | 480 000 |
| Brazil | 8 000 000 | 78.8 | 14 300 000 | 25.9 | 18 000 000 | 22.2 | 22 000 000 | 65.3 | 36 356 000 |
| Cayman Islands | .. | .. | .. | .. | .. | .. | .. | .. | .. |
| Chile | 3 102 200 | 15.2 | 3 575 000 | 11.9 | 4 000 000 | 7.5 | 4 300 000 | .. | .. |
| Colombia | 1 154 000 | 73.3 | 2 000 113 | 36.6 | 2 732 201 | 41.5 | 3 865 860 | 22.6 | 4 738 544 |
| Costa Rica | 384 000 | 112.4 | 815 745 | 10.3 | 900 000 | 11.1 | 1 000 000 | 10.0 | 1 100 000 |
| Cuba | 120 000 | 33.3 | 160 000 | -38.8 | 98 000 | 53.1 | 150 000 | 26.7 | 190 000 |
| Dominica | 9 000 | 38.9 | 12 500 | 36.0 | 17 000 | 20.6 | 20 500 | 26.8 | 26 000 |
| Dominican Rep. | 397 333 | 25.8 | 500 000 | 30.0 | 650 000 | 23.1 | 800 000 | 87.5 | 1 500 000 |
| Ecuador | 333 000 | 61.5 | 537 881 | 5.9 | 569 727 | 9.6 | 624 579 | -1.4 | 615 954 |
| El Salvador | 150 000 | 100.0 | 300 000 | 83.3 | 550 000 | 6.8 | 587 475 | 8.4 | 637 050 |
| French Guiana | 20 000 | 25.0 | 25 000 | 24.0 | 31 000 | 22.6 | 38 000 | 10.5 | 42 000 |
| Grenada | 5 200 | 188.5 | 15 000 | 26.7 | 19 000 | .. | 8 000 | .. | .. |
| Guadeloupe | 40 000 | 25.0 | 50 000 | 26.0 | 63 000 | 25.4 | 79 000 | 7.6 | 85 000 |
| Guatemala | 200 000 | 100.0 | 400 000 | 37.5 | 550 000 | 38.2 | 760 000 | 31.6 | 1 000 000 |
| Guyana | 100 000 | 25.0 | 125 000 | 12.0 | 140 000 | 3.6 | 145 000 | 10.3 | 160 000 |
| Haiti | 30 000 | 166.7 | 80 000 | 87.5 | 150 000 | 233.3 | 500 000 | 20.0 | 600 000 |
| Honduras | 90 000 | 87.3 | 168 560 | 10.1 | 185 510 | 21.3 | 225 000 | 15.6 | 260 000 |
| Jamaica | 100 000 | 500.0 | 600 000 | 33.3 | 800 000 | 33.4 | 1 067 000 | .. | .. |
| Martinique | 40 000 | 50.0 | 60 000 | 33.3 | 80 000 | 37.5 | 110 000 | 18.2 | 130 000 |
| Mexico | 7 410 124 | 45.3 | 10 764 715 | 13.5 | 12 218 830 | 14.9 | 14 036 475 | 32.7 | 18 622 509 |
| Netherlands Antilles | .. | .. | .. | .. | .. | .. | .. | .. | .. |
| Nicaragua | 75 000 | 20.0 | 90 000 | 11.1 | 100 000 | 25.0 | 125 000 | 12.0 | 140 000 |
| Panama | 121 425 | 19.4 | 144 963 | 19.4 | 173 085 | 13.6 | 196 548 | 4.9 | 206 178 |
| Paraguay | 60 000 | 66.7 | 100 000 | 20.0 | 120 000 | 66.7 | 200 000 | 0.0 | 200 000 |
| Peru | 2 000 000 | 20.0 | 2 400 000 | 18.8 | 2 850 000 | 13.0 | 3 220 000 | 42.9 | 4 600 000 |
| Saint Kitts and Nevis | 3 600 | 177.8 | 10 000 | .. | .. | .. | .. | .. | .. |
| Saint Lucia | 13 000 | .. | .. | .. | 34 000 | 61.8 | 55 000 | .. | .. |
| St. Vincent and the Grenadines | 5 500 | 9.1 | 6 000 | 16.7 | 7 000 | 14.3 | 8 000 | 25.0 | 10 000 |
| Suriname | 14 520 | 37.7 | 20 000 | 15.0 | 23 000 | 30.4 | 30 000 | 6.7 | 32 000 |
| Trinidad and Tobago | 120 000 | 15.0 | 138 000 | 10.9 | 153 000 | 4.6 | 160 000 | .. | .. |
| Uruguay | 370 000 | 2.7 | 380 000 | 39.5 | 530 000 | 7.0 | 567 175 | 17.8 | 668 000 |
| Venezuela | 1 153 000 | 7.9 | 1 244 000 | 55.5 | 1 935 000 | 14.1 | 2 207 000 | 50.1 | 3 313 000 |
| Virgin Islands (US) | 20 000 | 50.0 | 30 000 | .. | .. | .. | .. | .. | .. |
| **OCEANIA** | | | | | | | | | |
| American Samoa | .. | .. | .. | .. | .. | .. | .. | .. | .. |

## Table 1.16 *(Continued)*

| | 2001 | % change 2001–2002 | 2002 | % change 2002–2003 | 2003 | % change 2003–2004 | 2004 | % change 2004–2005 | 2005 |
|---|---|---|---|---|---|---|---|---|---|
| Fiji | 15 000 | 233.3 | 50 000 | 10.0 | 55 000 | 10.9 | 61 000 | 6.6 | 65 000 |
| French Polynesia | 15 000 | 33.3 | 20 000 | 75.0 | 35 000 | 28.6 | 45 000 | 22.2 | 55 000 |
| Kiribati | 2 000 | 0.0 | 2 000 | 0.0 | 2 000 | 0.0 | 2 000 | 0.0 | 2 000 |
| Marshall Islands | 0 900 | 38.9 | 1 250 | 12.0 | 1 400 | 42.9 | 2 000 | 10.0 | 2 200 |
| Micronesia (Fed. States of) | 5 000 | 20.0 | 6 000 | 66.7 | 10 000 | 20.0 | 12 000 | 16.7 | 14 000 |
| Nauru | 300 | .. | .. | .. | .. | .. | .. | .. | .. |
| New Caledonia | 40 000 | 25.0 | 50 000 | 20.0 | 60 000 | 16.7 | 70 000 | 8.6 | 76 000 |
| Northern Mariana Islands | .. | .. | .. | .. | .. | .. | .. | .. | .. |
| Palau | .. | .. | 4 000 | .. | .. | .. | .. | .. | .. |
| Papua New Guinea | 50 000 | 50.0 | 75 000 | 50.7 | 113 000 | 6.2 | 120 000 | 12.5 | 135 000 |
| Samoa | 3 000 | 33.3 | 4 000 | 25.0 | 5 000 | 10.0 | 5 500 | 9.1 | 6 000 |
| Solomon Islands | 2 000 | 10.0 | 2 200 | 13.6 | 2 500 | 20.0 | 3 000 | 33.3 | 4 000 |
| Tonga | 2 800 | 3.6 | 2 900 | 3.4 | 3 000 | 0.0 | 3 000 | 0.0 | 3 000 |
| Tuvalu | 1 000 | 25.0 | 1 250 | 44.0 | 1 800 | 66.7 | 3 000 | .. | .. |
| Vanuatu | 5 500 | 27.3 | 7 000 | 7.1 | 7 500 | 0.0 | 7 500 | 6.7 | 8 000 |
| TRANSITION ECONOMIES | | | | | | | | | |
| SOUTH-EAST EUROPE AND CIS | | | | | | | | | |
| Albania | 10 000 | 20.0 | 12 000 | 150.0 | 30 000 | 150.0 | 75 000 | 150.7 | 188 000 |
| Armenia | 50 000 | 20.0 | 60 000 | 133.3 | 140 000 | 7.1 | 150 000 | 7.3 | 161 000 |
| Azerbaijan | 25 000 | 1100.0 | 300 000 | 16.7 | 350 000 | 16.6 | 408 000 | 66.4 | 678 800 |
| Belarus | 430 263 | 87.9 | 808 481 | 72.2 | 1 391 903 | 76.8 | 2 461 093 | 37.9 | 3 394 421 |
| Bosnia and Herzegovina | 45 000 | 122.2 | 100 000 | 50.0 | 150 000 | 50.0 | 225 000 | 258.4 | 806 421 |
| Bulgaria | 605 000 | 4.1 | 630 000 | .. | .. | .. | 1 234 000 | 29.0 | 1 591 705 |
| Croatia | 518 000 | 52.3 | 789 000 | 28.5 | 1 014 000 | 30.9 | 1 327 700 | 9.3 | 1 451 100 |
| Georgia | 46 500 | 58.1 | 73 500 | 59.2 | 117 020 | 50.1 | 175 600 | .. | .. |
| Kazakhstan | 150 000 | 66.7 | 250 000 | 20.0 | 300 000 | 33.3 | 400 000 | .. | .. |
| Kyrgyzstan | 150 600 | 0.9 | 152 000 | 31.6 | 200 000 | 31.5 | 263 000 | 6.5 | 280 000 |
| Rep. of Moldova | 60 000 | 150.0 | 150 000 | 92.0 | 288 000 | 41.0 | 406 000 | .. | .. |
| Romania | 1 000 000 | 120.0 | 2 200 000 | 81.8 | 4 000 000 | 12.5 | 4 500 000 | .. | .. |
| Russian Federation | 4 300 000 | 39.5 | 6 000 000 | 100.0 | 12 000 000 | 54.2 | 18 500 000 | 17.8 | 21 800 000 |
| Serbia and Montenegro | 600 000 | 6.7 | 640 000 | 32.3 | 847 000 | 79.1 | 1 517 015 | .. | .. |
| Tajikistan | 3 200 | 9.4 | 3 500 | 17.7 | 4 120 | 21.4 | 5 000 | .. | .. |
| TFYR Macedonia | 70 000 | 42.9 | 100 000 | 26.0 | 126 000 | 26.2 | 159 000 | 0.6 | 159 889 |
| Turkmenistan | 8 000 | .. | .. | .. | 20 000 | 80.0 | 36 000 | .. | .. |
| Ukraine | 600 000 | 50.0 | 900 000 | 177.8 | 2 500 000 | 50.0 | 3 750 000 | 21.6 | 4 560 000 |
| Uzbekistan | 150 000 | 83.3 | 275 000 | 78.9 | 492 000 | 78.9 | 880 000 | .. | .. |

**Notes:** [a] The value for Internet users in Canada in 2005 is assumed.

*Source:* UNCTAD calculations based on the ITU World Telecommunication Indicators Database, 2006.

# Annex I

## Statistical Annex

### Table 1.17

## Internet penetration: Economies by level of development and by region

Internet users per 100 inhabitants

| | 2001 | % change 2001-2002 | 2002 | % change 2002-2003 | 2003 | % change 2003-2004 | 2004 | % change 2004-2005 | 2005 |
|---|---|---|---|---|---|---|---|---|---|
| DEVELOPED ECONOMIES | | | | | | | | | |
| ASIA | | | | | | | | | |
| Israel | 29.0 | 8.8 | 31.5 | 22.5 | 38.6 | 25.6 | 48.5 | .. | .. |
| Japan | 38.4 | 20.9 | 46.4 | 3.9 | 48.3 | 3.9 | 50.2 | 32.8 | 66.6 |
| EUROPE | | | | | | | | | |
| Andorra | .. | .. | .. | .. | 15.1 | 9.0 | 16.4 | 98.6 | 32.6 |
| Austria | 38.8 | 5.8 | 41.1 | 11.4 | 45.8 | 4.3 | 47.7 | 2.3 | 48.8 |
| Belgium | 31.0 | 6.0 | 32.8 | 17.4 | 38.5 | 4.8 | 40.4 | 14.1 | 46.1 |
| Cyprus | 18.8 | 38.3 | 26.0 | 17.6 | 30.6 | 17.8 | 36.1 | 8.2 | 39.0 |
| Czech Republic | 14.6 | 73.5 | 25.4 | 19.3 | 30.3 | -16.8 | 25.2 | 7.2 | 27.0 |
| Denmark (incl. Faroe Islands) | 42.9 | 3.7 | 44.5 | 3.5 | 46.1 | 9.5 | 50.5 | 4.4 | 52.7 |
| Estonia | 31.7 | 4.0 | 32.9 | 35.9 | 44.7 | 12.2 | 50.2 | 3.4 | 51.9 |
| Finland | 43.1 | 12.8 | 48.6 | 0.9 | 49.0 | 4.4 | 51.2 | 4.2 | 53.3 |
| France | 26.3 | 14.9 | 30.2 | 20.0 | 36.3 | 8.6 | 39.4 | 9.8 | 43.2 |
| Germany | 31.5 | 7.6 | 33.9 | 17.7 | 40.0 | 6.6 | 42.6 | 6.5 | 45.4 |
| Gibraltar | 22.3 | .. | .. | .. | .. | .. | 22.6 | .. | .. |
| Greece | 8.3 | 61.8 | 13.4 | 15.4 | 15.5 | 13.5 | 17.6 | 2.2 | 18.0 |
| Greenland | 35.5 | 24.7 | 44.3 | 23.7 | 54.8 | 22.2 | 66.9 | .. | .. |
| Guernsey | 38.9 | 19.5 | 46.4 | 9.6 | 50.9 | 8.7 | 55.4 | 8.0 | 59.8 |
| Hungary | 14.5 | 8.4 | 15.7 | 50.4 | 23.6 | 12.8 | 26.7 | 11.4 | 29.7 |
| Iceland | 60.6 | 7.5 | 65.1 | 3.5 | 67.4 | 14.7 | 77.3 | 13.3 | 87.6 |
| Ireland | 23.2 | 20.9 | 28.0 | 12.2 | 31.4 | -6.6 | 29.4 | -5.9 | 27.6 |
| Italy | 27.0 | 26.7 | 34.2 | 15.4 | 39.5 | 18.6 | 46.8 | 2.9 | 48.2 |
| Jersey | .. | .. | .. | .. | 22.8 | 34.8 | 30.8 | .. | .. |
| Latvia | 7.2 | 83.5 | 13.2 | .. | .. | .. | 34.9 | 27.8 | 44.6 |
| Liechtenstein | 45.2 | 32.0 | 59.6 | -1.0 | 59.0 | 9.0 | 64.3 | .. | .. |
| Lithuania | 7.2 | 100.8 | 14.4 | 39.6 | 20.1 | 39.6 | 28.1 | 26.7 | 35.6 |
| Luxembourg | 36.3 | 1.8 | 36.9 | 1.7 | 37.5 | 57.3 | 59.0 | 14.8 | 67.8 |
| Malta | 17.8 | 14.3 | 20.3 | 18.8 | 24.1 | 15.7 | 27.9 | 13.5 | 31.7 |
| Netherlands | 31.6 | 1.6 | 32.1 | 1.5 | 32.6 | 15.3 | 37.6 | 18.2 | 44.4 |
| Norway | 29.1 | 5.4 | 30.7 | 12.6 | 34.6 | 12.6 | 39.0 | 88.8 | 73.6 |
| Poland | 9.8 | 133.8 | 23.0 | 1.1 | 23.2 | 0.4 | 23.3 | 11.2 | 26.0 |

## Table 1.17 (Continued)

| | 2001 | % change 2001-2002 | 2002 | % change 2002-2003 | 2003 | % change 2003-2004 | 2004 | % change 2004-2005 | 2005 |
|---|---|---|---|---|---|---|---|---|---|
| Portugal | 18.1 | 21.2 | 21.9 | 17.3 | 25.7 | 9.8 | 28.3 | -0.9 | 28.0 |
| San Marino | 50.9 | 2.6 | 52.3 | 0.1 | 52.4 | 2.7 | 53.8 | .. | .. |
| Slovakia | 12.5 | 28.0 | 16.0 | 59.5 | 25.5 | 65.5 | 42.1 | 9.9 | 46.3 |
| Slovenia | 30.5 | 25.0 | 38.1 | 6.7 | 40.7 | 18.7 | 48.3 | 14.8 | 55.4 |
| Spain | 18.0 | 5.1 | 18.9 | 23.0 | 23.2 | 44.7 | 33.6 | 4.5 | 35.1 |
| Sweden | 51.7 | 11.0 | 57.4 | 9.9 | 63.0 | 19.7 | 75.5 | 0.9 | 76.2 |
| Switzerland | 38.9 | 6.9 | 41.6 | 13.1 | 47.1 | 2.7 | 48.3 | 5.5 | 51.0 |
| United Kingdom | 33.6 | 25.8 | 42.3 | 3.7 | 43.9 | 7.6 | 47.2 | 1.2 | 47.8 |
| **NORTH AMERICA** | | | | | | | | | |
| Canada[a] | 45.2 | 7.5 | 48.5 | 14.6 | 55.6 | 12.5 | 62.6 | 0.0 | 62.6 |
| United States (incl. Puerto Rico and Guam) | 49.3 | 10.3 | 54.4 | 0.7 | 54.8 | 13.4 | 62.1 | .. | .. |
| **OCEANIA** | | | | | | | | | |
| Australia | 39.9 | 34.8 | 53.8 | 6.4 | 57.3 | 13.8 | 65.2 | 8.0 | 70.4 |
| New Zealand | 45.7 | 7.1 | 48.9 | 9.3 | 53.5 | 10.2 | 58.9 | 16.1 | 68.4 |
| **DEVELOPING ECONOMIES** | | | | | | | | | |
| **AFRICA** | | | | | | | | | |
| Algeria | 0.6 | 146.3 | 1.6 | 28.0 | 2.0 | 127.3 | 4.6 | 26.1 | 5.8 |
| Angola | 0.1 | 99.3 | 0.3 | 99.0 | 0.6 | 98.9 | 1.1 | -0.6 | 1.1 |
| Benin | 0.3 | 93.7 | 0.7 | 35.5 | 0.9 | 38.3 | 1.2 | 311.8 | 5.0 |
| Botswana | 2.8 | 19.6 | 3.4 | -0.0 | 3.4 | 0.1 | 3.4 | 0.2 | 3.4 |
| Burkina Faso | 0.2 | 27.4 | 0.2 | 85.9 | 0.4 | 7.3 | 0.4 | 17.7 | 0.5 |
| Burundi | 0.1 | 11.2 | 0.1 | 69.6 | 0.2 | 72.6 | 0.3 | 54.4 | 0.5 |
| Cameroon | 0.3 | 30.8 | 0.4 | 63.6 | 0.6 | 66.9 | 1.1 | 44.5 | 1.5 |
| Cape Verde | 2.6 | 30.2 | 3.4 | 22.1 | 4.1 | 22.1 | 5.0 | -2.3 | 4.9 |
| Central African Rep. | 0.1 | 64.4 | 0.1 | 18.5 | 0.2 | 48.1 | 0.2 | 20.7 | 0.3 |
| Chad | 0.0 | 261.8 | 0.2 | 93.0 | 0.3 | 12.8 | 0.4 | 10.8 | 0.4 |
| Comoros | 0.3 | 24.6 | 0.4 | 52.2 | 0.7 | 55.9 | 1.0 | 143.5 | 2.5 |
| Congo | 0.0 | 384.9 | 0.1 | 191.1 | 0.4 | 133.0 | 0.9 | 34.9 | 1.3 |
| Côte d'Ivoire | 0.4 | 26.5 | 0.5 | 53.2 | 0.8 | 12.6 | 0.9 | 23.1 | 1.1 |
| Democratic Republic of the Congo | 0.0 | 711.2 | 0.1 | .. | .. | .. | 0.2 | 21.3 | 0.2 |
| Djibouti | 0.5 | 33.3 | 0.6 | 41.6 | 0.8 | 35.9 | 1.2 | 9.2 | 1.3 |
| Egypt | 0.9 | 210.6 | 2.7 | 54.9 | 4.2 | 27.5 | 5.4 | 25.8 | 6.8 |
| Equatorial Guinea | 0.2 | 95.4 | 0.4 | 62.9 | 0.6 | 62.9 | 1.0 | 36.9 | 1.4 |
| Eritrea | 0.2 | 43.5 | 0.2 | 0.9 | 0.2 | 404.2 | 1.2 | 34.6 | 1.6 |
| Ethiopia | 0.0 | 95.1 | 0.1 | 46.4 | 0.1 | 47.1 | 0.1 | 41.7 | 0.2 |

## Table 1.17 *(Continued)*

| | 2001 | % change 2001-2002 | 2002 | % change 2002-2003 | 2003 | % change 2003-2004 | 2004 | % change 2004-2005 | 2005 |
|---|---|---|---|---|---|---|---|---|---|
| Gabon | 1.3 | 44.5 | 1.9 | 37.8 | 2.6 | 12.5 | 2.9 | 64.9 | 4.8 |
| Gambia | 1.3 | 34.8 | 1.8 | 36.1 | 2.4 | 36.2 | 3.3 | .. | .. |
| Ghana | 0.2 | 315.8 | 0.8 | 43.9 | 1.2 | 44.1 | 1.7 | 6.8 | 1.8 |
| Guinea | 0.2 | 128.3 | 0.4 | 11.8 | 0.4 | 12.5 | 0.5 | 6.4 | 0.5 |
| Guinea-Bissau | 0.3 | 239.6 | 1.0 | 31.6 | 1.3 | 32.8 | 1.7 | 15.7 | 2.0 |
| Kenya | 0.6 | 95.8 | 1.2 | 144.7 | 3.1 | 3.2 | 3.2 | 2.9 | 3.2 |
| Lesotho | 0.3 | 319.1 | 1.2 | 42.8 | 1.7 | 43.5 | 2.4 | .. | .. |
| Liberia | 0.0 | .. | .. | .. | .. | .. | .. | .. | .. |
| Libyan Arab Jamahiriya | 0.4 | 512.8 | 2.3 | 25.5 | 2.8 | 25.6 | 3.6 | .. | .. |
| Madagascar | 0.2 | 52.8 | 0.3 | 24.7 | 0.4 | 24.2 | 0.5 | 8.2 | 0.5 |
| Malawi | 0.2 | 31.9 | 0.2 | 30.4 | 0.3 | 25.4 | 0.4 | 11.3 | 0.4 |
| Mali | 0.2 | 21.3 | 0.2 | 35.8 | 0.3 | 38.6 | 0.4 | 16.5 | 0.4 |
| Mauritania | 0.3 | 38.6 | 0.4 | 16.4 | 0.4 | 13.2 | 0.5 | 38.7 | 0.7 |
| Mauritius | 8.9 | 16.8 | 10.3 | 18.8 | 12.3 | 18.9 | 14.6 | .. | .. |
| Mayotte | .. | .. | .. | .. | .. | .. | .. | .. | .. |
| Morocco | 1.3 | 72.1 | 2.2 | 40.5 | 3.2 | 244.4 | 10.9 | 29.4 | 14.1 |
| Mozambique | 0.1 | 64.2 | 0.2 | 63.6 | 0.3 | 63.8 | 0.4 | .. | .. |
| Namibia | 0.1 | 9.8 | 0.1 | 28.5 | 0.1 | 14.1 | 0.1 | .. | .. |
| Niger | 0.1 | 20.8 | 0.1 | 22.4 | 0.1 | 22.1 | 0.2 | 16.9 | 0.2 |
| Nigeria | 0.1 | 257.0 | 0.3 | 74.6 | 0.6 | 130.8 | 1.4 | 176.5 | 3.8 |
| Reunion | 16.3 | 22.9 | 20.0 | 18.1 | 23.6 | 9.4 | 25.9 | 8.4 | 28.0 |
| Rwanda | 0.2 | 21.6 | 0.3 | 22.0 | 0.4 | 20.9 | 0.4 | 29.3 | 0.6 |
| Sao Tome and Principe | 6.3 | 19.5 | 7.5 | 33.2 | 10.0 | 30.3 | 13.1 | .. | .. |
| Senegal | 0.9 | 2.5 | 1.0 | 109.2 | 2.0 | 109.2 | 4.2 | 9.4 | 4.6 |
| Seychelles | 11.6 | 29.3 | 15.0 | 1.3 | 15.2 | 65.1 | 25.0 | 4.0 | 26.0 |
| Sierra Leone | 0.1 | 9.4 | 0.2 | 7.5 | 0.2 | 6.6 | 0.2 | .. | .. |
| Somalia | 1.2 | -2.0 | 1.2 | 1.3 | 1.2 | .. | .. | .. | 1.1 |
| South Africa | 6.3 | 6.3 | 6.7 | 6.4 | 7.1 | 6.6 | 7.6 | 42.3 | 10.8 |
| Sudan | 0.4 | 96.2 | 0.9 | 206.6 | 2.7 | 19.4 | 3.2 | 140.8 | 7.7 |
| Swaziland | 1.4 | 42.3 | 1.9 | 34.8 | 2.6 | 33.4 | 3.5 | .. | .. |
| Syrian Arab Republic | 0.3 | 493.2 | 2.1 | 63.0 | 3.4 | 27.9 | 4.3 | 34.2 | 5.8 |
| Togo | 2.7 | 29.7 | 3.5 | 2.3 | 3.6 | 2.6 | 3.7 | 32.3 | 4.9 |
| Tunisia | 4.2 | 21.9 | 5.2 | 23.3 | 6.4 | 31.1 | 8.4 | 13.0 | 9.4 |
| Uganda | 0.2 | 61.2 | 0.4 | 20.8 | 0.5 | 54.5 | 0.7 | 141.4 | 1.7 |
| United Republic of Tanzania | 0.2 | 30.7 | 0.2 | 206.5 | 0.7 | 30.7 | 0.9 | .. | .. |
| Zambia | 0.2 | 106.0 | 0.5 | 106.3 | 1.0 | 106.6 | 2.0 | .. | .. |
| Zimbabwe | 0.8 | 396.6 | 3.9 | 59.0 | 6.2 | 1.9 | 6.3 | 21.3 | 7.7 |

## Table 1.17 *(Continued)*

| | 2001 | % change 2001-2002 | 2002 | % change 2002-2003 | 2003 | % change 2003-2004 | 2004 | % change 2004-2005 | 2005 |
|---|---|---|---|---|---|---|---|---|---|
| Afghanistan | .. | .. | 0.0 | 1803.1 | 0.1 | 19.1 | 0.1 | 14.8 | 0.1 |
| Bahrain | 14.6 | 20.8 | 17.6 | 20.4 | 21.3 | 0.4 | 21.3 | -0.0 | 21.3 |
| Bangladesh | 0.1 | 7.6 | 0.2 | 16.9 | 0.2 | 21.2 | 0.2 | 21.1 | 0.3 |
| Bhutan | 0.3 | 95.7 | 0.5 | 46.8 | 0.7 | 30.5 | 0.9 | 22.3 | 1.2 |
| Brunei Darussalam | 10.3 | .. | .. | .. | 13.4 | 14.1 | 15.3 | 13.5 | 17.4 |
| Cambodia | 0.1 | 194.1 | 0.2 | 14.4 | 0.3 | 14.9 | 0.3 | .. | .. |
| China | 2.7 | 74.2 | 4.7 | 33.7 | 6.2 | 17.5 | 7.3 | 17.4 | 8.6 |
| Dem. People's Rep. of Korea | .. | .. | .. | .. | .. | .. | .. | .. | .. |
| Hong Kong (China) | 38.7 | 10.9 | 42.9 | 8.8 | 46.7 | 7.1 | 50.0 | 0.2 | 50.1 |
| India | 0.7 | 133.1 | 1.6 | 9.8 | 1.7 | 86.5 | 3.2 | 68.9 | 5.4 |
| Indonesia | 2.0 | 5.8 | 2.1 | 77.3 | 3.7 | 37.2 | 5.1 | 40.8 | 7.2 |
| Iran (Islamic Rep. of) | 1.5 | 212.5 | 4.7 | 50.2 | 7.0 | 13.5 | 8.0 | 26.0 | 10.1 |
| Iraq | 0.0 | 94.4 | 0.1 | 16.7 | 0.1 | 16.8 | 0.1 | .. | .. |
| Jordan | 4.6 | 27.7 | 5.8 | 40.4 | 8.2 | 38.0 | 11.3 | .. | .. |
| Kuwait | 8.5 | 20.0 | 10.3 | 119.0 | 22.5 | 2.5 | 23.0 | 13.2 | 26.1 |
| Lao PDR | 0.2 | 46.5 | 0.3 | 23.8 | 0.3 | 7.5 | 0.4 | 21.2 | 0.4 |
| Lebanon | 7.6 | 52.3 | 11.5 | 23.7 | 14.3 | 18.8 | 16.9 | 15.5 | 19.6 |
| Macao (China) | 22.6 | 13.0 | 25.5 | 3.6 | 26.4 | 24.2 | 32.8 | 12.6 | 36.9 |
| Malaysia | 27.0 | 21.1 | 32.7 | 8.1 | 35.4 | 12.2 | 39.7 | 9.5 | 43.5 |
| Maldives | 3.4 | 46.2 | 4.9 | 10.5 | 5.4 | 9.0 | 5.9 | .. | .. |
| Mongolia | 1.5 | 23.2 | 1.9 | 183.7 | 5.3 | 38.1 | 7.3 | 31.9 | 9.6 |
| Myanmar | 0.1 | 144.9 | 0.1 | 9.8 | 0.1 | 123.1 | 0.3 | 20.2 | 0.4 |
| Nepal | 0.2 | 30.3 | 0.3 | 22.2 | 0.4 | 17.3 | 0.4 | -8.3 | 0.4 |
| Oman | 4.9 | 48.7 | 7.2 | 15.8 | 8.4 | 15.6 | 9.7 | 14.8 | 11.1 |
| Pakistan | 0.3 | 95.9 | 0.7 | 684.3 | 5.3 | 22.6 | 6.5 | 2.9 | 6.6 |
| Palestine | 1.8 | 69.4 | 3.1 | 33.8 | 4.2 | 6.9 | 4.5 | 47.1 | 6.6 |
| Philippines | 2.6 | 71.7 | 4.4 | 12.2 | 5.0 | 8.0 | 5.4 | .. | .. |
| Qatar | 6.2 | 63.8 | 10.2 | 88.2 | 19.2 | 10.6 | 21.2 | 26.9 | 26.9 |
| Rep. of Korea | 51.8 | 7.2 | 55.6 | 10.8 | 61.6 | 7.7 | 66.3 | 4.2 | 69.0 |
| Saudi Arabia | 4.6 | 35.8 | 6.2 | 2.9 | 6.4 | 3.0 | 6.6 | .. | .. |
| Singapore | 41.5 | 21.6 | 50.4 | 0.3 | 50.6 | 12.0 | 56.7 | .. | .. |
| Sri Lanka | 0.7 | 32.1 | 1.0 | 23.9 | 1.2 | 11.0 | 1.4 | .. | .. |
| Taiwan Province of China | 35.0 | 36.3 | 47.7 | 9.0 | 52.0 | 3.6 | 53.9 | 7.8 | 58.1 |
| Thailand | 5.7 | 34.5 | 7.7 | 24.5 | 9.5 | 14.6 | 10.9 | 0.8 | 11.0 |
| Turkey | 5.1 | 21.1 | 6.1 | 37.6 | 8.4 | 68.1 | 14.2 | 54.5 | 21.9 |
| United Arab Emirates | 28.0 | 11.8 | 31.3 | -91.3 | 2.7 | 957.4 | 28.9 | 7.5 | 31.1 |

## Table 1.17 *(Continued)*

| | 2001 | % change 2001-2002 | 2002 | % change 2002-2003 | 2003 | % change 2003-2004 | 2004 | % change 2004-2005 | 2005 |
|---|---|---|---|---|---|---|---|---|---|
| Viet Nam | 1.3 | 46.5 | 1.9 | 103.7 | 3.8 | 102.0 | 7.6 | 66.6 | 12.7 |
| Yemen | 0.1 | 470.1 | 0.5 | 16.3 | 0.6 | 45.4 | 0.9 | .. | .. |
| **LATIN AMERICA AND THE CARIBBEAN** | | | | | | | | | |
| Antigua and Barbuda | 9.0 | 41.0 | 12.7 | 38.3 | 17.6 | 41.2 | 24.8 | 43.3 | 35.6 |
| Argentina | 9.8 | 11.2 | 10.9 | 9.4 | 11.9 | 34.5 | 16.0 | 10.5 | 17.7 |
| Aruba | 25.6 | .. | .. | .. | .. | .. | .. | .. | .. |
| Bahamas | 5.5 | 249.6 | 19.3 | 38.1 | 26.7 | 9.2 | 29.2 | 9.3 | 31.9 |
| Barbados | 5.6 | 99.5 | 11.2 | 232.5 | 37.3 | 49.6 | 55.8 | 6.4 | 59.4 |
| Belize | 7.3 | 35.9 | 9.9 | 17.5 | 11.6 | 14.3 | 13.2 | 6.4 | 14.1 |
| Bermuda | 47.5 | .. | .. | .. | 56.5 | 7.9 | 61.0 | 7.3 | 65.4 |
| Bolivia | 2.1 | 47.0 | 3.1 | 12.6 | 3.5 | 26.5 | 4.4 | 17.7 | 5.2 |
| Brazil | 4.5 | 76.2 | 8.0 | 24.1 | 9.9 | 20.6 | 12.0 | 63.0 | 19.5 |
| Cayman Islands | .. | .. | .. | .. | .. | .. | .. | .. | .. |
| Chile | 19.9 | 13.9 | 22.7 | 10.7 | 25.1 | 6.3 | 26.7 | .. | .. |
| Colombia | 2.7 | 70.5 | 4.6 | 34.5 | 6.2 | 39.3 | 8.6 | 20.7 | 10.4 |
| Costa Rica | 9.6 | 108.2 | 19.9 | 8.2 | 21.5 | 9.1 | 23.5 | 8.1 | 25.4 |
| Cuba | 1.1 | 33.0 | 1.4 | -38.9 | .9 | 52.7 | 1.3 | 26.4 | 1.7 |
| Dominica | 11.5 | 38.6 | 16.0 | 35.8 | 21.7 | 20.3 | 26.1 | 26.2 | 32.9 |
| Dominican Rep. | 4.7 | 24.0 | 5.9 | 28.1 | 7.5 | 21.3 | 9.1 | 84.8 | 16.9 |
| Ecuador | 2.7 | 59.2 | 4.2 | 4.4 | 4.4 | 8.1 | 4.8 | -2.8 | 4.7 |
| El Salvador | 2.3 | 96.3 | 4.6 | 80.0 | 8.3 | 4.9 | 8.7 | 6.6 | 9.3 |
| French Guiana | 11.8 | 21.7 | 14.4 | 20.9 | 17.4 | 19.6 | 20.8 | 7.9 | 22.5 |
| Grenada | 5.1 | 188.3 | 14.7 | 26.5 | 18.6 | -58.0 | 7.8 | .. | .. |
| Guadeloupe | 9.2 | 23.9 | 11.4 | 24.9 | 14.3 | 24.4 | 17.8 | 6.8 | 19.0 |
| Guatemala | 1.7 | 95.3 | 3.4 | 34.2 | 4.6 | 34.9 | 6.2 | 28.4 | 7.9 |
| Guyana | 13.4 | 24.7 | 16.7 | 11.8 | 18.7 | 3.4 | 19.3 | 10.2 | 21.3 |
| Haiti | 0.4 | 162.9 | 1.0 | 84.8 | 1.8 | 228.6 | 5.9 | 18.3 | 7.0 |
| Honduras | 1.4 | 83.0 | 2.5 | 7.6 | 2.7 | 18.6 | 3.2 | 13.0 | 3.6 |
| Jamaica | 3.8 | 496.8 | 22.9 | 32.7 | 30.5 | 32.8 | 40.4 | .. | .. |
| Martinique | 10.3 | 49.2 | 15.4 | 32.6 | 20.4 | 36.8 | 27.9 | 17.7 | 32.8 |
| Mexico | 7.3 | 43.3 | 10.5 | 12.0 | 11.7 | 13.4 | 13.3 | 31.0 | 17.4 |
| Netherlands Antilles | .. | .. | .. | .. | .. | .. | .. | .. | .. |
| Nicaragua | 1.5 | 17.6 | 1.7 | 8.9 | 1.9 | 22.5 | 2.3 | 9.7 | 2.6 |
| Panama | 4.0 | 17.2 | 4.7 | 17.2 | 5.5 | 11.5 | 6.2 | 3.1 | 6.4 |
| Paraguay | 1.1 | 62.7 | 1.7 | 17.2 | 2.0 | 62.8 | 3.3 | -2.3 | 3.2 |
| Peru | 7.6 | 18.2 | 9.0 | 17.0 | 10.5 | 11.3 | 11.7 | 40.8 | 16.4 |
| Saint Kitts and Nevis | 8.8 | 175.0 | 24.3 | .. | .. | .. | .. | .. | .. |

## Table 1.17 (Continued)

| | 2001 | % change 2001-2002 | 2002 | % change 2002-2003 | 2003 | % change 2003-2004 | 2004 | % change 2004-2005 | 2005 |
|---|---|---|---|---|---|---|---|---|---|
| Saint Lucia | 8.4 | .. | .. | .. | 21.5 | 60.5 | 34.5 | .. | .. |
| Saint Vincent and the Grenadines | 4.7 | 8.5 | 5.1 | 16.0 | 5.9 | 13.7 | 6.8 | 24.3 | 8.4 |
| Suriname | 3.3 | 36.7 | 4.5 | 14.2 | 5.2 | 29.6 | 6.7 | 6.0 | 7.1 |
| Trinidad and Tobago | 9.3 | 14.6 | 10.7 | 10.5 | 11.8 | 4.3 | 12.3 | .. | .. |
| Uruguay | 11.0 | 2.0 | 11.2 | 38.5 | 15.5 | 6.3 | 16.5 | 17.0 | 19.3 |
| Venezuela | 4.6 | 5.9 | 4.9 | 52.7 | 7.5 | 12.0 | 8.4 | 47.5 | 12.4 |
| Virgin Islands (US) | 18.0 | 49.7 | 26.9 | .. | .. | .. | .. | .. | .. |
| **OCEANIA** | | | | | | | | | |
| American Samoa | .. | .. | .. | .. | .. | .. | .. | .. | .. |
| Fiji | 1.8 | 230.2 | 6.1 | 9.0 | 6.6 | 10.0 | 7.3 | 5.7 | 7.7 |
| French Polynesia | 6.2 | 31.1 | 8.2 | 72.1 | 14.1 | 26.5 | 17.8 | 20.4 | 21.4 |
| Kiribati | 2.2 | -2.1 | 2.1 | -2.0 | 2.1 | -2.0 | 2.1 | -2.0 | 2.0 |
| Marshall Islands | 1.7 | 34.3 | 2.3 | 7.8 | 2.4 | 37.4 | 3.3 | 6.0 | 3.6 |
| Micronesia (Fed. States of) | 4.7 | 19.3 | 5.6 | 65.4 | 9.2 | 19.1 | 10.9 | 15.8 | 12.7 |
| Nauru | 0.0 | .. | .. | .. | .. | .. | .. | .. | .. |
| New Caledonia | 18.4 | 22.6 | 22.6 | 17.7 | 26.6 | 14.5 | 30.4 | 5.4 | 32.1 |
| Northern Mariana Islands | .. | .. | .. | .. | .. | .. | .. | .. | .. |
| Palau | .. | .. | 20.3 | .. | .. | .. | .. | .. | .. |
| Papua New Guinea | 0.9 | 46.8 | 1.4 | 37.1 | 1.9 | 12.0 | 2.1 | 10.3 | 2.3 |
| Samoa | 1.7 | 32.1 | 2.2 | 24.0 | 2.7 | 9.2 | 3.0 | 8.4 | 3.2 |
| Solomon Islands | 0.5 | 7.1 | 0.5 | 10.7 | 0.6 | 16.9 | 0.6 | 30.0 | 0.8 |
| Tonga | 2.8 | 3.1 | 2.9 | 3.0 | 3.0 | -0.4 | 2.9 | -0.3 | 2.9 |
| Tuvalu | 9.8 | 24.3 | 12.1 | 43.3 | 17.4 | 65.9 | 28.9 | .. | .. |
| Vanuatu | 2.8 | 24.7 | 3.5 | 5.0 | 3.7 | -1.9 | 3.6 | 4.6 | 3.8 |
| **TRANSITION ECONOMIES** | | | | | | | | | |
| **SOUTH-EAST EUROPE AND CIS** | | | | | | | | | |
| Albania | 0.3 | 19.6 | 0.4 | 148.7 | 1.0 | 148.6 | 2.4 | 149.2 | 6.0 |
| Armenia | 1.6 | 20.6 | 2.0 | 134.3 | 4.6 | 7.5 | 5.0 | 7.7 | 5.3 |
| Azerbaijan | 0.3 | 1092.4 | 3.6 | 15.9 | 4.2 | 15.8 | 4.9 | 65.3 | 8.1 |
| Belarus | 4.3 | 88.9 | 8.1 | 73.1 | 14.1 | 77.8 | 25.1 | 38.7 | 34.8 |
| Bosnia and Herzegovina | 1.2 | 121.1 | 2.6 | 50.1 | 3.8 | 50.3 | 5.8 | 258.6 | 20.6 |
| Bulgaria | 7.6 | 4.8 | 8.0 | .. | .. | .. | 15.9 | 29.9 | 20.6 |
| Croatia | 11.5 | 52.1 | 17.5 | 28.0 | 22.4 | 30.4 | 29.2 | 9.0 | 31.9 |
| Georgia | 1.0 | 59.8 | 1.6 | 60.9 | 2.6 | 51.6 | 3.9 | .. | .. |
| Kazakhstan | 1.0 | 67.3 | 1.7 | 20.2 | 2.0 | 33.5 | 2.7 | .. | .. |
| Kyrgyzstan | 3.0 | -0.3 | 3.0 | 30.0 | 3.9 | 30.0 | 5.1 | 5.2 | 5.3 |
| Rep. of Moldova | 1.4 | 150.9 | 3.5 | 92.6 | 6.8 | 41.4 | 9.6 | .. | .. |

## Table 1.17 *(Continued)*

| | 2001 | % change 2001-2002 | 2002 | % change 2002-2003 | 2003 | % change 2003-2004 | 2004 | % change 2004-2005 | 2005 |
|---|---|---|---|---|---|---|---|---|---|
| Romania | 4.5 | 120.8 | 10.0 | 82.5 | 18.3 | 12.9 | 20.7 | .. | .. |
| Russian Federation | 2.9 | 40.2 | 4.1 | 101.0 | 8.3 | 54.9 | 12.9 | 18.4 | 15.2 |
| Serbia and Montenegro | 5.7 | 6.8 | 6.1 | 32.4 | 8.1 | 79.2 | 14.4 | .. | .. |
| Tajikistan | 0.1 | 8.2 | 0.1 | 16.5 | 0.1 | 20.0 | 0.1 | .. | .. |
| TFYR Macedonia | 3.5 | 42.5 | 4.9 | 25.7 | 6.2 | 25.9 | 7.8 | 0.4 | 7.9 |
| Turkmenistan | 0.2 | .. | .. | .. | 0.4 | 77.4 | 0.8 | .. | .. |
| Ukraine | 1.2 | 51.7 | 1.9 | 180.9 | 5.3 | 51.7 | 8.0 | 22.9 | 9.8 |
| Uzbekistan | 0.6 | 80.7 | 1.1 | 76.3 | 1.9 | 76.3 | 3.4 | .. | .. |

**Notes:** a The value for Internet penetration in Canada in 2005 is assumed.

*Source:* UNCTAD calculations based on the ITU World Telecommunication Indicators Database, 2006.

## Annex I

## Statistical Annex

## Table 1.18

## Broadband subscribers: Economies by level of development and by region

| | 2001 | % change 2001-2002 | 2002 | % change 2002-2003 | 2003 | % change 2003-2004 | 2004 | % change 2004-2005 | 2005 |
|---|---|---|---|---|---|---|---|---|---|
| | | | | DEVELOPED ECONOMIES | | | | | |
| **ASIA** | | | | | | | | | |
| Israel | 38 000 | 468.9 | 216 163 | 192.9 | 633 100 | 54.8 | 980 000 | 25.5 | 1 229 626 |
| Japan | 3 835 000 | 145.0 | 9 397 426 | 58.7 | 14 917 165 | 31.1 | 19 557 146 | 14.4 | 22 365 148 |
| **EUROPE** | | | | | | | | | |
| Andorra | .. | .. | 1 148 | 213.7 | 3 601 | 74.5 | 6 282 | 64.6 | 10 341 |
| Austria | 320 600 | 68.3 | 539 500 | 11.4 | 601 000 | 36.4 | 820 000 | 43.4 | 1 176 000 |
| Belgium | 458 759 | 77.7 | 815 418 | 52.4 | 1 242 928 | 30.1 | 1 617 185 | 24.0 | 2 004 859 |
| Cyprus | 2 500 | 135.2 | 5 879 | 70.7 | 10 033 | 33.2 | 13 368 | 99.6 | 26 684 |
| Czech Republic | 6 200 | 146.8 | 15 300 | 126.7 | 34 690 | 580.3 | 235 996 | 89.7 | 447 682 |
| Denmark (incl. Faroe Islands) | 223 276 | 102.1 | 451 297 | 59.2 | 718 299 | 42.1 | 1 020 893 | 32.9 | 1 356 283 |
| Estonia | 17 261 | 164.8 | 45 700 | 97.6 | 90 300 | 23.7 | 111 699 | 60.4 | 179 200 |
| Finland | 52 000 | 426.0 | 273 500 | 79.6 | 491 100 | 62.9 | 800 000 | 46.8 | 1 174 200 |
| France | 601 500 | 179.8 | 1 682 992 | 112.1 | 3 569 381 | 83.9 | 6 562 541 | 44.2 | 9 465 600 |
| Germany | 2 100 000 | 52.6 | 3 205 000 | 40.4 | 4 500 000 | 53.3 | 6 900 000 | 55.1 | 10 700 000 |
| Gibraltar | .. | .. | 225 | .. | .. | .. | .. | .. | .. |
| Greece | .. | .. | .. | .. | 10 476 | 391.2 | 51 455 | 211.2 | 160 113 |
| Greenland | .. | .. | .. | .. | .. | .. | .. | .. | .. |
| Guernsey | .. | .. | .. | .. | .. | .. | .. | .. | .. |
| Hungary | 20 000 | 457.3 | 111 458 | 137.1 | 264 311 | 55.6 | 411 171 | 58.5 | 651 689 |
| Iceland | 10 424 | 132.8 | 24 270 | 66.5 | 40 419 | 36.4 | 55 112 | 41.6 | 78 017 |
| Ireland | .. | .. | 10 600 | 294.3 | 41 800 | 263.9 | 152 100 | 78.0 | 270 700 |
| Italy | 390 000 | 117.9 | 850 000 | 164.7 | 2 250 000 | 97.8 | 4 450 000 | 52.4 | 6 780 000 |
| Jersey | .. | .. | .. | .. | .. | .. | .. | .. | .. |
| Latvia | 3 235 | 209.1 | 10 000 | 95.3 | 19 533 | 151.6 | 49 147 | 430.6 | 260 770 |
| Liechtenstein | .. | .. | .. | .. | .. | .. | .. | .. | .. |
| Lithuania | 2 427 | 724.1 | 20 000 | 234.0 | 66 790 | 93.2 | 129 051 | 81.4 | 234 081 |
| Luxembourg | 1 215 | 368.9 | 5 697 | 169.5 | 15 351 | 137.8 | 36 500 | 92.1 | 70 100 |
| Malta | 9 157 | 93.1 | 17 679 | 28.6 | 22 736 | 65.6 | 37 642 | 18.7 | 44 672 |
| Netherlands | 466 200 | 129.3 | 1 068 966 | 86.0 | 1 988 000 | 61.3 | 3 206 000 | 27.9 | 4 100 000 |
| Norway | 88 541 | 131.9 | 205 307 | 94.2 | 398 758 | 68.4 | 671 666 | 47.6 | 991 352 |
| Poland | 12 000 | 914.0 | 121 684 | 60.9 | 195 752 | 314.7 | 811 796 | 53.2 | 1 243 949 |
| Portugal | 96 324 | 172.8 | 262 789 | 91.5 | 503 128 | 70.6 | 858 419 | 41.2 | 1 212 034 |

## Table 1.18 (Continued)

| | 2001 | % change 2001-2002 | 2002 | % change 2002-2003 | 2003 | % change 2003-2004 | 2004 | % change 2004-2005 | 2005 |
|---|---|---|---|---|---|---|---|---|---|
| San Marino | .. | .. | .. | .. | 600 | .. | .. | .. | .. |
| Slovakia | .. | .. | .. | .. | 7 708 | 538.1 | 49 188 | 181.7 | 138 569 |
| Slovenia | 5 500 | 931.5 | 56 735 | 2.2 | 57 992 | 98.4 | 115 069 | 47.7 | 169 950 |
| Spain | 430 055 | 190.1 | 1 247 496 | 76.5 | 2 202 000 | 56.3 | 3 441 630 | 45.1 | 4 994 274 |
| Sweden | 356 500 | 100.9 | 716 085 | 10.7 | 793 000 | 56.0 | 1 237 000 | 56.1 | 1 931 000 |
| Switzerland | 140 000 | 225.2 | 455 220 | 72.2 | 783 874 | 55.3 | 1 217 000 | 41.8 | 1 725 446 |
| United Kingdom | 501 000 | 263.5 | 1 821 000 | 110.0 | 3 824 500 | 86.4 | 7 130 500 | 33.8 | 9 539 900 |
| **NORTH AMERICA** | | | | | | | | | |
| Canada | 2 836 000 | 23.9 | 3 515 000 | 28.4 | 4 513 000 | 20.0 | 5 416 000 | 23.8 | 6 706 699 |
| United States (incl. Puerto Rico and Guam) | 12 794 562 | 55.6 | 19 904 281 | 41.8 | 28 230 149 | 34.2 | 37 890 646 | 30.4 | 49 391 060 |
| **OCEANIA** | | | | | | | | | |
| Australia | 122 800 | 110.2 | 258 100 | 100.2 | 516 800 | 98.4 | 1 025 500 | 105.1 | 2 102 800 |
| New Zealand | 17 267 | 151.9 | 43 500 | 90.8 | 83 000 | 131.0 | 191 695 | 72.7 | 331 000 |
| **DEVELOPING ECONOMIES** | | | | | | | | | |
| **AFRICA** | | | | | | | | | |
| Algeria | .. | .. | .. | .. | .. | .. | 36 000 | 441.7 | 195 000 |
| Angola | .. | .. | .. | .. | .. | .. | .. | .. | .. |
| Benin | .. | .. | 21 | 0.0 | 21 | 285.7 | 81 | 142.0 | 196 |
| Botswana | .. | .. | .. | .. | .. | .. | .. | .. | .. |
| Burkina Faso | .. | .. | 50 | 190.0 | 145 | 6.2 | 154 | 68.8 | 260 |
| Burundi | .. | .. | .. | .. | .. | .. | .. | .. | .. |
| Cameroon | .. | .. | .. | .. | .. | .. | .. | .. | .. |
| Cape Verde | .. | .. | .. | .. | .. | .. | 283 | 231.1 | 937 |
| Central African Rep. | .. | .. | .. | .. | .. | .. | .. | .. | .. |
| Chad | .. | .. | .. | .. | .. | .. | .. | .. | .. |
| Comoros | .. | .. | .. | .. | .. | .. | 1 | 300.0 | 4 |
| Congo | .. | .. | .. | .. | .. | .. | .. | .. | .. |
| Côte d'Ivoire | .. | .. | .. | .. | 1 000 | -17.4 | 826 | .. | .. |
| Democratic Republic of the Congo | .. | .. | .. | .. | .. | .. | 1 450 | 3.4 | 1 500 |
| Djibouti | .. | .. | .. | .. | .. | .. | .. | .. | 42 |
| Egypt | .. | .. | 937 | 417.6 | 4 850 | 879.5 | 47 504 | 139.0 | 113 526 |
| Equatorial Guinea | .. | .. | .. | .. | .. | .. | .. | .. | .. |
| Eritrea | .. | .. | .. | .. | .. | .. | .. | .. | .. |
| Ethiopia | .. | .. | .. | .. | 57 | .. | .. | .. | .. |
| Gabon | .. | .. | .. | .. | 170 | 282.4 | 650 | 133.1 | 1 515 |
| Gambia | .. | .. | .. | .. | .. | .. | .. | .. | 71 |

## Table 1.18 *(Continued)*

| | 2001 | % change 2001-2002 | 2002 | % change 2002-2003 | 2003 | % change 2003-2004 | 2004 | % change 2004-2005 | 2005 |
|---|---|---|---|---|---|---|---|---|---|
| Ghana | .. | .. | .. | .. | .. | .. | .. | .. | 1 904 |
| Guinea | .. | .. | .. | .. | .. | .. | .. | .. | .. |
| Guinea-Bissau | .. | .. | .. | .. | .. | .. | .. | .. | .. |
| Kenya | .. | .. | .. | .. | .. | .. | .. | .. | .. |
| Lesotho | .. | .. | .. | .. | .. | .. | .. | .. | 45 |
| Liberia | .. | .. | .. | .. | .. | .. | .. | .. | .. |
| Libyan Arab Jamahiriya | .. | .. | .. | .. | .. | .. | .. | .. | .. |
| Madagascar | .. | .. | .. | .. | .. | .. | .. | .. | .. |
| Malawi | .. | .. | .. | .. | 69 | 100.0 | 138 | 192.8 | 404 |
| Mali | .. | .. | .. | .. | .. | .. | .. | .. | .. |
| Mauritania | .. | .. | .. | .. | .. | .. | .. | .. | 164 |
| Mauritius | .. | .. | 285 | 315.8 | 1 185 | 128.5 | 2 708 | .. | .. |
| Mayotte | .. | .. | .. | .. | .. | .. | .. | .. | .. |
| Morocco | .. | .. | 2 000 | 35.6 | 2 712 | 2284.2 | 64 660 | 285.3 | 249 138 |
| Mozambique | .. | .. | .. | .. | .. | .. | .. | .. | .. |
| Namibia | .. | .. | .. | .. | .. | .. | .. | .. | .. |
| Niger | .. | .. | .. | .. | .. | .. | 77 | 175.3 | 212 |
| Nigeria | .. | .. | .. | .. | .. | .. | .. | .. | 500 |
| Reunion | .. | .. | .. | .. | .. | .. | 56 536 | .. | .. |
| Rwanda | .. | .. | .. | .. | .. | .. | .. | .. | .. |
| Sao Tome and Principe | .. | .. | .. | .. | .. | .. | .. | .. | .. |
| Senegal | .. | .. | 1 200 | 75.0 | 2 100 | 264.9 | 7 663 | 140.1 | 18 396 |
| Seychelles | .. | .. | .. | .. | .. | .. | 349 | 64.8 | 575 |
| Sierra Leone | .. | .. | .. | .. | .. | .. | .. | .. | .. |
| Somalia | .. | .. | .. | .. | .. | .. | .. | .. | .. |
| South Africa | .. | .. | 2 669 | 661.1 | 20 313 | 195.4 | 60 000 | 175.5 | 165 290 |
| Sudan | .. | .. | .. | .. | .. | .. | 1 400 | 28.6 | 1 800 |
| Swaziland | .. | .. | .. | .. | .. | .. | .. | .. | .. |
| Syrian Arab Republic | .. | .. | .. | .. | .. | .. | 600 | .. | .. |
| Togo | .. | .. | .. | .. | .. | .. | .. | .. | .. |
| Tunisia | .. | .. | .. | .. | .. | .. | 2 839 | 480.9 | 16 491 |
| Uganda | .. | .. | .. | .. | 2 590 | .. | .. | .. | .. |
| United Republic of Tanzania | .. | .. | .. | .. | .. | .. | .. | .. | .. |
| Zambia | 31 | 54.8 | 48 | 89.6 | 91 | 174.7 | 250 | 0.0 | 250 |
| Zimbabwe | .. | .. | .. | .. | 4 618 | 94.2 | 8 967 | 13.6 | 10 185 |
| **ASIA** | | | | | | | | | |
| Afghanistan | .. | .. | .. | .. | .. | .. | 200 | 10.0 | 220 |

## Table 1.18 *(Continued)*

| | 2001 | % change 2001-2002 | 2002 | % change 2002-2003 | 2003 | % change 2003-2004 | 2004 | % change 2004-2005 | 2005 |
|---|---|---|---|---|---|---|---|---|---|
| Bahrain | 1 176 | 323.5 | 4 980 | 95.5 | 9 737 | .. | .. | .. | .. |
| Bangladesh | .. | .. | .. | .. | .. | .. | .. | .. | .. |
| Bhutan | .. | .. | .. | .. | .. | .. | .. | .. | .. |
| Brunei Darussalam | .. | .. | .. | .. | .. | .. | .. | .. | .. |
| Cambodia | .. | .. | 50 | 738.0 | 419 | .. | .. | .. | .. |
| China | 339 510 | 1480.8 | 5 367 000 | 107.7 | 11 147 000 | 123.2 | 24 875 000 | 50.8 | 37 504 000 |
| Dem. People's Rep. of Korea | .. | .. | .. | .. | .. | .. | .. | .. | .. |
| Hong Kong (China) | 716 435 | 45.0 | 1 038 995 | 22.0 | 1 267 966 | 19.9 | 1 519 837 | 9.2 | 1 659 098 |
| India | 50 000 | 64.8 | 82 409 | 70.3 | 140 362 | 67.4 | 235 000 | 453.2 | 1 300 000 |
| Indonesia | 15 000 | 155.3 | 38 300 | .. | .. | .. | .. | .. | .. |
| Iran (Islamic Rep. of) | 661 | 2346.4 | 16 171 | 9.5 | 17 700 | .. | .. | .. | .. |
| Iraq | .. | .. | .. | .. | .. | .. | .. | .. | .. |
| Jordan | 409 | 676.8 | 3 177 | 57.3 | 4 996 | 108.6 | 10 424 | .. | .. |
| Kuwait | 5 000 | 110.0 | 10 500 | 23.8 | 13 000 | 53.8 | 20 000 | .. | .. |
| Lao PDR | .. | .. | .. | .. | .. | .. | 550 | -69.1 | 170 |
| Lebanon | .. | .. | 35 000 | 100.0 | 70 000 | 14.3 | 80 000 | 62.5 | 130 000 |
| Macao (China) | 9 786 | 73.2 | 16 954 | 63.6 | 27 744 | 63.0 | 45 218 | 50.4 | 68 030 |
| Malaysia | 4 000 | 382.6 | 19 302 | 472.0 | 110 406 | 128.9 | 252 701 | 94.2 | 490 630 |
| Maldives | .. | .. | 190 | 164.7 | 503 | 42.5 | 717 | 191.6 | 2 091 |
| Mongolia | 49 | 83.7 | 90 | 455.6 | 500 | 80.0 | 900 | 100.0 | 1 800 |
| Myanmar | .. | .. | .. | .. | .. | .. | .. | .. | 119 |
| Nepal | .. | .. | .. | .. | .. | .. | .. | .. | .. |
| Oman | .. | .. | 97 | 40.2 | 136 | 391.2 | 668 | 1154.2 | 8 378 |
| Pakistan | .. | .. | .. | .. | .. | .. | .. | .. | 44 600 |
| Palestine | .. | .. | .. | .. | .. | .. | .. | .. | 7 665 |
| Philippines | 10 000 | 110.0 | 21 000 | 161.9 | 55 000 | .. | .. | .. | .. |
| Qatar | .. | .. | 228 | 1211.8 | 2 991 | 256.1 | 10 652 | 136.3 | 25 168 |
| Rep. of Korea | 7 806 000 | 33.3 | 10 405 486 | 7.4 | 11 178 499 | 6.6 | 11 921 440 | 2.3 | 12 190 711 |
| Saudi Arabia | 1 000 | 128.7 | 2 287 | 267.3 | 8 400 | 134.5 | 19 700 | .. | .. |
| Singapore | 151 000 | 78.8 | 270 000 | 56.2 | 421 700 | 21.5 | 512 400 | 29.9 | 665 500 |
| Sri Lanka | 327 | 81.0 | 592 | 477.2 | 3 417 | .. | .. | .. | 14 072 |
| Taiwan Province of China | 1 133 000 | 85.3 | 2 100 000 | 44.9 | 3 043 273 | 23.3 | 3 751 214 | 22.7 | 4 602 223 |
| Thailand | 1 613 | 829.9 | 15 000 | 200.0 | 45 000 | .. | .. | .. | .. |
| Turkey | 10 915 | 94.3 | 21 205 | 840.0 | 199 324 | 189.9 | 577 931 | 175.1 | 1 589 768 |
| United Arab Emirates | 7 754 | 108.6 | 16 177 | 84.4 | 29 831 | 86.2 | 55 541 | 131.3 | 128 493 |
| Viet Nam | .. | .. | 1 076 | 753.2 | 9 180 | 474.2 | 52 709 | 298.5 | 210 024 |
| Yemen | .. | .. | .. | .. | .. | .. | .. | .. | .. |

## Table 1.18 *(Continued)*

| | 2001 | % change 2001-2002 | 2002 | % change 2002-2003 | 2003 | % change 2003-2004 | 2004 | % change 2004-2005 | 2005 |
|---|---|---|---|---|---|---|---|---|---|
| **LATIN AMERICA AND THE CARIBBEAN** | | | | | | | | | |
| Antigua and Barbuda | .. | .. | .. | .. | .. | .. | .. | .. | .. |
| Argentina | 85 000 | 35.3 | 115 000 | 104.0 | 234 625 | 112.0 | 497 513 | 69.0 | 841 000 |
| Aruba | .. | .. | .. | .. | .. | .. | .. | .. | .. |
| Bahamas | .. | .. | 7 540 | 45.1 | 10 941 | 17.0 | 12 803 | .. | .. |
| Barbados | .. | .. | .. | .. | 27 319 | .. | .. | .. | 31 942 |
| Belize | .. | .. | .. | .. | 940 | 200.7 | 2 827 | 51.4 | 4 280 |
| Bermuda | .. | .. | .. | .. | .. | .. | .. | .. | .. |
| Bolivia | .. | .. | 3 330 | 72.4 | 5 740 | 52.0 | 8 723 | 23.7 | 10 788 |
| Brazil | 331 000 | 120.8 | 731 000 | 64.0 | 1 199 000 | 88.2 | 2 256 000 | 46.5 | 3 304 000 |
| Cayman Islands | .. | .. | .. | .. | .. | .. | .. | .. | .. |
| Chile | 66 722 | 182.4 | 188 454 | 86.9 | 352 234 | 36.0 | 478 883 | 47.9 | 708 358 |
| Colombia | 13 830 | 152.3 | 34 888 | 84.7 | 64 436 | 97.3 | 127 113 | 150.7 | 318 683 |
| Costa Rica | .. | .. | 363 | 3998.6 | 14 878 | 87.7 | 27 931 | .. | .. |
| Cuba | .. | .. | .. | .. | .. | .. | .. | .. | .. |
| Dominica | 175 | 1178.9 | 2 238 | 18.5 | 2 651 | 22.7 | 3 253 | .. | .. |
| Dominican Rep. | .. | .. | .. | .. | .. | .. | 37 257 | 76.8 | 65 856 |
| Ecuador | .. | .. | .. | .. | .. | .. | 11 620 | 130.5 | 26 786 |
| El Salvador | .. | .. | .. | .. | .. | .. | 29 321 | 44.3 | 42 314 |
| French Guiana | .. | .. | .. | .. | .. | .. | .. | .. | .. |
| Grenada | .. | .. | 563 | .. | .. | .. | 609 | .. | .. |
| Guadeloupe | .. | .. | .. | .. | .. | .. | .. | .. | .. |
| Guatemala | .. | .. | .. | .. | .. | .. | .. | .. | 27 106 |
| Guyana | .. | .. | .. | .. | .. | .. | .. | .. | 2 000 |
| Haiti | .. | .. | .. | .. | .. | .. | .. | .. | .. |
| Honduras | .. | .. | .. | .. | .. | .. | .. | .. | .. |
| Jamaica | .. | .. | 9 000 | .. | .. | .. | .. | .. | .. |
| Martinique | .. | .. | .. | .. | 6 000 | .. | .. | .. | .. |
| Mexico | 50 000 | 363.0 | 231 486 | 85.1 | 428 378 | 142.2 | 1 037 455 | 122.1 | 2 304 520 |
| Netherlands Antilles | .. | .. | .. | .. | .. | .. | .. | .. | .. |
| Nicaragua | 1 604 | 44.6 | 2 319 | 89.9 | 4 403 | 13.6 | 5 001 | 110.6 | 10 534 |
| Panama | 4 040 | 202.8 | 12 235 | 22.9 | 15 039 | 11.4 | 16 746 | 4.9 | 17 567 |
| Paraguay | 300 | 66.7 | 500 | 0.0 | 500 | .. | .. | .. | 5 600 |
| Peru | 7 237 | 375.3 | 34 400 | 172.4 | 93 695 | 47.6 | 138 277 | 152.8 | 349 582 |
| Saint Kitts and Nevis | .. | .. | 500 | .. | .. | .. | .. | .. | .. |
| Saint Lucia | .. | .. | .. | .. | .. | .. | .. | .. | .. |
| Saint Vincent and the Grenadines | 81 | 1240.7 | 1 086 | 5.5 | 1 146 | 15.2 | 1 320 | 176.3 | 3 647 |

## Table 1.18 *(Continued)*

| | 2001 | % change 2001-2002 | 2002 | % change 2002-2003 | 2003 | % change 2003-2004 | 2004 | % change 2004-2005 | 2005 |
|---|---|---|---|---|---|---|---|---|---|
| Suriname | .. | .. | 94 | 129.8 | 216 | 94.4 | 420 | 138.3 | 1 001 |
| Trinidad and Tobago | .. | .. | 95 | 830.5 | 884 | 378.8 | 4 233 | 155.2 | 10 803 |
| Uruguay | 1 371 | .. | .. | .. | .. | .. | 27 000 | 126.6 | 61 186 |
| Venezuela | 36 636 | 113.3 | 78 151 | .. | 116 997 | .. | 210 303 | 69.7 | 356 898 |
| Virgin Islands (US) | .. | .. | .. | .. | .. | .. | .. | .. | .. |
| **OCEANIA** | | | | | | | | | |
| American Samoa | .. | .. | .. | .. | .. | .. | .. | .. | .. |
| Fiji | .. | .. | .. | .. | .. | .. | .. | .. | .. |
| French Polynesia | .. | .. | .. | .. | 946 | 359.9 | 4 351 | 152.8 | 11 000 |
| Kiribati | .. | .. | .. | .. | .. | .. | .. | .. | .. |
| Marshall Islands | .. | .. | .. | .. | .. | .. | .. | .. | .. |
| Micronesia (Fed. States of) | .. | .. | .. | .. | .. | .. | .. | .. | .. |
| Nauru | .. | .. | .. | .. | .. | .. | .. | .. | .. |
| New Caledonia | 132 | 430.3 | 700 | 138.3 | 1 668 | 208.5 | 5 146 | 86.6 | 9 600 |
| Northern Mariana Islands | .. | .. | .. | .. | .. | .. | .. | .. | .. |
| Palau | .. | .. | .. | .. | .. | .. | .. | .. | .. |
| Papua New Guinea | .. | .. | .. | .. | .. | .. | .. | .. | .. |
| Samoa | .. | .. | .. | .. | .. | .. | .. | .. | .. |
| Solomon Islands | .. | .. | 108 | 89.8 | 205 | -2.4 | 200 | 125.0 | 450 |
| Tonga | .. | .. | 11 | .. | .. | .. | .. | .. | .. |
| Tuvalu | .. | .. | .. | .. | .. | .. | .. | .. | .. |
| Vanuatu | .. | .. | .. | .. | 15 | 53.3 | 23 | .. | .. |
| **TRANSITION ECONOMIES** | | | | | | | | | |
| **SOUTH-EAST EUROPE AND CIS** | | | | | | | | | |
| Albania | .. | .. | .. | .. | .. | .. | .. | .. | .. |
| Armenia | .. | .. | 8 | 25.0 | 10 | 9 900.0 | 1 000 | .. | .. |
| Azerbaijan | .. | .. | .. | .. | .. | .. | 900 | 142.7 | 2 184 |
| Belarus | .. | .. | 20 | 515.0 | 123 | 509.8 | 750 | 108.5 | 1 564 |
| Bosnia and Herzegovina | .. | .. | 213 | .. | .. | .. | 6 637 | 106.4 | 13 702 |
| Bulgaria | .. | .. | .. | .. | .. | .. | 1 291 | .. | .. |
| Croatia | .. | .. | 12 000 | .. | .. | .. | 26 800 | 235.1 | 89 800 |
| Georgia | .. | .. | 920 | 53.3 | 1 410 | .. | .. | .. | .. |
| Kazakhstan | .. | .. | .. | .. | .. | .. | 1 997 | .. | .. |
| Kyrgyzstan | .. | .. | 36 | .. | 139 | .. | 1 907 | 28.9 | 2 459 |
| Rep. of Moldova | .. | .. | 418 | 42.8 | 597 | 306.9 | 2 429 | 328.0 | 10 395 |
| Romania | 6 000 | 163.3 | 15 800 | 1141.2 | 196 106 | 95.2 | 382 783 | 96.2 | 751 060 |
| Russian Federation | .. | .. | 11 000 | .. | .. | .. | 675 000 | 135.4 | 1 589 000 |

## Table 1.18 *(Continued)*

|  | 2001 | % change 2001-2002 | 2002 | % change 2002-2003 | 2003 | % change 2003-2004 | 2004 | % change 2004-2005 | 2005 |
|---|---|---|---|---|---|---|---|---|---|
| Serbia and Montenegro | .. | .. | .. | .. | .. | .. | .. | .. | .. |
| Tajikistan | .. | .. | .. | .. | .. | .. | .. | .. | .. |
| TFYR Macedonia | .. | .. | .. | .. | .. | .. | .. | .. | 12 436 |
| Turkmenistan | .. | .. | .. | .. | .. | .. | .. | .. | .. |
| Ukraine | .. | .. | .. | .. | .. | .. | .. | .. | .. |
| Uzbekistan | .. | .. | .. | .. | 2 757 | .. | .. | .. | .. |

*Source:* UNCTAD calculations based on the ITU World Telecommunication Indicators Database, 2006.

## Annex I

## Statistical Annex

## Table 1.19

## Broadband penetration: Economies by level of development and by region

Broadband subscribers per 100 inhabitants

| | 2001 | % change 2001-2002 | 2002 | % change 2002-2003 | 2003 | % change 2003-2004 | 2004 | % change 2004-2005 | 2005 |
|---|---|---|---|---|---|---|---|---|---|
| DEVELOPED ECONOMIES | | | | | | | | | |
| ASIA | | | | | | | | | |
| Israel | 0.6 | 457.2 | 3.4 | 187.1 | 9.8 | 51.8 | 14.8 | 23.2 | 18.3 |
| Japan | 3.0 | 144.6 | 7.4 | 58.5 | 11.7 | 30.9 | 15.3 | 14.2 | 17.5 |
| EUROPE | | | | | | | | | |
| Andorra | .. | .. | 1.7 | 212.3 | 5.4 | 73.7 | 9.4 | 64.1 | 15.4 |
| Austria | 3.6 | 40.6 | 5.0 | 47.4 | 7.4 | 36.1 | 10.0 | 43.1 | 14.4 |
| Belgium | 4.5 | 89.2 | 8.4 | 42.2 | 12.0 | 29.9 | 15.6 | 23.7 | 19.2 |
| Cyprus | 0.3 | 132.2 | 0.7 | 68.6 | 1.2 | 31.7 | 1.6 | 97.4 | 3.2 |
| Czech Republic | 0.1 | 147.0 | 0.1 | 126.9 | 0.3 | 580.9 | 2.3 | 89.9 | 4.4 |
| Denmark (incl. Faroe Islands) | 4.1 | 101.4 | 8.3 | 58.6 | 13.2 | 41.7 | 18.7 | 32.4 | 24.8 |
| Estonia | 1.3 | 166.4 | 3.4 | 98.6 | 6.7 | 24.3 | 8.4 | 61.1 | 13.5 |
| Finland | 1.0 | 424.5 | 5.3 | 79.0 | 9.4 | 62.4 | 15.3 | 46.4 | 22.4 |
| France | 1.0 | 178.7 | 2.8 | 111.2 | 5.9 | 83.1 | 10.9 | 43.7 | 15.6 |
| Germany | 2.5 | 52.5 | 3.9 | 40.3 | 5.4 | 53.2 | 8.3 | 55.0 | 12.9 |
| Gibraltar | .. | .. | 0.8 | .. | .. | .. | .. | .. | .. |
| Greece | .. | .. | .. | .. | 0.1 | 390.1 | 0.5 | 210.6 | 1.4 |
| Greenland | .. | .. | .. | .. | .. | .. | .. | .. | .. |
| Guernsey | .. | .. | .. | .. | .. | .. | .. | .. | .. |
| Hungary | 0.2 | 458.7 | 1.1 | 137.7 | 2.6 | 56.0 | 4.1 | 58.9 | 6.5 |
| Iceland | 3.7 | 130.6 | 8.5 | 65.0 | 14.0 | 35.1 | 18.9 | 40.3 | 26.5 |
| Ireland | .. | .. | 0.3 | 287.1 | 1.0 | 257.4 | 3.7 | 75.0 | 6.5 |
| Italy | 0.7 | 117.6 | 1.5 | 164.3 | 3.9 | 97.5 | 7.7 | 52.2 | 11.7 |
| Jersey | .. | .. | .. | .. | .. | .. | .. | .. | .. |
| Latvia | 0.1 | 211.0 | 0.4 | 96.4 | 0.8 | 152.9 | 2.1 | 433.2 | 11.3 |
| Liechtenstein | .. | .. | .. | .. | .. | .. | .. | .. | .. |
| Lithuania | 0.1 | 727.5 | 0.6 | 235.1 | 1.9 | 93.9 | 3.7 | 82.0 | 6.8 |
| Luxembourg | 0.3 | 362.6 | 1.3 | 165.9 | 3.4 | 134.7 | 8.0 | 89.6 | 15.1 |
| Malta | 2.3 | 92.1 | 4.5 | 28.0 | 5.7 | 64.8 | 9.4 | 18.1 | 11.1 |
| Netherlands | 1.9 | 124.4 | 4.2 | 82.1 | 7.6 | 58.0 | 12.1 | 25.3 | 15.1 |
| Norway | 2.0 | 130.6 | 4.5 | 93.2 | 8.7 | 67.6 | 14.6 | 46.9 | 21.5 |
| Poland | 0.0 | 914.6 | 0.3 | 61.0 | 0.5 | 315.0 | 2.1 | 53.4 | 3.2 |

## Table 1.19 *(Continued)*

| | 2001 | % change 2001-2002 | 2002 | % change 2002-2003 | 2003 | % change 2003-2004 | 2004 | % change 2004-2005 | 2005 |
|---|---|---|---|---|---|---|---|---|---|
| Portugal | 0.9 | 171.4 | 2.5 | 90.4 | 4.8 | 69.7 | 8.2 | 40.5 | 11.5 |
| San Marino | .. | .. | .. | .. | 2.2 | .. | .. | .. | .. |
| Slovakia | .. | .. | .. | .. | 0.1 | 538.2 | 0.9 | 181.7 | 2.6 |
| Slovenia | 0.3 | 931.4 | 2.9 | 2.2 | 2.9 | 98.4 | 5.8 | 47.7 | 8.6 |
| Spain | 1.0 | 186.6 | 3.0 | 74.3 | 5.2 | 54.5 | 8.1 | 43.7 | 11.6 |
| Sweden | 4.0 | 100.1 | 8.0 | 10.3 | 8.8 | 55.3 | 13.7 | 55.5 | 21.4 |
| Switzerland | 1.9 | 224.3 | 6.3 | 71.8 | 10.8 | 55.0 | 16.8 | 41.5 | 23.8 |
| United Kingdom | 0.9 | 262.2 | 3.1 | 109.3 | 6.5 | 85.8 | 12.0 | 33.4 | 16.0 |
| **NORTH AMERICA** | | | | | | | | | |
| Canada | 9.2 | 22.7 | 11.2 | 27.1 | 14.3 | 18.8 | 16.9 | 22.6 | 20.8 |
| United States (incl. Puerto Rico and Guam) | 4.4 | 54.1 | 6.8 | 40.5 | 9.5 | 33.0 | 12.7 | 29.1 | 16.3 |
| **OCEANIA** | | | | | | | | | |
| Australia | 0.6 | 104.3 | 1.3 | 105.3 | 2.6 | 96.3 | 5.1 | 102.9 | 10.4 |
| New Zealand | 0.4 | 149.1 | 1.1 | 88.6 | 2.1 | 128.4 | 4.8 | 71.0 | 8.2 |
| **DEVELOPING ECONOMIES** | | | | | | | | | |
| **AFRICA** | | | | | | | | | |
| Algeria | .. | .. | .. | .. | .. | .. | 0.1 | 433.5 | 0.6 |
| Angola | .. | .. | .. | .. | .. | .. | .. | .. | .. |
| Benin | .. | .. | .. | .. | 0.0 | 1 207.4 | 0.0 | 134.5 | 0.0 |
| Botswana | .. | .. | .. | .. | .. | .. | .. | .. | .. |
| Burkina Faso | .. | .. | 0.0 | 180.8 | 0.0 | 2.9 | 0.0 | 63.6 | 0.0 |
| Burundi | .. | .. | .. | .. | .. | .. | .. | .. | .. |
| Cameroon | .. | .. | .. | .. | .. | .. | .. | .. | .. |
| Cape Verde | .. | .. | .. | .. | .. | .. | 0.1 | 223.5 | 0.2 |
| Central African Rep. | .. | .. | .. | .. | .. | .. | .. | .. | .. |
| Chad | .. | .. | .. | .. | .. | .. | .. | .. | .. |
| Comoros | .. | .. | .. | .. | .. | .. | 0.0 | 289.7 | 0.0 |
| Congo | .. | .. | .. | .. | .. | .. | .. | .. | .. |
| Côte d'Ivoire | .. | .. | .. | .. | .. | .. | 0.0 | .. | .. |
| Democratic Repubic of the Congo | .. | .. | .. | .. | .. | .. | 0.0 | 0.4 | 0.0 |
| Djibouti | .. | .. | .. | .. | .. | .. | .. | .. | 0.0 |
| Egypt | .. | .. | 0.0 | 407.8 | 0.0 | 860.9 | 0.1 | 134.5 | 0.2 |
| Equatorial Guinea | .. | .. | .. | .. | .. | .. | .. | .. | .. |
| Eritrea | .. | .. | .. | .. | .. | .. | .. | .. | .. |
| Ethiopia | .. | .. | .. | .. | .. | .. | .. | .. | .. |
| Gabon | .. | .. | .. | .. | 0.0 | 1 179.9 | 0.0 | 129.5 | 0.1 |

## Table 1.19 *(Continued)*

| | 2001 | % change 2001-2002 | 2002 | % change 2002-2003 | 2003 | % change 2003-2004 | 2004 | % change 2004-2005 | 2005 |
|---|---|---|---|---|---|---|---|---|---|
| Gambia | .. | .. | .. | .. | .. | .. | .. | .. | 0.0 |
| Ghana | .. | .. | .. | .. | .. | .. | .. | .. | 0.0 |
| Guinea | .. | .. | .. | .. | .. | .. | .. | .. | .. |
| Guinea-Bissau | .. | .. | .. | .. | .. | .. | .. | .. | .. |
| Kenya | .. | .. | .. | .. | .. | .. | .. | .. | .. |
| Lesotho | .. | .. | .. | .. | .. | .. | .. | .. | 0.0 |
| Liberia | .. | .. | .. | .. | .. | .. | .. | .. | .. |
| Libyan Arab Jamahiriya | .. | .. | .. | .. | .. | .. | .. | .. | .. |
| Madagascar | .. | .. | .. | .. | .. | .. | .. | .. | .. |
| Malawi | .. | .. | .. | .. | 0.0 | 95.7 | 0.0 | 186.5 | 0.0 |
| Mali | .. | .. | .. | .. | .. | .. | .. | .. | .. |
| Mauritania | .. | .. | .. | .. | .. | .. | .. | .. | 0.0 |
| Mauritius | .. | .. | 0.0 | 311.8 | 0.1 | 126.4 | 0.2 | .. | .. |
| Mayotte | .. | .. | .. | .. | .. | .. | .. | .. | .. |
| Morocco | .. | .. | .. | .. | 0.0 | 2245.7 | 0.2 | 279.2 | 0.8 |
| Mozambique | .. | .. | .. | .. | .. | .. | .. | .. | .. |
| Namibia | .. | .. | .. | .. | .. | .. | .. | .. | .. |
| Niger | .. | .. | .. | .. | .. | .. | 0.0 | 166.3 | 0.0 |
| Nigeria | .. | .. | .. | .. | .. | .. | .. | .. | 0.0 |
| Reunion | .. | .. | .. | .. | .. | .. | 7.3 | .. | .. |
| Rwanda | .. | .. | .. | .. | .. | .. | .. | .. | .. |
| Sao Tome and Principe | .. | .. | .. | .. | .. | .. | .. | .. | .. |
| Senegal | .. | .. | 0.0 | 70.9 | 0.0 | 256.3 | 0.1 | 134.5 | 0.2 |
| Seychelles | .. | .. | .. | .. | .. | .. | 0.4 | 63.2 | 0.7 |
| Sierra Leone | .. | .. | .. | .. | .. | .. | .. | .. | .. |
| Somalia | .. | .. | .. | .. | .. | .. | .. | .. | .. |
| South Africa | .. | .. | 0.0 | 655.3 | 0.0 | 193.6 | 0.1 | 174.2 | 0.3 |
| Sudan | .. | .. | .. | .. | .. | .. | 0.0 | 26.1 | 0.0 |
| Swaziland | .. | .. | .. | .. | .. | .. | .. | .. | .. |
| Syrian Arab Republic | .. | .. | .. | .. | .. | .. | 0.0 | .. | .. |
| Togo | .. | .. | .. | .. | .. | .. | .. | .. | .. |
| Tunisia | .. | .. | 0.0 | 885.3 | 0.0 | 8.4 | 0.0 | 474.7 | 0.2 |
| Uganda | .. | .. | .. | .. | .. | .. | .. | .. | .. |
| United Republic of Tanzania | .. | .. | .. | .. | .. | .. | .. | .. | .. |
| Zambia | .. | .. | .. | .. | 0.0 | 170.2 | 0.0 | -1.6 | 0.0 |
| Zimbabwe | .. | .. | .. | .. | 0.0 | 159.5 | 0.1 | 12.9 | 0.1 |
| ASIA | | | | | | | | | |
| Afghanistan | .. | .. | .. | .. | .. | .. | 0.0 | 5.3 | 0.0 |

**Table 1.19** *(Continued)*

| | 2001 | % change 2001-2002 | 2002 | % change 2002-2003 | 2003 | % change 2003-2004 | 2004 | % change 2004-2005 | 2005 |
|---|---|---|---|---|---|---|---|---|---|
| Bahrain | 0.2 | 316.8 | 0.7 | 92.8 | 1.4 | .. | .. | .. | .. |
| Bangladesh | .. | .. | .. | .. | .. | .. | .. | .. | .. |
| Bhutan | .. | .. | .. | .. | .. | .. | .. | .. | .. |
| Brunei Darussalam | .. | .. | .. | .. | .. | .. | .. | .. | .. |
| Cambodia | .. | .. | 0.0 | 721.7 | 0.0 | .. | .. | .. | .. |
| China | 0.0 | 1470.2 | 0.4 | 106.4 | 0.9 | 121.8 | 1.9 | 49.9 | 2.9 |
| Dem. People's Rep. of Korea | .. | .. | .. | .. | .. | .. | .. | .. | .. |
| Hong Kong (China) | 10.7 | 43.3 | 15.3 | 20.6 | 18.4 | 18.5 | 21.8 | 8.0 | 23.6 |
| India | 0.0 | 62.2 | 0.0 | 67.7 | 0.0 | 64.9 | 0.0 | 445.0 | 0.1 |
| Indonesia | 0.0 | 152.1 | 0.0 | .. | .. | .. | .. | .. | .. |
| Iran (Islamic Rep. of) | 0.0 | 2325.1 | 0.0 | 8.5 | 0.0 | .. | .. | .. | .. |
| Iraq | .. | .. | .. | .. | .. | .. | .. | .. | .. |
| Jordan | 0.0 | 654.9 | 0.1 | 52.9 | 0.1 | 103.1 | 0.2 | .. | .. |
| Kuwait | 16.6 | 32.7 | 22.0 | 7.0 | 23.6 | -96.7 | 0.8 | .. | .. |
| Lao PDR | .. | .. | .. | .. | 0.5 | .. | 0.0 | -69.8 | 0.0 |
| Lebanon | .. | .. | .. | .. | .. | .. | 2.3 | 60.8 | 3.6 |
| Macao (China) | .. | .. | 1.0 | 98.0 | 2.0 | 395.1 | 9.9 | 49.5 | 14.8 |
| Malaysia | 2.2 | 71.9 | 3.8 | 62.5 | 6.1 | -83.4 | 1.0 | 90.7 | 1.9 |
| Maldives | .. | .. | 0.1 | 461.1 | 0.5 | -50.6 | 0.2 | 184.5 | 0.6 |
| Mongolia | .. | .. | 0.1 | 158.2 | 0.2 | -79.6 | 0.0 | 96.7 | 0.1 |
| Myanmar | .. | .. | .. | .. | .. | .. | .. | .. | 0.0 |
| Nepal | .. | .. | .. | .. | .. | .. | .. | .. | .. |
| Oman | .. | .. | .. | .. | .. | .. | 0.0 | 1138.0 | 0.3 |
| Pakistan | .. | .. | .. | .. | .. | .. | .. | .. | 0.0 |
| Palestine | .. | .. | .. | .. | .. | .. | .. | .. | 0.2 |
| Philippines | .. | .. | .. | .. | .. | .. | .. | .. | .. |
| Qatar | .. | .. | 0.0 | 0 157.1 | 0.1 | 1898.4 | 1.4 | 125.8 | 3.1 |
| Rep. of Korea | .. | .. | 0.0 | 1127.8 | 0.4 | 6034.0 | 25.0 | 1.9 | 25.5 |
| Saudi Arabia | 0.0 | 122.5 | 0.0 | 257.5 | 0.0 | 128.4 | 0.1 | .. | .. |
| Singapore | 3.7 | 76.0 | 6.5 | 54.1 | 10.0 | 20.0 | 12.0 | 28.3 | 15.4 |
| Sri Lanka | 0.0 | 79.4 | 0.0 | 472.1 | 0.0 | .. | .. | .. | 0.1 |
| Taiwan Province of China | 5.1 | 84.3 | 9.3 | 44.3 | 13.5 | 22.8 | 16.6 | 22.2 | 20.2 |
| Thailand | 0.0 | 821.5 | 0.0 | 197.3 | 0.1 | .. | .. | .. | .. |
| Turkey | 0.0 | 91.5 | 0.0 | 827.1 | 0.3 | 186.1 | 0.8 | 171.4 | 2.2 |
| United Arab Emirates | 0.2 | 93.7 | 0.4 | 71.8 | 0.7 | 75.2 | 1.3 | 120.5 | 2.9 |
| Viet Nam | .. | .. | .. | .. | 0.0 | 466.4 | 0.1 | 293.2 | 0.2 |
| Yemen | .. | .. | .. | .. | .. | .. | .. | .. | .. |

## Table 1.19 *(Continued)*

| | 2001 | % change 2001-2002 | 2002 | % change 2002-2003 | 2003 | % change 2003-2004 | 2004 | % change 2004-2005 | 2005 |
|---|---|---|---|---|---|---|---|---|---|
| **LATIN AMERICA AND THE CARIBBEAN** | | | | | | | | | |
| Antigua and Barbuda | .. | .. | .. | .. | .. | .. | .. | .. | .. |
| Argentina | 0.2 | 34.0 | 0.3 | 102.1 | 0.6 | 110.0 | 1.3 | 67.4 | 2.2 |
| Aruba | .. | .. | .. | .. | .. | .. | .. | .. | .. |
| Bahamas | .. | .. | 2.4 | 43.1 | 3.5 | 15.4 | 4.0 | .. | .. |
| Barbados | .. | .. | .. | .. | 10.2 | .. | .. | .. | 11.8 |
| Belize | .. | .. | .. | .. | 0.4 | 194.5 | 1.1 | 48.4 | 1.6 |
| Bermuda | .. | .. | .. | .. | .. | .. | .. | .. | .. |
| Bolivia | .. | .. | .. | .. | .. | .. | 0.1 | 21.3 | 0.1 |
| Brazil | 0.2 | 117.7 | 0.4 | 61.7 | 0.7 | 85.6 | 1.2 | 44.5 | 1.8 |
| Cayman Islands | .. | .. | .. | .. | .. | .. | .. | .. | .. |
| Chile | 0.4 | 179.2 | 1.2 | 84.9 | 2.2 | 34.5 | 3.0 | 46.4 | 4.3 |
| Colombia | 0.0 | 148.2 | 0.1 | 81.8 | 0.1 | 94.2 | 0.3 | 146.9 | 0.7 |
| Costa Rica | .. | .. | 0.0 | 3920.7 | 0.4 | 84.3 | 0.7 | .. | .. |
| Cuba | .. | .. | .. | .. | .. | .. | .. | .. | .. |
| Dominica | 0.2 | 1176.6 | 2.9 | 18.3 | 3.4 | 22.4 | 4.1 | .. | .. |
| Dominican Rep. | .. | .. | .. | .. | .. | .. | 0.4 | 74.2 | 0.7 |
| Ecuador | .. | .. | .. | .. | 0.1 | 65.6 | 0.1 | 127.2 | 0.2 |
| El Salvador | .. | .. | .. | .. | 0.3 | 47.0 | 0.4 | 41.8 | 0.6 |
| French Guiana | .. | .. | .. | .. | .. | .. | .. | .. | .. |
| Grenada | .. | .. | 0.6 | .. | .. | .. | 0.6 | .. | .. |
| Guadeloupe | .. | .. | .. | .. | .. | .. | .. | .. | .. |
| Guatemala | .. | .. | .. | .. | .. | .. | .. | .. | .. |
| Guyana | .. | .. | .. | .. | .. | .. | .. | .. | .. |
| Haiti | .. | .. | .. | .. | .. | .. | .. | .. | .. |
| Honduras | .. | .. | .. | .. | .. | .. | .. | .. | .. |
| Jamaica | .. | .. | .. | .. | .. | .. | .. | .. | .. |
| Martinique | .. | .. | .. | .. | 1.5 | .. | .. | .. | .. |
| Mexico | 0.0 | 356.6 | 0.2 | 82.6 | 0.4 | 139.1 | 1.0 | 119.4 | 2.2 |
| Netherlands Antilles | .. | .. | .. | .. | .. | .. | .. | .. | .. |
| Nicaragua | 0.0 | 41.7 | 0.0 | 86.1 | 0.1 | 11.3 | 0.1 | 106.4 | 0.2 |
| Panama | 0.1 | 197.3 | 0.4 | 20.7 | 0.5 | 9.4 | 0.5 | 3.1 | 0.5 |
| Paraguay | 0.0 | 62.7 | 0.0 | -2.3 | 0.0 | .. | .. | .. | 0.1 |
| Peru | 0.0 | 368.2 | 0.1 | 168.4 | 0.3 | 45.4 | 0.5 | 149.1 | 1.2 |
| Saint Kitts and Nevis | .. | .. | 1.2 | .. | .. | .. | .. | .. | .. |
| Saint Lucia | .. | .. | .. | .. | .. | .. | .. | .. | .. |
| Saint Vincent and the Grenadines | 0.1 | 1 233.7 | 0.9 | 5.0 | 1.0 | 14.6 | 1.1 | 174.8 | 3.1 |

## Table 1.19 *(Continued)*

| | 2001 | % change 2001-2002 | 2002 | % change 2002-2003 | 2003 | % change 2003-2004 | 2004 | % change 2004-2005 | 2005 |
|---|---|---|---|---|---|---|---|---|---|
| Suriname | .. | .. | 0.0 | 128.3 | 0.0 | 93.2 | 0.1 | 136.9 | 0.2 |
| Trinidad and Tobago | .. | .. | 0.0 | 827.6 | 0.1 | 377.4 | 0.3 | 154.4 | 0.8 |
| Uruguay | .. | .. | .. | .. | .. | .. | 0.8 | 125.1 | 1.8 |
| Venezuela | 0.1 | 109.4 | 0.3 | .. | .. | .. | 0.8 | 66.7 | 1.3 |
| Virgin Islands (US) | .. | .. | .. | .. | .. | .. | .. | .. | .. |
| **OCEANIA** | | | | | | | | | |
| American Samoa | .. | .. | .. | .. | .. | .. | .. | .. | .. |
| Fiji | .. | .. | .. | .. | .. | .. | .. | .. | .. |
| French Polynesia | .. | .. | .. | .. | 0.4 | 375.7 | 1.7 | 149.0 | 4.3 |
| Kiribati | .. | .. | .. | .. | .. | .. | .. | .. | .. |
| Marshall Islands | .. | .. | .. | .. | .. | .. | .. | .. | .. |
| Micronesia (Fed. States of) | .. | .. | .. | .. | .. | .. | .. | .. | .. |
| Nauru | .. | .. | .. | .. | .. | .. | .. | .. | .. |
| New Caledonia | 0.1 | 426.8 | 0.4 | 135.8 | 0.9 | 205.0 | 2.8 | 84.7 | 5.3 |
| Northern Mariana Islands | .. | .. | .. | .. | .. | .. | .. | .. | .. |
| Palau | .. | .. | .. | .. | .. | .. | .. | .. | .. |
| Papua New Guinea | .. | .. | .. | .. | .. | .. | .. | .. | .. |
| Samoa | .. | .. | .. | .. | .. | .. | .. | .. | .. |
| Solomon Islands | .. | .. | 0.0 | 84.9 | 0.0 | -4.9 | 0.0 | 119.4 | 0.1 |
| Tonga | .. | .. | 0.0 | .. | .. | .. | .. | .. | .. |
| Tuvalu | .. | .. | .. | .. | .. | .. | .. | .. | .. |
| Vanuatu | .. | .. | .. | .. | 0.0 | 50.4 | 0.0 | .. | .. |
| **TRANSITION ECONOMIES** | | | | | | | | | |
| **SOUTH-EAST EUROPE AND CIS** | | | | | | | | | |
| Albania | .. | .. | .. | .. | .. | .. | .. | .. | .. |
| Armenia | .. | .. | 0.0 | 67.4 | 0.0 | 9936.7 | 0.0 | .. | .. |
| Azerbaijan | .. | .. | .. | .. | .. | .. | 0.0 | 141.0 | 0.0 |
| Belarus | .. | .. | 0.0 | 518.4 | 0.0 | 513.2 | 0.0 | 109.7 | 0.0 |
| Bosnia and Herzegovina | .. | .. | .. | .. | .. | .. | 0.2 | 106.6 | 0.4 |
| Bulgaria | .. | .. | .. | .. | .. | .. | 0.0 | .. | .. |
| Croatia | .. | .. | 0.3 | .. | .. | .. | 0.6 | 234.2 | 2.0 |
| Georgia | .. | .. | 0.0 | 54.9 | 0.0 | .. | .. | .. | .. |
| Kazakhstan | .. | .. | .. | .. | .. | .. | 0.0 | .. | .. |
| Kyrgyzstan | .. | .. | .. | .. | .. | .. | 0.0 | 27.5 | 0.0 |
| Rep. of Moldova | .. | .. | 0.0 | 148.6 | 0.0 | 308.2 | 0.1 | 329.2 | 0.2 |
| Romania | 0.0 | 1 673.3 | 0.1 | 828.3 | 0.9 | 95.9 | 1.8 | 96.9 | 3.5 |
| Russian Federation | .. | .. | .. | .. | .. | .. | 0.5 | 136.6 | 1.1 |

## Table 1.19 *(Continued)*

| | 2001 | % change 2001-2002 | 2002 | % change 2002-2003 | 2003 | % change 2003-2004 | 2004 | % change 2004-2005 | 2005 |
|---|---|---|---|---|---|---|---|---|---|
| Serbia and Montenegro | .. | .. | .. | .. | .. | .. | .. | .. | .. |
| Tajikistan | .. | .. | .. | .. | .. | .. | .. | .. | .. |
| TFYR Macedonia | .. | .. | .. | .. | .. | .. | .. | .. | 0.6 |
| Turkmenistan | .. | .. | .. | .. | .. | .. | .. | .. | .. |
| Ukraine | .. | .. | .. | .. | .. | .. | .. | .. | .. |
| Uzbekistan | .. | .. | .. | .. | .. | .. | .. | .. | .. |

Source: UNCTAD calculations based on the ITU World Telecommunication Indicators Database, 2006.

## Table 1.20 – Core indicators on use of ICT by businesses and on the ICT sector, selected economies, 2005 or latest available year

Enterprises with 10 or more employees

| | Reference Year | Proportion of: | | | | Proportion of enterprises: | | | | Proportion of enterprises accesing the Internet by: | | | | |
|---|---|---|---|---|---|---|---|---|---|---|---|---|---|---|
| | | Enterprises using computers | Employees using computers | Enterprises using Internet | Employees using Internet | With a website | With an intranet | Receiving orders over the Internet | Placing orders over the Internet | Analogue modem | ISDN | Fixed line connection under 2 Mbps | Fixed line connection of 2 Mbps or more | Other modes of access |
| | | B1 | B2 | B3 | B4 | B5 | B6 | B7 | B8 | B9.a | B9.b | B9.c | B9.d | B9.e |
| Andorra | 2005 | 72.9 | 62.0 | 63.0 | 44.5 | 30.8 | .. | 26.2 | 25.0 | 18.3 | .. | .. | .. | 44.7 |
| Argentina | 2004 | 97.1 | 38.0 | 93.6 | 21.5 | 57.2 | 43.0 | 37.4 | 36.5 | 20.2 | 4.8 | .. | .. | 70.2 |
| Azerbaijan | 2005 | 45.2 | 9.5 | 8.3 | 1.8 | 2.8 | 5.8 | .. | .. | 5.3 | 0.4 | 0.8 | 0.5 | 1.4 |
| Belarus | 2005 | 83.6 | .. | 37.6 | .. | 10.2 | .. | .. | .. | .. | .. | .. | .. | .. |
| Brazil | 2005 | 98.8 | 38.3 | 95.1 | 28.4 | 56.2 | 38.5 | 27.1 | 28.5 | 42.9 | 10.4 | 12.8 | 2.5 | 69.9 |
| Bulgaria | 2004 | 85.0 | 14.3 | 62.6 | 9.1 | 24.3 | 28.2 | 2.9 | 7.0 | 24.8 | 6.0 | 5.3 | 3.3 | 39.1 |
| Cameroon | 2005 | 67.8 | .. | 25.1 | .. | 12.1 | 12.3 | .. | .. | 19.0 | .. | 19.8 | .. | .. |
| Chile | 2003 | 24.7 | .. | 20.3 | .. | 8.6 | 4.6 | 1.2 | 1.8 | 5.9 | 2.1 | 8.6 | 15.5 | .. |
| China | 2005 | .. | .. | 67.6 | .. | 22.3 | .. | 9.1 | 8.1 | 6.2 | 4.3 | .. | .. | .. |
| Costa Rica | 2004 | 80.7 | .. | 69.9 | .. | 10.3 | .. | .. | .. | .. | .. | .. | .. | .. |
| Cuba | 2005 | 99.1 | 60.1 | 60.3 | 6.8 | 17.5 | 34.5 | 0.8 | 2.7 | 36.5 | 0.0 | 23.5 | 0.2 | 0.1 |
| Hong Kong (China) | 2005 | 90.2 | 55.0 | 84.8 | 43.0 | 40.5 | 26.2 | 3.3 | 18.5 | 3.2 | .. | 77.7 | 9.1 | 11.8 |
| India | 2003 | 61.3 | .. | .. | .. | .. | .. | .. | .. | .. | .. | .. | .. | .. |
| Kazakhstan | 2005 | 73.6 | .. | 45.5 | .. | 8.4 | .. | 13.1 | 13.7 | .. | .. | .. | .. | .. |
| Kyrgystan | 2005 | .. | .. | 25.1 | .. | 8.4 | .. | .. | .. | .. | .. | .. | .. | .. |
| Macao (China) | 2003 | 75.6 | .. | 69.1 | .. | 17.8 | .. | 7.4 | 8.9 | 14.3 | .. | 7.6 | 78.1 | .. |
| Mexico | 2003 | 73.1 | .. | 55.4 | .. | 7.2 | .. | .. | .. | .. | .. | .. | .. | .. |
| Moldova | 2003 | .. | .. | .. | .. | 9.3 | .. | .. | .. | .. | .. | .. | .. | .. |
| Morocco | 2005 | .. | .. | 90.6 | 14.2 | 46.7 | 34.4 | 5.2 | 9.0 | 7.5 | .. | 63.2 | 22.2 | 1.4 |
| Panama | 2002 | 81.0 | 24.6 | 65.7 | .. | .. | .. | 23.1 | 29.7 | .. | .. | .. | .. | .. |
| Paraguay | 2002 | .. | .. | 5.7 | .. | .. | 22.0 | .. | .. | .. | .. | .. | .. | .. |
| Philippines | 2001 | 87.9 | .. | 62.4 | .. | .. | .. | .. | .. | .. | .. | .. | .. | .. |
| Qatar | 2005 | 84.4 | .. | 68.4 | .. | 67.8 | 38.2 | 34.9 | 28.3 | .. | .. | .. | .. | .. |
| Rep. of Korea | 2004 | 95.6 | .. | 94.0 | .. | 38.9 | 35.2 | 6.8 | 23.9 | .. | .. | .. | 92.2 | 1.9 |
| Romania | 2004 | 80.0 | 16.7 | 52.3 | 9.2 | 19.9 | 15.4 | 5.4 | 2.6 | 24.2 | 6.2 | 4.0 | 2.2 | 16.6 |
| Russian Federation | 2004 | 96.6 | 27.7 | 68.2 | 10.9 | 24.0 | .. | 20.2 | 23.2 | .. | .. | 27.3 | .. | .. |
| Singapore | 2005 | 92.8 | .. | 91.0 | .. | 68.3 | 74.1 | 13.5 | 30.8 | 24.6 | 22.5 | 66.4 | 17.4 | 13.7 |
| Thailand | 2005 | 86.8 | .. | 64.1 | .. | 32.7 | .. | 7.2 | 8.7 | 40.4 | 3.4 | .. | 18.7 | 12.9 |

*Source:* UNCTAD e-business database, 2006

## Table 1.20 (Continued)

| | Proportion of enterprises with: | | Proportion of enterprises using the Internet for: | | | | | | | | |
|---|---|---|---|---|---|---|---|---|---|---|---|
| | Local Area Network (LAN) | An extranet | Sending and receiving e-mail | Information about goods or services | Information from public authorities | Other information searches or research | Internet banking or financial services | Transacting with public authorities | Providing customer services | Delivering products online | Other types of activity |
| | B10 | B11 | B12.a | B12.b.i | B12.b.ii | B12.b.iii | B12.c | B12.d | B12.e | B12.f | B12.g |
| Andorra | 25.7 | .. | .. | .. | .. | 44.7 | 38.9 | 15.7 | .. | .. | .. |
| Argentina | 71.1 | 13.0 | 90.2 | 71.5 | 73.9 | 85.4 | 69.1 | 46.7 | 35.5 | 4.5 | 7.6 |
| Azerbaijan | 11.5 | 9.2 | .. | .. | 1.3 | .. | 2.5 | 1.6 | .. | .. | 5.3 |
| Belarus | 41.1 | .. | .. | .. | .. | .. | .. | .. | .. | .. | .. |
| Brazil | 82.8 | 21.9 | 65.4 | .. | 61.6 | 72.8 | 75.1 | 28.5 | 46.4 | .. | 41.5 |
| Bulgaria | 44.9 | 3.6 | .. | .. | 29.5 | 22.2 | 26.5 | 32.4 | 3.7 | 1.1 | .. |
| Cameroon | 15.0 | 0.4 | 12.3 | 1.7 | 7.3 | 9.8 | .. | 7.3 | 1.7 | 1.7 | .. |
| Chile | 4.6 | 1.5 | 18.4 | .. | .. | .. | .. | .. | .. | .. | .. |
| China | 46.0 | .. | 56.4 | 41.9 | 44.0 | 39.2 | .. | 28.9 | 26.5 | 7.2 | .. |
| Costa Rica | .. | .. | 68.5 | .. | .. | .. | .. | .. | .. | .. | .. |
| Cuba | .. | 59.1 | .. | .. | .. | .. | .. | .. | 1.8 | 0.5 | .. |
| Hong Kong (China) | 61.1 | 7.6 | 82.8 | 81.5 | 60.1 | .. | 27.4 | .. | 17.6 | 34.8 | 41.0 |
| India | .. | .. | .. | .. | .. | .. | .. | .. | .. | .. | .. |
| Kazakhstan | 27.8 | .. | 40.8 | 28.6 | .. | 39.4 | .. | .. | 20.4 | .. | 42.0 |
| Kyrgystan | 15.8 | .. | 20.3 | .. | 2.1 | .. | .. | .. | .. | 1.6 | .. |
| Macao (China) | .. | .. | 41.8 | 32.7 | .. | .. | .. | 7.4 | .. | .. | 2.0 |
| Mexico | 38.0 | .. | .. | .. | .. | .. | .. | .. | .. | .. | .. |
| Moldova | 68.0 | .. | .. | .. | .. | .. | .. | .. | .. | .. | .. |
| Morocco | .. | .. | 87.3 | 83.5 | 66.0 | 82.5 | 34.9 | 24.5 | 44.3 | 9.0 | 46.2 |
| Panama | 57.6 | .. | .. | .. | .. | .. | .. | .. | .. | .. | .. |
| Paraguay | .. | .. | 15.1 | .. | .. | .. | .. | .. | .. | .. | .. |
| Philippines | 54.9 | 5.1 | .. | .. | .. | .. | .. | .. | .. | .. | .. |
| Qatar | .. | .. | .. | .. | .. | .. | .. | .. | .. | .. | .. |
| Rep. of Korea | 64.6 | .. | .. | .. | .. | .. | .. | .. | .. | .. | .. |
| Romania | 31.0 | 10.0 | .. | .. | 28.3 | .. | 25.4 | 10.4 | .. | 1.9 | .. |
| Russian Federation | 70.6 | 12.5 | 64.7 | 44.3 | 27.2 | 63.3 | .. | .. | 3.9 | 4.3 | .. |
| Singapore | 74.1 | 35.8 | 84.4 | 84.9 | .. | .. | 58.3 | .. | .. | 37.7 | .. |
| Thailand | .. | .. | 51.6 | .. | .. | 56.3 | 5.5 | .. | .. | .. | .. |

*Source:* UNCTAD e-business database, 2006

**Notes:**

**Andorra:** *Enterprises with 0-9 employees accounted for 82 per cent of the sample. Survey does not cover enterprises larger than 250 employees. Table 1.20 only reflects enterprises with 10-249 employees. There is no breakdown by ISIC.*

**Argentina:** *Enterprises with 0-9 employees accounted for 4.4 per cent of the sample. Survey of ISIC D only. Innovation Survey 2004.*

**Azerbaijan:** *Enterprises with 0-9 employees accounted for 64.8 per cent of the sample. Table 1.20 only reflects enterprises with 10 or more employees. Census of ISIC C, D, E, F, G, H, I, J, K, L, M, N, O by NACE Rev 2 or ISIC Rev 1. Excludes category A, B (NACE) and G staff under 5 workers.*

**Belarus:** *There is no breakdown by number of employees or ISIC. Sampling frame was composed of "organizations of all branches of economy, excluding public organizations, public safety and defense organizations, and "small business" enterprises"*

**Brazil:** *For indicator B9.e, other modes of access include "DSL, Wide Band and mobile narrow band". Survey of ISIC D, F, G, H, I, K, O.*

**Bulgaria:** *Survey of ISIC D, E, F, G, H, I60, I64, K70, K72, O.*

**Cameroon:** *Enterprises with 0-9 employees accounted for 39 per cent of the sample. Table 1.20 only reflects enterprises with 10 or more employees. Survey of ISIC A, E, F, G50, G51, I60, I63, I64, J, K72, K74, L, M, N, O.*

**Chile:** *There is no breakdown by number of employees, so sample could include enterprises with 0-9 employees. Structural surveys of ISIC C13, D, E401, G50-52, K70-72, K74, O90-93, and H55.*

**China:** *There is no breakdown by number of employees, so sample could include enterprises with 0-9 employees. Survey of ISIC C, D, E, F, G, H, I, J, K70.*

**Costa Rica:** *Enterprises with 0-9 employees accounted for 39 per cent of the sample. Survey does not cover enterprises larger than 250 employees. Table 1.20 only reflects enterprises with 10-249 employees. There is no breakdown by ISIC.*

**Cuba:** *Enterprises with 0-9 employees accounted for less than 1 per cent of the sample. Table 1.20 only reflects enterprises with 10 or more employees. Survey excludes ISIC P.*

**Hong Kong (China):** *Enterprises with 0-9 employees accounted for 87.7 per cent of sampling frame. Table 1.20 only reflects enterprises with 10 or more employees. Survey excludes ISIC A, B, C.*

**India:** *Enterprises with 0-9 employees accounted for 13.9 per cent of the sample. Table 1.20 only reflects enterprises with 10 or more employees.*

**Kazakhstan:** *Enterprises with 0-9 employees accounted for 34.3 per cent of the sample. Table 1.20 only reflects enterprises with 10 or more employees. Survey of ISIC A, C, D, E, F, K72, K73, M.*

**Kyrgystan:** *Of enterprises with computers. Enterprises with 0-9 employees accounted for 21.8 per cent of the sample. Table 1.20 only reflects enterprises with 10 or more employees. Survey excludes ISIC P.*

**Macao (China):** *Enterprises with 0-9 employees accounted for 88.2 per cent of the sample. Table 1.20 only reflects enterprises with 10 or more employees. Survey of ISIC C, D, E, F, G 50-52, H, I60-64, K74, O.*

**Mexico:** *Source is OECD database: "data refer to enterprises with 50 or more employees and include: Manufacturing, Services and Construction."*

**Moldova:** *There is no breakdown by number of employees, so sample could include enterprises with 0-9 employees. Statistical census of legal persons, wich detain informational assets and informational system.*

**Morocco:** *Enterprises with 0-9 employees accounted for 14.9 per cent of the sample. Table 1.20 only reflects enterprises with 10 or more employees. Survey excludes ISIC L, M, N.*

**Panama:** *Enterprises with 0-9 employees accounted for 87.4 per cent of sampling frame. Table 1.20 only reflects enterprises with 10 or more employees. Survey excludes ISIC L,P.*

**Paraguay:** *Enterprises with 0-9 employees accounted for 83.1 per cent of sampling frame. Table 1.20 only reflects enterprises with 10 or more employees. Survey of ISIC D only.*

**Philippines:** *Refers to enterprises with 20 or more employees. Survey excludes ISIC P.*

**Qatar:** *Enterprises with 0-9 employees accounted for 48.2 per cent of sampling frame. Table 1.20 only reflects enterprises with 10 or more employees. Survey excludes ISIC A, B, K73, L, P.*

**Rep. of Korea:** *Indicator B9.d includes xDSL, dedicated line and cable modem. Indicator B9.e includes dial-up modem, satellite etc. Survey excludes ISIC P and Q.*

**Romania:** *Enterprises with 0-9 employees accounted for 81.3 per cent of sampling frame. Table 1.20 only reflects enterprises with 10 or more employees. Survey of C, D, E, F, G50-52, H, I60-64, K70-74, O.*

**Russian Federation:** *Enterprises with 0-49 employees accounted for 54 per cent of sample. Table 1.20 only reflects enterprises with 50 or more employees. Survey excludes P.*

**Singapore:** *Enterprises with 0-49 employees accounted for 68.3 per cent of sample. Survey of ISIC D, G, H, I, J, M, N.*

**Thailand:** *Enterprises with 0-9 employees accounted for 96.3 per cent of sampling frame. Table 1.20 only reflects enterprises with 10 or more employees. Survey of D, F, G50-52, H, I60, I63, K70-74.*

# Annex I

## Statistical annex

### Table 1.21

## Exports of ICT-enabled services by country, 2000–2003 (million $)

|  | 2000 | % change 2000–2001 | 2001 | % change 2001–2002 | 2002 | % change 2002–2003 | 2003 |
|---|---|---|---|---|---|---|---|
| Afghanistan | .. | .. | .. | .. | .. | .. | .. |
| Albania | 22 | 49.5 | 33 | 39.9 | 46 | 116.1 | 100 |
| Algeria | .. | .. | .. | .. | .. | .. | .. |
| Angola | 251 | -24.7 | 189 | -19 | 153 | -10.6 | 137 |
| Anguilla | 5 | 8 | 6 | -1.2 | 6 | .. | .. |
| Antigua and Barbuda | 52 | -9 | 47 | -20.9 | 38 | .. | .. |
| Argentina | 631 | 48.2 | 935 | -2.5 | 911 | 25.8 | 1 147 |
| Armenia | 29 | 49.4 | 43 | -0.9 | 42 | 8 | 46 |
| Aruba | 96 | 5.5 | 101 | 10 | 111 | 19.1 | 132 |
| Australia | 5 385 | -24.3 | 4 077 | 13.9 | 4 642 | 18.4 | 5 497 |
| Austria | 16 123 | 5.8 | 17 055 | 1.2 | 17 264 | 15.5 | 19 946 |
| Azerbaijan | 47 | -4.7 | 45 | 12.6 | 50 | 161.7 | 132 |
| Bahamas | 141 | -4.8 | 134 | 1.3 | 136 | -15 | 115 |
| Bahrain | 79 | -18.7 | 64 | 28.6 | 83 | -35.3 | 54 |
| Bangladesh | 141 | -12.5 | 124 | 26.5 | 156 | 70.3 | 266 |
| Barbados | 305 | 1.7 | 310 | 3.7 | 321 | 5.5 | 339 |
| Belarus | 270 | -11.8 | 238 | 33.5 | 318 | -7.6 | 294 |
| Belgium | .. | .. | .. | .. | 19 331 | 19.8 | 23 157 |
| Belize | 19 | 3 | 19 | 7 | 21 | 11.8 | 23 |
| Benin | 31 | -8.8 | 29 | .. | .. | .. | .. |
| Bolivia | 89 | -11.5 | 78 | 0.3 | 79 | 9.7 | 86 |
| Bosnia and Herzegovina | 112 | 7 | 120 | 15 | 138 | 19.9 | 166 |
| Botswana | 31 | 16.7 | 36 | 57.2 | 57 | .. | .. |
| Brazil | 5 514 | 0.6 | 5 548 | -5.5 | 5 244 | 0.3 | 5 260 |
| Bulgaria | 373 | 11.5 | 415 | -6.8 | 387 | 15.2 | 446 |
| Burkina Faso | 5 | 49.8 | 8 | .. | .. | .. | .. |
| Burundi | 0 | 145.1 | 1 | 71.1 | 2 | -53 | 1 |
| Cambodia | 47 | 5.7 | 50 | 8 | 54 | -14.1 | 46 |
| Cameroon | .. | .. | .. | .. | .. | .. | .. |
| Canada | 20 736 | -2.6 | 20 197 | 4.1 | 21 026 | 13.3 | 23 820 |
| Cape Verde | 15 | 7.2 | 16 | 2.3 | 16 | 22.3 | 20 |
| Central African Republic | .. | .. | .. | .. | .. | .. | .. |
| Chad | .. | .. | .. | .. | .. | .. | .. |

## Table 1.21 *(Continued)*

| | 2000 | % change 2000–2001 | 2001 | % change 2001–2002 | 2002 | % change 2002–2003 | 2003 |
|---|---|---|---|---|---|---|---|
| Chile | 988 | -0.9 | 978 | 23.9 | 1 212 | 12.6 | 1 364 |
| China | 9 642 | 0 | 9 644 | 24.7 | 12 030 | 64.4 | 19 773 |
| Colombia | 366 | -7.5 | 339 | -13.6 | 293 | 15.7 | 338 |
| Comoros | .. | .. | .. | .. | .. | .. | .. |
| Congo | 84 | -10.6 | 75 | 26.4 | 95 | -40.4 | 57 |
| Costa Rica | 351 | 30.2 | 457 | -4.4 | 437 | 4.3 | 455 |
| Côte d'Ivoire | 271 | 28.7 | 348 | -2.1 | 341 | 7.5 | 366 |
| Croatia | 543 | 33.8 | 726 | 17.3 | 851 | 20.4 | 1 025 |
| Cyprus | 1 090 | 15.1 | 1 254 | 3.1 | 1 293 | 12.3 | 1 452 |
| Czech Republic | 2 221 | 1.8 | 2 261 | -2.4 | 2 206 | -12.9 | 1 922 |
| Denmark | 9 260 | 6.3 | 9 843 | 10.6 | 10 887 | 13.7 | 12 378 |
| Djibouti | .. | .. | .. | .. | .. | .. | .. |
| Dominica | 32 | -33.5 | 21 | 25.7 | 27 | .. | .. |
| Dominican Republic | 211 | -25.1 | 158 | 1.1 | 160 | 2.1 | 163 |
| Ecuador | 101 | 19.2 | 121 | 7.5 | 130 | 6.7 | 139 |
| Egypt | 2 604 | -18 | 2 136 | 12.1 | 2 394 | 14.1 | 2 733 |
| El Salvador | 194 | -10.1 | 174 | -1.5 | 171 | 6.8 | 183 |
| Equatorial Guinea | .. | .. | .. | .. | .. | .. | .. |
| Eritrea | 10 | .. | .. | .. | .. | .. | .. |
| Estonia | 228 | 14.6 | 261 | 2.7 | 268 | 71.5 | 460 |
| Ethiopia | 104 | -0.1 | 104 | 22.6 | 128 | 37.3 | 176 |
| Faeroe Islands | 10 | -12.2 | 9 | 73.3 | 15 | -51.2 | 8 |
| Fiji | .. | .. | .. | .. | .. | .. | .. |
| Finland | 2 663 | -7.8 | 2 454 | 18.3 | 2 902 | 21.6 | 3 528 |
| France | 27 933 | 9.3 | 30 517 | 1.8 | 31 057 | 19 | 36 968 |
| Gabon | .. | .. | .. | .. | .. | .. | .. |
| Gambia | .. | .. | .. | .. | .. | .. | .. |
| Georgia | 7 | 72.2 | 12 | 255.4 | 44 | 31.5 | 58 |
| Germany | 36 849 | 12 | 41 279 | 17.7 | 48 567 | 21.4 | 58 938 |
| Ghana | 57 | 6.5 | 61 | 9 | 66 | 11.6 | 74 |
| Greece | 1 805 | 2.5 | 1 851 | 3.2 | 1 911 | 25.8 | 2 404 |
| Grenada | 48 | -22.2 | 37 | -17.3 | 31 | .. | .. |
| Guatemala | 137 | 107 | 284 | 12.2 | 319 | -27.5 | 231 |
| Guinea | 5 | 439.6 | 28 | -79.3 | 6 | 18.1 | 7 |
| Guinea-Bissau | .. | .. | 1 | 370.1 | 4 | -39.8 | 2 |
| Guyana | 89 | 19.9 | 107 | 11.1 | 119 | 21.4 | 145 |

## Table 1.21 *(Continued)*

| | 2000 | % change 2000–2001 | 2001 | % change 2001–2002 | 2002 | % change 2002–2003 | 2003 |
|---|---|---|---|---|---|---|---|
| Haiti | 30 | -40 | 18 | 11.1 | 20 | 15 | 23 |
| Honduras | 122 | 0.5 | 122 | -4 | 117 | 4.9 | 123 |
| Hong Kong (China) | 19 652 | 6.9 | 21 003 | 4 | 21 846 | 10.3 | 24 087 |
| Hungary | 1 486 | 42.2 | 2 113 | 29.2 | 2 730 | 22.1 | 3 334 |
| Iceland | 190 | 32 | 250 | -1.5 | 247 | 17.7 | 290 |
| India | 10 090 | 13.8 | 11 486 | 16 | 13 318 | 19.1 | 15 859 |
| Indonesia | 86 | -1.2 | 85 | 107.1 | 176 | 42.2 | 250 |
| Iran, Islamic Rep. of | 185 | .. | .. | .. | .. | .. | .. |
| Ireland | 14 331 | 32.4 | 18 977 | 24.5 | 23 629 | 34.8 | 31 853 |
| Israel | 7 869 | -9.4 | 7 129 | -3.7 | 6 863 | 12.4 | 7 713 |
| Italy | 17 867 | 19.4 | 21 331 | 1.5 | 21 658 | 23.2 | 26 691 |
| Jamaica | 327 | -12.9 | 285 | 6.6 | 304 | -10.7 | 271 |
| Japan | 33 483 | -5.1 | 31 769 | 5.5 | 33 526 | 7.5 | 36 033 |
| Jordan | 577 | -25.2 | 431 | -8.5 | 395 | -13 | 344 |
| Kazakhstan | 88 | -4.6 | 83 | 48.6 | 124 | 86.4 | 231 |
| Kenya | 33 | 64.4 | 54 | -38 | 34 | 13.5 | 38 |
| Kiribati | .. | .. | .. | .. | .. | .. | .. |
| Kuwait | 91 | 0.0 | 91 | 36.9 | 125 | 4.7 | 131 |
| Kyrgyzstan | 22 | 9.7 | 24 | 75 | 42 | -9.1 | 38 |
| Lao People's Dem. Rep. | .. | .. | .. | .. | .. | .. | .. |
| Latvia | 239 | 10.2 | 263 | 10.2 | 290 | 20.8 | 350 |
| Lesotho | 12 | -5.9 | 11 | -3.4 | 11 | 35.6 | 15 |
| Liberia | .. | .. | .. | .. | .. | .. | .. |
| Libyan Arab Jamahiriya | 28 | 35.7 | 38 | 39.5 | 53 | 24.5 | 66 |
| Lithuania | 155 | 38.2 | 214 | 23.5 | 265 | 1.6 | 269 |
| Luxembourg | 17 039 | -2.9 | 16 542 | -2.3 | 16 156 | 23.7 | 19 987 |
| Macao (China) | .. | .. | .. | .. | 168 | 25 | 210 |
| Madagascar | 121 | -29.8 | 85 | -18 | 70 | -47 | 37 |
| Malawi | .. | .. | .. | .. | .. | .. | .. |
| Malaysia | 5 684 | -22.9 | 4 381 | -0.6 | 4 354 | 4 | 4 528 |
| Maldives | 4 | -6.3 | 4 | 30 | 5 | 32.8 | 7 |
| Mali | 17 | 18.3 | 20 | 20.6 | 25 | 27.2 | 31 |
| Malta | 177 | 4.6 | 185 | 13.5 | 210 | 3.8 | 218 |
| Mauritania | .. | .. | .. | .. | .. | .. | .. |
| Mauritius | 292 | 22.2 | 356 | -29 | 253 | -5.7 | 239 |
| Mexico | 3 903 | -26.5 | 2 867 | -13.7 | 2 473 | -19 | 2 003 |

### Table 1.21 *(Continued)*

| | 2000 | % change 2000–2001 | 2001 | % change 2001–2002 | 2002 | % change 2002–2003 | 2003 |
|---|---|---|---|---|---|---|---|
| Mongolia | 8 | 331.6 | 34 | -71.2 | 10 | .. | .. |
| Montserrat | 5 | -22.9 | 4 | -5.9 | 4 | .. | .. |
| Morocco | 330 | 65.1 | 544 | 23.5 | 672 | 48 | 995 |
| Mozambique | 154 | -16.8 | 128 | 10.4 | 141 | -28.9 | 100 |
| Myanmar | 221 | -6 | 207 | -12 | 183 | -23.9 | 139 |
| Namibia | 16 | -30.7 | 11 | -15.3 | 10 | 24 | 12 |
| Nepal | 191 | -41.5 | 112 | -53 | 53 | 27.5 | 67 |
| Netherlands | 21 796 | 3.6 | 22 578 | 17.8 | 26 603 | 12.3 | 29 879 |
| Netherlands Antilles | 636 | -1.7 | 625 | -5.8 | 589 | 10.7 | 652 |
| New Zealand | 868 | -5.5 | 820 | 10.8 | 909 | 12.4 | 1 021 |
| Nicaragua | 28 | -3.5 | 27 | -6.3 | 26 | 12.1 | 29 |
| Niger | .. | .. | .. | .. | .. | .. | .. |
| Nigeria | .. | .. | .. | .. | .. | .. | .. |
| Norway | 5 556 | -9.0 | 5 058 | 10.8 | 5 606 | 16.2 | 6 517 |
| Oman | 36 | -38.3 | 22 | 6.3 | 24 | -16.1 | 20 |
| Pakistan | 363 | 9.1 | 396 | 53.3 | 607 | -15.3 | 514 |
| Panama | 351 | -0.3 | 350 | 48.3 | 519 | 1.6 | 527 |
| Papua New Guinea | 224 | 15.7 | 259 | .. | .. | .. | .. |
| Paraguay | 431 | -14.4 | 369 | 8.4 | 400 | 2.8 | 411 |
| Peru | 340 | 3.8 | 353 | -5.1 | 335 | -2.6 | 326 |
| Philippines | 813 | -18.1 | 666 | -5.4 | 630 | 22.4 | 771 |
| Poland | 1 977 | 0.4 | 1 985 | -4.5 | 1 896 | 25.3 | 2 375 |
| Portugal | 2 045 | -1.7 | 2 011 | 18.3 | 2 378 | 20.4 | 2 862 |
| Republic of Korea | 9 196 | -8.0 | 8 457 | -3.6 | 8 155 | 13.0 | 9 213 |
| Republic of Moldova | 32 | 15.5 | 37 | 27.2 | 47 | 5.7 | 49 |
| Romania | 699 | 8.6 | 759 | 26.7 | 962 | 28.9 | 1 240 |
| Russian Federation | 2 410 | .. | .. | .. | 3 096 | 42.7 | 4 418 |
| Rwanda | 3 | 21.4 | 4 | 3.4 | 4 | .. | .. |
| Saint Kitts and Nevis | 25 | -18.8 | 20 | -8 | 18 | .. | .. |
| Saint Lucia | 29 | -3.0 | 28 | -6.9 | 26 | .. | .. |
| Saint Vincent and the Grenadines | 38 | 3.7 | 40 | 5.7 | 42 | .. | .. |
| Samoa | .. | .. | .. | .. | .. | .. | .. |
| Sao Tome and Principe | 3 | -13.7 | 2 | 4.3 | 3 | .. | .. |
| Saudi Arabia | 4 779 | 4.8 | 5 008 | 3.4 | 5 177 | 10.4 | 5 713 |
| Senegal | 133 | -2.3 | 130 | 17 | 153 | .. | .. |
| Seychelles | 10 | 58.0 | 16 | -6.3 | 15 | .. | .. |

## Table 1.21 *(Continued)*

| | 2000 | % change 2000–2001 | 2001 | % change 2001–2002 | 2002 | % change 2002–2003 | 2003 |
|---|---|---|---|---|---|---|---|
| Sierra Leone | 11 | 26.0 | 13 | -97.1 | 0 | 696.4 | 3 |
| Singapore | 12 053 | 5.6 | 12 730 | 3.9 | 13 232 | 10.6 | 14 639 |
| Slovakia | 723 | .. | .. | .. | 836 | 8.5 | 907 |
| Slovenia | 363 | 6.0 | 385 | 38.4 | 533 | 11.3 | 593 |
| Solomon Islands | .. | .. | .. | .. | .. | .. | .. |
| Somalia | .. | .. | .. | .. | .. | .. | .. |
| South Africa | 1 029 | -22.2 | 801 | -21.2 | 631 | 39.8 | 882 |
| Spain | 13 843 | 14.1 | 15 798 | 13.7 | 17 969 | 22.8 | 22 067 |
| Sri Lanka | 268 | 160.2 | 696 | -51.8 | 335 | 8.0 | 362 |
| Sudan | 3 | 37.5 | 4 | 27.7 | 6 | -28.8 | 4 |
| Suriname | 32 | -29.5 | 23 | -62.3 | 9 | 151.7 | 22 |
| Swaziland | 156 | -51.3 | 76 | 0.0 | 76 | .. | .. |
| Sweden | 10 913 | 6.6 | 11 637 | 15.2 | 13 406 | 35.1 | 18 118 |
| Switzerland | 15 415 | -8 | 14 181 | 25.5 | 17 803 | 13.1 | 20 128 |
| Syrian Arab Republic | 153 | 5.2 | 161 | -21.1 | 127 | 63.8 | 208 |
| Taiwan Province of China | 11 912 | -1.4 | 11 745 | 11.3 | 13 068 | 19 | 15 546 |
| Tajikistan | .. | .. | .. | .. | 12 | 27.7 | 15 |
| TFYR Macedonia | 116 | -34.3 | 76 | 22.2 | 93 | 30.4 | 122 |
| Thailand | 2 822 | -11.3 | 2 504 | 55.5 | 3 894 | 6.5 | 4 147 |
| Togo | 27 | -4.5 | 26 | 28.8 | 33 | -0.5 | 33 |
| Tonga | .. | .. | 7 | -11.6 | 6 | .. | .. |
| Trinidad and Tobago | 123 | 26.2 | 155 | -0.9 | 154 | .. | .. |
| Tunisia | 352 | 4.7 | 369 | 2.5 | 378 | 8.5 | 411 |
| Turkey | 8 553 | -49.9 | 4 284 | -39.3 | 2 599 | 10 | 2 859 |
| Turkmenistan | .. | .. | .. | .. | .. | .. | .. |
| Uganda | 8 | 70.9 | 14 | 9.8 | 15 | 275.6 | 57 |
| Ukraine | 448 | -25 | 336 | 13.7 | 382 | 34.3 | 513 |
| United Kingdom | 77 247 | 3.6 | 79 998 | 13.7 | 90 932 | 15.1 | 104 636 |
| United Republic of Tanzania | 142 | -3.5 | 137 | -19.3 | 110 | .. | .. |
| United States | 127 615 | 2 | 130 126 | 8.2 | 140 769 | 8.9 | 153 316 |
| Uruguay | 161 | 9.2 | 176 | -36.9 | 111 | 5.4 | 117 |
| Vanuatu | 33 | 18.9 | 39 | -64.8 | 14 | 27.1 | 17 |
| Venezuela | 260 | -7.3 | 241 | -27.4 | 175 | -12.6 | 153 |
| Viet Nam | .. | .. | .. | .. | .. | .. | .. |
| Yemen | 80 | -15.6 | 68 | 5.2 | 71 | -24.6 | 54 |
| Zambia | 5 | .. | .. | .. | .. | .. | .. |
| Zimbabwe | .. | .. | .. | .. | .. | .. | .. |

## Table 1.21 *(Continued)*

| ICT-enabled service exports by region (million USD) | 2000 | % change 2000–2001 | 2001 | % change 2001–2002 | 2002 | % change 2002–2003 | 2003 |
|---|---|---|---|---|---|---|---|
| Developed economies | 508 803 | 3.9 | 528 650 | 11.3 | 588 157 | 17.5 | 690 968 |
| Asia | 41 351 | -6.4 | 38 694 | 2.4 | 39 628 | 10.4 | 43 746 |
| Europe | 312 342 | 7 | 334 056 | 13.7 | 379 697 | 21.3 | 460 473 |
| North America | 148 857 | 1.4 | 151 003 | 8.1 | 163 282 | 10.4 | 180 231 |
| Oceania | 6 253 | -21.7 | 4 897 | 13.3 | 5 551 | 17.4 | 6 518 |
| Developing economies | 112 177 | -4.2 | 107 426 | 5.8 | 113 625 | 20 | 136 389 |
| Africa | 7 923 | -8 | 7 292 | 10.5 | 8 058 | 27.3 | 10 260 |
| Asia | 87 782 | -3.9 | 84 332 | 7.2 | 90 385 | 22.8 | 111 014 |
| Latin America and the Caribbean | 16 215 | -4.4 | 15 498 | -2.2 | 15 162 | -0.4 | 15 097 |
| Oceania | 256 | 18.7 | 304 | -93.5 | 20 | -11.9 | 17 |
| South-East Europe and CIS | 5 217 | -0.2 | 5 205 | 27.6 | 6 639 | 33.9 | 8 891 |
| World | 626 209 | 2.4 | 641 296 | 10.5 | 708 444 | 18 | 836 249 |

*Source:* UNCTAD calculations based on IMF BOP data

# Annex I

## Statistical Annex

## Table 1.22

## Exports of ICT-enabled services by sector and country, 2003 (million $)

|  | Communication | Computer and information | Insurance | Financial | Royalties and licence fees | Other business | Personal, cultural and recreational | Total ICT-enabled services |
|---|---|---|---|---|---|---|---|---|
| Afghanistan | .. | .. | .. | .. | .. | .. | .. | .. |
| Albania | 48 | 1 | 3 | 21 | 5 | 18 | 5 | **100** |
| Algeria | .. | .. | .. | .. | .. | .. | .. | .. |
| Angola | .. | .. | 0 | .. | .. | 135 | 1 | **137** |
| Anguilla | .. | .. | .. | .. | .. | .. | .. | .. |
| Antigua and Barbuda | .. | .. | .. | .. | .. | .. | .. | .. |
| Argentina | 148 | 153 | .. | 1 | 48 | 689 | 107 | **1 147** |
| Armenia | 17 | 11 | 7 | 2 | .. | 7 | 2 | **46** |
| Aruba | 12 | 0 | 0 | 3 | .. | 117 | .. | **132** |
| Australia | 611 | 720 | 441 | 645 | 401 | 2 302 | 376 | **5 497** |
| Austria | 669 | 188 | 1 739 | 995 | 155 | 15 936 | 265 | **19 946** |
| Azerbaijan | 22 | .. | 5 | .. | .. | 102 | 2 | **132** |
| Bahamas | .. | .. | .. | .. | .. | 115 | .. | **115** |
| Bahrain | .. | .. | .. | .. | .. | 54 | .. | **54** |
| Bangladesh | 71 | 5 | 4 | 28 | 0 | 153 | 4 | **266** |
| Barbados | 32 | 18 | 90 | 74 | 1 | 124 | 1 | **339** |
| Belarus | 70 | 17 | 1 | 2 | 1 | 200 | 2 | **294** |
| Belgium | 1 861 | 2 118 | 743 | 2 529 | 878 | 14 664 | 362 | **23 157** |
| Belize | 6 | 98 145 | 98 145 | 98 145 | 98 145 | 17 | 98 145 | **23** |
| Benin | .. | .. | .. | .. | .. | .. | .. | .. |
| Bolivia | 27 | 0 | 38 | 12 | 2 | 7 | 1 | **86** |
| Bosnia and Herzegovina | 87 | .. | 2 | 9 | .. | 68 | .. | **166** |
| Botswana | .. | .. | .. | .. | .. | .. | .. | .. |
| Brazil | 449 | 29 | 124 | 363 | 108 | 4 133 | 54 | **5 260** |
| Bulgaria | 45 | 15 | 18 | 18 | 5 | 308 | 37 | **446** |
| Burkina Faso | .. | .. | .. | .. | .. | .. | .. | .. |
| Burundi | .. | .. | 0 | .. | .. | 1 | .. | **1** |
| Cambodia | 39 | .. | .. | .. | .. | 7 | 1 | **46** |
| Cameroon | .. | .. | .. | .. | .. | .. | .. | .. |
| Canada | 1 776 | 2 788 | 3 414 | 1 038 | 2 854 | 10 336 | 1 614 | **23 820** |
| Cape Verde | 15 | 0 | 1 | 0 | 0 | 4 | 0 | **20** |
| Central African Republic | .. | .. | .. | .. | .. | .. | .. | .. |

## Table 1.22 *(Continued)*

| | Communication | Computer and information | Insurance | Financial | Royalties and licence fees | Other business | Personal, cultural and recreational | Total ICT-enabled services |
|---|---|---|---|---|---|---|---|---|
| Chad | .. | .. | .. | .. | .. | .. | .. | .. |
| Chile | 133 | 81 | 145 | 28 | 45 | 864 | 68 | **1 364** |
| China | 638 | 1 102 | 313 | 152 | 107 | 17 427 | 33 | **19 773** |
| Colombia | 136 | 16 | .. | 36 | 6 | 113 | 31 | **338** |
| Comoros | .. | .. | .. | .. | .. | .. | .. | .. |
| Congo | 3 | .. | 1 | .. | .. | 53 | .. | **57** |
| Costa Rica | 23 | 167 | .. | 5 | 0 | 261 | 0 | **455** |
| Côte d'Ivoire | 71 | 2 | 38 | 47 | .. | 208 | 0 | **366** |
| Croatia | 213 | 62 | 20 | 48 | 35 | 615 | 33 | **1 025** |
| Cyprus | 51 | 92 | 34 | 190 | 15 | 1 059 | 10 | **1 452** |
| Czech Republic | 104 | 77 | 1 | 174 | 50 | 1 406 | 111 | **1 922** |
| Denmark | .. | .. | .. | .. | .. | 12 378 | .. | **12 378** |
| Djibouti | .. | .. | .. | .. | .. | .. | .. | .. |
| Dominica | .. | .. | .. | .. | .. | .. | .. | .. |
| Dominican Republic | 104 | 18 | .. | .. | .. | 41 | .. | **163** |
| Ecuador | 103 | .. | 2 | .. | .. | .. | 34 | **139** |
| Egypt | 309 | 23 | 37 | 80 | 121 | 2 092 | 72 | **2 733** |
| El Salvador | 123 | 0 | 31 | 3 | 0 | 25 | .. | **183** |
| Equatorial Guinea | .. | .. | .. | .. | .. | .. | .. | .. |
| Eritrea | .. | .. | .. | .. | .. | .. | .. | .. |
| Estonia | 39 | 31 | 15 | 16 | 5 | 352 | 2 | **460** |
| Ethiopia | 21 | 0 | 1 | 5 | .. | 148 | 1 | **176** |
| Faeroe Islands | 2 | 0 | 3 | 0 | 0 | 1 | 1 | **8** |
| Fiji | .. | .. | .. | .. | .. | .. | .. | .. |
| Finland | 226 | 565 | 50 | 36 | 502 | 2 118 | 32 | **3 528** |
| France | 2 500 | 1 256 | 2 074 | 1 071 | 4 066 | 24 133 | 1 868 | **36 968** |
| Gabon | .. | .. | .. | .. | .. | .. | .. | .. |
| Gambia | .. | .. | .. | .. | .. | .. | .. | .. |
| Georgia | 24 | .. | 10 | 10 | 6 | 7 | 0 | **58** |
| Germany | 2 665 | 6 680 | 6 763 | 4 253 | 4 453 | 33 120 | 1 004 | **58 938** |
| Ghana | .. | .. | 7 | .. | .. | 67 | .. | **74** |
| Greece | 322 | 136 | 199 | 85 | 18 | 1 310 | 334 | **2 404** |
| Grenada | .. | .. | .. | .. | .. | .. | .. | .. |
| Guatemala | 9 | 2 | 59 | 5 | .. | 156 | 1 | **231** |
| Guinea | 0 | .. | 0 | .. | 0 | 6 | .. | **7** |
| Guinea-Bissau | 0 | .. | 0 | 1 | .. | 2 | .. | **2** |

## Table 1.22 *(Continued)*

| | Communication | Computer and information | Insurance | Financial | Royalties and licence fees | Other business | Personal, cultural and recreational | Total ICT-enabled services |
|---|---|---|---|---|---|---|---|---|
| Guyana | 26 | 4 | 9 | 63 | 32 | 10 | .. | **145** |
| Haiti | 23 | .. | .. | .. | .. | .. | .. | **23** |
| Honduras | 83 | .. | 18 | .. | .. | 22 | .. | **123** |
| Hong Kong (China) | 756 | 245 | 394 | 2 833 | 341 | 19 382 | 137 | **24 087** |
| Hungary | 208 | 244 | 33 | 191 | 313 | 1 519 | 825 | **3 334** |
| Iceland | 8 | 43 | 7 | 1 | .. | 227 | 4 | **290** |
| India | 1 066 | 11 366 | 409 | 392 | 25 | 2 601 | .. | **15 859** |
| Indonesia | 248 | .. | 3 | .. | .. | .. | .. | **250** |
| Iran, Islamic Rep. of | .. | .. | .. | .. | .. | .. | .. | **..** |
| Ireland | 1 159 | 14 372 | 5 245 | 3 727 | 206 | 6 743 | 400 | **31 853** |
| Israel | 171 | 3 657 | 16 | .. | 425 | 3 445 | .. | **7 713** |
| Italy | 1 894 | 501 | 1 157 | 893 | 525 | 21 000 | 720 | **26 691** |
| Jamaica | 143 | 36 | 7 | 26 | 12 | 26 | 20 | **271** |
| Japan | 662 | 1 076 | 373 | 3 471 | 12 271 | 18 042 | 140 | **36 033** |
| Jordan | .. | .. | .. | .. | .. | 344 | .. | **344** |
| Kazakhstan | 61 | 1 | 2 | 14 | 0 | 154 | 0 | **231** |
| Kenya | 15 | 0 | 11 | .. | 12 | .. | 0 | **38** |
| Kiribati | .. | .. | .. | .. | .. | .. | .. | **..** |
| Kuwait | .. | .. | 84 | .. | .. | 47 | .. | **131** |
| Kyrgyzstan | 9 | 1 | 1 | 1 | 2 | 19 | 5 | **38** |
| Lao People's Dem. Rep. | .. | .. | .. | .. | .. | .. | .. | **..** |
| Latvia | 36 | 33 | 10 | 93 | 4 | 171 | 3 | **350** |
| Lesotho | .. | .. | 0 | .. | 15 | 0 | .. | **15** |
| Liberia | .. | .. | .. | .. | .. | .. | .. | **..** |
| Libyan Arab Jamahiriya | 11 | .. | 55 | .. | .. | .. | .. | **66** |
| Lithuania | 60 | 29 | 0 | 7 | 1 | 155 | 18 | **269** |
| Luxembourg | 811 | 1 137 | 1 248 | 14 245 | 119 | 2 262 | 165 | **19 987** |
| Macao (China) | 45 | .. | 19 | 23 | .. | 122 | .. | **210** |
| Madagascar | 6 | 1 | 1 | 2 | 1 | 25 | 0 | **37** |
| Malawi | .. | .. | .. | .. | .. | .. | .. | **..** |
| Malaysia | 201 | 216 | 223 | 109 | 20 | 1 924 | 1 835 | **4 528** |
| Maldives | .. | .. | 0 | .. | 6 | 1 | .. | **7** |
| Mali | 12 | .. | 1 | 2 | .. | 16 | 0 | **31** |
| Malta | 25 | 4 | 18 | .. | 0 | 172 | .. | **218** |
| Mauritania | .. | .. | .. | .. | .. | .. | .. | **..** |
| Mauritius | 21 | 9 | 9 | 13 | .. | 182 | 5 | **239** |

## Table 1.22 *(Continued)*

| | Communication | Computer and information | Insurance | Financial | Royalties and licence fees | Other business | Personal, cultural and recreational | Total ICT-enabled services |
|---|---|---|---|---|---|---|---|---|
| Mexico | 423 | .. | 1 163 | .. | 84 | 41 | 293 | **2 003** |
| Mongolia | .. | .. | .. | .. | .. | .. | .. | **..** |
| Montserrat | .. | .. | .. | .. | .. | .. | .. | **..** |
| Morocco | 250 | .. | 76 | .. | 26 | 643 | .. | **995** |
| Mozambique | 7 | 0 | 1 | 4 | 15 | 73 | 0 | **100** |
| Myanmar | .. | .. | .. | .. | .. | 139 | 0 | **139** |
| Namibia | 9 | 0 | 0 | 0 | .. | 3 | .. | **12** |
| Nepal | 17 | .. | 1 | .. | .. | 49 | .. | **67** |
| Netherlands | 1 530 | 2 054 | 626 | 1 032 | 1 885 | 22 045 | 708 | **29 879** |
| Netherlands Antilles | 9 | 1 | .. | 3 | 1 | 637 | 1 | **652** |
| New Zealand | 180 | 98 | 41 | 20 | 118 | 494 | 69 | **1 021** |
| Nicaragua | 26 | .. | 2 | .. | .. | .. | .. | **29** |
| Niger | .. | .. | .. | .. | .. | .. | .. | **..** |
| Nigeria | .. | .. | .. | .. | .. | .. | .. | **..** |
| Norway | 300 | 373 | 359 | 552 | 195 | 4 529 | 210 | **6 517** |
| Oman | 15 | .. | 5 | .. | .. | .. | .. | **20** |
| Pakistan | 190 | 34 | 22 | 12 | 8 | 247 | 1 | **514** |
| Panama | 46 | .. | 19 | 295 | .. | 167 | .. | **527** |
| Papua New Guinea | .. | .. | .. | .. | .. | .. | .. | **..** |
| Paraguay | 13 | 0 | 20 | 6 | 193 | 178 | .. | **411** |
| Peru | 79 | .. | 88 | .. | 2 | 157 | .. | **326** |
| Philippines | 433 | 28 | 12 | 38 | 4 | 247 | 9 | **771** |
| Poland | 243 | 134 | 219 | 161 | 28 | 1 532 | 58 | **2 375** |
| Portugal | 361 | 109 | 94 | 160 | 36 | 1 967 | 135 | **2 862** |
| Republic of Korea | 343 | 30 | 71 | 696 | 1 325 | 6 672 | 76 | **9 213** |
| Republic of Moldova | 24 | 1 | 2 | 2 | 1 | 18 | 1 | **49** |
| Romania | 238 | 108 | 48 | 51 | 3 | 674 | 118 | **1 240** |
| Russian Federation | 443 | 175 | 148 | 176 | 174 | 3 177 | 125 | **4 418** |
| Rwanda | .. | .. | .. | .. | .. | .. | .. | **..** |
| Saint Kitts and Nevis | .. | .. | .. | .. | .. | .. | .. | **..** |
| Saint Lucia | .. | .. | .. | .. | .. | .. | .. | **..** |
| Saint Vincent and the Grenadines | .. | .. | .. | .. | .. | .. | .. | **..** |
| Samoa | .. | .. | .. | .. | .. | .. | .. | **..** |
| Sao Tome and Principe | .. | .. | .. | .. | .. | .. | .. | **..** |
| Saudi Arabia | .. | .. | .. | .. | .. | 5 713 | .. | **5 713** |
| Senegal | .. | .. | .. | .. | .. | .. | .. | **..** |

## Table 1.22 *(Continued)*

| | Communication | Computer and information | Insurance | Financial | Royalties and licence fees | Other business | Personal, cultural and recreational | Total ICT-enabled services |
|---|---|---|---|---|---|---|---|---|
| Seychelles | .. | .. | .. | .. | .. | .. | .. | .. |
| Sierra Leone | 3 | .. | 0 | 0 | 0 | 0 | .. | 3 |
| Singapore | .. | 319 | 874 | 1 803 | 197 | 11 426 | 20 | 14 639 |
| Slovakia | 76 | 84 | 18 | 58 | 50 | 552 | 69 | 907 |
| Slovenia | 70 | 88 | 8 | 19 | 11 | 375 | 21 | 593 |
| Solomon Islands | .. | .. | .. | .. | .. | .. | .. | .. |
| Somalia | .. | .. | .. | .. | .. | .. | .. | .. |
| South Africa | 56 | .. | 323 | .. | 49 | 453 | .. | 882 |
| Spain | 1 032 | 2 916 | 1 346 | 1 900 | 539 | 13 511 | 824 | 22 067 |
| Sri Lanka | 53 | 80 | 48 | .. | .. | 182 | .. | 362 |
| Sudan | 3 | .. | .. | 1 | .. | 0 | 0 | 4 |
| Suriname | .. | .. | 0 | .. | .. | 22 | .. | 22 |
| Swaziland | .. | .. | .. | .. | .. | .. | .. | .. |
| Sweden | 815 | 1 993 | 732 | 886 | 2 336 | 11 148 | 208 | 18 118 |
| Switzerland | 955 | .. | 3 542 | 8 387 | .. | 7 241 | 4 | 20 128 |
| Syrian Arab Republic | 40 | 50 | 1 | 22 | .. | 95 | .. | 208 |
| Taiwan Province of China | 338 | 110 | 451 | 863 | 215 | 13 529 | 40 | 15 546 |
| Tajikistan | 10 | 0 | .. | 2 | 1 | 2 | .. | 15 |
| TFYR Macedonia | 41 | 5 | 2 | 3 | 2 | 65 | 4 | 122 |
| Thailand | 148 | .. | 134 | .. | 7 | 3 858 | .. | 4 147 |
| Togo | 9 | 1 | 0 | 0 | .. | 23 | .. | 33 |
| Tonga | .. | .. | .. | .. | .. | .. | .. | .. |
| Trinidad and Tobago | .. | .. | .. | .. | .. | .. | .. | .. |
| Tunisia | 9 | 19 | 20 | 55 | 18 | 283 | 5 | 411 |
| Turkey | 224 | .. | 211 | 291 | .. | 1 352 | 781 | 2 859 |
| Turkmenistan | .. | .. | .. | .. | .. | .. | .. | .. |
| Uganda | 17 | 4 | 3 | 15 | 4 | 14 | .. | 57 |
| Ukraine | 83 | 17 | 14 | 20 | 14 | 361 | 4 | 513 |
| United Kingdom | 3 396 | 7 893 | 10 966 | 22 065 | 10 245 | 47 322 | 2 750 | 104 636 |
| United Republic of Tanzania | .. | .. | .. | .. | .. | .. | .. | .. |
| United States | 5 719 | 5 431 | 4 877 | 17 637 | 48 227 | 64 074 | 7 351 | 153 316 |
| Uruguay | 23 | 14 | 6 | 58 | .. | 16 | .. | 117 |
| Vanuatu | 3 | .. | .. | 9 | .. | 6 | .. | 17 |
| Venezuela | 48 | 6 | 2 | .. | .. | 92 | 5 | 153 |
| Viet Nam | .. | .. | .. | .. | .. | .. | .. | .. |
| Yemen | 43 | .. | .. | .. | .. | 10 | .. | 54 |

### Table 1.22 *(Continued)*

| | Communication | Computer and information | Insurance | Financial | Royalties and licence fees | Other business | Personal, cultural and recreational | Total ICT-enabled services |
|---|---|---|---|---|---|---|---|---|
| Zambia | .. | .. | .. | .. | .. | .. | .. | .. |
| Zimbabwe | .. | .. | .. | .. | .. | .. | .. | .. |

| World exports of ICT-enabled services in 2003 (million USD) | 829 625 |
|---|---|
| Communications services | 39 976 |
| Computer and information services | 71 524 |
| Insurance services | 52 382 |
| Financial services | 95 391 |
| Royalties and licence fees services | 94 231 |
| Other business services | 451 484 |
| Personal, cultural and recreational services | 24 637 |
| Non-ICT-enabled services | 1 007 236 |

*Source*: IMF BOP data

# Annex I

## Table 1.23

## Exports of computer and information services by country, 2000–2003 ($)

| | 2000 | % change 2000–2001 | 2001 | % change 2001–2002 | 2002 | % change 2002–2003 | 2003 |
|---|---|---|---|---|---|---|---|
| Albania | 2 200 000 | .. | .. | .. | 550 000 | 114.8 | 1 181 600 |
| Argentina | 147 106 000 | 28.4 | 188 912 000 | -39.1 | 115 056 000 | 32.6 | 152 616 000 |
| Armenia | 1 970 000 | 324.0 | 8 352 000 | 17.9 | 9 850 000 | 11.8 | 11 009 300 |
| Aruba | 391 061 | -28.6 | 279 330 | .. | .. | .. | 335 196 |
| Australia | 469 625 000 | -9.0 | 427 572 000 | 39.6 | 596 853 000 | 20.6 | 719 911 000 |
| Austria | 134 854 000 | -2.9 | 130 956 000 | 6.8 | 139 922 000 | 34.4 | 188 034 000 |
| Bangladesh | 3 243 270 | -22.8 | 2 503 150 | 25.6 | 3 143 810 | 62.5 | 5 108 450 |
| Barbados | 17 350 000 | 0.6 | 17 450 000 | 0.9 | 17 600 000 | 2.6 | 18 050 000 |
| Belarus | 4 500 000 | 48.9 | 6 700 000 | 83.6 | 12 300 000 | 41.5 | 17 400 000 |
| Belgium | .. | .. | .. | .. | 1 773 720 000 | 18.7 | 2 105 310 000 |
| Bolivia | 400 000 | 0.0 | 400 000 | 0.0 | 400 000 | 0.0 | 400 000 |
| Botswana | 21 365 | 1725.4 | 389 991 | 347.5 | 1 745 110 | -20.2 | 1 391 920 |
| Brazil | 33 971 000 | -20.6 | 26 966 000 | 35.1 | 36 418 000 | -20.2 | 29 071 000 |
| Bulgaria | 5 088 800 | 143.9 | 12 412 000 | -40.5 | 7 389 800 | 100.3 | 14 800 000 |
| Burkina Faso | 1 405 | 1259.8 | 19 099 | .. | .. | .. | .. |
| Canada | 2 428 410 000 | -4.0 | 2 330 850 000 | -2.1 | 2 282 810 000 | 22.1 | 2 787 780 000 |
| Cape Verde | 79 567 | 20.6 | 95 995 | -70.2 | 28 594 | 52.2 | 43 514 |
| Chile | 33 400 000 | 28.3 | 42 837 900 | 46.8 | 62 900 000 | 29.4 | 81 400 000 |
| China | 355 947 000 | 29.5 | 461 000 000 | 38.4 | 638 167 000 | 72.7 | 1102 180 000 |
| Colombia | 3 833 030 | 96.2 | 7 521 900 | -21.1 | 5 938 420 | 177.6 | 16 484 200 |
| Costa Rica | 59 653 100 | 109.0 | 124 650 000 | 23.1 | 153 436 000 | 8.7 | 166 761 000 |
| Côte d'Ivoire | 182 590 | -2.9 | 177 344 | 1760.7 | 3 299 910 | -51.1 | 1 613 900 |
| Croatia | 33 490 500 | 30.7 | 43 765 300 | 4.4 | 45 688 600 | 36.1 | 62 160 500 |
| Cyprus | 57 839 800 | 50.0 | 86 763 500 | 19.9 | 104 013 000 | -17.5 | 85 760 100 |
| Czech Republic | 94 679 100 | 29.6 | 122 716 000 | 17.5 | 144 224 000 | -46.9 | 76 600 900 |
| Dominican Republic | .. | .. | .. | .. | 17 800 000 | -1.1 | 17 600 000 |
| Egypt | 23 000 000 | -3.5 | 22 200 000 | 22.5 | 27 200 000 | -16.5 | 22 700 000 |
| El Salvador | 3 900 000 | -94.9 | 200 000 | -50.0 | 100 000 | 300.0 | 400 000 |
| Eritrea | 31 132 | .. | .. | .. | .. | .. | .. |
| Estonia | 21 175 300 | 9.8 | 23 256 200 | 4.4 | 24 268 600 | 28.1 | 31 099 600 |
| Ethiopia | 404 999 | 405.6 | 2 047 760 | -69.7 | 620 917 | -49.5 | 313 538 |
| Faeroe Islands | 180 000 | 5.6 | 190 000 | 36.8 | 260 000 | -11.5 | 230 000 |
| Finland | 203 128 000 | 49.8 | 304 370 000 | 66.2 | 505 824 000 | 11.7 | 565 056 000 |
| France | 803 433 000 | 39.7 | 1 122 610 000 | 5.8 | 1 188 220 000 | 5.7 | 1 256 130 000 |
| Gabon | 1 706 520 | -50.8 | 840 338 | -26.4 | 618 375 | 233.1 | 2 059 530 |
| Germany | 3 798 150 000 | 26.5 | 4 804 960 000 | 15.1 | 5 531 210 000 | 21.0 | 6 693 720 000 |
| Greece | 88 800 000 | -7.7 | 82 000 000 | -2.4 | 80 026 000 | 69.1 | 135 291 000 |
| Guatemala | 3 700 000 | 30.0 | 4 811 670 | 49.8 | 7 210 240 | -74.3 | 1 856 500 |

## Table 1.23 *(Continued)*

| | 2000 | % change 2000–2001 | 2001 | % change 2001–2002 | 2002 | % change 2002–2003 | 2003 |
|---|---|---|---|---|---|---|---|
| Guinea | .. | .. | 134 000 | -70.1 | 40 000 | .. | .. |
| Guyana | 500 000 | 260.0 | 1 800 000 | 138.9 | 4 300 000 | -4.7 | 4 100 000 |
| Hong Kong (China) | 59 681 000 | 158.0 | 153 999 000 | 34.8 | 207 593 000 | 18.2 | 245 436 000 |
| Hungary | 120 948 000 | 45.1 | 175 514 000 | 13.8 | 199 648 000 | 22.1 | 243 765 000 |
| Iceland | 29 480 800 | -7.8 | 27 188 700 | 44.1 | 39 190 000 | 12.9 | 44 240 400 |
| India | 4 727 390 000 | 56.7 | 7 407 380 000 | 20.0 | 8 889 330 000 | 27.9 | 11 365 700 000 |
| Ireland | 7 489 690 000 | 19.2 | 8 925 660 000 | 17.0 | 10 447 100 000 | 36.3 | 14 237 800 000 |
| Israel | 4 246 100 000 | -18.3 | 3 470 800 000 | -9.4 | 3 143 300 000 | 16.3 | 3 656 500 000 |
| Italy | 447 586 000 | -21.7 | 350 635 000 | 10.7 | 388 017 000 | 29.1 | 501 080 000 |
| Jamaica | 40 400 000 | -9.4 | 36 600 000 | -6.7 | 34 140 000 | 5.4 | 36 000 000 |
| Japan | 1 569 320 000 | -10.0 | 1 413 120 000 | -19.3 | 1 140 170 000 | -5.7 | 1 075 520 000 |
| Kazakhstan | 1 087 410 | -56.4 | 474 100 | -64.0 | 170 880 | 223.3 | 0 552 416 |
| Kenya | 370 421 | -9.8 | 334 151 | 103.8 | 681 150 | -99.7 | 0 1 712 |
| Kyrgyzstan | 473 757 | 0.7 | 477 239 | 36.3 | 650 651 | 128.1 | 1 484 380 |
| Latvia | 20 216 200 | 8.3 | 21 892 900 | 13.3 | 24 812 000 | 31.9 | 32 725 500 |
| Lebanon | .. | .. | .. | | 12 593 | -75.7 | 0 3 064 |
| Lithuania | 15 495 000 | 56.0 | 24 175 000 | -22.2 | 18 806 100 | 52.3 | 28 638 500 |
| Luxembourg | 172 179 000 | 0.1 | 172 410 000 | 79.2 | 309 015 000 | 291.1 | 1 208 560 000 |
| Madagascar | .. | .. | .. | .. | .. | .. | 715 742 |
| Malaysia | 81 578 900 | 116.1 | 176 316 000 | 3.0 | 181 579 000 | 19.0 | 216 000 000 |
| Mali | .. | .. | .. | .. | 117 649 | .. | .. |
| Malta | 3 442 750 | -7.4 | 3 187 000 | 10.0 | 3 504 620 | 44.8 | 5 076 430 |
| Mauritius | 2 817 420 | 116.4 | 6 097 940 | 2.0 | 6 217 450 | 47.4 | 9 162 000 |
| Mongolia | .. | .. | .. | .. | 925 590 | 94.5 | 1 800 000 |
| Mozambique | .. | .. | .. | .. | 0 986 | 692.4 | 7 813 |
| Namibia | 512 279 | .. | .. | .. | .. | .. | 26 856 |
| Netherlands | 1 166 300 000 | -25.9 | 863 731 000 | 64.7 | 1 422 490 000 | 102.8 | 2 884 340 000 |
| Netherlands Antilles | 2 011 170 | -23.6 | 1 535 750 | -37.4 | 960 894 | 40.1 | 1 346 370 |
| New Zealand | 79 782 800 | -1.9 | 78 268 300 | 23.6 | 96 725 600 | 1.7 | 98 329 200 |
| Niger | 14 045 | 385.6 | 68 209 | 34.6 | 91 824 | 113.6 | 196 146 |
| Norway | 660 314 000 | -10.8 | 589 015 000 | -48.9 | 300 880 000 | 24.1 | 373 277 000 |
| Pakistan | 22 000 000 | -13.6 | 19 000 000 | 10.5 | 21 000 000 | 61.9 | 34 000 000 |
| Paraguay | 400 000 | -25.0 | 300 000 | 33.3 | 400 000 | -50.0 | 200 000 |
| Philippines | 76 000 000 | -71.1 | 22 000 000 | -4.5 | 21 000 000 | 33.3 | 28 000 000 |
| Poland | 61 000 000 | 37.7 | 84 000 000 | 17.9 | 99 000 000 | 35.4 | 134 000 000 |
| Portugal | 74 891 600 | -19.1 | 60 555 200 | 27.7 | 77 346 000 | 41.2 | 109 175 000 |
| Republic of Korea | 10 600 000 | 51.9 | 16 100 000 | 21.1 | 19 500 000 | 52.3 | 29 700 000 |
| Rep. of Moldova | 570 000 | -29.8 | 400 000 | 117.5 | 870 000 | 36.8 | 1 190 000 |
| Romania | 44 000 000 | 13.6 | 50 000 000 | 56.0 | 78 000 000 | 38.5 | 108 000 000 |
| Russian Federation | 59 170 000 | 116.3 | 127 990 000 | 7.3 | 137 300 000 | 27.4 | 174 970 000 |
| Saint Lucia | 5 000 000 | -30.0 | 3 500 000 | -30.5 | 2 433 330 | .. | .. |

## Table 1.23 *(Continued)*

| | 2000 | % change 2000–2001 | 2001 | % change 2001–2002 | 2002 | % change 2002–2003 | 2003 |
|---|---|---|---|---|---|---|---|
| Senegal | 16 855 | 1454.0 | 261 923 | -90.1 | 25 825 | 193.1 | 75 705 |
| Singapore | 247 204 000 | 26.1 | 311 612 000 | 13.3 | 353 061 000 | -5.4 | 334 144 000 |
| Slovakia | 51 916 300 | .. | .. | .. | 71 009 300 | 17.9 | 83 746 800 |
| Slovenia | 53 920 000 | 18.9 | 64 090 000 | 24.5 | 79 772 000 | 10.8 | 88 378 500 |
| Spain | 2 043 160 000 | 6.6 | 2 177 810 000 | 14.3 | 2 490 110 000 | 17.0 | 2 913 370 000 |
| Sri Lanka | .. | .. | 65 960 000 | -24.2 | 50 000 100 | 30.0 | 64 999 900 |
| Sudan | .. | .. | .. | .. | 460 000 | .. | .. |
| Swaziland | 1 873 250 | -19.4 | 1 510 020 | -24.6 | 1 138 440 | 5.4 | 1 200 300 |
| Sweden | 1 190 920 000 | 20.3 | 1 432 980 000 | 2.7 | 1 471 560 000 | 35.5 | 1 993 310 000 |
| Syrian Arab Republic | .. | .. | .. | .. | .. | .. | 50 000 000 |
| Tajikistan | .. | .. | .. | .. | 7 300 | -84.9 | 1 100 |
| TFYR Macedonia | 1 036 400 | 52.7 | 1 582 800 | 23.2 | 1 950 450 | 134.0 | 4 564 740 |
| Togo | .. | .. | 95 493 | -74.5 | 24 391 | 2044.5 | 523 055 |
| Tunisia | 19 698 200 | 5.9 | 20 852 000 | -12.3 | 18 287 500 | 6.1 | 19 403 000 |
| Uganda | .. | .. | .. | .. | 648 359 | 554.7 | 4 244 640 |
| Ukraine | 6 000 000 | 16.7 | 7 000 000 | 42.9 | 10 000 000 | 70.0 | 17 000 000 |
| United Kingdom | 4 321 480 000 | 8.4 | 4 682 790 000 | 23.2 | 5 770 140 000 | 36.8 | 7 892 540 000 |
| United Republic of Tanzania | 500 001 | 8.7 | 543 667 | 30.0 | 707 037 | -71.0 | 204 854 |
| United States | 5 622 000 000 | -3.5 | 5 423 100 000 | -0.6 | 5 393 100 000 | 18.7 | 6 404 100 000 |
| Uruguay | 10 000 000 | 44.0 | 14 400 000 | -5.6 | 13 600 000 | -14.7 | 11 600 000 |
| Venezuela | 7 000 000 | 0.0 | 7 000 000 | 0.0 | 7 000 000 | -14.3 | 6 000 000 |
| World | 45 489 523 096 | 11.7 | 50 822 941 869 | 11.3 | 56 588 732 394 | 29.3 | 73 152 884 872 |
| Developed economies | 39 326 046 650 | 5.3 | 41 393 085 800 | 9.6 | 45 357 046 220 | 29.3 | 58 653 394 930 |
| Asia | 5 815 420 000 | -16.0 | 4 883 920 000 | -12.3 | 4 283 470 000 | 10.5 | 4 732 020 000 |
| Europe | 24 910 808 850 | 13.4 | 28 249 375 500 | 15.8 | 32 704 087 620 | 34.3 | 43 911 254 730 |
| North America | 8 050 410 000 | -3.7 | 7 753 950 000 | -1.0 | 7 675 910 000 | 19.7 | 9 191 880 000 |
| Oceania | 549 407 800 | -7.9 | 505 840 300 | 37.1 | 693 578 600 | 18.0 | 818 240 200 |
| Developing economies | 6 003 889 579 | 52.7 | 9 170 702 630 | 19.2 | 10 926 958 493 | 28.9 | 14 085 175 906 |
| Africa | 51 230 048 | 8.7 | 55 667 930 | 11.3 | 61 953 517 | 3.1 | 63 884 226 |
| Asia | 5 583 644 170 | 54.7 | 8 635 870 150 | 20.3 | 10 385 312 093 | 29.8 | 13 477 071 414 |
| Latin America and the Caribbean | 369 015 361 | 29.8 | 479 164 550 | 0.1 | 479 692 884 | 13.5 | 544 220 266 |
| Oceania | 0 | 0.0 | 0 | 0.0 | 0 | 0.0 | 0 |
| South-East Europe and CIS | 159 586 867 | 62.4 | 259 153 439 | 17.6 | 304 727 681 | 36.0 | 414 314 036 |

*Source*: UNCTAD calculations based on IMF BOP data.

# Annex II

# THE ORBICOM CONCEPTUAL FRAMEWORK

The research presented in section E of this chapter is based on the conceptual framework and methodology developed by the Orbicom Digital Divide project. Crucial to the project is the development of a composite index (ICT Opportunity Index) based on a number of ICT-related indicators that define the "infostate" of a country (Orbicom, 2005).

The Orbicom conceptual framework distinguishes between ICT productive and consumptive functions, denominated "infodensity" and "info-use" respectively.

ICT productive functions are understood to be indicative of productive capacity (both quantitative and qualitative) and include ICT capital and labour stocks; this is defined in the model as "infodensity". ICT capital includes network infrastructure, such as that related to main telephone lines, cable connectivity and the Internet, as well as ICT machinery and equipment (a total of eight indicators). ICT labour stocks are measured by the level of skills in the labour force, and in relation to basic literacy and school enrolment at different levels (a total of four indicators). They are not limited to ICT skills, but include overall levels of skills and education, which are considered indispensable for the functioning of knowledge-based societies.

## Chart 1.41

## Orbicom conceptual framework of Infostates

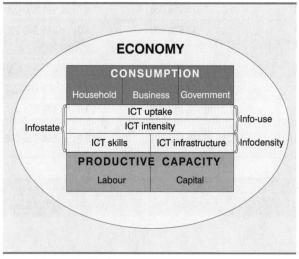

*Source:* Orbicom (2003)

ICT capital and labour stocks are assumed to expand over time and have no upward boundary. Furthermore, ICTs are assumed to affect factor growth, technological change and productivity gains. The notion of ICT networks deserves particular mention since networks create externalities — that is, their benefits increase with the number of users.

The ICT consumptive functions are understood as the "consumptive capacity" of people or the use of ICTs, comprising ICT uptake (such as telephones, PCs or Internet users per 100 inhabitants) and ICT intensity (such as broadband users and international phone traffic per capita). The consumptive part of the framework is called "info-use" (see chart 1.41 for a presentation of the framework).

As shown in chart 1.41, the "infostate" index is simply an aggregate of "info-use" and "infodensity". The model then defines the digital divide as the difference between countries' infostates.

The conceptual model was translated into an empirical, operational model, using statistical indicators, and creating a reference year (2001) and hypothetical country as benchmarks to quantify the evolution of the digital divide.

The analysis carried out by UNCTAD refers to "infodensity" only. Infodensity is assumed to be more relevant to measuring the impact of ICTs on economic growth (GDP per capita), which relies primarily on the expansion of productive capacity in a country, and less on the expansion of consumption.

In the Orbicom model, infodensity is expressed in relative terms; each country is allocated an infodensity index, which is calculated as follows:

$$Infodensity = \sqrt[k]{\prod_{i=1}^{k} I_{n,t}^{i,j(c)}} \text{, with k=2.}$$

The model is based on a number of statistical indicators and hence relies on existing data; the latest database includes time series covering the period 1995–2003. While data for up to 193 countries exist, 153 countries are included in the infodensity time series, representing 96 per cent of the global population in 2003.

## Table 1.24
## Country grouping by Infodensity levels

| Group A | Infodensity 2003 | Group B | Infodensity 2003 | Group C | Infodensity 2003 | Group D | Infodensity 2003 | Group E | Infodensity 2003 |
|---|---|---|---|---|---|---|---|---|---|
| Denmark | 246 | Slovenia | 166 | Bulgaria | 112 | Samoa | 82 | Kenya | 34 |
| Sweden | 242 | Czech Republic | 160 | Brazil | 111 | Ukraine | 82 | Djibouti | 32 |
| Netherlands | 238 | Estonia | 160 | Mexico | 99 | Belarus | 76 | Lesotho | 32 |
| Finland | 238 | Hungary | 159 | Russian Federation | 95 | Kazakhstan | 70 | Tajikistan | 32 |
| Norway | 234 | Spain | 156 | Turkey | 95 | Paraguay | 69 | Côte d'Ivoire | 32 |
| Switzerland | 219 | Portugal | 155 | Trinidad & Tobago | 94 | Georgia | 67 | Lao People's Dem. Rep. | 31 |
| United States | 212 | Italy | 151 | Romania | 92 | Bolivia | 67 | Sudan | 28 |
| United Kingdom | 210 | Malta | 150 | Malaysia | 91 | Fiji | 67 | Zambia | 27 |
| Belgium | 208 | Slovakia | 142 | Dominican Rep. | 90 | Philippines | 66 | Cameroon | 27 |
| Austria | 203 | Greece | 141 | Mauritius | 89 | Botswana | 64 | Pakistan | 26 |
| Canada | 201 | Latvia | 136 | Serbia & Montenegro | 87 | Namibia | 63 | Mauritania | 26 |
| Iceland | 200 | Poland | 135 | South Africa | 87 | Guyana | 63 | Senegal | 26 |
| Australia | 197 | Cyprus | 133 | Lebanon | 86 | Ecuador | 61 | Ghana | 25 |
| Luxembourg | 194 | Lithuania | 133 | Kuwait | 85 | Guatemala | 59 | Benin | 25 |
| Ireland | 190 | Qatar | 132 | Belize | 84 | Armenia | 56 | Congo | 24 |
| Germany | 186 | Uruguay | 126 | Panama | 83 | Oman | 55 | Uganda | 24 |
| Hong Kong (China) | 185 | Argentina | 124 | Costa Rica | 82 | Albania | 54 | Rwanda | 24 |
| France | 181 | Brunei Darussalam | 121 | Thailand | 82 | Kyrgyzstan | 53 | Cambodia | 23 |
| Singapore | 180 | Chile | 119 | Colombia | 80 | Mongolia | 52 | United Republic of Tanzania | 23 |
| Israel | 178 | Croatia | 117 | Rep. of Moldova | 79 | Swaziland | 51 | Yemen | 23 |
| New Zealand | 177 | United Arab Emirates | 108 | Jamaica | 79 | Nicaragua | 51 | Mozambique | 23 |
| Japan | 177 | Macao (China) | 105 | Venezuela | 74 | Indonesia | 48 | Madagascar | 21 |
| Rep. of Korea | 171 | Bahamas | 103 | Peru | 71 | Iran | 47 | Papua New Guinea | 21 |
| | | Bahrain | 98 | Jordan | 69 | Gabon | 47 | Nigeria | 21 |
| | | Barbados | 96 | Saudi Arabia | 67 | Tunisia | 47 | Bangladesh | 21 |
| | | | | El Salvador | 64 | Sri Lanka | 45 | Haiti | 20 |
| | | | | China | 62 | Egypt | 44 | Nepal | 20 |
| | | | | | | Honduras | 42 | Malawi | 18 |
| | | | | | | Morocco | 41 | Guinea | 17 |
| | | | | | | Zimbabwe | 39 | Mali | 15 |
| | | | | | | Libyan Arab Jamahiriya | 39 | Myanmar | 15 |
| | | | | | | Algeria | 36 | Burkina Faso | 14 |
| | | | | | | Cuba | 35 | Angola | 12 |
| | | | | | | Syrian Arab Republic | 35 | Liberia | 11 |
| | | | | | | Gambia | 35 | Central African Rep. | 11 |
| | | | | | | India | 34 | Chad | 11 |
| | | | | | | Viet Nam | 31 | Dem. Rep. of the Congo | 10 |
| | | | | | | Togo | 29 | Ethiopia | 10 |
| | | | | | | | | Eritrea | 10 |
| | | | | | | | | Niger | 8 |

*Source:* UNCTAD and Orbicom (2005)

# Annex III

## Table 1.25

## Breakdown of the computer and related service sector

| WTO classification | Provisional UNCPC Description |
|---|---|
| B. Computer and related services (under the superior aggregation Business services) | Division 84. Computer and related services (under Section 8. Business services) |
| 1.B.a. Consultancy services related to the installation of computer hardware (CPC 841) | 841. *Consultancy services related to the installation of computer hardware:* Assistance services to clients in the installation of computer hardware (i.e. physical equipment) and computer networks. |
| 1.B.b. Software implementation services (CPC 842) | 842. *Software implementation services:* All services involving consultancy services on software, and development and implementation of software. The term "software" may be defined as the sets of instructions required to make computers work and communicate. A number of different programs may be developed for specific applications (application software), and the customer may have a choice of using ready-made programs off the shelf (packaged software), developing specific programs for particular requirements (customized software) or using a combination of the two.<br><br>84210. *Systems and software consulting services:* Services of a general nature prior to the development of data processing systems and applications (management services, project planning services, etc.)<br><br>84220. *Systems analysis services:* Include analysis of the clients' needs, defining functional specification, and setting up the team. Also involved are project management, technical coordination and integration and definition of the systems architecture.<br><br>84230. *Systems design services:* Include technical solutions, with respect to methodology, quality-assurance, choice of equipment software packages or new technologies, etc.<br><br>84240. *Programming services:* Include the implementation phase, i.e. writing and debugging programs, conducting tests, and editing documentation.<br><br>84250. *Systems maintenance services:* Include consulting and technical assistance services of software products in use, rewriting or changing existing programs or systems, and maintaining up-to-date software documentation and manuals. Also included are specialist works, e.g. conversions. |
| 1.B.c. Data processing services (CPC 843) | 843. *Data processing services:*<br><br>84310. *Input preparation services:* Data recording services such as key punching, optical scanning or other methods for data entry.<br><br>84320. *Data-processing and tabulation services:* Services such as data processing and tabulation services, computer calculating services, and rental services of computer time.<br><br>84330. *Time-sharing services:* This seems to be the same type of services as 84320. Computer time only is bought; if it is bought from the customer's premises, telecommunications services are also bought. Data processing or tabulation services may also be bought from a service bureau. In both cases the services might be time sharing processed. Thus, there is no clear distinction between 84320 and 84330.<br><br>84390. *Other data processing services:* Services which manage the full operations of a customer's facilities under contract: computer-room environmental quality control services; management services of in-place computer equipment combinations; and management services of computer work flows and distributions. |
| 1.B.d. Data base services (CPC 844) | 84400. *Data base services:* All services provided from primarily structured databases through a communication network. Exclusions: Data and message transmission services (e.g. network operation services, value-added network services) are classified in class 7523 (Data and message transmission services). Documentation services consisting in information retrieval from databases are classified in subclass 96311 (Library services). |
| 1.B.e. Other (CPC 845+849) | 84500. *Maintenance and repair services of office machinery and equipment including computers:* Repair and maintenance services of office machinery, computers and related equipment.<br><br>849. *Other computer services:*<br><br>84910. *Data preparation services:* Data preparation services for clients not involving data processing services.<br><br>84990. *Other computer services n.e.c.:* Other computer related services, not elsewhere classified, e.g. training services for staff of clients, and other professional computer services. |

*Sources:* Document S/C/W/45, Background Note by the WTO Secretariat (July 1998) – page 3, figure 1; *Detailed structure and explanatory notes* of Provisional CPC code 84, http://unstats.un.org/unsd/cr/registry/regcs.asp?Cl=9&Lg=1&Co=84

# Annex IV

## Table 1.26

Mode 1 and Mode 3 market access commitments for computer
and related services (WTO, GATS)

| WTO members | Mode 1 Limitations on market access |
|---|---|
| Albania | None |
| Angola | Not included in the list |
| Antigua and Barbuda | None |
| Argentina | None |
| Armenia | None |
| Australia | None |
| Austria | None |
| Bahrain | Not included in the list |
| Bangladesh | Not included in the list |
| Barbados | None |
| Belgium | None |
| Belize | Not included in the list |
| Benin | Not included in the list |
| Bolivia | Not included in the list |
| Botswana | Unbound |
| Brazil | Not included in the list |
| Brunei Darussalam | None |
| Bulgaria | None |
| Burkina Faso | Not included in the list |
| Burundi | Not included in the list |
| Cambodia | None |
| Cameroon | Not included in the list |
| Canada | None |
| Central African Republic | Not included in the list |
| Chad | Not included in the list |
| Chile | Not included in the list |
| China | None |
| Chinese Taipei | None |
| Colombia | Unbound |
| Congo | Not included in the list |
| Costa Rica | Unbound |
| Côte d'Ivoire | Not included in the list |

## Table 1.26 *(Continued)*

| WTO members | Mode 1 Limitations on market access |
|---|---|
| Croatia | None |
| Cuba | None |
| Cyprus | None |
| Czech Republic | None |
| Dem. Rep. of the Congo | Not included in the list |
| Denmark | None |
| Djibouti | Not included in the list |
| Dominica | Not included in the list |
| Dominican Republic | Unbound |
| Ecuador | Unbound |
| Egypt | Not included in the list |
| El Salvador | None |
| Estonia | None |
| Fiji | Not included in the list |
| Finland | None |
| France | None |
| Gabon | Not included in the list |
| Gambia | None |
| Georgia | None - computer and related services except CPC 8499 |
| Georgia | Unbound - CPC 8499 |
| Germany | None |
| Ghana | Not included in the list |
| Greece | None |
| Grenada | Not included in the list |
| Guatemala | None |
| Guinea | Not included in the list |
| Guinea-Bissau | Not included in the list |
| Guyana | Not included in the list |
| Haiti | Not included in the list |
| Honduras | None |
| Hong Kong (China) | Partial |
| Hungary | None |
| Iceland | None |
| India | Unbound |
| Indonesia | None - CPC 84330 |
| Indonesia | Unbound - computer and related services CPC 841 AND 842 |
| Ireland | None |

## Table 1.26 *(Continued)*

| WTO members | Mode 1 Limitations on market access |
| --- | --- |
| Israel | None |
| Italy | None |
| Jamaica | None |
| Japan | None |
| Jordan | None |
| Kenya | Not included in the list |
| Kuwait | Unbound |
| Kyrgyzstan | None |
| Latvia | None |
| Lesotho | None |
| Liechtenstein | None |
| Lithuania | None |
| Luxembourg | None |
| Macao (China) | Not included in the list |
| Madagascar | Not included in the list |
| Malawi | Not included in the list |
| Malaysia | None |
| Maldives | None |
| Mali | Not included in the list |
| Malta | None |
| Mauritania | Not included in the list |
| Mauritius | Not included in the list |
| Mexico | None |
| Mongolia | Not included in the list |
| Morocco | Unbound |
| Mozambique | Not included in the list |
| Myanmar | Not included in the list |
| Namibia | Not included in the list |
| Nepal | None |
| Netherlands | None |
| Netherlands Antilles | Not included in the list |
| New Zealand | None |
| Nicaragua | Unbound |
| Niger | Not included in the list |
| Nigeria | Not included in the list |
| Norway | None |
| Oman | None |

**Table 1.26** *(Continued)*

| WTO members | Mode 1 Limitations on market access |
| --- | --- |
| Pakistan | Unbound |
| Panama | None |
| Papua New Guinea | None |
| Paraguay | Not included in the list |
| Peru | Not included in the list |
| Philippines | Not included in the list |
| Poland | None |
| Portugal | None |
| Qatar | Unbound |
| Republic of Korea | None |
| Rep. Of Moldova | None |
| Romania | None |
| Rwanda | Not included in the list |
| Saint Kitts and Nevis | Not included in the list |
| Saint Lucia | Not included in the list |
| Saint Vincent and the Grenadines | Not included in the list |
| Saudi Arabia | None |
| Senegal | Not included in the list |
| Sierra Leone | None |
| Singapore | None |
| Slovakia | None |
| Slovenia | None |
| Solomon Islands | Not included in the list |
| South Africa | None |
| Spain | None |
| Sri Lanka | Not included in the list |
| Suriname | Not included in the list |
| Swaziland | None |
| Sweden | None |
| Switzerland | None |
| TFYR Macedonia | None |
| Thailand | Unbound |
| Togo | Not included in the list |
| Trinidad and Tobago | None |
| Tunisia | Not included in the list |
| Turkey | Partial |
| Uganda | Not included in the list |

## Table 1.26 *(Continued)*

| WTO members | Mode 1 Limitations on market access |
|---|---|
| United Arab Emirates | None |
| United Kingdom | None |
| United Republic of Tanzania | Not included in the list |
| United States | None |
| Uruguay | None |
| Venezuela | Partial |

## Mode 3 market access commitments for computer and related services (WTO, GATS)

| Country | Mode 3 Limitations on market access |
|---|---|
| Albania | None |
| Angola | Not included in the list |
| Antigua and Barbuda | Partial |
| Argentina | None |
| Armenia | None |
| Australia | None |
| Austria | None |
| Bahrain | Not included in the list |
| Bangladesh | Not included in the list |
| Barbados | None |
| Belgium | None |
| Belize | Not included in the list |
| Benin | Not included in the list |
| Bolivia | Not included in the list |
| Botswana | None |
| Brazil | Not included in the list |
| Brunei Darussalam | Partial |
| Bulgaria | None |
| Burkina Faso | Not included in the list |
| Burundi | Not included in the list |
| Cambodia | None |
| Cameroon | Not included in the list |
| Canada | None |
| Central African Republic | Not included in the list |
| Chad | Not included in the list |
| Chile | Not included in the list |
| China | None - computer and related services CPC 841 and CPC 8431 to 8433 |

**Table 1.26** *(Continued)*

| Country | Mode 3 Limitations on market access |
| --- | --- |
| China | Partial - CPC 8421 to 8425 |
| Chinese Taipei | None |
| Colombia | None |
| Congo | Not included in the list |
| Costa Rica | Unbound |
| Côte d'Ivoire | Not included in the list |
| Croatia | None |
| Cuba | None |
| Cyprus | None |
| Czech Republic | None |
| Dem. Rep. of the Congo | Not included in the list |
| Denmark | None |
| Djibouti | Not included in the list |
| Dominica | Not included in the list |
| Dominican Republic | None |
| Ecuador | None |
| Egypt | Not included in the list |
| El Salvador | None |
| Estonia | None |
| Fiji | Not included in the list |
| Finland | None |
| France | None |
| Gabon | Not included in the list |
| Gambia | Partial |
| Georgia | None |
| Germany | None |
| Ghana | Not included in the list |
| Greece | None |
| Grenada | Not included in the list |
| Guatemala | None |
| Guinea | Not included in the list |
| Guinea-Bissau | Not included in the list |
| Guyana | Not included in the list |
| Haiti | Not included in the list |
| Honduras | None |
| Hong Kong (China) | None |
| Hungary | None |

## Table 1.26 *(Continued)*

| Country | Mode 3 Limitations on market access |
| --- | --- |
| Iceland | None |
| India | Partial |
| Indonesia | Partial |
| Ireland | None |
| Israel | None |
| Italy | None |
| Jamaica | Partial |
| Japan | None |
| Jordan | None |
| Kenya | Not included in the list |
| Kuwait | None |
| Kyrgyzstan | None |
| Latvia | None |
| Lesotho | None |
| Liechtenstein | None |
| Lithuania | None |
| Luxembourg | None |
| Macao (China) | Not included in the list |
| Madagascar | Not included in the list |
| Malawi | Not included in the list |
| Malaysia | Partial - computer and related services CPC 841, CPC 842, except software development, plus |
| Malaysia | None - CPC 842[1] |
| Maldives | None |
| Mali | Not included in the list |
| Malta | None |
| Mauritania | Not included in the list |
| Mauritius | Not included in the list |
| Mexico | Partial |
| Mongolia | Not included in the list |
| Morocco | None |
| Mozambique | Not included in the list |
| Myanmar | Not included in the list |
| Namibia | Not included in the list |
| Nepal | Partial |
| Netherlands | None |
| Netherlands Antilles | Not included in the list |
| New Zealand | None |

## Table 1.26 *(Continued)*

| Country | Mode 3 Limitations on market access |
| --- | --- |
| Nicaragua | None |
| Niger | Not included in the list |
| Nigeria | Not included in the list |
| Norway | None |
| Oman | Partial |
| Pakistan | None |
| Panama | Partial |
| Papua New Guinea | None |
| Paraguay | Not included in the list |
| Peru | Not included in the list |
| Philippines | Not included in the list |
| Poland | None |
| Portugal | None |
| Qatar | None |
| Republic of Korea | None |
| Rep. Of Moldova | None |
| Romania | None |
| Rwanda | Not included in the list |
| Saint Kitts and Nevis | Not included in the list |
| Saint Lucia | Not included in the list |
| Saint Vincent and the Grenadines | Not included in the list |
| Saudi Arabia | None |
| Senegal | Not included in the list |
| Sierra Leone | None |
| Singapore | None |
| Slovakia | None |
| Slovenia | None |
| Solomon Islands | Not included in the list |
| South Africa | None |
| Spain | None |
| Sri Lanka | Not included in the list |
| Suriname | Not included in the list |
| Swaziland | None |
| Sweden | None |
| Switzerland | None |
| TFYR Macedonia | None |
| Thailand | Partial |

## Table 1.26 *(Continued)*

| Country | Mode 3 Limitations on market access |
|---|---|
| Togo | Not included in the list |
| Trinidad and Tobago | None |
| Tunisia | Not included in the list |
| Turkey | Partial |
| Uganda | Not included in the list |
| United Arab Emirates | None |
| United Kingdom | None |
| United Republic of Tanzania | Not included in the list |
| United States | None |
| Uruguay | None |
| Venezuela | None |
| Zambia | Not included in the list |
| Zimbabwe | Not included in the list |

**Note:**

[1] Specifically, computer software development services covering development of new software for general application, including ready-made software packaged for general application.

*Source:* UNCTAD based on WTO Services Database (http://tsdb.wto.org/wto/WTOHomepublic.htm)

# References

Annamalai K and Rao S (2003). *What Works: ITC's E-Choupal and Profitable Rural Transformation*, a *What Works* Case Study of the World Resources Institute, University of Michigan. http://www.digitaldividend.org/case/case.htm

Austin RD and Bradley SP, eds. (2005). *The Broadband Explosion: Leading Thinkers on the Promise of a Truly Interactive World*. Boston: Harvard Business School Press.

Barro RJ (1997). *Determinants of Economic Growth: A Cross-Country Empirical Study*, Cambridge, MA, MIT Press.

Barro RJ and X Sala-i-Martin (1995). *Economic Growth*. McGraw-Hill, New York.

Bloom N, Sadun R and van Reenen J (2006). *It ain't what you do, it's the way that you do I.T. - testing explanations of productivity growth using US transplants*, London: mimeo, Centre for Economic Performance, London School of Economics.

Boufeas G, Halaris I and Kokkinou A (2004). *Business plans for the development of e-business in Greece: An appraisal*, UNCT Occasional Papers Series No. 5/2004, Athens: United Nations Thessaloniki Centre for Public Service Professionalism.

Brazilian Internet Steering Committee (CGI) (2006). *Survey on the Use of the Information and Communication Technologies in Brazil 2005*.

Chakrabarty SK, Ghandi P and Kaka NF (2006). The untapped market for offshore services, *The McKinsey Quarterly*, No. 2.

Clayton T (2006). *ICT Investment, Use and Economic Impact: Summary of UK ICT Productivity Findings to October 2005*, presentation at the OECD Impact Workshop, May 2006.

Clayton, T and Goodridge P (2004). E-business and labour productivity in manufacturing and services, *Economic Trends*, 609, pp. 47–53.

Crespi G, Criscuolo C and Haskel J (2006). *Information Technology, Organisational Change and Productivity Growth: Evidence from UK Firms*, Working Paper No. 558, Department of Economics, Queen Mary University of London, London.

Dunning JH, Kim CS and Lin JD (2001). Incorporating trade into the investment development Path: A case study of Korea and Taiwan, *Oxford Development Studies*, 29, 2, pp. 145–154.

E-Business Watch (2005). The European E-Business Report, 2005 edition, Luxembourg: Office for Official Publications of the European Communities.

Economic and Social Commission for Western Asia (ESCWA) (2005). *Regional Profile of the Information Society in Western Asia — 2005*. E/ESCWA/ITCD/2005/6. New York and Geneva: United Nations.

European Commission (2005a). *The 2005 European e-Business Readiness Index*, DG Joint Research Centre, Institute for the Protection and Security of Citizens, 7 November.

European Commission (2005b). *Information Society Benchmarking Report 2005*, available on the Internet: http://europa.eu.int/information_society/eeurope/2005/index_en.htm [2006-06-16].

European Competitive Telecommunications Association (ECTA) (2006). *ECTA Broadband Scorecard Q4 2005*, http://www.ectaportal.com/en/basic.php?id=245&sw=broadband, accessed May 2006.

Farooqui S and Sadun R (2006). *Broadband Availability, Use and Impact on Returns to ICT in UK Firms*, presentation at the OECD Impact Workshop, May 2006.

Ferguson CH (2004). *The Broadband Problem: Anatomy of a Market Failure and a Policy Dilemma*, Washington DC: Brookings Institution Press.

Fornefeld M, Oefinger P and Braulke T (2006). *Gesamtwirtschaftliche Auswirkungen der Breitbandnutzung.* Study for the German Ministry for Economics and Technology, http://www.bitkom.org/files/documents/BITKOM_Studie_Breitbandnutzung.pdf

Freund CL and Weinhold D (2002). The Internet and International trade in services, *American Economic Review*, vol. 92, no. 2, pp. 236–240.

Gillett SE, Lehr WH, Osorio CA and Sirbu MA (2006). *Measuring Broadband's Economic Impact.* Report for the US Department of Commerce, Economic Development Administration, February. http://cfp.mit.edu/groups/broadband/docs/2006/Measuring_bb_econ_impact-final.pdf.

Grupo de Análisis y Prospectiva del Sector de las Telecomunicaciones (GAPTEL) (2004). *Banda Ancha.* Madrid: Red.es. Available on the Internet: http://observatorio.red.es/gaptel/informes/trimestrales.html.

Herander MG and Saavedra LA (2005). Exports and the structure of immigrant-based networks: The role of geographic proximity, *Review of Economics and Statistics*, vol. 87, no. 2, pp. 323–335.

Infocomm Development Authority of Singapore (IDA) (2005). *Measuring Infocomm Usage by Companies, 2005*, available on the Internet: http://www.ida.gov.sg/idaweb/factfigure/infopage.jsp?infopagecategory=&infopageid=I3833&versionid=1.

International Federation of the Phonographic Industry (IFPI) (2006). *Digital Music Report 2006.* London: IFPI. http://www.ifpi.org/site-content/library/digital-music-report-2006.pdf.

ITU (2006). *World Telecommunications Development Report 2006: Measuring ICT for Social and Economic Development.* Geneva: International Telecommunication Union.

Jennings, R (2006). European Music Download Forecast: 2006 to 2011. *Forrester Trends*, 2006-03-27, available on the Internet: http://www.forrester.com/Research/Document/Excerpt/0,7211,38733,00.html.

Jorgenson DW, Ho MS and Stiroh KJ (2005). *Information Technology and the American Growth Ressurgence*, Cambridge, MA, MIT Press.

Kelley CM and McCarthy C (2006). *The Chinese and Australians Soak Up Broadband*, available on the Internet: http://www.forrester.com/Research/Document/Excerpt/0,7211,39378,00.html.

Krugman, P (1995). *Growing world trade: Causes and consequences*, Brookings Papers on Economic Activity No. 1, Washington DC: Brookings Institution.

Lopez, MD (2006). The State of Internet Access. *Forrester Trends*, 2006-04-07, available on the Internet: http://www.forrester.com/Research/Document/Excerpt/0,7211,38510,00.html.

Manual on Statistics of International Trade in Services, 2002, United Nations, European Commission, International Monetary Fund, Organization for Economic Co-operation and Development, UNCTAD and World Trade Organization.

Maliranta M and Rouvinen P (2004). *Informational Mobility and Productivity: Finnish Evidence*, Discussion Paper No. 919, Research Institute of the Finnish Economy, Helsinki.

McKinsey Global Institute (2003). Offshoring: Is it a win-win game?, available on the Internet: http://www. mckinsey.com/mgi/reports/pdfs/login.aspx?ReturnUrl=%2fmgi%2freports%2fpdfs%2foffshore%2fOffs horing_MGI_Perspective.pdf

OECD (2002). *Measuring the Information Economy*, Paris: OECD. http://www.oecd.org/dataoecd/16/14/1835738. pdf

OECD (2003). *ICT and Economic Growth Evidence from OECD Countries, Industries and Firms*, Paris: OECD.

OECD (2004). *ICT, E-Business and SMEs*. Paper for the OECD Conference of Ministers Responsible for SMEs, Istanbul, 3–5 June 2004.

OECD (2005a). *Information Technology Outlook 2004*, Paris: OECD.

OECD (2005b). *OECD Communications Outlook 2005*, Paris: OECD.

OECD (2005c). *Science, Technology and Industry Scoreboard 2005*, Paris: OECD.

OECD (2005d). *OECD Compendium of Productivity Indicators*, Paris: OECD.

OECD (2006). *Information Technology Outlook*, Paris: OECD.

Orbicom (2003). Monitoring the Digital Divide…and Beyond, Quebec: National Research Council of Canada.

Orbicom (2005). From the Digital Divide to Digital Opportunities: Measuring Infostates for Development, Quebec: National Research Council of Canada.

Parker A and Takahashi S (2006). European IT outsourcing deals: 2005 review. Forrester Trends, 2006-04-04, available on the Internet: http://www.forrester.com/Research/Document/Excerpt/0,7211,38700,00.html

Partnership on Measuring ICT for Development (2005). Core ICT Indicators. http://measuring-ict.unctad.org/

Pyramid Research (2006). *The world's mobile subscriber base will pass the 2.5bn subscriber mark; The interesting fact is how it will get there*, available on the Internet: http://www.pyramidresearch.com/pa_jan12_pred.htm, accessed May 2006.

Solow RM (1957). Technical Change and the Aggregate Production Function, *Review of Economics and Statistics*, vol. 39, no. 3, pp. 312–320.

Statistics Canada (2006). *Measuring ICT impacts at Statistics Canada*, paper presented by Bryon van Tol at the OECD WPIIS Meeting, May 2006, Paris.

UNCTAD (2002). *E-Commerce and Development Report 2002*, New York and Geneva: United Nations.

UNCTAD (2003). *World Investment Report 2003*, New York and Geneva: United Nations.

UNCTAD (2004). *World Investment Report 2004*, New York and Geneva: United Nations.

UNCTAD (2005). *World Investment Report 2005*, New York and Geneva: United Nations.

United States Department of Commerce (2003). International Services: Cross-Border Trade in 2002 and Sales through Affiliates in 2001; Washington DC: US Department of Commerce Bureau of Economic Analysis.

US Census Bureau (2006). 2004 E-commerce Multi-sector Report. Posted in May 2006 at http://www.census. gov/eos/www/ebusiness614.htm.

Waverman L, Meschi M and Fuss M (2005). The Impact of Telecoms on Economic Growth in Developing Countries, Vodafone Policy Paper Series, 2 (2005), pp. 10–23.

Whisler A and Saksena A (2003): Igniting the next broadband revolution, *Accenture Outlook Journal*, January 2003, available on the Internet: http://www.accenture.com/Global/Research_and_Insights/Outlook/By_Alphabet/IgnitingRevolution.htm, accessed May 2006.

World Bank (2005): *E-development: From excitement to effectiveness*. Washington, DC: World Bank.

World Bank (2006). *Information and Communications for Development: Global Trends and Policies*. Washington, DC: World Bank.

World Trade Organization (WTO) (2001). *Guidelines for the scheduling of specific commitments under the GATS*, Geneva: WTO.

World Trade Organization (WTO) (2005). *World trade developments in 2004 and prospects for 2005*, Geneva: WTO.

Wunsch-Vincent S (2005). *WTO, E-commerce and Information Technologies*, UN ICT Task Force Series, No. VII, New York: United Nations ICT Task Force.

Zhu K, Xu S and Kraemer K (2006). The global diffusion and convergence of e-commerce: Cross-Country Analyses, in: Kraemer K, Dedrick J, Melville N and Zhu K, *Global E-Commerce: Impacts of National Environments and Policy*, Cambridge: Cambridge University Press, ch. 10.

# Notes

1.  Although developing Oceania apparently presents the highest growth rate from 2004–2005, it should be noted that data for most countries are missing for 2004; countries also depart from a lower base than Africa.

2.  See http://www.pyramidresearch.com/pa_jan12_pred.htm.

3.  This does not include peer-to-peer music file sharing.

4.  Data on Internet users worldwide take into account all kinds of users in all types of locations, and in countries with no Internet use surveys, figures are estimated on the basis of the number of Internet subscribers, with a multiplier for each country.

5.  These countries also account for 35.3 per cent of the population in the whole of Europe (including South-East Europe and CIS countries), 54.1 per cent of the population in developed Europe and 55.5 per cent of the population in the EU25.

6.  In 2004, the financial sector had 97 per cent penetration or more for the six countries reporting on this industry. Of the 21 OECD countries able to report on wholesale trade and the real estate, renting and business services sectors, 14 had Internet penetration rates of over 90 per cent for both (including Belgium, Denmark, Finland and Sweden). The retail sector had slightly lower penetration except in Finland, Denmark, Sweden, Canada and Switzerland (all had more than 90 per cent).

7.  Germany conducted a different survey for the financial services sector because of its structural differences with other industries. Thus it is not always included in average values stated for all enterprises. (Information Technology in Enterprises and Households 2005, Federal Statistical Office of Germany).

8.  Enterprise data for 2005 are not available for France, Malta and Portugal.

9.  This is a Spearman rank correlation, which measures the strength of the associations between two variables. A coefficient between 0.5 and 1 shows a strong positive correlation.

10. Broadband access is defined as being equal to, or greater than, 256 Kbps, as the sum of the capacity in both directions (Partnership on Measuring ICT for Development, 2005).

11. The digital divide is apparent in the differences in the international Internet bandwidth available to developed and developing economies and its cost. For example, in 2004 Denmark had more than twice the bandwidth of the whole Latin American and Caribbean region. For a discussion on international Internet backbone connectivity and related issues for developing countries, see chapter 2 of the *Information Economy Report 2005*.

12. See OECD Broadband Statistics, December 2005, at http://www.oecd.org/document/39/0,2340,en_2649_34223_36459431_1_1_1_1,00.html.

13. See the "Bridging the Broadband Gap", COM(2006) 129 final, Commission of the European Communities, Communication from the Commission to the Council, the European Parliament, European Economic and Social Committee and the Committee of the Regions. Brussels, 20 March 2006.

14. The *Digital Divide Forum Report: Broadband access and public support in under-served areas* of the Commission of the European Communities does an excellent analysis of the urban–rural broadband divide in Europe and proposes policy actions to bridge this divide. http://europa.eu.int/information_society/eeurope/i2010/docs/implementation/ddf_report_final.pdf.

15. VSAT can be used for Internet access in places that cannot get ADSL or cable Internet access for geographical or other reasons that affect last-mile connectivity, for example remote or rural areas. Satellite bandwidth is scalable from speeds below 1 Mbit/s up to 45 Mbit/s.

16. Uganda and other East African countries are developing the Eastern Africa Submarine Cable System (EASSy) project with the aim of improving international connectivity. For more information see http://eassy.org.

17. European Commission Press Release IP/06/755, "State aid: Commission endorses public funding to bridge broadband communications gap in Latvia", Brussels, 8 June 2006.

18. See Ferguson (2004) and the exchange of letters in Foreign Affairs of Adam Segal (November/December 2004), Thomas Bleha (May/June 2005), and Philip J. Weiser and Thomas Bleha (September/October 2005).

19. In the absence of economic output data at the community level, the study measured broadband impact through other economic variables: employment, salaries, rent, and industry structure or mix.

20. The exceptions are Italy, Hungary and Greece, with less than 20 per cent.

21. Some EU countries show a slight decline from 2004 to 2005, which may be due to the statistical margin of error as well as changes in survey methodology.

22. Detailed data for 2003 on e-business activities in enterprises for a selection of OECD countries are available in IER 2005.

23. See chapter 2 of the *E-Commerce and Development Report 2004* on e-business and SMEs.

24. This was found to be the case with online purchases and sales.

25. See http://www.oecd.org/dataoecd/34/37/2771153.pdf for the detailed definition of the ICT sector.

26. As defined in OECD (2004), ICT specialists have the ability to develop, operate and maintain ICT systems, while ICT users are competent users of generic or more advanced tools, without having ICTs as their main job.

27. The definition differs from the OECD ICT sector definition; it includes information equipment manufacturing and information services.

28. Outsourcing is defined as the contracting out of non-core operations from the internal production of a company to a third party specializing in that operation. Operations can be transferred within the same country (domestic outsourcing) or abroad (international outsourcing). Offshoring is defined as the location or transfer of activities abroad. It can be done internally by moving services from a parent company to its foreign affiliates (sometimes referred to as "captive offshoring", involving FDI, to differentiate it from offshoring to third parties). It is different from the concept of outsourcing, which always involves a third party, but not necessarily a transfer abroad. Offshoring and outsourcing overlap only when the activities in question are outsourced internationally to third-party services providers (UNCTAD, 2004). For more information on business process outsourcing see chapter 5 of UNCTAD's *E-commerce and Development Report 2003*).

29. See box 1 for more information.

30. The authors used data on the number of top-level domain names.

31.  For more information on ICT policies see chapters 2 and 3 of this publication.

32.  Detailed country tables are provided in the statistical annex (annex I).

33.  See table 1.8 for a list of the services included.

34.  For more information see chapter 8 of UNCTAD's *E-commerce and Development Report 2002.*

35.  See section 3 for more detailed information.

36.  For more on computer and information service exports see part 3 of this section.

37.  Particularly high 2000–2003 growth rates for financial service exports were calculated for Cape Verde, Mali, Madagascar, Côte d'Ivoire and Tunisia.

38.  2004 values were available only for the developed countries. The growth rates shown in chart 1.25 are therefore CAGR calculations on a five-year basis, 2000–2004.

39.  "Other commercial services" include ICT-enabled services, together with construction services.

40.  Together with the European Commission, the International Monetary Fund, the Organisation for Economic Co-operation and Development, and the World Trade Organization.

41.  Electronic deliveries are also transmitted from a distance, although not all through Mode 1.

42.  UNCTAD estimates of world trade in services, February 2006 version.

43.  Japan was an exception, with a very high share of foreign affiliates' outward sales vis-à-vis BOP exports (8.5 in 2002), but with a fluctuating evolution of both FATS and BOP outflows of services during 1995–2002.

44.  With 6.2 as compared with 1.1 for the country ranking next, namely Costa Rica.

45.  Data on WTO members' market access commitments draws on the WTO services schedules available at http://www.wto.org/english/tratop_e/serv_e/serv_commitments_e.htm.

46.  The GNS/W/120 list based on the CPC, Version 1.0.

47.  News agency and other information provision services included in the BOP item are not covered by the same GATS commitments. Also, computer facilities management and data processing services provided on line are covered separately by WTO commitments on telecommunication services (The Manual, 2002).

48.  Exceptions are indicated with stripes in the chart.

49.  Similar to no market access.

50.  See, for example, the submission of the European Commission proposing that WTO members make commitments at the two-digit level of the CPC, GATS Council, Special Session. Communication from the EC and their Member States, GATS 2000: Computer and Related Services (CPC 84) - Addendum, S/CSS/W/34/Add.1 (15 July 2002).

51.  Communication from India, Proposed Liberalization of Movement of Professionals under GATS, S/CSS/W/12 (24 November 2000) and Negotiating Proposal on Computers and Related Services, S/CSS/W/141/Corr.1 (11 April 2002).

52.  The chapter will focus on the quantitative measurement of ICT impact, based on official statistical data sources only. It will not delve into research using qualitative approaches, such as surveys measuring the *perceived* impact of ICTs on businesses or individuals (e.g. through direct questions such as "In your view, …" or "Do you think/expect that …"). Chapter 2 of the ECDR 2003 provides a detailed overview of the literature on ICT and economic performance.

53.  Based on a presentation by OECD at the WPIIS Expert Group on ICT Impact, Paris, 4 May 2006.

54.  The research results presented here are discussed in detail in Orbicom (2005).

55.  Recent work on the impact of ICTs on economic growth in Latin America has been carried out by Prof. Nauro F. Campos of Brunel University West London. See http://www.itu.int/osg/spu/dtis/documents/presentations/campos.ppt.

56.  Other composite ICT indexes include the World Economic Forum (WEF) Network Readiness Index, the ITU Digital Access Index and Digital Opportunity Index, the UNCTAD Index of ICT Diffusion and the Economic Intelligence Unit (EIU) e-readiness ranking.

57.  As shown by the positive and statistically significant $a5,t$ coefficients.

# Chapter 2

# REVIEWING NATIONAL ICT POLICIES
# FOR THE INFORMATION ECONOMY

## A.  Assessing the role of ICTs in development

During the past decade, ICTs have become part of many developing countries' development plans and poverty reduction strategies. Those countries have designed and are implementing national ICT policies to reach overall development goals, recognizing the potential of new technologies in fostering economic and social development. Concretely, Governments have formulated one or several ICT strategies or "master plans"[1] over the years and set goals to ensure the effective deployment and use of ICTs in their country for the benefit of their citizens and enterprises.

To support developing countries in their efforts to develop their information societies, international organizations, regional groupings and international forums have anchored ICT for development in their work programmes, while donors have been increasingly mainstreaming ICTs into their development aid programmes as a strategic, cross-cutting tool in support of countries' own development plans. The World Summit on the Information Society (WSIS) outcome documents highlighted the vital role of Governments in developing national "e-strategies" and encouraged all Governments to further the penetration of ICTs in their national development plans. The Tunis Agenda for the Information Society, encourages Governments *"to elaborate, as appropriate, comprehensive, forward-looking and sustainable national e-strategies, including ICT strategies and sectoral e-strategies as appropriate, as an integral part of national development plans and poverty reduction strategies, as soon as possible and before 2010".*[2]

UNCTAD research has shown that as of June 2006, out of 181 developing and transition countries and territories, 80 (44 per cent) had already adopted a national ICT plan and 36 (20 per cent) were in the

### Chart 2.1

### National ICT plans in developing and transition countries and territories, 2006

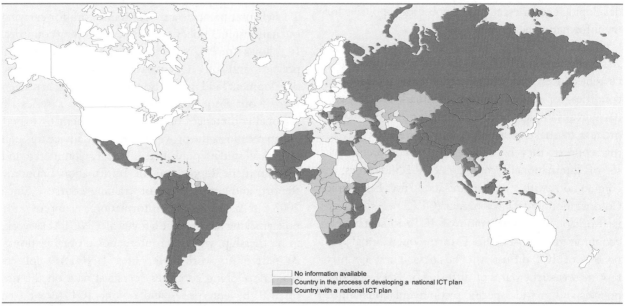

No information available
Country in the process of developing a national ICT plan
Country with a national ICT plan

*Source:* UNCTAD's questionnaire and Internet research.[3]

process of designing one (chart 2.1 percent and annex II). While the map in chart 2.1 does not feature OECD member countries with the exception of Mexico, the Republic of Korea and Turkey, most of them have put in place one or several national ICT plans.

## 1. A call for national ICT policy reviews

Given the large number of countries, even in the developing world, that have established national ICT plans and policies, the question arises as to the impact of these policies. How can we assess the impact of ICT policies on the development of the information and knowledge-based economy? What are the main barriers that hamper the implementation of ICT policies? What are successful policies that could perhaps be multiplied, scaled up and replicated? While Governments have been formulating and implementing ICT plans and policies during the past few years, there is now a need to review the status of their plans and understand the impact they have had so far on their economies and societies, and to allow decision makers to formulate new policies. ICT policies are dynamic tools that must be continuously updated in order to keep up with national, international and technological developments.

In recent years much attention at the international level has been paid to so-called e-readiness assessments, leading to the development of a range of assessment tools by various organizations to measure a country's e-readiness.[4] At the same time, little has been done to assess the implementation of national ICT policies in developing countries, and more specifically policies for the information economy.

Assessing national ICT policies and their impact is a current concern in most countries. Several developed countries, for example Austria, Denmark and Norway, have already implemented a systematic policy evaluation process to make policy decisions more effective. In this context, they have developed a comprehensive set of internationally comparable ICT indicators, in conjunction with the Organisation for Economic Co-operation and Development (OECD). As part of its work on the contribution of ICTs to sustainable economic growth,[5] the OECD carries out national peer reviews of ICT diffusion to business. These country reports review the status of diffusion of ICTs, describe policies and provide specific recommendations aimed at ICT uptake in enterprises.

While the information economy is becoming a reality in developed countries, little is known about the extent to which the spread of ICTs fosters growth and development in the developing world. Only a handful of countries (for example, Chile, Cuba, Dominican Republic, Egypt, Nepal, Oman, Republic of Korea, Rwanda, Syrian Arab Republic and Thailand) have so far carried out an assessment of their national ICT plans. The format and scope of their evaluation vary, but their assessments are all motivated by the need to ensure that appropriate revisions of priority policies and recommendations are formulated in preparation for new ICT plans to accelerate their socio-economic development.

By conducting an ICT policy review, Governments will be able to:

- Understand the policy challenges and opportunities which ICTs present for the information economy, and quantify the main achievements regarding the implementation of a number of ICT policy measures as foreseen in the national ICT plan;

- Identify critical success factors, best practices and conditions, as well as reasons for failure to be able to adjust and reform ICT policies;

- Formulate new and targeted policy decisions to support and accelerate ICT penetration with Government, businesses and the community.

## 2. UNCTAD's proposal for ICT policy reviews

This chapter presents a model framework for carrying out national ICT policy reviews in developing countries. It follows from UNCTAD's ongoing work on ICT policies and on ICT measurement for economic development and trade. So far, this work has been carried out through the organization of a series of regional conferences on ICT policies, thematic expert group meetings, the provision of policy advice through analytical studies published in the E-Commerce and Development Report and the Information Economy Report, and the delivery of training courses.[6] Since 2003, measuring the information economy for policymaking has become a focus of UNCTAD's work, in partnership with other international organizations.[7] As part of its work in this area, UNCTAD collects from developing countries statistical data on the use of ICT by enterprises and on the ICT sector (see chapter 1).

In the *E-Commerce and Development Report 2003*, UNCTAD introduced a model framework for the formulation of a national ICT strategy which focuses on the special concerns of developing countries, recognizing that elements and priorities of national ICT strategies might differ between developed and developing countries. The Report identified key areas and sectors of policy action and elaborated the elements and priorities of national ICT strategies for developing countries.

Based on the 2003 model framework, the review methodology presented in this chapter will focus on policies related to the information economy, including the overall business and economic environment, enterprise development and the development of the ICT industry. Emphasis is placed on the ICT policy actions that are undertaken to promote economic growth and development and the adoption of ICTs by Government and the business sector. An ICT policy review can be used as a road map for Governments as they develop their participation in the information economy. Reviews can also help developing countries to learn from each other's experiences. Box 2.1 provides further details about the proposed model review.

The model proposes a framework for reporting and monitoring the implementation and institutional mechanisms that affect the success of ICT-based policies. This will help Governments guide their reviews, identify the main strengths and weaknesses of their policies and, eventually, revise and adjust them to ensure the enabling conditions for the development of the information economy. Chart 2.2 summarizes the proposed review model framework. It focuses on three main components:

- A **review of the general economic environment and ICT diffusion** to assess the extent to which ICTs are available and used in the country;

- An **assessment of the key policy components** of the national ICT master plan and their implementation: ICT infrastructure, legal and regulatory framework, the development of ICT human resources (capacity building), and the development of sector-specific policies and ICT applications to promote e-business, e-government, ICT-related trade and investment policies, and technological innovation;

- An **assessment of the institutional framework**, implementation mechanisms and the roles of each stakeholder.

On the basis of the proposed framework, section C of this chapter will describe how national ICT policies could be assessed, using selected developing countries

---

## Box 2.1

## UNCTAD ICT policy reviews

As part of its technical cooperation activities, UNCTAD offers to carry out full-fledged country reviews to help developing countries adjust their ICT policies and implementation mechanisms aimed at developing the information and knowledge-based economy.

The reviews would assess the implementation of the national ICT master plans within the context of UNCTAD's mandate to examine how ICT and e-business development issues have been operationalized in country development strategies and to identify policies and programmes favouring the development of the information economy. In this context, specific e-business policies and cross-cutting policies that are intimately linked to the development of the information economy,[1] such as telecommunications infrastructure, legal and regulatory issues, and human resources, would be evaluated. Other components that form an integral part of an ICT national master plan, such as sectoral policies related to ICT and social development, including health and culture, could be added in partnership with other relevant organizations (e.g. WHO, UNESCO). The review methodology is intended to help policymakers, donors and the general public to assess the achievements of ICT policies and the current status of the information economy in a country, as well as to make recommendations on policy priorities.

ICT policy reviews would be carried out at the request of and in close cooperation with member States and subject to available funding. The review process would take the form of the compilation of an evaluation report prepared by UNCTAD in consultation with the national authority of the requesting member State. The process involves field missions, the active participation of the relevant stakeholders during interviews and the organization of workshops to discuss the evaluation of ICT policies related to the information economy and the recommendations of appropriate policy options, as well as indicators of achievement for future policy measures. Details on the methodological framework for carrying out the review will be part of a separate UNCTAD document and not included in this Report. Further information will be available at www.unctad.org/ecommerce.

[1] See chapter 3, ICT strategies for development, ECDR, 2003, available at www.unctad.org/ecommerce.

## Chart 2.2

## UNCTAD's ICT policy review model framework

**Assessment of existing ICT master plan**

| **ICT environment** | **ICT policy framework** | **Implementation and institutional framework** |
|---|---|---|

**ICT uptake and use indicators**

ICT infrastructure and access
Access to, and use of, ICTs by households and individuals
Use of ICTs by businesses
ICT sector and trade in ICT goods and services
Other ICT indicators

Objectives and priority areas and strategic approach
ICT infrastructure development
Legal and regulatory framework
Development of ICT human resources/skills
Business development
E-government
ICT-related trade and investment policies
Technological innovation (R&D)

Integration of ICT policies within national development plans/PRSP
Institutional set-up for implementation of national ICT policy master plan
Financial resources
Monitoring the implementation of ICT policies

Transparent and continuous consultation process with all stakeholders during the review process

**Indicators of achievement – identification of success factors, best practices, lessons learned and challenges ahead**

**Policy recommendations**

**Revised ICT master plan/policies**

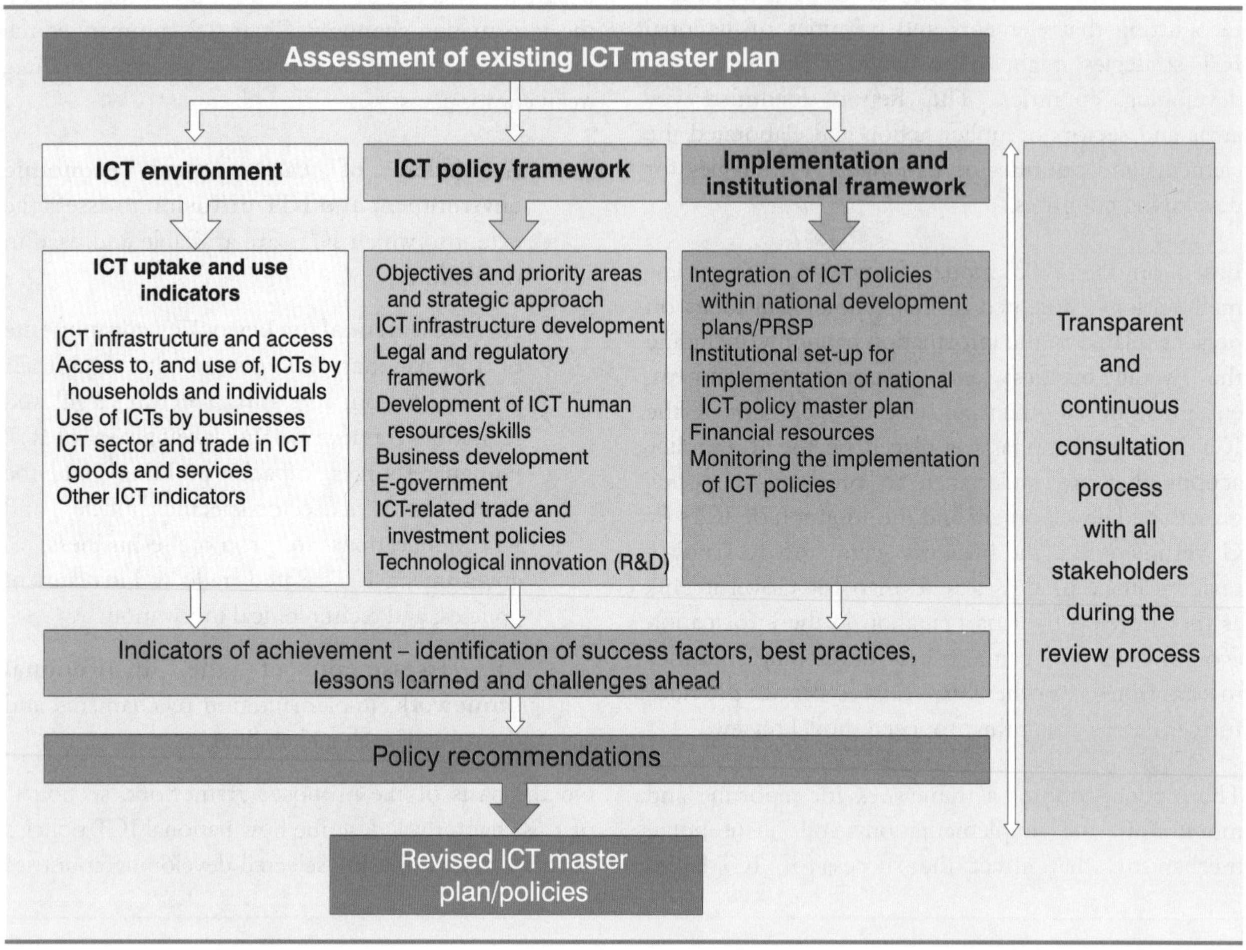

as examples. Lessons learned from implementation mechanisms and major achievements will be used to shed light on best practices and successful ICT policies.

In preparing this chapter, UNCTAD carried out in-depth research on developing and transition countries' status as regards formulating and implementing a national ICT master plan. For this purpose, it collected and analysed information on the ICT plans and policies of 181 developing and transition countries and territories (for an overview of the status of national ICT plan and policies, see annex II). The information is based on extensive Internet research (information provided by the websites of developing countries' Governments and on a questionnaire that was sent out to collect information on national ICT master plans and to enquire whether they had been already assessed).[8]

## B.    ICT policy review model framework

### 1.    Overview of the social and economic setting

The first section of the ICT policy review restates the objectives of an active or proposed national ICT policy. It reviews the policy against the backdrop of the economic, demographic and social environment in the country. It points out factors that can affect the implementation of the national ICT policies, and then provides a short overview of the major national economic and social key indicators at the time of the preparation of the ICT master plan, and at the time of the review. The purpose of the overview is to present the overall context in which the information economy in the country is evolving.

## 2. ICT environment: ICT uptake and use indicators

This part of the review provides an overview of a country's ICT uptake focusing on the current status of ICT penetration for different economic actors (industry sectors, companies and households). As part of the national ICT plan, it is critical for Governments to set measurable targets which then need to be assessed. Through their national statistical offices, ministries or telecommunications operators, Governments should collect ICT data on a regular basis to:

- Measure the success of the formulation and implementation of ICT policies;

- Identify the effectiveness of such policies;

- Establish links between ICT policies and the performance of specific sectors, such as telecommunications, and the development of information economies;

- Monitor ICT growth and use over time; and

- Carry out research and analysis on the impact of ICTs on productivity, growth, enterprise development and trade.

Below are four sets of internationally agreed upon core indicators (see annex I and chapter 1)[9] that are suggested as a reference tool to complement the existing methodological framework in a country. The list of indicators can be adapted to the needs of individual countries, depending on their own economic and social challenges. They focus on ICT infrastructure, and ICT access and use by businesses, households and individuals, as well as on the ICT sector and trade in ICT goods. These indicators help policymakers to assess the changes that have occurred over the years as a result of their policies and plans.

### Core indicators on ICT infrastructure and access

Developing countries have made the deployment of ICT infrastructure and universal ICT access a top priority in their ICT master plan, as a prerequisite for participating in the information economy. Many of them are starting to collect data on infrastructure and access to ICTs. These ICT infrastructure and access indicators correspond to individual use and measure accessibility in terms of people. For instance, those indicators include, per capita measures, fixed telephone lines, mobile cellular subscribers, Internet subscribers,

and so forth. Collecting such data helps Governments to monitor, inter alia, the advancement of ICT teledensity, geographical coverage, quality of services, communication costs and bandwidth availability.

### Core indicators on access to, and use of, ICT by households and individuals

Internet public awareness campaigns and advances in access to telecommunications through policymaking can be evaluated by collecting data on access to, and use of, ICT by households. For instance, core indicators on access to, and use of, ICT by households and individuals include the proportion of households with a radio, a TV, a fixed line telephone, a mobile cellular telephone and a computer with Internet access at home. Among those indicators, information on the type of activities carried out by households helps in assessing the frequency and volume of business-to-consumer e-commerce activities.

### Core indicators on the use of ICT by businesses

In addition to measuring computer penetration in the private sector, the actual level of use of computer systems to support e-business organizational activities and operations helps measure the level of development of the information economy in a country. The *E-Commerce and Development Report 2004*[10] noted that a large number of SMEs in developing countries have access to the Internet but have not yet integrated ICTs into their business functions. In most cases, computers are mainly used to carry out basic computing work such as word processing and e-mail. The Report stressed the lack of available statistical data on e-business and the implications that this may have for ICT-related policymaking. In this regard, it is essential to monitor progress in the use of high-end value-added applications, as well as the Internet. This could be done by using the core indicators on the use of ICT by business, which include the proportion of businesses using computers, those using the Internet, and proportion of businesses with a Web presence, with an intranet, receiving orders over the Internet or placing orders over the Internet.

### Core indicators on the ICT sector and trade in ICT goods and services

Developing countries have recently focused on the development of the ICT sector in order to diversify their economies, to respond to demand from developed countries for ICT-enabled services, to be less dependent on ICT goods and services imports, and to develop local human capabilities and generate job opportunities for the development of the information economy. The ICT sector core indicators that are considered in the review include the proportion of the total business sector workforce involved in the ICT sector and the value added in the ICT sector (as a percentage of total business sector value added) in a country.

Trade in ICT goods and services is among the most dynamic sectors of international trade (see chapter 1). For developing countries, exports of ICT-enabled services provide new opportunities for economic growth and employment creation, including through the continuous increase of outsourcing. Therefore, the review analyses developments in imports and exports of ICT goods and ICT-enabled services.

### Other ICT indicators

In addition to the core ICT indicators recommended by the international community, national ICT policy reviews assess the development of other information society indicators, such as ICT skills and computer literacy, the level of investment in ICTs, and indicators related to e-government and education, security and trust. The choice of indicators considered in the review is made on a country basis and reflects the particularities of the country under review.

## 3.   Assessment of ICT policy framework

This part of the review examines national ICT policies which have been put in place by the Government and discusses whether they have been successful in terms of meeting initial goals. It identifies the components of a national ICT plan, priority actions, sectors concerned, targets and relevant projects. If necessary, it also recommends how the policies can be improved.

The primary focus is on the review of policies implemented to accelerate ICT diffusion in a country and identify successful achievements as well as bottlenecks. In particular the review outlines specific reforms aimed at providing a more enabling business environment for SMEs. The main objective is to identify lessons learned as well as challenges ahead. Specific recommendations on action needed to achieve the policy objectives are provided.

### Objectives, priority areas and strategic approach

Each country, with its specific economic, social and legal context, is facing unique challenges regarding its ICT diffusion and use. Consequently, a national ICT master plan setting the overall direction and parameters for different areas of activities should address a country's specific needs and identify priorities accordingly. Related key objectives should address the identified areas of priorities and include quantitative results that make the master plan's long-term implications measurable.

The strategic approach to implementing the ICT plan defines key programmes and areas of activities in order to achieve the defined objectives and goals for the main policy components, such as ICT infrastructure, the legal and regulatory framework and the development of ICT human resources.

The process of the ICT policy formulation should be transparent and involve all stakeholders. ICT policies should be well structured and clearly formulated.

This part of the review closely examines the following issues related to policy formulation:

- Identification of a country's specific needs and areas of priority;

- Definition of ICT policy direction and key objectives;

- Focus of ICT plan;

- Key areas of activity;

- Indicators of achievement;

- Process of ICT policy formulation.

### ICT infrastructure development

Developing an affordable information and communication network infrastructure and applications is central to building the information economy. All countries have recognized the critical importance of the telecommunications sector in their ICT master plans. The Governments' objective is to ensure that the country has a competitive telecommunications industry which delivers reliable and affordable services and products for the economic and social benefit of citizens. Many Governments in developing countries have in recent years facilitated the introduction of competition into a telecommunications industry traditionally structured around monopolies. The development and deployment of ICTs are changing the structure of the industry, favouring the appearance of private operators offering advanced telecommunications networks and services.

In particular, the performance of the ICT sector itself is dependent on ICT policy measures that address the particular needs of ICT-sector firms and foster an enabling ICT environment. Policy measures can make an essential contribution to the national and international business environment, as well as to corporate strategies and enterprise performance, and hence the overall competitiveness of companies. If Governments define the enhancement of national software and IT services as a priority concern, the promotion of the ICT sector firms must also be a priority within a national ICT

master plan. Corresponding policy measures should enhance the ICT infrastructure with regard to access, pricing and local content, and they should be related to providing finance, skills and education. Moreover, they should encourage the development of a strong and competitive ICT sector in enabling ICT companies to enhance their competitiveness, at both the national and the international level.[11]

As part of the review, the effectiveness of policy measures on ICT infrastructure development is assessed and the challenges that remain in closing the connectivity and accessibility gaps are identified. The review closely examines the following issues:

---

## Box 2.2

## ICT infrastructure development in Nepal

Nepal's first National Communications Policy was adopted in 1992, and the Nepal Telecommunications Authority was established in 1997. In 1999, the National Policy was modified in order to initiate the liberalization of the Nepalese telecom sector, by encouraging the participation of the private sector. The same year, telephone penetration grew by 22 per cent.[1] In 2004, the telecommunication sector had been fully opened to private service providers and competition, through open licensing and by restructuring the State-owned operator. Some notable results were:

- Growth in the total telephone penetration rate from 1.4 per cent in August 2002 to 3.1 per cent (2 per cent for fixed lines and 1.1 per cent for mobiles) in July 2005;[2]

- Growth in the number of distributed (fixed) lines, which increased from approximately 65,000 in 1992 to over 470,212 in January 2006;[3]

- A mobile phone service was launched in 1999, and in January 2006 there were already over 99,000 post-paid and 200,000 pre-paid mobile subscribers. The network is now fully digital and offers full national and international direct dialing services.

Nepal's *Information Technology Policy 2004* states the policy measures to further the development of the ICT infrastructure in order to continue the progress made under the *IT Policy 2000*.

*Provide Internet facilities*

- Starting with very low levels, Internet connectivity grew by 150–160 per cent per annum between 1995 and 2002.

- There was a rapid fall in the cost of Internet access ($0.20 per minute in 1995 to $0.20 per hour in 2004). Unlimited Internet access via dial-up cost $70 per month in 1998, which fell to $10 per month in 2004.

- There are about 200,000 Internet users, of whom 40,000 are subscribers. In 1999, there were about 290 domain names registered under ".np", and close to 4,600 at the beginning of 2004.

*Develop virtual and physical Information Technology Parks*

- With the active participation of the private sector, the construction of the IT Park was completed and it is now in operation.

- With assistance from the Indian Government, the construction of an optical fibre link (the East–West Highway, 880 km) between Katmandu and Southern Indian terrestrial networks is nearly complete.

The growth in the telecommunications sector has been heavily skewed in favour of urban areas, in particular the Katmandu valley, which accounts for two thirds of the total number of telephone connections in the country. To remedy to this situation, around 200 telecentres in rural and sub-urban areas were set up in 11 districts.

---

[1]  High Level Commission for Information Technology of Nepal (2005).

[2]  http://www.itu.int/ITU-D/ict/informationsharing/index.html.

[3]  Nepal Telecommunications Authority, Management Information System (MIS) Report, http://www.nta.gov.np/mis_report.html.

## Table 2.1

## Egypt's major telecom infrastructure indicators

| Telecommunications Infrastructure Indicators | | | | |
|---|---|---|---|---|
| Indicator | October 1999 | March 2004 | March 2005 | December 2005 |
| Exchange capacity (million) | 6.4 | 11.6 | 12.1 | 12.7 |
| No. of telephone fixed lines (million) | 4.9 | 9.1 | 9.6 | 10.4 |
| No. of public phone booths | 13 305 | 48 983 | 54 346 | 55 700 |
| No. of mobile phone subscribers (million) | 0.654 | 6.1 | 8.6 | 14 |
| No. of Internet users (million) | 0.3 | 3.15 | 4.3 | 5 |
| No. of PCs (million) | 0.85 | 1.7 | 2 | 2.54 |
| Total number of IT companies | 266 | | 1 374 | 1 716 |

Source: Arab Republic of Egypt (2006).

- Telecommunications market (access, affordability, etc.);

- Deployment of broadband access network, fibre optic backbone networks, and increased access points for the Internet;

- Investment incentives;

- International and regional cooperation for infrastructure development;

- Resources;

- Technical and legal capacities to implement these policies;

- Coordination between public and private stakeholders;

- ICT sector.

As an example, box 2.2 – on the ICT policies related to infrastructure development in Nepal – presents some achievements in developing ICT use in the country by citizens and enterprises.

The Egyptian Information Society Initiative in the past five years has also taken significant steps forward in the modernization of ICT infrastructure. *Access to the Internet and Related Services* is one of the three main pillars that the Egyptian Government has established, where policy and development are currently concentrated (together with Research and Development and Maintaining Regulatory Policies). Table 2.1 presents some major telecommunication infrastructure indicators.

The following case study illustrates how liberal policies such as privatization and opening up to trade can be successfully blended with other trade policy instruments to ensure more social and economic benefits. Taking as an example Peru's telecommunications service sector from 1992 to 2004, the study combines elements of trade (subsidization), competition and broader economic policy.

### Legal and regulatory framework

An enabling legal and regulatory framework is one of the key policy pillars of an information-based economy – and one of the key elements of a national ICT plan.

An appropriate legislative framework is fundamental for any electronic commercial transaction, ensuring that the latter is legally valid, binding and enforceable. It builds confidence in the electronic transmission of sensitive information, creating trust between commercial partners and providing security for customers. It is a facilitator of domestic and international electronic trade, controlling and regulating the use of ICT-enabled services and ensuring legal protection for the provider and users in the global market.[12] Strengthening the trust framework, including information and network security, authentication and privacy, is a prerequisite for the growth of ICT uptake by businesses and the development of e-business.

Telecommunications regulations are essential in promoting telecommunications access, fostering

---

### Box 2.3

## Peru: Subsidizing the universal provision of telecom and Internet services at minimum cost

Following the 1992 privatization of the incumbent, Peruvians living in rural areas were still provided with very little access to basic telecom services.[1] In order to address this market failure, the Peruvian Government intervened to extend public fixed voice telephony and Internet access to the rural areas, seeking to achieve universal access in the long run. For this purpose, a special fund (Fondo de Inversión en Telecomunicaciones, FITEL) was established in 1993 for the purpose of subsidizing private telecom companies to provide service for targeted rural areas. The fund started to function in 1999 and was financed by a 1 per cent mandatory levy on the gross operating revenues of telecom companies. The positive aspects of Peru's initiative are the following:

- The fund is managed by an independent regulator, OSIPTEL, as opposed to government-dependent bodies. It made it more accountable to stakeholders since the moneys could not be transferred for other policy objectives.

- OSIPTEL was also in charge of attracting private investments in the Peruvian telecom sector. Foreign services suppliers were guaranteed the same level of fair treatment as their domestic counterparts.

- The subsidy scheme relied on a market distribution system, which minimized the cost of service provision. Private companies bid for the lowest subsidy to provide service in a given area, where they obtained a 20-year concession. For the pilot project (2000), the winning bid required a subsidy 74 per cent lower than the previous offer by the incumbent operator and 50 per cent lower than the mobilized funds.

- Following consultations with stakeholders and comprehensive assessments, the first projects focused on rural localities with 500 to 3,000 inhabitants. The challenge was to best allocate subdivisions in those areas to favour competition between providers, but without compromising economic viability. This approach had potential disadvantages for the smaller localities, for women and for the disabled (see chapter 2 for a discussion of telecentres' failure to address all aspects of poverty). However, disadvantages should be balanced against the scarcity of financial resources, and the intention to gradually expand the scope of the policy.

- OSIPTEL was also aiming to make the service provision to rural areas a stand-alone profitable commercial activity by the end of the 20-year concession. Therefore, the subsidy was granted only for the first five years, in periodic instalments and conditional on the provision of a minimum contracted service (including as measured by quality standards). Fines were collected when the provider under-delivered.

Several projects were conducted successfully. During the first stage (1999), 4,938 villages gained access to the telecom infrastructure and benefits accrued to 3.9 million inhabitants. In the targeted area, this improved the proportion of people with telephone access from 48 per cent in 1999 to 88 per cent in 2000. During the second stage (2000–2002), another 1.8 million people and 1,616 villages benefited. The last project was initiated in 2001 with a view to extending access to telephone and Internet for rural health establishments.

According to the OECD (2004), there are as many as 60 developed and developing countries in the world currently implementing or planning to put in place a universal access fund.

---

[1] *Sources:* OECD (2004), Intelecon Research (2005), Cannock (2001), Maddens (2005), World Bank (2002) and the OSIPTEL website.

---

competitive markets and attracting investment. Regulations and policies creating an overall enabling economic and business environment are important facilitators of foreign investment, as well as of ICT adoption by domestic business entities. In this regard, trade and investment policies, standard setting, banking and finance are important areas.

An ICT policy review examines policy measures related to the following:

- National regulatory institutions;

- Telecommunications regulations;

- Investment regulations;

- E-commerce laws (digital signatures, intellectual property laws, etc.);

- E-payment (see box 2.4);

- Trade policies (e.g. import duties in IT products; signatory to the Information Technology Agreement).

Box 2.4 gives an example of how a government policy has led to an increase in online payments.

## Box 2.4

## Tunisia's e-Dinar initiative

Credit cards operations have appeared only recently in Tunisia, and thus a majority of Tunisians still cannot make online payments. To address this problem and to promote e-commerce, Tunisia has issued a virtual currency, the electronic Dinar or "*e-Dinar*", also called the electronic purse. Created in August 2000 by the Ministry of Communication Technologies, it consists of an anonymous and virtual account, rechargeable through prepaid cards (with different values) that can be bought in Tunisian post offices. Various merchant websites (about 200) are connected to the "*e-Dinar*" platform, and offer different types of products and services, such as university registration, payment of national taxes, online bookings and payments (flights, hotels, car rentals). The Tunisian Post Portal[1] itself integrates 14 websites that offer e-commerce possibilities (Web Telegram, e-learning, stamps, flowers, etc.). In 2005, 54,000 persons used the "*e-Dinar*" system (with a total of 61, 288 cards sold[2]) to make online payments, compared with 3,000 users registered in 2001.[3] The platform was certified by Visa International and MasterCard in 2005.

*Source:* Chaffai El Sghaier (2006).

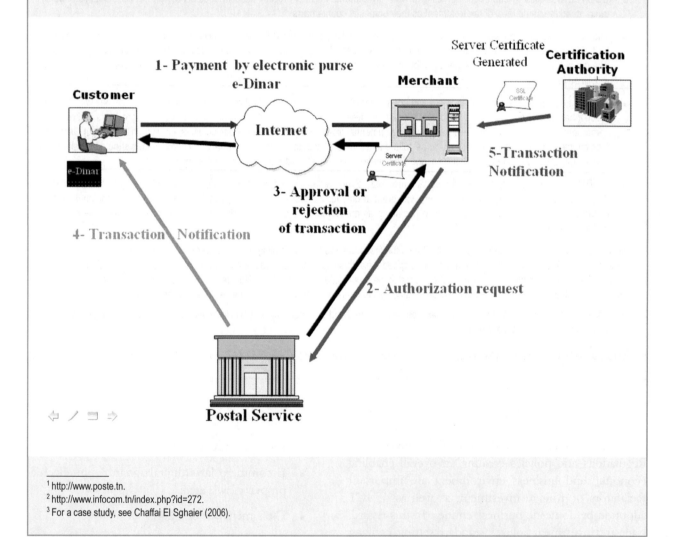

[1] http://www.poste.tn.
[2] http://www.infocom.tn/index.php?id=272.
[3] For a case study, see Chaffai El Sghaier (2006).

### Development of ICT human resources/skills

ICT skills are a fundamental enabler for actively participating in, and benefiting fully from, the information economy. Knowledge creation is vital for both the production and the use of ICTs. Many countries have introduced ICT training in the public and private sector, in ministries and related institutions, and in schools to increase educational opportunities and augment the supply of ICT graduates.

The ICT review looks at the policy measures aimed at developing:

- ICT skills in primary and secondary schools;

- IT graduates and programmes (universities);

- Training projects to enhance the IT workforce in the public sector (including ministries and NGOs) and the business community;

- Incentives for private sector companies to organize/support IT capacity building.

Box 2.5 presents the actions and results of Rwanda's first ICT plan and policy review in the field of development of ICT human resources.

### Business development

In their ICT plans, some countries have designed and are implementing specific policies to increase the diffusion of ICTs to SMEs to encourage their participation in the global economy. The development of e-business is carried out in cooperation with the business sector to identify the needs of SMEs, offer training programmes and improve their capacity on a continuous basis for use and innovation in the available technologies (see *E-Commerce and Development Report 2004*, chapter 4). Another important area for developing countries relates

---

## Box 2.5

## Review of the development of ICT human resources in Rwanda

The Rwanda Information Technology Authority (RITA),[1] started in 2001, is the national coordinating body to support the development and the implementation of Rwanda's first ICT Plan (National Information and Communications Infrastructure Plan, NICI, 2001–2005). Human resources development was one of the pillars of the NICI Plan and various programmes and initiatives were implemented in different areas. Following are some of the policy measures on human resources development that were implemented:

- National Human Resource Development Agency (NHRDA) was set up in 2002 to monitor national human resources needs, to mobilize funds and to develop appropriate training structures.

- Various ministries and public sector organizations put in place training to develop skills within the civil service *(special basic computing and Internet use training programme, special professional-level ICT training programmes)*. IT literacy will become an essential requirement for all future civil servants.

- A programme was put in place to enrol students in ICT-related courses and to add ICT courses to all types of degrees and diplomas within the National University of Rwanda (NUR), the Kigali Institute of Science Technology and Management (KIST), the Kigali Institute of Education (KIE) and other institutions of higher learning.

- A national programme was deployed to increase the use of ICTs in universities and colleges. It included the implementation of *Computer Science* or *Computing Departments* in universities, initiatives to increase the number of ICT students, availability of Internet access, the creation of a Rwandan Academic and Research Network (RARN), and the setting-up of ICT R&D centres within universities.

- Specific programmes were implemented to increase the enrolment of women in ICT-related higher education and professions.

- To increase the number of computers in schools, various programmes and policies were prepared, such as tax policy instruments (to facilitate the import of computers and related equipment), the forthcoming obligation for ministries, public agencies and public sector organizations to give their old computers to schools, and the implementation of the *Adopt-and-Sponsor a School*[2] initiative.

- A specific initiative has been implemented to ensure the IT literacy of teachers, via the creation of a *Train-the-IT Teachers (TITT) Certificate Programme*. During the first NICI Plan, about 3,000 teachers were trained.[3]

As a result of these measures, some progress has been made, especially in providing computer access in schools. For instance, in 2001, only one school (primary and secondary schools included) in the whole country had a computer. In 2005, 1,138 out of the 2,300 primary schools had one, and 100 of these schools had two.[4] However, a review carried out in 2005 identified the lack of qualified human resources as one of the main barriers to the implementation of the NICI Plan. As at June 2005, RITA had achieved only 26 per cent of the plan in five years.[5] The revised plan will have to put more emphasis on building ICT capacities.

---

[1] http://www.rita.gov.rw/about.htm.

[2] This specific initiative aims at looking for sponsors within the private sector, civil society and international agencies involved in Rwanda. These sponsors provide computers, resources and educational facilities to a school they have «adopted».

[3] Review of the implementation of the Rwanda ICT4D/NICI-2005 Plan, http://www.uneca.org/aisi/nici/Documents/The%20NICI-2005%20Plan%20Review-Final%20Report.pdf.

[4] Review of the implementation of the Rwanda ICT4D/NICI-2005 Plan, http://www.uneca.org/aisi/nici/Documents/The%20NICI-2005%20Plan%20Review-Final%20Report.pdf.

[5] http://africa.rights.apc.org/index.shtml?apc=21873n21845e_1&x=194393.

to the development of the ICT sector to improve their local capabilities and to diversify their economies by producing ICT goods and services.

The review examines the policies related to the following:

- Promoting the use of ICTs and e-business by enterprises (text processing, e-mails, e-business processes);

- SME capacity building;

- Financing SMEs (venture capital);

- Public procurement;

- Online e-business sectoral initiatives (e-market-places).

Box 2.6 presents some specific initiatives implemented by Nepal to encourage the participation of all businesses, including SMEs, in the global economy.

### E-government

In many developing countries, Governments are the main users, enablers and pioneers of ICT diffusion. E-government consists of the following electronic interactions: government-to-government (G2G), government-to-business (G2B) and government-to-citizen (G2C). Governments can provide non-commercial and commercial services to optimize administration costs and deliver better and more efficient services to their citizens, and stimulate the efficiency of their operations.[13] The Tunis Agenda for the Information Society noted the increasing use of ICTs by Governments and encouraged countries that have not yet done so to develop e-government programmes and policies. It encouraged the development and implementation of e-government applications based on open standards. Working on infrastructure and uniform standards for interchange of data between administrations will help streamline G2G and G2C communications. Challenges to e-government applications are often a combination of both policy and technology issues. Interoperable open standards among different government departments are the prerequisite for a seamless information flow and integration within e-government operations.

According to the latest UNDESA E-government readiness survey, published in 2005, 179 out of 191 member States had a website presence. A few countries utilized the full potential of e-government to provide information and services to their citizens, and transactional services online remained limited mostly to the developed countries.[14]

The review examines the policy measures aimed at developing:

- E-government non-commercial and commercial services;

- E- procurement;

- E-business systems.

Box 2.7 presents the actions undertaken by South Africa in the field of development of e-government, with a unique Initiative, called the "*Batho Pele Initiative*".

---

## Box 2.6

## National ICT plan and e-business development in Nepal

As part of the policy measures to foster the development of e-business in Nepal, the Government has planned to transform traditional industries into ICT-enabled businesses.

The Rural–Urban Partnership Programme (www.rupp.org.np) runs a B2B site (www.b2b.com.np) promoting business transactions among entrepreneurs, and also aims to establish regional linkages among 12 partner municipalities. Nepali e-Haat Bazaar is the national B2B e-commerce marketplace, a single electronic gateway to promote market linkages within the country and with the international markets.

The Government has set up business incubators (www.incubation.org.np) to develop SMEs (June 2005) and was planning to allocate a budget for the development of business incubation in order to gear up developmental and business activities. The Government also developed web portals and B2B marketplaces in selected market segments, such as:

- AgriPriceNepal (http://AgriPriceNepal.com) provides comprehensive agricultural commodity intelligence to traders.

- The enterprise site www.thamel.com, which provides information on business in the Thamel area of Katmandu, won the Worlds Bank's Tony Zeitoun Award for successful entrepreneurship and innovation in 2003.

---

## Box 2.7

## South Africa: The "Batho Pele Initiative"

South Africa's e-government policy is led by the Centre for Public Service Innovation (CPSI), created in 2001 to "*enable the South African Public Service to be able to effectively implement innovative ideas in its quest for improved service delivery*[1]" in partnership with the Department of Public Service and Administration[2] and the State Information Technology Agency.[3]

In this context, the "*Batho Pele Initiative*[4]" – or "People First Initiative" – has been established to provide a single entry point to government services and information, and to enhance the quality and accessibility of those services.

A Government Portal index page has been put in place (see www.gov.za), and provides online access to a large number of services and information. Services available online are dedicated to personal life events (such as birth, education, disability, citizenship, etc.), to organization – specific needs (such as taxes, intellectual property issues and other business issues), and to foreign nationals (people who want to move to, work in or visit South Africa).

Detailed information, steps to follow and downloadable administrative forms are available on the Portal. For instance, people can register a birth, renew their driving licence, apply for registration as a voter, apply for water and electricity, apply for VAT registration, register as a service provider/supplier for government, register a copyright, apply for naturalization, apply for a study permit, or apply for a visa, and so forth.

This project is planned to be extended to citizens living in poor or remote areas, via public information terminals available in post offices, and via an increasing number of community centres.

---

[1] http://www.itweb.co.za/office/sita/0108310825.htm.
[2] http://www.dpsa.gov.za/.
[3] http://www.sita.co.za/.
[4] http://www.info.gov.za/aboutgovt/publicadmin/bathopele.htm.

---

The following case study illustrates how the evaluation of Chile's electronic procurement system, which was near to failure, in 2002 and the consequent development and implementation of a strategic plan helped to make the platform a model of success.

### ICT-related trade and investment policies

Trade and investment policies play an important role in helping countries take advantage of the benefits offered by the information economy. They are critical to ensuring the growth and dissemination of ICT products and services, the development of an affordable and high-quality ICT infrastructure, and the development of human resources and technological innovation needed to advance a knowledge-based economy.

Policies that enhance international trade in ICT-related products and services range from a reduction of import and export duties on ICT goods, and the promotion of outsourcing of ICT-enabled services, to the liberalization of information and communication services. The WTO Information Technology Agreement has significantly reduced import duties on IT products of WTO member States. However, in some countries, high import duties on certain ICT products still keep prices artificially high in the domestic market and remain an obstacle to the development of the local information economy.

A policy framework that promotes open markets, competition and private-sector investment will attract companies not only in ICT-related industries but other sectors that support and benefit from the information economy. Proactive ICT-related investment policies include financial or/and non-financial incentives or the promotion of national and foreign investment via tax incentives, unlimited employment of foreign workers or guarantee of loans. To create an investment-friendly environment, the establishment of a legal framework that protects intellectual property rights is also critical.

A well-known example from South Asia is the Malaysian Super Corridor,[15] which is a key component of the Malaysian ICT plan. It is a dedicated 15 x 50 km corridor located 30 km south of Kuala Lumpur and hosting (in 2006) more than 900 ICT companies,[16] including national SMEs in the ICT industry. To attract the targeted companies, the Malaysian Government has committed itself to, inter alia, (1) a bill of guarantees, (2) a world-class infrastructure, (3) a suite of cyber laws, and (4) financial, as well as non-financial, incentives. Similar examples exist in other Asian countries, and in some developing countries in Latin America.

## Box 2.8

## Chile's e-government system: A best practice model

Chile's e-government system is regarded as the most advanced in Latin America and as best practice – not only for its variety of services and information, but also for the high degree of usability, efficiency and transparency.[1] In particular, the electronic procurement platform of the Chilean Government, ChileCompra,[2] is a centralized public sector procurement and contracts system that benefits both government agencies and private companies. According to the World Bank (2004), "*Chile has adopted a well thought and comprehensive strategy and action plan for procurement of goods and services that is a best practice example to be followed*". Moreover, it is recognized that ChileCompra has brought a high degree of transparency to public procurement.

However, in its early years (1998–2002) "*ChileCompra failed to take off*" (Gobierno de Chile, 2002). An evaluation of the platform in 2002[3] identified the underlying reasons: (1) a lack of leadership and political commitment within the implementation process; (2) a lack of awareness of the importance of public procurement among public agencies; (3) a lack of professionals in procurement and use of technologies; and (4) a cultural resistance to e-commerce tools. Furthermore, the platform itself revealed deficiencies such as misclassification of business areas or late postings. In 2002, only 9 out of 257 public agencies and 577 out of 6,193 suppliers were regular users of ChileCompra.

How could ChileCompra develop from a near-failure into a model of success? One of the driving forces to reinvigorate the project was the evaluation and the development and implementation of the Public Procurement System Strategic Plan 2002–2004. The plan is embedded in Chile's overall Digital Agenda 2004–2006 and reveals a realistic strategy to relaunch the online platform, with a clearly defined vision, mission and objectives, and specific action lines.

The strategy fosters small companies and regional participation, provides for more training and technical assistance, and includes the redesign of the platform in order to increase usability, security and standards – and client satisfaction. Furthermore, it defines appropriate indicators that will regularly evaluate the achievement of goals. For example, the achievement of "e-government promotion" and "e-commerce promotion" goals was defined in terms of numbers of member public agencies and member suppliers. Thus, the platform should have been joined by 250 government institutions as buying entities and by 10,000 providers on the supply side by the end of 2004. In point of fact, 879 public agencies and municipalities and more than 100,000 providers were registered by 2004.[4]

Further factors for success were a strong commitment by the Chilean president to promote the system, and the enactment of the Electronic Signature Law (2002) and the Government Procurement Law (2003). The latter established ChileCompra as the electronic procurement platform for all governmental agencies (regional, provincial and municipal) and the Armed Forces, and provided for a large increase in the number of users.[5] Another revitalizing factor was the Pro-Growth Policy Agenda of 2002, a key road map plan of the Ministry of Economy that prioritized the improvement of transparency and efficiency in the public sector, and set out a commitment to develop an electronic market. Furthermore, bilateral trade agreements with the United States and the EU forced Chile to provide foreign companies with access to its government procurement scheme.

---

[1] United Nations (2004, p.35).

[2] See http://www.chilecompra.cl.

[3] Dagnino (2004).

[4] Digital Agenda Technical Secretariat, Digital Agenda: Main Achievements, April 2005 (English version), http://www.agendadigital.cl/aws00/servlet/aawsconver?2,,115006.

[5] Gobierno de Chile, Digital Agenda 2004–2006 (English version), http://www.presidencyofchile.cl/upload_documentos/Digital_Agenda_2004-2006.pdf.

---

This part of the ICT policy review thus looks at policy measures aimed at:

- Increasing trade in ICT-related goods and services;

- Attracting FDI in ICT-related industries (investment incentives, taxation, regulations);

- Promoting specific economic sectors and activities, for example business process outsourcing.

### Technological innovation (research and development)

Science and technological innovation is acknowledged as an essential contributor to the overall social and economic development of a country: not only might it help solve problems which a country is facing (e.g. in providing infrastructure), but also it can be regarded as a *base* for economic development. As stated in a report by the UN Millennium Project Task Force on Science, Technology and Innovation, "*technological innovation is* ...

*not simply a matter of installing devices, but of transforming society and its value systems*.[17] The Tunis Agenda for the Information Society recognizes the enabling role of an international and domestic policy environment for encouraging investment and innovation, and the driving forces of the private sector and civil society[18] for innovation and private investment.

Given the increasing scientific gap between developed and developing countries, Governments need to become more active.[19] Moreover, *"the risk of a scientific divide arises when leading decision makers fail to regard science as a priority economic and human investment"*.[20] Governments play a crucial role not only in providing the legal environment, but also in encouraging the private sector in the field of technology and innovation – through goal-oriented policies, for example, as successfully pursued by Brazil.

A country's research and innovation capacity depends on the interaction between all stakeholders, complementing each other – the public sector as well as the private sector, civil society and academia. The greater the integration and interaction of and among stakeholders, the more successful a system of research and innovation will be. Developing countries, however, often reveal a lack of integration capacities.[21] Here, Governments play a crucial role in creating research networks, at national, regional and international levels. Moreover, the nature of innovation calls for long-term oriented, consistent policies.

In this regard, the review examines:

- Policy measures that aim at developing capabilities through research and development programmes;

---

## Box 2.9

## ICT policy with focus on ICT R&D: The case of Thailand

One of the key strategies defined in Thailand's ICT Master Plan 2002–2006 is to strengthen ICT research and development (R&D).[1] This Master Plan is linked to the Ninth National Economic and Social Development Plan as well as to the National Information Technology Policy 2001–2010 (which is built on the principles of *building up human capital, promoting innovation and investing in information infrastructure,* and *promoting the information industry*).

The Master Plan's ICT R&D strategy involves the participation of the public and private sector as well as educational institutions. Among its overall goals are "80 per cent of locally made PCs used in the country by 2004" and "at least 70 per cent of total developers should be software developers who can use network computing technology or web services by 2004". Furthermore, the plan defines several areas of activities contributing to goal achievement, including the promotion of R&D for products with potential commercialization. The strategy also identifies the roles and responsibilities of the agencies involved. Goal achievement is linked to a specific time frame of operation as a basis for the monitoring and evaluation process.

Could Thailand's ICT R&D strategy reach its goals? On the basis of data available as of June 2006, the general increase in R&D expenditures as percentages of GDP from 0.1 per cent in 1999 to 0.3 per cent in 2003 indicates a development in the right direction.[2] A survey published by the National Research Council of Thailand (NRCT) on Thailand's R&D expenditure and personnel in 2001 compared Thailand's R&D expenditures as percentages of GDP (0.2 per cent) with those of other countries, and noted that expenditures were below those of the United States and many Asian and European countries. Thailand's IT market has expanded, continuously with an average annual growth rate of 17 per cent between 1999 and 2004. In 2001, 45 per cent of R&D personnel were researchers (25,100 persons). The figure for Thailand's full-time equivalent research personnel was 3.9 per 10,000 inhabitants, also below that of other countries (7.5 in China and 4.3 in Malaysia). There were no data available indicating the development of R&D personnel within the last few years.

In its executive summary of the Strategy and Action Plan Development 2005–2007, Thailand's Office of the National Research Council identifies two key limitations to the development of a knowledge-based society in Thailand in the past.[3] The first is the lack of coherence in terms of policy directions and objectives and hence of research strategies, goals, resources allocation and systematic evaluation. The second limitation is a lack of cooperation among the research community and stakeholders from the private and public sector, as well as civil society. Accordingly, the recent overall strategy of the NRCT tries to address those obstacles.

Thailand seems to be making progress in terms of ICT R&D development itself, but also in terms of measuring its progress as a basis for monitoring and evaluation procedures. Furthermore, the NRCT has made an effort to analyse Thailand's R&D development in an international context. It also tries to identify, address and overcome non-measurable policy obstacles. Thailand's efforts to assess the national ICT R&D developments at different levels provide a good example for a country's ICT policy review practice – and illustrate the challenges of a long-standing and gradual process of implementing sustainable policy assessment measures.

---

[1] National Electronics and Computer Technology Center of Thailand (2003).

[2] All figures from National Research Council of Thailand. See http://www.nrct.net/eng/.

[3] See http://www.nrct.net/eng/downloads/strategy05_07.doc.

- Key incentives which support industry investment in research and development, such as tax rebates or exemption.

Box 2.9 highlights Thailand's ICT research and development policy, which is part of the country's ICT master plan and integrates indicators for measuring the achievement of goals.

## 4. Assessment of the institutional framework and implementation mechanisms

This part of the national ICT policy review considers the adequacy of implementation mechanisms and institutional framework and the extent to which changes have to be made to implement the policies contained in the ICT master plan.

The lack of efficient institutional framework and consultations with all stakeholders are the major bottlenecks for a limited implementation of ICT programmes. At the government level, for example, the various stakeholders involved in preparing and implementing policies should regularly hold consultations to review the situation and any difficulties they may encounter.

Consequently, the focus is on the role of the main bodies that formulate, implement and monitor ICT plans, through the collaboration of all stakeholders in the Government, civil society and also the private sector, with the involvement of the latter encouraging the adoption of ICT policy and the use of new technologies.

### Integration of ICT policies within national development plans

The need to embrace ICTs as tools for sustainable development and to mainstream them into overall national development plans has been stressed in different forums, notably the WSIS. The review analyses the link between the national ICT plan and the overall national development and poverty alleviation plans, and considers the degree of integration of ICT policies into such plans. Indeed, many developing countries have anchored them in major policy plans such as national development plans and Poverty Reduction Strategy Papers (PRSPs). According to a study published by OECD in January 2004,[22] only 13 countries in the 34 PRSPs analysed included ICTs as an independent strategic component for poverty

reduction. But in all countries except three, ICTs (sometimes limited to telecommunications) are always mentioned in the document as a significant component of the poverty reduction strategy. Nevertheless, some efforts have to be made to fully integrate ICT policies within national development or poverty reduction plans. For an analysis of pro-poor ICT policies, see chapter 3 of this Report.

Box 2.10 presents the case of The Gambia, where the national ICT plan fully supports the objectives set out in the national PRSP (The Republic of the Gambia Strategy for Poverty Alleviation was adopted in 2002), and provides an illustration of the integration of an ICT national policy within the national development and poverty reduction plans.

Institutional set-up for implementation mechanisms of national ICT policy master plan

Implementation mechanisms are a prerequisite for ensuring the efficient execution of a national ICT plan.

This part of the review looks at:

- Policy coordination and participating institutions;

- The role of stakeholders and partnerships;

- The implementation mechanisms;

- The challenges and lessons learned.

Examples of successful ICT policies formulation and implementation worldwide show that one critical factor has been a strategic political leadership involvement through the lead of one policymaker at the highest level (President or Prime Minister), an institution or a group of institutions.

Furthermore, the adoption of an institutionalized multi-stakeholder approach allowing all relevant stakeholders to participate in and contribute to the formulation and implementation of the ICT policy is essential. It will promote a strong commitment by all stakeholders and close cooperation among them, and will enhance the integration of the ICT policy into all levels.

For example, the development of Chile's Digital Agenda 2004–2006 brought together government agencies and institutions – among them the Ministries of the Interior, Economics, Finance, Education, Justice and Health – business organizations, academia and civil society. In total, more than 170 persons worked together for ten months to define Chile's Digital Agenda.[23]

## Box 2.10

## The Gambia: Integrating national ICT and poverty alleviation plans

As mentioned in the National Strategy for Poverty Alleviation,[1] *"Research and development of Information and Communication Technology (ICT) applications in development is a major priority of Government, and has resulted in the setting up of a Department of State to that effect. ICT application in Health, Government and Communications in Rural Areas will be systematically explored as an adequate strategy to improve service delivery through the introduction of telemedicine, e-government opportunities and development of rural telecentres."*

In order to achieve the development objectives, and to maximize the poverty alleviation impact of ICT, the National Information Society Infrastructure (NICI)[2] Policy, currently being developed, supports the ambitions of the PSRP through ICT-led plans of action and initiatives. The following table[3] illustrates some of the major ICT initiatives proposed for reaching the PRSP objectives.

| PRSP objective | NICI policy & plans |
|---|---|
| **1. Enhancing the productive capacity of the poor** | |
| a. Promoting labour-saving devices for women | Rural multimedia centres for women |
| b. Providing access to credit | Credit/loan opportunities information online |
| c. Reorganizing agricultural R&D to encourage labour-intensive agriculture and development of small ruminant | Agricultural information systems for rural community information centres |
| **2. Enhancing access to and the performance of social services** | |
| a. Expanding access to basic social services in rural areas | Launching e-government initiatives/providing access at local area councils |
| b. Delivering responsive social programmes to the poor | |
| c. Enhancing sustainability and quality of social services | |
| **3. Local-level capacity building** | |
| a. A political and legislative framework for decentralization | Local government leadership training for local government representatives |
| b. Empowerment of local government authorities to assume decentralized responsibilities | |
| **4. Promoting participatory communications processes** | |
| a. Enhancing participation beyond consultation | Planning feedback/local government representative links up to the National Assembly level |
| b. Addressing gender at national and local levels | Rural multimedia centres for women as the participatory hub/link to the national development processes/programmes |
| c. Institutionalizing dialogue between government, civil society and donors | NGO/CSO link through NGO associations (e.g. TAGNO, Action Aid in The Gambia) |

*Source:* Baharul Islam (2005).

---

[1] See http://poverty2.forumone.com/files/12016_GambiaPRSP.pdf.
[2] See http://www.uneca.org/aisi/NICI/.
[3] See Baharul Islam (2005).

## Box 2.11

## Achieving the Ghana ICT for accelerated development policy

In 2005, the Government of Ghana adopted the Ghana ICT for Accelerated Development Policy, which is intended to be integrated within the Government's three-pronged development strategy, which revolves around the development and enhancement of the human resource capacity, the renewal of the private sector and the strengthening of good governance.

The adoption of the national policy follows an extensive nationwide consultative process that was intended to associate all stakeholders in order to build a national consensus on the key policy and plan development issues, and on the implementation process. A *National ICT Policy and Plan Development Committee*[1] was launched in August 2002, with the aim of developing an integrated ICT-led socio-economic development policy and a corresponding plan, on the basis of an *"extensive national consultative exercise"*.[2]

This consultative exercise took the Committee to seven regions for briefings, public lectures and conferences, and to meet with a large number of public and private sector stakeholder organizations, including Parliament, the Council of State, the National House of Chiefs, ministries, universities, polytechnics, private sector companies, telecom operators, ICT service providers, labour organizations, security agencies, regional coordinating councils, UN organizations and other development partners.[3] Fifty-one meetings and presentations (usually on a daily basis) were conducted in the country between August 2002 to May 2003, with about 800 persons involved, as well as the entire student population.[4] A major result of this process was to facilitate the ownership of the policy and of its implementation process, and to implement a plan that takes into account the needs and suggestions of national key socio-economic actors.

---

[1] See http://www.ict.gov.gh/.

[2] See http://www.ict.gov.gh/.

[3] Statement by the Minister of Communication on the ICT policy for Ghana, http://moc.gov.gh/moc/PDFs/Statement%20on%20the%20ICT%20Policy%20for %20Ghana.pdf.

[4] The full list of organizations, agencies, institutions and individuals consulted is available in the *Integrated ICT-led Socio-economic Development Policy and Plan Development Framework for Ghana* document, available on the UNECA website, http://www.uneca.org/aisi/NICI/Ghana/ghana_consulted.htm, pp. 186–207.

---

Box 2.11 presents the case of the *Ghana ICT for accelerated development policy*, where an extensive nationwide consultative process was conducted.

### Financial resources

National ICT plans are subject to the resources available and hence the need to assess regularly whether the priorities are still the same and whether the best use is made of the funds being allocated. Policy measures must be continuously examined to see whether there are more efficient ways of accomplishing the same ends and whether the measures are still effective over time. An important aspect of evaluating current policy measures is the potential to leverage existing resources and to reallocate funds. The information on the financial resources allocated to various policies and programmes should be available so that it is possible to budget and to keep transparent records of costs arising from ICT development programmes in order to increase the efficiency of policymaking.

According to the World Bank's report *Information and Communications for Development 2006*, the majority of ICT plans do not specify the budgetary mechanism of the implementation process (40 per cent of 40 selected national ICT plans did not provide any budget information).[24]

For example, in Thailand's ICT Master Plan 2002–2006, it is mentioned that "*there must be a mechanism to link the operational plan with the budget as well as human resources plans. The framework and guidelines to assess the operational plan as well as ICT projects of government agencies should be established, by cooperation among the central agencies including … the budget bureau, and the Office of Civil Service Commission*".[25] However, it does not specify the concrete budgetary mechanism, but expects government agencies in charge of the implementation process to define their own five-year implementation plan, including a budgetary mechanism.

In general, the definition of a budgetary mechanism creates transparency and assigns roles and responsibilities to the government bodies involved. Lack of a budgetary mechanism within the ICT policy framework could lead to the unsuccessful implementation of an ICT plan. Lack of budget responsibility and planning might create budget constraints and the risk that the implementation process might be delayed or not finished at all.

This part of the review looks at:

- Allocation of resources;

- External and internal resources;

- Deployment of budgetary resources;

- Assignment of roles and responsibilities;

- Control mechanism.

### Monitoring the implementation of ICT policies

To monitor and review ICT policies, transparent and continuous policy coordination and discussion with all stakeholders (Government, business associations, chambers of commerce, academia, civil society, etc.) are essential, as well as the involvement of national statistical offices (NSOs) for data collection. In most developing countries, data are still scarce, not up-to-date or inconsistent. It is therefore highly recommended that a coordination entity (e.g. an NSO) be appointed to use standard indicators and to regularly conduct surveys (see chapter 1 on ICT indicators for development).

National ICT master plans should include monitoring and evaluation procedures, and identify institutions responsible. A study by the World Bank (2006) reveals that the majority of the 40 selected national ICT plans do not specify the monitoring and evaluation process.

An example of a developing country that has included monitoring in its national ICT plan is Thailand.

### Chart 2.3

### Relationship between Thailand's National ICT Master Plan and the ICT plans of ministries and departments

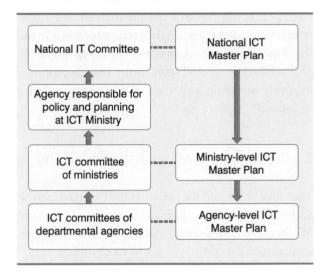

Source: National Electronics and Computer Technology Center (2003, p. 82).

Thailand's ICT Master Plan 2002–2006 provides that the ministries and departments as well as other government agencies involved in the implementation process have to create an ICT committee that oversees their ICT Master Plan and its implementation process. The committee is obliged to report the progress of implementation every six months to the next-higher-level committee. Chart 2.3 outlines the relationship between the National ICT Master Plan and the organizational ICT Master Plans of the ministries or government agencies concerned, as well as the monitoring of plans at each level.

### Chart 2.4

### Chile's Public Procurement System Strategic Plan, 2002–2004

| Goal | Indicator | Baseline situation as of October 2002 | Goal to December 2003 | Goal to December 2004 |
|------|-----------|------------------|------------------|------------------|
| E-government promotion | Member public agencies (using the system at least once a year) | 144 | 200 | 250 |
| E-commerce promotion | Suppliers generating at least 1 offer a year in the system | 2 907 | 5 000 | 10 000 |
| Platt form Quality | ChileCompra users satisfaction: maximum grade 7.0 | 4.9 | 5.5 | 6.0 |

Source: Gobierno de Chile (2002).

National ICT master plans should also map defined goals with indicators and include a time frame to measure the progress of implementation. Chart 2.4 presents, by way of example, the proposed goal achievement of Chile's Public Procurement System Strategic Plan. Each goal is mapped to a specific indictor and a time frame; this makes the goal achievement measurable and therefore transparent. Such an operational definition of goal achievement could serve as the basic component of the monitoring and evaluation process within a national ICT master plan.

## 5.  Evaluation and recommendations

The final part of the national ICT policy review analyses key lessons learned from the assessment of the country's policies as well as the measures, implementation and coordination mechanisms.

Each country has unique circumstances and conditions characterizing its ICT diffusion and therefore specific needs that require to be addressed within a national ICT master plan. Against that background, this part outlines the strengths and weaknesses of a national ICT master plan and identifies opportunities and threats for the implementation process. Furthermore, it makes in-depth recommendations on specific policy measures as well as on the institutional and implementation mechanisms. Regarding the latter, it recommends in particular how to optimize the monitoring and evaluation process in order to guarantee a sustainable policy.

## C.   Concluding remarks and recommendations

This chapter has presented a model ICT policy review framework for developing countries, which consists of three major components:

- A review of the global ICT environment (e.g. ICT access and use);

- An assessment of the main ICT policy areas (e.g. ICT infrastructure development, the legal and regulatory environment, the development of ICT human resources, e-business and e-government, ICT-related trade and investment policies, and technological innovation); and

- An assessment of the institutional framework and the implementation mechanisms (e.g. the integration of ICT policies within national development plans, the institutional set-up, the financial resources and the monitoring mechanisms).

Using selected developing country examples, the chapter illustrated how specific ICT policies could be monitored and assessed. There is a wide range of stages at which countries are with respect to their ICT policymaking. Although many countries have adopted national ICT plans, only a few have already carried out an ICT policy review or are in the process of doing so. Since there are no international guidelines for developing countries to define and implement such a review, the model framework presented here is a first step in that direction. The proposed framework is a generic model that could be used as a basis by developing countries. It will have to be adapted to the needs of each country, and could include additional elements to reflect specific national aspects not covered by the model.

Potential challenges related to the use of the proposed model review may include:

- The limited availability of information related to the implementation of policy measures, including data, achievements and failures;

- The lack of defined indicators of achievements, both qualitative and quantitative, which can be used to benchmark and assess ICT policies;

- The lack of commitment on the part of the relevant stakeholders in charge of policy planning and implementation to provide information, as well as their lack of willingness to conduct self-appraisals;

- Potential institutional conflicts among different (public and private) stakeholders; and

- The limited participation of relevant stakeholders in the evaluation process.

- Developing countries that are considering carrying out an ICT policy review should pay attention to the following:

- Planning the adequate timing of the review is essential. Time requirements vary and are subject to the demand of each country, while largely depending on the progress made in the implementation of the ICT master plan.

- Clearly defining policy objectives and indicators of achievements at the time the policy decisions are made is vital for assessing the success of a measure and planning future policy decisions; policymakers need to be able to establish such evaluation indicators and they should work closely with NSOs to obtain relevant statistical data.

- Committing financial resources is a prerequisite for undertaking a review.

- Promoting a multi-stakeholder process helps temper potential conflicts between stakeholders and increases the commitment of all involved.

A sustainable, long-term-oriented national ICT master plan calls for the implementation of continuous monitoring and evaluation procedures at different levels. As illustrated by the example of Thailand, the implementation process itself is a comprehensive and gradual process which cannot be realized overnight. It is in the nature of policy reviews that they demand a continuing and sustainable commitment by all relevant stakeholders. Policymakers should guarantee this through the definition of clear monitoring and evaluation procedures, including a realistic time frame, the creation of budgetary mechanisms and the assignment of roles and responsibilities. These notions apply to all countries, regardless of how advanced their

ICT policy and review process is:

- Countries that are at an early stage in formulating and developing their ICT master plan can already start anticipating an ICT policy review by ensuring the integration of monitoring and evaluation procedures into their master plan.

- Countries whose national ICT master plan is at an advanced stage should review their monitoring and evaluation procedures and try to optimize them on an ongoing basis.

- Countries that have already defined monitoring and evaluation procedures should make sure that reviews are carried out regularly, including the measurement of related ICT indicators.

National ICT policy reviews help policymakers revise and formulate policies taking into account the evolution of ICTs and their impact on the information economy, in the context of their overall development plans and poverty reduction strategies. UNCTAD highly recommends developing countries to carry out ICT policy reviews to continuously adjust their ICT plans, policies and implementation mechanisms. To support these efforts, UNCTAD, as part of its technical cooperation activities, offers to carry out complete national ICT policy reviews, at the request of and in close cooperation with member States (see box 2.1).

## Annex I

## Core ICT indicators[27].

(a) Core indicators on ICT infrastructure and access

| Basic core | |
|---|---|
| A1 | Fixed telephone lines per 100 inhabitants |
| A2 | Mobile cellular subscribers per 100 inhabitants |
| A3 | Computers per 100 inhabitants |
| A4 | Internet subscribers per 100 inhabitants |
| A5 | Broadband Internet subscribers per 100 inhabitants |
| A6 | International Internet bandwidth per inhabitant |
| A7 | Percentage of population covered by mobile cellular telephony |
| A8 | Internet access tariffs (20 hours per month), in $, and as a percentage of per capita income |
| A9 | Mobile cellular tariffs (100 minutes of use per month), in $, and as a percentage of per capita income |
| A10 | Percentage of localities with public Internet access centres (PIACs) by number of inhabitants (rural/urban) |
| Extended core | |
| A11 | Radio sets per 100 inhabitants |
| A12 | Television sets per 100 inhabitants |

(b) Core indicators on access to, and use of, ICT by households and individuals

| Basic core | |
|---|---|
| HH1 | Proportion of households with a radio |
| HH2 | Proportion of households with a TV |
| HH3 | Proportion of households with a fixed line telephone |
| HH4 | Proportion of households with a mobile cellular telephone |
| HH5 | Proportion of households with a computer |
| HH6 | Proportion of individuals who used a computer (from any location) in the last 12 months |
| HH7 | Proportion of households with Internet access at home |
| HH8 | Proportion of individuals who used the Internet (from any location) in the last 12 months |

| HH9 | Location of individual use of the Internet in the last 12 months |
|---|---|
| | At home |
| | At work |
| | Place of education |
| | At another person's home |
| | Community Internet access facility (specific denomination depends on national practices) |
| | Commercial Internet access facility (specific denomination depends on national practices) |
| | Others |
| HH10 | Internet activities undertaken by individuals in the last 12 months |
| | *Getting information* |
| | About goods or services |
| | Related to health or health services |
| | From government organizations/public authorities via websites or e-mail |
| | Other information or general Web browsing |
| | *Communicating* |
| | *Purchasing or ordering goods or services* |
| | *Internet banking* |
| | *Education or learning activities* |
| | *Dealing with government organizations/public authorities* |
| | *Leisure activities* |
| | Playing/downloading video or computer games |
| | Downloading movies, music or software |
| | Reading/downloading electronic books, newspapers or magazines |
| | Other leisure activities |

**Extended core**

| HH11 | Proportion of individuals with use of a mobile telephone |
|---|---|
| HH12 | Proportion of households with access to the Internet by type of access |
| | Categories should allow an aggregation to narrowband and broadband, where broadband excludes slower speed technologies, such as dial-up modem, ISDN and most 2G mobile phone access. Broadband will usually have an advertised download speed of at least 256 kbit/s. |
| HH13 | Frequency of individual access to the Internet in the last 12 months (from any location) |
| | At least once a day |
| | At least once a week but not every day |
| | At least once a month but not every week |
| | Less than once a month |

(c) Core indicators on the use of ICT by businesses

| Basic core | |
|---|---|
| B1 | Proportion of businesses using computers |
| B2 | Proportion of employees using computers |
| B3 | Proportion of businesses using the Internet |
| B4 | Proportion of employees using the Internet |
| B5 | Proportion of businesses with a Web presence |
| B6 | Proportion of businesses with an intranet |
| B7 | Proportion of businesses receiving orders over the Internet |
| B8 | Proportion of businesses placing orders over the Internet |
| **Extended core** | |
| B9 | Proportion of businesses using the Internet by type of access<br><br>Categories should allow an aggregation to narrowband and broadband, where broadband excludes slower speed technologies, such as dial-up modem, ISDN and most 2G mobile phone access. Broadband will usually have an advertised download speed of at least 256 kbit/s. |
| B10 | Proportion of businesses with a local area network (LAN) |
| B11 | Proportion of businesses with an extranet |
| B12 | Proportion of businesses using the Internet by type of activity<br><br>Sending and receiving e-mail<br>Getting information<br>   About goods or services<br>   From government organizations/public authorities via websites or e-mail<br>   Other information searches or research activities<br>Performing Internet banking or accessing other financial services<br>Dealing with government organizations/public authorities<br>Providing customer services<br>Delivering products online |

(d) Core indicators on ICT sector and trade in ICT goods

| Basic core | |
|---|---|
| ICT1 | Proportion of total business sector workforce involved in the ICT sector |
| ICT2 | Value added in the ICT sector (as a percentage of total business sector value added) |
| ICT3 | ICT goods imports as a percentage of total imports |
| ICT4 | ICT goods exports as a percentage of total exports |

# Annex II

## National ICT plans in developing and transition countries and territories, 2006

| Country/territory | Date | Title of the national ICT plan | Status of the plan |
|---|---|---|---|
| Afghanistan | 2003 | Information and Communication Technologies (ICT) Policy | Under development |
| Albania | 2003 | National Information and Communication Technologies Strategy | Approved |
| Algeria | 2000 | Law n. 2000–03 | Approved |
| Angola | | | Under development |
| Anguilla | 2002 | A Strategic Framework for an Information Economy for Anguilla (Draft) | Under development |
| Antigua and Barbuda | | Information and Communication Technologies (ICTs) Draft Policy | Under development |
| Argentina | 2002 | Estrategia Nacional para la Sociedad de la Información | Approved |
| Armenia | 2001 | ICT Master Strategy for Republic of Armenia | Approved |
| Azerbaijan | 2002 | National Information and Communication Technologies Strategy for the Development of the Republic of Azerbaijan (2003–2012) | Approved |
| Bahamas | 2003 | Policy Statement on Electronic Commerce and the Bahamian Digital Agenda | Approved |
| Bangladesh | 2002 | ICT Policy of Bangladesh | Approved |
| Barbados | 2005 | Barbados' National ICT Strategic Plan (Draft) | Under development |
| Benin | 2000 | Plan de développement de l'Infrastructure d'information et de communication du Bénin 2000–2004 (NICI Plan) | Approved |
| Benin | 2002 | Bénin 2005: Une société de l'Information solidaire, épanouie et ouverte | Approved |
| Bhutan | 1999 | Bhutan Information Technology Strategy (BITS) | Approved |
| Bhutan | 2001 | ICT Master Plan for Bhutan | Approved |
| Bhutan | 2004 | Bhutan Information and Communications Technology Policy and Strategies (BIPS) | Approved |
| Bolivia | 2002 | Estrategia Nacional para la transición hacia una Sociedad de la Información boliviana | Approved |

## Annex II *(continued)*

| | | | |
|---|---|---|---|
| **Bosnia and Herzegovina** | 2004 | Policy, Strategy and Action Plan for the Development of an Information Society in Bosnia and Herzegovina | Approved |
| **Botswana** | | | Under development |
| **Brazil** | 2000 | Information Society in Brazil, Green Book | Approved |
| **Brunei Darussalam** | 2000 | National IT Strategic Plan – IT 2000 and Beyond | Approved |
| | 2005 | Brunei Darussalam Information Society: Strategy Paper | Under development |
| **Bulgaria** | 1999 | National Program for the Information Society Development (IS) | Approved |
| **Burkina Faso** | 1999 | Plan de développement de l'Infrastructure d'information et de communication du Burkina Faso 2000–2004 (NICI Plan) | Approved |
| **Burundi** | 2002 | Projet de stratégie nationale de développement des Technologies de l'Information et de la Communication au Burundi | Approved |
| **Cambodia** | 2004 | Draft ICT Policy Cambodia | Under development |
| **Cameroon** | | | Under development |
| **Cape Verde** | 2000 | Plan National de Développement d'Infrastructure des Technologies d'Information et Communication | Approved |
| **Central African Republic** | | | Under development |
| **Chad** | | | Under development |
| **Chile** | 2003 | Agenda Digital | Approved |
| **China** | 2005 | State Informatization Development Strategy (2006–2020) | Approved |
| **Colombia** | 2000 | Agenda de Conectividad CONPES 3072 | Approved |
| **Comoros** | 2004 | Lettre de politique de développement des Nouvelles Technologies de l'Information et de la Communication (NTIC) 2004–2008 | Approved |
| **Congo** | 2004 | Stratégie nationale pour le développement des TICs au Congo | Under development |
| **Costa Rica** | 2001 | Agenda Digital | Approved |
| **Côte d'Ivoire** | 2000 | Plan de Développement de l'Infrastructure Nationale de l'Information et de la Communication 2000–2005 | Approved |

## Annex II *(continued)*

| | | | |
|---|---|---|---|
| **Croatia** | 2002 | Information and communication technology – Croatia in the 21st century | Approved |
| **Cuba** | 1997 | Lineamientos Estrategicos de Informatización de la Sociedad | Approved |
| **Democratic Republic of the Congo** | | | Under development |
| **Djibouti** | 2003 | Djibouti National ICT Strategy and accompanying Action Plan | Approved |
| **Dominica** | 2005 | Estrategia Nacional para la Sociedad de la Información | Under development |
| **Dominican Republic** | 2003 | Estrategia Nacional para la Sociedad de la Información Dominicana: e-dominicana | Approved |
| **Ecuador** | 2002 | Agenda Nacional de Conectividad Plan de Acción 2005–2010 | Approved |
| **Egypt** | 1999 | National Plan for Communications and Information Technology, incorporates revised Egypt Information Society Initiative (EISI) | Approved |
| **El Salvador** | 2000 | Política Nacional de Informática | Under development |
| **Ethiopia** | 1999 | | Under development |
| **Gabon** | | | Under development |
| **Gambia** | | | Under development |
| **Georgia** | | | Under development |
| **Ghana** | 2005 | The Ghana ICT for Accelerated Development (ICT4AD) Policy | Approved |
| **Grenada** | 2002 | Information and Communication Technology: A Strategy and Action Plan for Grenada 2001–2005 | Approved |
| **Guatemala** | | Propuesta hacia la Iniciativa de la Sociedad de la Información en Guatemala | Under development |
| **Guinea** | 2000 | Plan de développement de l'infrastructure nationale d'information et de communication de la République de Guinée 2001–2004 | Approved |
| **Guyana** | 2001 | Draft Guyana IT Policy | Under development |

## Annex II *(continued)*

| | | | |
|---|---|---|---|
| **Hong Kong (China)** | 1998 | Digital 21 IT Strategy (1998) | Approved |
| | 2001 | Digital 21 IT Strategy (2001) | Approved |
| | 2004 | Digital 21 IT Strategy (2004) | Approved |
| **India** | 1998 | IT Action Plan I: Software; IT Action Plan II: Hardware; and IT Action Plan III: Long-term National IT Policy | Approved |
| **Indonesia** | 2001 | 2001 ICT Policy Framework | Approved |
| **Islamic Republic of Iran** | 2002 | TAKFA — Extension of Application of ICTs in Iran | Approved |
| **Jamaica** | 2002 | A Five Years Strategic Information Technology Plan for Jamaica | Approved |
| **Jordan** | 1999 | REACH | Approved |
| **Kazakhstan** | | | Under develoment |
| **Kenya** | 2006 | Kenya ICT Policy | Approved |
| **Kyrgyzstan** | 2002 | National Strategy Information and Communication Technologies for Development in the Kyrgyz Republic | Approved |
| | 2003 | National ICT Action Plan | Approved |
| **Lao People's Democratic Republic** | | | Under Development |
| **Lebanon** | 2004 | National e-Strategy for Lebanon | Approved |
| **Lesotho** | 2005 | Lesotho ICT Implementation Plan | Approved |
| **Madagascar** | 2005 | Stratégie Nationale des TIC pour le développement | Approved |
| **Malawi** | 2003 | An Integrated ICT-led Socio-Economic Development Policy for Malawi | Approved |
| **Malaysia** | 1996 | The National IT Agenda (NITA) | Approved |
| **Maldives** | 2003 | | Under development |
| **Mali** | 2005 | NICI Policy and Plan documents | Approved |

## Annex II *(continued)*

| | | | |
|---|---|---|---|
| **Mauritania** | 1999 | Plan de développement de l'Infrastructure nationale d'Information et de Communication: 1999–2002 | Approved |
| **Mauritius** | 1998 | National IT Strategy Plan (NITSP) | Approved |
| **Mexico** | 2000 | Sistema Nacional e-México | Approved |
| **Mongolia** | 2000 | National Vision for ICT development of Mongolia up to 2010 ("ICT Vision 2010") | Approved |
| **Morocco** | 2001 | Stratégie Maroc 2005 | Approved |
| **Mozambique** | 2002 | Draft Policy for Information and Communication Technologies | Approved |
| **Myanmar** | 2005 | Myanmar ICT Development Master Plan/Action Plan (draft) | Under development |
| **Namibia** | 2002 | Information and Communication Technology Policy for the Republic of Namibia | Under development |
| **Nepal** | 2000 | Information Technology Policy, 2057 (2000) | Approved |
| **Nicaragua** | 2005 | Estrategia nacional de desarrollo TIC | Approved |
| **Nigeria** | 2000 | Nigerian National Policy for Information Technology (IT) | Approved |
| **Oman** | 2003 | Digital Oman Government Strategy | Approved |
| **Pakistan** | 2000 | 2000 IT Policy & Action Plan | Approved |
| **Panama** | 2003 | Programa e-Panamá | Approved |
| **Peru** | 2001 | Lineamientos de politicas generales para promover la masificación de Internet en el Perú | Approved |
| | 2001 | e-Perú: Propuestas para un plan de acción para el acceso democratico a la Sociedad de la Información y el conocimiento | Approved |
| **Philippines** | 1994 | National Information Technology Plan 2000 | Approved |
| | 1998 | IT21 | Approved |
| | 2003 | e-Philippines: ITECC Strategic Roadmap | Approved |

## Annex II *(continued)*

| | | | |
|---|---|---|---|
| **Qatar** | 2005 | Qatar National ICT Strategy | Approved |
| **Republic of Korea** | 1996 | First Master Plan for Informatization Promotion | Approved |
| | 1999 | CYBER KOREA 21 (Second Master Plan of Infomatization Promotion) | Approved |
| | 2002 | e-Korea Vision 2006 (The Third Master Plan for Informatization) | Approved |
| | 2003 | Broadband IT KOREA VISION 2007 (Revision of the Third Master Plan for Informatization Promotion) | Approved |
| **Republic of Moldova** | 2005 | National Strategy on Building Information Society – "e-Moldova" (2005–2010) | Approved |
| **Romania** | 2002 | National Strategy for the New Economy and the Implementation of the Information Society | Approved |
| **Russian Federation** | 2002 | Electronic Russia (2002–2010) | Approved |
| **Rwanda** | 2001 | An Integrated ICT-led Socio-Economic Development Policy and Plan for Rwanda: 2001–2005 | Approved |
| **Samoa** | 2002 | ICT Policy and Strategic Plan | Approved |
| **Saudi Arabia** | | The National IT Plan (NITP) | Under development |
| **Serbia** | 2005 | National Strategy for an Information Society in Serbia | Under development |
| **Sierra Leone** | | | Under development |
| **Singapore** | 1980 | National Computerisation Plan | Approved |
| | 1986 | National IT Plan | Approved |
| | 1992 | IT2000 | Approved |
| | 2000 | Infocomm 21 | Approved |
| | 2003 | Connected Singapore | Approved |
| | 2006 | iN2015 | Approved |
| **South Africa** | | Strategic Plan 2005–2008 | Approved |

## Annex II *(continued)*

| | | | |
|---|---|---|---|
| **Sri Lanka** | 2005 | e-Sri Lanka Development Project | Approved |
| **Swaziland** | | | Under development |
| **Syrian Arab Republic** | 2006 | National ICT Strategy for Socio-economic Development | Approved |
| **Tajikistan** | 2003 | ICT for Development of the Republic of Tajikistan | Approved |
| **Thailand** | 1996 | IT 2000 Policy (1996–2000) | Approved |
| | 2002 | IT 2010 Policy (2001–2010), National Information and Communication Technoloy (ICT) Master Plan (2002–2006) | Approved |
| **TFYR Macedonia** | 2005 | National Information Society Policy | Approved |
| | 2005 | National Strategy for Information Society Development and Action Plan of the Republic of Macedonia | Approved |
| **Trinidad and Tobago** | 2003 | National ICT Strategy | Approved |
| **Tunisia** | | Stratégie Nationale | Approved |
| **Turkey** | 2005 | | Under development |
| **Uganda** | | | Under development |
| **Ukraine** | 2003 | National Strategy for Information Society Development in Ukraine | Under development |
| **United Republic of Tanzania** | 2003 | Tanzanian National ICT Policy | Approved |
| **Uruguay** | 1999 | Uruguayan National E-Commerce Strategy | Approved |
| **Uzbekistan** | | | Under development |
| **Venezuela** | 2001 | Plan Nacional de Tecnologías de Información | Approved |
| **Viet Nam** | 2002 | Master Plan for Information Technology Use and Development in Vietnam by 2005 | Approved |
| **Yemen** | 2003 | Information Technology Master Plan for Yemen (Draft) | Under development |
| **Zambia** | | | Under development |

## Annex II *(continued)*

| | | | |
|---|---|---|---|
| **Zimbabwe** | | | Under development |

*Source:* Questionnaire sent by UNCTAD to developing countries to collect information on their national ICT master plans and to enquire whether those have been already assessed and extensive Internet research on developing countries' ICT plans and policies. Please note that countries without an explicit ICT master plan are not included in this table, although they might have developed specific sector policies such as e-government programmes.

# References and bibliography

Arab Republic of Egypt, Ministry of Communications and Information Technology (2006). Egypt's best practices in ICT.

Baharul Islam K.M. (2005). National ICT Policies and Plans towards Poverty Reduction: Emerging Trends and Issues, http://www.uneca.org/disd/events/accra/Poverty/ICT%20for%20Poverty%20Reduction-%20Paper%20by%20Baharul%20Islam.pdf.

Bridges (2005). E-readiness assessment: Who is doing what and where?, http://www.bridges.org/ereadiness/where.html.

Cannock G. (2001). Expanding rural telephony: Output-based contracts for pay-phones in Peru, http://www.gpoba.org/docs/06ch1.pdf.

Chaffai El Sghaier G. (2006). Case Study: The Tunisian e-Dinar, ICT, Trade and Economic Growth Forum, Addis Ababa, 14–16 March 2006, http://www.uneca.org/e-trade/main.html.

Dagnino A. (2004). Chile Compra EGP experience, International Conference on e-GP: Lessons Learned, 26–28 October 2004, http://www.mdb-egp.org/data/international.htm.

De Ferranti D., Perry G.E., Gill I.S. et al. (2003). Closing the Gap in Education and Technology, Washington, DC, World Bank.

ECLAC (2003). Building an Information Society: A Latin American and Caribbean Perspective, Santiago de Chile, http://www.eclac.cl.

Gobierno de Chile (2002). Public Procurement System Strategic Plan 2002–2004, https://www.chilecompra.cl/Portal/acerca/fr_acerca_eng.html.

High Level Commission for Information Technology of Nepal (2005). A Fact Book on the Information and Communications Technology Sector of Nepal, http://www.hlcit.gov.np/downloads.php.

Intelcon Research (2005). Universal Access Funds and Service Funds: Insights and experience of international best practice, http://www.inteleconresearch.com/pdf/050713%20-%20universal%20access%20and%20universal%20service%20funds%20v3.pdf.

Inter-American Development Bank (2005). The Role of Information and Communication Technology in Building Trust in Governance: Toward Effectiveness and Results, Tunis, http://csrc.lse.ac.uk/research/IADB_report.pdf.

ITU (2005). Report on the WSIS Stocktaking, http://www.itu.int/wsis/stocktaking/index.html.

ITU (2006a). Frequently asked questions with regard to the World Summit on the Information Society and the associated process, http://www.itu.int/wsis/basic/faqs.asp.

ITU (2006b). ICT indicators: Data and statistics on the ICT/telecommunication sector, http://www.itu.int/ITU-D/ict/informationsharing/index.html.

Maddens S. (2005). The Cost and Funding of Universal Access, presentation in Abuja, 25 February 2005.

Mann C.L. (2004). Information Technology and E-Commerce in Tunisia: Domestic and international challenges and the role for the financial system, report for a project funded by the Commercial Law Democratic Program, US Department of Commerce and the Association of Professional Bankers, Tunisia.

Mena C.L. (2005). ICT as a part of Chile's Strategy for Development: Present Issues and Challenges, Ministry of Economics, Chile,

http://www.ccti-mexcor.org/work/ccti_archivos/lanzamiento_presentaciones/Leonardo_Mena.pdf.

Meso P., Checchi R., Sevcik G., Loch K. and Straub D. (2006). Knowledge Spheres and the Diffusion of National IT Policies, *Electronic Journal on Information Systems in Developing Countries*, Volume 23 (2006), http://www.ejisdc.org/ojs/viewissue.php?id=151.

National Electronics and Computer Technology Center of Thailand (2003). Thailand Information and Communication Technology Master Plan (2002-2006), www.nectec.or.th/pld/masterplan/document/ICT_Masterplan_Eng.pdf.

Nepal Telecommunications Authority (2006). Management Information System (MIS), http://www.nta.gov.np/mis_report.html.

*New Times* (2005). Rwanda: Government to constitute new ICT body, APC Africa ICT Policy Monitor, http://africa.rights.apc.org/index.shtml?apc=21873n21845e_1&x=194393.

OECD (2004a). ICT Diffusion to Business: Peer Review, Country Reports, http://www.oecd.org/document/6/0,2340,en_2649_33757_34227910_1_1_1_1,00.html.

OECD (2004b). Leveraging Telecommunication Policies for Pro-Poor Growth, Universal Access Funds with Minimum-Subsidy Auctions, (Karine Perset).

OECD (2006). ICT use by businesses: Revised OECD Model Survey, http://www.oecd.org/dataoecd/58/7/35867672.pdf.

Orbicom, IDRC, UNDP-APDIP (2005). *Digital Review of Asia Pacific 2005/2006*, Penang, Southbound.

Partnership on Measuring ICT for Development (2005). Core ICT Indicators, http://www.itu.int/ITU-D/ict/partnership/material/CoreICTIndicators.pdf or http://measuring-ict.unctad.org/.

Republic of the Gambia (2002). Strategy for Poverty Alleviation, http://poverty2.forumone.com/files/12016_GambiaPRSP.pdf.

Republic of Ghana (2003). The Ghana ICT for Accelerated Development (ICT4AD) Policy, http://www.uneca.org/aisi/ NICI/Ghana/ghana_consulted.htm.

Rwanda (2005). Review of the implementation of the Rwanda ICT4D/NICI-2005 Plan, http://www.uneca.org/aisi/nici/ Documents/The%20NICI-2005%20Plan%20Review-Final%20Report.pdf.

Sagasti F. (2004). *Knowledge and Innovation for Development: The Sisyphus Challenge of the 21st Century*, Cheltenham, UK, Edward Elgar Publishing.

Tunis Agenda for the Information Society, http://www.itu.int/wsis/docs2/tunis/off/6rev1.html.

United Nations (2004). *Global E-Government Readiness Report 2004: Toward Access for Opportunity*, New York, http://unpan1. un.org/intradoc/groups/public/documents/UN/UNPAN019207.pdf.

United Nations (2005). *Global E-government Readiness Report: From E-government to E-inclusion*, New York, http://www.unpan. org/egovernment5.asp.

UN Millennium Project, Task Force on Science, Technology and Innovation (2005). *Innovation: Applying knowledge in development*, London and Sterling, VA/USA, Earthscan.

UNCTAD (2003). *E-Commerce and Development Report 2003*. United Nations publication, New York and Geneva, http://www. unctad.org/ecommerce.

UNCTAD (2004). *E-Commerce and Development Report 2004*. United Nations publication, New York and Geneva, http://www. unctad.org/ecommerce.

UNCTAD (2005). *World Investment Report 2005. Transnational Corporations and the Internationalization of R&D,* chapter VII, The role of national policies, http://www.unctad.org/Templates/WebFlyer.asp?intItemID=3489&lang=1.

UNDP-APDIP (2004). *An overview of ICT policies and e-strategies of select Asian economies*, New Delhi, Elsevier.

UNDP-APDIP (2005). *ICT policy formulation and e-strategy development: A comprehensive guidebook*, New Delhi, Elsevier.

UNESCO (2005). *UNESCO World Report: Towards Knowledge Societies*, Paris, http://www.unesco.org/publications.

UNESCO Bangkok (2005). *Information Policies in Asia: A Review of Information and Communication Policies in the Asian Region*, Bangkok, http://www2.unescobkk.org/elib/publications/076/Inf_policy.pdf.

World Bank (2002). Universally Bad Service: Providing infrastructure services to rural and poor urban consumers (G.R.G. Clarke and S.J. Wallstern), Policy Research Working paper 2868.

World Bank (2004). Chile: Country Procurement Assessment Report, http://www.worldbank.org.

World Bank (2005a). *E-development: From excitement to effectiveness*, Washington DC, http://www-wds.worldbank.org/servlet/ WDSContentServer/WDSP/IB/2005/11/08/000090341_20051108163202/Rendered/PDF/341470EDevelopment. pdf.

World Bank (2005b). E-Strategies: Monitoring and Evaluation Toolkit, http://www.worldbank.org/ict/.

World Bank (2006). *Information and Communications for Development 2006: Global trends and policies,* Washington DC, www.worldbank.org/ic4d.

# Notes

1.   There is no internationally agreed terminology concerning national government activities on ICTs. Terms such as ICT or e-strategies, programmes, plans and policies are often used interchangeably. Similarly, names of national ICT plans feature all of the above-mentioned terms. In this chapter, we will refer to national ICT "plans" as the documents containing the countries' strategies and policies, and ICT "policies" as the core components describing the measures implemented to enhance access to, use and impact of, ICTs. The proposed national ICT policy reviews will cover an assessment of both the measures and the related implementation mechanisms.

2.   Tunis Agenda for the Information Society, http://www.itu.int/wsis/docs2/tunis/off/6rev1.html.

3.   See annex II.

4.   For a description of e-readiness assessment tools, see http://www.bridges.org/ereadiness/where.html.

5.   http://www.oecd.org/sti/information-economy.

6.   More information is available at http://www.unctad.org/ecommerce.

7.   More information available at http://measuring-ict.unctad.org.

8.   UNCTAD received questionnaire responses from the following 29 countries: Afghanistan, Belize, Brunei, Chile, Cuba, the Democratic Republic of the Congo, the Dominican Republic, Egypt, Ethiopia, Ghana, Guyana, Lesotho, Madagascar, Mauritius, Mexico, Montenegro, Morocco, Oman, Philippines, Qatar, the Republic of Korea, Romania, Sri Lanka, Sudan, Swaziland, the Syrian Arab Republic, Thailand, Trinidad and Tobago, and Ukraine. Out of those countries, 11 had already carried out a review, and 1 country was in the process of doing so. However, there is no information available on the complexity of those reviews.

9.   For more information and a methodological approach on ICT core indicators, refer to the publication on core ICT indicators, Partnership on Measuring ICT for Development, available at http://measuring-ict. unctad.org/QuickPlace/measuring-ict/Main.nsf/h_Index/21B143B6971D3863C12570C70037130A/ ?OpenDocument&Form=h_PageUI.

10.   Chapter 2, E-business and SMEs, ECDR 2004, available at  http:/www.unctad.org/ecommerce.

11.   See also *E-Commerce and Development Report 2004,* chapter 7, A case study on Tunisia's ICT sector and related policies.

12.   See also *E-Commerce and Development Report 2003,* chapter 3, ICT strategies for development, available at http:/ www.unctad.org/ecommerce.

13.   For more on e-government, see ECDR 2004, at http://www.unctad.org/ecommerce.

14.   http://www.unpan.org/egovernment5.asp.

15.   http://www.mdec.com.my/.

16.   Pioneer Companies with MSC Status:  Sun Microsystems, Telekom Malaysia MSC, MIMOS and NTT MSC. Others with MSC Status: Microsoft, Oracle MSC, HP, Netscape, Ericsson, Intel MSC, MEASAT, Sumitomo, NEC, NCR, Lotus, Digital Equipment, EDS, Nortel, Siemens, Fujitsu, DHL, Astro, ICON, Sapura, Sime, Motorola, Binariang, Newbridge, IBM, Lotus, ATI, BT Multimedia, Lucent Technologies, Bridgestone, Nokia, EDS, MCSB, Unisys, etc., http://www.mdc.com.my/cs/company/default.asp.

17. UN Millennium Project, Task Force on Science, Technology and Innovation (2005, p. 15), referring to Sagasti (2004).

18. In this context, one example might be the initiative of the Science and Development Network (http:www. scidev.net), which aims at providing information and recommendations about how science and technology can contribute to economic and social development.

19. For a more in-depth discussion on the role of national policies in R&D, see UNCTAD (2005).

20. UNESCO (2005, p. 100).

21. UNESCO (2005, p. 99).

22. OECD Informal Expert Meeting on ICTs for Poverty Reduction (7 July 2004), ICTs in Poverty Reduction Strategy Paper (PRSPs) as of January 2004.

23. Mena (2005).

24. World Bank (2006, p. 93).

25. National Electronics and Computer Technology Center (2003, p. 81).

26. National Electronics and Computer Technology Center (2003, p. 81).

27. Partnership on Measuring ICT for Development, available at http://measuring-ict.unctad.org/QuickPlace/ measuring-ict/Main.nsf/h_Index/21B143B6971D3863C12570C70037130A/?OpenDocument&Form=h_ PageUI.

# CHAPTER 3

# PRO-POOR ICT POLICIES AND PRACTICES

## A. Introduction

Information and communication technologies (ICTs) have opened up new opportunities to alleviate poverty and have changed the way in which poverty reduction efforts take place.

There are many examples of how ICTs are enhancing the livelihoods of people living in poverty. In Bolivia, agricultural and market price information shared through the radio and the Internet is giving small producers more negotiating power and is increasing the efficiency of their production methods (International Institute for Communication and Development (IICD), 2005). ICTs are bringing valuable environmental information to rural populations, including weather forecasts for agriculture and fisheries or early warnings on natural disasters.

ICTs provide increased opportunities to access health and education services and are reducing the vulnerabilities to sickness and unemployment of people living in poverty. For instance, in Ginnack, a remote island village on the Gambia River, nurses use a digital camera to take pictures of symptoms for examination by a doctor in a nearby town (Harris, 2004). In Brazil's urban slums, the Committee to Democratize Information Technology[1] has trained more than 25,000 young students every year in ICT skills that give them better opportunities for jobs, education and life changes (Harris, 2004).

Governments and civil society organizations are becoming more effective in their poverty reduction efforts by using ICTs to manage knowledge, share best practices and communicate more effectively. In India, the computerization of land ownership is allowing farmers cheaper and quicker access to statements of land holdings.[2] Civil society organizations are, on behalf of the poor, mobilizing support through the Internet. ICTs are being used to draw attention to the needs of those living in poverty and to lobby policymakers. In Sierra Leone, women's groups are broadcasting their concerns and needs through radio (see box 3.5).

However, the extent to which ICTs can contribute to poverty reduction is contested. Different misconceptions surround the role of ICTs in poverty reduction and their contribution to the Millennium Development Goals: from "ICTs are not relevant for poverty reduction" to "Telecentres are reducing poverty" (see box 3.1). The aim of this chapter is to help clarify those misconceptions and review to what extent, and how, ICTs can help alleviate poverty.

Although ICTs offer vast development opportunities, those most in need of ICTs (low income groups, rural communities, women, people with no formal education) often have the least access to them. Women in almost every country fall behind in access to, use of and profit from the Internet. They "represent less than 10 per cent of the Internet users in Guinea and Djibouti, less than 20 per cent in Nepal, and less than one-quarter in India" (Huyer et al., 2005). People living in rural

---

### Box 3.1

### Misconceptions about ICTs and poverty

"ICTs are not useful for poverty reduction".

"ICTs for development efforts are supporting poverty reduction".

"Competitive markets will bring ICTs for all".

"Telecentres are reducing poverty".

"ICT policies are gender-neutral".

"Increased Internet penetration will bring an increased proportion of women online".

areas are also often neglected. "In 2004, only 1,000 of the 142,000 Senegalese villages were connected to the telephone network, and most fixed lines (63 per cent) were concentrated in its capital Dakar, which represents only a quarter of the population" (Sagna, 2005). And usually only the better educated have the most chances of using the Internet. For instance, "in Chile, 89 per cent of Internet users have tertiary education" (UNDP, 2001). Furthermore, if people living in poverty cannot benefit from ICTs, there will be another missed opportunity to achieve the Millennium Development Goals and halve poverty by 2015.

The following analysis looks at the latest thinking and practices regarding the use of ICTs for poverty reduction, focusing particularly on ICT policies and programmes aimed at the poor. It aims at informing policymakers about best practices and providing recommendations for institutional development in order to further ICTs for poverty reduction. The leading questions are:

- What does the term "pro-poor ICTs" mean?

- Which are the best-practice pro-poor ICT policies and interventions?

- Which framework can be used to assess whether a given ICT intervention is pro-poor?

- Which institutional handicaps are hindering the use of ICTs for poverty alleviation?

- How can international organizations, national Governments and civil society further support pro-poor ICTs?

The chapter starts by examining the concept of ICTs for poverty reduction and pro-poor ICTs. Section C reviews current thinking, illustrated with best-practice examples, on pro-poor ICT strategies and actions, and analyses the validity of the above-mentioned ICT misconceptions. Section D critically reviews current institutional handicaps that prevent the stronger development and implementation of pro-poor ICT policies and programmes. Section E provides a framework to help policymakers and other actors include a strong pro-poor component in their ICT policies and interventions. Section F offers fundamental policy recommendations for institutional development to promote ICTs for poverty reduction. To illustrate the different concepts and the framework, two case studies will be used throughout the chapter: the TIC Bolivia Country Programme (see box 3.4) and the Development through Radio programme for women in Sierra Leone (see box 3.5).

## B.   The concept of pro-poor ICTs

Throughout history poverty has been defined and measured in diverse ways based on diverse assumptions. It is important to understand the different definitions, as they have different implications for poverty reduction policies and for how ICTs can contribute to poverty alleviation. Box 3.2 summarizes the definitions of poverty and the related policy approaches to alleviate it.

The monetary approach to poverty is often used in macroeconomic studies because it is easy to measure and to use in modelling. However, it leaves out of the analysis many other factors that influence poverty (education, health, political space, security etc.). The capability approach is valuable for considering these multiple variables, but its measuring is limited by the arbitrariness of the basic capabilities chosen and the sets of data available. Social exclusion approaches (which concentrate on understanding how individuals or groups are excluded from their community) and social institutions (which focus on designing and implementing policies according to beneficiaries' own perceptions of their needs) also attempt to address the various dimensions of poverty but both are difficult to compare across communities and countries – what works in one community will not necessarily work in another community. Participatory approaches, favoured in the design and implementation of poverty reduction programmes, are also questioned with regard to who participates, how representative they are and how to deal with disagreements (Ruggeri Laderchi et al., 2003; OU, 2005a).

Today (and in this chapter), poverty is broadly understood as multidimensional, not merely material, deprivation encompassing a lack of essential needs (lack of income, lack of access to health and education) as well as increased insecurity and vulnerability to external events, and powerlessness to voice concerns and introduce change (World Bank, 2001; SIDA, 2005). Poverty reduction involves expanding the "capabilities that a person has, that is, the substantive freedoms he or she enjoys to lead the kind of life he or she has reason to value" (Sen, 1999, p. 87).

Thus, this chapter will be based on the capability approach and will examine how ICTs can expand the capabilities of the poor. But it will also consider two major contributions from the social exclusion approach – understanding the process by which multiple deprivation occurs –, and the participative

## Box 3.2

## Key poverty concepts[3]

**Four different approaches to poverty alleviation.**

- *Monetary poverty*: A shortfall in consumption (or income) from a poverty line.

    Approach: Policies promoting economic growth and the distribution of income

    Measured by: People living on under $1 a day (extreme poverty)

    People living on under $2 a day (poverty)

- *Capability poverty*: Restriction of the "capabilities that a person has, that is, the substantive freedoms he or she enjoys" (Sen, 1999)

    Approach: Promote multiple capabilities (health, education, political space etc.)

    Measured by:  UNDP Human Development Index

    UNDP Human Poverty Index

- *Social exclusion*: "Process through which individuals or groups are wholly or partially excluded from full participation in the society in which they live" (European Foundation, 1995)

    Approach: Understand the process by which multiple deprivation occurs

    Measured by: The "Poverty Audit" White Paper (set of indicators)

    The Millennium Poverty and Social Exclusion Survey

- *Participatory methods*: Get people themselves to participate in decisions about what it means to be poor and the magnitude of poverty (Chambers, 1997)

    Approach: Use participatory processes

    Measured by: Participatory poverty assessments

**Two measures of poverty alleviation**

- *Absolute poverty alleviation:* The position of those living in poverty improves
    Approach: Promote overall economic growth and development

- *Relative poverty alleviation:* The position of the poor improves at a higher rate than that of the general population
    Approach: Redistribution and reducing inequality

---

[3] For further examination of the concept of poverty see Maxwell (1999)

*Source:* IDRC (2003); Sen (1999); Ruggeri Laderchi et al. (2003); Lessof and Jowell (2000); SIDA (2005).

method, namely the importance of people who live in poverty participating in poverty reduction processes.

In dealing with the impact that ICTs have on poverty, it is crucial to accept that "Poverty is the result of economic, political and social processes that interact with each other and frequently reinforce each other ... requiring a broader, more comprehensive strategy to fight it" (World Bank, 2001 p. 6). It is also crucial to acknowledge that efforts to reduce poverty must question who benefits as well as who is excluded from a policy or intervention (OU, 2005a, p. 89), and should be aimed at addressing power inequality by providing the poor with the necessary policy space.

Policy space concerns institutions and discourses, as well as practices that influence decision-making and programme implementation (Engberg-Pedersen and Webster, 2002).

This chapter differentiates between development and poverty alleviation endeavours. Development efforts aim at enhancing the capabilities of a society at large, whereas poverty reduction goes one step further by aiming to enhance the capabilities of the poor. Poverty reduction efforts focus on reducing inequality, promoting economic opportunities and security for the poor, fostering their health and education, and empowering people living in poverty.

Moreover, within the capability approach to poverty alleviation, how these efforts take place is also important,[4] including developing the agency of the poor by nourishing participatory and people-centred approaches, promoting partnerships, and supporting sustainable, differentiated (characteristics of poverty and appropriate policy responses differ among different groups of the poor) and dynamic approaches.

What, then, is the impact of ICTs on poverty alleviation? The general impact of ICTs on development is now acknowledged. They provide access and means to exploit information and create knowledge. They are helping accelerate productivity gains and access to health information or educational services, and are modifying the way people learn and interact, and exchange and voice their interests. The question today is, how are ICTs expanding the capabilities of the poor? How can ICTs support poverty reduction efforts such as those related to the Millennium Development Goals or national poverty reduction strategies?

ICTs have the potential to contribute to poverty reduction, by:[5]

(1) Supporting general growth and development processes, such as increased productivity or improved labour utilization;

(2) Enhancing efficiencies in specific sectors, such as rural livelihoods or infrastructure;

(3) Complementing specific pro-poor activities, such as supporting rural health extension programmes or micro-credit activities;

(4) Directly enhancing poor livelihoods; and

(5) Helping address barriers to poverty reduction, such as corruption or natural vulnerabilities.

The first two dimensions refer to the general contribution that ICTs can make to general economic growth and social development, but it should be noted that "in some cases the poor benefit proportionally less than the non poor" (OECD, 2005). The last three dimensions, however, specifically deal with poor livelihoods (UNDP APDIP, 2005).

Governments have built up and put in place ICT strategies for development (**ICT4D**), which have focused on creating an enabling environment for the broad uptake of ICTs. But for ICTs to also accrue for poverty reduction, more specific actions are needed. These specific efforts directed at ensuring that people living in poverty can also benefit from ICTs and at ensuring that ICTs help reduce poverty are recognized as ICTs for poverty reduction (**ICT4P**) (IDRC, 2003). Within these efforts there are ICT policies and programmes aimed at groups of people living in poverty, such as rural communities, disabled people and women, which are known as **pro-poor ICT policies and programmes** (see box 3.3 for an outline of these concepts). While the borderlines dividing these three categories are blurred, it is important to point out that not all ICTs for development efforts address the needs of people living in poverty.

Developing a common understanding of what poverty and pro-poor ICTs mean is a first step towards alleviating poverty. Then, it is necessary to be familiar with which are best practices in pro-poor ICT approaches.

---

## Box 3.3

## ICT4D, ICT4P and pro-poor ICT policies and programmes

**ICT4D:** Harnessing ICTs for economic growth and broad development.

*Example:* Policies to develop ICT infrastructure.

- **ICT4P:** More focused efforts to bring ICT access and its benefits to poor communities (*Pro-poor ICTs*) and using ICTs in ways which support poverty reduction.

  *Example:* A programme that uses ICTs to share knowledge on poverty issues, such as an Internet website providing health professionals with valuable information on local epidemics.

  - **Pro-poor ICT policies and programmes:** Those ICT policies and programmes aimed at people living in poverty (rural communities, marginalized groups etc.).

    *Example:* Policies or programmes providing affordable ICT access, the necessary skills and relevant content to women living in poor communities.

## C.   Current thinking and realities regarding pro-poor ICTs

This section presents the current thinking on ICTs for poverty reduction based on a review of the existing literature and case examples. This review is complemented by a discussion of best practices in two areas of major concern for reducing poverty, namely gender and rural development, in order to offer more insights regarding the impact and experience of pro-poor ICT interventions and to test some of the theoretical thinking.

### ICTs as a tool for poverty reduction

Literature and policy strategies[6] identify ICTs as a tool for poverty reduction, rather than an end in itself. ICTs have the capability to make poverty reduction activities more efficient. For example, by collecting and processing information in rural areas, health extension programmes can better assess and monitor health, and thus take the appropriate actions. The goal is to reduce morbidity and mortality, and to make citizens healthier through basic health education rather than having well equipped extension workers. Governments are responsible for fostering growth, reducing inequalities and providing security in the best way possible, and ICTs are a tool and strategy but not the objective.

### ICTs are necessary but insufficient for poverty alleviation

To extend the capabilities of the poor and to ensure that they can benefit from ICTs other conditions are also needed. UNDP APDIP (2005) points to conditions that are needed both at the government level and at the level of programme implementers. Some of these conditions include the existence of an enabling environment, political will, and ICT and other basic infrastructure, as well as management and technical skills.

### Pro-poor ICT efforts must be embedded in poverty reduction initiatives

If ICTs are to be a tool for development and poverty reduction, ICT strategies must be consistent with poverty reduction strategies. Pro-poor ICT policies make more sense if they are part of a national Poverty Reduction Strategy Paper (PRSP) or other national development strategies, which reflect the commitment that a national Government makes to reduce poverty. A PRSP, a concept promoted by the World Bank and the International Monetary Fund, is a long-term national strategy developed through broad consultation, which provides guidance to Governments and donors on a country's priorities for poverty reduction. Chapter 2 shows the case of The Gambia, whose national ICT strategy supports the objectives of its national PRSP. The UN system, as a major player in poverty reduction efforts, may also consider incorporating ICTs into its national assessments (Common Country Assessment (CCA)) and strategies (United Nations Development Assistance Framework (UNDAF)).

Mainstreaming ICTs into development and poverty reduction policies means looking at how ICTs can help achieve agreed poverty reduction objectives: how they can assist with the achievement of secondary education objectives, how they can support primary health care or the control of key infectious diseases, how they can help with the development of key economic sectors, how they can facilitate national governance, and so forth.

The World Bank, as part of its support to governments in putting in place PRSPs, has developed a number of suggestions about how ICTs should be incorporated into PRSPs, including promoting access to ICTs by reducing supply and demand constraints, incorporating ICTs into the broader governance reform agenda, prioritizing, and monitoring and evaluating in order to understand ICTs' impact on poverty reduction (World Bank PRSP Sourcebook, chapter 24).

However, in practical terms, it is not so straightforward to include ICTs in national poverty reduction strategies. For instance, the United Nations system's national assessments and strategies (CCA/UNDAF) have concentrated on social and humanitarian issues and their economic content, and the inclusion of ICT considerations has been limited, partly because of the excessively modest contribution of the United Nations entities with limited country-level presence, such as DESA, UNCTAD and the regional commissions (United Nations, 2004, para. 88).

Moreover, PRSPs' effectiveness in reducing poverty is still questioned. While PRSPs may have promoted improved policy processes, there are still practical issues – for example, the extent of participation, ownership, timing and resources provided – and substantive concerns (for instance, about the impact of the extended conditionality and the underlying macroeconomic framework). There are also more fundamental questions about the actual ownership of donor-driven processes and the effectiveness of participatory processes in committing Governments to efficient poverty reduction policies (Booth, 2005).

### ICT-related interventions should be based on poverty reduction principles

"ICT enthusiasts … must ensure that poverty-reduction good practice is incorporated into any ICT initiative" (OECD, 2005, p. 14) Good practice includes developing a comprehensive approach, promoting the participation of beneficiaries, making sure that the programme or policy is relevant to the local context, and guaranteeing the accountability of policymakers, donors and programme implementers. Multidisciplinary approaches involving different actors have the advantage of providing further resources and strength to the ICT policy or programme. Involving beneficiaries in the design, implementation and evaluation of ICT programmes can yield increased and sustainable results. Adapting good ICT programmes to the local context, needs and resources available is a way to help increase the impact and sustainability of the programme. And only when donors, Governments, the private sector and non-profit organizations are accountable to the beneficiaries for the policies and programmes they adhere to and implement (or not), will there be long-lasting results.

ICTs will not by themselves turn bad development into good development, but can reinforce good development practices (Harris, 2004). For example, establishing an online forum will not necessarily reinforce communications among different stakeholders, and hence development, if there is no interest in open dialogue.

### Addressing sustainability: A major concern

The financial, technical, institutional and sociocultural sustainability of ICT programmes continues to be a major concern in the design of ICT policies and programmes and their impact on poverty alleviation. Financial sustainability concerns require that there be a focus on self-financing programmes so as to not distort competition, and in the hope that it will bring better services. However, the self-financing objectives clash with the very low income that poor communities have, in particular, for infrastructural programmes that require large investments. The fast pace of change

in ICTs requires continuous investments to upgrade equipment and skills in order to continue to benefit from them. Culturally, the demands of working in partnership and involving beneficiaries as well as the competing objectives of donors, policymakers and other stakeholders also endanger the sustainability of ICT policies and programmes.

Governments and donors tend to promote ICT programmes that will ultimately be able to continue without external financial or staffing support.[8] And while the design, implementation and evaluation of policies and programmes should take into account programme sustainability, this should not jeopardize the primary objective of reducing poverty, by for example asking for fees that the poor cannot afford. Innovative approaches, such as sharing connection costs or providing multiple services, are often required in order to ensure financial sustainability and also that the poorer benefit from the ICT programme.

The choice of technology and software is crucial for the technical sustainability of ICT programmes. The use of low-cost, simple and traditional technologies is often recommended (World Bank, 2002; Gerster and Zimmermann, 2005), one reason for this being its advantages in building capacities, as well as the use of free and open source software (FOSS) since it allows the adaptation of the software to future needs and does not require an onerous upgrade of software or hardware (UNCTAD, 2003).

Different initiatives,[9] such as the Indian Simputer, the Jhai PC,[10] the $100 laptop supported by MIT Lab[11] and the Brazilian PC Conectado,[12] are developing or making available low-cost (even free[13]) computers. At first sight, these programmes appeal to pro-poor ICT efforts to offer affordable computers to poor people. However, a closer look shows that each model has substantially different objectives and strategies – from making computers commercially available to wholesaling them only to Governments for their use by schoolchildren, and from designing low-cost and durable hardware to providing incentives such as tax-free computers – and, therefore, the initiatives may achieve different results.

From a poverty alleviation perspective, the success of any of these schemes should be judged on the extent to which the production efforts are accompanied by complementary efforts aimed at making them available, affordable and meaningful to the poorest people. Cheap computers alone will not benefit the poor. Computers may not necessarily reach the poor and, without further support (to ensure that the necessary IT, reading or language skills, relevant content and access to the Internet and electricity are available), they may not enhance the capabilities of a poor community.

The **Pro-poor ICTs Framework** (see section E) can help assess the extent to which a particular low-cost computer initiative may be supporting poverty reduction by pointing to major questions, including the following: Who will benefit? Who will retain control (i.e. regarding hardware/software development)? Who will provide training and support? How will it affect current power structures? How will it impact on the local ICT (both manufacturing and services) sector?

### *Different technologies contribute differently to poverty reduction*

Different technologies have different characteristics and thus have different impacts on the poor. The impact that radio or television, for example, have on the poor is unlike that of the Internet. While radio and television are mostly one-way communication tools, the Internet allows for two-way, synchronous and asynchronous, interaction managed by the user. On the other hand, illiterate people may better benefit from mobiles, radio or TV educational programmes than from access to the Internet. For example, mobile phones have allowed telephone access for smaller entrepreneurs in Africa and are proving to be a valuable business tool.[14]

More significant is how innovative pro-poor ICT approaches are maximizing the impact of different technologies by combining them (Mathison, 2005; Girard, 2005). In low-income countries, as more people have access to radio than to computers, local development programmes aiming at serving rural information needs, such as the Kothmale Community Radio Internet Project in Sri Lanka,[15] use the Internet to search for information and the radio to disseminate it. In this project, listeners can send questions to the radio (i.e. via the post or telephone), and the radio station team looks for the answers on the Internet, translates them into the local language and broadcasts them.

### *Expand impact by scaling up thriving pro-poor ICT projects*

There is now some experience of pro-poor ICT programmes at the micro level, and an increased interest in finding ways to multiply and scale up good practices and amplify the impact that successful pilot projects have in alleviating poverty. How can successful ICT programmes be replicated in other areas? What actions and policies can support the scaling up of ICT programmes for the poor?

Gerster and Zimmermann (2005) provide four basic recommendations for scaling up ICT programmes:

1. The promotion of an enabling ICT policy environment;

2. High priority assigned to ICTs for poverty reduction;

3. Appropriate technology choices; and

4. Mobilization of additional public and private resources.

### *Support needed at all levels*

If ICTs are to contribute to poverty alleviation, action is needed at different levels. Governments are expected to provide the enabling environment for the uptake and use of ICTs by, inter alia, putting in place the necessary mechanisms to ensure that ICT infrastructure reaches the poor communities; the private sector is expected to contribute to the deployment of infrastructure as well as the provision of services; and civil society is expected to manage programmes, advocate, and promote grass-roots knowledge. Given the large costs involved, donor Governments also have a role in supporting ICT programmes that benefit the poor and in mainstreaming ICTs in their donor strategies.

In this regard, multi-stakeholder partnerships involving civil society, the private sector and Governments are seen as fundamental in being able to respond to the need for resources and the complexity of tasks (Gerster and Zimmermann, 2005).

### *Policies and programmes must be context-specific*

The effectiveness and the sustainability of pro-poor ICT initiatives depend on their being able to consider and adapt to the sociocultural, legal, political and economic context. One-size-fits-all approaches for the uptake and use of ICTs run the danger of not being adapted to the reality of the poor and not serving their needs. Pro-poor ICT approaches have to be linked to the local context. A review by the Overseas Development Institute (Chapman and Slaymaker, 2002) of ICTs in rural development stresses the need for flexible and decentralized models for using ICTs. As a study (Gov3, 2005) of government schemes to increase adoption of home computers shows, simply transferring an approach from one country to another does not guarantee immediate success.

### Focused research on pro-poor ICTs is essential

Qualitative and quantitative research on the impact of ICTs for poverty reduction, and on which pro-poor ICT policies and programmes are most effective, help policymakers, donors and civil society in their decisions. Case studies have shown how ICT programmes work for the poor. Some macro analyses reveal the status of the digital divide. However, there is insufficient research focused on pro-poor ICTs.[16] More information is needed in order to understand how to scale up ICT programmes, what is the impact of ICTs on the lives of the poor, and what are the negative externalities that ICT4D initiatives may have on the poor. For a deeper and more thorough analysis, it is necessary to have empirical studies on the relationship between ICTs and poverty; to have information and research disaggregated by gender, rural/urban and other poor communities as well as by different types of technologies; to study the micro and macro impacts; and to examine the links and integration of ICT strategies with poverty reduction strategies.[17]

So far, we have discussed current views on pro-poor ICTs from a general perspective. However, the poor are a broad category. The following section will therefore provide further insights regarding how ICTs can enhance the capabilities of two categories of people living in poverty: the rural poor and poor women.

## 1. ICTs benefiting the rural poor

Most of the poor live in rural areas,[18] which are areas the least likely to enjoy access to ICTs. For instance, in 2002, 97 per cent of Internet users in Indonesia and 90 per cent in the Philippines lived in urban areas.[19] The newer ICTs arrive first in the main cities, and often never get to rural areas,[20] thus creating a tension between the opportunity to integrate citizens into global society which is offered by ICTs and the threat of exclusion through the strengthening of the hegemony of the elite and widening of the urban–rural divide[21].

Although a couple of pages cannot do justice to the existing knowledge about ICTs for rural development,

the next paragraphs highlight various attempts to bridge the rural digital divide and current thinking in this field.

Populations living in rural areas particularly suffer from structural infrastructure deficiencies, which condition their access to ICTs. National Governments have been undertaking during the last decade a plethora of efforts to create an enabling environment and a competitive telecommunications sector, including the privatization of the incumbent telecommunications agency, the liberalization of the market and the creation of an independent regulator. Additionally, since it is clear that market mechanisms alone will not provide affordable universal access[22] (see Spence, 2005; OECD, 2004b), Governments have established different universal access mechanisms to ensure that non-profitable areas are also served. Regulation for universal access is yet to provide positive and wide-reaching results in many countries[23] for a variety of reasons: several countries are still in the process of fully adopting regulatory measures; implementation has been feeble, particularly because of weak institutions; and over-regulation is preventing alternative flexible options such as VoIP and radio bands for community radio (Spence, 2005) from operating efficiently. As telecommunications infrastructure will generally benefit the better-off first, ensuring that it also services the poor requires continued and progressive efforts, in terms of policy, regulation and implementation, to provide increased access, at affordable rates, to existing and newer technologies.

For the provision of universal access, one of the approaches receiving most attention is the so-called competitive bidding for Universal Access funds,[24] whereby operators bid to service rural zones and are compensated for doing so. This approach, already successful, in terms of meeting universal access targets, in several Latin American countries[25] and currently being tested in Uganda, supports a competitive telecommunications sector while at the same time ensuring that unprofitable areas are also connected. However, its implementation requires a strong institution able to administer the fund independently, with the knowledge necessary for designing the auction and identifying less attractive regions in order to bundle them with more attractive ones, as well as able to monitor and evaluate the services delivered, and take the necessary measures if the obligations are not fulfilled.

General recommendations to develop ICT infrastructure for poverty reduction include taking a rural-client approach that focuses on the needs of rural communities, providing the necessary space for initiative to take place through decentralization, and encouraging experimentation with different mechanisms (ODI, 2002).

The other major instruments to provide universal access to ICTs are public access models such as telecentres or mobile access points. These instruments, developed by private entrepreneurs and by not-for-profit players, exist in a myriad of forms (from new for-profit telecentres to the integration of ICTs in existing community centres/programmes or the creation of a computer laboratory in a school), and they offer different types of services (communication, information, education and community development) to different extents. The advantage of public access models lies in their ability to bring ICTs to a larger number of users, but it is important to note their different approaches and impact on poverty reduction. Models range from private to community-owned telecentres:[26] at one extreme, private entrepreneurship models are promoted for encouraging financially sustainable projects through natural selection (Schware, 2003); at the other extreme, community-based networks "potentially [offer] significantly larger benefits, especially in a development context" (Ó Siochrú and Girard, 2005, p. 12) as they mobilize resources, require a lower return on investment, any surplus is reinvested in the programme, their services and applications are based on needs, and they contribute to further development activities (Ó Siochrú and Girard, 2005).

If telecentres are to be catalysts for poverty reduction they need to be used by and serve the needs of those living in poverty, including rural populations, women or illiterate citizens. A study of telecentres[27] in five African countries[28] (Etta and Parvyn-Wamahiu, 2003) showed that users only represented a small percentage of the population and that there were disadvantages based on age, gender, education, literacy levels and socioeconomic levels. The barriers to using the telecentres included the following: the high cost of services, particularly important for women, the unemployed, students and poor community members; inadequate physical facilities with no privacy; poor management of the telecentre, including lack of trained staff; limited opening hours; inappropriate location, which increases safety concerns and transport costs; poor publicity for the telecentres and the services offered; and the perception that telecentres are places for the educated, given that most Internet content available is in English. More importantly, telecentres were mainly used for social purposes (communication and entertainment), professional and economic purposes being of

secondary importance. In this regard, if the objective is to bring the information economy to the rural communities, it will be worth considering where access to ICTs should be provided (for example, an existing agricultural information centre may be a more suitable option than the creation of a separate centre).

Thus, the notion that telecentres are reducing poverty is a misconception. Telecentres, and other ICT initiatives, can contribute to poverty reduction when accompanied by poverty alleviation efforts that open the telecentre to the poor, supply them with relevant and accessible content, provide additional support (such as ICT skills training) and ensure that the telecentre is well managed, maintained and sustainable. The expansion of ICTs through existing development initiatives and structures, such as the Grameen mobile phone scheme in Bangladesh, where local women earn an income from renting mobile phone services (Chapman et al., 2003, p. 19), is facilitating their uptake as well as more directly serving poverty reduction objectives by, inter alia, providing women with a job opportunity.

The poverty dimension should be included in the design and evaluation of telecentres and other ICT programmes. Are the poor using the telecentre? If so, for what purposes? How is it changing their livelihoods? What could be done to ensure that the poor benefit from the programme? Issues such as the location of the telecentre, who manages it, community ownership, opening hours, cost of services, and the content and format of material available have a direct impact on who can benefit from the telecentre. Moreover, perceptions and awareness are also important. Often telecentres are perceived as being relevant only to educated men. Evaluating[29] these aspects and introducing simple measures can make a considerable difference: allocating special times for women, employing female staff, having longer opening hours, having different types of materials, and, more importantly, materials of direct relevance to poor communities, and providing basic ICT literacy training increase the participation of the poor and the impact that ICT programmes have on alleviating poverty.

As mentioned earlier, scaling up good practices and successfully working at the meso level (that is, being able to efficiently work with other organizations between the micro and macro environments) expand the positive contribution of ICTs to reducing poverty and reduce inequality by increasing the opportunities to access and use ICTs. For instance, a study of information services in China found that it was "difficult for information services to produce large-scale effects because of

---

## Box 3.4

## The TIC Bolivia Country Programme (www.ticbolivia.net)

The TIC Bolivia Country Programme supported by the International Institute for Communication and Development (IICD) aims at helping local communities develop sector-wide ICT strategies, design and implement projects, and improve their ICT skills and knowledge. The programme comprises fifteen projects in three sectors (agriculture and rural development, education and governance) carried out by partner organizations. These implementing partners also collaborate with each other to share what they have learned and build an enabling environment for ICTs in Bolivia, without which the projects could not succeed. The main forum for this sharing of experiences is Red TICBolivia, a national ICT network. Through this platform, partners raise awareness about the relevance of ICTs for the country's development, lobby ministries about the importance of considering ICTs in their sector policies, and search for practical and affordable connectivity solutions in rural areas. The partners often undertake evaluation and training together in order to learn from each other's experiences.

The programme activities in the agricultural sector provide access to ICTs and agricultural information and help the Ministry of Agriculture develop and implement an ICT strategy for the agricultural sector. A users' questionnaire reveals that 58 per cent of respondents experienced a direct positive economic impact, mainly because better access to market price information had improved their negotiation position and also because it had increased the efficiency of their production methods.

---

*Source:* IICD (2005).

limited organisation among farmers" (Yongling, 2004). A recent review of an ICT programme in Bolivia (see box 3.4) working at the meso level and mainly in rural areas finds that building institutional and ICT capacities, that is complementing technical training with the development of management skills, is essential, and that involving end users early and often is necessary in order to ensure that the project meets the needs of the beneficiaries and to enable them to take ownership. Also, the review suggests that strategic alliances be cultivated with other organizations in order to pool resources (and, for example, share satellite services costs); that there be more effective lobbying and learning from each other; that there be engagement with policymakers and that elements of the projects (such as negotiating the expansion of telecentres and ICT training) be embedded at the regional and national levels to support long-lasting results and scale up good practice.

Some of the main challenges that the ICT Bolivia programme still faces, and which those developing pro-poor ICT programmes may take into account, are the following: reaching target groups (that is, the poorest communities and women), working with less experienced local partner organizations and managing the difficulties of working in a multi-stakeholder environment. Moreover, the programme constantly has to find and retain qualified staff and address financial sustainability.

This chapter will now discuss how ICTs can enhance the capabilities of women and men, and how women and girls continue to benefit less. It will also provide an overview of best practices to ensure that ICT policies and programmes include a gender perspective.

## 2. Women, gender and ICTs

Women are a central figure in poverty and its alleviation. Among poor people women are in the majority. But women are also one of the main actors in poverty reduction – empowering women means providing opportunities for them, and also their children and families. And because *"women are not likely to benefit equitably from such [ICT] projects unless special efforts are made to (i) identify their situation and needs and (ii) take effective action to incorporate their participation"* (Hafkin, 2002a), this section is devoted to reviewing the impact of ICT policies and programmes on women and poverty reduction.

ICTs can be a tool for the empowerment of women and gender equality. Women in post-war Sierra Leone are using the radio (see box 3.5) to express their needs and collectively find solutions to their problems. Through this medium, these women have been trained and sensitized regarding HIV/AIDS and have received support in establishing market centres (Wambui, 2005). ICTs are also offering women new working opportunities, enabling them to become small business owners or work in ICT-enabled services.[30] In education, new ICTs allow the adaptation of learning processes and contents to the needs of women.

However, the information society poses challenges as well as opportunities for women that are different from those for men, based on their different roles and positions in the family and society (UNCTAD, 2002).

Often, women continue to benefit less than men from ICTs. Women have less access to technologies,

---

## Box 3.5

## Development through Radio in Sierra Leone

In accordance with best practices in southern Africa, the Development through Radio (DTR) project in Sierra Leone uses radios to voice the needs of poor women with no access to community radio. It is run for and by women and the Forum of Conscience (FOC), a human rights NGO, is the facilitator of the project. Women meet to discuss education, health issues, entrepreneurship and democratization, as well as inputs to the Truth and Reconciliation Commission. The issues are determined, examined and agreed upon by the communities. The discussions are audio/video-taped and sent to the FOC's DTR coordinator, who writes a synopsis and contacts relevant policymakers and NGOs for responses to the specific issues raised. The taped discussions and responses are sent to commercial community radio stations, which edit and broadcast them at a discount price thanks to the support of Radio Netherlands.

ICT infrastructure in Sierra Leone is in dire need of reform. Internet cafes and mobile telephones, present in Freetown, have yet to arrive in rural areas. Moreover, Internet connection is slow, expensive and hindered by power cuts. FOC has computers in all its offices but suffers from a lack of Internet access and frequent power cuts. Nevertheless, Reuters Digital Vision Programme has supported the digitization of the audio and video recordings as well as the development of a dedicated website (www.dtronline.org), undertaken in the United States in consultation with FOC, for further dissemination. Regarding radio technologies, annual licences for single-channel radio stations cost $2,000, an exceedingly large sum for poor communities in Sierra Leone to be able to afford.

*Sources:* Wambui (2005), World Bank (2005); Government of Sierra Leone (2005); Caulker (2006); US Department of State (2003).

---

## Box 3.6

## Gender and FOSS

Only 2 per cent of FOSS developers are women, compared with an average 25 per cent in the software development industry. Consequently, the software developed may not satisfy women's specific needs.

The factors that exclude women from participating in the FOSS community are underwritten by a culture dynamic, which views technology as an autonomous field, separate from people:

- Women are actively (if unconsciously) excluded because of the importance given to individual agency.

- Women are treated either as strangers or are assumed to be male and thus made invisible.

- Using and developing FOSS requires lengthy learning time and long hours of work, and women face difficulties in devoting a large amount of unwaged time to learning and developing and tend to engage later in their lives with computers.

- FOSS rewards the production of code, and associated skills, rather than software; and thus attributes a lower value to activities in which women often engage, such as interface design or documentation.

- Aggressive talk accepted in FOSS projects as a way to develop reputation, is off-putting for newcomers, exacerbating the confidence difficulties women tend to have as a result of lower levels of previous computer experience.

How can Governments promote increased participation of women in FOSS projects? The following possibilities exist:

- Providing tangible resources to help women devote time to software development activities;

- Fostering the participation of girls in FOSS at an early stage;

- Supporting existing efforts in the FOSS community to increase female participation, such as specialized FOSS user and development communities for women (i.e. LinuxChix, Debianwomen and Ubuntuwomen);[1]

- Encouraging a greater variety of working methods in the production of software, including through the modification of procurement criteria;

- Creating a greater understanding, including among leaders, of women's contribution to technology.

---

[1] www.linuxchix.org, www.debianwomen.org, https://wiki.ubuntu.com/UbuntuWomen

*Source:* Cinco (2006); FLOSSPOLS (2006).

especially the newer technologies; they use ICTs less often, spend less time and engage in less diverse uses; and they are less likely to work in the ICT sector, particularly in higher positions (Huyer et al., 2005). For example, in Viet Nam, women represent 25 per cent of the software workforce, and their work is concentrated in execution tasks, while men concentrate in conception tasks, with a related pay differential (Le Anh Phanm Lobb[31]). Even in the development of free and open source software (FOSS), which is considered more appropriate for poverty reduction efforts,[32] the unequal participation of women is notorious (see box 3.6).

A recent and extensive study on women in the information society (Huyer et al., 2005) shows that "the gender [digital] divide is large and widespread ... and is more pronounced in developing economies – although there are some exceptions" such as the Philippines, Mongolia and Thailand, where female Internet use exceeds male use. It also argues that the gender digital divide is specific to the context. For example, it explains the prominent female Internet use in the Philippines by the fact that English is the working language, Internet content thus being accessible, and that women participate actively in economic and political life.

Moreover, the gender digital divide is not necessarily linked to the overall divide. For instance, the proportion of female Internet users does not necessarily expand with increased Internet penetration. As chart 3.1 shows, the proportion of female Internet users varies enormously even in countries with similar Internet penetration rates. For example, the proportion of female users (40 per cent) in the Netherlands is identical to that for Brazil or Mexico despite the fact that the

### Chart 3.1

### Relationship between Internet penetration and proportion of female Internet users

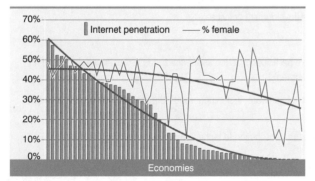

*Source:* Huyer et al. (2005, p. 144) based on ITU, World Telecommunications Indicators 2004, and selected national sources.

overall penetration in the Netherlands approaches 60 per cent, whereas in Brazil and Mexico it is less than 5 per cent (Huyer et al., 2005).

The barriers that women have to confront in order to participate in the information society are well known: women have lower levels of education and ICT literacy; sociocultural norms hamper their access to and use of ICTs; they have less access to technologies and finance; and the content available, including through media, is less relevant to women (UNCTAD, 2002; Hafkin, 2002b).

How these barriers can be dealt with depends on different world views and approaches to women and technology, which range from considering technology inherently neutral (women in technology) to viewing technology as part of the masculine project of domination and control of women (eco-feminist approach) through understanding the role of technology as cultural processes that can be negotiated and transformed (gendered approach). For a summary of the different approaches to women and technology, see box 3.7.

Because of its appropriateness to the capabilities approach for poverty alleviation, and in consonance with current discourses,[33] this chapter focuses on the gender approach and on how ICTs can expand the capabilities of poor women and girls. "*Engendering ICTs* is the process of identifying and removing gender disparities in the access to and use of ICTs, as well as of adapting ICTs to the special needs, constraints, and opportunities of women" (World Bank Gender ICT Toolkit[34]).

The roles of men and women roles and their relationships are socially embedded and institutionally constructed. Moreover, women, depending on their education, class, ethnicity, age or race, use and benefit differently from ICTs. Thus, ICT policies and programmes should be specific to the targeted women and men and adapted to the specific context of their roles and relationships. How can ICTs help women and girls living in poverty generate income or have better access to health in their particular context?

Efforts to reduce gender inequality in ICTs include the implementation of special programmes targeted at women and girls, and the mainstreaming of gender in overall policies and programmes. Mainstreaming gender in ICTs means doing a gender analysis and including a gender perspective across ICT policies and programmes. So far, "the vast majority of ICT applications that address gender are women-only

---

# Box 3.7

## Different views on women and technology

- **Women in technology:** Technology is inherently neutral.

- **Marxism:** Women's exclusion from technology due to the gender division of labour and the historical and cultural view of technology as masculine. Technology reflects male power as well as capitalist domination.

- **Eco-feminism:** Technology as part of the male project of domination and control of women.

- **Third-world perspective:** Challenges Western systems of knowledge and technology as these colonize and displace local knowledge and experience.

- **Gender ICTs:** Technology as cultural processes, which can be negotiated and transformed. Technology is neither inherently neutral nor masculine.

---

*Source:* Wood (2000).

projects" (Chamberlain, 2002, p. 12). Moreover, there is a difference between practical programmes that focus on providing women with further access to ICTs and more strategic programmes that use ICTs to empower women and change the roles and relationships of men and women. ICT activities for women have been most effective in addressing poverty issues "when they go beyond issues of access and infrastructure to consider the larger social context and power relations" (Gurumurthy, 2004), an example of this being the Development through Radio programme in Sierra Leone, where women are provided not only with access to radio but more importantly with a tool to make their voices heard.

ICT policies are not gender-neutral.[35] They impact (albeit to various degrees) on women and men differently. Gender issues include issues affecting access to and use of ICTs and specific gender issues in ICT policy, such as the extent to which a proposed telecommunications modernization provides infrastructure that is affordable for most women. For an elaboration of gender issues in ICT policy, based on the work of Jorge (2000), see annex 1.

The third meeting of the ITU Working Group on Gender Issues[36] identified five common priorities across all regions: affordability, training, content, local language and access. Other essential areas (Chamberlain, 2002) include creating awareness at all levels among policymakers and implementers; promoting female participation in ICT policymaking and ICT programme management, and involving women in the design, implementation and evaluation of policies and programmes;[37] and the development of industrial policy essential for encouraging women

to further develop their careers in the ICT sector throughout their working life.

Although Governments have adopted gender policies at the international level, their implementation is not obvious. Many ICT activities and policies – of markets, governments and NGOs – are still gender-blind.[38] Only few countries have gendered their ICT policies, and there is no strategy for the implementation of most policies. Mozambique's ICT policy approved in 2000 included gender aspects, while its 2002 implementation strategy "proved disappointing on the incorporation of gender issues" (Hafkin, 2002b, p. 16).

To monitor and evaluate the impact of ICTs on men and women, it is important to develop indicators and collect data on gender and ICTs. Having data disaggregated by gender is one step, but it is also necessary to undertake studies (such as the FOSSPOLS study on FOSS and gender mentioned in box 3.6) to better understand how ICTs affect women and men differently. The Gender and Evaluation Methodology (GEM) for the Internet and ICTs is a tool for designing and evaluating ICT programmes focused on assessing the effect that an ICT programme or policy has on women's empowerment. Additionally, Heeks et al. (2005) are proposing a more holistic approach to evaluate ICT programmes promoting women's entrepreneurship that analyses ICTs' impact from three standpoints: gender, enterprise and livelihoods.

Gender and ICTs are an area that requires further exploration as well as critical analysis, and to which UNCTAD could continue to contribute. UNCTAD can help develop a greater understanding of the impact that ICTs and e-business have on women and men and their economic activities through its analytical work and its work on measuring the information economy (see chapter 1). It can also support Governments in conducting a gender analysis and reviewing the gender aspects of their ICT policies. Furthermore, it can promote dialogue and awareness among policymakers regarding gender and e-business issues.

# D.   Institutional barriers

The current thinking on recommended ICT policies and programmes for poverty alleviation having been reviewed, this section looks at the obstacles to their implementation. Why are ICT policies not yet fully effective for poverty reduction? Why do many of the practices not mirror discourses?

First of all, **international debates and their outcomes are not focused on ICTs for poverty reduction**. When ICTs are discussed among other poverty issues, such as in the context of the Millennium Development Goals, their role is often seen as less relevant than other pressing concerns such as improving health or education. At the same time, issues of a technical/sectoral nature rather than poverty reduction efforts dominate the international ICT agenda. For example, the preparation, outcomes and follow-up of the World Summit on the Information Society (WSIS), while recognising the potential of ICTs to promote the development goals of the Millennium Declaration (para. 2 of the Geneva Declaration of Principles), do not have a focused discussion on poverty reduction. It centres rather on the role of stakeholders, infrastructure, access, capacity building, building confidence, the enabling environment, applications, cultural diversity, media and international cooperation.[39] Poverty alleviation is a multidimensional effort but because poverty is not a stand-alone issue for discussion, ICTs for poverty reduction efforts have lower visibility. An expanded analysis of the relevance of WSIS for poverty alleviation is provided in section E(c).

Secondly, the **cross-cutting nature of ICTs for poverty reduction**, where different disciplines are involved in the technological dimension (i.e. infrastructure, content, business, legal environment) and in the development one (health, women, rural development, poverty, human rights), makes it more difficult to have focused discussions, research and measurement on ICT4P.

**Broad international commitments on ICTs and development**, such as the outcomes of the WSIS, **have to be translated into national policy and practice.** Their impact on poverty reduction is shaped by local institutions as well as by the motivations and power of the different stakeholders. The WSIS commitments do not include an implementation strategy, nor have they been allocated specific resources. For example, while the Geneva Declaration of Principles endorses the promotion of gender equality and the empowerment of women, "the outcomes fall short of providing specific directions and action plans for the building of a gender-just information society" (Gurumurthy, 2004).

**The implementation of pro-poor ICT policies and programmes is not easy.** A gender analysis of various case studies of multi-donor ICT interventions reveals that all of the projects had gender issues, but these were rarely articulated in the product design and implementation. Even in a best-practice example of an ICT course that effectively trained women in ICTs, management and gender, the programme could not ensure that, upon their return home, they would be able to make use of their newly gained skills (Hafkin, 2002a). Ideally, the programme should make sure that women are able to access and use ICTs once the training is completed, and, where appropriate, provide them with opportunities to work/study using their new skills.

**There is limited availability of quantitative measurement and qualitative assessments of ICTs for poverty alleviation** (Gerster and Zimmermann, 2005). Strong evidence on the impact of ICTs on poverty reduction is limited, because of the cross-cutting reality of ICTs, because of the multidimensional nature of ICTs and because of the difficulty in measuring their impact. In general, ICT measurements are scarce: regarding gender and ICTs, for example, there is no comparable systematic measurement (Huyer et al. 2005). And qualitative research is also necessary in order to assess the (positive and negative) impact that ICTs have on poverty (Mathison, 2005). "Sector-wide or region-wide assessments of the ICT contribution to poverty reduction hardly exist or remain vague" (Gerster and Zimmermann, 2005).

**Scaling up successful ICT projects** to expand the impact of ICTs on poverty reduction **involves more than replicating good projects**. It requires taking successful projects to another level of commitment, adapting systems, structures and budgets, adopting new policies and changing practice (Klinmahorm and Ireland, 1992). The TIC Bolivia programme exemplifies how scaling up the impact of individual telecentre requires working and learning with other organizations, developing management capacities, and obtaining political support and further resources, as well as lobbying ministries to adapt policies and create an enabling environment (IICD, 2005).

Institutionally, there is **little accountability or incentive to coordinate ICT strategies and poverty reduction policies**. For instance, at the national level many developing countries are preparing Poverty Reduction Strategy Papers (PRSPs) and, while some have now incorporated ICTs into their PRSPs, few have effectively mainstreamed ICTs into them (Gerster and Zimmermann, 2005; SIDA, 2005). As of January 2004, 34 PRSPs had been developed, of which only 13 considered ICTs a strategic component, 18 considered them a sector or tool and 3 did not mention ICTs at all in PRSPs (OECD, 2004a). Similarly, it is argued that "the mainstreaming approach to gender ... has had modest impact primarily because it is seldom well-resourced and non-compliance to gender policy is tolerated" (KIT, 2005, p. 17)

**Contested discourses continue to influence policies and practices.** The capability approach to poverty reduction is a different development paradigm from that proposed by the "orthodox market-based approach"[40]. While the latter relies mainly on development outcomes generated by the operation of markets, the former assigns a larger role to the collective action of Governments, communities and markets to expand the capabilities of the poor. And while there is a convergence of views on the role that different stakeholders can play in society, there are still conflict areas that continue to be negotiated. A case in point is the financing of the information society. There is still much disagreement about the financial mechanisms to support ICT4P and about the extent to which pro-poor ICT programmes need to be financially sustainable. For instance, if telecentres are to benefit people living in poverty, a financial sustainability objective should not jeopardize poverty reduction efforts. As stated in paragraph 17 of the Chennai Statement (2005), "The drive for up-scaling and sustainability can itself become a challenge, as it may cause a drift away from a focus on the poorest".

**Working with other organizations is not easy**. Multi-stakeholder approaches have many virtues, but practical implementation is not one of them. "Multi-stakeholderism" means cooperating with other organizations that have diverse economic and human

endowments and whose own mission/vision may, at times, be contradictory. Working with others requires time and effort, leadership skills, financial resources, a shared vision and a great deal of confidence. Time is required in order to allow for discussions and participation, and to develop trust. As evidenced in the TIC Bolivia network programme, a major challenge in multi-stakeholder approaches is to manage the friction among the different parties.

Finally, but not less relevant, is the fact that the extent to which ICTs can empower people living in poverty depends upon **how power imbalances are dealt with.** For ICTs to make a difference, people with weaker positions must be able to participate fully in the negotiation and the implementation of ICT policies and programmes. They must be provided with the necessary means, including financial resources, time and support, to be able to organize themselves and advocate for their needs. For example, women or other groups of people living in poverty need to be given the chance and time to understand, experiment and learn about ICTs as well as to discover what ICTs can provide for them. In practical terms, this may be done by providing financial support over a longer period of time, by including early in the programme a phase to allow women to experiment with ICTs, and by providing women with a say in, and flexibility to modify, the programme after they have discovered what ICTs can provide for them.

There are different approaches to deal with power imbalances: from self-empowerment – when those in weaker positions mobilize themselves[41] – to outside support for those living in poverty through participatory and facilitative approaches,[42] or a combination of both.[43] Self-empowerment approaches focus on the beneficiaries, but they overlook the fact that those at disadvantage may have neither the possibility nor the capacity to create change. For instance, in the specific case of ICTs, poor communities may have never worked with a computer and it should not be expected that they will demand access to computers without being familiarised with them. On the other hand, participation and facilitation approaches are questioned about the extent to which those in a weaker position have the capacity to fully participate, and to voice and defend their needs, and those in a facilitative role can speak on behalf of the poor.[44]

Power may be formal or informal, is acquired from different sources and evolves over time, and a first step to address poverty issues is to discern who has power (formal or informal) and who has a voice, both as groups and as individuals. For instance, within rural communities, residents of the main village may be able to access ICTs better than those in smaller villages. Some basic approaches to balance negotiations include acknowledging power imbalances and the benefits of balanced dialogues, setting concrete objectives, and providing the necessary means for participation.

Power imbalances are part of the larger socioeconomic environment. But power inequities in the area of ICTs do not exactly reproduce general socio-economic imbalances. For example, non-English speakers are more at a disadvantage in the information society than they may be in the context of society as a whole. Nor may the same approaches to deal with power imbalances be appropriate to follow. For instance, ICTs are not backed up by specific enforceable human rights legislation, such as the right to education established by the Universal Declaration of Human Rights. Moreover, ICTs are providing a new way to deal with power imbalances: open approaches, in terms of software and content, are changing power balances and providing the opportunity for more people to participate in the information economy.

These obstacles are institutional failures hampering the adoption of the best pro-poor ICTs policies and practices, and the conclusions of this chapter will provide some recommendations on institutional development to increase the impact of ICTs on people living in poverty.

## E.   Framework to understand, question and propose pro-poor ICT policies and interventions

This chapter has offered a review of current thinking on ICT policies and programmes for poverty reduction, including the need for an increased focus on ICT4P and for embedding pro-poor ICT efforts in poverty reduction initiatives and principles. This section presents a framework to examine the poverty alleviation focus of a given ICT strategy or policy, in the belief that questioning to what extent an ICT intervention is pro-poor contributes to the achievement of the Millennium Development Goals.

The framework, expanded from Rao's (2003) *8 Cs Framework for Analysis and Planning ICT interventions*, presents twelve parameters that define the extent to which an ICT policy or programme is effectively

supporting poverty reduction, and which should be taken into account when designing or evaluating pro-poor ICT policies and interventions. Rao's original 8 Cs are Connectivity, Content, Community, Commerce, Capacity, Culture, Cooperation, and Capital; and four additional Cs have been added to review to what extent: (1) ICT policies and practices are adapted to the local context (Context); (2) the policy or programme is sustainable (Continuity); (3) beneficiaries have a say in the policy or programme (Control); and (4) the policy or programme is coherent with other poverty reduction policies and programmes (Coherence). Table 3.1 explains each of the parameters.

The framework is a tool to analyse current policies and practices and their impact on poverty reduction. It helps in the asking of questions. While the discussion in this chapter already offers some guidelines on what are desirable courses of action and institutional barriers, the framework does not impose or propose specific actions, as these are to be examined and negotiated within each specific context.

This 12 Cs framework (see chart 3.2) highlights the multiple influence layers that shape actions: macro (international/national), meso (interaction between organizations and institutions, the interplay between the macro and micro level) and micro (local). The macro level looks at how the international agenda (including the WSIS outcomes, trade agreements or development assistance policies) and national processes (such as Poverty Reduction Strategy Papers or National ICT strategies) influence each of the parameters. By way of example, to what extent does a donor's support influence the *continuity* of the TIC Bolivia programme or the cooperation among different stakeholders? Or to what extent does Bolivia's national ICT strategy support affordable technology (*connectivity*) for rural communities living in poverty? The meso level looks at the interaction between institutions and organizations and how their initiatives influence the expansion of pro-poor policies and practices regarding each of the parameters. For example, to what extent is the network TIC Bolivia (*cooperation*) supporting the poor in using ICTs for developing their capabilities? The micro level looks at how an individual programme features in each of the parameters. For instance, who benefits (*community*), and who does not, from a particular telecentre?

The framework also sets aside a space in which to question the assumptions, to reflect on what is the ultimate goal and to highlight the conflicts behind each parameter. Visions and assumptions frame

# Table 3.1

# The 12 Cs of the pro-poor ICTs framework

| 12 Cs | Key issues | Questions |
|---|---|---|
| Connectivity | - Infrastructure & technology (hw/sw) accessible & affordable | Extent to which the planned infrastructure and technology ensure the people living in poverty can use and afford them. |
| Content | - Relevant<br>- Accessible<br>- Beneficiaries involved | Extent to which the content is relevant to the needs of the targeted population.<br>Can women and men access and use it to meet their needs?<br>Is it available in the local language & accessible to non-literate and ICT-illiterate people?<br>Do beneficiaries participate in the development of the content? |
| Community | - Who benefits?<br>- Beneficiaries participate | Who should be the target group?<br>How do the different stakeholders participate in the programme?<br>Are beneficiaries taking part in the design and implementation of the programme?<br>How will the intervention affect the different groups (women, men, old, young, illiterate, etc.) of the community? |
| Commerce | - Supports livelihoods | Does the planned intervention sustain the livelihoods of the beneficiaries?<br>To what extent does it support the economic activities of the beneficiaries? |
| Capacity | - Beneficiaries' capacity<br>- Organizations' capacity | Do beneficiaries have, or can they acquire, the capacity to participate in the programme?<br>Do the organizations involved have the (financial and organizational) capacity to develop and implement the programme? |
| Culture | - Supportive culture<br>- Learning promoted | Is there a forward-looking and supportive culture for using ICTs for poverty reduction? |
| Cooperation | - Stakeholders cooperation favourable | To what extent is the cooperation among the different stakeholders favourable to ICTs for poverty alleviation? |
| Capital | - Financial sustainability | Are there sufficient financial resources? |
| Context | - Adapted to context<br>- Influences context | Is the policy or programme adapted to the local context?<br>Is the intervention able to influence changes for a more favourable context for using ICTs for poverty alleviation? |
| Continuity | - Monitoring and evaluation<br>- Flexible, promotes learning<br>- Potential for increased impact<br>- Socially sustainable | Does the policy or programme incorporate a monitoring and evaluation component?<br>Does it promote learning and allow flexibility for adaptation?<br>Could the ICT programme be scaled up?<br>To what extent is it socially sustainable? |
| Control | - Beneficiaries' ownership<br>- Stakeholders accountable | Do beneficiaries have ownership of the policy or programme?<br>Do beneficiaries have a say in the design, implementation and evaluation of the policy or programme?<br>Are the different stakeholders accountable? |
| Coherence | - Pro-poor | To what extent is the ICT policy or programme consistent with other pro-poor policies and interventions? |

*Source:* UNCTAD, based on Rao (2003).

responses. For example, the TIC Bolivia programme's goal regarding the *connectivity* parameter (see chart 3.3) is to bring ICT access to the rural community on the assumption that the best way to do so is through existing agricultural centres. Being aware of the assumptions is an opportunity to review the extent to which the vision will be achieved and what are potential areas of conflict. In this case, where the agricultural information centres are, who uses them and how are used will have an impact on the programme. Often conflicts arise between two competing objectives, such as how to reach the poorest while having the widest possible impact. This frame, like the logical framework used in development interventions, tries to highlight the coherence between different levels of action and assumptions, and it can be used in a participatory manner. The additional features of this framework facilitate a comprehensive approach to ICTs for poverty reduction.

The advantages of this framework are the following: (1) it can be used at different levels, for specific contexts and specific target poor communities;(2) it forces people to think about issues relevant to the poor, and not about functional ones, such as the legal framework and the budget, and takes into account ICTs' cross-cutting nature; (3) it highlights linkages between different levels of action – macro, meso and micro;[45] and (4) it draws attention to assumptions, conflicts and visions.

Conversely, the disadvantages of the model are the following: (1) it is not structured as an e-strategy or in the way ministries or institutions are used to, (2) it does not provide solutions – it is up to the user to fill the

matrix and to discover the assumptions and conflicts; and (3) its ambition to provide a holistic view makes the framework come across as rather dense.

The following three examples illustrate how this framework is useful for:

(a) Reflecting on how the ICT programme for rural development in Bolivia is addressing the needs of the rural communities (chart 3.3);

(b) Examining how the Development through Radio programme is addressing the needs of poor women in Sierra Leone (chart 3.4);

(c) Reflecting on the World Summit on the Information Society policy discussions, its outcomes and its links to poverty reduction.

### (a)   Agriculture and the rural development sector of IICD's Bolivia ICT Country Programme (chart 3.3)

The nature of the programme means that the framework is largely focused on the meso level. However, it also looks at how the macro level, that is the national context and international agreements and initiatives, has an influence on the impact of ICTs in rural Bolivia – for example, how the programme is aligned with the Millennium Development Goals or how intellectual property rights may be affecting the access to content. The micro level looks at the impact and characteristics of the individual projects and within specific communities. To what extent is the project on market access or the project promoting ecological

### Chart 3.2 – 12 Cs pro-poor ICTs framework

#### Framework to understand, question and propose pro-poor ICT policies and interventions

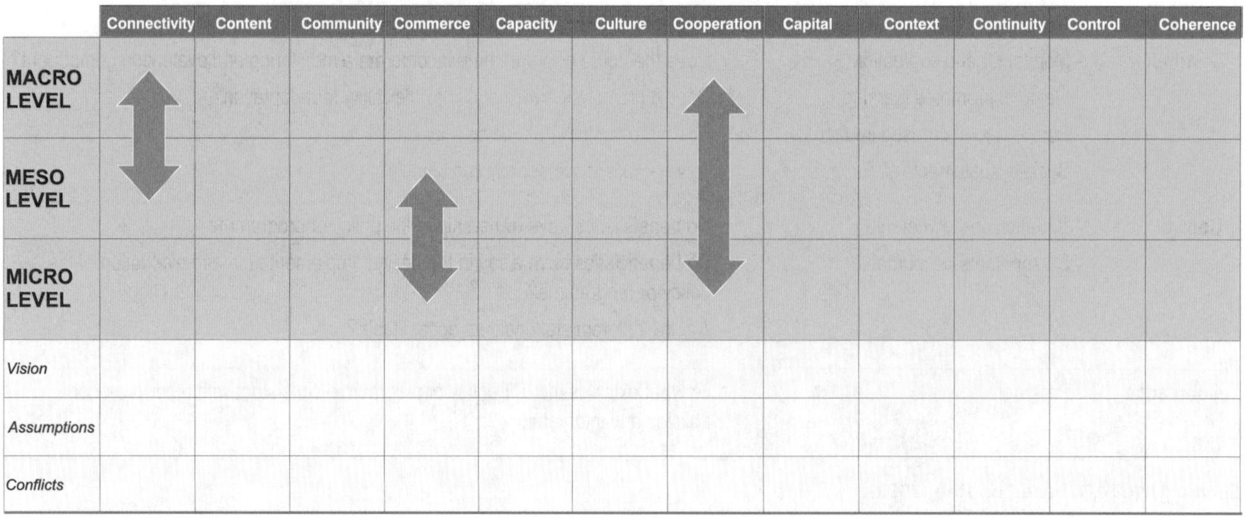

| | Connectivity | Content | Community | Commerce | Capacity | Culture | Cooperation | Capital | Context | Continuity | Control | Coherence |
|---|---|---|---|---|---|---|---|---|---|---|---|---|
| **MACRO LEVEL** | | | | | | | | | | | | |
| **MESO LEVEL** | | | | | | | | | | | | |
| **MICRO LEVEL** | | | | | | | | | | | | |
| *Vision* | | | | | | | | | | | | |
| *Assumptions* | | | | | | | | | | | | |
| *Conflicts* | | | | | | | | | | | | |

*Source:* UNCTAD, based on Rao (2003).

## Chart 3.3

### 12 Cs Pro-poor ICTs framework – ICTs and rural communities: The case of the TIC Bolivia programme

| | Connectivity | Content | Community | Commerce | Capacity | Culture | Cooperation | Capital | Context | Continuity | Control | Coherence |
|---|---|---|---|---|---|---|---|---|---|---|---|---|
| **MACRO LEVEL** | ICT strategy: eTIC / PRSP'01: ICTs not mentioned / Basic telecom agreement? / Telecoms liberalized in '01 | Impact of intellectual property rights? | ↔ | ↔ | Supporting Ministry of Agriculture in designing sectoral ICT strategy | ↔ | Supports Ministry of Agriculture in developing an e-strategy / Donor assistance | Donor assistance | ↔ | ↔ | ↔ | Supports pro-poor views in national ICT policy processes / Supports PRSP / MDGs |
| **MESO LEVEL** IICD's Bolivia ITC country programme: Agriculture & rural component / National context | Combines computers and radio / Uses innovative connectivity arrangements to bring costs down / Software used? | Relevant to agricultural livelihoods / Which content? / Languages covered? / Accessibility? / Produced by whom? | Reaching target groups: women, poorer rural communities, smaller SMEs | Supports farmers' access to markets. / Acknowledged impact | Developing organizational capacities / Dependence on IICD | Has created a supportive culture | Promotes cooperation of many different stakeholders / Managing stakeholders' relations | Dependence on IICD | IICD supports development of an enabling environment | Owned & run independently by well-established organizations / Projects embedded by policymakers at the sector level / Evaluation | Evaluation of impact on poor is limited | ↔ |
| **MICRO LEVEL** Local telecentres | Tries to promote women's access to telecentres | In the local language / Relevant to women? / Relevant to small farmers? | 75% of users are male / Engages beneficiaries? | 58% of beneficiaries have benefited from a direct positive economic impact | Development of org. capacities / Finding and retaining qualified staff | Different cultures, similarities/differences? Which programme elements need to be culturally specific? | Managing stakeholders' relations | Financial sustainability / Users find costs high | Unstable politics | Integrated into existing organizations / Evaluation per project? | ↔ | Supports local initiatives |
| *Vision* | Bring ICT access to rural community | | Support rural livelihoods | Support agricultural livelihoods | Local organizations can make use of ICTs | Create supportive culture for use of ICTs | Organizations work together to maximize ICTs | Financially supportive | | | | |
| *Assumptions* | ICTs in agric. Information centres best option | | | Access to information | Once trained, organizations will be ready | | Organizations can work together | Creative ICT arrangements can work | | | | |
| *Conflicts* | Where ICTs are located, who uses them and how are used impact on poverty reduction | Multiple languages / High levels of illiteracy | Reach the poorest while having as wide an impact as possible | Whose livelihoods? Smaller, producers livelihoods? Women? | Retaining staff | Multiple different cultures and languages | Inter-organizational relations are not always straightforward | Time-consuming / Trust is essential | Multiple different contexts. One-fits-all-solutions may not be appropriate | | | |

*Sources:* IICD (2005), Bolivia Poverty Reduction Strategy and UNCTAD analysis.

**Notes:** # = paragraph; blank spaces = parameters for which information is not available, and which may be worth exploring; yellow highlight with red font = achievements or areas that support poverty reduction; red highlight = areas that require attention if ICTs are to support poverty reduction.

exports increasing the capabilities of the poor? To what extent is the programme effective in a specific community? Managers of individual projects would be interested in reviewing the impact of their project in their own community. In chart 3.3 only the major benefits and concerns have been highlighted.

This framework, in addition to the challenging areas mentioned in the report (see earlier description in section C.1.), highlights two areas that may be worth acting upon:

- The introduction of ICTs into national poverty reduction strategies; for instance, the Bolivian Poverty Reduction Strategy (2001) does not include any reference to ICTs;

- Specific evaluation of how ICTs are impacting on the poorer groups in rural communities, and how they are affecting the roles and responsibilities of men and women.

Moreover, the framework highlights areas in which it would be worth having more information:

- Content: What content is available? Who produces it? Is it relevant to the smaller producers? Is it relevant to other people living in rural areas but not working in agriculture? Is it relevant to women's needs? Can they access it?

- Local context: How do the programmes deal with different communities and the various cultures and languages? When is a broad approach appropriate? Which interventions need to be customized?

- Connectivity: Which software is being used? Is it appropriate?

- How does the international agenda (trade agreements, intellectual property rights, etc.) affect Bolivia's use of ICTs for rural **development**

### (b) Development through Radio programme in Sierra Leone: ICTs addressing the needs of poor women (chart 3.4).

The Development through Radio programme in Sierra Leone (see box 3.5 and chart 3.4) is an example of how basic but widespread and affordable technology can empower poor women by making their needs heard and influencing policymakers and donors. The case study shows many of the elements earlier described

as best practice in pro-poor ICT programmes: it is based on an existing poverty reduction effort, in which women themselves participate; it uses basic and affordable technology; it drives to increase its influence by working through a network of women; and there is monitoring of the impact of the programme on poverty reduction (see following up of responses by policymakers).

However, there are questions about the national environment, including how current regulation (i.e. high licence fees) and the political climate hinder the use of new technologies for poverty reduction; about the sustainability of the programme (i.e. how the programme could be expanded or to reduce its dependence on the Forum of Conscience); and about the sustainability of the digitization of the information and availability on the web.

The framework also highlights the conflict regarding the role of men and their involvement in programmes aimed at addressing women's needs. While best practice in addressing women's needs suggests that both women and men should be involved, in this particular context experience suggested that it was best to develop a women-only programme.

Moving on from national perspectives, we will now examine ICT policy debates in a global setting.

### (c) Outcomes of the World Summit on the Information Society and the needs of the poor

The second phase of the World Summit on the Information Society (WSIS) closed in Tunis in November 2005. While it is still too early say what its impact on development and poverty reduction will be, a preliminary assessment of the relevance of the policy discussions and the outcomes to poverty reduction can inform the follow-up to the Summit and its implementation.

Broadly speaking, the WSIS has developed a higher level of awareness of the opportunities and challenges that ICTs offer for development in general and provided a focal discussion forum for issues that are considered and negotiated in different international organizations. Moreover, the WSIS has introduced a new way of undertaking intergovernmental debates, where non-State actors – that is, representatives from the private and not-for-profit sectors – have also the opportunity to participate in the process.

The WSIS outcomes make reference to the contribution that ICTs can make to the attainment

## Chart 3.4

## 12 Cs Pro-poor ICTs framework – Gender and ICTs, Sierra Leone

| | Connectivity | Content | Community | Commerce | Capacity | Culture | Cooperation | Capital | Context | Continuity | Control | Coherence |
|---|---|---|---|---|---|---|---|---|---|---|---|---|
| **MACRO LEVEL** The national context: Policies and practices | No ICT strategy. Radio regulation exorbitant licences fees. Telecom: State monopoly. ICT component in PRSP is vague | ⟷ | Already best practice in other African context | No enabling environment for e-commerce | ⟷ | Post-war reconstruction | Shift geography of aid. In war time: east & south regions. After: north reg. Cooperation very political | ⟷ | Pre-election period. | ⟷ | Post-war context | Coherent with national priorities MDGs, security, and governance quality |
| **MESO LEVEL** Development through radio (Sierra Leone) programme coordination | Provides access to those with no radio community access. Website done abroad | Content produced by women. Web & digitization brings visibility to FOC | Meets rural women's needs, both literate and illiterate. Role of men widely discussed. Expansion to areas with no radio access? | Programmes' vision: use ICTs for selling articles produced by women online | FOC seems to be well established. No training provided to women for editing content | Supportive women's groups. Promotion of learning but not on ICTs | Cooperation among FOC, commercial community radios, Radio Netherlands & Digital Vision Programme | Sustainable. Some groups would require radio transmitter resources | Adapted to a context with low presence of new ICTs | Following up responses of policy-makers. Scaled-up programme. Overwhelming demand on FOC & DTRP coordinator | Women control their own groups. No ownership of website. What if external support is discontinued? | Support development efforts. Use of the website when no access by women |
| **MICRO LEVEL** Individual women's group | Not all groups have radio transmitter | Produced by women locally and available in local content. Benefit of web for women? | Women participate. Men? Eastern groups: resent unmet promises | Received relevant assistance for productive activities. Trained to do business. East: Gained skills irrelevant to job oppor. | Some groups (Rorinka) on early stages of mobilization | Some groups still need to develop | | ⟷ | Programme adapted to local context and women's needs | Assistance for training centre | Local women control radio and ownership of their groups | Eastern groups lacking development support |
| *Vision* | *Affordable. Widespread use & coverage* | *Relevant to women's needs* | *Community needs met* | *Increased food security* | *Women's group help bring development* | *Empowered women* | *Programme will develop through cooperation with others* | *Programme works with minimum resources* | | *Move information online* | *Women manage & own the programme* | *Programme helps address women's basic needs* |
| *Assumptions* | *Radio available everywhere* | *Women produce relevant content* | *Women suffice* | *New business opportunities* | *FOC have the capacity* | *Women mobilize* | *Partner provides support* | *Minimal resources needed* | *Reconstruction will continue* | *PC access, ICT skills, literate, external aid, needs met* | *Women have the tools to manage the programme* | |
| *Conflicts* | *Radio still not everywhere* | *Management of different local languages?* | *Role of men* | *Livelihoods link missing sometimes* | *What if FOC's capacity ends?* | *Time needed for groups to develop* | *What if SLBS does not cooperate?* | *Resources still needed for radio transmit.* | *Political abuse vs. political support of the programme* | *Website sustainability* | *Ownership of digitization and website* | *Further support always needed* |

*Sources:* Wambui (2005); World Bank (2005); Government of Sierra Leone (2005); Caulker (2006) and UNCTAD analysis.

**Notes:** # = paragraph; blank spaces= parameters for which information is not available, and which may be worth exploring; yellow highlight with red font = achievements or areas that support poverty reduction; red highlight = areas that require attention if ICTs are to support poverty reduction.

of the Millennium Development Goals and other International Development Goals, and take up poverty reduction concerns and the promotion of pro-poor ICTs. For example, paragraphs 20 and 23 of the Tunis Commitment state that "we shall pay particular attention to the special needs of marginalised and vulnerable groups of society" and that "we reaffirm our commitment to women's empowerment and to a gender equality perspective". However, the outcomes do not specifically address how this should happen, and this remains the contentious and unsolved issue of the debate. For example, how should all these commitments be financed? And how will powerless women be empowered? As these questions are left open, the risk of limited or biased implementation increases. Notwithstanding, the WSIS documents also make reference to some best practices on ICTs for poverty reduction, including the integration of national e-strategies into national development plans[46] and mainstreaming ICTs into official development assistance strategies.

While the WSIS outcomes acknowledge the fact that ICTs can be instrumental in supporting poverty reduction efforts, they do not indicate how this should be achieved, with what resources, and how it will be supported and enforced. The commitments are usually too general to deal with the specific problems of the poor. A serious problem is the lack of adequate financial mechanisms available for developing countries to benefit from the information society[47] in general, and for poverty reduction in particular. This makes the full implementation of the WSIS commitments more difficult.

The Tunis Agenda for the Information Society provides a guide for implementation and follow-up. For example, paragraphs 83, 97, 98, 101, 102, 105, 108 and 110 recommend a multi-stakeholder approach. However, in practical terms, while the WSIS outcomes acknowledge that Governments are not the only actors in poverty reduction, and the critical role that the private sector and non-governmental organizations have to play in promoting the information society, for civil society actors "governments have accepted 'multi-stakeholderism' in the texts but not in their hearts and practices" (NGLS, 2005).

A revised report on the WSIS stocktaking of ICT activities (WSIS Executive Secretariat, 2005) estimates that 70 per cent of the project activities are relevant to the goals of the Millennium Declaration. However, it should be noted that only 18.5 per cent are directly relevant to poverty reduction (Goal 1, "Eradicate Poverty and Hunger").

The above paragraphs provide some different views on the WSIS outcomes. WSIS stakeholders may wish to further use the framework to explore the extent to which the WSIS policy discussions and outcomes are relevant to poverty reduction.

## F.   Making ICTs work for the poor: Institutional development recommendations

ICTs are a tool for poverty reduction. ICTs are inter alia providing women with new working opportunities, enabling them to make their needs heard and helping agricultural organizations share knowledge. ICTs are necessary – as Amartya Sen puts it, "the availability and use of this technology is no longer optional"[48] – but insufficient for poverty alleviation: other efforts, including the provision of basic and ICT infrastructure, and developing organizational capacities and information management and technical skills, are also needed. Pro-poor ICT policies and programmes must be embedded in poverty reduction strategies and programmes, and be based on poverty reduction principles. For instance, telecentres provide benefits to people living in poverty when men and women can fully participate and benefit, and relevant content is accessible.

Different technologies, from radio to computers, have different contributions to make to poverty reduction, and innovative approaches opt for combining various technologies to maximize the benefits of ICTs. Financial and social sustainability issues continue to be major concerns because of pressures for self-financing, the high cost of technologies and their evolving nature. The market alone will not bring ICTs to the poor, and while creating an enabling environment is a major approach for addressing the needs of the poor it should also be acknowledged that additional financial provision is often still needed. Support is needed at all levels, from policymakers to create an enabling environment, to donors' assistance focusing on poverty reduction efforts, and civil society organizations taking up the challenge of using ICTs for poverty reduction. Similarly, research and evaluations are needed at all stages to understand what works and what does not.

Pro-poor ICT policies and programmes are most effective when they are context-specific and address beneficiaries' specific needs through the appropriate approaches. The implementation of best practices still requires that they be adapted to each context. At the same time, to scale up the impact of ICTs, interventions must be able to change the status quo by embedding pro-poor ICT programmes in policies and by changing practices.

Strong institutions are needed so that significant benefit may be derived from best practices and lessons learned: institutions able to focus ICT debates, policies, actions and research on reducing poverty and able to understand and manage the cross-cutting nature of ICTs; public administrations able to translate broad policy commitments into specific commitments and action; organisations that are motivated and remain accountable for their action; institutions that are open to continued dialogue and that reflect on the real impact that ICT discourses, policies and practices have on the poor; organizations that work effectively with each other and develop a consensus about how to use ICTs for poverty reduction; and leaders able to encourage people living in poverty to participate in the design and implementation of interventions and effectively use ICTs for poverty reduction.

To make ICTs work for poverty alleviation, institutional development is required at all levels: "The potential for ICTs in future rural development strategies will depend on the ability of those strategies to transcend institutional boundaries and control, and therefore be inclusive of community level institutions, private sector organisations, NGOs and a variety of new and old media channels" (ODI, 2002).

What follows are some suggestions for institutional development addressed to policymakers and programme designers, including the donor community and civil society actors, which seek to make a difference with regard to using ICTs for poverty alleviation.

- Focus on ICTs for poverty reduction. Emphasize poverty alleviation in ICT dialogue, policies, assistance, interventions and research. Encourage and participate in pro-poor ICT debates and discourses, including in the context of the follow-up to, and implementation of, the World Summit on the Information Society and promote agreement on what pro-poor ICT means. Design and implement sound policies, adopt and adapt best practices, and support approaches, including participation and decentralization, that enable the poor to be heard and participate actively.

- Mainstream ICTs effectively into national and sectoral poverty reduction policies and programmes, while being aware of the cross-cutting nature of pro-poor ICTs. Mainstream ICTs also into development assistance programmes, which may include building institutional capacities by training staff on ICT issues for poverty reduction and sharing best practices. Donors should also consider the importance of funding ICT infrastructure and other infrastructure favouring poor communities, particularly in least developed countries.

- Understand the poverty implications and gendered nature of ICT policies and programmes. Carry out poverty and gender analysis of ICT policies and undertake country reviews of ICT4P policies and programmes across sectors and issues areas. In this regard, the 12 Cs framework can contribute to mapping the impact of policies and programmes on poor communities and indicate priority intervention areas. Additionally, collect data disaggregated by sex, age, education and geography to help identify who is benefiting or not from ICTs, and measure the impact of ICT interventions on the poor. Monitor progress and regularly evaluate the impact of ICT policies and programmes on the poor so as to revise strategies and improve their effectiveness.

- Promote the scaling up of successful programmes by providing an enabling environment and encouraging the development of pro-poor ICT networks. Support local governments and sectoral agencies adopting pro-poor ICT policies and practices, including through fostering awareness of ICT and poverty issues. Promote the development of organizational capacities that help organizations work with other stakeholders in partnership. Support learning approaches by providing programmes with long-term support and by allowing flexibility to adapt the programmes to the needs of the poor.

This chapter has demonstrated that, and how, ICT policies and programmes can contribute to poverty reduction. It has asked critical questions and provided instruments to encourage dialogues and practices with the aim of promoting ICT policies and programmes that contribute to the achievement of the Millennium Development Goals. Now, it is the turn of policymakers and other stakeholders to put these recommendations into practice.

# Annex I

# Gender issues in ICT policy

| ICT aspect | Gender equality issue |
|---|---|
| Network modernization | • The proposed modernization will provide infrastructure that is affordable to most women. |
| Network architecture | • Equipment and service providers can offer cost-effective and appropriate solutions for the majority of women. |
| Network deployment | • Choices of network infrastructure can be made that cater for the majority, focusing on universal access to ICTs instead of expensive high-capacity specialized access.<br><br>• Affordable wireless alternatives can ensure low-cost access.<br><br>• Women need to be included in the training when new technologies are implemented.<br><br>• The location of infrastructure will facilitate access for women. |
| Infrastructure | • Infrastructure needs to be developed throughout the country in areas where many women live.<br><br>• Provisions need to be made for high-technology applications in areas where many women live outside the capital and major cities.<br><br>• Gender awareness is essential in planning and implementing infrastructure because social, economic and/or cultural constraints may prevent women from accessing ICTs even when these are available in their communities. |
| Technology choice | • Affordability of service is a key issue for women. If technology choices are limited, this can keep new entrants out of the market and limit the introduction of technologies that might reduce costs (for example, many developing countries ban Wi-Fi Internet and VOIP (Voice Over Internet Protocol) telephony).<br><br>• Limiting the choice of mobile standards (for example, GSM, CDMA) can prevent fragmentation of markets during the initial stages; however, continued insistence on such standards can block the entry of mobile technologies that are cheap and effective for underserved areas.<br><br>• Assessments need to be undertaken to determine appropriate technology choices: who will use the technology and for what purpose.<br><br>• It is important to promote and support user-friendly technology, particularly in the context of low literacy levels. |
| Sector liberalization | • Opening the telecoms and ICT sector to competition can bring in needed investment and force down end-user prices to make access more affordable, notably to women (however, monopoly system operators understandably dispute this fact). |
| Tariff policy | • High customs duties on mobile telephones and computer equipment, as well as high prices for telephone service, are deterrents to women users (this includes both import duties and taxes on computer equipment and pricing schemes for communication services).<br><br>• Many countries are rebalancing international and domestic tariffs to eliminate existing subsidies, most frequently for local service. This rebalancing has meant higher rates for local calls in many places, which hit poor women the hardest. Although it is expected that competition will lower prices in the long run, in the interim many users cannot afford local service. Among the ways to compensate for rebalancing costs is the application of tariffs based on forward-looking costs and regional (rural versus urban) tariffs. |

| Regulation | • Regulators do not set policy but rather help in its implementation. Regulation is a vital area for advocates of gender equality in ICTs because it produces a set of rules for market behaviour: who can provide what service and under what conditions. Regulation also sets the framework for achieving desirable outcomes established by national policy, particularly in the two areas of the greatest interest to ICTs and the empowerment of women (universal access and affordable services). Gender proponents need to focus on regulation. |
|---|---|
| Independent regulators | • An independent regulator can compel profit-driven private sector players to meet social and gender-policy objectives such as universal access (see below).<br><br>• In return for granting licences, regulators can compel service providers to offer service to underserved areas where women predominate.<br><br>• Because regulators have the authority to set service priorities, gender-equality advocates need to lobby to ensure that service to poor women in rural areas is a priority.<br><br>• Regulators can provide funds for research, development and testing of ICTs that will serve women.<br><br>• Those that secure licences, particularly for cellular phones, are often required to fulfil community service obligations. Elements that promote gender equality could be written into these obligations. |
| Regulatory frameworks | • Regulatory frameworks can permit the resale of mobile phone services, which are often profitable businesses for women to establish.<br><br>• Regulatory frameworks can reduce licensing fees, spectrum prices and interconnection charges, and can thus make ICTs more accessible to women. |
| Licensing | • If fees for telecommunications, Internet service providers (ISPs) and mobile service licences are high, these costs will be passed on to users, limiting affordability to women and the poor. High fees increase the cost of telephone and ICT services, discouraging women-owned communications businesses (including telecentres, phone-fax-Internet shops and mobile telephones).<br><br>• A certain number of telecommunications licences need to be allocated to women-owned businesses or businesses with women in management positions.<br><br>• A gender-equality licensing policy could waive licence fees for communications businesses run by women entrepreneurs or businesses that provide services to underserved areas, particularly where women are concentrated.<br><br>• Fees could be reduced for operators with gender-equity and pro-handicapped employment policies.<br><br>• Licences can obligate providers to offer discounted service to certain customers, such as poor women in rural areas.<br><br>• Licensing procedures need to be transparent so that women applicants can have ready access to the information.<br><br>• Licence awards can contain conditions that promote gender analysis and mainstreaming for the company. |
| Universal access | • Universal access concerns the establishment of telecommunications development funds and other programmes that are funded by carrier fees and other revenues collected by regulators, and used to facilitate the expansion of access to the underserved. Because telecoms development funds reflect important policy and set the rules for implementation of ICT projects in underserved areas, they deserve great attention from gender advocates. |

| | |
|---|---|
| | • Develop gender-aware universal access policies that stress public access points as an alternative to more capital-intensive choices (one line per home) and ensure that the locations of public access points are gender-sensitive (not in bars or auto shops). |
| **Universal service obligations** | • Universal service is a specific obligation that regulators require of operators in return for licences. Under universal service obligations, regulators can mandate the provision of telecentres in underserved areas. Telecentre plans need to take into account the different needs of men and women in the communities concerned.<br><br>• Gender advocates could lobby to incorporate gender-based issues into universal service rules. In most places this has not yet happened.<br><br>• Demands could include that service to underserved areas be delivered to reflect the male–female distribution in the population and that priority be given to disadvantaged women such as single mothers, widows and handicapped women. Service providers could be mandated to offer telephone subsidies or price packages targeted at rural women, the handicapped and the aged. |
| **Radio frequency spectrum** | • This issue also involves fees and licences. Lower fees will encourage applicants to provide services to new markets, including women. Licences need to be equally and transparently distributed, so that women-owned business and businesses that serve women have a chance to secure licences. In several African countries where the Government maintains a monopoly on radio frequencies, public–private access to radio frequency is still an issue. In a number of places, women-run community radio stations have obtained licences. |
| **Research and development and innovation** | • Incentives could be directed at encouraging women to engage in ICT research and innovation.<br><br>• Tools and software need to be developed using local languages.<br><br>• Research and development of technologies for the illiterate and neo-literate need to be encouraged.<br><br>• Research efforts and programmes that promote women innovators could be subsidized.<br><br>• Scholarships and grant programmes for women in science and technology could be created.<br><br>• Technology programmes will promote and accept women's participation.<br><br>• Technical programmes at universities could be created and supported by providing grants or scholarships for women students and researchers. |
| **Systems for learning and training** | • Women need to have equal access to technical training.<br><br>• Programmes need to be supported to train women in technical and management programmes, and to provide internships. |
| **Software and applications** | • Women will have a say in what applications are being promoted in order to ensure that they are usable by and accessible to many women. Policies need to support open source software and operating systems that can make software available to communities with limited budgets. |
| **Building technological capacity** | • Opportunities will be extended to women as well as men. Mechanisms need to be provided to encourage women to enter these fields. Female teachers will act as role models for young girls.<br><br>• Training opportunities need to be available not only for technology professionals but also for non-professionals to use ICTs. |

| ICT industry development and labour policies | • Encouragement and incentives need to be given to encourage women to enter all segments of the ICT labour force, not just the assembly-line positions they have dominated in the past.<br><br>• Enabling policy can encourage the establishment of teleworking, which has provided jobs for many women. |
|---|---|
| ICT business development and e-commerce | • Enabling legislation for e-commerce will encourage women entrepreneurs.<br><br>• Small ICT-related businesses that can be owned by women and women's groups need to be encouraged.<br><br>• Telecentres can provide economic opportunities for women and need to be promoted as business opportunities for women owners.<br><br>• A number of telecommunications licences need to be allocated to women-owned businesses.<br><br>• Carriers could be obligated to do a certain percentage of business with women-owned businesses.<br><br>• Training programmes could be promoted to establish ICT-related business opportunities (for example, e-commerce, telecentres, and wireless company ownership). |
| E-government | • Women can benefit from e-government services, such as on-line access to land and voter registration and licence applications, particularly when they would normally have to travel to the capital city to obtain these services. |

*Source:* Based on Jorge (2000).

# References

APC (2006). Pushing and prodding, goading and hand-holding. Reflection from the Association for Progressive Communications at the conclusion of the World Summit on the Information Society, 14 February 2006.

Arun S., Heeks R. and Morgan S. (2004) ICT initiatives, Women and Work in Developing Countries: Reinforcing or Changing Gender Inequalities in South India? Working Paper No. 20. Development Informatics. Institute for Development Policy and Management. University of Manchester. Available at www.sed.manchester.ac.uk/idpm/publications/wp/di/index.htm

Badshah A., Khan S. and Garrido M. (eds.) (2003). Connected for Development: Information Kiosks and Sustainability. UN ICT Task Force Series 4.

Benson T. (2005). *Brazil: Free Software's Biggest and Best Friend. New York Times.* 29 March 2005.

Booth D. (2005). Missing Links in the Politics of Development: Learning from the PRSP Experiment. Working Paper 256. Overseas Development Institute, London, October 2005. Available online at www.odi.org.uk/publications/working_papers/wp256.pdf.

Brown, M.M. (2001) Can ICTs Address the Needs of the Poor?, A Commentary from UNDP, June 2001. http://www.undp.org/dpa/choices/2001/june/j4e.pdf

Castelo Branco Correia J. (2000). From Paulo Freire to Clodomir Sandos de Morais: from critical to organizational consciousness, in Carmen, R. and Sobrado, M. (eds.), A Future for the Excluded. Job Creation and Income Generation by the Poor: Clodomir Santos de Morais and the Organisation Workshop, London and New York, Zed Books, pp. 39 – 49 as reproduced by the Open University (2005b).

Caulker J. (2006). Interview between the author and J. Caulker, manager of the programme, 18 May 2006.

Chamberlain L. (2002). Considerations for Gender Advocacy vis-à-vis ICT Policy and Strategy. Expert Group Meeting on "Information and Communication Technologies and their impact on and use as an instrument for the advancement and empowerment of women", EGM/ICT/2002/OP.2, 5 November 2002.

Chambers R. (1997) Whose Reality Counts? Putting the First Last. London, Intermediate Technology Publications, in Ruggeri Laderchi (2003).

Chapman R. and Slaymaker T. (2002). ICTs and Rural Development: Review of the Literature, Current Interventions and Opportunities for Action. ODI Working Paper 192, November 2002.

Chapman R., Slaymaker T. and Young J. (2003). Livelihoods Approaches to Information and Communication in Support of Rural Poverty Elimination and Food Security. ODI Research and Policy in Development (RAPID).

Chennai Statement (2005). Chennai Statement on Up-scaling Pro-Poor ICT policies and practices. January 2005. Chennai, India.

Cinco C. (2006). We assume FOSS benefits all equally. But does it really? 27 February 2006, www.genderit.org.

Engberg-Pedersen L. and Webster N. (2002) 'Introduction to political space', in Webster, N. and Engberg-Pedersen, L. (eds) *In the Name of the Poor. Contesting Political Space for Poverty Reduction*, London, Zed Books, p.7 as compiled in Open University (2005a)

Etta F. and Parvyn-Wamahiu S. (eds.) (2003). Information and Communication Technologies for Development in Africa: Vol 2. The experience with Community Telecentres. Available at www.idrc.ca.

European Foundation (1995). Public Welfare Services and Social Exclusion: the Development of Consumer Oriented Intitiaves in the European Union. Dublin, The European Foundation in Ruggeri Laderchi (2003)

FLOSSPOLS (2006). Gender: Integrated Report of Findings. Free/Libre and Open Source Software: Policy Support. Cambridge, March 2006.

Fukuda-Parr S. (2003) The Human Development Paradigm: Operationalizing Sen's Ideas on Capabilities in Feminist Economics 9 (2 –3), Routledge, pp. 301–317

Gerster R. and Zimmermann S. (2005). Up-scaling Pro-Poor ICT-Policies and Practices. A Review of Experience With Emphasis on Low Income Countries in Asia and Africa. SDC and M S Swaminathan Research Foundation, Richterswil, January 2005.

Girard B. (2005). Internet, Radio and Network Extension, in Mahan A.K. and Melody W. H. (eds.), Stimulating Investment in Network Development: Roles for Regulators. Report on the World Dialogue on Regulation. Available at www.regulateonline.org.

Gov3 (2005). Achieving Digital Inclusion. Government Best Practice on Increasing Household Adoption of Computers. Intel White Paper Volume 1, January 2005, available at www.intel.com.

Government of Bolivia (2001). Bolivia Poverty Reduction Strategy, 10 May 2001.

Government of Sierra Leone (2005). Poverty Reduction Strategy Paper, 9 February 2005.

Gurumurthy A. (2004). Gender and ICTs. Overview Report. Bridge Development-Gender. Institute of Development Studies, September 2004.

Gustainiene A. (2005) Gender-focussed ICT policy making. GenderIT.org, 27 July 2005. Available at www.genderit. org.

Hafkin N.J. (2002a). Are ICTs Gender Neutral? A Gender Analysis of Six Case Studies of Multi-Donor ICT Projects. UN/INSTRAW Virtual Seminar Series on Gender and ICTs. Seminar One, 1–12 July 2002.

Hafkin N.J. (2002b) Gender Issues in ICT Policy in Developing Countries: An Overview. Expert Group Meeting on "Information and Communication Technologies and their impact on and use as an instrument for the advancement and empowerment of women", EGM/ICT/2002/EP.1, 25 October 2002.

Harris R. (2004). Information and Communication Technologies for Poverty Alleviation. E-Primers for the Information Economy, Society and Polity. UNDP-APDIP.

Heeks R., Arun S. and Morgan S. (2005). Researching Women's ICT-Based Enterprise for Development: Methods, Tools and Lessons from Fieldwork. IDPM, University of Manchester, UK, available at www. womenictenterprise.org.

Huyer S. et al. (2005). Women in the Information Society, in Sciadas (ed.) *(2005) From the Digital Divide to Digital Opportunities: Measuring Infostates for Development.* Orbicom. Montreal (Quebec), Canada.

IDRC (2003). Information and Communication Technologies (ICTs) for Poverty Reduction: When, Where and How? Background Paper: Discussion, Research, Collaboration, by R. Spence, 18 July 2003, available at http:// www.idrc.ca/en/ev-53023-201-1-DO_TOPIC.html.

IFAD (2001). Rural Poverty Report 2001: Key messages, available at www.ifad.org/poverty/presentation/1.htm.

IICD (2005). The TIC Bolivia Country programme. The impact of IICD support for poverty reduction and development using ICTS, 2000-2004. International Institute for Communication and Development.

ITU (1998). World Telecommunication Development Report. Universal Access. March 1998. Executive summary available at www.itu.int/ITU-D/ict/publications/wtdr_98/index.html.

ITU (2004) Third Meeting of the Working Group on Gender Issues. Final Report. Document WGGI. ITU Headquarters, Geneva, 30 June –2 July 2004, July 2004

Jorge S. (2000). Gender Perspectives in Telecommunications Policy: A curriculum proposal. ITU, Geneva, as compiled in the World Bank's Engendering ICT toolkit at www.worldbank.org.

Klinmahorm S. and Ireland K. (1992). NGO-government collaboration in Bangkok, in Edwards M. and Hulme D. (eds.), *Making a Difference: NGOs and Development in a Changing World*, pp. 60–69 Earthscan

Lessof C. and Jowell R. (2000). Measuring Social Exclusion. Working Paper Number 84, Centre for Research into Elections and Social Trends, September 2000.

Mathison S. (2005). Digital Dividends for the Poor. ICT for Poverty Reduction in Asia. Global Knowledge Partnership.

Maxwell S. (1999). The Meaning and Measurement of Poverty, ODI Poverty Briefing paper, London, Overseas Development Institute as in Open University (2005a)

Michiels S. I. and Van Crowder L. (2001). Discovering the "Magic Box": Local Appropriation of Information and Communication Technologies (ICTs). Available at www.fao.org/sd/2001/KN0602a_en.htm.

NGLS (2005). World Summit on the Information Society Tunis Phase: Committing to Solutions. NGLS Roundup 125. United Nations Non-Governmental Liaison Service, December 2005.

Nyaki Adeya C. (2002). ICTs and poverty. A literature review. Available at http://www.idrc.ca/acacia/ev-24718-201-1-DO_TOPIC.html.

Ó Siochrú S. and Girard B. (2005). Community-based networks and innovative technologies: New models to serve and empower the poor. A report for UNDP. Series: Making ICT Work for the Poor. Available at http://pro-poor-ict.net.

ODI (2002). ICTs and Rural Development: Review of the Literature, Current Interventions and Opportunities for Action. Working Paper 192, November 2002.

OECD (2004a). Informal Expert Meeting on ICTs for Poverty Reduction, 7 July 2004.

OECD (2004b). Leveraging Telecommunications Policies for Pro-Poor Growth. Universal Access Funds with Minimum-Subsidy Auctions. DAC Network on Poverty Reduction. DCD/DAC/POVNET(2004)13, Berlin 27–29 October 2004 .

OECD (2005). Good Practice Paper on ICTS for Economic Growth and Poverty Reduction. Document WSIS-II/PC-3/CONTR/1-E, 13 April 2005. Available at www.oecd.org.

Open University (2005a). Institutional Development: Theory, Policy and Practice. TU872 Institutional Development: Conflicts, Values and Meanings.

Open University (2005b). Part 3 Readings. TU872 Institutional Development: Conflicts, Values and Meanings.

Pascal Zachary G. (2004). Black star: Ghana, information technology and development in Africa. First Monday, Issue 9/3. 12 February, available at www.firstmonday.org/issues/issue9_3/zachary/index.html.

Pereira Gomes R., Lakhani S. and Woodman J. (2002). PRSP – Politics, Power and Poverty. A Civil Society Perspective. Economic Policy Empowerment Programme. European Network on Debt and Development (EURODAD). Available online at www.trocaire.org

Rahnema M. (1992). Participation, in Sachs W. (ed.) The Development Dictionary: A Guide to Knolwedge and Power, London and New Jersey, Zed Books Ltd, pp. 116–131, as reproduced by the Open University (2005b).

Rao M. (2003). The nature of the information society: A developing world perspective, in Goodrick J. (ed.) *Visions of the Information Society*, ITU, available at www.itu.int/visions.

Ruggeri Laderchi C.R., Saith R. and Stewart F. (2003). Does it matter that we don't agree on the definition of poverty? A comparison of four approaches. Working Paper Number 107, Queen Elizabeth House, University of Oxford, May 2003.

Sagna O. (2005). Senegal. Chapter 5, Regional Perspectives, in Sciadas (ed.) *From the Digital Divide to Digital Opportunities: Measuring Infostates for Development*. Orbicom, Montreal (Quebec), Canada, p. 73.

Schware R. (2003). Private Sector Kiosks and Government Incentives: What Works and What is Sustainable in Badshah et al. (eds.) Connected for Development: Information Kiosks and Sustainability. UN ICT Task Force Series 4.

Sen A. (1999). *Development as Freedom*. Oxford University Press. Oxford, UK, p. 87.

SIDA (2005). ICTs for Poverty Alleviation: Basic Tool and Enabling Sector. November 2005.

Spence R. (2003). Information and Communciations Technologie (ICTs) for Poverty Reduction: When, Where and How? Background paper: Discussion, Research, Collaboration IDRC

Spence R. (2005). Epilogue. Pro-poor, Pro-market ICT Policy and Regulation: Global Initiative, Scaling up in Mahan A.K and Melody W.H. (eds.), Stimulating Investment in Network Development: Roles for Regulators. Report on the World Dialogue on Regulation. Available at www.regulateonline.org.

Task Force on Financial Mechanism on Universal Access (2004). Financing ICT: A review of trends and an analysis of gaps and promising practices. Report of the Task Force on Financial Mechanism on Universal Access, 22 December, available at http://www.itu.int/wsis/tffm/final-report.pdf.

UNCTAD (2002) Chapter 3 Gender, e-commerce and Development. *E-Commerce and Development Report 2002*, available at www.unctad.org/ecommerce.

UNCTAD (2003). Chapter 3 Free and open source software: Implications for ICT policy and development, *E-Commerce and Development Report 2003* available at www.unctad.org/ecommerce.

UNCTAD (2004). Trade and Gender. Opportunities and Challenges for Developing Countries. United Nations, Geneva.

UNCTAD (2005). *Information and Economy Report 2005* available at www.unctad.org/ecommerce

UNDP (2001). Human Development Report 2001. Making New Technologies Work for Human Development p. 40.

UNDP APDIP (2005). ICT for Poverty Reduction: "Necessary but Insufficient". A State of the Art Review. Available at www.unapdip.net.

United Nations (2004). Triennial Comprehensive Policy Review of Operational Activities for Development of the United Nations System. Report of the Secretary-General. General Assembly. Economic and Social Council A/58/85- E/2004/68, 28 May 2004.

US Department of State (2003). Sierra Leone. Country Reports on Human Rights Practices 2002. Bureau of Democracy, Human Rights, and Labor. 31 March 2003.

Wambui M. (2005). Development through Radio: A Case Study from Sierra Leone, pp. 51–60 in KIT (2005), Gender and ICTs for Development. A Global Sourcebook. KIT, The Netherlands and Oxfam, UK available at www.oxfam.org.uk.

Whyte A. (2000). Assessing Community Telecentres: Guidelines for Researches. IDRC. Available at http://www.idrc.ca/en/ev-9415-201-1-DO_TOPIC.html#beginning.

Wood, P. (2000). 'Putting Beijing online: women working in information and communication technologies: experiences from the APC Women's Networking Support Programme', Philippines: APC Women's Networking Support Programme in Gurmurthy (2004)

World Bank (2001). *World Development Report 2000/2001. Attacking Poverty*. Available at www.worldbank.org.

World Bank (2002). A Source Book for Poverty Reduction Strategies. October 2002. Available at www.worldbank.org/poverty.

World Bank (2005). Republic of Sierra Leone. Joint IDA-IMF Staff Advisory Note on the Poverty Reduction Strategy Paper, 13 April 2005.

World Bank PRSP Sourcebook. Chapter 24. Available online at http://povlibrary.worldbank.org/files/4414_chap24.pdf.

WSIS (2003). Declaration of Principles. World Summit on the Information Society, 12 December 2003. WSIS-03/GENEVA/DOC/4-E.

WSIS Executive Secretariat (2005). Revised Report on the WSIS Stocktaking, Document WSIS-II/PC-3/DOC/3-E, 30 August 2005.

Yongling Z. (2004). Information Services in Rural China Field Surveys and Findings, in Riggs M., Hazelman M. and Weike L. (eds.), FAO Bangkok, available at www.fao.org

# Notes

1.  A Brazilian non-governmental organization.

2.  See the India project, ICT and Rural Development, at www.chathamhouse.org.uk.

3.  For further examination of the concept of poverty see Maxwell (1999).

4.  See Sustainable Livelihoods approach principles in Chapman et al. (2003).

5.  Based on OECD's (2005) five dimensions in which ICTs contribute to pro-poor economic growth, but the dimensions have been broadened to emphasize poverty as multiple, rather than just economic, deprivation.

6.  As an example see Brown (2001) in Nyaki Adeya (2002); Mathison (2005); WSIS Declaration of Principles (WSIS, 2003)

7.  See Pereira Gomes et al. (2002).

8.  Swedish International Development Cooperation Agency (SIDA, 2005).

9.  See a list of different initiatives in www.infodev.org/section/programs/mainstreaming_icts/info_devices/devices_list.

10. For information on the Jhai Computer and the Indian Simputer see chapter 3 of UNCTAD (2003), p. 71–72

11. For an overview of the characteristics and critics of the $100 laptop see http://en.wikipedia.org/wiki/$100_laptop and http://wiki.laptop.org/index.php/OLPC_myths.

12. See www.softwarelivre.gov.br or Benson (2005).

13. See the Asiatotal computer in www.asiatotal.net.

14. For further information see chapter 1 in UNCTAD (2005).

15. See www.kothmale.org. and www.unesco.org/webworld/netaid/com/sri_lanka.html.

16. Spence (2003); Nyaki Adeya (2002).

17. See Michiels and Van Crowder (2001) in Chapman et al. (2003), who stress the need for improved monitoring and evaluation especially with regard to impact on the economic and social livelihoods of communities, or see UNDP APDIP (2005).

18. 800 million of the 1.2 billion of people living in extreme poverty live in rural areas (IFAD, 2001).

19. ASEAN statistics available at www.aseanconnect.gov.my.

20. Bridges.org,  Spanning the Digital Divide: Understanding and Tackling the Issues.

21. For an example see the study of ICTs in Ghana carried out by Zachary (2004).

22. Note that universal access – where a telephone, and more broadly access to ICT services including the Internet, should be within a reasonable distance of everyone – is defined in different ways "from a telephone within less than five kilometre in Brazil to a thirty minute travelling distance to a phone in South Africa" (ITU, 1998).

23. See Report of the Task Force on Financial Mechanism on Universal Access "experience with Universal Access Funds to date is mixed" p. 54 or OECD (2004) for a summary of the results of different universal access mechanisms.

24. For further information on this and other universal access approaches see OECD (2004).

25. Chile, Peru, Guatemala, Colombia and the Dominican Republic.

26. For further elaboration of the importance of community-based networks see Ó Siochrú and Girard (2005) and for other examples on telecentre models and experiences see Badshah et al. (2003).

27. The telecentres studied were under private (individual) ownership, private NGO or CBO ownership or trusteeship. The study did not include public facilities.

28. Mali, Mozambique, Uganda, South Africa and Senegal.

29. For guidelines on how to evaluate telecentres see Whyte (2000).

30. For a review of e-commerce and ICT-related opportunities for women see UNCTAD (2002) and chapter 14 " The role of Information Technology in the promotion of gender equality", in UNCTAD (2004).

31. See Le Anh Phanm Lobb's Gender and Software Work in Vietnam presentation in http://siteresources. worldbank.org/INTGENDER/Resources/GenderandSoftwareWorkJan24.pdf

32. For further information on free and open source software, see chapter 4 Free and open source software: Implications for ICT policy and development, in UNCTAD (2002).

33. World Bank and UNDP.

34. The World Bank's Engendering ICT Toolkit available at *www.worldbank.org.*

35. Note here that ICT policies are classified as either gendered or gender-blind. Calling an ICT policy neutral is misleading because policies have an impact on women, which is different from that on men.

36. ITU (2004).

37. See, for example, how and to what extent the Government of Albania included women in the elaboration of its national ICT strategy in Gustainiene (2005).

38. See Arun et al. (2004) for a comparison of two ICT initatives in India, one gender-blind and the other gender-focused.

39. These are the action lines of the Geneva Plan of Action, www.itu.int/wsis.

40. See Fukuda-Parr (2003) for a comparison of both approaches.

41. See Freire's "conscientization approach" as reviewed in Open University (2005a).

42. See Chambers' proposition for those with relative power to hand over the stick as reviewed in Open University (2005a).

43. Such as Santos de Morai's "Organisation Workshops", which promote self-organization on the basis of support from outside facilitators. See in Castelo Branco Correia (2000).

44. See Rahmena's strong critique of participation in Rahnema (1992).

45.   Arrows are used to question missing links or inconsistencies between different levels.

46.   See paragraph 100a of the Tunis Agenda for the Information Society.

47.   See, for example, APC (2006).

48.   A Dialogue on ICTs and Poverty: The Harvard Forum, information available at http://web.idrc.ca/en/ev-46261-201-1-DO_TOPIC.html.

# Chapter 4

# ICTs IN THE OIL SECTOR:
# IMPLICATIONS FOR DEVELOPING ECONOMIES

## A. Introduction

Oil is the main non-renewable source of energy that is currently "fuelling" the world economy. In spite of many efforts to develop renewable energy sources, which have been further stimulated by major increases in international crude oil prices during last few years, the share of such sources in global energy consumption is still marginal. Conventional wisdom suggests that the world economy will continue to be highly dependent on oil and gas: while in coming decades the share of gas might increase considerably and eventually surpass that of oil, the latter will still play a major role in the world energy balance.

Increased oil prices, together with global warming, are considered to be a change of first order for the world economy. In particular, the oil industry itself has an impact on the use of information and communication technologies (ICTs) in the global economy. Higher oil prices increase the risk of squeezing information technology (IT) budgets in oil-using industries. In particular, they can affect oil-importing developing countries with regard to their increased consumption and their often limited capacity to respond to oil price shocks. On the other hand, increased revenues of energy producers give oil-producing countries an opportunity to increase their investments in IT. At the same time they will increase support for high-tech energy conservation efforts and for the production of alternative renewable energy sources (Bartels, 2006).

ICTs play a major role in increasing productivity and cutting costs in many sectors of the economy (UNCTAD, 2003a). And given the expectation of high oil prices for long periods of time, the question arises as to whether more efficient production and more equitable distribution of this valuable energy resource are possible, inter alia, through the active use of modern ICTs. To what extent can ICTs help increase efficiencies in the production and allocation of crude oil and its products?

This is in particular pertinent to developing and transition countries whether they are oil exporters, or major or low-income oil importers. Oil exporters are interested in maximizing the benefits of using ICTs. Oil importers, as they further increase their oil consumption, particularly China and India, are interested in being able to buy petroleum[1] at better prices and use it effectively. Reducing price volatility is especially important for developing countries' importers, from low-income economies, as they have more difficulties in coping with oil price shocks. Thus, determining the role of ICTs in the oil sector could be crucial for better assessing the economic development perspectives of developing countries in the coming decades.

ICTs and modern petroleum technologies (which are also becoming information - intensive technologies) provide new opportunities to improve economic performance at all stages of the oil supply chain. These technologies influence both upstream operations (exploration and production of crude oil) and downstream operations (transportation, refining of crude oil and distribution of oil products). For example, in upstream operations, ICTs and related technologies may provide possibilities for expanding proven crude oil reserves, improving the rate of crude oil extraction from existing wells, and providing further means to discover new wells, and so forth.

Understanding to what extent new ICTs and related technologies might help to extend the lifespan of proven oil reserves and help to find new ones will provide more predictability about future oil supply; it could also be a stabilizing factor helping to allay investors and consumers' fears, and could contribute to putting downward pressure on oil prices.

The use of ICTs in the oil industry is not only relevant for international oil companies (IOCs) in their competitive drive to stay in the forefront of technological progress, but also has also direct implications for national oil companies (NOCs) in OPEC and other oil-exporting countries. Unlike in the 1970's, the major national oil companies in the OPEC region as well as in other countries have matured, accumulated considerable financial resources and know-how, and are ambitious to compete with IOCs also in the use of ICTs. However, they still have to address issues such as the lack of skilled human resources, and the need for increased knowledge of cutting-edge technologies, and business processes. The NOCs in some developing countries face the challenge of keeping up with new technologies, including ICTs. But to upgrade technologies they need first to put in place basic infrastructure and earmark enough financial resources to upgrade their technological capabilities.

Oil trading in spot markets started in the early 1980s, creating modern futures markets and becoming the dominant mode of trading of oil. It is hard to overstate the role of ICTs in oil spot and futures markets and in the changes that occurred. The number of participants in the physical oil supply chain is limited, but the emerging e-marketplaces are generating further competition within the oil industry. In addition to oil and its derivatives, oil equipment and technology are increasingly offered for sale online. E-marketplaces might still provide increased efficiencies in the distribution and marketing of oil products and related equipment. ICTs are helping in the exchange of information and better interaction among oil companies and between them and their equipment, technologies and services suppliers.

The chapter starts by reviewing the state of play in the international petroleum market. Section C identifies ICT-driven efficiency gains in both upstream and downstream stages of the global petroleum industry, drawing on the experience and concerns of developing countries. Section D reviews the electronic trading methods of major oil exchanges and emerging oil and related-product e-marketplaces. Section E identifies the means of increasing the effectiveness of the petroleum industry and opportunities for its further diversification in oil-exporting developing and transition economies, as well as possibilities to improve the production and distribution of oil products in oil-importing countries. To conclude, the chapter provides some policy recommendations.

## B.    International petroleum market: The state of play

In spite of serious energy conservation measures taken primarily by OECD countries, resulting in nearly

halving the energy intensity of their per capita incomes, the world economy continues to witness an increase in demand for oil. One of the driving forces here is the demand from major developing economies, primarily China and India, where energy and, in particular, oil consumption is increasing in both absolute and relative terms. Thus, China imports 3 mb/d (million barrels per day) of crude oil, which represent half of its domestic consumption. While China's share in the global oil market is still 8 per cent, since 2000 it has captured 30 per cent of the growth in global oil demand. As a result of such growth in China, India and other Asian countries, Asia, which in the 1970s consumed only half of the amount consumed by the North American market, surpassed North America as the principal oil-consuming region of the world. However, the United States' per capita oil consumption is still twice as much as in Europe and several times higher than in Asia, and its imports of around 12 mb/d are approximately equal to the crude oil production of all former USSR countries (CERA, 2006; Yergin, 2006).

As chart 1 shows, world oil demand may rise from 77.7 mb/d in 2002 to nearly 85 mb/d in 2006 and that in spite of more than tripling of prices since 2002 from around $20 to around $70 per barrel of crude oil.[2] According to the International Energy Agency (IEA) as well as similar forecasts of the Organization of the Petroleum Exporting Countries (OPEC), by 2030 oil demand might reach 120 mb/d, with the transportation sector as the main user of its products (IEA 2002, 2005a; OPEC, 2006).

The recent decline in stocks of oil in importing countries highlights a situation of nearly full capacity utilization in the oil industry and exerts upward

### Chart 4.1

### Global oil supply and demand

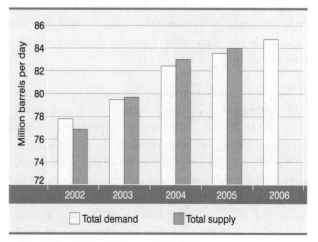

Source: IEA, Oil Market Report, 12 May 2006.

pressure on oil prices in the spot and futures market. More importantly, the political climate in respect of the Islamic Republic of Iran and shortfalls in production of crude oil in Nigeria, Venezuela and Iraq, as well as the impact of Hurricane Katrina on the US Gulf coast, also add upward pressure on oil prices. On the other hand, the recovery of Russian oil production is notable, representing almost 40 per cent of the global crude oil production increase since 2000. However, various internal policy problems and insufficient investment limit the production of Russian crude oil (Hill, 2004).

Current tight supply and demand conditions that increase the prices of oil products are also due to a mismatch between global petroleum refining capacities and their product mix, and an actual demand for oil products. As a result of underinvestment during the period of low oil prices (1980s–1990s), there is a shortage of capacities to convert heavier crudes into highly demanded middle distillates such as diesel, jet fuel and heating oil (Franssen, 2005). That in turn increases the premium paid for lighter grades of crude oil. The profitability margins (that is, the price difference between the crude oil input and the oil products) of the main refining centres has dramatically increased

in 2005–2006.[3] Meantime, the spare capacities in the global oil refining industry are still at the unprecedented low level of 3mb/d.[4]

The volatility of oil prices in spot and futures oil markets is also a result of the heightened reactions by speculators who recently switched part of their hedge funds investment from financial to commodity derivatives, thus creating a liquidity overhang in commodity exchanges.[5]

OPEC countries[6] produce around 40 per cent of the world crude oil and other related liquids (that is, 3 mb/d) and they dominate in the world demand for oil.[7] Additionally, by coordinating their production and export strategies through production quotas (28 mb/d in 2005), OPEC countries dominate the oil trade flows. Another major oil exporter is the Russian Federation, and the rest of non-OPEC oil exporters (including from the former USSR, Latin America and Africa) still play a marginal role (see table 4.1).

Given the fact that all spare capacities of 1.8 mb/d, that is less than 2 per cent of global supply, are located in Saudi Arabia (see table 4.2), OPEC countries have additional power to balance demand needs if

### Table 4.1

### Geography of crude oil and oil products trade in 2005 (mb/d)

|  | Crude imports | Product imports | Crude exports | Products exports |
|---|---|---|---|---|
| **United States** | 10 055 | 3 470 | 38 | 1 091 |
| **Canada** | 934 | 276 | 1 643 | 558 |
| **Mexico** |  | 328 | 1 956 | 109 |
| **S & Central America** | 657 | 399 | 2 201 | 1 327 |
| **Europe** | 10 537 | 2 724 | 765 | 1 384 |
| **Former USSR** |  | 92 | 5 374 | 1 702 |
| **Middle East** | 205 | 134 | 17 329 | 2 492 |
| **North Africa** | 179 | 169 | 2 462 | 608 |
| **West Africa** | 58 | 186 | 4 191 | 167 |
| **East and Southern Africa** | 548 | 117 | 249 | 17 |
| **Australasia** | 488 | 234 | 145 | 77 |
| **China** | 2 552 | 832 | 135 | 293 |
| **Japan** | 4 225 | 999 |  | 107 |
| **Other Asia-Pacific** | 7 420 | 2 086 | 930 | 1 388 |
| **Unidentified** |  |  | 442 | 727 |
| **Total world** | 37 859 | 12 047 | 37 859 | 12 047 |

*Source:* BP Statistical Review of World Energy, June 2006

### Table 4.2

### OPEC vis-a-vis the rest of world supply (mb/d)

|  | 7 January 2005 | May 2006 | | |
|---|---|---|---|---|
|  | OPEC 10 quota | Production | Capacity | Surplus capacity |
| Algeria | 894 | 1 380 | 1 380 | 0 |
| Indonesia | 1 451 | 900 | 900 | 0 |
| Iran  (Islamic Rep. of) | 4 110 | 3 800 | 3 800 | 0 |
| Kuwait | 2 247 | 2 525 | 2 525 | 0 |
| Libyan Arab Jamahiriya | 1 500 | 1 680 | 1 680 | 0 |
| Nigeria | 2 306 | 2 150 | 2 150 | 0 |
| Qatar | 726 | 800 | 800 | 0 |
| Saudi Arabia | 9 099 | 9 200 | 10 500–1 000 | 1 300–1 800 |
| United Arab Emirates | 2 444 | 2 500 | 2 500 | 0 |
| Venezuela | 3 223 | 2 500 | 2 500 | 0 |
| OPEC 10 | 28 000 | 27 435 | 28 735–29 235 | 1 300–1 800 |
| Iraq |  | 1 900 | 1 900 | 0 |
| Crude oil total |  | 29 335 | 30 635–31 135 | 1 300–1 800 |
| Other liquids |  | 3 998 |  |  |
| Total OPEC supply |  | 33 333 |  |  |

Sources: IEA and OPEC

marginal and unexpected increases occur.[8] It is also important to remember that after nationalization of the oil fields by OPEC in the 1970s the lion's share of the world's proven reserves is on the balance sheets of the NOCs of such key OPEC members as Saudi Arabia, the Islamic Republic of Iran, Iraq, Kuwait and Abu Dhabi.

At the same time the higher oil prices are playing their classic role: on the supply side they bring into the stream crude oil from more expensive oil fields and its derivatives from tar sands and other fossil fuels, as well as stimulating production from alternative energy sources, while on the demand side they further squeeze purchasing power and encourage energy conservation measures. Thus, on the basis of the current level of prices, the potential increase in the international petroleum industry's productive capacity in the coming decade is estimated at between 20 and 25 per cent (Yergin, 2006). The annualized cost of crude oil for the buyers may have already surpassed $2 trillion. In the principal consuming regions the crude oil price represents less than half of the cost that the end users are paying for oil products (the rest going to refining, distribution, marketing and taxes). This suggests that these elements are also crucial for the efficient use and allocation of oil.

The recent major increases in oil prices are reminiscent of the oil price increases during the famous first and second oil crises of 1973–1974 and 1979–1980. However, unlike in the 1970s, this terms-of-trade shock represents a smaller share of GDP, financial markets and international trade. As a result, the global economy shows greater resilience and is still characterized by dynamic growth rates coupled with relatively low inflation and interest rates (IMF, 2006b). The fact that increased oil bills for consuming industries and households do not translate so far into lower demand reflects also the low short-term price elasticity of oil consumption. At the same time, in spite of a longer-term relative decrease in demand for oil in developed countries, its steady increase in selected developing and transition economies might create possibilities for further energy crises and price increases.

Ensuring that supply will keep pace with demand involves a massive scale of investment in primarily exploration and production of oil, representing around 80 per cent of the capital costs of the oil supply chain. According to the IEA (2003), to meet the demand, investments in crude oil and its products supply chain should be close to $1 trillion during the current decade, and for supply to exceed demand they would have to increase further in the next two decades.

So far, the recent decreases in reserve replacement rates to less than 100 per cent in some major IOCs mean that the latter were pumping more oil than they were able to add to their proven reserves. While IOCs are trying to improve the proven reserve profiles of their existing oil fields by increasing their oil recovery rate through the use of new technologies, including ICTs, they are not equally successful in finding new oil, especially outside existing major oil-producing areas. Attempts by some IOCs to improve on reserve replacement rates by buying companies or participating in the ownership of oil wells in-oil producing developing countries help to improve the position of a given company vis-a-vis its competitors and the value of its shares, but not overall proven crude oil reserves.[9]

Already in the 1970s the higher oil prices triggered supply–side competition and, as a result, expansion in the exploitation of more costly and difficult oilfields through the use of newer technologies (Indjikian, 1983). Currently, ICTs are introducing major changes in the oil supply chain. They represent a larger part of the capital structure of the oil industry and are also embedded in oil-related technologies. Moreover, moving from the exploration of conventional oil to its extraction from tar sands, or its conversion from gas and coal, increases the technological intensity of the oil-manufacturing process. Oil derived from those sources and especially heavy oil, mainly contained in tar sands, might dramatically increase the volume of global recoverable oil reserves. And here the question relates not only to the oil price that would make those projects viable, but also to the application of new more powerful technologies such as a sophisticated steam injection process, making it possible to increase the heavy oil recovery rate from 6 to 40 per cent.[10]

As was the case in the 1970s, the oil-exporting countries are experiencing a considerable increase in their export revenues owing to the increased oil prices. That will open up new investment opportunities to upgrade the capital stock in both upstream and downstream oil sectors of those countries. The increase in prices will also trigger more oil production by non-OPEC exporters competing with low-cost OPEC oil for the market share. As a result, oil fields in countries such as Angola and VietNam or Azerbaijan and Kazakhstan will become more attractive for further exploration and exploitation. As the following sections will show, the development of modern oil technologies, coupled with more intensive use of ICTs, allows the exploitation of more difficult oil fields, including offshore and deepwater ones, which is particularly interesting for developing countries such as those mentioned above.

The current high level and volatility of oil prices further increase the possibility of financial crises. Low-income oil-importing developing countries that are not major exporters of other commodities or dynamic exporters of manufactures and services particularly face the burden of further balance-of-payments difficulties and increased current account and fiscal deficits as a result of such terms-of-trade shocks. The IMF and other multilateral and bilateral donors are called on to protect low-income countries from sharply increased oil import bills. The introduction of the newly proposed Exogenous Shocks Facility as a part of IMF emergency lending could be used to cover oil price shocks as well as other external shocks such as natural disasters and armed conflicts (Bunte, 2005). This facility would have a conditionality similar to that of Poverty Reduction and Growth Facility (PGRF), and thus be more concessional than other mechanisms such as the IMF Compensatory Financial Facility (IMF, 2006a).

Nevertheless, this chapter, rather than exploring how to overcome financial constraints, will focus on how developing countries can make better use of technologies, and, in particular, ICTs, in order to make the distribution of oil products more efficient and hence less costly for end users.

## C.    ICTs and their impact on the oil supply chain

The capital-intensive and labour-saving nature of the oil industry helps to explain the very high levels of company revenues per employee. In the case of leading oil companies this indicator can reach several million dollars. The information revolution further increases the role of automation, computation, modelling and other analysis methods, and has scaled up the use of ICTs in the petroleum industry, both upstream and downstream. Although all major IOCs and NOCs were vertically integrated companies and were trying to optimize resource flows and investments and integrate operations from exploration to distribution of oil products, they lacked the necessary instruments to achieve that objective. ICTs, through modern software and their capacities to find optimal solutions for complex systems containing multiple inputs and variables, might increase efficiency in the petroleum industry.

Given the capital-intensive nature of the oil sector, the main part of investment goes to oil-specific technologies, with ICTs still in the process of gaining relative importance in technology related investment. In this regard, it is important to make a distinction between the use of basic ICTs such as e-mail and the Internet and the use of more sophisticated ICT solutions such as integrated data networks or censor devices measuring the drilling and extraction processes. The basic ICT solutions are increasingly standardized and are used extensively by IOCs as well as NOCs in developing countries. The more sophisticated ICT solutions have so far been fully installed only in leading IOCs but are becoming more and more important within the oil sector. Thus, it is estimated that the oil majors, including BP, Conoco-Phillips, Chevron, Exxon-Mobil, Shell, that is the five descendants of the famous seven sisters (Sampson, 1975), as well as ENI and Total, spend over $10 billion a year on ICTs in all their oil and gas operations, including upstream, downstream and petrochemicals.

When implementing ICT solutions in the oil sector there are several conditions that need to be fulfilled. The first concerns the ability to have sufficient capital to invest in new technologies including ICTs. Second, the human and logistical infrastructure has to be in place so that it is possible to apply and work with the new technology. The third condition is the functionality and adequacy of the technology that one would like to apply. Linking the second and third elements is essential as these technologies cannot stand on their own, and sufficient expertise and ability to adjust business processes need to be within the reach of organizations. For example, employees need to be able to easily interpret data flowing in from control systems, integrate and transform those data into knowledge and share and mix different bits of the knowledge of various experts in order to take quick collective decisions on the optimization of business processes.

An indicator showing the increased adoption of ICTs by oil companies is the amount of hardware and software per employee. The better performance of new oil equipment, as far as its measuring and computing features are concerned, also indicates the growing information-intensive nature of the equipment and its integration with ICTs within more holistic business architectures and processes. Increased efficiency in using ICTs might contribute to the extension of proven reserves beyond existing levels, and increase the rate of extraction of crude oil from existing wells and products from crude oil. Competitive pressures from producers of alternative energy sources might also drive technological advances, implying the increased use of ICTs.

While IOCs have a vertically integrated structures that manages all upstream and downstream operations, there are oil companies specializing in parts of those operations or just oil trading. Among vertically integrated or specialized oil or transportation companies there are both private and public companies. The presence of both types of proprietary systems in the international petroleum industry reflects the policies of various Governments regarding natural monopolies and the role of oil in the national economy. In that respect, identifying the impact of ICTs' use in the oil-sector of oil exporting developing countries might be of particular importance.

The advent of modern Internet-based ICTs in the 1990s increased the interest of oil-sector players in assessing the impact of ICTs on the industry and the prospects for competitive benefits that their extensive use might bring about. Apart from analysis undertaken within major IOCs, a number of private consultants (Accenture, Aupec, Compass, Gartner, Forrester, Hackett), as well as technology vendors (Halliburton, IBM, Schlumberger, EDS, Siemens), are systematically exploring the possibilities for more extensive use of ICTs and related new technologies in the oil sector. The responsive attitude of oil companies to surveys conducted by specialized consultants is driven by their desire to keep pace with their peers. With the aid of confidentiality agreements to preserve their anonymity and competitive advantages, they share information willingly with specialized oil consultants to trace the use of ICTs within different peer groups in the oil industry. These studies also permit them to compare the performance indicators of oil or oil-product producers operating in different regions and countries.

Major NOCs from leading developing oil exporters are equally interested in improving production methods and increasing their market shares in downstream operations and are becoming more open in participating in peer reviews and thus learning more from the best practices not only of IOCs but also of other NOCs. That was one of the conclusions of recent major research by the United Kingdom's Royal Institute of International Affairs, analysing the activities and performance of five major NOCs, namely Saudi Arabia's Aramco, the Kuwait Oil Company (KOC), the Abu Dhabi National Oil Company (ADNOC), the National Iranian Oil Company (NIOC) and Algeria's Sonatrach (Marcel and Mitchell, 2006).

Specialized energy consultants normally provide confidential benchmarking services to IOCs and to some NOCs to assess the efficiency of ICTs in particular business functions[11] or for specific aspects of ICT services.[12] The data supplied are then analysed statistically to determine the best explanatory variables for measuring efficiency and other management decision indicators. On the basis of such data, various key performance indicators or metrics are constructed using normalizing or explanatory measures.

For ICT services as a whole a key cost driver is the number of access points, measured as the total number of desktops, including PCs, laptops and technical workstations. The common ICT performance indicator is the total ICT operating cost divided by the total number of desktops. The senior management of IOCs are often more concerned about the effectiveness of their ICT services. When that is the objective of measurement, the normalizing measures are likely to be oil production, sales volume, asset value or profitability. The numerators (or top line date) for many of the key financial performance indicators are usually total ICT spending or costs and its components, operating expenses and investment spending. To understand the ICT intensity of operations at the level of the whole company a measure computing the percentage of total company expenditure devoted to ICTs is used. As a result of such surveys, a participating oil company has a better idea regarding the use of ICTs, on the basis of comparison with its peers and with companies in other

regions. This information helps in the decision-making process regarding future resource commitments to ICTs (Rose, 2002).

ICTs are increasingly considered to be a commodity for the production of goods or services (such as electricity). While previously analysis of the use of ICTs and its impact on economic performance consisted mainly in comparing peers in a single industry, linking ICTs to commodities now makes it possible to compare the oil industry with other industries. Comparing the oil industry with, for example, the organization of business by financial service providers might encourage the use of ICTs in the former. Such an approach might be complicated by the uniqueness of applications and related hardware to carry out technological operations in a given industry. For example, the geophysics applications are technology-specific to the oil industry.

The following subsections will explore in more detail the use of ICTs in upstream and downstream operations, which is schematically presented in chart 4.2.

## 1.   ICTs and upstream operations

The main challenge of upstream operations that include exploration and production (E&P) of crude oil is to extend the life of this depleting resource.

## Chart 4.2

## ICTs in the oil value chain

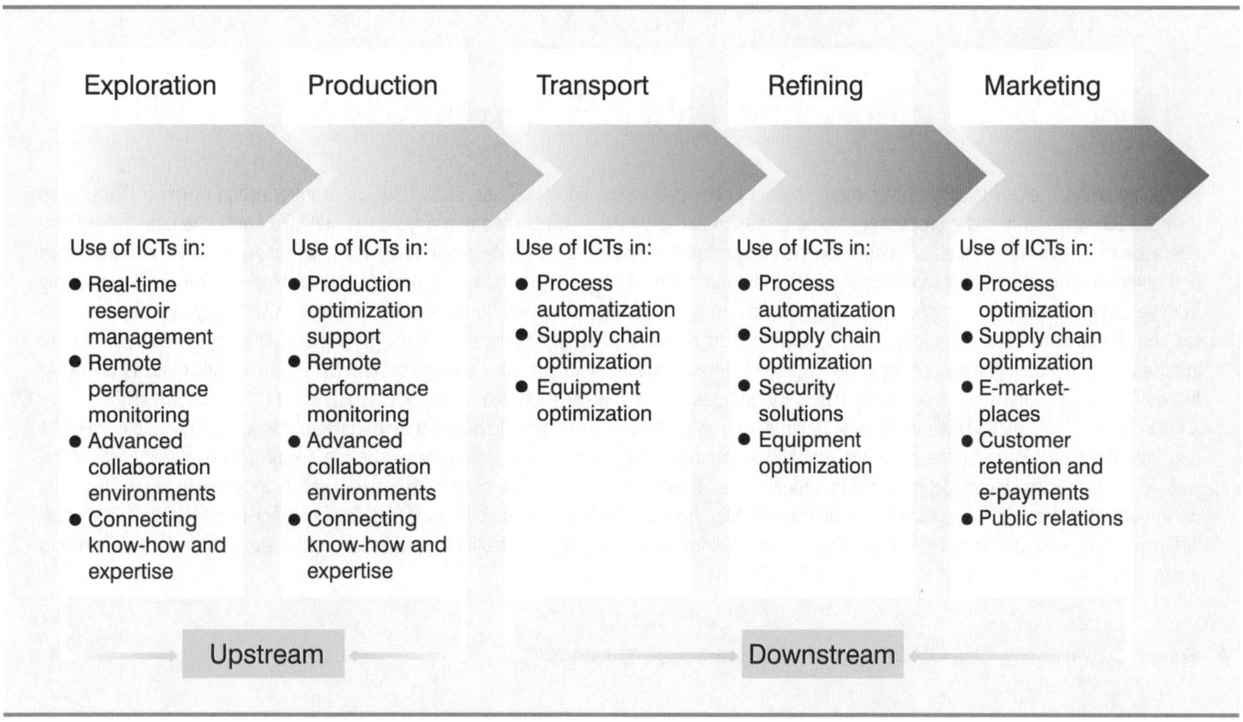

| Exploration | Production | Transport | Refining | Marketing |
|---|---|---|---|---|
| Use of ICTs in: | Use of ICTs in: | Use of ICTs in: | Use of ICTs in: | Use of ICTs in: |
| • Real-time reservoir management<br>• Remote performance monitoring<br>• Advanced collaboration environments<br>• Connecting know-how and expertise | • Production optimization support<br>• Remote performance monitoring<br>• Advanced collaboration environments<br>• Connecting know-how and expertise | • Process automatization<br>• Supply chain optimization<br>• Equipment optimization | • Process automatization<br>• Supply chain optimization<br>• Security solutions<br>• Equipment optimization | • Process optimization<br>• Supply chain optimization<br>• E-market-places<br>• Customer retention and e-payments<br>• Public relations |

Upstream                                                      Downstream

ICTs are becoming more and more important for the upstream operations of the oil industry. Because of the increasing demand for oil and the difficulties in keeping up with this demand from the supply side, the sector is facing the challenge of increasing production and improving oil recovery rates. This situation has caused the oil sector to invest more and more in research and development, and as a result, improved drilling and extraction technologies have been introduced. These new technologies can be divided into two categories. The first one is purely mechanical, focusing on better drilling and extraction instruments such as "horizontal drilling", a drilling process where the pipes are horizontally inserted into the oilfield. This makes it possible to cover a broader area than with vertical drilling. The second category of technologies is based on providing information during the processes. This is done by using monitoring devices in drilling and extraction processes in order to steer them in such a way that maximum productivity and oil recovery are achieved. These new technologies are becoming indispensable as the share of easy oil from the Middle East is decreasing and difficult oil such as offshore oilfields in deep water is replacing it to keep up with demand. The increasing importance of difficult oil has led to the emergence of a new kind of oilfield that is highly digitalized.

Apart from going for new oilfields, a key challenge is to get more oil out of existing fields through the use of more sophisticated technologies that make it possible to "visualize" the oil wells and recover more oil than the current techniques permit. ICTs' role here is hard to overstate as they make it possible to collect massive amounts of data concerning oilfields, with consecutive transfer and manipulation of those data in sophisticated models that in their turn support decision-making as far as the optimal oil recovery methods are concerned. Oilfields are increasingly becoming a part of an ICT network at company level, as all of them are increasingly connected through the Internet and monitored in a quasi-real-time regime. All elements of oilfields, including the oil wells, pumps, pipelines, rigs, production platforms and compression facilities, are interlinked, each having its own IP address. The greatest computing needs for interpreting elements of oil-well-related data derive from so-called 3D/4D seismic search methods that by using downhole sensors make it possible to visualize subsurface fluid flow in three or four dimensions, time being the fourth such dimension. At the same time, major IOCs continue to work on improvements in those methods, trying to acquire seismic data in substantially higher resolution.

The US petroleum industry is one of the largest users of the computing capacity provided by major IT companies such as IBM. They provide capacity to geoservice companies or similar departments of IOCs to manipulate data of prospective and existing wells using the 3D seismic technology which makes it possible to monitor changes in oil fields and to provide

---

## Box 4.1

## Managing oilfields electronically

Managing oilfields electronically from remote centres is not only about improved use of technology or introduction of more IT, but also changes the way in which the processes of oil exploration and production are carried out. A typical digital field implies remote control and operation of oil wells on a constant basis using the interpretation of near real-time data captured by sensors that are installed within oil wells and obtaining information about various physical and chemical parameters of the oil well. Computer-based models capture data not only from sensors but also from logging equipment and flow-rate measuring equipment. In the event of a problem with, say, a well production log, the oil company calls in the logging company (such as Schlumberger) to help interpret the log. All these different streams of data are integrated into a model that helps geologists, engineers, physicists and other company experts to work as a team to find solutions to ensure the well's optimal "behaviour". A computer model can suggest an optimal decision after trying out thousands of different possibilities. To get a value from all oilfields and their wells in an optimal way, an oil company will need to model their behaviour during their complete life cycle (i.e. from the beginning). In that case, the model will determine the initial control setting, based on the design and expected yield of the well. At the same time the model provides for modifications based on the actual flow of oil from a given well. If an experienced technologist disagrees with the model's suggestions, he or she can alter the decision and then feed the modified decision back into the model. The latter will incorporate such a change while proposing future solutions. Combining logical solutions provided by computers with the human ability to interpret is the synergy required to run a digital field.

*Source: Digital Energy Journal, issue 1, April 2006, and issue 2, June 2006.*

## Chart 4.3

## An ICT-based collaborative environment in oil upstream

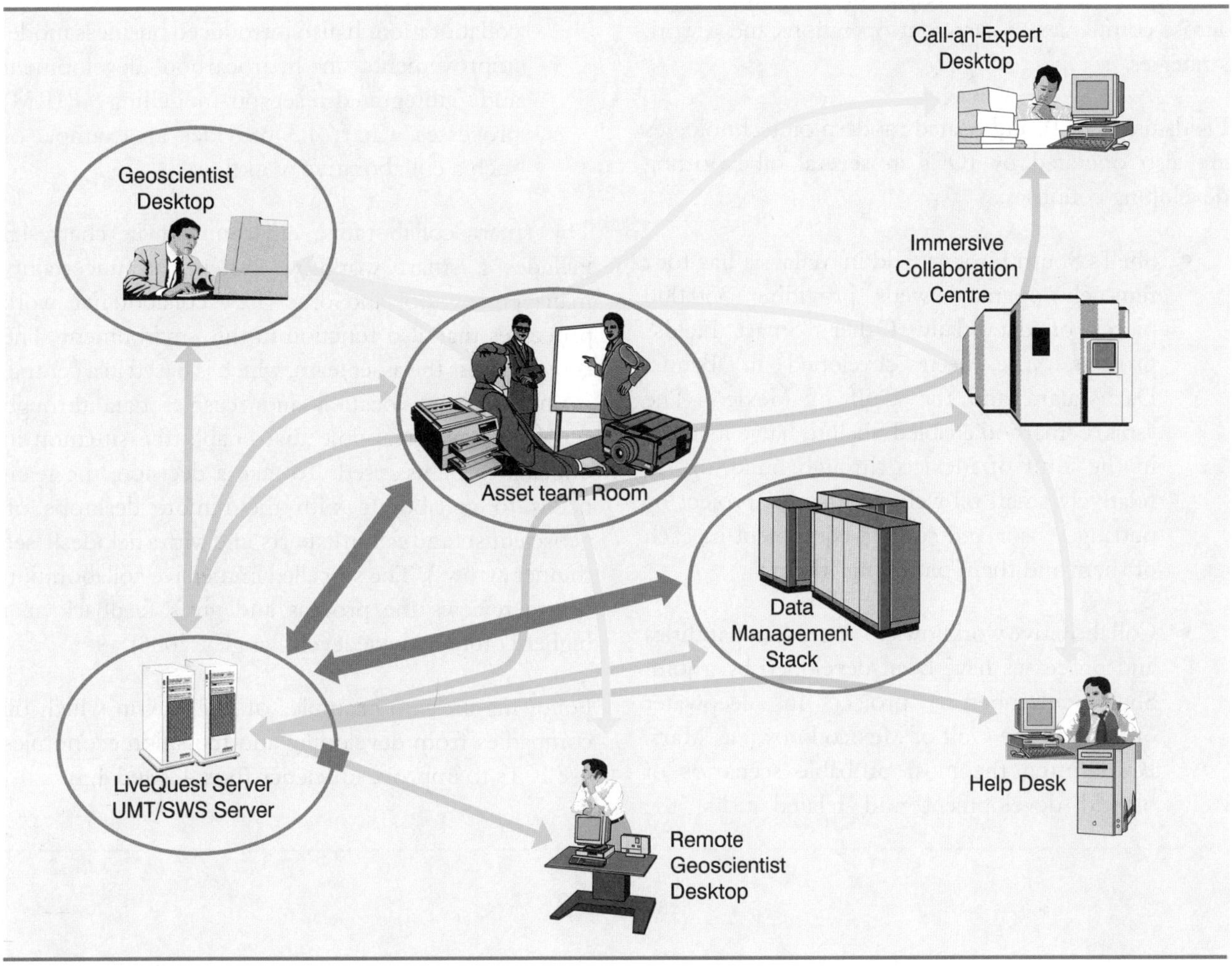

*Source:* Society of Petroleum engineers, Paper 99482.

data for further manipulation services to their clients. Such a large amount of quasi-real-time information creates a problem regarding its assimilation and the timely taking of complex decisions on the optimization of oil extraction.

There is a major need to manipulate data, especially in the case of horizontal drilling in hostile environments of difficult wells. By using logging while drilling, the data from the wells are transmitted to the experts, who then judge and take action to ensure the best drilling strategies and oil recovery methods. One such method consists in lowering a "logging tool" on the end of a wire line into a well, which makes it possible to visualize and monitor the actual drilling process, record rock and fluid properties and identify hydrocarbon zones in geological formations sometimes below the earth's crust. An interpretation of these measurements then makes it possible to locate and quantify potential depth zones intervals containing oil. Logging tools

developed over time measure the electrical, acoustic, radioactive, electromagnetic and other properties of the rocks and the fluids contained in them. Well logging is performed at various intervals during the drilling of the well as well as when the total depth of the well, which could be from 300 m to 8000 m, is drilled. Traditionally, logging was performed as the drilling tools were pulled out of the hole. Now ICTs enable data to be read using sensors in the drill-string. This saves time and money. The data, called a "Well Log", on the basis of which a decision is made are normally transmitted digitally and almost in real time to the main offices.

The departments of major oil companies responsible for the search for oil and optimization of exploration and production processes are now increasingly responsible for running so-called digital or smart or electronic fields. For example, Shell developed the "Smart Fields" program. Here smartness implies a technology-driven improvement in the business process that enables an appropriate level of intelligence to be applied to that process.[13] The idea is to build up integrated operations that bring together offshore and onshore work teams across companies to carry out operations and rework strategies.

Fields using ICTs and related modern oil technologies are also operated by IOCs in several oil-exporting developing countries.

- Shell's South Furious field in Malaysia has four remotely operated wells providing 350,000 pieces of data daily. Other "Smart Fields" projects have been developed in Brunei Darussalam and the Gulf of Mexico. The "smart" method enabled Shell to halve its costs in the Gulf of Mexico through bundling six relatively small oil wells in a single project by putting sensor and control equipment in each of them and then "plumbing" them.[14]

- Collaborative workflows to upgrade capabilities and processes have been developed by a joint Shell–Schlumberger project in deepwater oilfields in the Gulf of Mexico known as Mars. By defining the most probable scenarios of oilfield development and related risks, the

team in charge of those fields tried to identify the optimal use of resources. It used software solutions to evaluate scenarios and options, support decisions and provide architecture for collaboration. It also introduced business model improvements in hydrocarbon development and integrated-reservoir-modelling (IRM) processes. Chart 4.3 provides an example of such a collaborative workflow.

The smart collaborative environment in chart 4.3 includes a smart workflow system, an uncertainty management tool and other new collaborative work processes that also function in this environment. The central part is the asset team, which is based in a central, mainly onshore location and receives data through servers in near real-time that enable the situation in oilfields to be assessed. To take a decision, the team needs to collaborate with the remote desktops of geoscientists and call-in experts, and with a helpdesk (see thinner arrows). The so-called immersive collaboration centre reviews the process and gives feedback at a higher company-wide level (Langley, 2006).

Following are two examples of the way in which oil companies from developing and transition economies use ICTs to improve efficiency (box 4.2 and 4.3).

---

## Box 4.2

## ICT use by the Saudi Arabian national oil company

A striking example of the use of the most advanced IT systems to manage the oil upstream process is the Saudi Arabian NOC, Aramco. It is sitting on the largest oil reserve in the world and is also the world's largest producer and exporter of oil. It disposes of the recent models of CRAY, one of the largest computer systems in the world. Aramco uses them to manipulate enormous masses of data on oilfields' performance and reservoir characteristics in order to '"see into" the reservoirs in three dimensions, thus managing to achieve an optimal level for oil fields' production performance. It has also developed in-house so-called fractal deconvolution, an algorithm enabling improved resolution of seismic pictures. Other software, called DETECT, makes it possible to map out subsurface channels and see the thinnest and thickest parts of oil reservoirs. The company has installed a major integrated SAP software solution, to which 51,000 users in company locations worldwide have access. It supports about 80 per cent of Aramco's key business processes and has managed to absorb more than 250 legacy programs without compromising or disrupting company operations. Employees in remote areas are linked to each other through wireless local area networks (LANs). Access to wireless LANs also allows service and utility organizations to access company SAP applications, e-mail and the Internet. Since 2001, Aramco has also been using VSAT (very small aperture terminal) satellite technology to provide network connectivity for mobile field operations and remote company facilities. VSAT provides inter alia disaster recovery capabilities and back-up communications services to remote areas. The satellite communications enable timely use of information from rigs, field crews and marine vessels. They are available on all rigs, feeding advanced 3D visualization centres and thus enabling remote geo-steering systems for drilling operations through real-time drilling, data collection and monitoring. More sophisticated IT solutions that are feature-rich, real-time and multimedia-based are increasingly making inroads into company practices. According to its Chief Geophysicist, in the next five years Aramco is planning to quadruple its investment in oil exploration.[1] The company invests on a continuous basis in developing and enhancing the IT knowledge of the workforce so that it can adapt better to technological change. The company's ICT-related sophistication has been reflected in the several international awards that its website has received during the last few years.[2]

[1] "Saudi Aramco commits to technology automation" *Digital Energy Journal*, 16 May 2006
[2] See: www.saudiaramco.com

## Box 4.3

## ICT use by Russian oil companies

Another large oil producer is the Russian Federation, where oil is produced by a mix of government-controlled and private companies. Among the major Russian oil producers are Rosneft in which the Government is a majority shareholder, and other privately owned companies such as Lukoil, TNK-BP and Surgutneftegaz. Rosneft is using actively technologies to improve the flow rates of existing wells, as well as exploiting proven but as yet untapped reserves through development drilling with quite low levels of operating and capital expenditures. By using traditional well and modern well and reservoir management techniques, including artificial lift, hydrofracturing and waterflooding techniques the company achieves higher recovery rates from existing wells. Integrated production management software based on geological and simulation models using 2D and 3D seismic data of the key fields, makes it possible to identify those wells with the greatest potential and to allocate drilling, hydrofracturing and lifting resources to maximize the net present value of production in each field. At the same time Surgutneftegaz has designed a method for drilling horizontal wells that makes it possible to increase four or five times the rate of crude oil flow in comparison with wells drilled through the application of conventional technologies. All those technologies are monitored by ICTs related to those processes.[1] Other oil producers in the Russian Federation also use similar methods. At the same time the local oil-related technology and ICT producers are facing tough competition from international service companies and are having difficulty in winning contracts from Russian major oil companies.

[1] See www.rosneft.com; www.surgutneftegas.ru.

Many leading IT and process automation service providers are involved in helping IOCs and NOCs to make upstream operations an ICT-intensive process. While service operators and technology vendors propose various technological solutions, the oil companies are striving to design a single IT architecture for their upstream operations permitting them to operate like an integrated system. As a result, they request the help of service providers in achieving such a solution rather than selling their pieces of ICT equipment or applications. Within oil companies, while business units create and own data it is the responsibility of IT departments to manage those data in the most effective ways. The latter implies ensuring the security of data and its standardization across the company.

Aupec studies analyse the use of ICTs in upstream operations in a representative group of both IOCs and NOCs.[15] The average share of IT spending in total expenditures (including operating capital and project expenditures) was 7 per cent for 2004 and 8 per cent for 2005. These numbers compare well with the share of ICT expenditures in the GDP of the most developed economies. While more than two thirds of the IT budget goes to operating expenditure for running and maintaining the IT infrastructure, investments are also increasing. Also, one fifth of the operating expenses to maintain software applications are devoted to ERP support. While all employees have desktops and many of them have laptops, there is a tendency towards use of high-end PCs and workstations. Equally, companies use predominantly new servers (less than three years old), with Unix servers having a dominant position.

Linux use is increasing in the technical computing segment.[16]

From a developing and transition economy perspective, the adoption of ICTs and investment in them in the oil sector need to take into account a number of considerations.

First, ICTs are becoming extremely important to the oil industry. While pipes, rigs, pumps and large platforms are thought to be made up of low-tech bits and pieces, in reality they are monitored by ICTs and interact by relying on massive amounts of high-tech inputs – from exploration to drilling, development and production – using data management and manipulation, computer-aided design (CAD), supervisory control and data acquisition (SCADA), and so forth.   The above elements represent parts of increasingly integrated operations in the oil industry networked by ICTs that make it possible to communicate, monitor, compute, model and take decisions at the various levels of the upstream.

Second, given the remoteness of many oil-fields and their location outside the main telecommunications networks, access to sufficient bandwidth is of prime importance for IOCs and NOCs. This helps them maintain operations in a holistic way. Some of them use the services of satellite telecom providers to set up intra-company satellite telecommunication networks to link all their oilfields and manage them from the head or strategic regional offices. Companies operating in developing and transition oil-producing countries need to spend more on ICT infrastructure than is the case for North America and Europe, as they frequently need to build up their own infrastructures and cannot rely on local support.

Third, the diverging interests of various players and competition between different standards and programs sometimes limit the possibility of extending integrated operations throughout the industry. These difficulties become apparent when undertaking restructuring, standardization and simplification of installations and programs. Adapting to technological change also requires changing old working habits and labour composition and location. This is often done by moving control and measurement activities from offshore platforms to onshore locations, where virtual control and decision-making are increasingly taking place (Wahlen et al., 2005).

In order to maximize the impact of ICTs on oil upstream operations, developing and transition economies must continuously invest in ICTs and other technologies, and consider the additional barriers, such as limited local expertise, and the need for additional investment in infrastructure.

## 2.    ICTs and downstream operations

ICTs are also actively used in the downstream part of the oil supply chain, namely transportation and refining of crude oil as well as marketing and distribution of its products. As in upstream, here also the share of ICT expenditures in overall costs, including operational and capital expenditure, tends to be around 8 per cent.[17] Downstream operations constitute an information-intensive process that deals with different pieces of data on purchasing and delivery of crude, further refining and distribution of products. Those data include crude prices, inventory, storage and transport capacity, delivery costs, sourcing options and prices, oil products throughput and mix, and delivery to wholesale and retail points of sale. Similar logistical and data assimilation and decision-making problems arise in the case of petrochemicals production and distribution.

The main regulatory requirements that induce oil companies to use next-generation oil technologies more actively are those that impose a large-scale reduction of harmful emissions. As a result, the producers of oil products are constantly searching for products with the lowest possible $CO_2$ and other polluting emissions. Since vehicles and other means of transportation are

the main users of oil products, the possibilities of supplementing oil products with bio fuels or, synthetic fuels or combining combustion engines with electrical motors are among the possibilities to explore. "Fuel cell" is an emerging method for the production of clean energy from fossil fuel. It is an electrochemical device which combines hydrogen and oxygen to produce electricity. It does not require recharging and its only by-products are water and heat. Compared with combustion, this process is several times more efficient and less polluting. However, in spite of the introduction of new technologies and fuels, oil products remain unchallenged and their global consumption shows an upward trend.

Meanwhile the use of ICTs in refineries helps to improve technological processes and increases yields of lighter oil products with less harmful emissions. In transportation and distribution, ICTs make it possible to avoid losses and help to optimize the stocking and further delivery of oil products to users.

Given expectations of a high oil product demand, the world is not short of projects for building new refineries. However, according to Wood Mackenzie[18], most announced refinery projects in 2006 (500, of which 66 are for new refineries) will probably not be realized. As a result, capacity utilization in the industry will remain high and any additional supply capacity will be most probably absorbed by the increasing demand. At the same time the structure of demand will generate further investment in additional refining capacity and more upgrading of existing capacities. The main region that is expected to construct new refineries of a capacity of 1.5 mb/d and expand existing refineries by 2 mb/d is the Asia-Pacific region. Surprisingly, the North American region will concentrate on new projects of more than 1 mb/d, while the Middle East will concentrate on extension of existing refineries by 1.5 mb/d, adding a meagre 0.4 mb/d as new refineries. Another surprise is the fact that while Africa might expand its existing capacities by some 0.4 mb/d, even lower growth is expected in Latin America, Europe and the Russian Federation (Jamieson, 2006). At the same time, given the outdated nature of the technologies used in Russian refineries, which are biased towards heavy oil products, many companies are starting to invest to upgrade the refineries product mix towards lighter products and middle distillates.[19]

Efforts to increase refinery utilization were made in the period of low oil prices in the second half of the 1980s and 1990s, with a view to improving operating efficiencies and thus meeting the challenges of fall a in revenues and profits. Thus, between 1982 and 2002 the US refining industry increased its capacity utilization from 85 per cent to 93 per cent. It also managed to raise by 75 per cent the yield of light products from heavy crudes, considerably reduce crude and product inventories and double the average throughput per retail station. Such efficiency gains were due mostly to progress in using ICT tools. While the 1980s were characterized by the use of linear programming and modelling, which enabled economic processes to be assessed and plant operations to be optimized, the 1990s brought advances in distributed controls, in-line blending, maintenance management, logistics management and introduction of software systems of enterprise resource planning (ERP). Later on, the scale-up of electronic communications and transactions, as well as a wave of consolidations in the industry, added to the increase in operating efficiencies. However, the efficiency gains of that period did not result in increased net margins for the refineries, as the benefits were competed away and passed to customers (Miller et al., 2003).

At the same time, the mergers and acquisitions of the 1990s also increased the operational complexity of running large enterprises. Meanwhile competition and new methods of tracing inventories brought about a trend of decreasing inventories with related risks in supply shortfalls in the event of unexpected contraction of supply from crude oil producers. As mentioned above, modern refineries have also to face the clean fuel requirements and an increasing number of product specifications. Finding the optimal balance between those complexities and efficient and effective production of oil products is a major challenge and requires capital investment not only in modern deep oil cracking equipment, related storing and distribution facilities, but also in integrated downstream operations and management solutions based on the recent web - based ICT programmes. The challenge here is to move out from IT silos based on the priorities of individual departments or parts of the downstream value chain to a global functional model controlling in an integrated manner the work processes, information flows and performance indicators (Moore, 2005).

In other words, further expansion of refining capacities in various parts of the world should take place on the basis of modern information-intensive business processes characterized by intensive use of IT systems that manage transportation of crude, technologically advanced refining processes and further flow of oil products in the paradigm of optimized IT solutions for all stages of the downstream. Linkages between

information systems of various oil companies may also create possibilities to switch from competition to cooperation between oil product suppliers, especially if there are tight demand conditions and very high-capacity utilization.

As will be shown in following sections, the downstream operations are important for developing countries. Many oil exporters diversify their petroleum industry by investing in refinery and distribution not only in their own countries but also in countries importing their crude oil. Some oil-importing developing countries also have refineries. All of them should be concerned with improvement in oil products distribution systems. ICTs are becoming increasingly present in all those operations.

## D.    ICT contribution to increased efficiency in oil trading

### 1. Oil spot and futures markets

In the aftermath of the crises of the 1970s the oil market was the first to introduce on a large scale the spot and futures market as a method of trading, risk management and price discovery. The first oil futures contract using West Texan Intermediate (WTI) as a benchmark was launched in 1983.[20] As a result, in the early 1980s, the prices set previously by oil exporters were replaced by spot prices determined in the London and New York exchanges by both supply and demand. To cover the risks of price fluctuations and defaults on payments, the oil exchanges started to introduce derivative financial instruments such as futures and options. Soon the derivatives market became a major business, which greatly exceeded the volume of the physical market. Increased reliance on futures markets became the main method of determining the market price and managing risks related to price and exchange rate fluctuations. Eventually, the derivatives also determined the prices for oil products and petrochemicals.

Futures trading as a concept has been used since the late Middle Ages, when agricultural producers were managing the risk of price falls by setting contract prices in advance with their potential buyers. However, only the means provided by ICTs permitted futures trading to really take off. The use of electronic means made the price discovery process nearly instantaneous, making it possible to factor in market fundamentals, as well as positive and negative news, for setting current and expected prices of a commodity. However, it was only after the second oil crisis in the early 1980s that pricing started to move out from the so-called posted prices (set by OPEC members) to prices quoted in derivatives exchanges by spot and futures contracts. This oil trading mainly takes place in two principal energy exchanges – the New York Merchantile Exchange (NYMEX) and the International Commodity Exchange (ICE) of London[21]. Those exchanges had concentrated the highest levels of liquidity, which permits the efficient setting of oil futures and options. Operations here are regulated by exchange clearing houses which act as counterparts to every transaction and ensure that brokers honour their commitments. The exchanges cover themselves against the risk of default by pooling brokers' deposits in the clearing house. For example, in NYMEX, which is the largest energy futures exchange, the clearing-house safety net pooled a guarantee fund of $135 million and a default insurance fund of $ 100 million.[22]

Even if energy represents only 2 per cent of the global derivatives markets with financial products,[23] the traded values are growing at an impressive rate. Thus, during the first two months of 2006, 11.1 million oil futures contracts were traded in NYMEX. This represented an impressive 32.1 per cent increase in comparison with the same period in 2005. During the same period, the number of Brent futures contracts in ICE increased by 63.3 per cent to reach 6.4 million. New types of contracts also experienced rapid growth. For example, NYMEX recently launched the electronic mini crude oil contracts. From 2005 to 2006 their volume increased by 488.4 per cent to reach 1.6 million contracts. Interesting was also the dramatic growth of fuel oil contracts in the Shanghai Futures Exchange. Those contracts were launched in August 2004 and reached the impressive level of 2.2 million contracts in January–February 2006, with an 887.6 per cent increase on a yearly basis. There are derivatives exchanges also operating in developing and transition economies, including India, China, Mexico, Brazil and Taiwan Province of China. They are in full expansion and already trade several hundreds of millions of various contracts a year. One of the largest derivatives exchanges in the world is the Korea Exchange.[24]

Analysing the nuts and bolts of futures trading is not the aim of this chapter. However, a short description of its ICT use is provided. Oil futures markets are similar to stock exchanges where brokers agree on futures contracts through open outcry. The positions of the many bidders are then digitalized and communicated to the counterparts and the exchange clearing house.

However, to make trade happen, the broker needs to be physically present in the exchange.

This traditional type of futures market still exists in NYMEX, but no longer in ICE, which became an entirely electronic trading floor. Traders in ICE communicate with each other silently through Internet connection and ICE could therefore give up the trading floor in central London. In fact the fully electronic trading floor has a shorter transaction time. The increase in the speed and volume of transactions brought about a dramatic increase in the membership of ICE, streamlining access to a larger pool of buyers and sellers and a market with more liquidity. Also, ICE developed a service called ICE Data, which delivers online to more than 20,000 subscriber's data on the energy market, including prices, real-time quotes, trades, tick data, historical time series and technical analysis.[25] ICE's departure from the open outcry method induced NYMEX Europe to follow up by opening similar e-floors, first in Dublin and then in London.

At the same time, in June 2006, NYMEX agreed with the Chicago Merchantile Exchange (CME) to start trading energy futures on the CME Globex electronic trading platform.[26] This is one of the largest financial exchanges, with derivative instruments not only for commodities but also for segments of stock equity indexes, interest rates and individual equity. The new element of commodities futures in Globex was the addition of the energy and crude oil segment to the more traditional soft commodities traded in CME.

According to critics, the fully electronic market is more anonymous[27] and more rigid than the open outcry one. They also claim that, in order to be efficient, brokers need to have multiple screens to compensate for the flexibility of the open outcry.[28] The organizers of fully electronic exchanges are aware of this and equip brokers with all necessary ICT tools to ensure that electronic brokerage meets fully the requirements of clients.

Finally, it is known that the benchmarks[29] used in the main US and UK exchange markets refer to the local crude oil types such as WTI and Brent, which are lighter crudes. The only heavy crude that is used as a benchmark is the Dubai from the United Arab Emirates, which has lost importance with time. While world crude oil production shifts towards heavy or sour types of oil with higher sulphur content, the oil product mix demand faces stricter environmental regulations and therefore favours lighter products with very low sulphur content. As a result, it is increasingly difficult to ensure that the price discovery for heavy oils compares well with that of light oil benchmarks traded in NYMEX and ICE. As the Middle East and the Russian Federation are not only the main suppliers of oil but also the centres of heavy oil production, the rationale of focusing oil trading on light benchmarks is questionable. With increasing expertise in the functioning of derivative exchanges and with adequate financial resources, selected oil-exporting developing and transition economies could become new centres of spot and futures trading for energy and primarily crude oil. These new centres would introduce new benchmarks based on the main heavy crude types such as Urals and Dubai. That in turn may increase the ICT-related sophistication of oil-traders based in the main oil-producing regions.

## 2.   Other oil-related e-marketplaces

There are other major oil-trading platforms with Internet-based techniques for transacting mainly oil products, petrochemicals and also some crudes. However, such oil-related e-marketplaces are less visible than e-trading of, say, electricity. Analysis of their structure, business models and sources of financing make it possible to describe the role of Internet-and of Intranet-based e-marketplaces in the oil sector. There is also online trading of oil equipment, spare parts and the like(Geyer, 2003).

E-marketplaces for commodities have been well known for quite some time.[30] Here also buyers and sellers leverage information to make the exchange of products more efficient. However, after the first Internet boom many online trading initiatives in the oil sector were abandoned and the high expectations for e-marketplaces' performance could not be met. Over-investment, together with weak financial management, caused the failure of many of these e-marketplaces. The investments needed were larger than the expected cost reductions. However, some companies such as Intercontinental Exchange and Trade-Ranger continued operating in the market by betting on the long-term benefits of e-business and were ready to invest until the potential of e-marketplaces had been fully developed (Jones, 2003).

The participants in oil e-marketplaces include suppliers,[31] buyers,[32] traders, brokers, distributors, and industrial and private end-users. The varying needs and interests of the different actors, the increasing competitiveness in the sector and the complexity of

the oil supply chain itself have led to the emergence of various e-marketplaces.

The first type, the Power Exchanges, function like stock exchanges. This leads to an environment in which every participant can decide whether to sell or buy its commodity. Thanks to the electronic environment facilities, searching time can be reduced and efficiency gains can be achieved. Because of the nature of the oil market, orders have to be scheduled. This process of scheduling is accompanied by procedures for coping with potential imbalances in supply and demand. These e-exchanges also permit online financial settlements.

The second type, the e-procurement operations, can be regarded as the purchasing of commodities online. Services are designed to deal with the difficulties of complex supply chains, as can be seen in the oil sector. This is being achieved by fully automating the procurement process in a rule-based environment that is supposed to be beneficial to both buyers and sellers. The efficiency gains generated in these procurement e-marketplaces derive from the latter's ability to create sufficient liquidity, deals flow and collaboration arrangements, leading to cost reduction in the supply chain process. The procurement e-marketplace might be compared to a reverse auction process where buyers can place offers and make sellers compete. This leads to an environment in which every supplier can decide where to set its commodities price to get the order. Buyers, on the other hand, can decide what to buy taking into account the prices and amounts offered by suppliers. Meanwhile, given the limited number of players in the oil market, the IOCs are not yet considering e-marketplaces as important playing fields and as a result the emerging e-marketplaces do not yet have the financial backing of IOCs.

At the same time e-procurement and online trading of oil-related equipment are becoming increasingly popular. In many cases these e-marketplaces are a part of multifunctional platforms that also provide other services to customers in the oil industry. One of such platform, called Rigzone.com, together with a marketplace for various type of equipment, also provides information, directories, analysis and so forth.[33]

Selling and buying oil products and oil equipment in e-marketplaces could create competition and thus play a beneficial role, especially for oil-importing developing countries, which would be able to use such marketplaces as to benefit from better prices. For this, adequate ICT infrastructure and financial mechanisms need to be in place.

# E.   The development perspective

Developing and transition economies will probably not be in a position to use oil in the same way as industrialized countries for at least two reasons: the natural oil resources are limited and environmental concerns impose the use of sustainable development models. To both problems ICTs can provide solutions that go beyond the mere improved efficiency and productivity of the oil industry.

To effectively use ICTs in the petroleum industry and related sectors oil-exporting and oil-importing countries need to improve employees' knowledge and skills. The local oil companies are increasingly aware of this issue and engage more often in technology and human capital investments. They also need to learn to combine local R&D with technology transfer so as to make the most efficient use of both.

## 1.   Oil-exporting developing and transition economies

Thanks to increased demand for oil and high oil prices, emerging oil-exporting developing countries currently can have access to sufficient financial resources for their oil projects. However, they encounter many other challenges, including technical ones. The use of state-of-the-art ICT technologies in the oil sector is becoming more and more widespread. Developing countries are now facing the challenge of keeping up with technological developments in order to be able to derive maximum benefit from their oil reserves. As shown before, they need to meet several preconditions in order to do so. While IOCs are already working on integrating their ICTs with business processes and are adapting their human skills to carry out that task, NOCs and independent companies in developing countries are still struggling to get their infrastructure right and to improve access to modern ICTs. Larger NOCs from the Middle East and the Russian Federation are better positioned than the NOCs from other countries as they have enough financial resources to secure access to recent technologies and acquire the requisite experience and skills.

To secure access to new ICTs, the NOCs have basically two possibilities. They can either buy access to new technologies from service operators or they can cooperate with IOCs in exploiting their oilfields. They might acquire more experience and technology by working on pilot projects and other cooperative

arrangements with IOCs and to a lesser extent with NOCs from countries such as China, Malaysia, the Russian Federation and Saudi Arabia. Cooperative arrangements with IOCs have another advantage compared with working with service operators. Clauses for technology transfers and training of NOCs' staff can be inserted in the contracts on the terms of participation of IOCs in the oil production process. As a result, these new agreements are creating a solid legal base for acquiring and adapting the new technologies used by IOCs while the IOCs get access to new oilfields. IOCs can provide developing country NOCs with valuable experience regarding how to re-engineer processes and implement new technologies in an effective way.   Including adequate training programme requirements in agreements with IOCs is equally important for creating a skilled workforce to drive NOCs towards new technologies and ICTs.

Another of the major problems that developing countries have to resolve in their drive for more value-added activities is development of human capital and skilled labour.   In the oil industry those categories include qualified engineers and IT experts. The new work processes based on the use of new technology, including ICTs, need skills that are not easy to find in those countries. One way of addressing this issue would be for local companies to hire specialized skilled labour and consultants from abroad to train the local workforce while backing up local operations. Another way would be to leverage on the technology transfer clause in the contracts with foreign oil companies to ensure the transfer of technology and training and education of local staff. So far, NOCs have requested from IOCs more technology transfer than training for local personnel. Probably many prefer to use specialized independent consultants to train local staff without interference from their potential competitors.

Perceiving oil-exporting countries as a high political risk in terms of their reliability as oil suppliers has often more to do with geopolitical calculations than with economic analysis. The track record of oil-exporting countries shows the contrary. Unlike in the pre-OPEC times of concessions, today oil-exporting countries are fully exercising ownership rights to underground reserves. At the same time, they work in close cooperation and are parties to E&P agreements with IOCs. Those agreements may take the form of production sharing agreements (PSA), service contracts, buy-back deals and so forth.   Moreover, many oil-exporting countries, through their national oil companies, play a leading role in new discoveries and capital investment in E&P. For example, of the

$8.6 billion expected to be invested in E&P in Algeria during 2006–2010, more than 70 per cent will be invested by Sonatrach, the national oil company, while the rest will come from foreign partners. Sonatrach itself made six out of eight discoveries in 2005.[34] If it had not had the technological and financial capacity, Sonatrach would have been unable to take the lead in searching for oil. Moreover, being less constrained by the short-term reporting of results to shareholders, well-organized and modern national oil companies are able to cope with more risky investments in E&P and are reinvesting the resulting profits to improve the proven reserves/production ratios.

After the nationalization of oilfields by OPEC countries in the mid-1970s, the largest part of global oil reserves is under the control of NOCs. In recent decades the NOCs have accumulated not only financial resources but also know-how and diversification strategies by incorporating downstream and upstream operations both locally and internationally. At the same time, the NOCs with access to conventional technologies are increasingly aware of the need to introduce more actively the latest technologies, including ICTs. The latter are at the disposal of technology vendors and major IOCs. To produce oil in more complex and unconventional environments the NOCs will need to work within new IT-intensive collaborative processes and be able to better leverage new technologies.

According to comprehensive research on leading NOCs, the latter prefer to go for independent ways of building up modern business processes and technological capabilities For example, ADNOC, Saudi Aramco and Sonatrach are eager to participate in R&D of new technologies in order to gain an edge in the industry. As was mentioned in the section on ICTs and upstream operations, Saudi Aramco tries to build up its core competencies by addressing fundamental pillars such as technological excellence, people and processes. Looking into the future of the oil market, Aramco is also trying to innovate by developing for example, fossil-fuel-driven fuel cell technology. The emerging collaboration between NOCs to develop clean oil technology is also a part of their technological drive (Marcel and Mitchell, 2006).

An example of active use of ICTs is the National Iranian Oil Company (NIOC), a subsidiary of the Ministry of Petroleum (MOP). It is providing IT services to MOP and its other subsidiaries within the oil sector. The aim is to equip all operational and service units with modern ICTs permitting them to be competitive both in the Islamic Republic of Iran and abroad. NIOC plays the role of an ICP (with a plans to become an ASP) for all MOP subsidiaries in order to provide secure communications for all oil industry units. With more than 150 IT engineers and with a network centre connected to more than 300 access points in various parts of the country, it tries to run enterprise applications which improve communications and procedures within and between the various units in the upstream and downstream operations. It also plays the role of a consultant and provides management with information necessary for taking decisions. The ERP, e-commerce and other web-enabled applications are the elements of online activities of the producers of the Iranian crude oil, as well as of those of oil products and petrochemicals and their users.[35]

There is also an increasing South–South dimension in the oil companies' search for new oil. Sonatrach has been active in prospecting for oil in other developing countries such as Yemen. Being a major oil exporter, the Russian Federation actively encourages its companies to invest in upstream and downstream operations in other transition and developing economies. Major oil-importing developing countries such as China and India are increasingly participating in the search for oil in Africa. This is another dimension of South–South investments in the oil sector (see section on oil importers). All those national companies are competing quite actively with IOCs, proposing to host countries modern technological solutions on more competitive terms.

Finally, the benefits of a more effective use of ICTs in the oil sector should also spill over to other sectors of the economy in order to avoid the "Dutch disease" or, in other words, to avoid making other exports (especially manufactured goods) less competitive as a result of the windfall profits from the oil export sector and the appreciation of the national currency, which could hold back the diversification of the economy and even cause its de-industrialization. One way of countering the "Dutch disease" could be the dissemination in oil-exporting countries of the ICT-enabled efficiency gains, in particular improved corporate governance and organization, to the oil servicing sectors as well as other parts of the economy and especially to less competitive export and non-traded goods sectors. Such a spill over effect, together with flexible foreign exchange and monetary policies, could also keep prices and hence national currencies at competitive levels. It may also inter alia allow local oil services companies to be competitive while participating in bids and auctions of oil-producing companies seeking equipment, goods and services for their activities.

## 2.   Oil-importing developing and transition economies

While major emerging economies can sustain the financial shock due to the increase in oil prices, thanks to their flexibility and quite diversified exports base, the majority of middle and small oil-importing countries are facing major terms-of-trade losses and related multiple economic challenges. In 2005, while net official development assistance (ODA) stood at $106 billion, the outflow from the developing countries on the account of higher oil prices increased by $130 billion. Already in the year 2000, at the time of a much lower oil price increase, UNCTAD proposed that IFIs activate compensatory financing facilities in order to smooth the terms-of-trade shock for oil-importing developing countries.[36] The magnitude of the external shock this time was much greater. Thus, between 2003 and 2005, owing to the increase in oil prices, real incomes in oil-importing countries contracted by 3.6 per cent, while for some low-income countries the loss was much greater, totalling up to 10 per cent of their income (World Bank, 2006).

### Major developing net oil importers

As indicated at the beginning of chapter two major developing oil importers–China and India–are considered to be major competitors in the international oil markets and are thought to be among the driving forces behind the higher plateau of crude oil prices. Currently, around 60 per cent of Middle Eastern oil is flowing to Asia, including Japan, which is second to China in terms of absolute level of oil consumption (OPEC, 2004). In fact, China and India also have local oil production and their NOCs are moving fast up the ladder, catching up with IOCs as far as their corporate organization, technological sophistication and working methods are concerned.

The main Chinese NOC is the China Petroleum & Chemical Corporation, more than 50 per cent of whose shares are controlled by the Government. It showed an extremely impressive expansion of overall sales, both upstream and downstream, from around RMB 350 billion in 2002 to RMB 830 billion in 2005 (Sinopec Corp. 2005, p. 9). Its parent company, Sinopec Group, has developed major South–South oil investment projects including those in West and North Africa. It has been taking economic and political risks in acquiring international equity capital in crude oil production in various regions, and it is expected that

the oil produced from those sources will increase quite soon from 3 million tons to 10 million tons yearly. As soon as the issue of economic and political risks has become a matter of less concern, these assets will be transferred to Sinopec Corp.

With regard to using the local and imported crude oil in an efficient way, Sinopec Corp. stressed the use of ICTs as crucial in the development of resource and supply chain optimization systems, especially in downstream operations. Thus, it established an integrated optimization model at headquarters, followed by a single refinery and multi-period enterprise model, a crude spots procurement optimization model, a process mechanism model, and an integrated refinery and chemical enterprise model. The company IT infrastructure is constructed around a major ERP system covering key information-intensive elements such as supply chain, electronic commerce, seismic data processing, oil reservoir description, production scheduling optimization, advances process control and, IC refuelling card. By the end of 2005, 41 branches of Sinopec Corp. were using the ERP.[37]

In India the two major NOCs, the Oil and Natural Gas Corporation Ltd (ONGC) and Oil India Ltd (OIL), dominate the county's oil sector. While the Government is the main shareholder in both, they are also strategic partners through cross-ownership – that is, they own a part of each other's shares. While OIL is the downstream giant of India, ONGC is the largest Indian player in upstream and transportation (pipelines). Through its subsidiary, Indian Oil Technologies Limited (ITL), and its R&D Centre, OIL is trying to pioneer oil technology development in India. It has upgraded such technologies and technical expertise in the refining and lubricant sector as fluid catalytic cracking (FCC), hydro processing, catalysis, residue upgradation, distillation, simulation and modelling, lube processing, crude oil evaluation, process optimization, material failure analysis and remaining life assessment.[38] At the same time ONGC has one of the main virtual reality interpretation facilities and also one of the largest ERP implementation facilities.[39]

### Other oil importers

The small and medium-sized oil-importing developing countries have fewer possibilities to compensate for the increase in their oil bills through a corresponding increase in exports of goods and services, or accelerated economic growth, and are facing formidable challenges in adapting to the world of expensive oil. These countries include the overwhelming majority of least developed countries (LDCs). While the combined GDP of the 50 LDCs was around $260 billion in 2004 and could be a little higher for 2005 and 2006, the increased profits of oil majors or the-so-called five sisters represented around half of the overall value added produced by those countries.[40]

The main challenge for these oil importers is to find internal and external financial resources to finance the greatly inflated oil imports bill. They also face the need to improve the management of trading, transportation and distribution of oil products to consumers. Increased costs of acquisition of oil and oil products are in themselves a major deterrent and do not allow complacency about the costs related to oil distribution networks in those countries. However, to cut costs or diminish waste they also need upfront investments to replace the outdated technologies and storage capacities.

One of the main challenges for oil importers, and especially for small and medium-sized countries, is the development of a system of joint stockpiling and emergency sharing of oil. Stocks representing 30 days of imports are considered to be optimal. While in some countries Governments and the private sector stock only crude oil, in other countries it is a mix of crude oil and oil products. Moving oil storage from national to regional level makes the management of stocks a more complex task and by definition requires better organization of this framework. Since the regional framework represents a type of network, ICTs are the technologies that can ensure its efficient functioning provided that the established rules of the game do not face the risk of unilateral changes by individual members. Among developing countries this question has been discussed particularly in various Asian organizations and forums. However, the Asian countries are still at the stage of pledging to institute such an arrangement and have not yet started it (Shin, 2005).

Another major problem is the outdated nature of refining in many oil-importing developing countries. In the majority of cases the refining capacities are not using the modern cracking technologies, and the yield of light oil products out of imported crude oil is much lower than similar indicators for modern US and European refineries. While improving the existing oil products distribution network requires relatively incremental investments in ICTs to enable resource flow to be better tracked and losses to be diminished, the technological changes needed in refining and acquiring

related modern ICTs would require considerably larger investments.

Meanwhile many oil-importing developing countries are trying to use imported crude oil and oil products more effectively and are building up stocks. In trying to meet such targets as better organization of purchasing, inbound logistics and distribution of oil products many of them are endeavouring to improve the capacity to manage such processes with more active use of ICTs. In countries with relatively well-organized oil trading companies the latter are in a position to rely on local or international vendors of hardware and software and relative simple variants of ERP to organize streamlined versions of purchasing, transportation and distribution of oil products.

However, the financial resources at the disposal of oil-importing developing countries are further diminished by the increase in oil prices, and the financial assistance provided by international financial organizations, bilateral donors and oil-exporting countries is lagging far behind the actual need of those countries. At the same time, awareness of the need to help developing oil importers to face the challenges of streamlining their oil distribution networks, inter alia through the more efficient use of ICTs, is increasing among various groups of donors as well as the oil companies that are trying to sell oil products to those countries.

## F.   Conclusions and policy recommendations

Traditional crude oil will probably continue to play a crucial role in the future world energy balance for at least several decades. In the more distant future crude oil will derive not only from traditional oilfields but also from other oil-containing energy sources. Also, oil products will be increasingly used in conjunction with biofuels and electricity. That presents policy-makers as well as industry participants and consumer groups with the major task of ensuring a secure supply and efficient use of oil in the paradigm of sustainable development models. In that respect, a key question that should be addressed primarily by the international petroleum industry is how to ensure optimal ways of supplying oil and its products, in particular by using the possibilities provided by ICTs.

Better use of ICTs and related technologies in the oil sector might provide an approach to addressing the current difficult situation regarding oil supply in world energy markets and to achieving a more efficient use of existing oil resources. While ICTs and related technologies should help to locate new oil-fields, with greater accuracy and hence more effective capital expenditure, the issue of more efficient oil extraction from existing fields is no less important. Consequently, the main stakeholders, including the shareholders of IOCs, should espouse a longer-term strategic approach, including increased R&D efforts in the oil sector and reinvesting larger revenues from hydrocarbons in better production modes and reserve indicators.

Avoiding potential deterioration and supply shocks can be achieved only within the framework of well-defined and coordinated policies and practices that include the use of ICTs as a tool for integrating and optimizing business processes in both upstream and downstream operations. The benefits of such an approach are especially apparent for those countries that are lagging behind in the use of technologies as a means of improving their energy situation. The most vulnerable group in that respect are the oil-importing developing countries that have no means of compensating for the increases in the cost of oil by switching to alternative energy sources or by introducing effective conservation measures. Thus, it is equally apparent that well-designed international energy cooperation efforts should clearly include financial and technological support measures for those countries.

To improve the use of ICTs and new technologies the NOCs of the main oil-exporting developing countries should continue investing in ICT related know-how and business processes. Inserting technology transfer clauses in production sharing or other arrangements with IOCs could also be a part of their strategies. At the same time the technology transfer clauses in various types of contracts with IOCs could be the main way of acquiring oil technologies, including those related to ICTs, especially in the case of the new wave of non-OPEC oil exporters from developing and transition economies. Another way to make sure that the IOCs use state-of-art ICTs and other technologies while exploiting oil-fields and developing related infrastructure is to include such requirements in the national oil regulatory framework and ensure that oil operators are fulfilling them. As a result, foreign operators will make the necessary investments in new ICTs and other oil-related technologies while extracting oil in those countries.

Another approach, which is quite well utilized by NOCs from mainly OPEC countries, is based on

closer relations with oil service companies and oil technology and ICT-related vendors, and on closer ties with other oil industry consultants and experts. That makes it possible to set up competitive and integrated technology and ICT architecture within NOCs using means that are relatively independent of IOCs. The problem here is to compensate for the gaps in experience and adequate business processes within NOCs by more actively involving service and technology providers in following up the functioning of newly installed ICT and related technologies. At the same time more active cooperative arrangements for R&D with leading international companies and the involvement of experienced and in many cases retired oil engineers, technicians and corporate executives to help to use better those technologies could also be among the means of achieving a state of excellence in technology, business processes and human resources development.

At the same time oil-exporting countries' Governments may find that the reason for lagging behind is because NOCs, exploiting their special status, are not paying enough attention to the introduction of modern ICTs as a means of improving their corporate performance. To avoid such a situation, adequate regulatory and incentives mechanisms encouraging NOCs to participate more actively in, say downstream might be envisaged. For example, while Governments in many oil-exporting countries are the owners of oil wells, private capital investment, and hence competition, can be further promoted in downstream operations.

Similarly, possibilities for competition in purchasing and supplying oil products in both oil-exporting and oil-importing countries might lead local oil trading and distribution companies to streamline their corporate structures and use ICT more effectively. The issue of efficient use of transportation, storage and distribution networks in all countries, as well as refining in countries that do have such capacities, is becoming a major issue in improving the efficiency of the global oil supply chain. Further diversification of the oil sector in developing countries should take into account the most recent technological solutions in the oil-refining and petrochemicals industry which make it possible to enter as competitive participants in the higher-value-added levels of downstream operations both domestically and internationally.

Oil-importing developing countries that face severe financial problems in buying oil products need to receive financial and technical assistance in purchasing oil products and ensuring that they are transported, stored and distributed efficiently. To make that happen, there is an urgent need to change the focus from traditional IMF compensatory financing mechanisms to special new funds, for example to an enlarged Exogenous Shock Facility with active participation by various groups and types of donors. OPEC and other oil-exporting countries, as well as major oil companies, are in a position to provide considerable funding for such mechanisms. They should also consider playing a proactive role in defining the conditions attached to such a facility. Thus, better use of technologies, and especially ICTs, to streamline the distribution of oil and its products could be one of the recommendations while providing such a facility. In other words, one of the requirements while rendering financial assistance might be the use of part of that assistance to upgrade the ICT capabilities of oil refining and oil products distribution networks in oil-importing developing countries in order to achieve tangible results with regard to more efficient ways of supplying oil and its products to end users.

Such an approach should also be a part of national policies encouraging policy-makers and company executives in those countries to pay due attention to introducing corporate governance criteria that take into consideration the efficient use of ICTs in the distribution of oil products. However, this cannot be achieved unless international financing arrangements helping the most affected oil-importing countries are put in place. Considering better options for financing and using oil and its products should be an important responsibility of public and private decision makers in oil-importing countries. It should be also an important point for consideration by oil exporters, IFIs and the donor community at large.

# References and bibliography

Ait Laoussine Nordine and Gault John (2004). Foreign investment and public goals. Paper presented at the 9th International Energy Forum 2004, 22-24 May, Amsterdam, Netherlands.

Bartels Andrew (2006). Trends 2006: Six economic shifts affecting IT. Forrester, March 15.

Bunte Jonas (2005). Analysis of the new IMF Exogenous Shocks Facility (ESF). Paper for erlassjahr.de dated 5 December.

http://www.erlassjahr.de/content/publikationen/dokumente/20051205_esf_analysis.pdf

CERA (2005). The oil industry growth challenge: Expanding production capacity. Testimony by Robert Esser to the US House of Representatives, 12 December.

CERA (2006). The Global Context. Testimony by Daniel Yergin to the US House of Representatives Committee on Energy and Commerce, 4 May.

EIA (2006). *International Energy Outlook 2006*.

Shin Eui-Soon (2005) Joint stockpiling and emerging sharing of oil: Update on the situations in the ROK and on arrangements for regional cooperation in Northeast Asia. Presentation at the Asian Energy Security Workshop, Sampson 13-16 May.

Franssen Herman (2005). The end of cheap oil: Cyclical or structural change in the global oil market? *Middle East Economic Survey,* 7 February.

Geyer Gerda (2003). E-marketplaces in the Energy Sector. Norwegian Trade Council.

Hill Fiona (2004). Oil, gas and Russia's revival. Foreign Policy Centre, London, September.

IEA (2000). India-a growing international oil and gas player, March, Paris.

IEA (2002). *World Energy Outlook 2002*, Paris.

IEA (2003). *World Energy Investment Outlook 2003.* Insights. Paris.

IEA (2005a). *World Energy Outlook 2005.* Paris.

IEA (2005b). Energy technologies at the cutting edge. Paris.

IMF (2004). Review of the compensatory financing facility. Prepared by the Policy Development and Review Department, 18 February.

IMF (2006a). Guidance note on the Exogenous Shocks Facility. Prepared by Policy Development and Review Department, 27 January.

IMF (2006b). Oil prices and global imbalances, Chapter II, *World Economic Outlook,* April.

Indjikian Rouben (1983). OPEC in the world capitalist economy, monograph (in Russian), International Relations Publishers, Moscow.

Jamieson Aileen (2006). Refiners to see strong returns near-term despite looming capacity build-up. *Oil and Gas Journal,* 13 March, pp. 52–56.

Jones Matthew (2003). E-business: The second generation. World Petroleum Congress 2nd Regional Meeting and Exhibition, held December 8-11, 2003 in Doha, Qatar.

http://www.world-petroleum.org/isc2004/File%20014/089-93.pdf

Langley Diane (2006). Shaping the industry's approach to intelligent energy. *Journal of Petroleum Technology*, Society of Petroleum Engineers, March.

Marcel Valérie and Mitchell John V (2006). "Oil titans: National oil companies in the Middle East", monograph, Chatham House/Brookings.

Miller William J, Sakaguchi Jeffrey B and Gess Mark A (2003). Transforming the petroleum supply chain: "Fulfilling the Promise". Accenture.

Moore Chuck (2005). Maximizing value in the petroleum supply chain. Petroleum Review, 1 March. http://www.aspentech.com/publication_files/Petroleum%20Review%20May2005%20Supply%20Chain.pdf

Moore Cynthia et al. (2005). Hype cycle for the oil and gas industry, 2005. Gartner Industry Research, 29 July.

OPEC (2004). *Annual Statistical Bulletin*. Vienna.

OPEC (2006). OPEC long-term strategy. Vienna. http://www.opec.org/library/Special%20Publications/pdf/OPECLTS.pdf

Pahladsingh Shanti (2005). E-marketplaces in the energy & fuels sector. eMarketServices, The Netherlands. http://www.emarketservices.com/upload/Reports/Report050407_Energy.pdf

Peterson R D, S Yawanarajah, D Neisch and S James (2006). Improving the quality and efficiency of subsurface workflows. Paper (SPE Paper 99482-MS) presented at the Intelligent Energy 2006 conference, held 11-13 April 2006 in Amsterdam, The Netherlands.

Rose David (2002). Trends in information technology costs and investment levels in the oil industry. Publication of Aupec Ltd, Aberdeen, UK.

Sampson Anthony (1975). *The Seven Sisters: The Great Oil Companies and the World They Made*, London, Hodder and Stoughton.

Sinopec Corp. (2005). China Petroleum & Chemical Corporation, Annual Report.

Skinner Robert (2006). World energy trends: Recent developments and their implications for Arab countries. Oxford Institute for Energy Studies, May.

UNCTAD (2003a). ICT and economic performance: Implications for developing countries. Chapter 2, *E-Commerce and Development Report 2003*, New York and Geneva.

UNCTAD (2003b). Marketing developing-country agricultural exports via the Internet. Chapter 6, *E-Commerce and Development Report 2003*, New York and Geneva.

UNDP, UNDESA and World Energy Council (2004). Energy Resources and Technological Options. Part IV, World Energy Assessment Overview, 2004 Update.

Wahlen Mona et al. (2005). Report on the consequences of large-scale adoption of integrated operation on the Norwegian shelf for employees in the petroleum industry and on the opportunitits for creating new jobs in Norway. SINTEF HiT Final Report, 1 December.

World Bank (2006). Prospects for the global economy. Chapter 1, *Global Development Finance 2006*.

Yergin Daniel (2006). Ensuring energy security. *Foreign Affairs*, March/April.

# Notes

1. The terms petroleum and oil or crude oil have the same meaning and are used interchangeably.

2. See IEA, Oil Market Report, 12 May 2006, at *www.oilmarketreport.org*. One million barrels a day represent 50 million tons per year. At the same time 1 ton of crude oil is equal on average to 7.3 barrels, with higher indicators for light sorts of petroleum and lower ones for heavy crudes.

3. See *www.unctad.org/infocomm/francais/petrole/ecopol.htm*.

4. Oil and Gas Journal, 13 March 2006, p. 52.

5. IEA, Oil Market Report, 12 May 2006, p.15.

6. OPEC has 11 members:  Algeria, Indonesia, the Islamic Republic of Iran, Iraq, Kuwait, The Libyan Arab Jamahiriya, Nigeria, Qatar, Saudi Arabia, the United Arab Emirates and Venezuela. Iraq is currently not subject to quotas discipline.

7. See *www.oilmarketreport.org*.

8. IEA, Oil Market Report, 14 March 2006, p. 15.

9. *The Economist*, 15 April 2006, p. 67.

10. Steady as she goes: Why the world is not about to run out of oil, *The Economist*, 22 April 2006. http://www.economist.com/finance/displaystory.cfm?story_id=6823506.

11. Such as upstream exploration and production operations, technical computing, downstream refining, marketing and retail.

12. Such as distributed computing,  wide area networks and midrange computing.

13. What are smart fields?, *Digital Energy Journal*, April 2006.

14. Ibid.

15.. See http://www.aupec.com/

16. Ibid.

17. Ibid.

18.. See http://www.woodmacresearch.com/

19. Who is preparing the gasoline crisis? Argumenti I Fakti (in Russian), 19 April 2006.

20. http://www.nymex.com/energy_in_news.aspx?id=eincrudeprice.

21. Formerly International Petroleum Exchange -(IPE).

22. See http://www.nymex.com.

23. Interest rates and individual equity futures and options have the lion's share on the global derivatives markets.

24. Rebecca Holz, Trading volume: A remarkable start in 2006, *Futures Industry,* May/June 2006, pp. 10–13.

25. http://www.theice.com/market_data.jhtml.

26. http://www.nymex.com/hot_topics.aspx.

27. One does not see who is in the other part of the deal.

28. *Alexander's Gas and Oil Connection,* vol. 10, issue 21, 10 November 2005.

29. Types of crude oil around which are determined the international prices of other sorts of crude oil.

30. For more information on e-marketplaces for commodities see UNCTAD (2003b).

31. IOCs, NOCs, small and medium-sized independents in E&P, etc.

32. Independent refineries, small and medium-sized independents with a shortage in their own oil resources, IOCs, NOCs etc.

33. See www.rigzone.com.

34. *Oil and Gas Journal,* 6 March 2006 p. 28.

35. See http://www.nioc.com/computer_services/index.html.

36. UNCTAD urges "compensatory" funding for oil-importing developing countries, TAD/INF/PR/066 09/10/00. See http://www.unctad.org/Templates/Page.asp?intItemID=1528&lang=1.

37. See *http://english.sinopec.com.*

38. See *wwww.iocl.com*

39. See *www.ongcindia.com*

40. See *www.unctad.org, www.worldbank.org*

# Chapter 5

# ICTs, ENTERPRISES AND JOBS: WHAT POLICIES?

## A. Introduction

To understand the poverty effects of information and communication technologies (ICTs), it is necessary to know how these technologies alter labour markets. Ultimately, jobs are the only sustainable poverty eradication tool because they are the source of income both for the population through wages and for Governments through taxation. ICTs are important contributors to business performance. For this reason, policymakers must develop strategies to promote competitive enterprises (particularly small and medium-sized ones) that generate decent work (ILO, 2001). Effective enterprises require competent managers and productive workers. Human resource development is therefore an indispensable component of any ICT-related economic and social growth policy.

The benefits of *the information technology revolution are today unevenly distributed between the developed and developing countries and within societies.*[1] This "digital divide" is the result of prevailing social and economic inequalities within and between countries. A major concern is to adopt corrective policies so that this divide does not prolong and deepen existing socio-economic inequalities. The introduction of ICTs is not neutral. Without intervention, the greater use of ICTs can increase existing social and economic divides. This is true between and within countries. Social and equity issues must be considered. This is particularly true in the case of ICTs. Financial and human resources are required in order to exploit ICTs advantageously. This is true for an individual, for an enterprise and for an economy. Enterprises or persons that understand how to use information can exploit the comparative advantage bestowed by both hardware and software. Economies must face such a challenge too. In so doing, they become more competitive: ICTs thus leverage and amplify existing social and economic divides unless corrective action is taken. Countries with large human resource pools and solid social security systems have the capacity to adapt, to finance retraining and to cushion the costs of transformations. In so doing, they can increase their productivity and become more competitive, thus widening the gap between them and

less developed economies. The policy challenge is to ensure that the less privileged strata of society, of firms and of countries can benefit from the enhancements that new technologies provide.

It is in the developed world that many of the effects of ICTs on production processes and labour markets can be observed at this time. It is there that most investments have been made, and it is there that evidence is readily available. This is true both in industries that produce directly ICT goods and services and in other enterprises that use these to improve their performance. It is therefore important to emphasize that even if most of the evidence available reflects experiences in the developed countries, indirect and anecdotal information seems to indicate that the process is being replicated in the developing world. For example, while there do not seem to be standardized employment figures for Indian business services, the data on external trade in this sector would seem to suggest that employment there must have grown significantly (see chart 5.6). Similar output figures for other developing countries for which data are available tend to confirm this hypothesis. The first section of this chapter will review some of the factors that explain why ICTs have considerable effects on labour markets. The second will examine the technologically induced changes in the structure of the economy. The third section will show that the introduction of automation at the "factory" (or production) level has shifted employment away from production into managerial and other non-production employment and to the services sector. A common belief is that this results in offshoring: work previously carried out in high-cost areas is displaced to low-labour-cost economies. The fourth section, however, argues that the scant evidence available tends to *disprove* this notion. Indeed, the employment levels of skilled workers in many developing countries tend to show a trend of labour market segmentation similar to that seen in the developed economies. In all these countries there is evidence of an increase in either the employment or the wage levels of skilled workers and a fall in these same factors for others. It will be also argued in the fourth section that these changes are the result of technological change. The final section will examine some consequences of these shifts and the policies that countries will need to adopt in order to face the challenges posed by ICTs.

## B.   How do ICTs interact with the world of work?

ICTs are important factors in determining how, where, when and who works. They do so directly through the transformation of machinery and equipment used in the production of goods and services. Occupations have disappeared and been created: who had heard of web page designers some fifteen years ago? Similarly, how many typographers does industry need now? Clerical tasks carried out by telephonists, data entry personnel and secretaries have been changed beyond recognition. Indeed, repetitive tasks of increasing complexity can now be - and are being - automated at an ever more rapid pace.

The fall of microprocessor prices and the increase in their performance have led to rapid implementation of automation, the creation of powerful optimizing algorithms and data mining technologies. Thanks to these developments, new administrative and control processes are possible, permitting greater inventory and logistics management and new marketing processes. There is ample evidence already that, under specific conditions (Dorgan and Dowdy, 2004), investments in ICTs improve the productivity of firms (OECD, 2003; Indjikian and Siegel, 2005), ICTs become competitive tools and their use becomes indispensable. This poses a real challenge to developing countries, where there are few financial and human resources to implement the changes required in order to make full use of investments in those technologies.

The market effects of ICTs could be just as significant. The reduction of transaction and search costs has improved the performance of markets (Eggleston, Jensen and Zeckhauser, 2002). It is now possible for most firms to ascertain the prices charged by their competitors and to identify low-cost suppliers, thus improving their competitive position. This can, in turn, lead firms to assess their value chain and to identify those activities that could – or should – be subcontracted and those that give them a competitive edge. It also allows customers to find the best prices for the products or services they seek to acquire. The market operates in a more effective manner by increasing the number of actors that can operate in any market and by making prices of intermediary and final goods much more transparent.

The rapid growth of the Internet and the consequential reduction of transmission costs have made it possible and economical to transmit vast amounts of information across large distances. This, in turn, has allowed the trade in services that have permitted coordination and planning of production processes across both time and space. No longer is it necessary to have research and development teams physically near production or marketing teams; no longer do back-office tasks need to be near cost centres. A critical component of enterprises' strategies is now to determine what to subcontract and what to produce in-house. Globalization and technology have jointly made it possible not only to subcontract a number of activities, but also to do so at an international level: it is increasingly simpler to make jobs – rather than workers – migrate. ICTs have the potential to transform production methods, processes and management in all enterprises regardless of size and location. The transformation is, however, clearly evident in the IT industry itself, which has led in adopting significant structural changes in the recent past.

The transformations of production methods and processes do not, by any means, imply the loss of total jobs in an economy. They require a change in the structure of competencies. Unfortunately, the pace of change of productivity is often greater than that of the rate of transformation of the skill mix of a society, and this can lead to transitory rises in unemployment levels. Historically, however, technological change has led to productivity growth, greater innovation and, ultimately, increases in the standard of living (Broadberry and Irwin, 2005). The policy challenge is to speed up and facilitate the transformations required of the labour force and reduce the costs resulting from these changes. This must be considered for equity reasons and also to facilitate the adoption of new technologies. Workers who do not fear change and are equipped to benefit from it will be much more amenable to the adaptations resulting from the adoption of ICTs.

## C.   Economic "sector" shifts

During the Industrial Revolution productivity rose significantly in agriculture (Stokey, 2001) and there was a shift of employment and production from farms and households to "factories" (Mokyr, 2000; Piore and Sabel, 1990). It is very likely that the ICTs are currently having a similar effect, transferring activities from manufacturing to the *business* services sector: new production models rely on "high skill" activities such as design, research and development and supply chain management and marketing at the corporate level. The production of goods and services is subcontracted to first-tier producers (Auer, Besse and Méda, 2006). Services, particularly business services, can increasingly be traded.

Changes in the structure of production of goods and services can be divided into changes that alter the production processes within enterprises themselves and changes that lead to the suppression of activities within an enterprise and that are subsequently acquired in the marketplace – the "horizontalization" of enterprises. Many of the internal production changes result in productivity increases and changes in the demand for labour. These will be briefly examined in section E of this chapter, which will review available data on shifts from manufacturing to those services that were traditionally carried out within firms and are now increasingly subcontracted. Therefore, the changes that will be examined here concern manufacturing and financial intermediation, real estate, renting and business activities.

The definition of economic sectors and their dynamics must be viewed with some caution. The development of supply chains facilitated by highly effective data processing equipment and increased market openness

makes it possible to separate the pure production of goods (or services) from their design, marketing and distribution. This process is amplified by economies of scale, specialization and different innovation practices. Indeed, by making it possible to distribute goods and services over wider geographical areas it is possible to achieve much larger returns to scale. Thus, some enterprises can specialize in product development and marketing, while others thrive on process innovation. This increased specialization can modify the nature of firms, leading to possible errors of classification: when electronic industries subcontract the production of their goods and concentrate on design, marketing and supply chain management, do they belong to the "manufacturing" sector? The changes in the forms of distribution of content (music, text and cinema) will reduce the production of goods too. The production of tapes or compact disks is being replaced by the electronic distribution of content: is content a good or a service? The same might happen in the future with books. There is thus a need to explore the shift from the manufacturing to the business services sector and to the production of intangibles (content), taking into account that there are significant risks of mis-classification because of the changing nature of business and the absence of fine-grain, comparative data on the subject.

## Chart 5.1

### Output of business services and manufacturing output as a proportion of total output

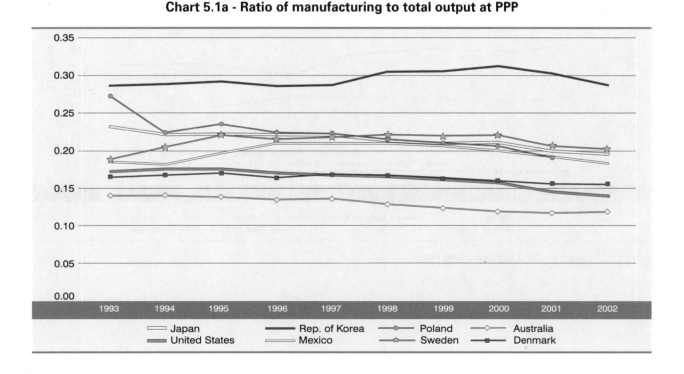

**Chart 5.1a - Ratio of manufacturing to total output at PPP**

**Chart 5.1b – Ratio of business services to total output at PPP**

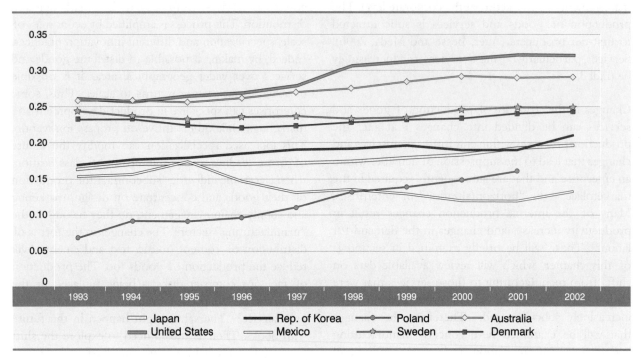

*Source:* ILO, based on UNSO and World Bank (World Development Indicators).

## Chart 5.2 – Employment levels

### Chart 5.2a – Manufacturing

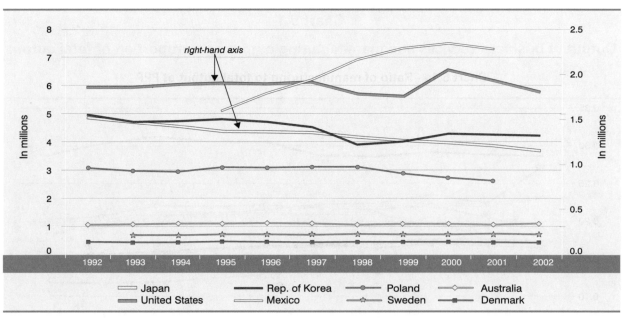

*Source:* ILO, based on UNSO and World Bank (WDI).

## Chart 5.2b – Business services

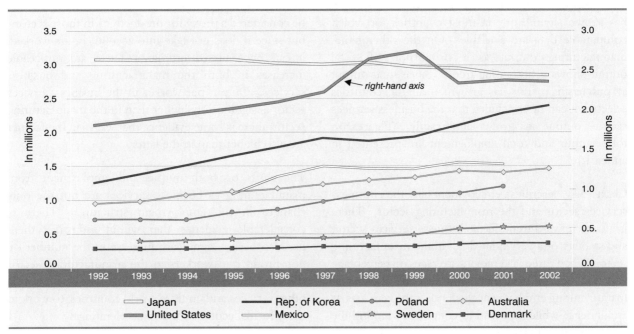

*Source:* ILO, based on UNSO and World Bank (WDI).

## Chart 5.3 – Smoothed average changes in employment levels

### Chart 5.3a – Changes in manufacturing employment

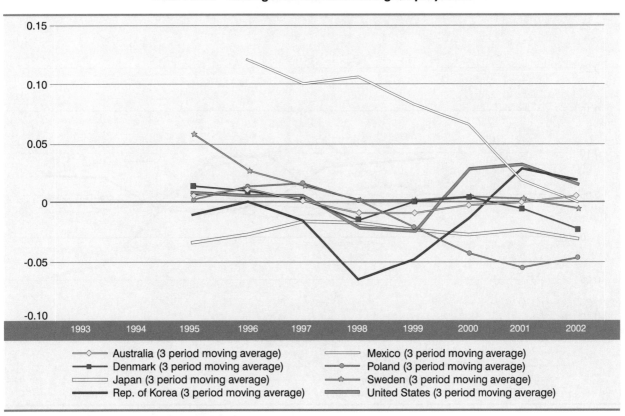

*Source:* ILO, based on UNSO and World Bank (WDI).

As chart 5.1[2] shows, the output of business services as a proportion of total output (figure on the right) has grown significantly in most countries for which comparable data are available.  On the other hand, manufacturing output as a proportion of total output shows a decreasing trend.  Since total output at purchasing parity has grown in all the countries selected, it can be concluded that the business services sector's output has grown significantly.  (Figures on total output and total employment are presented in annex 1.)

Chart 5.2 describes employment in the business services sector and the manufacturing sector.  There is a clear upward trend in the business services sector, and stability or a very limited fall in the manufacturing sector. When three-year moving averages of percentage variations are plotted, they show that the changes in manufacturing employment cluster near the zero axis or are under it, while they tend to concentrate around the 5 to 10 per cent ranges in business services – describing a level of stability in employment for the manufacturing sector and growth for the business services sector. Both Japan and the United States show negative smoothed employment growth rates in the business services sector, but this could probably be partly due to (or is a result of) the output employee ratios described below.

Chart 5.4 illustrates the output per worker in the manufacturing and business services sectors. (This can be considered a proxy for productivity in those sectors, but since it does not take into account hours worked, it can be a biased estimate.) There are noticeable increases in both the manufacturing and business services.  Output per worker in the business services sector is significantly higher than in the manufacturing sector: there is some evidence that wages in the former are also higher than in the latter.

The shifts of both output and employment from manufacturing to business services are not the only changes in the employment structure.  There is considerable evidence that within industries there has also been a significant increase in the number of non-production workers in the manufacturing sector (Berman, Bound and Machin, 1998).  The shift towards other services and, in third world countries, to work in the informal economy is also accelerating.

In conclusion, it could be said that technology has brought stability in the employment levels for the manufacturing sector and growth in the business services industries.  Output per worker in both these sectors is growing, but growth in manufacturing is lower than in the business services sector.  Unfortunately,

## Chart 5.3b – Changes in employment in business services

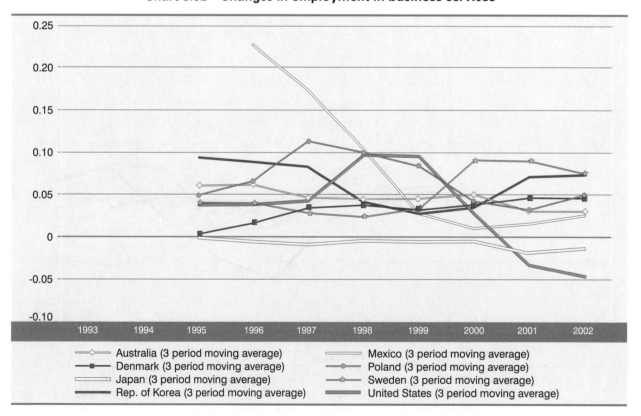

Source: ILO, based on UNSO and World Bank (World Development Indicators).

## Chart 5.4 – Output per worker (USD)

### Chart 5.4a – Manufacturing

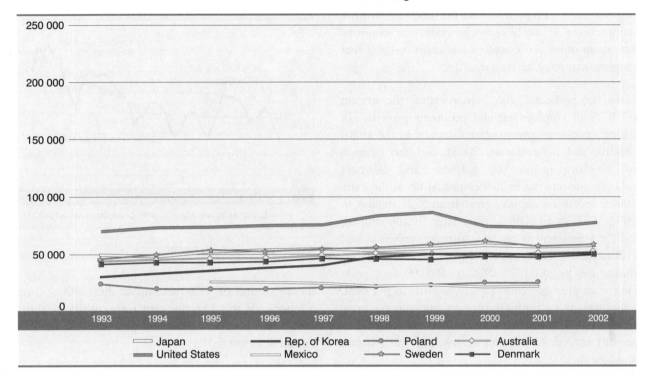

### Chart 5.4b – Business services

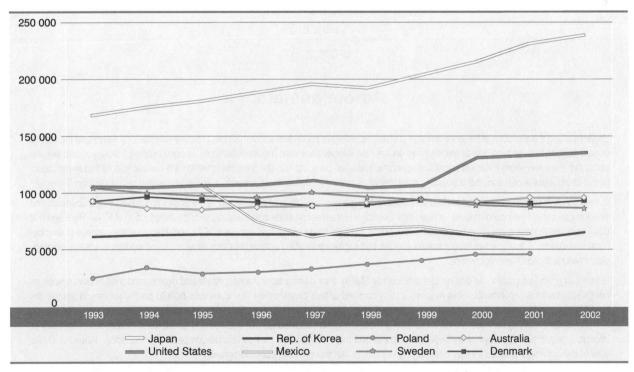

*Source:* ILO, based on UNSO and World Bank (World Development Indicators).

the picture is not complete since India and China, major beneficiaries of current economic trends that have showed significant export and output growth, do not have compatible statistics allowing further comparisons. It may be noted, however, that economic activity in these two countries has expanded and that employment must have increased too.

India, in particular, has demonstrated the impact of ICTs in employment and economic growth. In reality, economic growth started rapidly in the 1980s (Rodrik and Subramanian, 2005), and the creation of employment in the software and business process outsourcing industries picked up in the early 1990s. Software exports grew from $225 million in 1992–1993 to $3,010 six years later (Kambhampati, 2002). Employment in the software industry was estimated to have grown from 242,000 persons during the period 1999–2000 to 568,000 four years later – an average yearly growth rate of 18 per cent. Employment in business process outsourcing grew from 70,000 workers in 1999–2000 to 245,500, a growth rate of 42 per cent average per year (Kumar and Joseph, 2005).

Chart 5.5 shows the significant growth of the services sector in India (which includes the business sector) starting around 1983. This break roughly corresponds to the changes resulting from policy transformations as described by Rodrik and Arvind (2005). Business and communications were the largest contributors to this growth (an average growth rate of 13 per cent in

### Chart 5.5[3]

### Growth rate of services sector, India

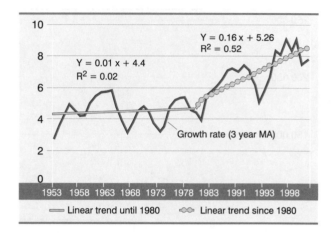

*Source:* Gordon and Gupta (2003).

the 1980s and of 19.8 per cent in the 1990s and of 6.1 per cent and 13.6 per cent respectively). A short comment on data sources and problems therein can be found in box 5.1

## D.   The geographical movement of jobs and workers

It was previously noted that low search and transaction costs associated with ICTs facilitated the development

## Box 5.1

## A note on data

Understanding the evolution of the economy and creating appropriate social and economic policy require information. Assessing the results of past policies to determine how to respond and design new interventions also requires statistics. In paraphrasing Solow, you can see the computer age everywhere except in social and economic statistics, particularly in the developing world. It is curious to note that the introduction of cheap data acquisition and processing machinery has not led to visible improvements in social and economic information there.

In common with others, labour markets can be influenced by greater availability of information. Enterprises can advertise job openings and workers can submit their candidatures for openings. Search and transaction costs could also fall with the introduction of ICTs. Here again, it must be noted that there are important divides: low-skilled workers tend to have less access to ICTs and, therefore, less access to employment information. Clearly, active labour market policies that capture available opportunities and allow unskilled workers to identify postings would reduce frictional unemployment.

In terms of policy, information on enterprises (particularly SMEs), their demography (births, growth and deaths) and their human resources needs substantial improvements. This requires a fairly comprehensive classification of occupations both to permit workers to assess demand for jobs and to determine individual career paths through training and retraining. Such data are also useful for programme education and professional training services. At the same time, a more fine grain classification of industries and an improved description of formality or informality would permit policymakers to define industrial and trade policies that play on relative competitive advantages. Indeed, a closer view of the dynamics of sectors helps in identifying key actors that can promote economic growth.

of global supply chains through the expansion of offshoring and foreign direct investment. This is, clearly, not a new phenomenon. In the manufacturing sector numerous industries have transferred activities to low-labour-cost economies over the last few decades. This has been done either through the establishment of wholly owned subsidiaries or, through outsourcing to external manufacturers within or outside national borders. Labour cost differentials can (sometimes) justify such outsourcing to external economies (which will be identified here as offshoring). Chart 5.6 presents estimates for the amount of services offshored in 2003.

Unfortunately, estimating the net employment effects of offshoring is not an easy task. In the first place, it is difficult to identify the net number of jobs lost due to subcontracting. The United States Department of Labor has carried out research to estimate the total employment affected by offshoring. This is described in table 5.1 (Brown, 2004), which analyses the nature of the separations of staff when enterprises with more than 50 or more workers lay off staff. In summary, only 26 per cent of closures and layoffs led to offshoring, but only 7 per cent were transferred outside the enterprise.

Some precautions must be taken in interpreting these data. They do not include employment *created* by foreign companies that outsource *to* the United States. They do not examine the growth in market share that can result from increased competitiveness, leading to rises in employment, and they do not take into account the rise in exports to low-income countries that are frequently the ones that benefit from the offshored jobs. (US exports to India, for example, doubled in five years (US Census Bureau, 2006).) Finally, they do not take into account employment changes in small and medium-sized entreprises (SMEs), which represent a large volume of total employment. Here again a review of production and labour statistics would be welcome (see box 5.1).

Preliminary data indicate that only 2 per cent of firms in Japan offshore. Tomiura - Marin (2004) estimates that 0.26 per cent of German jobs were lost to offshoring between 1990 and 2001 to the Central and Eastern European Countries. Kirkegaard (2005) estimates that in 2004 offshoring represented 0.14 per cent of the labour force in the European Union. Again, it is, unfortunately, not possible to identify the employment gains resulting from offshoring in developing countries. International trade figures, however, can provide an idea of the consequences of offshoring in the developing world. Exports from India increased by 12 per cent per year over the period 1993–2003 and those from China grew, on average, 17 per cent per year between 1997 and 2004. The ratio of commercial service exports to

## Chart 5.6

## Outsourcing volumes[4], 2003 (billion USD)

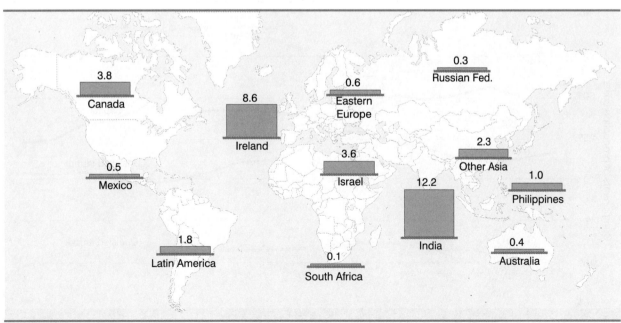

*Source:* Farrell D. et al. (2005).

## Table 5.1

## Employment and outsourcing (United States)

|  | Layoff actions | Separations |
|---|---|---|
| Total private non-farm sector (*) | 279 | 40 727 |
| **By location** | | |
| Out of country | 70 | 10 722 |
| Within company | 46 | 7 863 |
| Different company | 24 | 2 859 |
| Domestic relocations | 200 | 27 326 |
| Within company | 167 | 22 697 |
| Different company | 33 | 4 629 |
| Unable to assign | 9 | 2 679 |
| **By company** | | |
| Within company | 221 | 32 586 |
| Domestic | 167 | 22 697 |
| Out of country | 46 | 7 863 |
| Unable to assign | 8 | 2 026 |
| Different company | 58 | 8 141 |
| Domestic | 33 | 4 629 |
| Out of country | 24 | 2 859 |
| Unable to assign | 1 | 653 |

*(\*) excluding seasonal and vacation events with movement of work*

*Source:* US Census Bureau (2006).

## Chart 5.7

## Colombia production costs

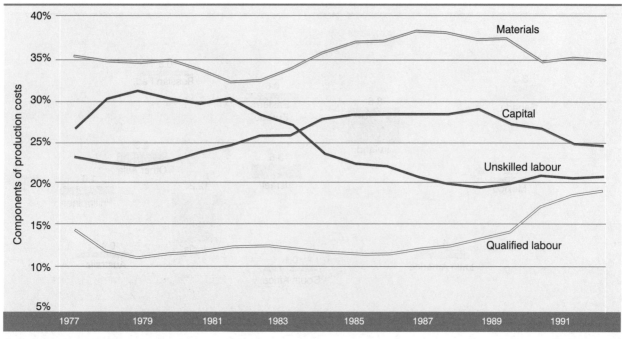

*Source:* Ramírez and Núñez (2000).

merchandise exports grew in the former from 23 per cent to 40 per cent, while it has remained fairly stable for the latter.

## E.   ICTs and the segmentation of the labour force

Chart 5.7[5] describes the evolution over time of the different cost components of manufacturing in Colombia. The fall in the participation of unskilled workers and the rise of skilled workers are noticeable: there is clearly an evolution in the composition of the labour market. Investment in technology and higher productivity led to a fall in total employment levels where the unskilled where the major losers. In fact, in decomposing the different components explaining the changes in employment, CEPAL (Gutiérrez, 2004) finds that technological change contributes positively – and sometimes significantly – in employment in the business services sector in Brazil, Colombia and Chile. The same effect is seen in the manufacturing sector in the latter two countries, while there is a negative impact in Brazil.

Turning to developed countries, in summarising research on the effects of technical change on the structure of salaries and jobs, Chennells and Van Reenen (1999) have concluded that there is considerable evidence that the introduction of technology tends to favour skilled labour in the United States, Canada and the United Kingdom through increased wage differentials (Handel, 2003). Unemployment of unskilled male workers was three and a half times larger than that of university graduates and five times greater for uneducated women (Maurin et al., 2001). In many instances, the technological factor behind these changes was the nature of computer use. In other developed countries where wage structures are more rigid, the increased reliance on technology tends to raise unemployment levels – predominantly among the unskilled segments of the population (Werner and Wijkander, 2000). There is also considerable evidence that the wage differentials of employed workers tend to increase in exporting countries and particularly developing ones (Marjit and Chakrabarti, 2004).

In effect, there is an increasing body of evidence indicating that both technology (in particular ICTs) and trade *increase* inequality. It might be worthwhile to see which of the two factors plays the more important

role. To stave off the competition from enterprises in the developing world seeking to leapfrog those in the industrialized economies, Thoenig and Verdier (2003) argue, enterprises in the latter will emphasize tacit know-how. In doing so, firms will find it much harder to acquire the knowledge needed to compete with their more innovative and productive rivals in the developed economies. The immediate effect of emphasizing implicit knowledge is an increase in skill requirements within enterprises. Competition (or potential competition) resulting from globalization will thus generate skill-biased employment, increasing the demand for qualified personnel. Firms in the developing countries face a similar situation. Here also the need to catch up with the competition will lead to the engagement of skilled staff, thus increasing the wage differentials between skilled and unskilled workers (Epifanit and Gancia, 2004).

An explanation at a microeconomic level of the relationships between the restructuring of the labour force and the diffusion of ICTs merits a detailed review because it can provide some pointers for human resources development policies. Occupations could be classified as communications-based, manual or analytical, on the one hand, and – roughly – routine or non-routine, on the other. Repetitive communications could be those carried out by telephonists; non-routine communication tasks include those performed by sales clerks, for example. Manual routine occupations could include car body painting or lathe operators. Medical assistants or janitors perform manual non-routine operations. Bank teller occupations are repetitive intellectual tasks while web page design or customer service personnel perform non-routine intellectual activities.

The classification has been made in order to identify whether tasks can be formally described as a finite set of predefined rules or actions or not. The more the rules or actions are defined, the more easily the task can be performed by digitally controlled machinery. On the basis of such a classification, Autor et al. (2003) conclude that *"Computer technology substitutes for workers in performing routine tasks that can be readily described with programmed rules, while complementing workers in executing nonroutine tasks demanding flexibility, creativity, generalized problem-solving capabilities, and complex communications".*[6] On the basis of this work, Levy and Murnane (2004) analysed the evolution of employment in the United States using the task classification described here. The results are presented in chart 5.8.[7] This clearly shows how the evolution of ICTs is segmenting the labour force and is leading to the replacement of workers doing tasks that can easily be programmed. This substitution

## Chart 5.8

## Evolution of employment in the United States

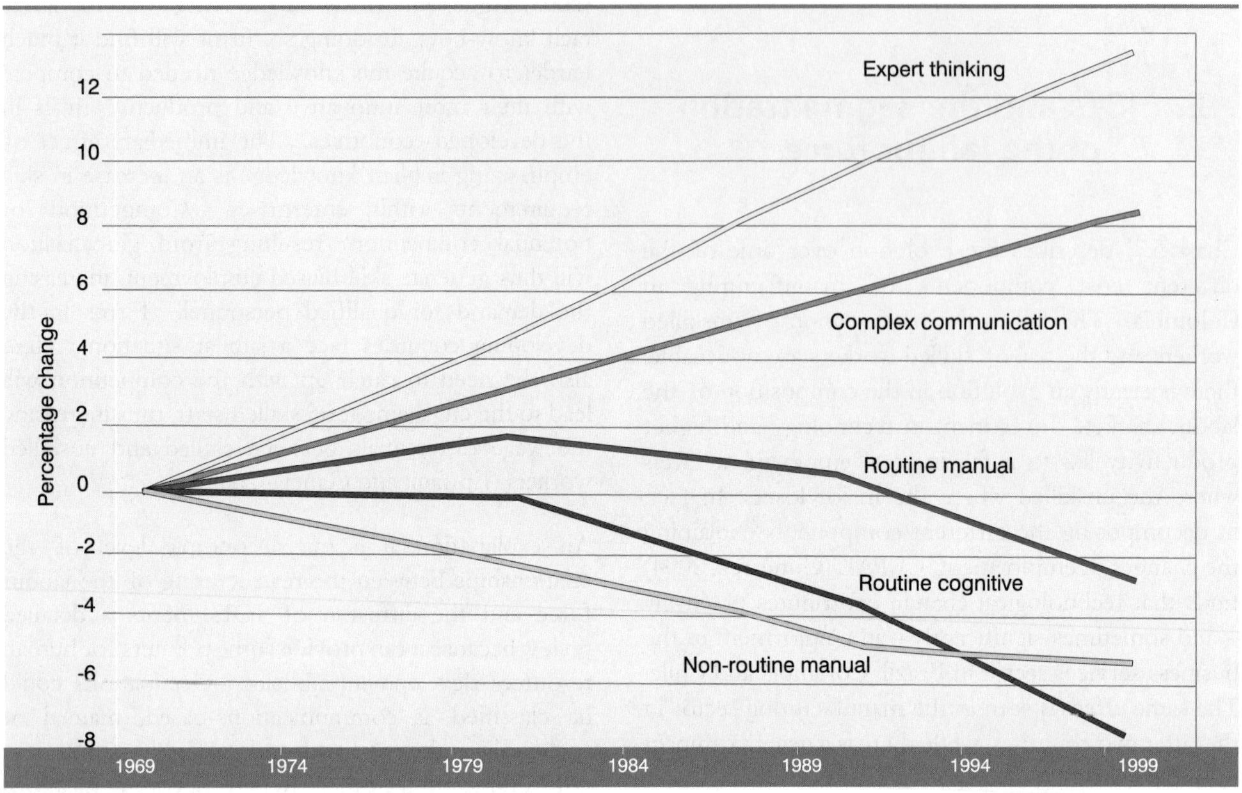

*Source:* Levy and Murnane (2004).

operates because the competitive advantage of workers lies in problem solving and communications rather than in performing repetitive tasks.

## F.   Enterprises and ICT strategies

Those enterprises that fail to adapt to the structural changes associated with globalization and ICTs might be marginalized if they fail to recognize the competitive advantage offered by technology and the economies of scale that are associated with larger markets. Moreover, it is increasingly clear that economic activity will increasingly be network-driven.  Subcontracting and supply management will be one source of competitive advantage.  ICTs provide the backbone for these networks and here again, investing in – and understanding the value of – ICTs is crucial.

Several paths can be taken to achieve social and economic progress through ICTs.  In the first, enterprises must be able to fully exploit the benefits of ICTs.  This implies ensuring that firms achieve

productivity increases through their investments in these technologies.  Much must be done in this domain. Accessibility (in terms of both infrastructure and affordability) must be achieved; security and trust must be established to ensure transaction trustworthiness; and, finally, managers and entrepreneurs must be able to develop the processes and create the organizations that will make efficient use of investments in ICTs. Development of appropriate local IT solutions and helping managers use these tools are a fundamental activity in this regard.

Efforts to identify competitive advantages should concentrate on both processing and manufacturing industries and should also revolve around business services. The enhancement of local supply chains that seek to increase local value added should be emphasized. Indeed, the increased reliance on outsourcing leads to the strengthening of productive networks. This seems to point to the need to revive industrial policies. This not only helps create local value added, but can also help disseminate new technologies when suppliers or customers request technologically advanced management support systems. For example, the identification of vertically integrated sectors and ways of increasing the value added at the local and national levels should become an industrial policy priority.

Because product life cycles shorten significantly in a highly competitive world, innovation becomes a critical component in the development and survival of firms. While innovation is frequently associated with product development, it can also be achieved in production processes, marketing and enterprise organisation. These do not depend, necessarily, on expensive research and development facilities.   There are numerous opportunities to create competitive firms relying on abundant local know-how provided that adequate policies are put in place to foster innovation. Experience has shown that "social capital" at the local level can promote innovation (Foray and Perez, 2000). It could therefore be useful to consider the implementation of local initiatives that strengthen local economic links, that enhance trust and cooperation among members of the community and that define practical action plans which promote decent employment within communities:   actions to increase cooperation and trust amongst economic, scientific, social and public actors must be undertaken to strengthen social capital, thereby enhancing innovation and productivity.

Human resource development is a fundamental prerequisite for adopting and using technology, and firm-level initiatives can make an important contribution. Uninformed people fear change.  Taking the time and effort to explain to workers the work-related implication of investments in technology helps to enlist their assistance and allay their fears. Indeed, it has been standard practice for some time in the development of any IT application to ensure the users' full participation in the process (Martin, 1990). This can be achieved through dialogue, through social security and through training.   Freedom of association and the possibility of initiating dialogue between employers and workers are central to this aim. Inevitably, there are workers who can lose their jobs in the adjustment process. Mechanisms to reduce the traumas of unemployment and aid in the transition to other employment would also limit resistance to change and can reduce the negative consequences of investments in ICTs.  This is the role of social security benefits.

Dialogue, training and reinforcing workers' adaptability will be of practical use only when associated with best practice in entrepreneurship. If efforts are deployed to train workers, there must be a similar endeavour to train managers. Employers must be able to understand the value of investing in new technologies and in human resources.  They must organize their enterprises to be able to compete in an increasingly open environment where survival depends on productivity and innovation. It is therefore indispensable to ensure that public authorities and entrepreneurs engage in extensive campaigns to emphasize the importance of modern management practices in ensuring an adequate return on investments in human resources and equipment.

## G. Conclusions

The growing use of ICTs creates, at the same time, a basis for a further widening of the development gap and global and local income inequality, and empowers developing countries, and their workers, firms and employees, to overcome such disparities. ICTs are a challenge and a solution for the developing world. They are depriving many developing countries of their main competitive advantage: cheap labour. To counter this trend, those countries must not only continue to adopt the use of ICTs, but also find ways to lead and innovate. For that to happen, an important thrust of any ICT policy must be directed to human resource development, especially that related to the labour force.

Special efforts must be made to strengthen SMEs. They are the enterprises that have the greatest difficulties in investing in ICTs, and they are the largest employers.  By improving the effectiveness of SMEs it will be possible to generate better employment.  Business development services that provide assistance in standard business practices but that can also furnish access to data processing and telecommunication equipment and technical assistance in ICTs would probably be a desirable practice provided that those services are economically sustainable.  Efforts to integrate them into supply chains and the industrial policies already mentioned clearly play an important role here.

A further policy conclusion would be that ICT adoption in the business services sector can be more efficient and effective from the viewpoint of overall economic policy and international competitiveness. Therefore, the developing world should carefully assess its industrial and employment policies to emphasize growth in business services rather than emphasizing the role of the manufacturing sector as a driver of growth and exports. Moreover, productivity improvements achieved in the developed world have given the latter (and some countries in transition) competitive advantages over developing economies that can be compensated for only in very limited circumstances by low production costs. Competition in globalized markets will force the developing economies to adopt increasingly technology based production processes, resulting in labour market changes described in this chapter.

Policymakers should concentrate their efforts on identifying the most significant factors enabling ICT adoption among employees, firms and households, while devising strategies to address the multitude of difficulties encountered in this process. However, on their own, ICT policies and strategies are insufficient and countries must strive to achieve a number of general enabling circumstances:

- Low inflation and low-debt monetary and fiscal policies;

- Enhanced economic integration;

- Property rights and contract enforcement systems that enhance trust; and

- Social cohesion, solidarity and political stability (Rodrik, 2004).

The differential competitive status of economies — associated with the adoption of new technologies and other managerial and logistics factors — would clearly be one such critical barrier to economic development. The adoption of ICTs requires actions in a number of fields: training workers to handle new technologies will be effective only if enterprises invest in them and succeed in generating favourable returns on investments in ICTs.

Product quality requirements and just-in-time inventory management throughout supply chains might be undermining the competitive advantage resulting from low-labour costs. In any case, a race towards the bottom based on low labour costs and increased reliance on non-formal forms of employment would end up being detrimental to economic growth and development. There is no alternative to a "high road" (WCSDG, 2004) development strategy where business and labour collaborate to achieve efficiency through innovative and efficient enterprises and concomitant decent employment. Indeed, enterprises will be able to compete in a networked economy by finding niche marketing, exploiting economies of scale, innovating and achieving greater productivity. Public policy must

help enterprises achieve these aims without unduly exacerbating social or economic divides.

The growth of informal economies is a significant barrier to the effective dissemination of ICTs. Informality frequently limits enterprises' ability to manage trust factors. They frequently have difficulty in accessing network-based financial transactions and contract enforcement or arbitration mechanisms. Their ability to manage and retain skilled personnel is limited, and so their productivity and quality control procedures are frequently found wanting. Since the informal economy is an important component in many economies, actions to "formalize" SMEs are a critical component of any ICT dissemination strategy. Actions to redress the cost benefit ratio of informality should be undertaken by increasing the benefits of formality rather than attempting to reduce costs: educating workers, and providing them with social security and appropriate wages, lead to social development and economic expansion.

Unless the workforce has the necessary skills to adapt and be creative, enterprises will not be able to enhance their productivity and innovation. Throughout this chapter it has been noted that ICTs are changing the nature of many tasks that have little to do directly with computers. Thus, the emphasis should not be placed exclusively on an elusive "computer literacy". New production processes and enterprises require five fundamental skills: literacy, numeracy, the capacity to learn, the capacity to communicate clearly and the capacity to work in teams.[8] These are not task specific, and they are skills rarely taught in professional training schools. These five critical competencies must be developed throughout life and particularly in the education system. In any event, workers would need to acquire these skills through the professional training institutions. Industry or task-specific skills would complete the competency profiles of workers. All social actors should review current education and training systems to empower workers in a new technological environment. Experience and formal knowledge will need to be certified to ensure greater mobility in the labour market. This implies changes in the techniques to deliver education and training (ICTs for education and training) but, more importantly, it requires changes in the content and methods of education and training (education and training for ICTs).

# Annex I

## Chart 5.9

## Total output (USD)

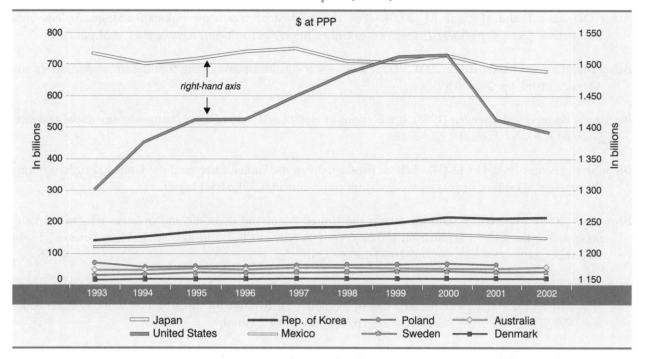

## Chart 5.10

## Total employment

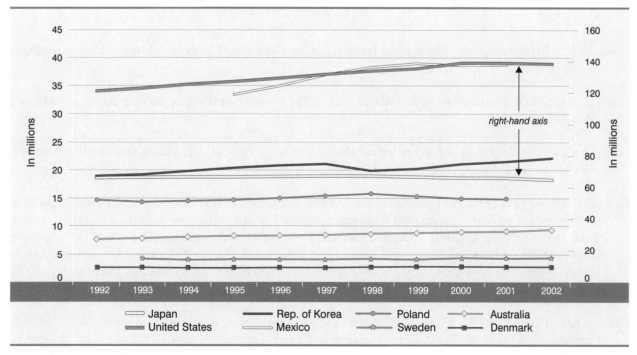

*Source:* ILO, based on UNSO and World Bank (World Development Indicators).

# References and bibliography

Auer P, Besse G and Méda D (eds.) (2006). Offshoring and the internationalization of employment: A challenge for a fair globalization? International Labour Organization/International Institute for Labour Studies/Ministère de l'emploi, de la cohésion sociale et du logement.

Autor DH, Levy F and Murnane RJ (2003). The skill content of recent technological change: An empirical exploration. *Quarterly Journal of Economics*, November. http://web.mit.edu/flevy/www/ALM.pdf.

Beladi Marjit S and Chakrabarti A (2004). Trade and wage inequality in developing countries. *Economic Inquiry*, vol. 42, no. 2, April, pp. 295–303(9).

Berman E, Bound J and Machin S (1998). Implications of skill-biased technological change: International evidence. *Quarterly Journal of Economics*, November.

Broadberry SN and Irwin DA (2004). Labour productivity in the United States and the United Kingdom during the nineteenth century, http://www.dartmouth.edu/~dirwin/C19USUK11a.pdf.

Brown SP (2004). Mass layoff statistics data in the United States and domestic and overseas relocation, paper presented at the EU-US Seminar on Offshoring of Services in ICT and Related Services, Brussels, 13–14 December, http://www.bls.gov/mls/mlsrelocation.pdf.

Chennells L and Van Reenen J (1999). Has technology hurt less skilled workers? An econometric survey of the effects of technical change on the structure of pay and jobs. Institute for Fiscal Studies Working Paper Series No. W99/27 (1999). http://ideas.repec.org/p/ifs/ifsewp/99-27.html.

Dorgan SJ and Dowdy JJ (2004). When IT lifts productivity, *McKinsey Quarterly*, no. 4.

Eggleston K, Jensen R and Zeckhauser R (2002). Information and communication technologies, markets and economic development, working paper, Economics Department, Tufts University and John F. Kennedy School of Government, Harvard University.

Epifanit P and Gancia GA (2002). The skill bias of world trade. University of Parma and CESPRI, CREI and UPF, November.

Ethier W (2002). Globalization, globalisation: Trade, technology and wages, Tinbergen Institute Discussion Paper No. 02-088/2.

Farrel D et al. (2005). The emerging global labour market: The demand for offshore talent in services. McKinsey Global Institute, p. 13.

Fernandez RM (2001). Skill-biased technological change and wage inequality: Evidence from a plant retooling, *American Journal of Sociology*, vol. 107, pp. 273–320.

Foray D and Perez LH (2000). The economics of open technology: Collective organization and individual claims in the "Fabrique Lyonnaise" during the Old Regime, prepared for the conference in honour of Paul A. David, Turin (Italy) [*in* Boari C (2001). Industrial Clusters, Focal Firms, and Economic Dynamism: A Perspective from Italy. World Bank Institute, http://siteresources.worldbank.org/, or O'Gorman C and Kautonen M (2000). Policies for New Prosperity: Promoting New Agglomerations of Knowledge Intensive Industries, http://www.uta.fi/.]

Gordon J and Gupta P (2003). Understanding India's services revolution, paper prepared for the IMF- NCAER Conference, A Tale of Two Giants: India's and China's Experience with Reform, 14–16 November, New Delhi.

Gutiérrez G (2004). Crecimiento económico, creación y erosión de empleo: un análisis intersectorial, CEPAL estudios estadísticos y prospectivos no. 29, Santiago de Chile, October.

Handel MJ (2003). Implications of Information Technology for Employment, Skills, and Wages: A Review of Recent Research. SRI International, Arlington, VA. http://www.sri.com/policy/csted/reports/sandt/it/Handel_IT_Employment_Main_Rept.pdf.

ILO (2001). Reducing the decent work deficit: A global challenge, Report of the Director-General submitted at the 89th Session of the International Labour Conference, Geneva, June.

Indjikian R and Siegel DS (2005). The impact of investment in IT on economic performance: Implications for developing countries, *World Development,* vol. 33, no. 5, pp. 681–700.

Kambhampati US (2002). The software industry and development: The case of India, *Progress in Development Studies* vol. 2, no. 1.

Kirkegaard JF (2005). Outsourcing and offshoring: Pushing the European Model over the hill, rather than off the cliff! Institute for International Economics, WP 05-1.

Kumar N and Joseph KJ (2005). Export of software and business process outsourcing from developing countries: Lessons from the Indian experience, *Asia-Pacific Trade and Investment Review,* vol. 1, no. 1, April.

Levy F and Murnane RJ (2004). The New Division of Labor: How computers are Creating the Next Job Market. Russell Sage Foundation, New York; Princeton University Press, Princeton and Oxford.

Mariacristina P, Santarelli E and Vivarelli M (2004). Technological and organizational changes as determinants of the skill bias: Evidence from a panel of Italian firms, http://www.ugr.es/~xxjei/JEI(13)(v1).pdf.

Marin D (2004). A nation of poets and thinkers: Less so with eastern enlargement? Austria and Germany, CEPR Discussion Paper 4358, http://ideas.repec.org/p/cpr/ceprdp/4358.html.

Martin J (1990). *Information Engineering, Book III, Design and Construction,* Prentice Hall, Englewood Cliffs.

Maurin E(CREST-INSEE), Thesmar D (INSEE) and Thoenig M (CERAS-CNRS) (2001). Mondialisation des échanges et emploi: Le rôle des exportations, September.

Mokyr J (2000a). The rise and fall of the factory system: Technology, firms, and households since the Industrial Revolution, paper prepared for the Carnegie-Rochester Conference on Macroeconomics, Pittsburgh, 17–19 November.

Mokyr J (2000b). Knowledge, technology, and economic growth during the Industrial Revolution, http://faculty.econ.northwestern.edu/faculty/mokyr/Groningen.pdf.

OECD (2003). *ICT and Economic Growth.* Paris.

Piore MJ and Sabel CF (1990). *The Second Industrial Divide: Possibilities for Prosperity.* Basic Books.

Ramírez JM and Núñez L (2000). Reformas, crecimiento, progreso técnico y empleo en Colombia, Proyecto Crecimiento, empleo y equidad: América Latina en los años noventa, Serie Reformas Económicas 59 (Parte II).

Rodrik D (2004). Rethinking growth policies in the developing world, draft of the Luca d'Agliano Lecture in Development Economics delivered on 8 October 2004 in Turin (Italy).

Rodrik D and Subramanian A (2005). From "Hindu growth" to productivity surge: The mystery of the Indian growth transition, International Monetary Fund, IMF Working Paper vol. 52, no. 2.

Stokey NL (2001). A quantitative model of the British industrial revolution, 1780–1850. Carnegie-Rochester Conference Series on Public Policy, vol. 55, issue 1, December, pp. 55–109.

Thoenig M and Verdier T (2003). A theory of defensive skill-biased innovation and globalization, *American Economic Review,* June.

Tomiura E (2004). Foreign outsourcing and firm-level characteristics: Evidence from Japanese manufacturers, http://hi-stat.ier.hit-u.ac.jp/research/discussion/2004/pdf/D04-64.pdf.

United States Census Bureau, Foreign Trade Statistics (2006). http://www.census.gov/foreign-trade/statistics/product/enduse/exports/c5330.html.

Werner R and Wijkander H (2000). Unemployment in Europe: Swimming against the tide of skill-biased technical progress without relative wage adjustment, http://www.ne.su.se/paper/wp00_09.pdf.

Wood A (1997). Openness and wage inequality in developing countries: The Latin American challenge to East Asian conventional wisdom, *World Bank Economic Review*, vol. 11, no. 1 pp. 33–57.

World Commission on the Social Dimension of Globalization (2004). A Fair Globalization: Creating Opportunities for All, ILO, February, p. 65.

# Notes

1.  Building the Information Society: A Global Challenge in the New Millennium (WSIS Geneva Declaration of Principles).

2.  Data for charts 5.1, 5.2, 5.3 and 5.4 were received from the UN Statistical Office. The sectoral classification corresponds to sub-group D (Manufacturing) and sub-groups J (Financial intermediation) and K (Real estate, renting and business activities) of the United Nations' International Standard Industrial Classification of All Economic Activities (ISIC), Third Revision. Series M, No. 4, Rev. 3. Output in those tables is presented in local currencies. Conversion factors for constant local currency and PPP are obtained from the implicit factors (from current to constant prices and from constant at local to constant at purchasing parity indices in the World Bank's World Development Indicators (WDI). The countries listed in the graphs correspond to series for which all data were available; unfortunately, employment and output statistics are either not available or do not exist under the required classification for most developing economies. It should be noted that no effort has been made to identify ICT-related industries on their own: investment in data processing and communication technologies shape many industries. The attempt made here is to describe the changes in two sectors widely believed to be influenced by both technology and globalization.

3.  Gordon and Gupta (2003).

4.  Farrel et al. (2005).

5.  Ramírez and Núñez (2000).

6.  Autor, Levy, and Murnane (2003).

7.  Levy and Murnane (2004).

8.  In an extensive follow-up of a plant restructuring, Roberto M. Fernandez (2001) notes that "the firm has moved from a situation where most jobs required only basic arithmetic ... to one where many (if not most) jobs ... require workers to be able to compute using decimals and to read a graph (e.g., a statistical process control graph). Language-related changes also seem modest, but in the direction of greater complexity." Fernandez RM (2001). Skill-biased technological change and wage inequality: Evidence from a plant retooling, *American Journal of Sociology*, vol. 107, pp. 273–320.

# Chapter 6

# SERVICE-ORIENTED ARCHITECTURE AND WEB SERVICES TECHNOLOGIES: TRENDS AND IMPLICATIONS FOR E-BUSINESS IN DEVELOPING COUNTRIES

## A. Introduction

ICTs, by making commercial transactions easier and cheaper to conduct over distances and by opening up new possibilities for business relationships, are among the driving forces of the wave of economic globalization that has taken place over the last decade. The central role of ICTs in this process has been reinforced by the development of production and distribution models that emphasize cooperation and fast information exchange among the various links in the value chain. For enterprises, particularly those in developing countries that may find themselves at earlier stages of internationalization, this means that their capacity to enter foreign markets is more and more dependent on their ability to use ICTs to integrate themselves into supply chains at regional and global levels. Efficient supply chain management is now central to the business model of the leading players in many industries, and ICTs play a fundamental role in it. Outsourcing, particularly in the services sector, is another important manifestation of globalization that could not have taken place without ICTs.

In both supply chain and outsourcing management, the power of ICTs to facilitate collaboration at every step of the processes through which value is created and exchanged has been fundamental. This chapter will describe in broad terms how such processes could be affected by the rapid development and deployment of Services-Oriented Architecture (SOA) and related Web services (WS) technologies. The issue of WS and the impact that these technologies could have on the development of e-business in developing countries was already touched on in the *E-commerce and Development Report 2003* as an emerging trend of significance for the future of e-business. Events since then seem to have confirmed this judgement, and the present chapter will make a more extensive examination of the issue of SOA and WS.

In simple terms (a more technically precise definition will be provided later on) WS can be described as technologies that enable automated interaction between computers. This interaction takes place over the Internet and involves transactions between computers that handle different business processes. Thus, a machine is able to feed into another one the information the latter needs, or conversely, it can formulate requests for information it needs for its own processes. This is made possible thanks to software that has been designed to use other software, the communication with which is based on Internet standards and protocols. A very simple example could be a catalogue in an SME's website that automatically updates prices in several currencies by checking periodically the latest exchange rates from a financial news service. Of course, the same logic could be applied to a much complex scenario involving any combination of business processes.

Systems operating in this way depend on the functionalities that other systems make available to them. Ideally, the level of dependence should be kept as low as possible in order to maximize the chances that different systems can interact with each other. Achieving such low levels of dependence is called "loose coupling", which is the goal pursued by SOA technologies. SOA is a software architectural style that aims at achieving loose coupling among interacting software agents.[1] In somewhat less abstract terms, SOA could be defined as a distributed software model "in which small, loosely coupled pieces of application functionality are published, consumed, and combined with other applications over a network."[2]

SOA and WS have the potential to become powerful instruments to enable enterprises to collaborate in shared business processes and provide the foundation of future supply chain strategies. Thus, technology proponents expect that WS will experience sustained, fast growth around the world.[3]

The main strength of SOA is considered to be the fact that, being based on industry-wide standards, these technologies allow for an easier integration than proprietary technologies and thus make cooperation among business partners or with third parties easier. At the same time, SOA implementation also seems to open possibilities for efficiency gains in intra-enterprise transactions. As better collaboration, both inside the enterprise and with business partners, and enhanced responsiveness to the external environment (customers, suppliers) and to internal conditions continue to gain importance as determinants of competitiveness, SOA and WS have a considerable transformative potential. More than a mere enhancement of an enterprise's ICTs capabilities, SOA implementations are said to involve true business-wide change, the result of which is a range of whole business processes being performed as automated services and integrated with those of the other entities in a company's "ecosystem": partners, suppliers, customers.

On the other hand, these claims are not fundamentally different from those made in the past about earlier technologies and sceptical voices can be clearly heard. They warn that much of the excitement about WS services may just be the latest example of IT vendor hype, and that businesses, particularly SMEs and developing country enterprises, should carefully examine the value proposition they are being offered by a particular WS implementation.[4] This chapter aims at providing interested decision makers in developing countries with some elements for undertaking that examination by providing an overview of these technologies, emphasizing whenever possible their implications from a developing country perspective.

SOA and WS will be considered in conjunction, as they are often so discussed – sometimes as though they were interchangeable terms. The reason for this is that although SOA and WS are two distinct concepts (SOA being a much older one than WS), WS explain much of the renewed attention being paid to SOA. WS represent a new development that makes SOA deployments easier and more productive. This chapter will approach the matter from two points of view. First, it will consider the significance of SOA and WS for the evolution of e-business technologies in general; then it will look at the role that they may play in changing international supply chains and what this can mean for developing country enterprises participating or aspiring to participate in them. Some issues concerning the role of open standards and the processes through which they are established will be presented. This will be followed by a succinct description of some experiences of the effects of SOA and WS on business performance.

The examination of the issues covered in this chapter leads to the conclusion that SOA and WS are likely to play a major role in the development of e-business. In terms of business strategies, SOA and WS will push in the direction of deeper levels of inter-business collaboration. This represents an opportunity for developing country enterprises as their participation in global supply chains could be facilitated and they could benefit from more opportunities for outsourcing. Therefore, developing country enterprises will increasingly need to familiarize themselves with SOA and WS technologies and should start their own investigation into the merits of investing in them. In this connection, the opportunities provided by free and open source platforms should be fully exploited. Another aspect that needs attention is the increased participation of users of SOA and WS technologies, particularly those from developing countries, in the standard-setting processes related SOA and WS.

From the point of view of policymakers in developing countries, the adoption of SOA and WS can be facilitated by taking the same steps as are often recommended for facilitation of the adoption of e-business practices in general. Two major issues in this regard are the reinforcement of relevant skills in the workforce and in the business community and the establishment of an environment of trust and security for e-business.

## B.    The business and technology forces behind the growth of Web services

By the end of 2002, according to IDC Research, only about 5 per cent of enterprises in the United States had completed a web services project, although 80 per cent of them were expected to do so in the next five years.[5] Two and a half years later IDC forecast that WS expenditure worldwide would grow from $2.3 billion in 2004 to $14.9 billion by 2009.[6] Other forecasts provide different estimates of the absolute size of the market for WS, but agree on the fact that this is an area of fast growth. For example, a study by the Radicati Group said that by the end of 2004 the market for WS would have reached $950 million and that it should grow to $6.2 billion by 2008.[7] According to that study, 52 per cent of the expenditure on WS in 2004 would take place in the United States, 39 per cent in Europe, 6 per cent in Asia-Pacific and 3 per cent in the rest of the world. More recently, a Gartner report estimated that the market for IT services related to WS would amount to $261 billion by 2008. The report added that this would represent a pervasive technology shift.[8]

From the technology point of view, WS implementations have now reached a level of maturity at which their cost-cutting potential has started to translate into bottom line figures, sufficient standards are now in place and security and management solutions are available. The next stage of SOA and WS can be expected to start developing in the short term, as enterprises move from point-to-point applications to broad application of SOA and WS inside the enterprise and in their interactions with business partners.   In fact, SOA and WS can already be described as two of the most significant developments in the field of e-business in recent years.

What makes SOA particularly attractive is its potential to add efficiency and flexibility to an enterprise's information technology assets. This potential, however, may not be fully realized without extensive re-examination of the way in which information technology is used by an enterprise, and the required investments can be considerable. The question to be answered, then, is how likely is it that the promise of SOA will be fulfilled. In addition, from the point of view of enterprises in the developing countries, there is also a need to consider how developing and implementing SOA and WS can help them remove the competitive disadvantage they face as a result of the lack of e-business capabilities. For a number of emerging economies, however, SOA and WS could conceivably be a positive factor in reinforcing their presence in international supply chains with the implications that this could have in terms of trade, investment and technology.

If the answer to these questions had to be formulated purely in terms of reductions in ICTs budgets, for most enterprises the case for moving towards SOA technologies today would perhaps not be a straightforward one, particularly in developing countries. However, another important consideration is that although SOA and WS are often presented as another IT "revolution", the reality is that they are perfectly suited to incremental adoption. This consideration is particularly relevant for smaller enterprises and for those from developing countries because, although these technologies are for the time being more commonly adopted by large, internationally-minded enterprises, the scalability of SOA and WS technologies makes them particularly suitable for adoption according to critical business priorities and

available budgets. As often, the pertinence of a change to SOA and WS hinges not on mere IT considerations but on their significance for overall business strategies.

From that point of view, there are strong forces for change in the way businesses organize themselves and interact with others (for example, supply and demand chain integration, and various forms of outsourcing) that support the idea that SOA and WS technologies should have a central role in the short- and medium-term evolution of e-business. From the technology standpoint, SOA and WS are manifestations of a renewed emphasis on distributed and network-based approaches to computing in which the network itself is the source of computing power. The following sections will therefore look at the technological and the business strategy underpinnings of SOA and WS.

## 1.   Technology background

The following paragraphs are intended to give the reader a broad understanding of the specificities of the approach to IT that SOA and WS technologies represent. These technologies are part of a more general paradigm known as distributed computing. The fundamental concept supporting distributed computing is the idea that the use of computing resources (processing power or storage capacity) can be optimized by pooling them in a network, rather than concentrating them at any given place. Computing resources can then be used where and when needed.

An important element of distributed computing systems is a category of software usually known as "middleware". Middleware is often defined as the elements that join different software components in a system, or that interface the software and the network (the slash in the client/server model). Middleware can be used to interconnect applications. In this case, its task normally consists in mediating between applications in order to manage data and/or to orchestrate business process flows. The applications in question frequently use different operating systems, data formats, networking protocols and so forth. The task of middleware is to reconcile all these elements.

Earlier examples of distributed computing include middleware platforms such as CORBA and DCOM, which also consider software resources as services available on a network.[9] What makes SOA different from these[10] is that it is both based on open standards and loosely coupled. In a tightly coupled architecture, both ends of a distributed computing link had to agree on the details of the API.[11] Loose coupling separates the participants in distributed computing interactions so that modifying the interface of one participant in the exchange does not break the other's. Secondly, earlier architectures were proprietary. SOA's reliance upon universally accepted standards such as XML and SOAP (Simple Object Access Protocol) provides broad interoperability among different vendors' solutions — the importance of the use of open standards will be elaborated on later in this section. The combination of these two core principles means that an enterprise can implement WS without having any knowledge of the consumers of those services, and vice versa.

In technical terms, a definition of SOA could be the following: "an application architecture in which all functions, or services, are defined using a description language and have invokable interfaces that are called to perform business processes. Interactions are independent of each other and of the interconnect protocols of the communicating devices (i.e., the infrastructure components that determine the communication system do not affect the interfaces)".[12] As explained in the introduction, SOA should be differentiated from the concept of Web services.[13]

There are many definitions of Web services. From the viewpoint of the functions they perform, they can be defined as "open standard (XML, SOAP, etc.) based Web applications that interact with other web applications for the purpose of exchanging data".[14] They have also been defined as "self-contained, modular, distributed, dynamic applications that can be described, published, located, or invoked over the network to create products, processes, and supply chains…"[15] On the basis of the protocols and standards that underpin Web services, they have been defined as "a standardized way of integrating applications that uses XML, SOAP, WSDL (Web Services Description Language), and UDDI (Universal Description Discovery and Integration) open standards over the Internet protocol. XML is used to tag the data (i.e. to specify how a document or part of it should be formatted), SOAP is used to transfer the data, WSDL is used for describing the services available and UDDI is used for listing what services are available".[16] An important characteristic of WS is reusability, which means that once a Web service is in place other Web services (or other applications) can find it and use it as a building block.

In order to automate business interactions between two different companies (or systems within the same organizations), the business processes in question have to be specified. This role is performed by the Business Process Execution Language (BPEL), which is an XML-based language. BPEL is based on Microsoft's XLANG and IBM's WSFL. Using BPEL different services can be put together into a given business process. The collaboration between several different Web services to define a new Web Service is called orchestration

## Chart 6.1

### WS protocol stack

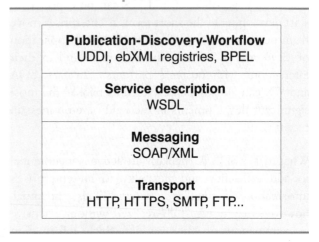

Chart 6.1 shows how various WS-related standards and specifications are applied at the different layers of a WS implementation (see the list of acronyms for an explanation of the other acronyms in chart 6.1).

## Chart 6.2

### A Web services architecture

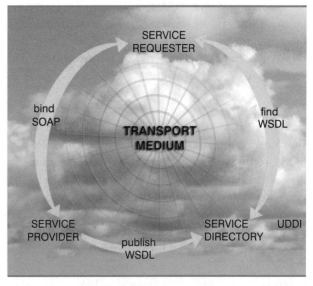

Chart 6.2 shows the individual components of a service-oriented architecture.

A Web services architecture must allow three sets of functions:

1. The dynamic discovery of registered services: looking for services that meet a particular need, provide certain information (for example, the price of a product, its physical characteristics, its time of production), and so forth.

2. The organization of services, so that one can easily understand what a service offers.

3. The description of services, including the formats and protocols that are needed in order to invoke the WS.

The service directory is where the information about the services that are available is stored. In order to publish the services they have on offer, service providers must make the necessary entries in the service directory. Service requesters use the service directory to find services that match their criteria (for example, a particular price level). This means that the service directory must include not only the classifications that are needed in order to perform a search, but also other information relevant for the business process where the service may be used (price or physical features of a product, etc.). When a service requester finds a service that matches its requirements, it binds to the service provider, using binding information maintained in the service directory. The binding information tells the service requester the protocol that it must use and the structure of the request messages and the resulting responses.

The format of messages that are exchanged between the service requestor, the service provider and the service directory is specified by SOAP; UDDI defines the structure and the contents of the service directory; and WSDL provides the capability to describe a WS service, without the need to have it formally standardized.

SOAP is a protocol for exchange of information in a decentralized, distributed environment using typed message exchange and remote invocation. It defines a mechanism for the communication with Web services over the Internet. It is an XML-based protocol that consists of three parts: (1) an envelope that defines a framework for describing what is in a message and how to process it; (2) a set of encoding rules for expressing instances of application-defined datatypes; and (3) a convention for representing remote procedure calls and responses. SOAP can potentially be built on top of any transport layer, for example an HTTP-based infrastructure.

UDDI is the definition of a set of services supporting the description and discovery of (1) businesses, organizations and other Web services providers; (2) the Web services they make available; and (3) the technical interfaces which may be used to access those services. UDDI provides information about the registration of service types and about the actual business data such as the name of the company offering the service, the type of service, taxonomies that classify the offered service, and references to those standard service types or to Web Services Description Language (WSDL) specifications.

WSDL is an XML format for describing network services based on a standard messaging layer such as SOAP. A WSDL document defines services as collections of network endpoints, or ports. A WSDL description of a Web service provides all the information needed to actually invoke it. A service is described by giving the port type to use, the kind of operations that the port type supports and the structure of the input and outcome messages.

## 2.   A simple model of WS implementation

How does all this translate into actual business operations? Let us assume that company A has decided to outsource some services in order to cut costs. After a UDDI directory has been chosen and consulted, several potential business partners that offer such services are identified and after which one most closely matches a set of criteria has been assessed, one is selected as the provider for the required services.

In abstract terms the service provider appears as a business partner that implements a collection of port types covering the required services. For its part, company A has to provide a port type with operations that work as "stubs"[17] and that are capable of communicating with the ports that provide the service on its partner's side. In fact, company A may decide to provide multiple port types that collectively cover these stubs — that is, company A becomes itself a service provider. For the service to be delivered, both participants have to make their respective operations communicate with each other. This is done through "plug links". A plug link identifies pairs of operations that communicate with each other, and describes which operation initiates this communication. A communication consists, for example, in the process of sending a request and receiving a response message.

When the corresponding service partners are plug-linked they can start working together. The plug-links that have been defined can be used to exchange messages. Then, it is necessary to establish an agreed order ("flow model") so that both sides of the transaction expect the same sequence of events.

Company A may later wish to change the business partner to which the services in question are outsourced, because, for example, its requirements have become more complex. In that case, the new requirements can be put into a query called locator, which is run against a service directory. The locator returns a list of qualifying service providers. From this list Company A chooses a new business partner that better serves its needs.

Company A may also decide to provide value-added functions to outdo its competitors. For this purpose it creates a global model, that is a new Web service that aggregates the services of multiple service providers. This new global Web service can be published in a UDDI directory, which will enable service requesters to search and find the new service.

## 3.  Web services and business strategies

Over the last two decades, fast technological change, the opening of a growing number of markets to international competition, deregulation and privatization, among other factors, have resulted in fundamental strategic and operational changes in business worldwide. Customers' expectations about the quality of products and services tend to converge globally at higher levels, strong competitive pressures push for faster innovation, and efficiency and increasingly globally minded shareholders demand world-class returns on investment.

In this environment, the capacity of enterprises to respond quickly and flexibly to changing market conditions becomes more important than ever. A consequence has been the implementation of intra- and inter-organizational changes that often involve the emergence of various kinds of strategic alliances and other forms of business collaboration.[18] More and more enterprises seek productivity gains by entering into networked organizational arrangements that have been described as "value networks".[19]

In sectors such as manufacturing or distribution, the effects of global supply chains on competition are

so intense that it has been argued that in some cases competition is no longer taking place among companies but among rival supply chains.[20] Competitive pressures provide incentives for participants in supply chains to cooperate more and more closely. A company's customers and suppliers tend to become more and more involved in processes that range from product specification to inventory management. This requires more integration of their respective information systems.

These processes are dependent on the deployment of management tools that rely on information technologies, both internally (Enterprise Resource Planning, order processing, floor shop management) and externally (from simple e-mail to communicate with customers and suppliers to Electronic Data Interchange (EDI), web-based marketplaces).

The supply chain provides a good example of how ICT-enabled interorganizational systems (IOS) can generate competitive advantage. This has been well documented, for example, as an ingredient of the competitive success of small and medium-sized computer equipment producers in Taiwan Province of China.[21] From the developing country perspective, this is particularly interesting as participation in global supply chains provides opportunities for export-led growth and progress up the technology and value ladder. The supply chain can be considered as a web of processes and facilities by means of which the material inputs required for its productive processes flow into an enterprise are transformed into intermediate or final goods and are then distributed to its customers. This increasingly requires deeper levels of cooperation with outside entities.

In modern, more tightly integrated supply chains the links between suppliers and manufacturers extend downwards to include distributors and retailers. The digitally-enabled supply chain solution typically allows the leading operator (say, the operator of an international chain of fashion stores with suppliers in both developed and developing countries) to access information about supply and demand flows for the various ranges of products so that it can maintain the best possible balance between them. This requires digital access to demand information from the retail points (sales and stocks) as well as from its manufacturing facilities and subcontractors, down in the supply chain.

The use of WS technologies in the supply chains should help businesses to engage in extensive data exchange with their business partners, regardless of their location, at a lower cost than with earlier technologies (for example, EDI). Data exchanges through WS technologies should also offer advantages compared with "traditional" just-in-time purchasing and vendor-managed inventory systems, which are normally implemented only with suppliers based in the close vicinity. In companies that apply best practice in this area, information moves back and forth along these chains in real time, adjusting the delivery so that it closely matches the needs of the customer, in location as well as in timing. These integrated chains will deliver all their potential efficiency gains only if synchronized, real-time interaction exists between the networks of all the actors that participate in them. WS technologies fit perfectly into this picture.

More and better information enables companies to better match demand and supply and thus improve efficiency. For example, inventory levels can be brought lower (an important counterbalance to the push for higher inventory levels that may be needed as companies increasingly turn to global sourcing, which involves longer lead times and higher risks of disruption caused by transport). The so-called bullwhip effect, which consists in the magnification of the fluctuations of demand caused by imperfect information as orders flow along the supply chain, could be eliminated or greatly reduced. The aggregate effect of the implementation of ICT-based solutions along the supply chain should be higher effectiveness and competitiveness in terms of product specification, prices and services. At the macro level WS could provide an example of how, by contributing to the reduction of information asymmetries, ICTs could play a role in the smoothing of the business cycle.

Technologies such as order management systems, enterprise resource planning (ERP) and supply chain management (SCM) applications are the main ICT underpinning modern supply chains. A further step in the digitalization of supply chain management it the use of IOS that connect them through Internet-based e-business systems. However, in developing countries only a few enterprises, even in industries that are closely integrated into global supply chains, have these capabilities. If one goes a step down in the chain, even fewer of their suppliers have them, and so digital integration of the supply chain is only partial at best, limited mostly to global operators and their larger developing country suppliers. The ability of these large and medium-sized developing country participants in global supply chains to trust their lower-tier suppliers to the required degree depends much less on technology

and more on organizational factors such as industry clustering, executive networks, business practices and interpersonal relationships.[22]

While downward flows carry information about product designs and orders, it is also possible to have information moving up the supply chain. For instance, smaller suppliers in the lower echelons tend to specialize in the particular input they produce. They can provide their larger customers with information about their product, in some case even results from high-value-added activities such as product research and development. Larger suppliers can also cooperate with global brand owners in product design and specification. These multidirectional flows of information along the supply chain create opportunities for efficiency enhancement through extensive automation along the chain, from global operator to the lower-level suppliers. For example, quality monitoring can be substantially improved thanks to IT. At the same time, automation can be seen by the global brand owners as opportunities to deal directly with lower-tier suppliers and thus squeeze out the larger suppliers. Such strategies could damage the traditional business networks that were critical to several developing country export strategies.[23]

The coexistence of multiple supply chain management systems based on EDI or Extensible Markup Language (XML) means that there is a useful integration role that could be played by WS. In the longer term, their use should extend to other business processes by enabling seamless, automatic interoperability between the software applications used in running every part of a business (procurement, production, sales and marketing, after-sales service, finance, human resources) with each other and with those of their customers and suppliers. Beyond that, WS will be an essential part of an economy in which "communication" between Internet-enabled objects (for example, a sensor in a machine that detects that a piece will need to be replaced soon and places an order with the supplier) will be increasingly important. Although the main impact of Web services will be on the operations of enterprises, there are also many possibilities for consumer-oriented applications. For instance, in the tourism sector — a key source of employment and foreign reserves for many developing countries — WS technologies could be used to create virtual travel agents that would combine access to reservation systems of airlines or railways, car rentals, hotels, travel-related content providers and so forth.

Outsourcing is another trend that makes the emergence of SOA and WS relevant for e-business development, and more so for developing countries, for which ICT-enabled outsourcing makes it possible to compete in a number of services that used to be closed to international competition.[24] Outsourcing is generally defined as the process by which enterprises, in order to focus on the activities and processes that constitute the core of their business, transfer non-core parts of their activities to outside partners. As these functions are transferred to specialists, more value can be generated in their performance. While outsourcing is most commonly conceived in this manner, other kinds of outsourcing are emerging too. For example, some enterprises are co-sourcing, that is pooling their non-core operations when no large-scale specialist exists. This can also be done internally, for example when affiliates of a transnational corporation concentrate their operations for a particular product or service in a single centre. In-sourcing consists in adopting best practice in a certain process and adding to efficiency gains by taking business from other companies (not direct competitors), with consequent benefits from economies of scale. In all these modalities the need to smoothly exchange information between computers running different operating systems and applications in distant locations and serving business processes that are the responsibility of different partners grows exponentially.

The adoption of WS technologies will be increasingly necessary in order to maintain competitiveness in several sectors and industries of importance to developing countries. For example, the ICT-producing sector, in which developing countries have a large and growing share of world trade, are rapidly adopting WS technologies. It can be expected that this trend will be replicated in a wide range of manufacturing activities of considerable importance in the developing world, including in areas such as textile and apparel. As for services, as mentioned above, more effective inter-enterprise collaboration through WS technologies could be of particular relevance to sectors such as business process outsourcing and tourism. Efficiency gains in transport and logistics operations through WS implementation could also represent a welcome contribution to the alleviation of the burden that these items represent for the operations of enterprises in many developing countries, in many of which inefficient transport and logistics make it impossible for enterprises to take advantage of the low cost of production. Finally, developing countries should consider the vast potential that WS and SOA technologies offer for the implementation of e-government services, both in those that are addressed in the business sector (for example, Customs) and in others that are fundamental for general development

objectives (health services). In addition to the list of industries above, which emphasizes sectors of greater importance for developing countries, other areas commonly cited as particularly likely to benefit from SOA and WS are the financial services, especially retail banking and insurance and distribution services.

Box 6.1 showcases a few examples of initiatives taken by Governments of developing countries that use service-oriented technologies in a wide range of areas. In some of them these technologies are used to facilitate G2B interaction, thus providing both an example and an incentive for private sector adoption of SOA.

---

### Box 6.1

### Developing-country public-sector adoption of SOA and WS

- In **Argentina**, the national tax agency has launched a project to facilitate the access of other agencies and enterprises to the information in its unified taxpayer database. The project was based on the World Wide Web Consortium (W3C) standards and other standards addressing different protocol layers and special security requirements. Inter-agency collaboration and improved internal management enabled the tax agency to provide real-time access and validation of information to users for different transactions in a secure environment.

- In **Chile**, an efficient mechanism is needed to exchange information among government agencies in order to implement recent legislation empowering citizens to access the information that the Government collects from them. For this, a Web-based information exchange platform is being developed using open XML for data exchange, SOAP and WS. The final objective is to have all public sector agencies participating in the platform.

- About 600,000 companies are expected to benefit from a project of the Government of **India** to provide them with online services such as company registration, payment of statutory fees and filing of tax returns. Following consultations with major technology players, an SOA was chosen for the project. The business needs of users are used to define the architecture's design. Transactions will be routed through a standards-based gateway to ensure interoperability. The implementation partner is compensated on the basis of a service-level agreement which defines quality of service requirements in terms of efficiency, user friendliness and user satisfaction.

*Source:* Berkman Center for Internet and Society at Harvard Law School (2005).

## C.   The crucial role of standards

As explained before, the technology undercurrent that is moving WS forward is the mounting popularity of distributed computing, which is closely linked to the emergence of the Internet as the main ICT platform. The reason for this is that the Internet's standards and protocols are designed to let computers using different operating systems work together well. In a similar fashion, what WS do is to apply the standards embodied in, for example, XML, to enable a computer to identify the resources it needs for a given task (for instance, a piece of software or a set of data), locate and access them through the network, formulate a request and deal with what is sent in response. This way the network operates as if it were a single powerful computer that, like a desktop PC, needs a sort of "operating system" to manage the flow of requests for resources. This role is played by platforms (or "application development environments") that provide developers with the instruments they need to write their Web service applications.

For WS to deliver their potential, services from one application vendor must be able to interoperate with those of another vendor, which may have been built on a different platform. In business terms this means that there must be a guarantee that the Web service that takes care of a company's inventory management can do business with the Web service that the supplier uses to handle orders. The standard-setting process is therefore critical for the development of WS. A service-oriented approach depends on open standards. Open standards ensure that the criteria and decisions are truly service-oriented and are not biased towards one platform or another. Without open standards the possibilities that SOA give enterprises to combine, replace and mix the components of their IT systems without the need to create specific code to interconnect would not materialize.

However, from the beginning of the emergence of WS technologies, standard setting has been a major issue of contention and there has been intense debate about and around the bodies in which it takes place. Critics have argued that in general WS specifications have been

---

### Box 6.2

### What makes a standard "open"?

"...a standard [is considered] to be open when it complies with all these elements:

- cannot be controlled by any single person or entity with any vested interests;

- evolved and managed in a transparent process open to all interested parties;

- platform independent, vendor neutral and usable for multiple implementations;

- openly published (including availability of specifications and supporting material);

- available royalty free or at minimal cost, with other restrictions (such as field of use and defensive suspension) offered on reasonable and non-discriminatory terms; and

- approved through due process by rough consensus among participants."

"Ten requirements that enable open standards:

1. Open Meeting — all may participate in the standards development process.

2. Consensus — all interests are discussed and agreement found, no domination.

3. Due Process — balloting and an appeals process may be used to find resolution.

4. Open IPR — how holders of IPR related to the standard make available their IPR.

5. One World — same standard for the same capability, world-wide.

6. Open Change — all changes are presented and agreed in a forum supporting the five requirements above.

7. Open Documents — committee drafts and completed standards documents are easily available for implementation and use.

8. Open Interface — supports proprietary advantage (implementation); each interface is not hidden or controlled (implementation); each interface of the implementation supports migration (use).

9. Open Access — objective conformance mechanisms for implementation testing and user evaluation.

10. On-going Support — standards are supported until user interest ceases rather than when implementer interest declines."

*Source:* Berkman Center for Internet & Society at Harvard Law School (2005) and Krechmer (2005).

biased in favour of large technology vendors, and that they do not properly reflect the interests of smaller players, particularly those from developing countries.[25] The criticism has been made that organizations such as OASIS, W3C and WS-I should not be considered proper standard-setting institutions and that their outputs are not real standards, but specifications that enjoy some level of consensus.[26] For these critics, those organizations lack full stakeholder involvement and openness, and their outputs are not freely available and implementable. For example, the claim that some of the world's largest IT companies deliberately undermined the development of the UN-supported ebXML is presented as an example of the way in which standard setting is skewed towards the interest of the largest corporations. From this viewpoint, although standard setting may be a formally open process, participation is costly and so the smaller player is "priced out of the standards game" and private considerations prevail over the public interest.

Criticisms such as those summarized above became particularly strong in February 2005, when OASIS announced a revised intellectual property rights policy that included three modes for standards work: Reasonable and Non Discriminatory Access (RAND); royalty-free on RAND terms; and royalty-free on limited terms.[27] For FOSS advocates the move would imply that the organization's standards could not be considered open. The response from OASIS was that none of the fully formalized OASIS standards required a royalty to be paid and that less than a dozen of the approximately hundred specifications under discussion at that point would have royalties. As for the W3C, after similar criticism of a proposal to allow companies to charge royalties for patented technologies they had contributed to its standards, it maintains a royalty-free policy.[28]

There are many alternative views, some stricter than others, about what defines an "open standard", two of which are summarized in box 6.2. It should be noted that for the authors of the first set of criteria for open standards, the output of the work of these entities would fall into the category of "open standards".

Regardless of the conceptual issues involved in the definition of a "standard", the role of formal, government-accredited standard-setting bodies in the field of ICT has diminished in importance over the last two decades at the national and global levels. The main reason for this is competition from private consortia (including entities requiring membership fees) and informal bodies, as a consequence of the

---

## Box 6.3

## Who's who in WS standard setting

The Organization for the Advancement of Structured Information Standards (OASIS, www.oasis-open.org) was founded in 1993 under the name SGML Open as a consortium of vendors and users devoted to developing guidelines for interoperability among products that support the Standard Generalized Markup Language (SGML). OASIS changed its name in 1998 to reflect an expanded scope of technical work, including the Extensible Markup Language (XML) and other related standards. It describes itself as "a not-for-profit, international consortium that drives the development, convergence, and adoption of e-business standards", and claims about 5,000 "participants" representing over 600 organizations and individual members in 100 countries. It has developed standards such as UDDI v.2, Web Services Security (WSS) and others (see annex I).

The World Wide Web Consortium (www.w3c.org) was created in 1994 and has published more than 90 standards, which it calls "W3C Recommendations", including Web services standards such as WSDL, UDDI and SOAP, and XML-based specifications. W3C is an inter-national consortium whose operations are hosted mainly by the Massachusetts Institute of Technology, the European Research Consortium in Informatics and Mathematics, and the Keio University of Japan. IT has a presence in 16 other locations, including three in developing countries (India, Republic of Korea and Morocco). Its nearly 400 members include businesses, government agencies, NGOs and academic and research institutions.

The Web Services Interoperability Organization (WS-I, www.ws-i.org) was created in February 2003 by a group of some of the leading global IT companies and is supported by major players in the WS field. Its purpose is to promote interoperability among Web services. The WS-I does not consider itself a standard-setting body in the sense that this term is normally understood, that is as a forum in which experts discuss successive versions of a proposed standard until consensus is reached and a standard is published. Instead, the WS-I produces technical guidelines to ensure that Web services products from different providers can work together. The WS-I offers a sort of Web services seal of approval, providing certification that Web services adhere to standards put out by other standards organizations, such as the World Wide Web Consortium (W3C), the Organization for the Advancement of Structured Information Standards (OASIS) and the Internet Engineering Task Force (IETF).

---

## Box 6.4

## A comparison between ebXML and Web services

Although Web services and ebXML rely on the same technologies (SOAP/XML), they follow different approaches, are suited to somewhat different purposes and are not yet interoperable.

In a Web services architecture, services are published on the Internet so that anyone who is interested can use them. A Web service is described, advertised and provided by the same organization. The requester finds the service and eventually binds to it. In the case of an ebXML implementation, business partners exchange predefined documents in an pre-agreed business process. This is a contract approach that can be bilateral or even multilateral. The trading partners must negotiate their profiles, agree on a contract and then conduct the business transaction.

Web services are designed in a bottom-up process: the specifications for the core requirements are implemented first (SOAP for messaging, UDDI for discovery, etc.) and then brought together to create the service. In ebXML the process is top-down: first the requirements of an e-business process are assessed and then the specifications to meet them are defined. While the bottom-up approach results in greater flexibility (thus allowing WS technologies to be useful for many non-business purposes), the top-down approach of ebXML may be more adequate for supporting specialized business transactions.

From the point of view of the protocols and specifications, ebXML has achieved maturity faster than WS. On the other hand, WS enjoy larger vendor support as they have a larger market and, as a consequence, all major players support the technology.

---

growing importance of private service providers and technology developers. The extent to which this trend has resulted in a suboptimal consideration of the public interest in ICT standard setting is open to discussion. It is also argued that the dominance of private interests in standardization also reduces the openness of standards by increasing IPR costs.[29]

In addition to the question of the marginal role that is left to the smaller stakeholders, the relationship among the larger players within the various WS-related bodies, and for some time also among the bodies themselves, was not always easy. For instance, Sun Microsystems was initially excluded from the board of the WS-I. The situation has evolved and a division of labour has been established between the major organizations, which are listed in box 6.3.

OASIS and the United Nations Centre for Trade Facilitation and Electronic Business (UN/CEFACT) have jointly developed a set of standards based on XML, the Electronic Business Extensible Markup Language (ebXML) that enables enterprises to conduct business over the Internet. Its objective is to provide an open, XML-based infrastructure that enables the global use of electronic business information in an interoperable, secure and consistent manner by all trading partners. The original project envisioned five layers of data specification, including XML standards for business processes, collaboration protocol agreements, core data components, messaging, and registries and repositories.[30] ebXML provides a standard means to use

the Internet to exchange business messages, conduct trading relationships, communicate data in common terms, and define and register business processes.[31]

In order to use ebXML, a "business process specification" (which describes how a business works) and a "business document" (which describes the information to be exchanged in the transaction) are needed. The business documents are exchanged using the ebXML Messaging Service, which is based on SOAP. The system is completed with ebXML registries, which are used to find information on potential partners that offer the required services.

### 1.   Main standards, openness and IT interoperability

Typically, an IOS is made up of a content platform, a delivery platform and a trading partner base.[32] In order to conduct business with their partners through their system, the members of an IOS need to have their private corporate data put into a format that the IOS can understand. This is the role of the content platform. The delivery platform is then used to physically move the data from the computers of an IOS member to those of another one. The data reach the counterparts in the trading partner base to which they were addressed. The degree of openness of an IOS will be determined by that of each of its constituent elements, ranging from the proprietary system, partially open (EDI) and open-based system (Internet-based).

In a proprietary IOS, data standards (content) and participation and access (trading partner base) tended to be under the control of one of the members (typically a large supplier or purchaser dealing with many smaller customers or suppliers). As a result, the systems tended to be highly customized and usable only for transactions with the dominant player: investing in the systems generated a lock-in effect for the smaller partners.

In the case of EDI, although some of the earlier data standards were proprietary, the most widely used ones were developed by open organizations (in particular, EDIFACT standards are approved and published by the United Nations). Thus, the content platform of EDI allows communications with a larger base of trading partners and is less prone to lock-in effects. However, in the typical case in which data transmission takes place over private value-added communications networks (VAN) the system cannot be said to be fully open.

XML provides an open platform for Internet-based inter-organizational systems. SOAP and WSDL may also be considered to be open standards content platforms. The Internet, as a globally accessible public network based on open standards and protocols, provides an open delivery platform. Enterprises that join in an Internet-based IOS with other partners enjoy the benefits of openness at the levels of both content and delivery and can theoretically extend their IOS to virtually any other firm in the world that has a computer with access to the Internet.

Zhu et al. (2005) includes a number of references to the existing literature about the differences between XML and EDI standards. It has been pointed out that cross-industry coordination is easier with XML-based standards, as these are often less complex, rigid and partner-specific.[33] XML standards are self-describing and significantly more user-friendly. Learning and applying XML standard requires less technical expertise than EDI. For all these reasons negotiating a business cooperation deal to be implemented through EDI-based technologies is considerably more costly and requires a longer-term perspective than doing so on the basis of XML standards.

The delivery platforms and communications protocols add another factor of differentiation. EDI normally used VANs with their own proprietary communications protocols. Interconnection with other VANs may imply the payment of additional charges or may even be plainly impossible. The Internet, on the contrary,

is based on protocols designed to ensure the global interoperability of the millions of networks of which it is made up. The consequences in terms of costs are significant, making XML-based systems much more affordable and suitable for small and medium-sized enterprises. Finally, there are important differences in the trading partner bases of EDI and XML-based standards. Internet-based IOS are open to a much broader partner base and thus have the potential to generate more significant network effects. In particular, thanks to the standards for the Universal Description Discovery and Integration Registry (UDDI) companies can search for unknown trading partners, while EDI implementations could happen only within an existing business relationship.

As products based on SOA and WS begin to enter the corporate mainstream, the more visible commitment of key technology providers should give enterprises the confidence to prepare for implementation of upcoming WS standards, as many real-world products based on these standards are now being developed. Annex I lists some of the most commonly cited WS-related specifications and standards.

For example, in 2005 IBM, Microsoft and a group of other technology providers, including Actional, BEA Systems, Computer Associates, Oracle, RSA Security and Verisign, announced that that they planned to place three key Web services security specifications under the control of the Organisation for the Advancement of Structured Information Standards (OASIS). The three specifications, all based on the core WS-Security, are:

- **WS-Trust** (which defines extensions for requesting security tokens and brokering trust relationships);

- **WS-SecureConversation** (which defines mechanisms for securing multiple messages);

- **WS-SecurityPolicy** (which defines security policy assertions for **WS-Security, WS-Trust** and **WS-SecureConversation**).

This move places fundamental WS specifications under the control of OASIS and reflects the growing maturity of WS security. Many of the basic elements of secure WS are now in place. The publication of these specifications as OASIS standards should help to advance interoperability, although further work, perhaps in the form of enhancements to the Web Services Interoperability (WS-I), may be required in order to help enterprises make their deployments as compatible as possible. Also, the basic security policy language is likely to require extensions, which will be implemented in both proprietary and future standard versions.

Open standards play an increasingly important role in the generation of the economic value that enterprises can derive from their participation in these business networks. The combination of open standards with application-level intelligence and "dumb" network is consistent with the Internet's underlying end-to-end principle. As chapter 7 of this Report shows, maintaining the integrity of the Internet's constituent layers is crucial for its potential to be fulfilled, including with regard to its business transformation aspects. Thus, while EDI had been available since the 1970s, it was the widespread adoption of Internet technologies (based on open standards such as the TCP/IP and XML) that accelerated the development of ICT-enabled inter-organizational systems (IOS).[34]

Enterprises that adopt open standards not only minimize their risk of being trapped in obsolete standards but also empower themselves to capture more of the economic benefits generated by the Internet. The importance of openness for SOA and WS technologies naturally leads to the consideration of how a closely related trend, namely the growing importance of free and open source software, may facilitate the adoption of SOA and WS technologies, especially in developing countries.

## 2. Free and open source software, SOA and WS

Free and open source software (FOSS) is an approach to software development whereby communities of developers create software through a public process and the resulting product is made available free of charge.[35] FOSS represents a major paradigm shift in the software industry, which is rapidly being adopted by many major middleware producers. For those companies, taking the FOSS approach ensures that their products will be of the highest quality, at least equivalent to that of commercial proprietary products. They build their business models around the sale of support and other services.

Like all other FOSS products, SOA and WS implemented on a FOSS platform make it possible for users to utilize the software without restrictions and without paying licence fees, as well as giving them the possibility to modify it and develop applications of it as they see it fit, and the possibility to distribute it to other users. Building WS on an open source platform also reduces concerns about vendor lock-in issues.

Of course, these features of FOSS-based WS are particularly interesting for developing countries.

The value of implementing SOA and WS increases exponentially with the number of services that are available on the SOA. Implementing a commercial, proprietary SOA normally involves the payment of fees that are proportional to the computing resources that are running the SOA infrastructure (number of computers and/or processing power). This means that going for a truly comprehensive SOA implementation that connects all the enterprise's services and applications can become rather expensive. If a FOSS platform is chosen, this restriction is lifted and the enterprise (or the public sector agency) can add as many services and applications to the SOA infrastructure as makes business sense.

A second interesting feature of FOSS is that vendor lock-in issues are alleviated. FOSS developers' communities have a strong culture of supporting the evolution of standards, which is particularly relevant in the case of SOA technologies. And they do not go out of business or change licensing models, thus leaving previous buyers stuck with technologies that are fast becoming obsolescent.

Another point of convergence between FOSS and SOA and WS is that standards are crucial for their successful implementation. FOSS production methods encourage the developing community to move towards standards. As shown by the listing in annex I, SOA and WS rely on the existence of an increasing number of standards. This makes it possible, and actually provides an incentive for the FOSS community, to develop solutions for SOA and WS. For developing countries FOSS platforms for SOA and WS also have the advantage that they may be able to benefit at no cost from solutions and updates that have been integrated into existing implementations and made available to the developing community.

The popularity of FOSS products such as Linus, Apache, MySQL and others indicates that the FOSS approach has been particularly productive in the systems and applications infrastructure layer. FOSS platforms using LAMP are among the more widespread platforms for the implementation of WS. LAMP stands for "Linux, Apache, MySQL and PHP", although the acronym is increasingly used to refer to WS built with any combination of FOSS products, such as Linux, FreeBSD/OpenBSD, Apache, Python, Perl, PHP, PostgreSQL and MySQL.

# Table 6.1

## Some open source projects relevant to SOA and WS

| Project | Description | More information |
|---|---|---|
| ActiveMQ | Java Message Service (JMS) provider | Activemq.codehaus.org |
| Axix | Web services connector for Java | ws.apache.org/axis |
| Celtix | Enterprise Service Bus (ESB) | Celtix.objectweb.org |
| JEMS | Suite of open source tools for SOA implementations | Www.jboss.org |
| JORAM | JMS implementation | Joram.objectweb.org |
| jUDDI | Java implementation of the UDDI specification for Web services | ws.apache.org/juddi |
| Mule | ESB messaging framework | mule.codehaus.org |
| open-esb | SUN-sponsored ESB | Open-esb.dev.java.net |
| openadaptor | Java/XML-based services connector | Www.openadaptor.org |
| OSMQ | Java message router, broker and middleware framework | www.bostonsg.com/osmq/index.html |
| RM4GS | Implementation of WS-RM, which provides reliable messaging for Web services | businessgrid.ipa.go.jp/rm4gs/index-en.html |
| Sandesha | Implementation of WS-RM, providing reliable messaging for Web services | ws.apache.org/sandesha/ |
| ServiceMix | An ESB and SOA toolkit | servicemix.org/site/home.html |
| Synapse | Web services connector | wiki.apache.org/incubator/SynapseProposal |
| UDDI4J | Discovery service client | uddi4j.sourceforge.net/ |

As of mid-June 2006, typing the words "web services" in the search engine of http://sourceforge.net (a site that hosts open source development projects) turns up 421 Web services projects. Increasingly, commercial vendors are themselves participating in open source projects, a trend that is likely to continue. As mentioned before, middleware vendors such as IBM, Sonic Software, IONA Technologies, SUN Microsystems and others have begun passing code to which they held proprietary rights on to open source projects. Table 6.1 lists just a few open source projects that are relevant to SOA.

FOSS platforms provide a significant opportunity for enterprises in developing countries to experiment with and gradually adopt SOA and WS technologies in an effective, secure and affordable manner. FOSS solutions offer tangible benefits that have been proven at the infrastructure layer and should receive full consideration by anyone interested in SOA and WS.

## D. Effects on e-business of SOA and WS deployments

According to a recent IDC Research report,[36] a clear focus for many of today's SOA implementation is the extension of information and business processes to new users (e.g. employees, partners, suppliers, customers and agencies). Other typical solutions include optimizing procurement, inventory and B2B information exchange processes, as well as sharing sales and financial information for use in planning, billing and credit processing. Many industry-specific use cases have been identified. For example, solutions within the health-care sector range from claims processing to bedside patient care.[37]

In general, companies tend to change to SOA as part of a medium- to long-term shift towards network-based IT solutions. However, there are also short-term benefits to be reaped. For instance, integration and compatibility across various retail channels can result in increased sales revenues, as they make it possible to more easily integrate demand-side information into the design and production processes.

Merger processes offer another example of how WS (as an initial step) and more sophisticated SOA implementations (at a later stage) can bring about substantial efficiency gains, in this case through the easier consolidation of databases and systems.

In retail financial services, the use of WS can result in significant cost reductions. For example, a leading North American bank added new functionality to existing Web-based customer application processes, achieving a consolidated view of customer account and

---

## Box 6.5

## An imaginary example of how to implement SOA

From its African home in Cornucopia, Bricks and Mortar Plc. (B&M) has grown into a global construction materials supplier with presence in six countries of West and South Asia and Latin America. Having accumulated a few years' experience with XML, B&M has launched a long-term SOA strategy in an effort to redesign its IT strategy to adapt it to the needs of its growing international activities. The goal is to create a single, cross-regional infrastructure to replace their rather fragmented base, and at the same time, to add IT capacity by sharing a larger part of the available resources. Another key objective was to enhance the efficiency of its supply chain management.

As is often the case with companies starting to experiment with the SOA model, it has taken about two years for B&M to have more than a few implementations running. However, the effort over these two years has served to sharply concentrate the company's IT policies on WS. B&M has established a policy to review its proposed WS implementations to make sure that they comply with the company's conditions and standards before they are published through the enterprise's registry. B&M continues to use traditional integration and middleware software while gradually deploying more and more WS solutions for areas such as development, security, management and business process orchestration.

In terms of concrete gains from the move towards SOA, B&M's IT management team are particularly pleased with the creation of a supply chain "control panel" that brings together information taken from applications from several vendors into a single view. They estimate that thanks to their decision to use SOA this project could be implemented with monetary savings in the region of 30 per cent and within much tighter deadlines. Equally important was the fact that this success story helped convince B&M's senior management to accelerate SOA and WS adoption in the company.

*Source:* UNCTAD elaboration of case studies published by SOA tool vendors.

---

credit information. This allowed the bank to retire half of its process locations and save several million dollars in costs. Another bank now allows online customer access to banking services previously available only to call centre agents. A US federal agency created a shared service centre to better manage inventories and handle logistical processes across its agency, customers and commercial trading partners. By implementing a seamless data architecture, it can more efficiently handle requisition approvals and updates, inventory searches and allocations, shipments and financial transactions.[38]

It is interesting to note that there is a wide diversity of reported reasons for adopting WS and SOA. Some organizations have targeted automating specific business functions and processes that were previously manual activities due to complexities in integrating fractured applications and systems. Others have opted to introduce SOA in non-mission-critical business functions in order to reduce the initial risk and ensure future investments. Box 6.5 presents the case of an imaginary enterprise, putting together information available about the experience of various enterprises in implementing SOA and WS in a developing country context.

Box 6.6 summarizes the motivations and expectations of an enterprise that plans to implement a SOA.

## 1. The transition to SOA

It is to be expected that not every aspect of an enterprise's systems will be immediately open to WS implementations. Normally, enterprises will not wish or need to completely reshape all their IT systems for that purpose. However, many companies, mostly in developed countries but also others based in developing countries, have started to implement WS to such an extent that they do need to put in place adequate SOAs.

This is not being made easier by the abundance of standards and the danger that there could be a divergence in this regard among major vendors. The response to these concerns tends to be that precisely because SOA allows the loose coupling of systems, each individual technology choice becomes intrinsically less risky. Enterprises that have taken a centralized approach to policy-making for SOA adoption are reported to have been more successful.[39] The teams of SOA experts that are thus created become a useful resource to identify best practice in the application of SOA and WS to key business processes. They also help build the enterprise's knowledge base about SOA, its impact on both IT systems and in overall business operations and how to identify the better candidate processes/services for the deployment of those technologies.

---

## Box 6.6

## The case of Asian Paints

Asian Paints is an Indian manufacturer of consumer and industrial paints with operations in 23 countries. It has experience in using IT to automate important business processes, including manufacturing, distribution and inventory management, and sees IT and particularly SOA as a means of differentiating itself from its competitors.

In 2000, Asian Paints decided to undertake a migration of critical systems from in-house-developed custom applications to vendor-provided solutions. An important reason for this move was the need to integrate internal systems with its supply chain business partners. The company currently uses XML to exchange information with its partners. The use of SOA technologies should in the future allow supply chain partners to obtain product and inventory information themselves rather than require Asian Paints to provide this information to them. WS and SOA standards are expected to broaden the range of interactions with supply chain partners and to lower their cost.

SOA-based applications will target better and more integrated supply-chain and production planning processes. Asian Paints also plans to add business process management, automated controls for compliance and specialized applications to support its painting services business with the new SOA architecture.

In order to maximize the value that could be generated by its SOA-based strategy, the company will need to convince its business partners to also take an SOA approach to their IT systems. Most of them do not currently use SOA/WS standards.

*Source:* IDC (2005).

Enterprises considering automating business processes through WS will not face any scarcity of commercial technology providers, either in developed or in developing countries. However, they should be aware that this is a field where experience about central issues such as performance, security and interoperability is still being accumulated at a fast pace. Therefore, before engaging in the process of change that WS and SOA involve it is important for enterprises to achieve a sufficient understanding of the standards and basic underpinnings of these technologies. They should also undertake their own investigation into the priorities for WS and SOA implementations and the necessary business process redesign.

## 2. Theory and practice

There is little doubt about the real positive impact that WS and SOA can make on competitiveness by facilitating integration of applications and collaboration

with business partners. For example, leading players in the B2C arena such as eBay and Amazon seem to have been able to make significant gains by implementing WS. Other companies claim that they have observed productivity gains, although this may be more in terms of additional capabilities than can be transformed into future benefits than of actual profits. In the United States, a survey of 437 companies made by the Yankee Group in 2004 found that 48 per cent of respondents had already implemented WS and another 39 per cent expected to do so in 2005. Seventy-one per cent said that they planned to increase spending on WS in 2005. The advantages most commonly quoted were improved ability to cooperate with business partners (77 per cent), reduced complexity in distributed applications (66 per cent), higher revenues (66 per cent) and lower application development costs (58 per cent). Security ranked at the top of the list of WS-related worries (72 per cent).[40]

Yet the experience of WS implementation so far shows that difficulties are bound to remain, for technical reasons but also, and more difficult to address, business reasons. The earlier WS adopters have tended to be large corporations. These are usually able to push their business partners to participate and eventually fix to a large extent the conditions under which their suppliers/customers engage in WS. For instance, a small company that intends to use eBay's WS to sell its products has no possibility of negotiating the WS that will apply to their transactions. All it can do is to adhere to the standards published by eBay. But even in these cases, applications used by different companies, even those used in the same business process, rarely include the same data or handle it in exactly the same way. Even minor data format disagreements (for example, the format in which decimals or dates are notated in an order) may involve extensive work before real systems integration can happen. There is no specific solution that WS can contribute to this problem.

As companies start to discuss solutions to these issues, the business problems of system integrations become apparent: decisions have to be made about the level of control each partner retains over its own information (some of which may be highly sensitive, i.e. customer data) and how much it provides to its partners. Details of financial and other business practices need to be agreed on, which may be challenging when the partners are based in countries with different business traditions and regulatory frameworks. For instance, at what time of the day is a transaction considered to have taken place the next business day? Or at what point in the history of the relationship with a customer are certain credit conditions granted? Resolving these issues can be time-consuming and expensive, even within different units of the same company.

In theory, WS should be equally applicable to transactions taking place inside a company or with external companies. In practice, it is more frequent to see them implemented for internal transactions. For inter-organizational links it is much more frequent to see WS used between enterprises that have a long record of cooperation and are technologically sophisticated. In terms of size, there are more examples of implementations among large corporations, although the case of WS relationships between large companies and their smaller suppliers is also frequent. But even in developed countries, smaller enterprises tend to cooperate using non-structured technologies such as e-mail and Web rather than structured ones such as EDI, XML and WS.[41]

In terms of the nature of the business processes to which WS are being applied so far, they tend to be the ones most simple and easiest to automate, such as the transmission of orders and the description of the items in a catalogue. In an evolutionary process WS are expected to extend their support to other more complex processes. However, for enterprises, particularly those with less experience in complex IT implementations, it is advisable to take an incremental approach to their adoption of WS.

There are a number of considerations that an enterprise should bear in mind when assessing the possibility of investing in a WS implementation. The first one is the kind of relationship it has with the business partners that are most likely to use the proposed WS. This includes not only the nature of the business relationship itself but also its time horizon. Then there is the issue of how data are going to be shared and who and how is going to handle a given segment of a business process, and how it is going to be handled. There are decisions to be made about the way in which the WS is going to be implemented: what processes are to be automated and if/how WS are to be extended to other business processes. Finally, there is the question of how the enterprise is going to handle the WS implementation so that at the end it has developed an additional competitive advantage and added to its knowledge base.

The preceding paragraphs made several references to the importance of work on security-related standards for WS.[42] WS may put outsiders in contact with systems that are at the core of the activity of an enterprise. This is a manifestation of a general trend towards greater openness of enterprises, in relation to both their customers and their suppliers. Normally, enterprises benefit from this greater openness, because they can be more responsive to their customers and receive better service from their partners. But it should not be forgotten that any interface with the outside world represents a risk of intrusion, ranging from the merely indiscreet to the seriously malicious. While the industry is taking significant steps to address security concerns, at this stage of the technology's maturity, and of the user's understanding of it, fully addressing security issues (including the implications for project scalability) should remain a central consideration of any major Web service implementation.

## E.    Conclusions and recommendations

The preceding sections of this chapter have shown how, for reasons that have to do with trends in the evolution of ICTs but also, and perhaps even more, with changes in business strategy, services-oriented architectures and Web services will have a major role in shaping e-business in the next few years. SOA will probably represent the next major wave of enterprise IT architectures, replacing in many instances the client/server model in its dominant role. Web services standards will play a central role in the materialization of this change, as they are what renders operative the networking, transport, security and other layers of SOA implementations.

In a wide range of industries, many of which (such as electronics, textiles, other manufactures and tourism) are of great importance for developing countries, competitiveness will be greatly influenced by the ability to integrate information systems inside the enterprise and with those of business partners. SOA and WS will be fundamental for this and enterprises need to be aware of these technologies, understand their underpinnings and put them into practice.

As wider deployment of SOA and WS technologies facilitates the achievement of deeper levels of collaboration among enterprises and across geographical boundaries, opportunities may arise for those from developing countries. These may come from easier participation in supply chains and from widened possibilities for outsourcing. Both increasingly require deeper levels of integration and interaction between the IT systems of enterprises. As companies share information better with their customers and suppliers, and IT enables them to cooperate at deeper levels, they can enhance product design and specification, customize production, improve quality, reduce stocks and become more responsive to changes in market conditions. In this context, SOA and WS may become a sort of global production infrastructure supporting a common organizational logic. The challenge for developing countries is to ensure that they become part of this global business infrastructure.

Decision makers in enterprises and in the public sector should be aware that interoperability is as much a business strategy issue as it is a technology one. Technology makes interoperability possible, but only if interoperability is incorporated into the business plans of the enterprises or public sector agencies concerned. Frequently, the main barriers to interoperability are not technical, and include issues such as the following:

Regulatory (or market-driven) limits on the nature of information that can be shared with business partners or, in the case of the public sector, on the kind of cooperation arrangements between different agencies;

Institutional and/or cultural boundaries that separate organizations in terms of information sharing or that generate resistance to perceived losses of control over information;

Lack of awareness about the services that are available and the ones that may contribute to a particular business need;

- Lack of managerial capacity;

- Fear of loss of intellectual property; and

- Concerns about security problems.

Therefore, besides technology, planning and implementation monitoring should address aspects such as the desired levels of information sharing, the changes that may be necessary in business processes and the upgrading of human skills, including at the managerial and strategy-setting levels.

In particular, Governments and enterprises should be aware that in a market environment increasingly marked by cooperation within, and competition among, networks, the capacity to generate and sustain trust among business partners and customers becomes a fundamental ingredient of success. Regulatory entities have a crucial role to play in this regard and Governments of developing countries should make sure that their enterprises are able to operate within a legal and regulatory framework that creates trust and facilitates ICT-enabled information sharing and collaboration.

Another consideration that should be incorporated into public policies in order to facilitate the adoption of services-oriented architectures and Web services relates to the role that public-sector agencies can play as early adopters and role models for the private sector. In addition to enhancing the effectiveness of public services, SOA and WS implementations in public-sector agencies can raise awareness about these technologies among the less internationally exposed enterprises and provide incentives for their adoption. In so doing, both public- and private-sector decision makers should give full consideration to FOSS platforms for SOA and WS. Governments should also consider establishing their own frameworks for IT interoperability.

Finally, this chapter has shown how without open standards, SOA and WS technologies lose much of their business transformation potential. However, many aspects of standard-setting in this, as in several other areas of ICTs, are currently outside the public sphere and dominated by a small number of private players — mostly technology vendors. Whether the interests of users and consumers, particularly those from developing countries, are adequately taken into account in these standard-setting processes is open to discussion. Government involvement is not necessarily a precondition for the development of open standards. But Governments, including those of developing countries, should pay adequate attention to those processes, and both as intensive IT users and in their function of protecting the public interest should provide input and feedback into the SOA and WS standard-setting processes, promote awareness about them among their private sector and facilitate the presence of private sector players from developing countries in the bodies that develop SOA and WS standards.

# Annex I

## Some Web services specifications and standards

### WS-TF (Web Service Transaction Framework)

| | |
|---|---|
| WS-Coordination | Protocol that coordinates activities in distributed environments. Enables existing systems to hide proprietary protocols and operate in an heterogeneous environment. |
| W S-Atomic Transaction | Coordinating protocol for handling well-known and accepted two-phase commit protocols. |
| WS-Business Activity | Defines protocols allowed to coordinate a business activity. |

### Metadata

| | |
|---|---|
| WS-Policy | Defines a base set of constructs that can be used and extended by other Web services specifications to describe a broad range of service requirements, preferences or capabilities. |
| UDDI | Universal Description, Discovery and Integration, used to locate Web services by enabling robust queries against rich metadata. |
| WSDL | Web Services Description Language standard, an XML format for describing network services as a set of endpoints operating on messages containing either document-oriented or procedure-oriented information. |
| WS-Discovery | Defines a multicast discovery protocol to locate services. |
| WS-Addressing | |

### Reliable Messaging

| | |
|---|---|
| WSRM | WS Reliable Messaging defines a mechanism to guarantee the delivery of messages to applications and Web services. |
| WS reliability 1.1 (WSRX) (OASIS Standard) | Idem (OASIS standard). |

### Security

| | |
|---|---|
| WSS v1.0 | Web Services Security describes mechanisms for message authentication including exchange of identification through profiles such as user name, X.509 certificates and Kerberos (OASIS Standard). |
| WS-SX | WS Secure exchange includes WS SecureConversation, WS-Trust and WS- SecurityPolicy (see below). |
| WS SecureConversation | Provides for the establishment and sharing of security contexts as well as a mechanism for deriving keys from security contexts. |
| WS-Trust | Defines mechanisms for establishing a trust relationship between Web services. Extends tokens that can be exchanged between trust domains. |
| WS-SecurityPolicy | Defines policy assertions that apply to Web services security (SOAP Message security, WS-Trust, WS-SecureConversation). |

### Management

| | |
|---|---|
| WSDM | Defines the means to provide management of services in a distributed environment. It comprises MOWS and MUWS (OASIS standard). |
| MOWS | Management of Webs Services, describes a mechanism for managing Webs services, including functional, resource and service management (OASIS standard). |
| MUWS | Management Using Web Services, describes the mechanism required to manage resources using Web services (OASIS standard). |

*Source:* http://www.networkcomputing.com/showArticle.jhtml?articleID=180205695

# References and bibliography

Aalst van der W M P (2003). Don't go with the flow. Web services composition standards exposed. IEEE Intelligent Systems, Jan/Feb issue. Available at http://is.tm.tue.nl/staff/wvdaalst/publications/p181.pdf.

Berkman Center for Internet and Society at Harvard Law School (2005). Roadmap for open ICT ecosystems. Available at http://cyber.law.harvard.edu/epolicy/roadmap.pdf

CIO Magazine (2004). Web services gain momentum. 15 November 2004. Available at http://www.cio.com/archive/111504/tl_numbers.html.

Cravens D W, Piercy NF and Shipp SH (1996). New organizational forms for competing in highly dynamic environments: The network paradigm. *British Journal of Management* 7 *(3), pp. 203–218.*

Ernst D (2000). Inter-organizational knowledge outsourcing: What permits small Taiwanese firms to Compete in the Computer Industry? *Asia Pacific Journal of Management,* vol. 17, issue 2, August, pp. 223–255. An unreviewed, unedited prepublication version is available at http://www.eastwestcenter.org/stored/pdfs/ECONwp001.pdf.

Greenspan A (2002). Testimony of Chairman Alan Greenspan: Federal Reserve Board's Semiannual Monetary Policy Report to the Congress before the Committee on Banking, Housing, and Urban Affairs. United States Senate, 7 March. http://www.federalreserve.gov/boarddocs/hh/2002/march/testimony.htm.

Gartner (2005). Gartner market Focus: Trends and forecasts for IT professional services for Web services and SOA, 2005, by Michele Cantara, 27 June.

IDC (2003). Web services are becoming reality: IT opportunity around Web services will reach $21 billion by 2007 according to IDC. Press release dated 4 February.

IDC Research (2005a). Press release, Consumption of Web services will greatly increase through 2009, IDC Finds. 14 July. Available at www.idc.com/getdoc.jsp?containerId=prUS00190705.

IDC Research (2005b). Business forces driving adoption of services oriented architecture. White paper sponsored by SAP AG. Available at http://www.sap.com/solutions/esa/pdf/BWP_AR_IDC_Service_Oriented_Architecture.pdf.

Johnston H R and Vitale M R (1988). Creating competitive advantage with interorganizational systems. *MIS Quarterly* 12:2, pp. 153–165.

Krechmer K (2003). Face the FACS (Formal Worldwide Regional and National Agencies for Communications Standardization). Paper presented at the Third IEEE Conference on Standardization and Innovation in Information Technology (SIIT 2003), 22 October, Delft, Netherlands. Available at http://www.csrstds.com/FACS.htm.

Krechmer K (2005). Open standard requirements. *International Journal of IT Standards and Standardization Research,* vol. 4 no. 1, January–June 2006. Available at http://www.csrstds.com/openstds.pdf.

Leyman F, Roller D and Schmidt M T (2002). Web services and business process management. *IBM Systems Journal,* vol. 41, no 2. Available at http://www.research.ibm.com/journal/sj/412/leymann.html.

Radicati Group (2004). Web Services Market 2004-2008. 1 September.

Stabell C B and Fjeldstad O D  (1998) Configuring Value For Competitive Advantage: On Chains, Shops, and Networks. *Strategic Management Journal*, vol. 19, pp. 413–437.

Stencil Group (2002). The laws of evolution: A pragmatic analysis of the emerging Web services market. April. Available at http://www.line56.com/research/download/stencil_evolution.pdf.

UNCTAD (2003). *E-commerce and Development Report 2003*.

UNCTAD (2005). *Information Economy Report 2005*.

Varian H et al. (2002). The net impact study. http://www.netimpactstudy.com/NetImpact_Study_Report.pdf.

Yang Y (2006). The Taiwanese notebook computer production network in China: Implication for upgrading of the Chinese electronics industry. CRITO consortium, http://www.pcic.merage.uci.edu/pubs/2006/TaiwaneseNotebook.pdf.

Zhu K et al. (2005). Migration to open-standard interorganizational systems: Network effects, switching costs and path dependency. Research Project Report. CRITO consortium., http://crito.uci.edu/pubs/2005/zhuKraemerGurbaxaniXu.pdf.

# Notes

1.  According to the IEEE Standard 1471-2000, architecture is defined as the fundamental organization of a system, embodied in its components, their relationship to each other and the principles governing its design and evolution.

2.  Stencil Group (2002).

3.  For example, see IDC Research (2005a).

4.  In 2003 Gartner predicted that about $1 billion would have been wasted on misguided Web services projects by 2007. See http://www.cio.com/archive/100103/standards.html.

5.  IDC Research (2003).

6.  IDC Research (2005a).

7.  Radicati Group (2004).

8.  Gartner (2005).

9.  CORBA stands for Common Object Request Broker Architecture. It is a standard that defines how applications written in various languages and running on different platforms can interoperate. DCOM stands for Distributed Component Object Model. This is a Microsoft proprietary technology that lets software components distributed among several interconnected computers communicate.

10. It should be noted that sometimes CORBA is considered a case of SOA implementation. See, for example, http://www-128.ibm.com/developerworks/webservices/newto/.

11. API, Application Programming Interface — an interface that lets one programme use facilities provided by another.

12. http://isp.webopedia.com/TERM/S/Service_Oriented_Architecture.html.

13. http://searchwebservices.techtarget.com/originalContent/0,289142,sid26_gci1044083,00.html for a long catalogue of possible definitions of SOA.

14. http://www.lucent.com/search/glossary/w-definitions.html.

15. http://publib.boulder.ibm.com/infocenter/wbihelp/v6rxmx/index.jsp?topic=/com.ibm.wbix_adapters. doc/doc/webservices/webservi10.htm.

16. http://isp.webopedia.com/TERM/W/Web_services.html.

17. A stub is a small program routine that substitutes for a longer, possibly remote, program. For example, a stub might be a program module that transfers procedure calls (RPCs) and responses between a client and a server. In Web services, a stub is an implementation of a Java interface generated from a WSDL document. http://publib.boulder.ibm.com/infocenter/adiehelp/index.jsp?topic=/com.ibm.wsinted.glossary. doc/topics/glossary.html.

18. See, for example, Cravens, Piercy and Shipp (1996).

19. See Greenspan (2002). Stabell and Fjeldstad (1998) define value networks as organizations that create value for customers by linking them together or mediating exchanges between them. See http://lef.csc.com/ foundation/library/value/RP01.asp. for a presentation of their concepts. See also http://www.vernaallee. com/value_networks/A_ValueNetworkApproach_white_paper.pdf for an alternative definition of value networks.

20.  *The Economist,* The physical Internet: A survey of logistics, 17 June 2006, p. 3.

21.  See Ernst (2000).

22.  Yang (2006).

23.  Ibid.

24.  See chapter 5 of UNCTAD (2003) for an extensive study of ICTs, their role in the expansion of business process outsourcing and the issues that this raises for developing countries.

25.  For a vocal argumentation along these lines, see "You call that a standard?", an interview with Professor Robert Glushko of the University of California at Berkeley, available at http://news.com.com/You+call+that+a+standard%3F/2008-1013_3-5200672.html?tag=guts_bi_7345. This interview generated an interesting online discussion and a considerable amount of criticism among XML developers, some of which is available at http://www.xml.com/lpt/a/2004/05/12/deviant.html.

26.  Ibid.

27.  See OASIS intellectual property policy at http://www.oasis-open.org/who/intellectualproperty.php.

28.  http://www.w3.org/Consortium/Patent-Policy-20040205/.

29.  See Krechmer (2003).

30.  See http://www.ebxml.org/geninfo.

31.  The Center for E-Commerce Infrastructure Development of Hong Kong (China) and the Department of Computer Science & Information Systems at the University of Hong Kong (China) sponsor the freebXML project, which was launched to promote development and adoption of ebXML-based open-source. See http//:www.freebxml.org.

32.  Johnston and Vitale (1988), quoted in Zhu (2005).

33.  The reason for the complexity and relative rigidity of EDI messages is that these standards were developed in a context of bandwidth scarcity in which efficiency in the transmission of information was at a premium.

34.  EDI standards define the format of messages and the communication protocol. Historically, EDI tended to be implemented over private networks.

35.  See UNCTAD (2003) for a comprehensive overview of the FOSS phenomenon and the benefits that developing countries could derive from a positive and proactive approach to FOSS.

36.  IDC (2005b).

37.  IDC (2005b).

38.  All examples in this paragraph are quoted from IDC (2005).

39.  IDC (2005b).

40.  CIO Magazine (2004).

41.  See "Confronting the reality of Web services," an interview with Professor A.P. McAfee, Harvard Business School Working Knowledge, 16 May 2005. Available at hbswk.hbs.edu/item.jhtml?id=4800&t=technology.

42.  See UNCTAD 2005 for a presentation of some key aspects of security in relation to the development of e-business.

# Chapter 7

# THE LAYERED INTERNET ARCHITECTURE: GOVERNANCE PRINCIPLES AND POLICIES

## A. Introduction

Internet governance matters because it can influence the economic and social opportunities for all peoples. Given the proven track record of the Internet as an innovation platform, it is only rational that Internet governance policy should be aimed at strengthening and improving this foundational characteristic. So far in human history, there has never been a flatter field for ambitious and competitive minds to stake their claim to technological fame and fortune. It is entirely feasible that the next Internet "killer application" may come from a developing country. Internet governance can assist this process. However, caution and deep reflection should be exercised, as misconceived policy or regulation can be harmful or even detrimental — usually to a disproportionate extent for developing countries.

The Internet governance debate is wide open. The World Summit on the Information Society (WSIS) succeeded in mainstreaming this important issue while perhaps disappointing only the most fervent optimists who may have hoped that a conclusive governance framework could have been established and set in motion. The WSIS events in Geneva and Tunis, as well as the Working Group on Internet Governance (WGIG), highlighted a diversity of views and approaches to the Internet governance issue. Perhaps the diversity was somewhat too diverse and therein lies one of the key challenges of the post-WSIS process.

What is needed in the continuation of the deliberations is convergence. However, it would be premature to seek convergence around prejudgement of an outcome. Today, and thanks to WSIS and WGIG, we have a better understanding of common terminologies and definitions. What we need to move forward is a set of criteria that will allow the development of policy and regulatory principles for Internet governance that are coherent and relevant to the Internet as a technological medium and that maintain its positive relationship with technological innovation and economic and social development.

The technical debate did not happen at WSIS and perhaps it would not have been timely. The priorities were clearly to establish "whether there are significant problems with existing governance mechanisms, and whether there are any pressing but unresolved issues that need to be tackled through international cooperation."[1] It is to be hoped that the Internet Governance Forum (IGF) — the post-WSIS successor to the WGIG — will provide a platform to engage technology and policy at the same time. This will not be an easy task as there are many public policy issues vying for the attention of the IGF. It is easy to reinterpret just about any action line from the WSIS final documents as being a governance issue, in addition to the fact that almost one third of the outcome deals explicitly with Internet governance.

This chapter proposes that Internet governance should be consistent with the layered nature of the Internet's technical architecture. More specifically, it should respect the layers principle and its corollaries. What does this mean? Unfortunately, attempting a definition at this point would be well nigh impossible. Similarly, restating the need for consistency and principles in more accessible terms can require oversimplifications that will obscure the issues at stake — and thus will be avoided. What this chapter proposes is to develop the notion of the layers principle and its relation to Internet governance from its particular elements to the point where its meaning becomes obvious. However, before going into technical and policy discussions, we will present several ideas that underscore the need for this discourse.

The layers principle is at the same time simple and opaque. The reason is that it requires an appreciation of the technology underlying the Internet protocol suite. It also requires an understanding that without the protocol, there is no Internet — in spite of all the wires, servers and networking hardware currently deployed. If we can govern well only what we understand, it follows that policymakers need to develop a sufficient technological understanding of the Internet protocol suite in order to establish quality in Internet governance.

Policymakers should go beyond understanding the economic and social implications of the Internet. They need to understand the technological Internet and how its structure is intimately related to social and economic issues and outcomes, in order to develop an effective framework of governance. Conversely, technologists need to understand that the issues of legitimacy and responsibility in governance are inseparable from efficacy. In a scenario reminiscent of the proverbial two cultures, policymakers and technologists should seek convergence. This is not unusual and we can identify similar developments in other current deliberations, such as poverty alleviation or climate change. Establishing a bridge between technologists and policymakers is therefore crucial to the positive and productive outcome of the Internet governance debate. However, rallying together in the abstract may be unproductive. Therein lies the value of developing a set of axiomatic principles upon which to focus the international debate on Internet governance.

This chapter does not suggest that the layers principle should become immovable and eternal Internet law. It does not suggest that it may be the only or most worthy principle — other principles can be developed, discussed and established. However, it does advance the idea that the layers principle and its corollaries are fundamental for establishing a rational and workable policy and regulatory framework for Internet governance. More broadly, this chapter advises policymakers that these principles are vital for building out an Internet that promotes economic democracy and innovation opportunity for all. This notion should be of particular concern for developing nations sizing up the development potential presented by information and communication technologies (ICTs). While wealthy nations could conceivably afford to occasionally use network technologies or implement governance policies that occasionally violate the layers principle, developing countries may find such a practice to be costly and detrimental to building their information societies and closing the digital divide.

The governance policy and regulatory concerns are important when we consider that eventually all ICTs will converge into the Internet (Werbach, 2002). The question is: do we recognize the value and contribution of the Internet and do we understand the role of its layered structure and open standards in permitting this amazing development of the global digital network? If we do, the only possible conclusion is that all other converging applications, such as broadcast and cable television, radio and telephony, should be guided to assimilate the Internet's qualities. Conversely, the

Internet should firmly resist becoming more like these old technologies and policy should support this. This also implies a move away from governing and regulating by type of service, infrastructure or geographical reach.[2] Most importantly, it entails a conscious decision to explore network communications layers as the basis for governance policy and regulation.

The discussion that follows owes much to the analysis developed by Werbach (2002, 2004) Solum and Chung (2003), Kruse, Yurcik and Lessig (2000) and Benkler (2000). After developing the concept of the layered Internet, the chapter will develop the layers principle while reflecting on supporting principles and corollaries and addressing criticism. The chapter will then examine more closely the nature of the layers principle from the perspective of its use in decision-making in policy and regulatory environments. The chapter will end with a discussion on the need for integrating the above notions into the post-WSIS Internet Governance Forum (IGF) process.

## B.    Layers and the Internet architecture

### 1.    Protocols and layers

The origin and development of the Internet have been explained and discussed in many reference sources. Readers are invited to consider, in particular, "A brief history of the Internet" (Internet Society, 2003)[3] for more details. This chapter will, however, avoid developing a historical perspective on the architecture of the Internet.

The Internet is still changing and its underlying technology and practical uses will evolve with increases in bandwidth and convergence of various delivery technologies and media, as well as with the development of new applications. The economics will change accordingly and interaction, and sometimes conflicts, between those that provide content, delivery pipes and attention will lead to new business models and environments. Attention providers — the online public audience at large — are of particular significance in this equation as online advertisement revenue continues to grow in importance for many enterprises.[4]

While nothing stays the same, the fundamental technical structure of the Internet acts as a springboard for change. More specifically, it is the Internet protocol suite that provides the stability of the Internet. It is often called the TCP/IP suite, a name combined from the abbreviations of the two most important components in the suite: the Transmission Control Protocol (TCP) and the Internet Protocol (IP). However, the TCP/IP suite also includes many other protocols such as those that are used for file transfer (FTP), e-mail transmission (SMTP) or hypertext transfer (HTML), to name but a few. Fortunately for the non-technical user, this multitude of contemporary protocols has become completely opaque, as many Internet applications, such as web browsers and e-mail clients, have been designed to engage any number and combination of these as required by the user. Annex I provides a selective list of Internet protocols.

The various protocols are often categorized in layers. Lower layers perform fundamental technical functions such as networking (establishing and maintaining connections among the many computers on the Internet) and transporting data. Upper layers provide application level functionality and rely on the lower layers to work reliably, but are purposefully independent. In a particular layer, functionally equivalent protocols, and the software applications that use them, can be substituted for one another without any adjustment being required in the protocols and applications that function in a layer above or below. This greatly reduces the complexity of the Internet protocol suite and increases its robustness, as its components are not forced into predefined linkages. Rather, they communicate and process data as needed in order to achieve a final functional outcome: access to a website, the reception of an Internet-based media stream such as Internet television, Voice over Internet Protocol (VoIP) or a secure remote connection to a database such as a reservation system for an airline. It is important to remember that the Internet transfers all data, be it e-mail messages, financial data or an Internet telephone conversation, by dividing up the data files or streams into smaller parcels, called data packets, labelling their order for reassembly at the destination computer and giving them origin and destination addresses. The Internet protocol suite will use a particular combination of protocols to channel these packets to their destination as efficiently as possible, reassemble them and present them to the user, and call for repeat sending of certain data packets if these are lost or arrive in a corrupted state.

From a technical perspective, four separate layers of Internet protocols are often cited, in addition to the fifth lowest layer — the physical network layer of optic fibre or metallic cables and radio links, hubs, repeaters,

and so forth. These are the data link layer, the network layer, the transport layer and the application layer. The TCP/IP suite merges the physical layer and the data link layer into a "host-to-network" layer and remains undefined in the suite as it varies from host to host and network to network (Tanenbaum, 1996).

The data link layer takes a raw digital transmission facility of the physical layer and transforms it into a connection that appears free of transmission errors. Senders break their data into data frames, transmit the frames sequentially, and processes the acknowledgement frames sent back by recipients. The data link layer corrects the errors and controls the flow of data between two adjacent nodes in a network. The network layer works to get data from the source network to the destination network. This generally involves routing packets that in their headers contain the sender's and recipients' Internet (IP) addresses across a network of networks — the Internet. The common protocol in the network layer is the Internet Protocol — the IP in the TCP/IP. The transport layer resides in between the application layer and the network layer and primarily provides the service of referencing applications on the senders' and the recipients' computers in order to provide coherence and reliability. It is the first end-to-end layer. All layers underneath the transport layer are concerned with connections of adjacent nodes in networks, while the transport layer is only concerned with the connection between the source and ultimate destination computers. The common protocol in this layer is the Transmission Control Protocol — the TCP in the TCP/IP. The TCP will typically ensure that data packets arrive correctly and in order, it will discard duplicate or corrupt packets and it will call for corrupted packets to be resent. Other transport layer protocols exist, besides the TCP, that are more suitable for telephony or streaming media. Finally, the application layer is the layer that most common Internet programs will work in, in order to communicate web pages, share files or data, or transmit or receive data streams. Chart 7.1 illustrates, in an analogy of communication between two businesses intermediated by a postal company, what happens at each layer of the Internet protocol suite.[5]

In many ways the layer structure described is similar to the International Organization for Standardization and the International Electrotechnical Commission standard Open Systems Interconnection (ISO/IEC OSI 7498-1 or just "OSI") model for networks.[6] It is also known as Recommendation X.200 of the International Telecommunication Union. The OSI was issued in 1984 and updated in 1994, and identifies

## Chart 7.1

## Internet protocol suite layers: A postal analogy

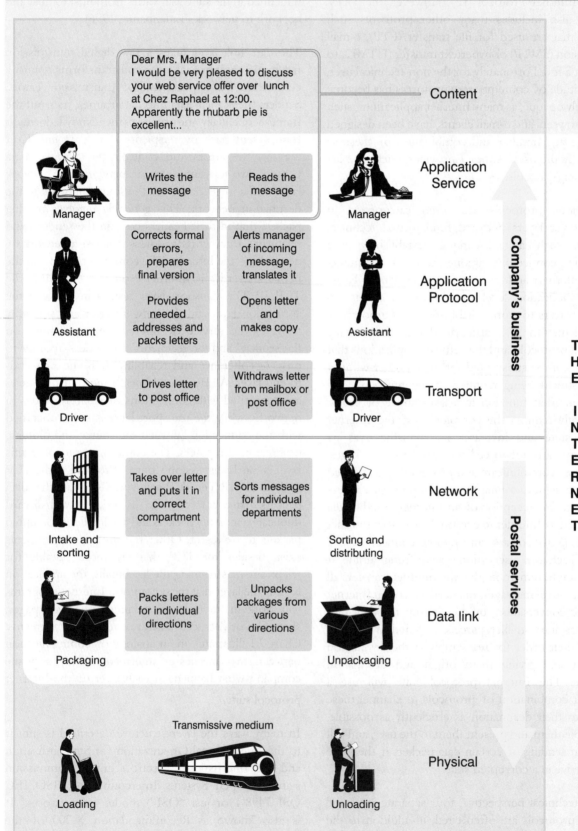

seven layers with similar properties and functions as the Internet protocol suite. Without going into technical detail, the Internet suite can be understood as a special case of the OSI, even though it preceded it in practice. The OSI model is often used as a general and more comprehensive reference model from which others could develop detailed interfaces, which in turn could become standards. A fuller description of the OSI model is provided in annex II.

## 2.   Internet layers and concepts

While the previous exposition of Internet layers and protocols is technically correct, analytically and from a policy and regulatory perspective, the discussion will need to redefine the layers in order to provide a conceptual, rather than technical, framework for exploring Internet governance issues. For the purpose of analysis, various authors have grouped the various layers slightly differently. This does not affect the analysis to a great extent, but it can create confusion. Thus it may be useful to review the various ways in which Internet layers have been bundled in recent literature.

Paralleling the technical definition of the Internet layers in section B.1 above, Solum and Chung (2003) define six layers: the physical layer, the link layer, the Internet Protocol layer, the transport layer, the application layer and the content layer. They note that the TCP/IP protocol suite is independent of the physical network hardware and that it is the link layer that is responsible for this freedom. The link layer exists in the form of device driver for a particular piece of network hardware. Using new hardware requires the development and installation of a new device driver that opens that hardware to the Internet protocol. In this way, the link layer enables the interconnection of the widest variety of disparate computer and network hardware, thus promoting competition and innovation. The Internet Protocol layer handles the movement of data packets around the network. The transport layer is where the files received from the application layer are broken up into data packets to be handed over to the Internet Protocol layer, and, moving in the opposite direction, the data packets received from the Internet Protocol layer are assembled into files to be delivered to the application layer. The application layer protocols are used to enable web communication, e-mail, file transfer and other functions more familiar to everyday Internet users.

Werbach (2002) suggests only four layers: the physical infrastructure layer, the logical layer, the applications layer and the content layer. Physical infrastructure consists of the underlying copper wire and optical fibre networks, terrestrial wireless and satellite communications. Setting up the physical layer usually requires substantial upfront investment. The owners, typically telecommunications companies, have often indicated that they are natural monopolies. While this is debatable, it has necessarily primed the physical layer as an obvious candidate for regulatory oversight and intervention.[7] The logical layer ensures the management and flow of data across the network. At the logical layer governance issues will typically be related to the functioning of the Domain Name System and the nature and role of bodies such as ICANN.[8] The application layer is where most end-user functions reside: web browser, Internet telephony, remote access to company Intranets, and so forth. Many of these applications used to be specialized services provided using proprietary infrastructure. Cable television or wired telephony are obvious examples. As the companies providing such services often own the physical infrastructure, and as the services are distinct, regulating by type of service seemed perfectly logical in the pre-Internet era. However, today this is becoming an increasingly dubious proposition given the ongoing technological assimilation of all services into the Internet. The content layer is the actual data or information made accessible by applications that depend on the logical layer as it uses the physical network to shift the content from providers to users. Historically, the regulatory treatment of content depended on the type of service — the content of a telephone conversation was often subject to different regulation from that of a television broadcast. However, the Internet does not distinguish between data packets of a VoIP or a video stream, and this causes regulatory conundrums. Is an e-mail circular to several hundred members of a particular club a private message or a broadcast?

Benkler (2000) proposes that we think of three layers. At the bottom of these three, there is the physical layer — the wires, cables and equipment that connect our computers. Above that is the logical layer that controls who gets access to what and what gets to run where; and above that, is the content layer — the actual substance of our communications. Each of the layers can vary in openness, ownership and control. The Internet is the most open digital communications network we have as its protocols and performance are neutral towards the contents of individual data packets, in spite of the fact that the physical network is largely privately owned and that there are many proprietary applications that are Internet-enabled. However, as the layers are effectively interdependent in the sense that we cannot

## Chart 7.2

## Conceptual layers of the Internet

| Technical layer | Conceptual layers according to... | | | Subject[1] | Governance issues |
|---|---|---|---|---|---|
| | *Solum and Chung* | *Werbach* | *Benkler and Lessig* | | |
| Content | Content | Content | Content | Text, data, graphics, audio, video, etc. | Spam, local content |
| Application services | Application layer | Application layer | Logical layer or the Code layer | Browsers, e-mail clients, anti-virus software, streaming media players, etc. | Data protection, privacy rights |
| Application protocols | | Logical layer | | HTTP, FTP, DNS, BitTorrent, etc. | Cybercrime |
| Transport (TCP) | Transport | | | TCP, UDP, etc. | DNS root server system |
| Network (IP) | Network | | | IP (IPv4, IPv6) etc. | IP addressing |
| Data link | Data Link | | | Ethernet, Wi-Fi | Stability |
| Physical network | Physical network | Physical network | Physical network | Binary transmission | Access, costs |

[1]For definitions of various protocol acronyms see Annex 1.

achieve a successful communication if one layer does not function or cooperate, it is entirely feasible to take control of a particular layer through another and without owning it. The most obvious example is making public domain material — the content layer — accessible with a proprietary application — the logical layer. If such an application has a dominant market share, it can restrict use of public domain content and any attempt to lift such restrictions are illegal under the World Intellectual Property Organization's Copyright Treaty and counterpart national laws, such as the United States' Digital Millennium Copyright Act and the European Copyright Directive.[9] While the openness of the Internet is a matter of technological choice and is achieved through its layered architecture and open protocols, governance policy and the accompanying regulatory regime can affect this openness, both positively and negatively.

The differences in the above definitions are about how much the middle layers — in between the physical network and the content — are bundled. Solum and Chung unbundled them completely, while Werbach bundles the link, protocol and transport layers but leaves out the application layer that prepares content for users. Benkler bundles everything, observing that it is all a set of software protocols and applications. Benkler's logical layer is equivalent to the "code" layer of Lessig (2001), whereby how it is designed and how it performs are the de facto law of the Internet, and governance issues will necessarily relate directly to who designs, manages and owns particular parts

of the "code" or logical layer. Recent developments show that control of the lowest physical layer also provides leverage for asserting governance. Network providers argue that high data volume applications, such as search engines, need to pay a premium for their disproportional use of bandwidth or that quality-sensitive services using streaming media desire and will pay a premium for transport priority, and suggest that their data will need to be tagged for priority, thus creating multiple data classes.[10]

Chart 7.2 gives a comparative overview of the different ways in which the layers can be rearranged into conceptual categories. The governance issues in the rightmost column are only indicative. Their actual placement in the layer should be the result of national and international policy processes and necessarily subject to ongoing examination. Technological progress, including the build-out of broadband networks as well as the development of new application protocols and services, may evolve particular concerns that are not apparent in the present circumstance. From a policy perspective, some issues may become irrelevant. Others may require relocation to different layers and new policy issues may arise as well.

## 3. Generating principles from layers

Establishing the relationship between the Internet architecture and governance should be treated as a matter of paralleling the layered structure with a corresponding policy and regulatory structure. The established linkages between technical layers and policy layers would serve as a kind of check and balance: social and political requirements, even when expressed legitimately, will need to consider the consequences. Similarly, any need for technical change should be subject to societal considerations. Requests and requirements would need to be debated and dealt with at the levels where they would be implemented. This empowers but also increases the shared responsibilities of the technological and political stakeholders in the process.

Not only is the understanding of Internet architecture essential to sound Internet governance, but also, vice versa, the development of new Internet technologies and innovation will need to embrace societal concerns as expressed through governance policy and practical regulation. Often, the issues will not be entirely new and will deal with the Internet versions of topics related to good governance and democracy, monopolies and antitrust law, problems of jurisdiction, intellectual property rights and many others. Besides the layers principle, a number of policy principles relating to Internet governance and policies have been advanced in the past and share many notions. However, they are not intellectually pedantic and, indeed, they may overlap or be directly derivative of each other or present a different viewpoint on the same or a similar issue.

The principle of layer-consistent Internet governance and the notion that minimizing of layer crossing in regulatory practice is a good thing, are often sourced to the work of Lessig (1999, 2001), where they appear as a discussion of the *code thesis* and the *end-to-end principle*. The *code thesis* states that the Internet is an artificial and engineered environment: humans design and implement it as they desire and to the extent that current software and hardware technology permits. The Internet does not have any natural properties. Its "inherent" nature is built into it through the design and implementation of its protocols and applications. For example, the only reason why the Internet seems to be exterritorial is because the logical layer does not distinguish data packets by geographical origin or destination.[11] This is a matter of how the protocols are written, and they can be redesigned to do otherwise. Thus, the sum of all the protocols and applications in the logical layer — the code — takes on some of the properties of a law, in the sense that it regulates the behaviour of Internet users.[12] Solum and Chung (2003) use the analogy of physical architecture — "just as the architecture of a building enables and encourages humans to move and congregate in certain ways, so the architecture of the Internet enables some activities by users and regulators while discouraging others".[13]

The *end-to-end principle* describes one of the key feature of the architecture of the Internet: the intelligence lives on the network periphery, in the application layer. In other words, functionality should be provided in the applications that are active in the application layer as used by users, but not by the network itself. This allows the logical layer to efficiently manage data transmission. The principle is sometimes described as a "stupid network" with "smart applications". As already noted, the logical layer does not, by design, discriminate or differentiate data traffic generated by different applications. Saltzer et al. (1981, 1998) argue that this lack of functionality encourages greater network reliability and decreases potential future costs of build-out and innovation.[14] Isenberg (1997) explains that the main advantages of the "stupid" Internet over the "smart" telephony network system derive from the fact that the Internet transport is neutral with intelligent and user-controlled endpoints. He also points out that its design is built on the notion of increasing and plentiful bandwidth and computing resources, while the transport is guided by the needs of the data – a particular combination of the many protocols and applications functioning in the logical layer will be engaged depending on the nature of the data being transported.

Most recently, the debate has continued through the discussion on *network neutrality*.[15] A network is neutral when it does not distinguish between the applications, or content, that depend on it, nor on the identity or nature of its users. Furthermore, entities operating a neutral network should not favour particular content or applications in order to gain a competitive advantage for certain types of services. If the Internet is to remain a platform for competing applications and content, it is important for the platform to remain neutral in order to ensure that competition is based on merit as expressed by users' preferences (Wu, 2005; Cerf, 2006). However, non-discrimination towards content and applications is a necessary but insufficient condition for network neutrality. A further condition is that of interconnection — network operators have the right to connect with other operators' networks and the obligation to accept connections and data from all other operators as well. A final requirement is that of open access. Not to be confused with similar issues in the technology and intellectual property debate, open access means that any end-user can connect to any other end-user, even when these are using a different network operator's infrastructure. Box 7.1 describes policy thinking and processes regarding the neutrality debate in the United States.

## Box 7.1

## Network neutrality in the United States: Policy processes and regulatory wisdom?

In February 2004, the Chairman of the Federal Communications Commission (FCC) of the United States, Michael Powell, proposed a set of non-discrimination principles. The principles of "Network Freedom" stated that Internet users in the United States must have the following four freedoms:

1.  Freedom to access content;

2.  Freedom to run applications;

3.  Freedom to attach devices;

4.  Freedom to obtain service plan information.

Later, in August 2005, his successor, Kevin Martin, restated these four freedoms in a FCC policy statement on "New Principles Preserve and Promote the Open and Interconnected Nature of Public Internet", as follows:

1.  Consumers are entitled to access the lawful Internet content of their choice;

2.  Consumers are entitled to run applications and services of their choice, subject to the needs of law enforcement;

3.  Consumers are entitled to connect their choice of legal devices that do not harm the network; and

4.  Consumers are entitled to competition among network providers, application and service providers, and content providers.

An often-cited positive case for network neutrality is when in early 2005 the FCC imposed fines on a local telephone carrier that was blocking voice-over IP service.[1] While awareness about the network neutrality issue has grown during the current debate, it is interesting to note that the United States Government has not codified this policy, but prefers that the FCC uses these principles in its ongoing policy activities. Clearly, policy may not need to translate into codified regulation, and recent developments proposing amendments to the United States Telecommunications Act of 1996 include advice to the FCC urging it to study and be alert to abusive business practices, such as discriminating against particular services, but do not propose specific language for network neutrality regulation.[2] However, during 2005, various civil society organizations and Internet-based businesses have been urging lawmakers to include Internet neutrality legislation in the revision of the Telecommunications Act, but without apparent success. The formal debate in the United States Senate is expected to resume in October 2005.[3]

---

[1] See the news story at http://news.com.com/2102-7352_3-5598633.html; the FCC decision is filed at http://hraunfoss.fcc.gov/edocs_public/attachmatch/DA-05-543A2.pdf.

[2] See http://commerce.senate.gov/pdf/06telcom.pdf.

[3] See http://news.com.com/Net+neutrality+fans+rally+in+25+cities/2100-1028_3-6111489.html

---

It is essential to keep in mind that the technological framework came first: most political, economic or sociological analysis has been an afterthought trying to make sense of the Internet, because it needs to be understood by policymakers in order to be governed. This holds true even if the policy conclusions mandate a deregulated approach. The effect of the layered structure of the Internet, first and foremost at a technical and functional level, is to liberate innovation and creativity on the Internet and substantively level the playing field for new entrants with designs and visions for ground-breaking uses and applications. Because the Internet's intelligence lives in the application layer, innovation is decentralized and the opportunity to devise new applications is available to all creative individuals with Internet access.

Unsurprisingly, many remarkable Internet projects, such as the Yahoo and Google portals, eBay.com, the Apache web server and Skype, to name but a few, started out as small projects conceived by motivated and creative individuals. End-to-end design, open protocols and transparent layers mean that innovators need only invest in developing software to run in the application layer. The application layer itself exists on every computer that has an Internet connection and does not enter into the cost of innovation. Innovators do not need to register their applications with any institution as the logical layer takes care of compatibility on its own — if innovators do not design their applications to respect the public TCP/IP protocols, their applications will simply not work. Box 7.2 highlights the importance of ensuring that the Internet continues to provide an open and accessible commercial development platform for technology companies and innovators from developing countries.

Entry barriers are further reduced because transparent layers turn consumers' computers into general-purpose Internet appliances. This means that a consumer need only invest in the software application itself in order to make use of it. This is in stark contrast to, say, the telephony system, where additional functionalities require the user to buy a more sophisticated telephone appliance or contact the telecom operator in order to subscribe and configure a centralized service, such as a voice mail box.

Another interesting issue is the notion of network effects, whereby the value of an application will increase with the number of users, all else staying the same. For any network technology there is a tipping point in the rate of adoption when application becomes sufficiently valuable to broaden its appeal from early adopters to ordinary users. Reducing the cost of adoption increases the likelihood that these networking effect gains will be realized, and realized earlier. If costs are too high for early adopters, the tipping point may never be reached. Thus the economic contribution of layer transparency and the end-to-end nature of the Internet are fundamental for innovation. Without it, motivation among inventors and investors would be lacking.

Nowhere is this more apparent than in the market for anti-virus and desktop security products. This particular product is interesting because security concerns have increased exponentially, with virtually every computer being connected to the Internet. A significant number of successful companies are not from the technology leader — the United States — and while their installed base and growth are unlikely to threaten and uncrown the market principals, Norton/Symantec and McAfee, their existence speaks of potential and possibilities. Table 7.1 provides a list of companies that are managing to compete with the dominant vendors precisely because the Internet provides a neutral, open

---

## Box 7.2

## Competition, choice and Internet governance [1]

The choice of the correct technology is fundamental to strengthening the ICT strategies of any company or institution. The Internet is central to making this choice because it allows Brazilian information technology companies to develop and innovate a range of products and services while relying on the established parameters of the Internet protocols. In this sense, the IT sector in Brazil is on equal terms with global ICT providers. Within our region, we can even generate advantages over global technology suppliers by providing a credible, secure and trustworthy relationship to our clients, built upon our long experience in the Brazilian information technology market. The Brazilian IT environment is a sophisticated and very competitive marketplace, reaching $12 billions in yearly sales volume. Almost all of the IT global players have operations in Brazil, increasing the level of local competition to higher standards.

The Internet governance issue is important for technology businesses that rely on the Internet protocols and network infrastructure being kept operational, transparent and non-discriminatory. This is important across all types of commercial activities, but in particular for application development, where highly trained teams are designated to develop and implement custom-made solutions and meet the requested technological requirements of domestic and international clients. In the application development, Brazilian software companies have developed strong competencies in several business areas, such as finance and bank automation, telecommunications, health and small and medium size enterprise business management software. Information technology security, e-business and e-government applications are also delivered to the highest international standards of quality and sophistication. While it is entirely feasible to produce such applications for proprietary data networks and protocols, developing and running them using the public protocols of the TCP/IP suite brings out the competitive advantages of Brazilian technology businesses and improves the scope of choice for its clients.

Therefore, Internet governance should work to secure open functionality and access to the Internet as a commercial data network and as an innovation catalyst. It should work to limit the danger posed by, and the harm done by negative by-products such as spam, cybercrime or viral attacks. It must do this in cooperation with the technology industry. Many of the problems may be mitigated, if not resolved, with specific and tailored applications or technology strategies that can be developed and delivered by the Brazilian software industry. Cooperation is particularly important in security issues because, in the final instance, software products and services will be dependent on the overall stability of the Internet.

---

[1] This commentary was provided by Djalma Petit, Coordinator General of Softex, Brazil. SOFTEX is a Public Interest Civil Society Organization that promotes the growth and extension of the Brazilian software industry. Its work is directed at creating business opportunities, attracting investors and consolidating the image of Brazil as a software producer and exporter.

## Table 7.1

### Selected examples of international anti-virus software producers

| Name | Country | Website |
|---|---|---|
| Virus Chaser | China | www.viruschaser.com.hk |
| Rising Anti-Virus Software | China | www.rising-global.com |
| F-Secure | Finland | www.f-secure.com |
| F-Prot | Iceland | www.f-prot.com |
| BitDefender | Romania | www.bitdefender.com |
| Doctor Web | Russian Federation | www.drweb.com |
| Kaspersky Anti-Virus | Russian Federation | www.kaspersky.com |
| NOD32 | Slovakia | www.eset.com/ |
| Panda | Spain | www.pandasoftware.com |

and layered communications platform — their clients can install and test alternative products without any concessions to hardware providers, existing suppliers of anti-virus or other software and, lastly, the physical network operators.

## 4.　Criticism of proposed principles

The arguments presented for developing governance policy principles, based on the notions of a layered, end-to-end and neutral Internet, are sometimes criticized as giving Governments an excuse to increase obtrusive and unnecessary regulation where market forces suffice. Moreover, Yoo (2004) argues that principles such as the end-to-end concept should not be necessarily translated into regulatory mandates as this could "become the source of, rather than the solution to, market failure. Such considerations are particularly problematic when the industry is undergoing dynamic technological change...". Regulating the Internet to conform to open standards and principles is often opposed by the operators of the physical layer. Arguments range from suggesting that network neutrality principles may translate into a more intrusive regulation of the Internet to the notion that codifying open protocols will disadvantage companies that want to differentiate their services by, among other things, using alternative proprietary protocols that will favour certain applications or services over others. For example, certain ISPs may want to specialize in e-mail services, while other would be more interested in providing streaming media, and others still may stay with providing generic Internet connectivity.

Critics will also argue that proposing additional or new regulation unnecessarily complicates the existing and fairly evolved regulatory frameworks for telecoms and goes against established regulatory modes that are, by and large, by type of service. This could require the re-regulation of all services, operators and communications infrastructures — a time-consuming activity with an ambiguous outcome. Finally, some critics maintain that the Internet has succeeded in becoming a global innovation platform and has outgrown and out-competed the proprietary data networks precisely because it has been free from government regulation, as opposed to the highly regulated telephony market. Thus, there is no real practical reason to explore the introduction of new regulation. On the contrary, any attempt by Governments to regulate the Internet, including by those with a genuine intention to preserve its neutrality, carries the risk of breaking it.

There are many ways to answer the criticisms and, indeed, several have already been pre-empted in the previous sections of the discussion. However, two issues need to be clarified in particular. The first is the notion that the Internet developed because it was not regulated or, at least, not overregulated. While the technological development was guided by practical concerns, the commercial build-out has been dependent on user demand that was fuelled by freedom of choice. These freedoms have been safeguarded precisely by telecom regulations that have ensured consumer access to competing ISPs, the possibility to use a wide range of competing hardware and software platforms, and a multiplicity of application, services and content. Such telecom regulation, often described as non-discrimination, is a precursor to Internet network neutrality and is still valid today as last-mile access to most consumers is physically dependent on the network operator that is often the historical incumbent and has a favourable, if not monopolistic, market position.

The second issue relates to the criticism that embracing a set of principles necessarily leads to their codification in some form of regulation. A basic principle for considering codification is that activities that result only in a certain loss should be formally regulated. However, this is not an exclusive principle. In this sense it is the law in many countries that automobile passengers must wear seat belts: there is no conceivable benefit at the level of society in not wearing one. Similarly, financial services companies are required to establish minimum capital reserves of various levels: avoiding this obligation will eventually lead to the failure of a number of institutions with consequences for clients, shareholders, staff and management. Policymakers should be aware that in between general principles and hard law there is a range of options and policy mixes that embrace varying degrees of education, policy awareness building, capacity building, economic incentives, self-regulation, supervisory activities and, finally, regulatory and legal processes. Whatever the policy tool, each and every one should be subject to review by referencing it to the layers principle and it corollaries.

## C.  Layers principle and policy concerns

### 1.  The layers principle as a policy source

Having, we hope, conveyed the wisdom of maintaining a layered, and therefore neutral, open and transparent Internet, we will now develop a more detailed exposition of the layers principle in order to enable policy conclusions for Internet governance to be drawn. The discussion will largely follow that of Solum and Chung (2003). In essence, the layers principle states as follows: respect the integrity of Internet layers. In other words, Internet governance policy and regulation should avoid interfering with and changing the layered nature of the Internet architecture. This principle can be devolved into two arguments: the principle of layer separation and the principle of minimization of layer crossing.

The principle of layer separation states that the separation between Internet layers as designed into its basic technological architecture must be maintained. This means that policy or regulation that would require one layer of the Internet to differentiate the handling of data on the basis of information available only at another layer should be disallowed. In practice, the principle of layer separation would proscribe any policy or regulation that requires network operators to filter and censor data packets coming from a particular application, such as VoIP, P2P file-sharing or e-mail.

The principle of minimizing layer crossing states that governing authorities primarily use or develop policy or regulation for content or activity for a particular layer that is meant to be implemented precisely at that same layer. However, as this may not always be feasible, governors should minimize the distance between the layer at which policy aims to produce an effect and the layer directly targeted by the policy or regulation. The notion of distance is related to the proximity of technological or conceptual Internet layers as explained in box 7.1 and chart 7.1. In this sense, the maximum distance would be that between the physical network layer and the content layer. Adjacent layers, such as the content and application layers, are "nearby". In this sense, the "greater the number of layers crossed, the worse the regulation; the fewer the layers crossed, the better the regulation".[16] An example of a policy that violates this principle would be a regulation addressing copyright issues by requiring action at the IP layer by blocking of certain Internet addresses. Another example would be addressing bandwidth congestion by blocking of port assignments that are used by high-bandwidth applications.

The layers principle does not intend to provide a general theory of Internet governance and relevant regulatory policy. It aims only to support governing authorities with two bottom-line parameters that need to be considered each and every time a particular governance policy or regulation is proposed. This begs the question: do we actually need a comprehensive theory of Internet governance and regulation? UNCTAD (2005) has argued that as the Internet is a platform for many existing human activities, in at least the first instance, the policy, governance and regulatory goals that apply to those activities as conducted outside the Internet should also apply to the Internet. Any comprehensive regulation of the Internet should be very proximate to the existing and accepted notions of legal and political theory in general. In this sense, redesigning policy and regulation for many activities that have to some degree moved online may be inefficient.

The layers principle should be a sufficient criterion for evaluating most policy or regulatory proposals for Internet governance. However, governing authorities should, especially when in doubt or when issues are ambiguous cross-reference with the related principles as presented in part C.3 of this chapter. Where layer violation is justified, governing authorities should choose that policy or regulation that proposes crossing the fewest layers in order to achieve the policy objective.

An alternative to associating Internet governance policy and regulation with the layers principle and related corollaries would be to establish judgement on a case-by-case basis, analysing the net outcome of the expected costs and benefits of a particular policy. While this approach may have a common-sense appeal, it also presents several problems. The first is that the cumulative impact of multiple decisions may be different from a mere sum of the individual impacts, and this notion may not enter the decision-making process. One possible reason could be the growth of network effects, during the period when individual decisions were taken, which substantially change the assumptions. While adjusting for changing assumptions may be workable for each policy case on its own, after a cumulative policy outcome has been reached, a full rollback of policy and regulation may prove difficult if the cumulative network effects are judged undesirable. The other is that the fundamental premises of the issue may be severely affected by the actual case-by-case judgements. For example, regulators may mandate one or several changes in the TCP/IP suite that decrease its layers separation and users may be able to develop a workaround or a tolerable compromise. However, the cumulative effect of a larger number of layer violations may produce a threshold that becomes a significant disincentive to programmers and innovators seeking to fix, upgrade or develop new applications and online activities.

A case-by-case approach may not be well suited where the risks to innovation due to a change in Internet architecture and as a result of policy or regulatory activity are very difficult to estimate. Compounding the problem is the lack of institutional and human capacity to consider the impact of Internet governance policy and regulation on its ability to provide an accessible ICT innovation platform. While understanding the purpose, structure and functions of the Internet architecture is not impossibly complicated, policymakers are more likely to make good decisions by respecting the layers principle as a general rule and cross-referencing it with its corollaries, while using a case-by-case assessment of the effects of particular policies and regulations as a component of, rather than a decisive input into, the policy process.

Developing such a capacity anywhere, and not the least in developing countries, would mean establishing national governance and regulatory institutions such as those found in the financial sector, medical profession or the food and pharmacological industry. The report of the WGIG specifically states that "resources have not been available to build capacity in a range of areas relevant to Internet management at the national level and to ensure effective participation in global Internet governance, particularly for developing countries".[17]

Aside from the usual problems of sources of funding, length of political decision-making processes and a pending debate on the scope and depth of assigned duties and powers, a particular problem is that the Internet is a general-purpose technology. Thus the governance problems would not have a specific sectoral focus but would, as noted earlier, face a diversity of issues from intellectual property disputes to electronic commerce security, and on to human rights problems such as freedom of speech and privacy. This would be unfeasible as it risks questioning the policy and regulatory authority of existing governing and legal institutions.

These notions extend to the international policy level as well. The post-WSIS governance debate continues through a newly founded institution, the Internet Governance Forum (IGF). The IGF should be supported in debating and establishing a set of principles for Internet policy and regulation. The layers principle and the associated principles of the end-to-end, transparent, open and neutral Internet should be considered foundational as they can ensure that the Internet remains an open and accessible innovation platform that promotes a democracy of opportunity not yet witnessed in the history of technological development.

## 2.    Policy concerns and perspectives

The established linkages between the technological Internet — its layers of open protocols and applications — and its rationalization through a set of principles need to be reconciled with existing governance policy and practice. A number of questions arise at this point. One is: how would new regulation interact with existing regulation? Looking at the layers, many countries should be able to identify regulation that could apply to the physical layer in the form of telecom regulation. Also, there may be regulation content either from the perspective of ethics, moral codes and conventions, privacy and freedom of expression, or by analogy with the perspective of broadcasting. Another question would be: does one codify the logical layer or behaviour in the logical layer? What are the actual Internet governance concerns? It may be worthwhile to consider the actual issues that have made Internet governance a major debating point at WSIS. Table 7.2 lists major issues of Internet governance concern in four Asian developing countries.

## D.   WSIS, Internet governance and principles

The discussions on Internet governance became a central focus during the WSIS process. The process itself consisted of two summit meetings, held in Geneva in December 2003 and in Tunis in June 2005, as well as of a series of preparatory meetings,[18] and, specifically on governance issues, the work and output of the Working Group on Internet Governance (WGIG) and the subsequent establishment of the Internet governance Forum (IGF).[19]

The Geneva summit in 2003 provided an unambiguous indication that Internet governance issues were clearly the domain of public policy as devised and implemented by Governments at a national level, and as negotiated and resolved among Governments at the international level.[20] In order to develop a framework and strategy

## Table 7.2

### Internet governance concerns in selected Asian countries and in the WSIS process

|  | Regional rank average | China % dissatisfied | China local rank | India % dissatisfied | India local rank | Pakistan % dissatisfied | Pakistan local rank | Thailand % dissatisfied | Thailand local rank | WSIS public policy concern |
|---|---|---|---|---|---|---|---|---|---|---|
| Cybercrime, online fraud | 1 | 100.0 | 1 | 95.0 | 2 | 89.3 | 3 | 96.4 | 2 | ✓ |
| Virus attacks | 2 | 100.0 | 2 | 94.4 | 3 | 90.9 | 1 | 98.2 | 1 | |
| Spam | 3 | 96.2 | 3 | 95.6 | 1 | 90.9 | 2 | 94.6 | 3 | ✓ |
| Illegal content | 4 | 84.9 | 5 | 84.9 | 4 | 85.1 | 4 | 78.6 | 4 | |
| Privacy online | 5 | 85.8 | 4 | 62.7 | 12 | 62.8 | 8 | 64.3 | 5 | ✓ |
| Availability and cost of Internet | 6 | 56.6 | 10 | 80.5 | 5 | 52.1 | 11 | 40.4 | 12 | |
| Wireless Internet: Spectrum and access | 7 | 55.7 | 11 | 66.0 | 11 | 63.6 | 7 | 54.4 | 6 | |
| Reliability and speed of Internet | 8 | 68.9 | 6 | 75.5 | 7 | 56.3 | 10 | 36.8 | 13 | ✓ |
| Online access to government information | 9 | 68.6 | 7 | 76.1 | 6 | 57.9 | 9 | 48.2 | 7 | |
| Availability of local language software | 10 | 26.9 | 21 | 60.4 | 13 | 48.8 | 13 | 43.9 | 9 | |
| Availability of local content | 11 | 32.7 | 20 | 53.2 | 16 | 44.5 | 16 | 45.6 | 8 | ✓ |
| e-Commerce payment systems | 12 | 60.6 | 8 | 58.5 | 15 | 50.0 | 12 | 35.1 | 15 | |
| Fair access to/protection of intellectual property | 13 | 59.4 | 9 | 67.9 | 8 | 70.9 | 5 | 43.9 | 10 | |
| Internet telephony (VoIP) | 14 | 49.1 | 14 | 66.5 | 10 | 68.6 | 6 | 35.7 | 14 | |
| Network interconnection/ backbone access | 15 | 41.5 | 16 | 39.2 | 17 | 48.7 | 14 | 30.4 | 19 | ✓ |
| ISP market conditions | 16 | 47.6 | 15 | 67.1 | 9 | 47.1 | 15 | 33.9 | 18 | |
| Secure server/encryption | 17 | 55.2 | 12 | 60.1 | 14 | 37.6 | 17 | 42.1 | 11 | |
| Access to technical standards and their adaptability | 18 | 36.2 | 19 | 34.0 | 19 | 35.7 | 19 | 35.1 | 17 | |
| Domain names with non-Roman character sets (IDN) | 19 | 40.0 | 18 | 34.2 | 18 | 36.4 | 18 | 35.1 | 16 | |
| Domain name management | 20 | 40.0 | 17 | 32.7 | 20 | 34.5 | 20 | 26.3 | 20 | ✓ |
| IP address allocation/management | 21 | 52.4 | 13 | 29.3 | 21 | 27.4 | 21 | 23.6 | 21 | ✓ |
| Own skills for using Internet | 22 | 9.5 | 22 | 13.3 | 22 | 4 | 22 | 3.5 | 22 | |

*Source: based on UNDP-Apdip (2005), WGIG (2005b).*

for the Internet governance deliberations, the Geneva summit established a temporary body — the WGIG — that was mandated to define Internet governance, to identify the most relevant governance issues, to develop a consensus on the roles and responsibilities of Governments, international organizations, the private sector and civil society from both developing and developed countries, and finally, to prepare a report as an input for the Tunis summit, which was held in June 2005.[21]

The work of the WGIG and the resulting report, together with the deliberations during the preparatory sessions and at the Tunis summit, further increased the profile of the Internet governance issue. While it can sometimes be difficult to judge the substance and quality of intergovernmental discussions on the basis of their documentary outputs, in terms of pure quantity the Tunis summit statements on Internet governance are roughly seven times longer than the Geneva outcome. In relative terms, the Internet governance component in the summit outcomes increased from around 4 per cent in Geneva to 30 per cent in Tunis.

A large number of analytical contributions were made in an attempt to provide a breadth of consideration, but also to influence the process. MacLean (2004) and Drake (2005) provided an insight into the detail of the concerns and discussions. They engaged the opinions of the direct participants in the WGIG and successfully drew attention to the large diversity of views and proposals and the varying principles and politics that underpin them. This was a positive contribution to the formal process and the outcomes of the WGIG and the Tunis summit in the sense that enquiring readers may seek out the root arguments and proponents for many of the positions taken, as well as the consequential compromises that became the foundation for the work of the IGF after WSIS. The WGIG also publicly released the background document, which was not negotiated and not subject to consensus acceptance, but served as the foundation of its final report.[22]

The WGIG final report, formally entitled the Report of the Working Group on Internet Governance, is a concise document focused on addressing a subcomponent of one key WSIS principle: the provision of a stable and secure infrastructure.[23] In its introduction it underscores the notion that "the WGIG was guided primarily by the key WSIS principles. In particular, the WSIS principle relating to the stable and secure functioning of the Internet was judged to be of paramount importance"[24]. It goes on to perform one of its key tasks — to define Internet governance:

> Internet governance is the development and application by Governments, the private sector and civil society, in their respective roles, of shared principles, norms, rules, decision-making procedures, and programmes that shape the evolution and use of the Internet.

The stated notion of shared principles, norms, rules and decision-making procedures does not, however, reappear to any significant extent in the continuation of the text, which is preoccupied with developing a list of Internet governance public policy issues and producing a proposal regarding who does what, addressed to governments, the private sector and civil society. This is not surprising given that the referential segment on principles in the WGIG background document is fairly brief, while admittedly to the point. In the main, it is the last bullet point of paragraph 24, and paragraph 25 that suggest the following:

> The end-to-end principle: the neutrality of the Internet, chiefly concerned with the effective transportation of packets, enables its intelligence to reside largely at the networks' ends through applications in computers, servers, mobile and other devices. This has enabled the development of a wide range of new ICT activities, industries and services "at the ends" and turns the Internet into an important tool within the wider context of economic and societal development. …Any proposal for change would have to assess whether any of these elements, which are important for the functioning of the Internet, would be affected in one way or another.

Thus the consideration of a set of principles for governance as a key public policy issue, which will serve as a reference framework for considering all other policy issues and can provide guidance as to acceptable or hazardous levels of policy interference in the Internet architecture, has been left open. It is now up to the successor to the WGIG — the IGF — to consider the need to re-establish the issue of instituting foundational principles for Internet governance. The first meeting of the IGF will start on 30 October 2006 in Athens. The provisional agenda calls for a debate on, among other issues, Internet governance and development, and in particular the notion of openness. While these can provide a handle to initiate discussions on establishing governing principles, at the time of writing it is difficult to predict how the deliberations will develop. The current UNCTAD Information Economy Report will be in print at the time of that meeting and may need to consider a follow-up to the IGF process in its 2007 edition.

## Table 7.3

## Thirteen DNS root servers

| Letter - Name | Operator | Location |
|:---:|:---|:---|
| A | VeriSign | Virginia, USA |
| B | ISI University of Southern California | California, USA |
| C | Cogent Communications | Distributed using anycast |
| D | University of Maryland | Maryland, USA |
| E | NASA | California, USA |
| F | Internet Systems Consortium | Distributed using anycast |
| G | US Department of Defense | Ohio, USA |
| H | US Army Research Lab. | Maryland, USA |
| I | Autonomica | Distributed using anycast |
| J | VeriSign | Distributed using anycast |
| K | RIPE NCC | Distributed using anycast |
| L | ICANN | California, USA |
| M | WIDE Project | Distributed using anycast |

Source: Internet Society (http://www.isoc.org/briefings/019/)

The Tunis summit itself, aside from considering the WGIG final report and mandating the IGF, conducted an energetic discussion on the Internet governance theme. Many delegations from developing countries felt that the United States Government, mainly through the relationship between its Department of Commerce and ICANN, had too much influence in managing the Internet.[25] Furthermore, some developing countries argued that the fact that the 13 domain name root servers were all located in the developed world — several are controlled by United States Government or military institutions — in itself posed a threat to the Internet's alleged global, open and accessible nature. Table 7.3 provides an illustrative list of DNS root server locations.

At first sight, it seems that few DNS root servers are located outside the United States. The M server is operated by the Widely Integrated Distributed Environment (WIDE) Project in Tokyo, and the K server is managed by Amsterdam-based Réseaux IP Européens Network Coordination Centre (RIPE NCC). Autonomica is based in Sweden. Several of the listed servers are using the anycast protocol to point to many addresses around the world, accessing 80 server locations in 34 countries, including many developing countries.[26] It is interesting to note that the anycast[27] protocol has been implemented without much ICANN involvement, without a formal policy process and without official consultations with the US Department of Commerce (Peake, 2004).

Developed countries, and in particular the United States, countered mainly by suggesting that the Internet governance system, narrowly defined as a set of technical coordination activities such as those carried out by ICANN, was not broken and therefore that while ICANN itself could benefit from reform, it did not need replacing with new or existing institutions, in particular not those from the United Nations system. They also affirmed their conviction that a deregulated, private-sector and market-based model for the build-out of the Internet was and would still be more efficient and effective than a top-down regulated environment aimed at balancing diverse national interests through regulatory measures that consider the Internet to be a public service.[28]

The compromise position was reached by adopting a set of agenda points. These had several outcomes. One was the previously noted establishment of a discussion platform, namely the IGF. Another was the introduction of a set of soft principles advocating that the Internet governance processes be multilateral, transparent, democratic and open to all stakeholders. These principles are positive and difficult to criticize. While they describe an ideal process of governance, they do not provide references for analysing concrete Internet policy or regulatory proposals. In this sense, they have crowded out the consideration of Internet-specific principles, such as the layers principle, the end-to-end principle or the network neutrality principle, discussed earlier in this chapter.

Finally, the process has produced a set of public policy issues. These are the administration of the root zone files and root server system of the Domain Name System (DNS), IP addressing, interconnection costs, Internet stability, security and cybercrime, spam, freedom of expression, meaningful participation in global policy development, data protection and privacy rights, consumer rights and multilingualism. While current at the time of writing, these issues may prove to be static and outdated because of technological development. Many also contain significant technological scope while the scope for policy reflection may be rather limited in the case of, say, spam, where there is a unanimous agreement that it is undesirable, the real problems being a lack of resources and capacity, rather than an evolved policy framework. The WSIS requested the IGF to consider these issues and present the discussions and outcome to the UN Secretary-General, who will report periodically to the UN member States on the Forum's operation.

While the WSIS and WGIG processes have produced a better understanding of Internet governance, what is needed is a point of convergence for the future deliberations of the IGF. A set of principles that would serve as policy and regulatory guidelines for Internet governance, such as the layers principle and its corollaries, are needed in particular if information society stakeholders see an advantage in further developing the Internet as a global, accessible and open communications platform and maintaining its positive relationship with technological innovation and economic and social development.

## E.   Conclusions and recommendations

The Internet is a truly remarkable technological platform. Barely a year goes by without our hearing yet again, of some extraordinary and innovative Internet development that is impacting on our social and economic life. Most recently, blogs have led the global media industry to re-examine its basic journalistic credos and principles. Wikis are redefining the scope and nature of communal knowledge development and have led to an examination of our understanding of encyclopaedic activities. Web services, discussed in some detail in chapter 6 of this report, may bring about a new burst of productivity growth among firms and economies. Online office software, torrent-based broadcasting, distributed always-on video telephony — what will be next?

A more interesting question is perhaps, who will be next? Individuals or small teams developed some of the most noteworthy Internet applications. These include Yahoo, eBay, Amazon, Google and Skype. Many free and open source software projects have been matured into world-class applications also by small teams, albeit with community support.[29] It is entirely conceivable that a globally important application will emerge from the sheds and bedrooms of tech-savvy youths from a developing country. Developing country Internet governance policy should therefore strategically support the build-out of national Internet infrastructure and should participate in strengthening its role as an open and accessible innovation platform through activities at national and international policy levels.

What all these technologies have in common is that they take advantage of several fundamental characteristics of the Internet. The first is that the TCP/IP suite takes care of itself. It is robust and reliable, but it does not interfere and treats all data equally — in fact, it cannot do otherwise because it lacks the necessary functionality and this is part of its purposeful design. The second is that it does not care about what applications are using it nor about the type of content they generate. The Internet does not care who the user is: it leaves this decision to the developer of the application. Finally, the Internet is a layered suite of public protocols where each layer performs a specific and separate function without concerning itself with the processes in other layers.

However, the Internet is a human product and its characteristics are not a given fact; rather, they are subject to change. While its present characteristics were designed by technologists, its future may be decided by governing authorities and policymakers. Thus, it is imperative that policymakers analogize the technical design values of the Internet into conceptual principles that define it and explain its success, from a social, political and economic perspective. Such principles can then be used in the process of governance. This may not be a simple notion nor an easily practicable process and many national and international political processes will shy away from this issue, preferring to deal with more observable manifestations such as problems with spam or cybercrime. To a certain extent, the Internet is a victim of its own success, having expanded so much and having become a locus of so many social and economic activities that Governments can no longer leave it alone. Society is moving online and with it its need to organize and govern.

Accepting that the need to govern the Internet is a given, a political fact of life, the question that follows is: how to go about it? A first and unavoidable step is to advance the dialogue between the technological and the political communities. This should be done at the national and international levels. Governments, in particularly those of developing and transition economies, should spare no effort to engage their scientific and academic communities, in particular those members that specialize in electronic and digital communications, and institutionalize a permanent dialogue on Internet governance issues. The learning process would be a two-way street. As much as policymakers may be unfamiliar with, say, the functions of various protocols residing in the transport layer, technologists may need to learn about issues of legitimacy, economic externalities and utilities above and beyond the concepts of technical functionality, effectiveness and efficiency. Such processes need to be reinforced at the level of international policy and the IGF needs to be challenged and supported in bringing the political and technological communities together in the Internet governance debate.

A further step for the IGF would be to formulate a key set of principles to serve as guidelines for Internet governance policy and regulation. This chapter proposes the layers principle because it reduces many other proposed principles to two arguments: does proposed policy require one layer to differentiate the handling of data based on information available in another layer, and does the proposed policy minimize the distance between the layer at which it is implemented and the layer where the outcomes are expected? However, many policymakers and technologists may choose instead, or in addition, the end-to-end principle or the network neutrality principle. They may also choose to develop a new principle from scratch or a derivative of existing notions. Whatever the case, this chapter suggest that policymakers should develop Internet governance policy based on a set of debated and agreed principles.

Finally, there will always be questions as to how far to go in codifying any of the proposed principles. The conventional wisdom is that activities that result only in a certain loss should be regulated. Does *not codifying* the Internet present society with situations of certain and unambiguous loss without any upside or possible benefits? This is a serious issue that will require much debate. At this point in time it would be safe to say that policymakers should consider the full spectrum of policy tools, including education, awareness and capacity building, economic incentives and self-regulation, before considering regulation.

Finally, the international community needs to extend the opportunity for technical cooperation on Internet governance issues to developing and transition economy countries and in particular to least developed countries. This will ensure that they fully benefit from the development opportunities provided by the Internet. It would also improve their ability to make a valuable contribution to the IGF and other international processes dealing with Internet governance in the post-WSIS era.

# Annex I

## A selective overview of protocols that make up the Internet protocol suite

| Acronym | Description | Layer level |
|---|---|---|
| ARP | The Address Resolution Protocol (ARP) is the method for finding a host's hardware address when only its Internet Protocol address is known. | Network |
| ATM | Asynchronous Transfer Mode (ATM) is a cell relay network protocol that encodes data traffic into small fixed-sized cells, instead of variable-sized packets as used in the Internet Protocol or Ethernet. | Link |
| BitTorrent | BitTorrent is a file sharing protocol designed to widely distribute large amounts of data without the corresponding large consumption in server and bandwidth resources. | Application |
| DCCP | The Datagram Congestion Control Protocol is a transport layer protocol used by applications with timing constraints on data delivery, such as streaming media and Internet telephony. | Transport |
| DNS | The domain name system/server translates domain names to IP addresses and thus provides a global redirection service for the Internet, and thus is essential for its use. | Application |
| Ethernet | Ethernet is a networking technology for local area networks that has been standardized as IEEE 802.3. | Link |
| Frame Relay | Frame relay is an efficient data transmission technique. While IP-based networks have gradually begun to displace frame relay, in areas lacking DSL and cable modem services frame relay "always-on" connections provide a possibility for high-speed access. | Link |
| FTP | File transfer protocol is used for exchanging files over any network that supports the TCP/IP protocol, such as the Internet or an intranet. | Application |
| HTTP | Hypertext Transfer Protocol is used to transfer Information on the World Wide Web by providing a standard for publishing and reading HTML pages. | Application |
| ICMP | The Internet Control Message Protocol is used to send error messages, indicating, for example, that a requested service is not available or that a host cannot be reached. | Network |
| IGMP | The Internet Group Management Protocol is used to manage multicast groups. It is used for online video and gaming. | Network |
| IMAP | The Internet Message Access allows a local client to access e-mail on a remote server. | Application |
| IP | Internet Protocol provides the service of communicable unique global addressing amongst computers. It is encapsulated in a data link layer protocol (e.g. Ethernet) and this relieves the data link layer of the need to provide this service. | Network |
| IRC | Internet Relay Chat provides instant communication over the Internet and was designed for discussion forums or one-on-one exchanges. | Application |
| NNTP | The Network News Transfer Protocol is used to read and post Usenet articles and to transfer news among news servers. | Application |
| POP3 | The Post Office Protocol version 3 is used by subscribers to Internet-based e-mail accounts to access their e-mail on their local computers. | Application |
| PPP | The Point-to-Point Protocol establishes a direct connection between two nodes and many Internet service providers use PPP to give customers dial-up or DSL access to the Internet. | Link |
| RTP | The Real-time Transport Protocol (or RTP) defines a standardized packet format for delivering audio and video over the Internet. | Application |
| RUDP | The Reliable User Datagram Protocol is a transport layer protocol designed as an extended functionality UDP protocol that can provide guaranteed-order packet delivery. | Transport |
| SCTP | SCTP can transport multiple message-streams and operates on whole messages instead of single bytes. | Transport |
| SIP | Session Initiation Protocol enables initiating, modifying and terminating Internet connections for multimedia applications such as audio, video, instant messaging, online games and virtual reality. | Application |
| SMTP | Simple Mail Transfer Protocol is the standard for e-mail and Internet fax transmissions across the Internet. | Application |

## Annex I *(continued)*

| SNMP | The simple network management protocol is used by network management systems for monitoring network devices for occurrences that require administrative attention. | Application |
|---|---|---|
| SSH | Secure SHell allows the establishment of a secure connection between two remote computers using public-key cryptography for authentication as well as confidentiality and data integrity. | Application |
| TCP | The Transmission Control Protocol is, together with the IP, a core protocol enabling exchange of data packets. It provides for reliable and in-order delivery, and enables multiple, concurrent applications to send data at the same time. | Transport |
| TELNET | The Telephone Network protocol provides a general, two-way communications facility and was designed to emulate a single terminal attached to the other computer using a telephone network. | Application |
| TLS/SSL | Transport Layer Security and Secure Socket Layer are cryptographic protocols for secure communications on the Internet. The protocols allow applications to communicate while decreasing the risk of eavesdropping, tampering and message forgery. | Application |
| UDP | The User Datagram Protocol allows programs on networked computers to send short messages, but it does not provide the reliability and ordering guarantees that TCP does. While packets may arrive out of order or go missing, UDP can be more efficient than TCP for time-sensitive applications. | Transport |
| Wi-Fi | Wi-Fi is a protocol enabling wireless local area networks (WLAN) based on the IEEE 802.11 specifications. Wi-Fi also allows connectivity in peer-to-peer mode; this makes it useful in consumer electronics and gaming applications. | Link |

## Annex II

The ISO/IEC Open Systems Interconnection model (OSI) is a framework describing how messages should be transmitted between any two points in a telecommunication network. It divides a telecommunications network into seven layers. When data pass only through a computer, on their way to a final destination, only the lower three layers — up to the network layer — are used. The OSI is a modular system that divides a complex set of functions into manageable and self-contained layers. In theory, this allows communication systems to independently develop and innovate applications at the various layers without a global redesign being mandated. The seven layers are:

Layer 1: The physical layer conveys the bit stream through the network at the electrical and mechanical level. It provides the hardware means of sending and receiving data on a carrier.

Layer 2: The data-link layer provides synchronization for the physical level and furnishes transmission protocol knowledge and management.

Layer 3: The network layer handles the routing and forwarding of the data. This means sending data in the right direction to the right destination on outgoing transmissions and receiving incoming transmissions at the packet level.

Layer 4: The transport layer manages the end-to-end control — for example, determining whether all packets have arrived — and error-checking. It ensures complete data transfer.

Layer 5: The session layer sets up, coordinates and terminates conversations, exchanges and dialogues between the applications at each end. It deals with session and connection coordination.

Layer 6: The presentation layer is usually part of an operating system which converts incoming and outgoing data from one presentation format to another. It is sometimes called the syntax layer.

Layer 7: The application layer is the layer at which communication partners are identified, quality of service is identified, user authentication and privacy are considered, and any constraints on data syntax are identified.

OSI represents a design paradigm for packet-switched network architecture and reflects the increasing level of use of such technologies. From a practical perspective, while extensive effort was invested in its promotion, OSI did not become a popular implementation, as it was not accepted by the communications industry, which favoured the TCP/IP suite.

# References

Benkler Y (2000). From consumers to users: Shifting deeper structures of regulation toward sustainable commons and user access, *Federal Communications Law Journal* , vol. 52, no. 3.
http://www.law.indiana.edu/fclj/pubs/v52/no3/benkler1.pdf

Cerf V (2006). Network neutrality, presented at the hearing of the US Senate Committee on Commerce, Science, and Transportation.
http://commerce.senate.gov/pdf/cerf-020706.pdf

DiLorenzo TJ (1996). The myth of the natural monopoly, *Review of Austrian Economics,* vol. 9, no. 2.
http://www.mises.org/journals/rae/pdf/rae9_2_3.pdf

Drake W (2004). Reframing Internet governance discourse: Fifteen baseline propositions, Memo #2 for the Social Science Research Council's Research Network on IT and Governance.
http://www.ssrc.org/programs/itic/publications/Drake2.pdf

Drake W, ed. (2005). Reforming Internet governance: Perspectives from the WGIG, United Nations Task Force Series 12.
http://www.wgig.org/docs/book/WGIG_book.pdf

Interent Society (2003). A brief history of the Internet.
http://www.isoc.org/internet/history/brief.shtml

Isenberg D (1997). Rise of the stupid network: Why the intelligent network was once a good idea, but isn't anymore, Computer Telephony.
http://www.hyperorg.com/misc/stupidnet.html

Kruse H, Yurcik W, Lessig L (2000). The InterNAT: Policy Implications of the Internet Architecture Debate, Telecommunications Policy Research Conference - Agenda 2000.
http://www.tprc.org/abstracts00/internatpap.pdf

Lessig L (1999). *Code and Other Laws of Cyberspace*, Basic Books.

Lessig L (2001). *The Future of Ideas: The Fate of the Commons in a Connected World*, Vintage Books.

MacLean D, ed. (2004). Internet governance: A grand collaboration, United Nations Task Force Series 5.
http://www.epol-net.org/pport/pdf/465794058.pdf

Mitchell WJ (1995). City of Bits: Space, Place, and the Infobahn. MIT Press.

Peake A (2004). Internet governance and the World Summit on the Information Society (WSIS), Association for Progressive Communications (APC).
http://rights.apc.org/documents/governance.pdf

Saltzer JH, Reed DP and Clark DD (1981). End-to-end arguments in system design, *ACM Transactions in Computer Systems* vol. 2, no. 4, November 1984.
http://web.mit.edu/Saltzer/www/publications/endtoend/endtoend.txt

Saltzer JH, Reed DP and Clark DD (1998). Active networking and end-to-end Arguments, IEEE Network vol. 12, no. 3, May/June.
http://web.mit.edu/Saltzer/www/publications/endtoend/ANe2ecomment.html

Solum B and Chung M (2003). The layers principle: Internet architecture and the Law, Public Law and Legal Theory Research Paper 55, University of San Diego School of Law, California.
http://papers.ssrn.com/sol3/papers.cfm?abstract_id=416263

Tanenbaum AS (1996). Computer Networks (3rd Ed), Prentice-Hall Inc.

UNCTAD (2002). *E-Commerce and Development Report 2002*, UNCTAD/SDTE/ECB/2.
http://r0.unctad.org/ecommerce/ecommerce_en/edr02_en.htm

UNCTAD (2003). *E-Commerce and Development Report 2003*, UNCTAD/SDTE/ECB/2003/1.
http://r0.unctad.org/ecommerce/docs/edr03_en/ecdr03.htm

UNCTAD (2005). *Information Economy Report 2005*: *E-commerce and development*, UNCTAD/SDTE/ ECB/2005/1.
http://www.unctad.org/en/docs/sdteecb20051_en.pdf

UNDP-APDIP (2005). *Internet Governance: Asia-Pacific perspectives,* Elsevier.
http://www.apdip.net/publications/ict4d/igovperspectives.pdf

Werbach K (2004). Breaking the ice: Rethinking telecommunications law for the digital age, *Journal on Telecommunications and High-Tech Law*, 2005.
http://werbach.com/docs/breaking_the_ice.pdf

Werbach K (2002). A layered model for Internet policy, *Journal on Telecommunications and High-Tech Law*, vol. 1, no. 37.
http://papers.ssrn.com/sol3/papers.cfm?abstract_id=648581

WGIG (2005a). Report of the Working Group on Internet Governance.
http://www.wgig.org/docs/WGIGREPORT.pdf or
http://www.wgig.org/docs/WGIGREPORT.odt

WGIG (2005b). Background report of the Working Group on Internet Governance.
http://www.wgig.org/docs/BackgroundReport.pdf or
http://www.wgig.org/docs/Background-Report.htm

Wu T (2005). Network neutrality, broadband discrimination, *Journal of Telecommunications and High Technology Law*, vol. 2.
http://papers.ssrn.com/sol3/papers.cfm?abstract_id=388863

Yoo CS (2004). Would mandating broadband network neutrality help or hurt competition? A comment on the end-to-end debate, Vanderbilt University Law School Law & Economics Working Paper Number 04-04.
http://papers.ssrn.com/sol3/papers.cfm?abstract_id=495502

# Notes

1.  See Drake (2004).

2.  Mobile telephony is a typical example: providers will have a licence for a specified type of service, such as GPRS or 3G, in a particular region or country, and will use identifiable infrastructure.

3.  See http://www.isoc.org/internet/history/brief.shtml .

4.  In June 2005, an Interactive Advertising Bureau and PricewaterhouseCoopers survey estimated that Internet advertising totalled over $2.8 billion for the first quarter of 2005; this made it the highest reported quarter in nine consecutive growth quarters and represented a 26 per cent increase over the first quarter of 2004 (http://www.iab.net/news/pr_2005_6_6.asp). For a more detailed discussion of online advertising see "Online Advertising Landscape, Europe" and "The Decade in Online Advertising, 1994-2004"; http://www.doubleclick.com/us/knowledge_central/ .

5.  The diagram is derived from a graphic presenting the OSI reference model. The original was produced by Josef Sábl for Wikipedia and is available under the GNU Public Licence at http://en.wikipedia.org/wiki/Image:Rm-osi_parallel.png .

6.  The full specification can be accessed at http://standards.iso.org/ittf/PubliclyAvailableStandards/s020269_ISO_IEC_7498-1_1994(E).zip.

7.  DiLorenzo (1996) argues that monopolies in the telephony sector were created through government regulation instead of being a result of market failure.

8.  See UNCTAD (2002), chapter 2, "The domain name system and issues for developing countries".

9.  See http://www.wipo.int/treaties/en/ip/wct/trtdocs_wo033.html, http://www.copyright.gov/legislation/dmca.pdf , and http://eur-lex.europa.eu/LexUriServ/LexUriServ.do?uri=CELEX:32001L0029:EN:HTML

10. See http://news.com.com/2102-1028_3-6058223.html .

11. This is not entirely correct. Data travelling on the Internet have origin and destination IP addresses associated with it; thus one can see where data come from, as the IP numbers give at least an approximate indication of where users may be located. However, the Internet uses these data only to manage the routing and transporting of the data. It is the applications that the data reach that then choose to interpret and use the data from a geographical perspective. For example, Apple iTunes refuses to sell music downloads to users not residing in the same domicile as the regional portal. Therefore, only French residents can do business with iTunes.fr. However, while the iTunes.fr website is an Internet-enabled e-commerce application, it is not strictly speaking the Internet — it merely uses the Internet. It is up to the website manager or programmer to choose to consider IP number information. The Internet itself does not do this other than in respect of routing and transporting data.

12. Lessig (1991, p. 5) ascribes the "code is law" notion to Mitchell (1995).

13. See Solum and Chung (2003, p. 13).

14. More specifically, Saltzer et al. (1998) state that "building complex function into a network implicitly optimizes the network for one set of uses while substantially increasing the cost of a set of potentially valuable uses that may be unknown or unpredictable at design time. A case in point: had the original Internet design... Preserving low-cost options to innovate outside the network, while keeping the core network services and functions simple and cheap, has been shown to have very substantial value."

15.    See http://search.news.com/search?q=internet+neutrality .

16.    See Solum and Chung (2003, p. 32, second para.).

17.    WGIG (2005a, p. 6, para. 20).

18.    The WSIS Second phase Prepcom-3 was the locus for developing the Internet governance debate in between the Geneva and Tunis summits; see http://www.itu.int/wsis/preparatory2/pc3/index.html .

19.    For comprehensive documentation see the WSIS portal at http://www.itu.int/wsis/.

20.    See Annex 3: Geneva Declaration of Principles, article 49.1.

21.    In November 2004, Secretary-General Kofi Annan appointed 40 individuals from government, the private sector and civil society to the WGIG. However, many more people attended the WGIG consultations in Geneva, contributing their views and knowledge. Lists of participants, and papers and presentations submitted, are available at the WGIG website at http://www.wgig.org .

22.    See WGIG Background Report at http://www.wgig.org/.

23.    See WGIG Final Report at http://www.wgig.org/.

24.    See WGIG (2005a), page 3, para. 6.

25.    See  http://rights.apc.org.au/wsis/2005/03/report_wsis_prepcom2.php , http://news.com.com/U.N.+says+its+plans+are+misunderstood/2008-1028_3-5959117.html , http://www.infotoday.com/newsbreaks/nb051121-1.shtml , or http://www.worldsummit2005.de/en/web/796.htm. Also see the Memorandum of Understanding Between the Department of Commerce and the Internet Corporation for Assigned Names and Numbers (ICANN) at http://www.ntia.doc.gov/ntiahome/domainname/icann.htm .

26.    See the Internet Society's "DNS root name servers explained for non-experts" at  http://www.isoc.org/briefings/019/ as well as Root-servers.org for a complete list of server locations at http://www.root-servers.org/.

27.    Anycast is a network technology that routes data traffic to the "nearest" or "best" destination in accordance with the routing topology.  It can be used to provide redundancy and load sharing for particular Internet functions, such as DNS root servers;  see http://www.net.cmu.edu/pres/anycast/.

28.    An excellent description of United States policy can be found in Ambassador David A. Gross' testimony before the Senate Committee on Commerce, Science, and Transportation; see http://www.state.gov/e/eb/rls/rm/36700.htm .

29.    See UNCTAD (2003) for a detailed analysis of the free software phenomenon.

# Chapter 8

# LAWS AND CONTRACTS IN AN E-COMMERCE ENVIRONMENT

## A. Introduction

Most legal systems have developed over many years and comprise a myriad of laws and regulations as well as judicial decision-making. While laws and regulations rarely expressly require the use of paper, they often use terminology that seems to presume the use of paper and other physical acts, phrases such as "under the hand of" and "on the face of". As a consequence, when organizations shift from paper-based communication techniques to electronic methods, there is often uncertainty about how existing laws will treat data messages in terms of validity, enforceability and admissibility. This legal uncertainty is an obstacle to the adoption of e-commerce and therefore many Governments have amended or supplemented existing laws in order to address it.

This chapter examines the legal nature of communications and data messages in electronic commerce. Considerable international harmonization has been achieved in this field, on the basis of a series of initiatives by the United Nations Commission on International Trade Law (UNCITRAL). The most significant of these was the adoption of the United Nations Convention on the Use of Electronic Communications in International Contracts, which was formally adopted in November 2005 and opened for signature in January 2006. The provisions of this Convention will be examined in relation to the conclusion of contracts through data messages and fulfilling requirements of form with data messages. Consideration will also be given to the experience of developing countries in amending their domestic legal framework to reflect the needs of an electronic commerce environment.

While the legal discussion on the specific aspects of the UN Convention that will be examined in this chapter is applicable to all countries, regardless of their level of development, it is worthwhile to note the relevance of the UN Convention for developing countries. It has the potential to facilitate international electronic commerce, which can open the doors to new markets and become a source of economic growth. Some developing countries will require awareness-raising and technical assistance in order to accept and implement the Convention. Such awareness-raising and assistance should take place in the context of international efforts to reduce the digital divide.

## B. EDI and trading partner agreements

While electronic contracting has become especially relevant as a result of the Internet revolution since the mid-1990s, electronic business has existed before in a business-to-business context through the use of Electronic Data Interchange (EDI). EDI consists of standard business messages being transmitted from one computer to another computer. It differs from the use of regular e-mail in that it is based on a standard or code that is agreed upon by two parties, enabling the automated processing of the content of a message without human intervention. Over time, a variety of EDI standards have been developed, at industry, national and international levels, including the United Nations UN/EDIFACT standard.[1]

Since the parties to an EDI transaction must rely on using the same EDI messaging standard, parties generally enter into a "trading partner agreement", in which they agree on the EDI standard and additional provisions regarding the treatment and validity of the data messages being exchanged. The trading partner agreement may be a separate agreement or may be integrated into a master purchase agreement containing the substantive provisions of the sales–purchase relationship between the parties. Since the 1990s, a number of model trading partner agreements have been developed on a national, regional or international level. In 2000, for example, the United Nations Centre for Trade Facilitation and Electronic Business (UN/CEFACT) adopted a model Electronic Commerce Agreement.[2]

This agreement provides an overview of the issues facing the establishment of a paperless EDI system and is designed to contribute "to the building of trust between business entities".   In the trading partner agreement, the parties can address the specific issues of electronic contracting, such as when a person is bound by a message or by erroneous electronic messages.   Generally, by entering into the trading partner agreement, the parties would agree that they consider contracts concluded electronically via EDI to be valid and enforceable obligations between them.

In the absence of an appropriate statutory regime, private law mechanisms, such as contractual agreements, made between the parties to a transaction but recognized and enforceable before the courts, are an important means of addressing the legal uncertainties of doing business electronically.

## C.   UNCITRAL initiatives

An important concern of many countries is that traditional legal frameworks may prove to be a barrier to increased global electronic trade.   As early as 1985, UNCITRAL and the United Nations General Assembly called upon all Governments to review legal requirements for a handwritten signature or other paper-based requirements for trade-related documents in order to permit, where appropriate, the use of electronic technologies.[3] States were slow to respond, and UNCITRAL ultimately concluded that paper-based requirements combined with the lack of harmonization in the rules applicable to electronic commerce constituted a substantial barrier to international trade, and that uniform rules for electronic commerce were necessary.

In 1992, UNCITRAL embarked upon the preparation of legal rules on the subject and gave its final approval to the resulting Model Law on Electronic Commerce, which was eventually adopted by the General Assembly in December 1996.[4] The Model Law has proved a great success, as a basis for national law reform initiatives (see box 8.1), as well as for encouraging similar initiatives in other intergovernmental forums. In November 2002, for example, a meeting of the Commonwealth law ministers, representing 53 developed and developing countries, approved a Model Law on Electronic Transactions and a Model Law on Electronic Evidence.[5]

The main objective of the UNCITRAL Model Law was to offer national legislators a set of internationally acceptable rules allowing a number of legal obstacles to be removed and a more secure legal environment to

be created for electronic commerce.  The UNCITRAL Model Law is not an international treaty and does not therefore constitute positive law. Instead, it was drafted to provide a guide for individual countries in preparing their own national legislative response. National legislators and policymakers are not required to adopt in its entirety (or reject in its entirety) the UNCITRAL Model Law.  Instead, national legislatures may modify it to meet concrete needs or concerns of their jurisdictions.    This flexibility fosters the adoption of the core provisions of the UNCITRAL Model Law, which promotes the development of an international system of national electronic contracting legislation that, although not identical, is similar in structure and content. UNCITRAL has also published a Guide to Enactment of the UNCITRAL Model Law on Electronic Commerce,[6] which provides national policymakers with background and explanatory information to assist them in using the Model Law.

---

### Box 8.1

### UNCITRAL Model Law on Electronic Commerce (1996)

Legislation implementing provisions of the Model Law has been adopted in:

Australia (1999), China (2004), Colombia* (1999), Dominican Republic* (2002), Ecuador* (2002), France (2000), India* (2000), Ireland (2000), Jordan (2001), Mauritius (2000), Mexico (2000), New Zealand (2002), Pakistan (2002), Panama* (2001), Philippines (2000), Republic of Korea (1999), Singapore (1998), Slovenia (2000), South Africa* (2002), Sri Lanka (2006), Thailand (2002) and Venezuela (2001).

The Model Law has also been adopted in:

The Bailiwick of Guernsey (2000), the Bailiwick of Jersey (2000) and the Isle of Man (2000), all Crown Dependencies of the United Kingdom of Great Britain and Northern Ireland; in Bermuda (1999), Cayman Islands (2000), and the Turks and Caicos Islands (2000), overseas territories of the United Kingdom of Great Britain and Northern Ireland; and in the Hong Kong Special Administrative Region of China (2000).

Uniform legislation influenced by the Model Law and the principles on which it is based has been prepared in:

The United States of America (Uniform Electronic Transactions Act, adopted in 1999 by the National Conference of Commissioners on Uniform State Law);

Canada (Uniform Electronic Commerce Act, adopted in 1999 by the Uniform Law Conference of Canada).

* Except for the provisions on certification and electronic signatures.

Source: www.uncitral.org.

## 1. Model Law on Electronic Signatures

Building on the success of the Model Law as a precedent for national law reform, UNCITRAL adopted in 2001 a Model Law on Electronic Signatures,[7] which builds on the signature provision in the 1996 Model Law. From a legal and security perspective, signatures provide two key elements — authentication and integrity. The use of such techniques is seen as critical to the widespread adoption of electronic commerce, particularly in terms of meeting the requirements of Governments and regulatory authorities.

The 2001 Model Law addresses an issue raised in the 1996 Model Law concerning the reliability of an electronic signature. Article 7 of the 1996 Model Law states that an electronic signature shall satisfy a requirement for a signature where it meets two criteria: first, that the signature technique identifies the signatory and indicates his or her approval of the message content, which reflects the basic functions of a signature; and second, that the method used was "as reliable as was appropriate for the purpose", which reflects the security functionality of a signature.The 2001 Model Law addresses the issue of reliability by

## Box 8.2

## United Nations General Assembly Resolution 60/21, United Nations Convention on the Use of Electronic Communications in International Contracts

(December 2005)

*Considering* that problems created by uncertainties as to the legal value of electronic communications exchanged in the context of international contracts constitute an obstacle to international trade,

*Convinced* that the adoption of uniform rules to remove obstacles to the use of electronic communications in international contracts, including obstacles that might result from the operation of existing international trade law instruments, would enhance legal certainty and commercial predictability for international contracts and may help States gain access to modern trade routes,

*Recalling* that, at its thirty-fourth session, in 2001, the Commission decided to prepare an international instrument dealing with issues of electronic contracting, which should also aim at removing obstacles to electronic commerce in existing uniform law conventions and trade agreements, and entrusted its Working Group IV (Electronic Commerce) with the preparation of a draft,[1]

*Noting* that the Working Group devoted six sessions, from 2002 to 2004, to the preparation of the draft Convention on the Use of Electronic Communications in International Contracts, and that the Commission considered the draft Convention at its thirty-eighth session in 2005,[2]

*Being aware* that all States and interested international organizations were invited to participate in the preparation of the draft Convention at all the sessions of the Working Group and at the thirty-eighth session of the Commission, either as members or as observers, with a full opportunity to speak and make proposals,

*Noting with satisfaction* that the text of the draft Convention was circulated for comments before the thirty-eighth session of the Commission to all Governments and international organizations invited to attend the meetings of the Commission and the Working Group as observers, and that the comments received were before the Commission at its thirty-eighth session,[3]

*Taking note with satisfaction* of the decision of the Commission at its thirty-eighth session to submit the draft Convention to the General Assembly for its consideration,[4]

*Taking note* of the draft Convention approved by the Commission,[5]

1. *Expresses its appreciation* to the United Nations Commission on International Trade Law for preparing the draft Convention on the Use of Electronic Communications in International Contracts;[5]

2. *Adopts* the United Nations Convention on the Use of Electronic Communications in International Contracts, which is contained in the annex to the present resolution, and requests the Secretary-General to open it for signature;

3. *Calls upon* all Governments to consider becoming party to the Convention.

---

[1] Official records of the General Assembly, Fifty-sixth Session, Supplement No. 17 and corrigendum (A/56/17 and Corr. 3), paras. 291–295.

[2] Ibid., Sixtieth Session, Supplement No. 17 (A/60/17), chap. III.

[3] A/CN.9/578 and Add.1–17.

[4] Official Records of the General Assembly, Sixtieth Session, Supplement No. 17 (A/60/17), para. 167.

[5] Ibid., annex I.

laying down certain criteria that, if met by a particular form of electronic signature, would be presumed to be reliable for the purposes of Article 7. The 2001 Model Law also places behavioural obligations upon the signatory and the relaying party, as well as a third-party certification service provider (CSP). As such, the 2001 Model follows the stance taken in the European Union Directive on Electronic Signatures in 1999,[8] remaining technology-neutral whilst also promoting the role of CSPs in the establishment of trust and security in an electronic commerce environment.

## 2. United Nations Convention (2005)

While the Model Laws have been very influential in terms of encouraging harmonized law reform in the field of electronic commerce, they have no formal status as international legal instruments. Therefore, to promote and further facilitate law reform, the Commission in 2001, tasked its Working Group on Electronic Commerce with the drafting of an instrument of public international law. In November 2005 the Convention on the Use of Electronic Communications in International Contracts was adopted by the UN General Assembly,[9] and opened for signature on 16 January 2006 (see box 8.2). The first three signatories were from two least developed countries (LDCs) — Senegal and the Central African Republic — and from one developing county, Lebanon. Already, the Convention has been taken into consideration, together with the UNCITRAL Model Laws and regional laws, in preparing legislation on electronic transactions in Sri Lanka (see box 8.3)

The Convention prepared under the auspices of UNCITRAL[10] aims to enhance legal certainty and commercial predictability where electronic communications are used in relation to international contracts. It is intended to govern the formation and performance of contracts using electronic communications in international transactions. The range of subject matter addressed in the Convention is therefore narrower than that of the 1996 Model Law. Certain types of contracts are excluded from the Convention, for example, including contracts concluded for "personal, family or household purposes" and a range of finance-related agreements, such as inter-

## Box 8.3

## Sri Lanka - Legislating on electronic transactions

In 2003, the Sri Lankan Parliament adopted legislation establishing an agency, the Information and Communication Technology Agency of Sri Lanka (ICTA), with the specific remit of devising and implementing a strategy and programme of activities to promote an e-Sri Lanka development project, coordinating both public and private sector input. ICTA was granted statutory powers and functions, which include assisting in the development of a national policy on ICTs and taking steps to facilitate its implementation.

Law reform and regulation are an important element of the strategy, addressing three key areas: e-commerce legislation, data protection and computer crime. Subsequent to a joint Cabinet Memorandum of the Prime Minister, the Minister of Trade and Commerce, and the Minister of Science of Technology, ICTA facilitated the preparation of an e-Transactions Bill, which takes into consideration the UNCITRAL Model Laws and Convention, as well as regional laws. The resultant statute, the Electronic Transactions Act No. 19 of 2006, was finally adopted in May 2006.

The Act begins with a statement detailing the objectives of the Act:

" (a) to facilitate domestic and international electronic commerce by eliminating legal barriers and establishing legal certainty;

(b) to encourage the use of reliable forms of electronic commerce;

(c) to facilitate electronic filling of documents with Government and to promote efficient delivery of Government services by means of reliable forms of electronic communications;

and

(d) to promote public confidence in the authenticity, integrity and reliability of data messages and electronic communications."

Such declarations of intent not only offer comfort to the business community, both domestically and foreign investors, who wish to rely on the provisions of the Act; but would also provide important guidance to the judiciary if it is called upon to interpret the provisions of the Act.

Since legislative reforms can take several years to be enacted by Parliament, ICTA has been directed to introduce appropriate regulations under the ICT Act of 2003 in order to give legal effect to technology standards and facilitate e-transactions, with the participation of the Government and private sector stakeholders. Under the e-policy programme, it is envisaged that electronic laws will be in place within a period of three to four years.

bank payment systems and bills of lading (Article 2). In addition, issues concerning the evidential value of electronic communications are also not addressed in the Convention.

## General provisions

While the Convention is designed to form the basis of a statutory framework, it retains the concept of party autonomy (Article 3), such that trading partners have the freedom to agree, in contract, to operate in accordance with terms and procedures that differ from the provisions of the Convention. Thus, for example, a trading community operating under an EDI trading partner agreement that reflects the customs and practices of that particular industry would not be obliged to amend such an agreement.

Reflecting the Model Laws, the Convention utilizes a series of terms that underpin it. Electronic commerce, for example, is conducted through the exchange of a variety of electronic messages, called a "data message" under the Convention, Article 4(c).

"Data message" means information generated, sent, received or stored by electronic, magnetic, optical or similar means, including, but not limited to, electronic data interchange, electronic mail, telegram, telex or telecopy;

Alternative phrases have been used in national legislation, such as "electronic record" in the United States and "electronic document" in Canada. However, the Convention provides a standard language that can be adopted without need for further modification.

## Legal validity

A fundamental legal concern that a person will have when communicating electronically is whether such communications will be considered valid. Legal validity concerns arise from a number of different sources. First, it may simply be an issue in respect of the trading partner to whom a message is being sent: will the party accept my electronic message and act on it? As discussed above, EDI trading partner agreements are primarily designed to address questions of validity in this context. Second, there will be concerns that communications that pass between trading partners, but which are also required to be made by law, such as tax invoices, will be an acceptable record for the public

authority with responsibility for regulatory supervision. Third, communications that are made directly with public authorities, namely e-government applications, raise issues concerning the possibility and validity of sending such communications electronically. Fourth, there is the need for electronic communications to be acceptable in a court of law in the event of a dispute arising between trading partners or a claim being made by a third party affected by the electronic communication. The Convention is designed to contribute to the resolution of all these different validity concerns.

### (a) Legal recognition of electronic communications

Data messages may have a variety of legal consequences. Some may simply provide information, such as the arrival time of a shipment, which could give rise to a tortious action if the information-giver was negligent in respect of such information. A message may constitute a contractual offer or acceptance, binding the sender into a binding legal relationship. Alternatively, a message may evidence compliance with a contractual obligation. Some communications, rather than imposing legal obligations upon the parties, transfer certain legal rights between the parties, such as ownership under a bill of lading or share certificate. A data message may be required for regulatory purposes, such as revenue-related matters, for example an invoice indicating the amount of sales tax paid, which are imposed by law or public authorities. Finally, a message may require prior authority or a licence before it may be sent. Under European privacy laws, for example, organizations may require prior authority before transferring personal data to another country. A licence may be required from a rights-holder where the subject matter being communicated is protected by copyright.

Whatever the legal significance of a data message, there is a need to ensure that these communications or information are not deprived of their legal significance simply because the medium that is used for transmission or storage is electronic rather than paper-based. Consequently, most laws contain a declaratory statement that any document sent or stored through the use of electronic technologies is not rendered invalid because of its electronic form. Article 8(1) of the Convention provides that:

1. A communication or a contract shall not be denied validity or enforceability on the sole ground that it is in the form of an electronic communication.

## Box 8.4

## Legal recognition in ASEAN member States

The 10 ASEAN member States represent a broad range of economic development, from highly developed economies such as Singapore to LDCs such as the Lao People's Democratic Republic. In 2000, the ASEAN member States adopted an e-Asean Framework Agreement designed to encourage the take-up of electronic commerce within the region.

Article 5 of the Framework Agreement concerned the "facilitation of the growth of electronic commerce". Among the issues addressed was the need for laws based on international norms. In 2001, this was developed further into a Reference Framework for Electronic Commerce Legal Infrastructure, which outlined a range of legal measures that should be adopted, including the legal recognition of electronic transactions, as well as the facilitation of cross-border trade and the use and recognition of electronic signatures . At the 10th ASEAN summit in 2004, member States accepted a commitment to adopt such legal measures by 31 December 2008.

To date, six members have successfully adopted legislation on electronic commerce (Brunei Darussalam, Malaysia, Myanmar, Philippines, Singapore and Thailand), while the remaining four have draft legislation that has been prepared (Cambodia, Indonesia, Lao People's Democratic Republic and Viet Nam). All of these statutes reflect the 1996 Model Law.

2. Nothing in this Convention requires a party to use or accept electronic communications, but a party's agreement to do so may be inferred from the party's conduct.

The formulation chosen here makes it clear that while the form in which the information is sent or retained cannot be used as the grounds for denying it validity, it may be denied legal validity on other grounds. For example, a notice that does not contain the information required by applicable law may be invalidated on those grounds; if it contained the required information, however, it could not be invalidated on the grounds it was in electronic form.

Although this provision is simple, its importance cannot be overemphasized. The principle that it articulates, that of non-discrimination, is the cornerstone of most electronic commerce legislation. It stands for the proposition that the use of electronic technologies should not be used as an excuse for invalidating communications and records. As such, the provision gives the certainty to the participants in electronic commerce that what they are doing will be treated as valid and enforceable. ASEAN member States have recognized the importance of the legal recognition of electronic transactions is encouraging the take-up of electronic commerce in the region (see box 8.4).

### (b) Contract creation

The use of data messages to conclude contracts may raise numerous questions. First, is such a contract valid? Some types of contracts are subject to specific requirements of form, designed to protect particular

interests or persons. While Governments may permit certain types of contract to be concluded electronically, in the same way as oral contracts have been recognized as valid in many legal systems, others may continue to be executed in physical form. Second, can a data message be viewed as the expression of a party's will (a requirement in many jurisdictions), especially where there has been no human review or intervention? Third, what terms are incorporated into the contract? Fourth, when and where can a contract be deemed to have been concluded?

The Convention contains a series of interrelated provisions directed at different aspects of the process of concluding contracts. As already noted, Article 8(1) provides that an electronic contract shall not be denied validity solely on the grounds that it is in electronic form. The effect of this provision is twofold. On the one hand, it emphasizes that electronic contracts constitute binding obligations as much as any traditional contract as long as the requisite elements of a valid contract are in place. This clarification provides the reassurance and certainty necessary for commercial undertakings to rely on the enforceability of electronic contracts. Such reliance is important because it forms the cornerstone for such undertakings to adopt electronic contracting as their way of doing business and promote the growth of electronic commerce.

On the other hand, these provisions make it clear that the rules of electronic contracting do not replace the traditional contract requirements. For example, the use of electronic contracting to exchange an offer and acceptance would not result in an enforceable contract if applicable contract law requires consideration that is still lacking. This means that a country adopting the provisions of the Convention can merge those provisions easily with its existing contract law, whether the country has common law, civil law or another system of contract law. This is an important feature of virtually all proposed or enacted electronic commerce legislation: it augments existing law but does not displace substantive law. In so doing, it validates the use of electronic means of contracting, thereby giving the participants the certainty that they desire.

The Convention differs from the 1996 Model Law and other existing legislative initiatives that recognize that a jurisdiction may restrict certain types of legal agreement from being formed electronically. The Model Law does not detail such exceptions, leaving it, in Article 11(2), for each jurisdiction to specific the applicable areas. Within the European Union,[11] for example, an exhaustive list is detailed:

(a) contracts that create or transfer rights in real estate, except for rental rights;

(b) contracts requiring by law the involvement of courts, public authorities or professions exercising public authority;

(c) contracts of suretyship granted and on collateral securities furnished by persons acting for purposes outside their trade, business or profession

(d) contracts governed by family law or by the law of succession.

Similarly, Article 15 of the Commonwealth Model Law contains a general exclusion provision, which would enable particular forms of contractual arrangements to be excluded:

15. This Act does not apply to:

(a) the creation or transfer of interests in real property;

(b) negotiable instruments;

(c) documents of title;

(d) wills and trusts created by will; and

(e) any class of documents, transactions or rules of law excluded by regulation under this Act.

In those cases, the nature of the legal rights involved has acted as a restraint on the liberalization from traditional paper-based mechanisms.

## (c)  Electronic agents

With the progress of computer technology, it is possible to program computers to automatically issue and receive orders without specific human intervention through the use of so-called "electronic agents". An electronic agent is basically a computer program that can independently place or receive purchase orders, respond to electronic records or initiate other action, using applications such as Java and Microsoft's Active X. Traditionally, offers and acceptances were valid only if made on the basis of a human decision. Technology served merely as the tool of transmission. Therefore, under the principles of traditional contract law, the enforceability of contracts entered into by electronic agents was questionable.

The Convention, in contrast to the 1996 Model Law, contains in Article 12 an express provision regarding electronic agents:

A contract formed by the interaction of an automated message system and a natural person, or by the interaction of automated message systems, shall not be denied validity or enforceability on the sole ground that no natural person reviewed or intervened in each of the individual actions carried out by the automated message systems or the resulting contract.

However, national electronic contracting laws that do not contain explicit rules for electronic agents are often broad enough to implicitly include the conclusion of contracts through electronic agents.

## (d)  Incorporation by reference

In traditional contracts, the terms that comprise the agreement between the parties are either detailed in the body of the agreement or are implied in the contractual relationship by law (through statute or judicial precedent), custom and practice or the action of the parties. In addition, the parties may simply exchange their standard documentation, such as a purchase order, with terms and conditions of doing business detailed on the back of the documents (often in small grey print!), which are never actually agreed between the parties, although a court may be required to decide whose terms take precedent. However, where the parties have an ongoing trading relationship or operate within a particular sector, the terms and conditions of doing business are often referred to in a document, rather than expressed stated. Such incorporation of terms by reference is an important commercial practice, which needs to be replicated in an electronic environment and rendered legally valid.

The issue was addressed in the UNICTRAL Model Law through an amendment to the Law in 1998, incorporated as Article 5*bis*:

"Information shall not be denied legal effect, validity or enforceability solely on the grounds that it is not contained in the data message purporting to give rise to such legal effect, but is merely referred to in that data message."

However, the Convention does not replicate this provision, but instead addresses the issue under a general disclosure provision, discussed below.[12]

## Form requirements

As noted in the introduction, legal systems abound with terms and phrases that, while not expressly excluding the use of electronic communications, were clearly used in reference to physical documents and processes, such that uncertainties exist as to whether electronic alternatives are acceptable. Both the 1996 and 2001 Model Laws address such form requirements in considerable detail. These are replicated, in whole or part, in the Convention.

### (a)  Writing requirements

A legal system may require that certain contracts be concluded as and be embodied in a written document or in a specific form, or they may require that certain documents used in commerce (such as an invoice) be in writing. Such requirements may be contained in general interpretation statutes, where for example a "writing" is required to be "in visible form", potentially excluding contracts concluded through fully automated systems. In addition, the terminology used in legislation may create uncertainty about the validity of an electronic writing. Under EU consumer protection law, for example, certain information must be provided to consumer "in writing or *on another durable medium*".[13] Printing out a data message as a paper document may or may not satisfy these writing requirements, depending often on judicial interpretation. One advantage of e-commerce is the use and storage of a message in an electronic rather than a paper medium.

In such cases, it is questionable to what extent an electronic contract or message may fulfil these form requirements. Electronic commerce legislation will generally address this issue, otherwise there will be uncertainty as to whether an electronic message is valid and enforceable. Such uncertainty could significantly depress the use of e-commerce by commercial parties, particularly in business transactions where substantial amounts of money or goods are involved.

Governments have two basic options for dealing with this issue: (i) removing the form requirement altogether by changing the country's otherwise applicable substantive law (often but not exclusively the law of contract), or (ii) adapting the form requirement to e-commerce. One of the original reasons for these form requirements was to prevent, with regard to important contracts such as the sale of land, the commission of fraud through false claims of an oral promise. However, there may be other reasons for a form requirement, such as to alert a party to the legal significance and responsibility of entering into a contract or an evidentiary function to provide for predictability and clarity in the enforcement of an obligation set forth in a written contract. Therefore, a legal system may not wish to completely abrogate its form requirements under existing law. Nonetheless, as will be seen below, most e-commerce legislation operates on the assumption that all form requirements are covered and modified, unless otherwise specified in that legislation.

The alternative is to adapt the traditional form requirement to electronic contracts by providing a rule that electronic contracts may, in principle, be sufficient to satisfy the writing or form requirement. The Convention adopts this more flexible alternative, in Article 9(2):

Where the law requires that a communication or a contract should be in writing, or provides consequences for the absence of a writing, that requirement is met by an electronic communication if the information contained therein is accessible so as to be usable for subsequent reference.

The key to the Convention provision is that it be available and readable in the future. Accessibility means that the information should be readable, either by machine or by humans. There is no requirement that the information be available indefinitely or be unalterable; even paper can be destroyed or lost, and its contents changed.

Again, in contrast to the 1996 Model Law, the Convention does not provide for exclusions from this general facilitative provision. However, a jurisdiction may be expected to exempt contracts or documents in legal areas where the possibility and incentive for fraud or abuse are so high or where legal uncertainty would be so detrimental that there is still a need for a paper document  (for example, wills or real property transfers).

## (b)  Signature or signing requirements

In addition to requiring that information be in the form of a writing, laws and regulations may require that the writing be "signed". In some cases, this requirement may be expressly defined, either in a particular statute or under general interpretative legislative provisions. Obviously, if these requirements were applied so as to require pen and ink signatures made by hand, the effect would be to undermine attempts to validate electronic messages. As a result, most electronic commerce legislation deals with the validity of electronic signatures. Article 9(3) of the Convention provides that:

Where the law requires that a communication or a contract should be signed by a party, or provides consequences for the absence of a signature, that requirement is met in relation to an electronic communication if:

(a) A method is used to identify the party and to indicate that party's intention in respect of the information contained in the electronic communication;

and

(b) The method used is either:

(i) As reliable as appropriate for the purpose for which the electronic communication was generated or communicated, in the light of all the circumstances, including any relevant agreement; or

(ii) Proven in fact to have fulfilled the functions described in subparagraph (a) above, by itself or together with further evidence.

Part (a) of the definition defines the traditional legal functions of a signature that are to be fulfilled by the electronic signature: identification and validating the integrity of the message content. Under some legal systems a signature also indicates the signatory's intention to be bound by his or her signature. This has not been incorporated in the Convention, but has been adopted in some national rules.

In its treatment of signatures, the Convention simply looks at whether electronic signatures may satisfy

signature requirements in the law.   The approach exemplified is that of minimalism: that the legislation is operating primarily to validate and support but not regulate electronic commerce by providing for a functional equivalent for paper transactions.  It does not address other aspects of signatures, for example when a signature is "authentic" and in turn demonstrates that the writing on which it appears is authentic. This aspect was addressed by UNICTRAL in its Model Law on Electronic Signatures (2001), but has not been replicated in the Convention.

Rather than simply facilitating electronic signatures, the 2001 Model Law imposes a certain minimum standard upon signatures used in certain contexts. A similar approach has been adopted under the EU Signatures Directive. Under the Directive, differential legal recognition is given to two categories of signature: "electronic signatures" and "advanced electronic signatures". The latter category are considered to be more secure and therefore are granted beneficial legal presumptions in terms of satisfying a legal requirement for a handwritten signature and in terms of admissibility. There is considerable controversy in this field as to whether such differential legal treatment of electronic signatures is beneficial in terms of facilitating e-commerce. Concern has been expressed that some signature laws have granted beneficial legal recognition to a particular technological form of electronic signature, namely the public-key digital signature using a certification infrastructure. Such technology-specific legislation is seen as entrenching a technology that may be superseded in time, as a result of which the legislation would be rendered obsolete. However, for communications with administrations in certain e-government contexts, such as health, those standards may seem a necessary element for ensuring secure transmissions.

## (c)  Requirements for originals

When a person opens an envelope with a paper letter inside, unless there are extraordinary circumstances, the letter is the one placed there by the sender. The same may not be true with electronic communications. When a person "sends" an electronic message, it sends an exact duplicate of the message that was created; the sender can then delete what was created or store it. Every time an electronic message is sent, received, retrieved, stored or read, it is electronically replicated. Moreover, during the process of sending, receiving, storing or retrieving, the message will normally be "processed" through one or more software programs: to be compressed, decompressed, encrypted or formatted in the desirable form. As a result, to speak of an "original" electronic document is almost nonsensical.

Consequently, any legal requirement that an "original" be produced or retained is an insurmountable burden on e-commerce, unless that requirement is adapted for electronic messages. Thus, we find the following in Article 9(4) and (5) of the Convention:

4. Where the law requires that a communication or a contract should be made available or retained in its original form, or provides consequences for the absence of an original, that requirement is met in relation to an electronic communication if:

  (a) There exists a reliable assurance as to the integrity of the information it contains from the time when it was first generated in its final form, as an electronic communication or otherwise; and

  (b) Where it is required that the information it contains be made available, that information is capable of being displayed to the person to whom it is to be made available.

5. For the purposes of paragraph 4 (a):

  (a) The criteria for assessing integrity shall be whether the information has remained complete and unaltered, apart from the addition of any endorsement and any change that arises in the normal course of communication, storage and display;

  and

  (b) The standard of reliability required shall be assessed in the light of the purpose for which the information was generated and in the light of all the relevant circumstances.

This provision recognizes that the essence of "originality" requirements is the integrity of the information contained in the document, and that the information must not be compromised. What is "reliable" depends on all the relevant circumstances; no absolute definition exists. Thus, it is possible that a document which has all the essential information but has been stripped of the formatting information may still satisfy the requirements of an original, as long as the information is complete and unaltered.

## (d) Dematerialization of financial instruments

When data messages are sent instead of paper documents, the data message should be able to replicate the legal functionality of the paper it is replacing. Broadly speaking, such functionality can be divided into three categories. First, paper has an information function, conveying certain data to the recipient, such as the description of goods. Data messages are very good at representing every sort of information. Second, paper has an evidential function, evidencing the obligations of the parties and their compliance with such obligations. In most legal systems, for example, oral contracts are valid for many types of commercial contracts, although their evidential value may render such contracts unenforceable. Data messages are generally perceived as being evidentially somewhere between oral contracts and written documents. A third function of paper in certain contexts is a symbolic function — the paper somehow represents the information which it contains. The most common example relates to "negotiable" instruments, such as the use of bills of lading in international trade and share certificates under company legislation. With a negotiable instrument, the legal rights detailed in the document, such as title to specified goods, are transferred simply by delivery of the physical instrument. Replacing such a symbolic function through data messages is clearly a more significant challenge to lawmakers and organizations wishing to adopt e-commerce techniques. "Dematerialization" is the term commonly used to refer to procedures designed to replicate this symbolic function.

As a consequence of the negotiability feature, instruments such as bills of lading and share certificates have been heavily relied upon in the arrangement of commercial financing, particularly in international trade. Banks and finance houses will be willing to extend credit to an entity on the basis of security given to them in the form of negotiable instruments. In the event that the entity defaults on a transaction, the bank has possession of certain of the entity's assets represented by the instruments, which it can dispose of in order to recoup the loan. Such functionality will need to be replicated in an e-commerce environment, or the parties will continue to rely on the use of paper instruments.

To replicate the function of a negotiable instrument, any scenario of data messages will need to be able to evidence the obligation and evidence the chain of transfers in respect of that instrument. In a physical environment, the parties relied on the existence of an original document. In an e-commerce environment, originality has no real meaning since everything is a copy of copy, and it therefore has to be replaced by a secure and verifiable record of the transfers of data messages between various parties.

Full dematerialization, in the sense that the paper instrument is completely replaced by an exchange of data messages, is sometimes achieved after a period of partial dematerialization, where the physical instrument is retained but is "immobilized" — that is, it does not move between lawful holders, but is held by a trusted third party registry, which records any changes in ownership which occur and delivers the instrument, if required, to the final holder.

From a legal perspective, the validity of a dematerialized instrument may be achieved either through law reform or through the use of contractual mechanisms to bind the various parties involved. Law reform is clearly the preferred route in terms of establishing legal security and facilitating the adoption of e-commerce techniques. In terms of international trade, national legislation in many jurisdictions simply reflects international treaties governing such activities, such as the Hague Convention of 1924, which use terminology that can restrict the adoption of e-commerce techniques.

As well as the need to reform national and international laws, there has been a need to reform international custom and practice in the area. Such custom and practice have been codified by the International Chamber of Commerce (ICC) in various documents, such as INCOTERMS 2000 and the Uniform Customs and Practice for Documentary Credits (UCP) 500, on which many involved in international trade rely.[14] INCOTERMS was revised in 2000 to expressly recognize the use of data messages as replacements for paper documents.[15] The current UCP has been supplemented by the eUCP (2001), which is designed to redefine existing terminology, such as references to a document that "appears on its face" to be correct, in order to encompass electronic alternatives.

The UNCITRAL 1996 Model Law on Electronic Commerce expressly addresses such issues in Articles 16 and 17, providing that data messages should be accepted as an alternative to using a paper document. In stark contrast, however, the Convention expressly excludes the application of its provisions to such symbolic documents.[16]

## Regulating the contract creation process

As a general proposition, most electronic commerce legislation leaves in place underlying contract law on such issues as contract formation, enforceability, terms and remedies. There are a few instances, however, where there has been supplementation of that law, specifically in areas where there is a perceived need to deal with unique aspects of electronic commerce.

### (a) Disclosures

Article 13 of the Convention addresses the availability of contract terms:

> Nothing in this Convention affects the application of any rule of law that may require a party that negotiates some or all of the terms of a contract through the exchange of electronic communications to make available to the other party those electronic communications which contain the contractual terms in a particular manner, or relieves a party from the legal consequences of its failure to do so.

Generally, contract law requires that a party has had the opportunity to review the terms and conditions of a contract before being bound by it. In particular, if the parties have no prior contracting history and have no knowledge of each other's terms and conditions, the issue arises as to whether the party had the opportunity to review the terms and conditions before declaring its consent. Otherwise, the terms and conditions may not bind the party. This has special relevance for the Internet, where parties often contract without having dealt with each other previously.

There are various ways of disclosing the terms and conditions of a contract on the Internet. In a web-based environment, for example, the supplier will often present the customer with his standard terms of doing business during the course of the transaction process, obliging the customer to "click" his consent before proceeding with the transaction. Alternatively, the supplier may simply present a hypertext link to the customer, where the standard terms are detailed, and rely on implied consent from having provided the customer with the opportunity to review such terms. Such an approach may be vulnerable to challenge, however, depending on the placement of the link; if it is at the bottom of a web page, for example, the customer will be required to take the initiative and scoll down the page. Such transparency requirements directly impact on the way in which websites are designed.

## (b) Error correction

Mistakes arise in all forms of human endeavour, for example the wrong price for a product is given or the wrong quantity is ordered. How are such errors to be dealt with in an electronic commerce environment? Article 14 of the Convention provides as follows:

1. Where a natural person makes an input error in an electronic communication exchanged with the automated message system of another party and the automated message system does not provide the person with an opportunity to correct the error, that person, or the party on whose behalf that person was acting, has the right to withdraw the portion of the electronic communication in which the input error was made if:

   (a) The person, or the party on whose behalf that person was acting, notifies the other party of the error as soon as possible after having learned of the error and indicates that he or she made an error in the electronic communication; and

   (b) The person, or the party on whose behalf that person was acting, has not used or received any material benefit or value from the goods or services, if any, received from the other party.

2. Nothing in this article affects the application of any rule of law that may govern the consequences of any error other than as provided for in paragraph 1.

By restricting the protection to natural persons, the provision is primarily designed to protect the interests of consumers in a web-based environment, rather than B2B electronic commerce. In contrast to the 1996 Model Law,[17] the Convention does not address record retention and evidential issues; therefore, in the event of a dispute, there may continue to be uncertainties concerning the admissibility and probative value of the computer-derived evidence that either party may seek to rely upon.

## (c) Dispatch and receipt of electronic messages

One of the most significant characteristics of e-commerce is that geographical boundaries become irrelevant: people throughout the world can communicate quickly and easily, and many times may do so without knowledge of the location of the other party. While geography may be irrelevant for e-commerce, however, geography – and particularly the *place* where certain acts such as the dispatch or receipt of a communication occur – is still relevant to several legal issues in such areas as private international law (i.e. choice of law and forum) or contract creation. Moreover, determining the place of dispatch or receipt raises a variety of questions. Is the message sent when the "send" button is pushed, or is something else needed? Is a message received when my server receives it, it is put in my mailbox, I download it or I read it? These and similar questions require a clear, and consistent, answer. Therefore, many e-commerce laws contain provisions defining *when* and *where* dispatch and receipt occur. Again, these laws are virtually all drawn from, or similar to, Article 15 of the UNCITRAL Model Law, which has now been redrafted in Article 10 of the Convention:

1. The time of dispatch of an electronic communication is the time when it leaves an information system under the control of the originator or of the party who sent it on behalf of the originator or, if the electronic communication has not left an information system under the control of the originator or of the party who sent it on behalf of the originator, the time when the electronic communication is received.

2. The time of receipt of an electronic communication is the time when it becomes capable of being retrieved by the addressee at an electronic address designated by the addressee. The time of receipt of an electronic communication at another electronic address of the addressee is the time when it becomes capable of being retrieved by the addressee at that address and the addressee becomes aware that the electronic communication has been sent to that address. An electronic communication is presumed to be capable of being retrieved by the addressee when it reaches the addressee's electronic address.

3. An electronic communication is deemed to be dispatched at the place where the originator has its place of business and is deemed to be received at the place where the addressee has its place of business, as determined in accordance with article 6.

4. Paragraph 2 of this article applies notwithstanding that the place where the information system supporting an electronic address is located may be different from the place where the electronic

communication is deemed to be received under paragraph 3 of this article.

In each case, the question of "when" something is sent or received turns on whether the message is within the sphere controlled by the sender or the recipient. Thus, dispatch occurs when the message "enters an information system outside the control" of the sender. Similarly, where the recipient has designated a certain information system for receipt of messages, receipt occurs when the message enters that information system. However, if the recipient has not designated any such information system, no receipt occurs until the recipient actually receives it.

The "where" issue is more complicated. The difficulty with "where" something occurs is that the physical location of the parties at any relevant time (particularly with laptop use combined with cellular or wireless technology) may not only be constantly changing, but may also be unknown. Thus, any relationship between their location and the transaction may be fortuitous. Moreover, the location of the computers or systems processing the information may be equally irrelevant to the transaction. As a result, a data message is deemed dispatched at the place where the sender has its place of business, and is deemed received at the place where the recipient has its place of business. Both these locations are comparatively easy to ascertain; indeed, the Convention lays out in Article 6 rules for determining the parties' place of business:

1. For the purposes of this Convention, a party's place of business is presumed to be the location indicated by that party, unless another party demonstrates that the party making the indication does not have a place of business at that location.

2. If a party has not indicated a place of business and has more than one place of business, then the place of business for the purposes of this Convention is that which has the closest relationship to the relevant contract, having regard to the circumstances known to or contemplated by the parties at any time before or at the conclusion of the contract.

3. If a natural person does not have a place of business, reference is to be made to the person's habitual residence.

4. A location is not a place of business merely because that is: (a) where equipment and technology supporting an information system used by a party in connection with the formation of a contract are located; or (b) where the information system may be accessed by other parties.

5. The sole fact that a party makes use of a domain name or electronic mail address connected to a specific country does not create a presumption that its place of business is located in that country.

## D. Concluding remarks and policy recommendations

Electronic commerce systems generate a range of issues in respect of the validity, enforceability and admissibility of the data messages being exchanged.

This chapter has examined some salient aspects of the new UN Convention designed to facilitate and harmonize national approaches to addressing such issues. However, the Convention cannot, and is not intended to, address all issues raised by the development of electronic contracting. In this regard, one should bear in mind that electronic contracting is not an isolated area of law; rather, it constitutes a new and exciting opportunity to conduct business faster and in a more cost-efficient. This means that the types of issues and the resolution of these issues are framed specifically by the existing requirements of traditional contract law. For example, the fewer form requirements included in traditional contract law, the less intricate the rules for recognition of contracts in electronic format need to be. On the other hand, if existing law has very strict or elaborate form requirements for contracts and data messages, the e-commerce legislation may need to be more extensive in addressing how electronic contracts fit into such formalized systems. Therefore, at the outset, one should look at the issues addressed in the Convention and at other issues raised by e-commerce in the light of existing national law.

The wide acceptance of the UNCITRAL 1996 Model Law as a basis for e-commerce legislation in large as well as smaller countries is a testimony to its adaptability. The Convention attempts to build on the success of the UNCITRAL Model Law and enhance convergence of electronic contracting laws around the world. The countries or jurisdictions implementing the Convention will create similar electronic contracting legal systems. As a consequence, businesses from one of those countries or jurisdictions will quickly be familiar with the general rules of

---

# Box 8.5

## UNCTAD technical assistance on the legal aspects of e-commerce

UNCTAD can assist developing countries in addressing the legal aspects of e-commerce through the activities described below.

*1. Organization and delivery of a training course on the legal aspects of e-commerce*
The objective is to prepare lawmakers and government officials in all aspects to be considered for the drafting of e-commerce laws. The training course also targets entrepreneurs who wish to venture into e-commerce operations and who are not familiar with the legal environment for e-commerce.

### Programme outline:

Module 1: Regulating e-commerce

Module 2: The legal validity of data messages

Module 3: Consumer protection and e-commerce

Module 4: Protecting intellectual property assets

Module 5: Content regulation

Module 6: Taxing e-commerce

Module 7: Privacy online

Module 8: Securing e-commerce

*2. Policy advice*

- **Assessing the needs for law reform**

This consists in the preparation of a legal inventory of existing laws and regulations that need adaptation to accommodate e-commerce in cooperation with relevant ministries and institutions. This review aims to identify legal obstacles and uncertainties and propose appropriate amendments in the light of the current state of e-commerce development of individual beneficiary countries, bearing in mind regional electronic commerce laws and the broader international framework.
Feasibility missions to beneficiary countries can be organized to discuss and assess the needs for e-commerce law reform with all relevant stakeholders. A local counterpart is identified in cooperation with the relevant ministries and in some cases with local law firms in order to encourage a participatory approach.

- **Drafting e-commerce legislation**
A national stakeholders' meeting can be organized to discuss the findings and proposals as identified in the needs assessment phase.
On the basis of the assessment of the need for law reform, a draft of e-commerce legislation is prepared in consultation with government authorities involved in the preparation of electronic commerce laws, and there are consultations with all relevant stakeholders for final approval.
**Requesting UNCTAD's assistance**
Developing countries that would like to receive technical assistance on e-commerce law reform should send an official request to UNCTAD's Secretary-General by fax at +41 22 917 0042, with a copy to +41 22 917 0052.
For further information, see also:
- http://r0.unctad.org/ecommerce/ecommerce_en/ecomlaw.htm;
- http://r0.unctad.org/trainfortrade/tftpresentation/eu2/courses/eclen.htm.

---

electronic contracting in another of those countries or jurisdictions. Such familiarity, in turn, makes it easier for businesses to deal electronically with business partners in other countries or jurisdictions, which, after all, is what a large portion of e-commerce is about. The result could well be a significant increase in e-commerce, and private and government revenue, in those countries.

### Recommendations

The following highlights some policy considerations and recommendations that policymakers in developing countries may need to address when they consider reviewing their legal infrastructure to ensure that it is supportive of and conducive to the practice of electronic commerce:

- In reviewing their legal framework, Governments should give consideration to using the Model Law on Electronic Commerce and the Model Law on Electronic Signatures of the United Nations Commission on International Trade Law as a basis for preparing new laws or adjusting current laws. Consideration should also be given to the introduction of rules to provide certainty with regard to the legal effect of using specific technologies within a technologically neutral legal infrastructure.

- To remove obstacles to the use of electronic communications in international contracts, including obstacles that might result from the operation of existing international trade law instruments, Governments should consider becoming party to the United Nations Convention on the Use of Electronic Communications in International Contracts, 2005.

- Countries should ensure that national legislation facilitates the use of out-of-court dispute settlement schemes. In parallel, many countries should also consider investing more in modernizing their judicial system by training judges, increasing the number of judges, equipping their courts with up-to-date infrastructures and allowing them to proceed online if need be.

- Education and awareness should be treated as a priority by Governments and the international community. Thus, in response to its member States' requests for capacity building in the area of legal aspects of e-commerce, UNCTAD is offering training and advisory services for the preparation of an enabling legal and regulatory environment for e-commerce (see box 8.5).

# Notes

1. ISO 9735. See generally http://www.gefeg.com/jswg/.

2. Available at http://www.unece.org/cefact/recommendations/rec31/rec31_ecetrd257e.pdf.

3. Official Records of the General Assembly, Fortieth Session, Resolution A/40/17.

4. Official Records of the General Assembly, Fifty-first Session, Resolution A/51/628.

5. LMM(02)11 Revised. Available from www.thecommonwealth.org/.

6. Available at http://www.uncitral.org in English, French, Arabic, Chinese, Russian and Spanish.

7. Official Records of the General Assembly, Fifty-sixth Session, Resolution A/56/80. Available at http://www.uncitral.org in English, French, Arabic, Chinese, Russian and Spanish.

8. Directive 1999/93/EC "on a community framework for electronic signatures", OJ L 13/12, 19.1.2000.

9. Official Records of the General Assembly, Sixtieth Session, Resolution A/60/21. Available at http://www.uncitral.org in English, French, Arabic, Chinese, Russian and Spanish.

10. See text of the Convention in http://www.uncitral.org.

11. Directive 2000/31/EC on Certain Legal Aspects of Information Society Services, in Particular Electronic Commerce, in the Internal Market (the "e-commerce Directive"). Available at http://europa.eu.int/eur-lex.

12. At 3.2.4.1.

13. Directive 1997/7/EC "on the protection of consumers in respect of distance contracts", OJ L 144/19, 4.6.1997, at art. 5(1).

14. Available at http://www.iccwbo.org.

15. In 2000, UNCITRAL adopted a decision commending the use of Incoterms 2000 as a record of good international commercial practice.

16. Article 2(2).

17. Articles 9 and 10.